Bx 1584 LIN

Spanish Church and Society
1150-1300

Dr Peter Linehan

Peter Linehan

Spanish Church and Society
1150-1300

VARIORUM REPRINTS
London 1983

British Library CIP data   Linehan, Peter A.
  Spanish Church and society, 1150-1300.
  — (Collected studies series; CS184)
  1. Catholic church — Spain — History
  2. Spain — Religious life and customs
  I. Title
  282'.46   BX1584

  ISBN 0-86078-132-1

Copyright © 1983 by   Variorum Reprints

Published in Great Britain by   Variorum Reprints
  20 Pembridge Mews London W11 3EQ

Printed in Great Britain by   Galliard (Printers) Ltd
  Great Yarmouth Norfolk

  VARIORUM REPRINT CS184

CONTENTS

This volume contains a total of 336 pages

PREFACE

The nine essays reprinted in this volume were first published between 1969 and 1982. They represent part of a continuing endeavour to investigate a number of related themes with which I was occupied in *The Spanish Church and the Papacy in the Thirteenth Century* (Cambridge University Press, 1971). There I was concerned with thirteenth-century churchmen in their social and political setting, and in their dealings with popes and kings. Here, however, the context is almost exclusively peninsular. It has not proved practicable to include papers which dealt with the activities of Spaniards at the papal curia, and to that extent the popes remain offstage. Moreover, the volume has a pronounced Castilian-Leonese bias. The Church in the *Corona de Aragón* receives short shrift. The study of Abril of Urgel is as much about Galicia and León as it is about Catalonia. This imbalance reflects my own attempt to compensate for the relative neglect from which until very recently the ecclesiastical history of the western kingdoms had suffered in comparison with that of Aragon and Catalonia. This is less the case in 1983 than it was in 1969. Much important work has been and is being done on the churches of Castile and León, and I have taken the opportunity of referring to some of it in the section of Addenda and Corrigenda.* All but one of the following essays deal with the period from the mid-twelfth to the late thirteenth century. In the odd one out (I) — itself a preview of a larger study soon to be published — I stray beyond these limits in the hope of describing something of the setting in which the rest may be better understood.

For all that, I fear that I may not have done enough to shake the conviction of critics such as Padre I. de Villapadierna whose reading of *The Spanish Church and the Papacy* persuaded him that I was chiefly interested in describing 'con una animosidad mal disimulada . . . los lados negativos de la vida eclesiástica española' (*Collectanea Franciscana* 42 [1972] 209), and must instead rest content with the verdict of those whose judgement is based upon consideration of my handling of those issues with which I was then and am here concerned and who are not unduly dismayed by my failure to concentrate upon 'la religiosidad del pueblo, las obras sociales y culturales de la Iglesia, la aportación de evangelismo fresco por dominicos y franciscanos.'

I wish to express my sincere thanks for permission to reprint these essays to the editors and publishers of *Studies in Church History*, *Bulletin of Medieval Canon Law*, *Hispania Sacra*, *Anuario de Estudios Medievales*, *English Historical Review*, *Revista Española de Teología*, and *Fuentes y Estudios de Historia Leonesa*, as well as to Cambridge University Press in respect of essay IX. I seize this opportunity to acknowledge my sense of indebtedness, both personal and intellectual, to Walter Ullmann, for whose Festschrift that essay was written, and by whose recent death medieval studies everywhere have been so greatly impoverished. To those archivists in Spain who have permitted me to consult the treasures in their keeping, and to St John's College Cambridge and my colleagues there who have supported and assisted me over the years I extend my warmest thanks.

PETER LINEHAN

St John's College,
Cambridge
March 1983

---

* References to the Addenda and Corrigenda are indicated by daggers (†) in the margin by the passages concerned; where it was feasible, other corrections have been made in the texts themselves.

I

RELIGION, NATIONALISM AND NATIONAL IDENTITY IN MEDIEVAL SPAIN AND PORTUGAL

'A NO SER por el Clero, y en especial por el Episcopado
español', declared Vicente de Lafuente a century ago,
'España sería un país sin historia, pues la historia sin
escribir no es historia'.[1] Lafuente himself was a layman—though it
did not always show—with conventional views regarding the
'democratic tyranny' of his age which a spell as rector of Madrid
university during the student and other troubles of the mid-1870s
served only to reinforce. He found it odd that he rather than an
ecclesiastic should have written the first ecclesiastical history of
Spain.[2] A committee of churchmen had been formed in Rome for
the purpose in 1747, but it is too soon to report on the outcome of
that venture.[3] Lafuente's history, though more than a century old,
is still the only full-scale work of its kind by a Spaniard—'and since
that time there is not a single chronicle that I can discover; though
(like John of Salisbury in his day) I have found in church archives
notes of memorable events which could be of help to any future
writers who may appear'.[4] In presenting some of these notes here,
in the context of the theme of this conference, I find myself
altogether less daunted by the notion of nationalism, which a self-
respecting medievalist is expected fastidiously to eschew,[5] than
by the problem of how to evaluate the testimony of so many
witnesses, clerical and lay, medieval and modern. The difficulty
consists not in locating in the sources evidence of nationalism—or
rather of one of the competing, coexisting nationalisms—but in

[1] [Vicente de] Lafuente, [*Historia Eclesiástica de España*] 6 vols (2 ed Madrid 1873–5)
4, p 307.
[2] *Ibid* 1, p 1; 6, p 268; V. Cacho Viu, *La Institución Libre de Enseñanza* 1 (Madrid
1962) pp 214, 302–17.
[3] Lafuente 1, pp 285–92. Compare the general introduction by [R.] García Villoslada
to the projected five-volume [*Historia de la Iglesia en España*]—of which vols 1 (to
711) and 5 (since 1810) have so far appeared: 1 (Madrid 1979) pp xxiii–xxiv.
[4] *Historia Pontificalis*, ed and trans M. Chibnall (London/Edinburgh 1956) p 2.
[5] Compare K. F. Werner, 'Les nations et le sentiment national dans l'Europe
médiévale', *RH* 244 (1970) pp 285–304, esp pp 285–9.

I

evaluating sources which derive from a tradition wherein national myth-making has been accompanied by invention and forgery in the service of other loyalties both local and ecumenical, and in handling writers for whom faith and religion can serve as synonymous terms for Christianity in general and Spanish catholicism in particular.[6] Scratch any piece of evidence for our subject before about 1130, it sometimes seems to me, and out sheepishly will come that prince of falsifiers, bishop Pelayo of Oviedo, the ink still wet on his fingers. But at least historians are alert to Pelayo and aware of his loyalties.[7] It is the testimony and the actions of the rest, the mass of bishops and clerics, that are so perplexing. Were they what they were because, being to some degree literate, they reflected common opinions—or even formed them—or because, as the successors in title to the churchmen of Visigothic Spain, they were the servile accomplices of royal authority and licensed mouthpieces of the official line? I wish it were possible to treat history written by bishops as J. C. Russell does, as 'marked by a freedom from servility which might not have been expected in a court-patronised literature', but the all too evident continuity of conduct between the vast majority of Visigothic churchmen and the vast majority of their medieval successors makes this a difficult distinction to sustain.[8] The subject has resisted my attempt to treat it with conceptual sharpness at least in part because it can only be approached through a series of distorting mirrors, darkly. And, to add to this, I have been constrained by the limitations of this paper to provide a manifestly patchy and eclectic account of a subject which in some places would have an entire Institute devoted to its study.

[6] Compare the two English translations of the work of [Américo] Castro: 'Life was grounded in religion, and religion was the station from which, directly or indirectly, every activity emerged' [The] Structure of Spanish History, [transl E. L. King] (Princeton 1954) p 189); 'Life was grounded in faith, and faith was the origin, directly or indirectly, of every activity' The Spaniards[. An Introduction to their History, trans W. F. King and S. Margaretten] (Berkeley/Los Angeles/London 1971) p 456.
[7] [F. J. Fernández Conde, El Libro de los Testamentos de la Catedral de Oviedo (Rome 1971) pp 50–67, 367–72; idem, 'La obra del obispo ovetense D. Pelayo en la historiografía española, Boletín del Instituto de Estudios Asturianos 25 (Oviedo 1971) pp 249–91.
[8] 'Chroniclers of medieval Spain', Hispanic Review 6 (Philadelphia 1938) p 230. Compare C. Sánchez Albornoz, 'El Aula Regia y las asambleas políticas de los godos', CHE 5 (1946) p 86; [A.] Barbero and [M.] Vigil, La formación [del feudalismo en la Península Ibérica] (Barcelona 1978) p 290.

Religion and national identity in medieval Spain

The assertion of Lafuente that but for her churchmen Spain would have had no history, or that but for her Christian writers and tradition her history would have been a poor, sad and wretched affair, has always flowed easily from the pens of Spanish writers —and does so still.[9] Quevedo in the seventeenth century pressed the claim of a very particular churchman, Saint James himself, to be regarded and honoured as Spain's patron, as the man given by God 'when Spain was not' so that Spain might be. At the time Santiago was threatened.[10] (And I mention Santiago now because I will not be returning to him later). Periods of stress and national peril have never failed to elicit such exalted claims. Lecturing in 1935, Zacarías García Villada (whose murder in the following year truncated another ecclesiastical history) delivered himself of the view that he and his audience would have been 'Muslims and real Africans' had it not been for the intransigence of the voluntary martyrs of Córdoba in the mid-ninth century.[11] Echoes of Gibbon apart, past history was being pressed into the service of present politics. The sentiments were those of the street-corner, or the pulpit, rather than of (say) the Ecclesiastical History Society. So was the language: the Jews are described as moving by stealth to encompass the ruin of Visigothic Spain.[12] The victory four years later of the Nationalist cause—of *la cruzada nacional*—released a pent-up flood of invective disguised as history. In a volume in the series *Colección pro Ecclesia et Patria* published in 1942, Dom Justo Pérez de Urbel celebrated the Córdoba martyrs as having given their lives *por la fe y por la patria*, and Saint Isidore as a hero of Spanish nationalism—not, he insisted, a regionalist *de ideas estrechas y mente encanijada*; Isidore's special affection for Baetica notwithstanding, *su patria es la península entera*—and this without detriment

---

[9] '¡Qué pobre, triste y desolada se nos quedaría España!': García Villoslada, pp xlv-xlvi.

[10] 'Hízole Dios patron de España que ya no era, para cuando por su intercesion, por su dotrina y por su espada volviese á ser. Hízole patron de la fe que aun no teniamos, para que la tuviésmos': F. de Quevedo, *Su espada por Santiago* (1628), *Obras*, ed A. Fernández-Guerra y Orbe, B[iblioteca de] A[utores] E[spañoles] 48, 2 (Madrid 1859) p 445. For the context see T. D. Kendrick, *Saint James in Spain* (London 1960) pp 64-7.

[11] [Z] García Villada, [*El destino de España en la historia universal*] (2 ed Madrid 1940) p III.

[12] Ibid pp 82-3.

I

to his devotion to Rome.[13] On the strength of the etymological identity of 'Gotalandia, Cathalaunia, Cataluña' meaning the land of the Goths, Mons. José Rius Serra suggested in 1940 that *la restauración del ímperio de la Gocia podría ser una de las flechas de la nueva misión de España en el mundo*,[14] while Jewish pollution of the 'clean' Spanish people was the theme of Manuel Gaibrois Ballesteros—a layman whose interests subsequently shifted to Latin-American anthropology—but who in 1941 was at pains to establish the racial purity of archbishop Rodrigo of Toledo.[15]

The reason for mentioning the galvanised state of these four historians in the aftermath of Franco's victory is that three of them were held in the very highest regard within their profession; it is not that they were priests, though they were that too. Spanish churchmen enjoy no monopoly of the triumphalist interpretation of the medieval Spanish Church: it was Lafuente who in 1880 recommended the *imprimatur* for the book which, as Lannon has mentioned, more than any other has served as the arsenal of such material, Menéndez Pelayo's *Historia de los Heterodoxos Españoles*. Both were laymen, and it is in the latter's epilogue that one finds, stated in Mosaic language, the view that it was neither the sword nor learning that forged Spanish unity and kept it intact throughout the Middle Ages, but the faith, and that it was because of the Church, enshrining that faith, *que fuimos nación, y gran nación, en vez de muchedumbre de gentes colecticias*.[16] The influence of Menéndez Pelayo has been enormous, akin to that of William Cobbett and

[13].[J.] Pérez de Urbel, *El monasterio en la vida española de la Edad Media* (Barcelona 1942) pp 79, 76, and 5–6 on the subject of the debt of 'nuestra patria' to the medieval monks, and their role 'en el desarrollo de nuestra nacionalidad.' In the same year Dom Justo described Saint Isidore as 'el primer español' to have possessed 'una idea clara y fija de la unidad de España, y sin detrimento de la pureza y fervor de un universalismo católico': a revealing protestation: idem and T. Ortega, *San Isidoro (Antologia)* (Madrid 1942) p 34.
[14] J. Rius Serra, 'El derecho visigodo en Cataluña', S[panischen] F[orschungen der] G[örresgesellschaft] 8 (Münster 1940) p 67.
[15] References in [P. A.] Linehan, [*The*] *Spanish Church* [*and the Papacy in the Thirteenth Century*] (Cambridge 1971) p 15. Antisemitic sentiment in these years is described in C. C. Aronsfeld, *The Ghosts of 1492. Jewish aspects of the struggle for religious freedom in Spain 1848–1976* (New York 1979) pp 43–7.
[16] [M.] Menéndez Pelayo, [*Historia de los heterodoxos españoles,*] 1 ed Madrid 1880–82 (ed Biblioteca de Autores Cristianos, Madrid 1956) 2, p 1193. Lafuente's eulogistic appraisal as *censor eclesiástico* is repr. ibid 1, pp xiv–xvi. Menendez Pelayo's response in his second edn (1910) was to describe Lafuente's *Historia* as 'demasiado elemental' (*ibid* p 22). See below p 567ff.

Religion and national identity in medieval Spain

G. M. Trevelyan combined, reaching far beyond scholarly circles, although (or perhaps because) he was himself not a professional medievalist.[17] He has been the mighty battery upon whom many lesser lights have drawn. In his own lifetime he gave respectability to the views of such as M. Hernández Villaescusa, whose own nationalistic zeal was sufficient to make the fourteenth-century cardinal Gil de Albornoz the founder, no less, of the university of Bologna. For Hernández Villaescusa, however, nationalism was a secondary not the primary consideration; the heroes of the Reconquest fought for God, and only incidentally for *la patria*. The Reconquest was the work of the Church.[18] In the present century Menéndez Pidal, the pupil of Menéndez Pelayo and his successor in public esteem, has pronounced a similar judgment, although more modestly phrased and presented: it was *el libre y puro espíritu religioso, salvada en el Norte..que dió aliento y sentido nacional a la Reconquista*; without it Spain would have been *desnacionalizada*, islamicized like the countries across the Straits of Gibraltar.[19] Other explanations are lumped together as *la interpretación laica*, and rejected as *incompatible con el espíritu religioso de la época*.[20]

Consistent with this view of the past, though not essential to it, is the belief that the birth not only of a national church but of Spain itself occurred at the third council of Toledo in 589 when king Reccared announced his conversion to catholicism—providing the beginnings of the nation which the religious spirit preserved from extinction after 711.[21] Here we must touch on a controversy that has blazed for decades, consuming a wealth of energy which might have been more productively harnessed otherwise, between

[17] See V. Palacio Atard, *Menéndez Pelayo y la historia de España* (Valladolid 1956) pp 13, 44.
[18] '¿A quién debe España su gloriosa Reconquista? Al sentimiento religioso. ¿Quién alentó, purificó, dió forma y dirección conveniente y adecuada á este sentimiento? La Iglesia. Todas las proezas de la Reconquista, ya sociales, ya individuales, están marcadas con ese augusto sello. Se luchaba por Dios antes que por la Patria': [M.] Hernández Villaescusa, [*Recaredo y la unidad católica*] (Barcelona 1890) pp 343, 358.
[19] R. Menéndez Pidal, introduction to *Historia de España* (Madrid 1926) 1 p xxvii: quoted approvingly by García Villoslada, p xlv.
[20] Thus [J.] Goñi Gaztambide, [*Historia de la Bula de la Cruzada en España*] (Vitoria 1958) p 39, whose chapter 2 is entitled 'La Reconquista, Guerra Santa': also highly thought of by García Villoslada (pp xl-xli). That the 'finger of providence' guided Spain's destiny during these centuries is asserted by García Villada, p 108.
[21] '¿Cuando nace España? A mi entender, en el momento en que la Iglesia católica la recibe en sus brazos oficialmente y en cierto modo la bautiza en mayo del 589': García Villoslada, p xlii. Cf García Villada, p 104.

Claudio Sánchez-Albornoz and Américo Castro, maintaining respectively the reality of *la contextura vital hispana* before the Arabs came and essentially unaffected by their presence on the one hand, and on the other, the acculturative formation of Spain in the atmosphere of *convivencia* of Moors, Jews and Christians.[22] The wider ramifications of this debate need not concern us here, except to notice that, in the matter of the disputed 'Spanishness' of the Visigoths, (and all that that implies for the national significance of Reccared's conversion), the year 711 is the protagonists' 1066, and that the subject has been debated with all the passionate intensity of the Victorian giants in their pursuit of and repudiation of continuity. Anglo-Saxon historians cannot afford to adopt an attitude of lofty superiority to this aspect of the debate on 'Spanishness', while they themselves continue to play the game of hunting Freeman *redivivus* through other people's footnotes—though the task of drawing parallels between him and Round and Castro and Sánchez-Albornoz would be one for the comparative historian.[23] For all the bitterness of their disagreement, however—and, as P. E. Russell has observed, Sánchez-Albornoz does at times envisage a 'Nazi-like world of Jewish plots against the innocent Christian Spaniards, both in the Middle Ages, and, it is hinted, now'[24]—they do both assume an admixture of religion and nationalism in the reconquest, though they differ as to the proportion and the source of each ingredient.[25] At the very least, *la reconquista del solar nacional*

[22] Surveyed by H. Lapeyre, 'Deux interprétations de l'histoire d'Espagne: Américo Castro et Claudio Sánchez-Albornoz', *Annales* 20 (1965) pp 1015–37.

[23] [Roger] Collins has recently spoken of the 'moral or providential explanations' of the events of 711 as 'the kind of interpretations that were used of the closing years of the Anglo-Saxon kingdom and the Battle of Hastings during the last century, and today would rightly be greeted with ridicule': 'Mérida and Toledo [: 550–585]', [*in Visigothic Spain. New Approaches*] ed [E.] James (Oxford 1980) p 189. Compare E. John, 'Edward the Confessor and the Norman succession', *EHR* 94 (1979) p 254 n.1. John's view that 'to be intelligible the Norman Conquest needs to be understood as the climax of a crisis that had been going on for generations, not as a sudden bolt from the blue' (p 267) applies equally to 711, and suggests that a comparative study, both historical and historiographical, might be of interest. Freeman's remark to Canon Meyrick in 1891 may be noted in passing: 'History of the Church of Spain! That's a large undertaking!' W. R. W. Stephens, *The Life and Letters of E. A. Freeman*, 2 vols (London 1895) 2 p 448.

[24] P. E. Russell, 'The Nessus-shirt of Spanish history', *Bulletin of Hispanic Studies* 36 (Liverpool 1959) p 223.

[25] [C.] Sánchez-Albornoz, *España: un enigma histórico*, 2 vols (Buenos Aires 1956) 1 pp 249 (on 'la naturaleza nacional y "divinal"' of the Reconquest), 283–6 (on

Religion and national identity in medieval Spain

implicaba la guerra contra el enemigo de Cristo y de su Iglesia y ello daba matiz religioso a la contienda;[26] or, more positively put—as Fernando del Pulgar put it to queen Isabella at the end of the affair—the presence of the Moors provided the signal advantage not only of a just war, but of a holy war too, available without stirring from home.[27] So there is no denying that a religious content was present, even if some historians have denied its priority, noting that the movement was one of conquest rather than reconquest, having its origins in an area which had earlier successfully resisted Roman and Visigothic rule, and that Liébana, the epicentre of Christian resistance, had never acquired episcopal status;[28] others questioning its firmity of purpose since booty was preferred to the destruction of the enemy when Al-Andalus lay exposed in the mid-eleventh century;[29] and practitioners of the 'new kind of history' sometimes attaching greater significance to force (Menéndez Pelayo's iron) than to faith,[30] and to human resources, demography and the climate,[31] in their study of the seven and a half centuries after the fatal year 711.

Castro's estimate of the significance of Santiago), 303–11 (denying equivalence of Christian and Moorish zeal in respect of Holy War); Castro, *The Spaniards*, pp 449–56.

[26] Sánchez-Albornoz, *España: un enigma histórico*, 1, p 309.

[27] Compare [J. N.] Hillgarth, *The Spanish Kingdoms* [1250–1516,] 2 vols (Oxford 1976, 1978) 2, pp 372–4.

[28] Barbero and Vigil, *Sobre los orígenes sociales de la Reconquista* (Barcelona 1974) pp 78–9, 96 ('El fenómeno histórico llamado Reconquista no obedeció en sus orígenes a motivos puramente políticos y religiosos, puesto que como tal fenómeno existía ya mucho antes de la llegada de los musulmanes'); idem, *La formación*, pp 234–5, 259–60; G. Menéndez Pidal, 'Mozárabes y asturianos en la cultura de la Alta Edad Media', *B[oletín de la] R[eal] A[cademia de la] H[istoria]* 134 (Madrid, 1954) p 151. Compare the criticisms of Sánchez-Albornoz, 'Observaciones [a unas paginas sobre el inicio de la Reconquista', *CHE* 47–8 (1968)] pp 341–52; [C.–E.] Dufourcq, 'Notes de lecture', *Revue d'histoire et de civilisation du Maghreb* 4 (Rabat 1968) pp 74–8.

[29] I. de las Cagigas, *Minorias etnico-religiosas de la Edad Media española* I: 2 vols (Madrid 1948) 2, p 444.

[30] 'C'est la force des armes qui orienta l'histoire': Dufourcq, 'Berbérie et Ibérie médiévales: un problème de rupture', *RH* 240 (1968) p 323—although in the struggles of the twelfth and thirteenth centuries, he concedes, 'la religion devint un élément caractéristique, essentiel' (p 319). Compare Menéndez Pelayo: 'No elaboraron nuestro unidad el hierro de la conquista ni la sabiduria de los legisladores; la hicieron los dos apóstoles y los siete varones apostólicos.'

[31] [T. F.] Glick, [*Islamic and Christian Spain in the Early Middle Ages. Comparative perspectives on social and cultural formation*] (Princeton 1979) *passim*, esp pp 33–5;

The initial success of the invaders in that year and their over-running of almost the entire peninsula in the two that followed would be regarded as 'completely fabulous', Lafuente observed, if history did not prove it.[32]

The startling claim that history does *not* prove it—that the invasion of 711 is a myth fabricated a century later out of a trivial incident in a civil war between Catholics and Arians which spanned the period 589–800—has been effectively demolished by the results of research into the social structures of al-Andalus.[33] It must be said that the claim would be more difficult to disprove—though it would not be impossible to do so[34]—on the sole strength of purely Christian evidence from the north, for our knowledge of the events of the entire eighth century and most of the ninth derives from accounts which were written up no earlier than the 880s: a circumstance which keeps the beginnings of the Reconquest shrouded in mystery: *La idea central de la Reconquista surgió en la mente de un hombre culto en fecha imprecisa del siglo VIII.*[35] There has been much debate concerning the interrelationship of these chronicles—the so-called *Crónica Albeldense* and the two redactions of the *Crónica de Alfonso III*—and the hypothesis has been advanced of a now lost chronicle which may have been the common source of them all.[36] Amidst the recital of kings poisoned or eaten by bears, no clear view emerges of the rule of particular churchmen. But the

---

T. F. Ruiz, 'Expansion et changement: la conquête de Séville et la société castillane (1248–1350)', *Annales* 34 (1979) pp 548–9.

[32] Lafuente, 3, p 13.

[33] [I.] Olagüe, [*Les Arabes n'ont jamais envahi l'Espagne*] (Bordeaux 1969), *passim*, esp pp 232, 258; [P.] Guichard, *Structures sociales [*"orientales" et "occidentales" dans l'Espagne musulmane*]* (Paris/The Hague 1977): see my review in *Social History* 2 (London 1978) pp 377–9.

[34] Bitter regret at the fate of 'infelix Spania . . . condam deliciosa et nunc misera effecta' is expressed in the so-called *Cronica Mozárabe de 754* (ed T. Mommsen, *MGH AA*, 11, p 353), but the 'vehemently nationalist' author, though almost certainly a churchman, was evidently a Mozarab writing under Moorish domination. See [B.] Sánchez Alonso, [*Historia de la historiografía española,*] 2 ed (Madrid 1947) 1, pp 101–4; [M. C.] Díaz y Díaz, La historigrafía [hispana desde la invasión árabe hasta el año 1000',] in *De Isidoro al siglo XI* (Barcelona 1976) pp 207–9. The charter evidence of the Christian kingdom is analysed by L. Barrau-Dihigo, 'Étude sur les actes des rois asturiens (718–910)', *Revue hispanique* 46 (Paris 1919) pp 1–192.

[35] Sánchez-Albornoz, 'Observaciones' p 351.

[36] Idem, 'Una crónica asturiana perdida?', *Revista de Filología Hispánica* 7 (Buenos Aires-New York 1945) pp 105–46: reprinted in his *Investigaciones [sobre historio-*

Religion and national identity in medieval Spain

realm of the embattled Christians is defined as just that: *christ-ianorum regnum*, set against Muslim 'Spania', the affairs of which are ignored. The general identity of church and kingdom is tacitly assumed: during the reign of Alfonso III *ecclesia crescit, et regnum ampliatur.*[37] Despite the fact that the circumstances of Pelayo's emergence as leader seem to have been all too human, namely the unwelcome advances to which his sister had been subjected by the Arab governor of Gijón, the origins of *Asturorum regnum* are piously attributed to *divina providencia.*[38]

Because the territorial contest had unavoidable confessional implications it might not be thought remarkable that the clergy should have ensconced themselves as aiders and abettors of the Asturian monarchs during these centuries. But the association of *ecclesia* and *regnum* was not at all inevitable. The clergy received a bad press in the accounts furnished by these very chronicles of the collapse of the Visigothic kingdom; their sins and those of their kings were held to have caused Spain's ruin. Concerning the reign of Wittiza, the *Crónica Rotense*—written *in hac patria Asturiensium* and held to be the earlier version of the *Chronicle of Alfonso III* on † account of its inferior Latin, and because of its inferior Latin held to have been the work of a layman[39]—quotes a whole string of scriptural references on the subject of errant priests; and the later version, the *Crónica Ovetense*, although less insistently well-informed on the point, is also sufficiently emphatic: *Quia reges et*

---

grafía hispana medieval (siglos VIII al XII)] (Buenos Aires 1967) pp 111–60. The most revealing recent accounts of this and related matters are Díaz y Díaz, 'La historiografía, *SSSpoleto* 17.i (1970) pp 313–43 (repr. in his *De Isidoro al siglo XI*, pp 205–34), and Barbero and Vigil, 'La historiografía [de la época de Alfonso III]' *La formación*, pp 232–78.

[37] [M.] Gómez-Moreno, ['Las primeras crónicas de la Reconquista: el ciclo de Alfonso III',] *BRAH* 100 (1932) p 604; Barbero and Vigil, *La formación*, p 262. Compare [E.] Benito Ruano, 'La historiografía [en la Alta Edad Media española]', *CHE* 17 (1952) pp 71–4.

[38] Gómez-Moreno, p 601; [L.] Vázquez de Parga, 'La biblia [en el reino astur-leonés',] *SSSpoleto* 10 (1963) pp 278–9. For an anthropological interpretation of another liaison in the Christian camp, also with important political consequences, see Barbero and Vigil, 'La sucesión al trono [en el reino astur]' *La formación*, pp 349–51: here the analysis leads to Frazer's *Golden Bough* rather than to Holy Writ.

[39] Vázquez de Parga, 'La biblia' p 277. Gómez-Moreno (p 586) infers lay authorship- —'por sabio que pareciese'—of *Crónica Rotense* from the barbarity of its Latin. Thus too Sánchez-Albornoz, 'La redacción original de la Crónica de Alfonso III', *Investigaciones*, p 25.

*sacerdotes legem Domini derelinquerunt omnia agmina Gothorum Sar-
racenorum gladio perierunt.*[40] And their accounts of the very beginnings
of the Reconquest at Covadonga are even more damaging to the
attempt to identify *ecclesia* and *regnum* in a sense which would
accommodate priests and bishops. In both versions a bishop is the
villain of the piece: the 'perfidious' Oppa, bishop of Seville (or
Toledo) and brother (or son) of king Wittiza who advances from
the Moorish ranks bent upon cajoling Pelayo, the Asturians' elected
princeps, into surrendering. Chided by Oppa about the Christians'
prospects of success on that mountaintop when the whole Visigothic army had perished on the plain (thanks partly to Oppa's
treachery there, as the chronicler observes), Pelayo it is who raises
the flag. In a scriptural *tour de force*, he proceeds from Matthew 13
on the *ecclesia domini* as a mustard seed, by way of the ringing
declaration that *spes nostra Christus est, quod per istum modicum
monticulum, quem conspicis, sit Spanie salus et Gotorum gentis exercitus
reparatus*, to the playing of his trump card—a couple of verses of
Psalm 89. Whereupon battle commences and the Arabs incur losses
of 189,000 (and should the reader be predisposed to scepticism
about this, he is advised to remember the story of Moses and the
Red Sea).[41]

In the changes wrought upon the primitive *Crónica Rotense* by the
compiler of *Crónica Ovetense*, scholars have perceived a deliberate
attempt to disguise the earlier failings of the clergy.[42] Yet in neither
account of the crucial confrontation of Covadonga does their
representative Oppa emerge with any credit. It is a matter which
seems until recently not to have intrigued scholars, despite its
implications for attempts which would later be made to establish
by whatever means the continuity of medieval churchmen with
their Visigothic predecessors and with all that they had represented
in the Visigothic kingdom. It is possible of course that knowledge
of Oppa's perfidy was too widely disseminated for any attempt at
rehabilitation even to have been contemplated—or *ever* to have
been contemplated. But we do not know when and in what
circumstances the attempt was made to make the clergy *but not*

---

[40] *Crónica de Alfonso III*, ed A. Ubieto Arteta (Valencia 1961) pp 18–19.

[41] *Ibid* pp 28–35; Vázquez de Parga, 'La biblia' pp 279–80.

[42] Sánchez-Albornoz, *Investigaciones*, pp 31–7; [P.] David, *Études historiques [sur le
Galice et le Portugal du VIe au XIIe siècle]* (Lisbon–Paris 1947) p 320. Compare [J. A.]
Maravall, *El concepto de España [en la Edad Media]* (2 ed Madrid 1964) pp 305–9;
Díaz y Díaz, *De Isidoro al siglo XI*, pp 214–15.

Religion and national identity in medieval Spain

Oppa more respectable for the future by tampering with the account of the past—any more than we know for whose edification the whitewash was applied, for whom, that is, these writers thought they were writing. The hypothesis of Sánchez-Albornoz, however, that behind the associated chronicles of Alfonso III's reign lies a now lost common source composed perhaps during the reign of Charlemagne's contemporary, Alfonso II,[43] does provide a suitable context for these alleged happenings, and – though this is to build conjecture upon hypothesis—a context in which the exclusion of bishop Oppa from the retrospective amnesty would be explicable.[44] Alfonso's long reign (791–842) witnessed important developments which reflected and shaped the Christians' perception of their past and future. One was the elaboration of the neogothic myth: the programmatic recreation of 'the Gothic order as it had been at Toledo', the purpose of which was to establish at Oviedo Alfonso's continuity with the Visigothic rulers, as their legitimate heir—just as Leovigild had done at Toledo itself in the sixth century—and thereby to stake his claim to rule over the entire peninsula. The methods employed—or such of them as we know of—were artistic and ceremonial; visual expression was provided in ecclesiastical edifices.[45] Whether this development was indigenous to the Asturias, or had its origins in the initiative of emigré Mozarabic bishops from the south, it cannot be dissociated from either the second issue crucial for a land without a name or a permanent capital: the establishment of the shrine of Saint James at Compostela[46], or from the third: the Adoptionist controversy.

---

[43] Sánchez-Albornoz, *Investigaciones*, pp 116–18; Díaz y Díaz, *De Isidoro al siglo XI*, pp 215–16.

[44] Barbero and Vigil regard the chronicle's Oppa at Covadonga as 'el prototipo del obispo que ha pactado con los musulmanes', note the development of the historic Oppa (brother of Wittiza and bishop of Seville) into the chronicle's Oppa (son of Wittiza and bishop of Toledo), and suggest that he may have been the literary creation of Mozarabic clergy opposed to the type of alliance with the Muslim which Oppa here was represented as favouring; even that 'con la presencia de Oppas, Asturias se transforma en Toledo': *La formación*, pp 275–6. Compare Díaz y Díaz, *De Isidoro al siglo XI*, p 224.

[45] *Crónica Albeldense*, ed Gómez-Moreno, pp 602–3; [L. de] Valdeavellano, [*Historia de España*], I, 2 vols (4 ed Madrid 1968) I, pp 435–6; H. Schlunck, 'La iglesia de San Julián de los Prados (Oviedo) y la arquitectura de Alfonso el Casto', *Estudios sobre la monarquía asturiana. Colección de trabajos realizada con motivo del XI centenario de Alfonso II el Casto, celebrado en 1942* (2 ed Oviedo 1971) pp 405–65. On Leovigild's precedent see Collins, 'Mérida and Toledo', pp 212–14.

[46] L. Vázquez de Parga, J. M. Lacarra, J. Uría Ríu, *Las peregrinaciones a Santiago de Compostela*, 3 vols (Madrid 1948) I pp 39–46.

Spear-headed by Beatus of Liébana and Etherius, the orthodox revolt of the north provided churchmen there with an eminently respectable opportunity to declare themselves independent of the Mozarabic hierarchy of the south, whose very existence under Muslim rule served to obscure the clear and clean identification of the Asturian monarchy with the Christian cause—quite apart from any question of Adoptionism's alleged Arian content.[47] In a celebrated outburst, Elipand metropolitan of Toledo (who was already suffering harrassment at Roman hands) voiced his indignation at criticism from such a remote quarter: was it not unheard of for Liébana to lay down the law to Toledo?[48] We may ask another question here: what possibility was there in such circumstances of making an honest man of his predecessor at Toledo, Oppa the collaborationist representative of the Visigothic church?

Now how much of this was the work of churchmen *qua* churchmen rather than of churchmen *qua* royal propagandists is a matter for debate—as is the question of whether such a distinction would have had much meaning for contemporaries. Historians further complicate the matter by too confidently inferring clerical authorship of chronicles from their superior latinity, and then too readily claiming to have discovered the cause of any perceptible pro-clerical bias.[49] The difficulty of interpretation is not of course peculiar to ninth-century Asturias, nor until the papacy had developed sufficiently as a tool capable of prising clergy and king apart will there be any prospect of solving it. But if the rehabilitation of bishop Oppa was such a hopeless case in the ninth century, and beyond,[50] and the rewritten history of *Crónica Ovetense* was the best that could be done by those who held the pen while the

[47] Valdeavellano, I p 444; R. d'Abadal [i de Vinyals], *La batalla del Adopcionismo en la desintegración de la Iglesia visigoda* (Barcelona 1949).
[48] 'Nam nunquam est auditum ut Libanenses Toletanos docuissent': *PL* 96 (1854) col 918C; E. Amann, *L'Époque carolingienne*, FM 6 (Paris 1947) pp 130–34. Compare M. Ríu, 'Revisión del problema adopcionista en la diócesis de Urgel', *AEM* I (1964) pp 77–96. The 'anti-Toledanism' of Alfonso II's reign is remarked by Díaz y Díaz, *De Isidoro al siglo XI*, p 221.
[49] Above, n 39. Compare Díaz y Díaz, *De Isidoro al siglo XI*, p 222.
[50] See the version of Oppa's confrontation with Pelayo in the early twelfth-century *Historia Silense*, [ed J. Pérez de Urbel and A. González Ruíz-Zorrilla] (Madrid 1959) pp 132–4. As late as 1216–17 the archbishop of Braga's proctor at the papal curia could seek to damage Toledo's case by recalling 'quod Opa, quondam archiepiscopus Toletanus . . . apostavit cedens in sectam Mohabitarum et per eum amissa fuit tota Hyspania et recuperata per Bracarensem': [P.] Feige [, *Die Anfänge des portugiesischen Königtums und seiner Landeskirche*], *Spanischen Forschungen der*

Religion and national identity in medieval Spain

warriors rested on their spears, then the reinterpretation of the Visigothic past was uphill work indeed. 'It is', E. A. Thompson has remarked, 'scarcely possible to deny that throughout the seventh century, except in Erwig's reign, the bishops of Spain were supine supporters of the king'.[51] True, there were cases of seventh-century bishops who took a tough line with the king, but they were rare,[52] and something of their temporising esprit de corps can be discovered in the way in which they handled the delicate matter of the fate of the rebel Hermenegild at the hands of his Arian father Leovigild five years before Reccared's public conversion. Catholic martyr or thankless rebel? Contemporaries were in no doubt, at least in the record they left for posterity. Hermenegild's action was tyrannical, according to Johannes Biclarensis bishop of Gerona, while the author of the *Vitas SS. Patrum Emeretensium* mentions Hermenegild only incidentally in his description of Reccared's conversion, by removing the reference to martyrdom from the account which he borrowed from Gregory the Great.[53] Gregory's view that Hermenegild had died a martyr's death in the course of a religious war against an unjust and heretical father,[54] might have had some uncomfortable implications for these men. At any event, they did not espouse it. Nor did Isidore,[55] although at a later stage it would triumph and lead eventually to Hermenegild's canonisation at Philip II's insistence in 1586. Hermenegild's changing fortunes reveal something of Spanish churchmen's powers of self-analysis

---

Görresgesellschaft, I. Reihe: *Gesammelte Aufsätze zur Kulturgeschichte Spaniens*, 29 (Münster-in-W 1978) pp 85–436, at p 399.

[51] E. A. Thompson, *The Goths in Spain* (Oxford 1969) pp 316–17. Compare [J. M.] Lacarra, 'La iglesia visigoda [en el siglo VII y sus relaciones con Roma]', *SSSpoleto* 7. i (1960) pp 358–60, 373–5.

[52] Hillgarth, 'Popular religion in Visigothic Spain', James, *Visigothic Spain*, pp 40–41.

[53] *Chronicon Johannis Biclarensis*, ed J. Campos (Madrid 1960) pp 89, 91, 141–3; *Vitas . . . V.9.4*: 'qui [*scil*. Reccaredus] non patrem perfidum sed Christum dominum sequens ab Arianae haereseos pravitate conversus est'—substituting 'Christum dominum' for 'fratrem martyrem' in Gregory, *Dial*. 3. 31—cit. [E. A.] Thompson, '[The] Conversion [of the Visigoths to Catholicism]', *Nottingham Mediaeval Studies* 4 (Nottingham 1960) p 12. Compare J. Fontaine, 'Conversion et culture chez les Wisigoths d'Espagne', *SSSpoleto* 14 (1967) pp 109–12, 117–20, 143–4.

[54] Thompson, 'Conversion' pp 19–22; Hillgarth, 'Coins and Chronicles[: Propaganda in sixth-century Spain and the Byzantine background]', *Historia* 15 (Wiesbaden 1966) pp 491–501.

[55] [*Historia Gothorum*,] ed [T.] Mommsen, *MGH AA*, 11, p 287.

and state of self-confidence over that millennium;[56] as also does the list of other monarchs in whom successive centuries discovered saintly qualities—Pelayo (highly questionable), Fernando III (problematical but possible), and James I of Aragón, Fernando's contemporary and equal in battle, but nevertheless wholly implausible.[57]

'It is ironical', as J. N. Hillgarth has observed, 'that.....Isidore of Seville should have shared in the suppression of the truth (regarding Hermenegild), in the interest of the unity of the Kingdom.'[58] Whether or not this expression of his preconceptions should incline us to describe Isidore as a nationalist spokesman is another question, and one which continues to be much debated. How are we to interpret the fact that his celebrated *Laus Spaniae*, with its glorification of *mater Spania*—'*omnium terrarum, quaequae sunt ab occidu usque ad Indos, pulcherrima es, o sacra semperque felix principum gentiumque mater Spania*—is emblazoned at the beginning of a history which has as its title *Historia Gothorum* rather than *Historia Spaniae*? Is Isidore writing 'national' history or 'royal' history? Are we to understand his pronouncement as the expression of a new *comunidad hispánica*, itself the fruit of the religious unity achieved by Reccared's conversion? If we are—and if we are to view the Visigothic councils as bodies dedicated to furthering the unitary policies of the monarchs—then we must at least note that a consequence, or at least a concomitant of this was that this community's ecclesiastical relationship with Rome was formal at best, and towards the end of the century was distinctly strained. Reccared was in no hurry to inform the pontiff of his conversion, and seventh-century bishops did not hesitate to adopt a patronising tone in their meagre correspondence with successive popes, Braulio of Zaragoza for example advising Honorius I not to concern

[56] [J. N.] Garvin, [*The Vitas Sanctorum Patrum Emeretensium*] (Washington 1946) pp 490–91; J. Tamayo Salazar, *Anamnesis sive commemorationis sanctorum Hispanorum* . . ., I (Lyons 1652) pp 202–3, 2 p 580; J.-M. del Estal, 'Culto de Felipe II a San Hermenegildo', *La Ciudad de Dios* 174 (El Escorial 1961) pp 550–52; Linehan, *Spanish Church*, p 330. Compare R. de Maio, 'L'ideale eroico nei processi di canonizzazione della controriforma', in *Riforme e miti nella Chiesa del Cinquecento* (Naples 1973) pp 261–2.

[57] Maravall, *El concepto de España* pp 257–8 (Pelayo); Linehan, *Spanish Church* pp 331–3 (Fernando); [J.] Massó Torrents, ['Historiografia de Catalunya en català durant l'epoca nacional'], *Revue hispanique* 15 (1906) pp 546–7.

[58] 'Coins and Chronicles' p 501. If Collins is correct in his suggestion that Hermenegild had not converted to catholicism at the time of his rebellion, then the irony of the situation may be less—but not the interest of the treatment which it received at the hands of later writers: 'Mérida and Toledo' pp 215–18.

Religion and national identity in medieval Spain

himself about the bishops' apparent subservience to the king, and incidentally correcting a faulty biblical reference in the pope's own letter. Certainly there are no signs of that *obediencia castrense* to Rome which Sánchez-Albornoz regards as characteristic of later centuries, and which recent propagandists have strained so hard to detect.[59]

To some degree the debate over these issues must always remain unresolved because the participants cannot agree about defining the terms that they use. What matters more to us, however, is the use which could be made of Isidore, and which *was* made of him in the centuries after the rout of 711—a rout the very occurrence of which casts doubt on the claim that Isidore inspired an intellectual and spiritual renaissance in his lifetime.[60] True, Isidore continued to be read. But those who read him were whistling in the dark themes which only later could be orchestrated for full brass.[61] For nationalism has a geographical dimension as well as a historical one, and Isidore's significance can only be properly appreciated when set in the context of political reality. It is necessary therefore to consider briefly Spain's political developments.

[59] *Laus Spaniae*, ed Mommsen p 268; Hillgarth, 'Historiography in Visigothic Spain', *SSSpoleto* 17 (1969) pp 298–9, and F. Udina Martorell and J. Fontaine in *discussione*, *ibid* pp 345–50. Compare Lacarra, 'La iglesia visigoda' pp 353–84, and O. Bertolini in *discussione, ibid* p 406; Sánchez-Albornoz, *España: un enigma histórico* I pp 353, 357; Pérez de Urbel, above n 13; Hernández Villaescusa who contents himself with the assumption that the kings nominated bishops 'por una especie de delegación' from Rome (p 352). On Isidore's position see J. M. Wallace-Hadrill, *Early Germanic Kingship in England and on the Continent* (Oxford 1971) pp 53–5; Barbero and Vigil, 'El feudalismo visigodo', *La formación* pp 174–6; and for the view that the events of 589 witnessed 'la aparición de una verdadera Iglesia nacional, al margen no solo del Imperio de Oriente sino de la propria Roma', [J. A.] García de Cortazar, [*La Época medieval: Historia de España Alfaguara*], 2, (5 ed Madrid 1978) p 43.

[60] M. Cruz Hernández, 'San Isidoro y el problema de la "cultura" hispano-visigoda', *AEM* 3 (1966) pp 414, 422–3, commenting on J. Fontaine, *Isidore de Seville et la culture classique dans l'Espagne visigothique* (Paris 1959).

[61] The view that Isidore's writings express a vision of 'una nacionalidad naciente, pero ya inequívocamente diferenciada y autónoma' is found in J. L. Romero, 'San Isidoro de Sevilla. Su pensamiento históricopolítico y sus relaciones con la historia visigoda', *CHE* 8 (1947) pp 57–8; Maravall, *El concepto de España* pp 21–2. Compare L. Vázquez de Parga, 'Notas sobre la obra histórica de S. Isidro', *Isidoriana*, [ed M. C. Díaz y Díaz] (León 1961) p 106: 'No ha hecho, creo yo, historia nacional, sino dar una historia de pueblos no romanos, con independencia, y considerar en la *laus Hispaniae* a España unida al pueblo godo. Pero no hay propiamente concepto de nacionalidad.' For later use of Isidore see Díaz y Díaz, 'Isidoro en la Edad Media hispana', *Isidoriana* pp 345–87 (repr *De Isidoro al siglo XI*, pp 143–201).

The chroniclers of the twelfth century and later deplored those political divisions of Spain which had resulted from the Arab invasion, and the further sub-division of *regna*—the 'principle of fragmentation', as Maravall has called it, which is so marked a feature of Spain's medieval history, and which clerical authors regarded as divine punishment for the sins of men.[62] The Christian kings ruled over places not over peoples. The title *rex Hispanorum* would have implied rule over the Mozarabs of the south. They were kings 'not of a kingdom but of a space'. They lacked any 'corporative or organic concept' of a kingdom'.[63] As the travel posters affirm, 'Spain is different'. All is fluctuation and fragmentation. Squaring the unitary neogothic myth with political reality called for some virtuoso conceptual gymnastics. *Regnum Hispanie* survived only as a latent concept. without a *rex Hispanie* to rule over it. 'King' and 'kingdom' *no son absolutamente correlativos*. Political power was exercised by a number of princes, the plurality of 'kings and princes of Spain' to which both native and foreign writers so often refer, Maravall's *pululación de reyes*, occasional kings promiscuously coming and going, or all together subscribing the remarkable—in our eyes remarkable—document of 1153 :

> imperante domno Adefonso imperatore cum domna Rica imperatore uxore sua; domna Sancia infantissa cum fratre suo regnante; Sancius, rex similiter; Fernandus, rex similiter.[64]

One effect of all this was to limit the opportunities open to churchmen to establish a mediating role in the process of king-making. It is striking that the attributes of royalty should have come to enjoy less prominence than elsewhere in Europe in the very land which has provided the earliest recorded evidence of the practice of royal unction.[65]

---

[62] Maravall, *El concepto de España* pp 344, 355: 'Creo que es absolumente indispensable para entender nuestra Edad Media partir de ese principio de fragmentariedad'; Sánchez-Albornoz, 'La sucesión al trono [en los reinos de León y Castilla]', *Boletín de la Academia Argentina de Letras* 14 (Buenos Aires 1945) pp 35–124—repr in his *Estudios [sobre las instituciones medievales españolas]* (Mexico 1965) p 673.

[63] Maravall, *El concepto de España* pp 350, 351, 357, 359.

[64] *Ibid* pp 408–9, 388–99, 366, 380, 384, 369.

[65] [P. E.] Schramm [(trans L. Vázquez de Parga)], *Las insignias[de la realeza en la Edad Media española]* (Madrid 1960) p 63. On unction as 'el factor constitutivo o al menos confirmante de la legitimidad real' in the Visigothic period see J. Orlandis Rovira, 'La iglesia visigoda y las problemas de la sucesión al trono en el siglo VII', *SSSpoleto* 7. i (1960) pp 333–51, esp pp 349–51, and O. Bertolini, G. B. Picotti, L. Prosdocimi, J. M. Lacarra and G. P. Bognetti in *discussione, ibid* pp 385–95,

Religion and national identity in medieval Spain

For a century and a half after the death of Alfonso VII in 1157 no king of Castile was crowned.[66] In thirteenth-century Navarre Teobaldo II's attempt to introduce the practice of unction led to popular demand for the retention of the established practice of raising the king on his shield,[67] and in Aragón, despite the later tradition that in order to emphasise the papal role Innocent III in 1204 had intended to impose the crown on Pedro II with his feet—an attempt which the king foiled by providing an unmanoeverable crown of soft bread for the occasion—his son Jaime the Conqueror chose not to be crowned, and though later coronations at Zaragoza may have helped to establish that place as the kingdom's capital, Alfonso III was at pains to emphasise that his own coronation there by the bishop of Huesca in 1286 was not to be taken as implying that he had received his crown *tanquam ab ecclesia romana, nec pro ipsa ecclesia nec contra ecclesiam,* nor that any prejudice was thereby suffered by any other place in his kingdom.[68] The sword not the crown was the king of Aragon's distinctive emblem, and the ceremonial secured no political influence for churchmen whom Pedro III could forbid to enforce papal sentences against him *propter naturalitatem quam habetis nobiscum.*[69]

The churchman's role was to be that of acolyte rather than celebrant. This did not mean that their role was entirely passive—in times of crisis, in Castile in 1166 for example, they would move

398–404; A. Barbero de Aguilera, 'El pensamiento político visigodo y las primeras unciones regias en la Europa medieval', *Hispania* 30 (Madrid 1970) pp 245–326, esp pp 314–17. For developments after 711 see Barbero and Vigil, 'La sucesión al trono', *La formación*, p 290.

[66] Schramm, *Las insignias*, p 32. Alfonso X in the thirteenth century scoffed at the thaumaturgic pretensions of the kings of France and England: Maravall, ['Del regimen feudal al regimen corporativo en el pensamiento de Alfonso X'], *Estudios [de historia del pensamiento español]* (2 ed Madrid 1973) p 117.

[67] Lacarra, *Historia del reino de Navarra en la Edad Media* (Pamplona 1975) p 295 (compare pp 246–7); Schramm, 'Der König von Navarra (1035–1512)', *ZRG GAbt* 81 (1951) pp 144–9. I have not seen Lacarra's *El juramento de los reyes de Navarra (1234–1329)* (Madrid 1972).

[68] [B.] Palacios Martín, [*La coronación de los reyes de Aragón 1204–1410. Aportación al estudio de las estructuras medievales*] (Valencia 1975) pp 23, 77–81, 107–8, 308. The importance of the ceremonial of royal unction enacted there in establishing Toledo as the capital of Visigothic Spain is stressed by Collins, 'Julian of Toledo and the royal succession in late seventh-century Spain' in *Early Medieval Kingship*, ed P. H. Sawyer and I. N. Wood (Leeds 1977) pp 45–6.

[69] Palacios Martín pp 83–6; L. González Antón, *Las Uniones aragonesas y las Cortes del reino (1283–1301)* 2 vols (Zaragoza 1975) 1 pp 373–8, 438–40.

into the political vacuum 'to save the nation'.[70] Nor of course were they ever indifferent regarding the political outcome. Strong (but not too strong) central rule was in their best interests—or so archbishop Rodrigo of Toledo implied in his account of the part played by the prelates of the kingdom of León in the negotiations which led to the union of León with Castile in the person of Fernando III in 1230: *regni prelati, quorum interest regnum et sacerdotium contueri*[71] By then the realisation of Visigothic unity may have seemed to be within sight. Three centuries before, while postponing that outcome *sine die*, they busied themselves on a lower plane in the service of the monarch, fabricating false genealogies which connected him with the Visigothic rulers, introducing into charters and diplomas phrases which implied a new juridical theory of the ruler's full hereditary rights; deploying such imperial titles as *Ranimirus, Flavius, princeps magnus, basileus unctus, in regno fultus*, and blessing the king and his army before their campaigns,[72] or bolstering his political power by sanctifying it, bringing to ninth-century Oviedo (as to sixth-century Toledo) quantities of relics from the south, many the remains of venerable martyrs long dead, others of more recent origin. That market was buoyant and the competition international, but this was important work, and the significance of their acquisitions seems to have been crucial.[73]

Of the many puzzling features of the case of the voluntary martyrs of Córdoba in the 850s, none is more surprising than the fact reported of bishop Eulogius of Toledo that he had been partially awakened to the significance of Islam on reading a distorted life of Mohammed in the library of a Navarrese monastery, when, as has been said, 'he could have obtained more accurate information by asking any Muslim in the street'. For Ignacio Olagüe of course here is proof positive that the Arabs had never

[70] Below pp 190–91.
[71] *De Rebus Hispaniae*, 9. 14: ed F. Lorenzana, *PP Toletanorum quotquot extant Opera*, 3 (Madrid 1793, repr Valencia 1968) p 204.
[72] Sánchez-Albornoz, 'La sucesión al trono', *Estudios* p 663 (compare Barbero and Vigil, 'La sucesión al trono', *La formación* pp 279–353); A. Sánchez Candeira, *El "regnum-imperium" leonés hasta 1037* (Madrid 1951) passim, esp pp 11, 65 (Ramiro III *anno* 974); Sánchez-Albornoz, *España: un enigma histórico* 2, pp 373–80; Goñi Gaztambide pp 33–5.
[73] B. de Gaiffier, 'Les notices hispaniques dans le Martyrologe d'Usuard', *An Bol* 55 (1937) pp 268–83; *idem, Recherches d'hagiographie latine* (Brussels 1971) p 8. Compare Collins, 'Mérida and Toledo' p 214.

Religion and national identity in medieval Spain

invaded Spain.[74] The equally remarkable testimony of Paulus Alvarus—'apparently a layman' (but does that matter?)—that the Mozarabic Christians of Córdoba were so enthralled by Arabic culture that they despised or ignored their Christian heritage, is also open to doubt.[75] But it was that version of events that passed to the north, that interpretation of the martyrs' motives that was received together with the remains of Eulogius and Leocadia in 883 (and perhaps, it may be suggested, the conventional wisdom regarding bishop Oppa). We may shrink from the interpretation of García Villada or Pérez de Urbel, for whom Eulogius was chief of *un partido nacional* and endowed with *una generosa tendencia nacionalista*, but it would be difficult to deny all symbolic significance to the translation of their relics, quite apart from the effect of their collective self-sacrifice in establishing the belief that death at Muslim hands automatically counted as martyrdom.[76]

Two hundred years later, in 1063, another relic expedition brought off a further important coup, when the bishops of León and Astorga set off for the south in search of the remains of the third-century martyr Justa. What Ordoño of Astorga returned with from Seville were the remains of Isidore—the complete set apparently.[77] It should cause no surprise that movement between the two zones should have been so easy. It usually was, and thirty years after the collapse of the caliphate of Córdoba, the south was vulnerable as never before to Christian pressure. But the Christian leaders preferred to take booty—*parias*—from the subject Muslim

[74] *PL* 115 (1854) col 859; Glick p 176; Olagüe p 268: 'Si nous n'en avions d'autres, ce seul témoignage suffirait à ruiner la légende.' Compare E. P. Colbert, *The Martyrs of Córdoba (850–859): a study of the sources* (Washington 1962).

[75] *Indiculus luminosus*: *PL* 121 (1854) cols 555–6; [J.] Waltz, ['The significance of the voluntary martyrs of ninth-century Córdoba'], *The Muslim World* 60 (Hartford, Conn., 1970) p 155.

[76] García Villada, above p 163; Pérez de Urbel, *San Eulogio de Córdoba, o la vida andaluza en el siglo IX* (2 ed Madrid 1942) pp 124, 253: 'un gran símbolo. Por ella encomendaba la realización de su más grande anhelo a aquellos montañeses, fuertes e indomables, que habian conservado con toda su pureza la tradición española.' In the south of course 'la tradición española' was tainted: 'estos hombres estaban inficionados hasta la medula por el influjo de la nueva civilización' (p 252), whereas Eulogius and Leocadia were 'los dos campeones del españolismo tradicional' (p 249). Compare Waltz pp 232–5.

[77] *Historia Silense* pp 197–204; A. Vinayo González, 'Cuestiones histórico-críticas en torno a la traslación del cuerpo de San Isidoro', *Isidoriana* pp 285–98. The importance of possessing the complete remains is illustrated by Compostela's reaction when archbishop Mauricio of Braga acquired an extra head of Saint James in the Holy Land: David, *Études historiques* pp 475–7.

I

kingdom, to the enormous benefit of Cluny incidentally; and if any
churchman felt conscientious scruples about this his protest was not
recorded. The bringing to León of Isidore's remains in the year
after the kingdom of Toledo had for the first time accepted client
status vis à vis the king of León, almost amounted to a statement of
intent to postpone the prosecution of a decisive policy against
Seville and the south.[78] When the struggle was resumed Isidore
would be pressed into service both as saint and, improbably
enough, as *caudillo*. But the struggle, when resumed, would continue
fitfully for a matter of centuries; and part of the reason for that is
hinted at in the admission, albeit grudgingly made by the author of
the *Historia Silense*, that some trace of virtue was discernible in the
Moorish king of Seville.[79] The atmosphere of political tolerance and
burgeoning *convivencia* in which these events took place anticipates
the non-combative atmosphere which, alongside the military
exploits of the thirteenth century, would permit the nuns of Las
Huelgas to be tended by mudejar servants who had their own
mosque, and enjoy baths and the ministrations of Jewish physi-
cians: the side of the story, in short, which makes it so difficult to
regard the history of the Reconquest, whether an exclusively
religious phenomenon or not, as a total account of the history of
Christian Spain in the Middle Ages.[80]

The unidentified author of *Silense* compiled his account of Isidore's
translation some fifty or sixty years after the event, c.1118. He
marks (for us) some important developments. Regarded as the first
writer possessed of 'a complete vision of Spain as the object of the
historian's attention', he is notorious for the anti-French bias which
he reveals in his account of events from Charlemagne's time

[78] Lacarra, 'Aspectos económicos de la sumisión de los reinos de taifas, 1010–1102',
Homenaje a J. Vicens Vives (Barcelona 1965) pp 255–77; [C. J.] Bishko, 'Fernando I
y [los origenes de la alianza castellanoleonesa con] Cluny', *CHE* 47–8 (1968) pp
31–135, 49–50 (1969) pp 50–117, esp pp 47–8, 99–135; P. Segl, *Königtum und
Klosterreform in Spanien. Untersuchungen über die Cluniacenserklöster in Kastilien-León
vom Beginn des 11. bis zur Mitte des 12. Jahrhunderts* (Kallmünz 1974) pp 73–6;
Valdeavellano 2, p 285.
[79] L. López Santos, 'Isidoro en la literatura medioeval castellana', *Isidoriana* pp 402–8;
Historia Silense p 201: 'Expavit barbarus, et licud infidelis, virtutem tamen Domini
admirans . . .' Compare the editors' introduction (p 48) where the significance of
this admission seems to be misunderstood.
[80] L. Torres Balbas, *Algunos aspectos del mudejarismo urbano medieval* (Madrid 1954) pp
78–9.

Religion and national identity in medieval Spain

onwards: the *franci* were corruptible and their histories were false.[81] His cry of protest against the all-pervasive French influence of the period has been widely remarked. Whereas the nationalism of Beatus of Liébana and Paulus Alvarus had been apocalyptic and extra-terrestrial, his is firmly rooted in Spanish soil.[82] In him—with whom incidentally Hermenegild re-enters Spanish historiography wearing the martyr's crown[83]—the focus becomes sharper than at any time in the proceeding four centuries. Churchmen formerly have been vague and shadowy figures, their identity and their attitudes largely matters of conjecture. Only rarely can Lafuente's picture of the 'church of Spain' supporting 'the State' during those centuries be substantiated.[84] Through the eyes of the *Silense* author we begin to see matters rather more clearly, just as our field of vision is widened in these years by the inclusion of a new dimension: the papal dimension.

Although Catalonia and Aragón had always been more open to outside influences than had regions farther west, the entire peninsula had tended to be hermetically sealed in spiritual terms and consciously self-sufficient to a marked degree. The air of satisfaction with which modern Spanish writers have regarded the council of Coyanza (1055) faithfully reflects the spirit of the century to which it belongs. Although summoned by king Fernando I, in whose names its decrees were promulgated, and attended by lay magnates—all in true Visigothic style—the council of Coyanza is regarded as demonstrating that the eleventh-century Spanish church had no need of foreigners to reform it, and indeed stood in little need of reform from any quarter. The subject matter of its thirteen canons is taken as showing that there was less cause for remedial action here than elsewhere in Europe; satisfactory performance in all aspects of ecclesiastical practice and discipline is inferred from absence of reference to specific abuses.[85] The argu-

[81] Ed cit pp 129–30; Maravall, *El concepto de España* p 30.

[82] Díaz y Díaz, 'La historiografía' pp 219–21.

[83] Ed cit pp 115–16, reproducing the account of Gregory the Great (above n 53). The *Compilatio Ovetensis* of 883 (cit. Garvin p 488) had not gone so far.

[84] 'La Iglesia de España ha seguido la suerte del Estado en su próspera y adversa fortuna, alentando al combate, exhortando en la pelea, consolando en la derrota, y cortando las rencillas y discordias fraternales: en los escasos momentos de ócio ha manejado la pluma, mientras el guerrero descansaba apoyada en su lanza': Lafuente 3 pp 379–80.

[85] *Ibid* 3 p 290; Menéndez Pelayo 1 p 455; J. López Ortiz (bishop of Túy), 'La restauración de la cristiandad', [*El*] *Concilio de Coyanza* [*(Miscelanea)*] (León 1951)

ment from silence which provides such a favourable impression (and where in Europe would it not produce the same effect before the advent of the Gregorian reformers?) has proved impervious to the results of research into the text of the Coyanza decrees, research which has revealed that what historians have taken to be the authentic legislation of the council is in fact a product of the workshop of Pelayo of Oviedo, a reworking done seventy-odd years later. What is notable about the Pelagian version is that, apart from stressing the king's part in the council's proceedings, the reviser of the text of the decrees seems to have had two purposes in view which did not seem to him to be in any way incompatible: the promotion of Gregorian notions and of the interests of the see of Oviedo.[86] No particular desire to emphasize the nationalist (as against the royalist) content of the original decrees is apparent.[87]

The presence and absence of such preconceptions are relevant to consideration of the impact of the peninsular policies of Gregory VII. It is customary to observe here the confrontation of Spanish catholicism and Spanish nationalism—with the former prevailing as Spanish historians take pride in recalling.[88] Of course, Gregory's

---

pp 5, 11–12. Understanding of this subject began in earnest with A. García Gallo's fundamental monograph ['El Concilio de Coyanza. Contribución al estudio del derecho canónico español en la Alta Edad Media'], *Anuario de Historia del Derecho Español* 20 (Madrid 1950) pp 275–633—although he too assumes the absence of 'situaciones intolerables' (pp 364–6). The same assumption is present throughout the much-quoted work of R. Bidagor, *La "iglesia propria" en España. Estudio histórico-canónico* (Rome 1933) esp pp 82, 98, 115. Indeed, it held to *explain* the slow pace of reform during the twelfth century (p 157). For Bidagor the Visigothic regime is normative (pp 169–70) and its incompatibility with 'Gregorian' notions is not considered. Compare Lacarra, 'La iglesia visigoda' p 384: 'si . . . no se apartó de la Iglesia Universal en sus principios dogmáticos, ni recusó formalmente la autoridad del Romano Pontífice, de hecho vivió encerrada en sí misma'; and E. Magnou-Nortier, *La Société laïque et l'église dans la province ecclésiastique de Narbonne (zone cispyrénéenne) de la fin du VIIIe à la fin du XIe siècle* (Toulouse 1974) pp 447–518, for the experiences during these years of a closed society which was in many ways comparable.

[86] García Gallo pp 321–3; idem, 'Las redacciones de los decretos del Concilio de Coyanza', *Concilio de Coyanza* pp 25–39, esp pp 31–2; G. Martínez Díez, 'El concilio compostelano del reinado de Fernando I', *AEM* I (1964) pp 121–38, esp pp 133–5; O. Engels, 'Papsttum, Reconquista und Spanisches Landeskonzil im Hochmittelalter', *Annuarium Historiae Conciliorum* 1 (Amsterdam 1969) pp 276–87.

[87] García Gallo pp 298–9, 342–3: cc. VII.3; IX (on *Liber iudicum* and *Lex Gothica*). Compare c. XIV of the Pelagian redaction (absent from the earlier *redacción portuguesa*) confirming 'totos illos foros cunctis habitantibus in Legione quos dedit illis rex domnus Adefonsus' (*Ibid* p 302): a royalist interpolation indeed.

[88] 'El sentimiento católico, irresistible en la raza, se sobrepuso a todo instinto de

Religion and national identity in medieval Spain

claim to possession of the *regnum Hyspaniae* was, as has been said, 'grotesquely out of touch with the realities of the Reconquest'. More to the point, however, is the fact that neither in 1073 nor in 1077 did it succeed in eliciting any response from those to whom it was addressed.[89] Spanish churchmen did not need to regard this as a battle of conflicting loyalties. In the matter of the substitution of the Mozarabic rite by the Roman, in which Gregory again acted with characteristic heavy-handedness, there is indeed evidence of popular resistance—but it is evidence from a royal source, and it was the king who settled the matter, albeit to the pope's satisfaction, with his celebrated and decisive aphorism *alla van leyes do quieren reyes*.[90] It is perhaps no exaggeration to describe the response to Gregory's interventions as at best cosmetic. Nowhere in the peninsula do we find churchmen being drawn away from their accustomed allegiance. In Catalonia, indeed, it was precisely at this time, while the papacy was declaring against the practice, that bishops and abbots were entering into vassal relationships with the count of Barcelona and other laymen.[91] In Aragón meanwhile, king Pedro I made clear to Urban II his attitude to trouble-making reforming prelates who sought to introduce new-fangled theories behind his back while he was at the front fighting night and day against the enemies of the Cross. The king's letter contained an unmistakable warning to the pontiff: if Christendom's fight was to be fought in

---

orgullo nacional, por grande y legítimo que·fuese': Menéndez Pelayo 1 p 458; 'No todas las acciones de los Santos son santas, ni tiene el cristiano obligación de aceptar cada una de ellas en particular. ¿Quien hoy proclamará el papa infalible en política y quien podra igualmente defender la conducta de San Gregorio VII con respecto á España?': Lafuente 3 pp 363–4.

[89] H. E. J. Cowdrey, *The Cluniacs and the Gregorian Reform* (Oxford 1970) pp 221–2, 226. Compare David, *Études historiques* pp 377–82; Bishko, 'Fernando I y Cluny', *CHE* 49–50, pp 100–4.

[90] 'De Romano autem ritu quod tua iussione accepimus sciatis nostram terram admodum desolatam esse' (Alfonso VI to Hugh of Cluny, July 1077): David, *Études historiques* pp 402–3, 419–20. See also C. Morris, '*Judicium Dei*: the social and political significance of the ordeal in the eleventh century', *SCH* 12 (1975) pp 98–9; [C.] Servatius, [*Paschalis II. (1099–1118). Studien zu seiner Person und seiner Politik*] (Stuttgart 1979) pp 29–32.

[91] P. Bonnassie, *La Catalogne du milieu du Xe à la fin du XIe siècle* 2 vols (Toulouse 1975–6) 2 pp 701–5, esp p 703: 'Tout révérence gardée envers le successeur de Pierre, l'Eglise catalane n'admet, au temporel, d'autre chef que le comte de Barcelone et elle s'intègre naturellement au nouveau système gouvernemental que celui-ci met en place.'

Spain, then it must be fought on Spain's terms.[92]

The effect of reforms formulated by the papacy—or, as Fletcher has it, of 'what is loosely and unsatisfactorily called "reform"' —failed to disturb the relationship of king and bishop, or to introduce any significant irritant into that relationship, not because the formulation was imperfect but because the parties were deaf to influences outside.[93] The year 1085, then, was significant not for Gregory VII's death, but for Alfonso VI's conquest of Toledo—or 'pseudo-conquest', as it has been described by an historian who sees in it a manoeuvre engineered by the Mozarabic community judging their prospects to be better under Alfonso's rule not because he was Christian but because he was nearer at hand: so the Christians did not reconquer Toledo, just as the Arabs had never invaded Spain![94] Nevertheless, the event—or pseudo-event—certainly created new horizons for the king by his possession of the old Visigothic capital, and new problems in the matter of the treatment of the now subject Muslims. The religious and the political solutions exemplified in Talavera and Cisneros at the end of the fifteenth century had their protagonists four centuries earlier in archbishop Bernard of Toledo (prompted by queen Constance) and the king respectively. Alfonso VI was only deterred from his intention of burning the archbishop and queen for having forcibly converted the Toledo mosque to Christian use by the pleas of the 'prudent' Arabs themselves who, as the story was told by Rodrigo of Toledo in the thirteenth century, were fearful of further reprisals.[95]

The conquest of Toledo gave rise also to a series of problems particularly affecting churchmen, those connected with the issues of ecclesiastical primacy and provincial organisation.[96] To bolster

---

[92] P. Kehr, *Das Papsttum und die Königreiche Navarra und Aragon bis zur Mitte des XII Jahrhunderts, ADAW, PhH Kl* (Berlin 1929) pp 55–7.

[93] [R. A.] Fletcher, [*The Episcopate in the Kingdom of León in the Twelfth Century*] (Oxford 1978) cap 5, esp pp 184, 203.

[94] M. Criado del Val, *Teoría de Castilla la Nueva. La dualidad castellana en los orígenes del español* (Madrid 1960) pp 84–5, 100–101: 'su participación en la Reconquista será de distinto signo religioso que la de Castilla, y en algunos momentos no parecerá tener conciencia de ello' (p 100).

[95] *De Rebus Hispaniae*, 6. 24: ed Lorenzana pp 137–8; J. Orlandis, 'Un problema eclesiástico de la *Reconquista* española: la conversión de mezquitas en iglesias cristianas', *Mélanges offerts à Jean Dauvillier* (Toulouse 1979) pp 597–9. Compare Hillgarth, *The Spanish Kingdoms*, 2 pp 477–8.

[96] D. Mansilla, 'Disputas diocesanas entre Toledo, Braga y Compostela en los siglos XII al XV', *Anthologica Annua* 3 (Rome 1955) pp 89–143, esp pp 91–130; J. F.

Religion and national identity in medieval Spain

the claims of his church each prelate had recourse to the papacy and to forgery, whichever suited him better. Soon the whole issue was bedevilled by the so-called Division of Wamba, bishop Pelayo of Oviedo's re-working in the 1120s of an earlier fabrication which purported to be an authoritative description of the diocesan divisions made, at the bishops' request, by king Wamba in the seventh century.[97] Its influence was to be enormous. In the 1240s it was used by both Toledo and Tarragona in their battle for ecclesiastical control of Valencia, as one of the many evidences both genuine and spurious unearthed by their agents in libraries both within the peninsula and beyond[98] The real interest of the Gothic heritage to these men was here displayed, in an ecclesiastical dispute which was of supreme political and national significance to the kings of Castile and Aragón.[99] Neither monarch was prepared to permit Valencia to be ecclesiastically subject to the province controlled by the other and the other's metropolitan. The dangers and difficulties presented by ecclesiastical boundaries which were not concurrent with political boundaries was a subject on which the kings of Castile-León at least already possessed a century of experience, in their dealings with the count-kings of Portugal.

The first king of Portugal owed no part of his royal title to Portuguese churchmen: between July 1139 and April 1140 Afonso Henriques slipped from describing himself as *princeps* to *rex* parthenogenetically, as a matter of chancery practice merely, without acclamation, enthronement or coronation. Forty years later, at considerable expense, he secured papal recognition from Alexander III.[100] Ecclesiastical complications, however, remained, with the archbishop of Compostela claiming the obedience of all the Portu-

Rivera Recio, *La iglesia de Toledo en el siglo XII (1086–1208)* 2 vols (Rome 1966–76) I *passim*.

[97] Vázquez de Parga, *La División de Wamba[. Contribución al estudio de la historia y geografía eclesiásticas de la Edad Media española]* (Madrid 1943) esp pp 89–93; D. Mansilla, *Iglesia castellano-leonesa y curia romana en los tiempos del rey San Fernando* (Madrid 1945) pp 94–7, esp p 95 n 19.

[98] Vázquez de Parga, *La División de Wamba* p 46; V. Castell Maiques, 'Un elenco de códices de la Hispana del año 1239', *Anthologica Annua* 16 (1968) pp 329–43.

[99] R. I. Burns, 'Canon Law and the Reconquista: convergence and symbiosis in the kingdom of Valencia under Jaume the Conqueror (1213–1276)', *Proceedings of the Fifth International Congress of Medieval Canon Law (Salamanca, 21–25 September 1976)*, ed S. Kuttner and K. Pennington (Vatican City 1980) pp 398–402.

[100] Feige pp 244–5, 300–307.

guese bishops bar Oporto as falling within the ancient province of Lusitania (of which he, as successor to the authority of the unreconquered see of Mérida was head), and the archbishop of Toledo continuing to press for complete peninsular domination. The evidence submitted in 1198–9 by the archbishops of Braga and Compostela for control of the church of Zamora aptly illustrated the political dimension of ecclesiastical divisions. One witness recalled how Fernando II of León had sought to draw the suffragans of Braga from obedience to their archbishop because the latter intended to excommunicate him;[101] another remembered Fernando's pressure on the bishop of Zamora, politically his subject, to defect from Braga to Compostela *quia magis sibi debebat placere suum regnum decorare quam alterius.*[102] As to Compostela's claim to control of the Portuguese sees on the grounds that Braga was not possessed of metropolitan authority, Braga had 'old histories' to prove the opposite and no fewer than 144 witnesses—Braga men who would know the reason why.[103] The adversaries were seasoned litigants, canonists who knew every trick in the book and employed all manner of arguments ranging from geography to palaeography,[104] but the essence of Braga's case was this: by his *strenuitas* and other virtues Afonso Henriques had made a kingdom for himself which Rome recognised; Rome had formally excluded all foreign—that is, Leonese and Castilian—ecclesiastical jurisdiction from Portugal; the king by his victory over the Saracens had obtained the right to plant churches where he would; and—incidentally—the archbishop of Braga, having borne the heat and burden of battle, deserved to enjoy the fruits of victory.[105]

---

[101] *Ibid* p 384. At issue was the king's marriage within the forbidden degrees. See J. González, *Regesta de Fernando II* (Madrid 1943) pp 69–70, 112; Fletcher pp 195–203.

[102] Feige, pp 384–5.

[103] *Ibid* p 390.

[104] 'Ponit procurator Bracarensis, quod Bracara est in capite provinciarum Hyspanie habito respectu ad mare Oceanum, cui vicinior est Bracara quam Toleto. Respondet archiepiscopus Toletanus, quod non est in capite sed in fine'; Braga's protest that the papal privileges presented by Toledo 'non sint originalia sed confirmatoria tantum': *ibid* pp 399–400, 409.

[105] 'Accidit ergo quod olim domnus Alfonsus . . . qui antea infans vocabatur, interim terram illam dilatavit (. . .) regnum latum et spaciosum fecit et ab hac sacrosancta sede de infante meruit rex vocari, propter cuius strenuitatem et meritorum dotem concessionem a Romana ecclesia per privilegium obtinuit, quod nulla ecclesiastica persona (. . .) in regno suo iurisdicionem vel potestatem aliquam haberet nisi papa vel eius legatus. Obtinuit ius, quod quamcumque

Religion and national identity in medieval Spain

The case for a national church could hardly have been better
put—though Aragón and Castile claimed similar privileges for
their reconquering monarchs, in the forged bull of Urban II,[106] and
Alfonso X's claim to control episcopal elections as *Sennor natural de
la tierra ó son fundadas las eglesias*.[107] But it is arresting to find the case
being so eloquently put by an archbishop at the court of Innocent
III. The king of Portugal controlled the Portuguese church under
papal licence, because of not in spite of Portugal's feudal subjection
to Rome.[108] National considerations were invoked by the prelate in
order to beat off threats to ecclesiastical integrity: the suggestion
that Toledo enjoyed primatial authority throughout the whole
peninsula was scandalous both politically, because it implied the
subjection of the other *reges Hispaniae* to the king of Castile, and
also pastorally, because it demeaned the other metropolitans in the
estimation of *simplices et laicos*.[109]

For as long as national and ecclesiastical boundaries failed to
coincide, prelates would continue to have to endure some uncomfortable consequences. When, additionally, a century further on
and with papal influence on the wane, the bishops of Castile and
Portugal came to appreciate the distinct disadvantages of the
system of royal control which had been advocated by the
archbishop of Braga, and braved themselves to petition for relief
from royal exactions, it was *two* monarchs that they had to address.
But how very restrained they were when they did so, at Salamanca
in 1310. They did not aspire to hold anything so formal as a
council, because kings did not like councils. And they certainly did
not contemplate the use of canonical sanctions in their own

---

terram a Sarracenis occupasset, propter exaltacionem fidei, quam (. . .) christ-
ianos (. . .) dilataverat Sarracenos opprimendo et eos per archiepiscopum suum
Bracarensem ad fidem convertendo, cuicumque vellet, posset supponere ecclesie';
'(Bracarensis) archiepiscopus (*in captione*) illius terre multas expensas fecerat in
expeticione eundo cum rege, sicut mos et consuetudo est terre illius, et ob hoc
multas possessiones Bracarensis ecclesie pignerari obligavit, quas pro parte
nondum redimere potuit . . .': *ibid* 393–4.
[106] *Ibid* pp 335–7.
[107] Primera Partida, ley 5, tit. 17: *Alfonso X el Sabio. Primera Partida (manuscrito Add.
20.787 del British Museum)*, ed J. A. Arias Bonet (Valladolid 1975) p 77; Linehan,
Spanish Church p 108.
[108] 'Nec videmus causam, quare dominus papa tantam iniuriam nobis vellet facere,
cum etiam dampnum romane ecclesie procuraret. Preterea cum regnum Por-
tugalense sit eius et solvat ei annuatim duas marchas auri, quod non facit aliud
regnum in Hyspania . . .': Feige p 418.
[109] *Ibid* p 423.

defence.[110] As has been observed, religious nationalism and royal interventionism in the affairs of the church prospered in parallel.[111]

Viewed historically in its peninsular setting, the phenomenon under consideration may be said to have its origins in a failure to achieve on a political plane that restoration of the Visigothic system to which churchmen in an ecclesiastical context aspired. The view, widely held, throughout the Middle Ages, of the Moorish occupation, that it was trespass which left unaffected all rights enjoyed in the year 711 and created no new rights,[112] evidently constituted no problem for Afonso Henriques in 1139, nor for the archbishop of Braga in 1199. Yet it was to that very tradition the Portugese churchmen appealled at the siege of Lisbon in 1147, with the bishop of Porto learnedly defining the just war for the benefit of the horny-handed would-be crusaders from Dartmouth, and representing the issue not primarily as a religious struggle (though that aspect was stressed for effect and in order to justify their not proceeding to Jerusalem), but as a venture for the recovery of lost property,[113] and with the archbishop of Braga urging the Moors to return with all their chattels to the place from whence they had come—as if they had been there just a week rather than for the 358 years during which, by his calculations, they had retained *iniuste* the Christians' cities and possessions,[114] (If national characteristics were

---

[110] Linehan, '[The] Spanish Church revisited [: the episcopal *gravamina* of 1279]', *Authority and Power: Studies on Medieval Law and Government presented to Walter Ullmann on his seventieth birthday*, ed B. Tierney and P. Linehan (Cambridge 1980) p 127 and references cited there.

[111] 'En su conjunto *nacionalismo religioso* e intervencionismo regio en la Iglesia crecieron paralelamente': García de Cortazar p 491.

[112] 'Cual si ésta hubiera sido un accidente en la vida española, incapaz de crear derechos': Lacarra, 'La reconquista y repoblación del Valle del Ebro' in *La Reconquista española y la repoblación del país* (Zaragoza 1951) p 79. The notion persisted throughout the medieval period; see Fernando del Pulgar, cited Maravall, *El concepto de España* p 274. Compare B. Blanco González, *Del cortesano al discreto*, 1 (Madrid 1962) 374: 'por haber cristalizado prematuramente la unidad espiritual en tres conjuntos, Portugal, Castilla y Aragón, no se logró, ni en la Edad moderna, la unidad definitiva'.

[113] *De Expugnatione* [*Lyxbonensi*, ed C. W. David[(New York 1936) pp 76–80; E.–D. Hehl, *Kirche und Krieg im 12. Jahrhundert. Studien zu kanonischem Recht und politischer Wirklichkeit* (Stuttgart 1980) pp 259–61.

[114] '. . . cum omnibus sarcinis vestris, peccuniis, et pecculiis, cum mulieribus et infantibus, patriam Maurorum repeteritis unde venistis, linquentes nobis nostra': *De Expugnatione* pp 114–16. The archbishop's exogamous assumptions deserve consideration in the context of the work of Guichard (above n 33). As to his historical calculations, compare the altogether more sanguinary account of the Muslim occupation which in 1096 Pedro I of Aragón reckoned had already lasted

Religion and national identity in medieval Spain

exhibited on that occasion, and again at the siege of Silves in 1189, it was by the northerners whose sense of fair play was outraged by a Moorish attack on some Bretons out fishing, and who showed such marked interest in the fate of a prize mare in foal).[115]

For foreign consumption, as in 1147, it was politic for a peninsular prelate to stress the international dimension of the national venture—in order to derive benefit from the papally inspired crusading movement.[116] The relationship of the *Reconquista* to the eastern crusades is a large subject into which I cannot enter here—except just to say that Spaniards believed that there were lessons to be learned from the experiences of the Christians of Outremer, and in particular cautionary lessons about the fragility of success and the dangers of false optimism. 'Remember Damietta', warned the versifying Guillelmus Petri de Calciata in the mid-thirteenth century.[117] Thus they were able, kings and bishops alike, to foster pontifical anxiety, summoning up dreadful spectres of imminent disaster to the Christian cause in the west as in the east, unless the pope gave them a free hand with the resources of the Spanish church.[118] The papal dimension served to tighten the bonds which bound the national church to the crown.

It is not difficult to produce instances of churchmen in the eleventh, twelfth and thirteenth centuries performing on a national

---

for 460 years: A. Duran Gudiol, *Colección diplomática de la catedral de Huesca* (Zaragoza 1965) p 90. The formation of historical consciousness at this period deserves further study.

[115] *De Expugnatione* pp 140, 176. Forty-two years later, in 1189, the German author's account of the foreign crusaders' participation at the siege of Silves is harshly critical of the Portuguese: 'nec laborabant nec pugnabant, sed tantum insultabant nobis quod in vanum laboremus et quod inexpugnabilis esset munitio': *Narratio* [*de itinere navali peregrinorum Hierosolymam tendentium et Silviam capientium*], ed C. W. David, *Proceedings of the American Philosophical Society* 81 (Philadelphia 1939) pp 629–30. J. C. Russell suggests that Glanvill may have been the author of the 1147 account: 'Ranulf de Glanville', *Speculum* 45 (1970) p 74.

[116] 'Nulla ergo itineris incepti vos festinationis seducat occasio, quia non Iherosolimis fuisse sed bene interim invixisse laudabile est', in the words of the bishop of Porto in 1147: *De Expugnatione* p 78. The *Narratio* contains no mention of a similar plea, or the need for one, in 1189.

[117] 'Propter hoc satagite: vigiles estote/Maurorum insidias: o plebs cavetote/Quid egerit Corduba: olim mementote/Damiate insuper: cronicam scitote': 'Guillelmi Petri de Calciata rithmi de Iulia Romula seu Ispalensi urbe', ed D. Catalán and J. Gil, *AEM* 5 (1968) pp 549–57, v 91. See C. J. Bishko, 'The Spanish and Portuguese Reconquest, 1095–1492', *A History of the Crusades*, 3, ed K. M. Setton (Madison-London 1975) pp 396–456.

[118] Linehan, *Spanish Church*, chaps 6–9.

plane the public role of their Visigothic predecessors—both directly, for example promoting the peace movement or the cause of good money,[119] and incidentally by the imposition of more restrictive synodal legislation regarding the permitted number of godparents *pro removenda futura impedimenta matrimonii contrahendi inter liberos patrinorum*,[120] thereby providing conditions more favourable to the production of larger Christian families, as desired by the secular rulers.[121] *La iglesia*, in García de Cortazar's words, *se muestra en estos siglos [XI–XIII], en especial en el XIII, como un instrumento nacionalizante al servicio del poder político.*[122]

In times of crisis or political turmoil the role of churchmen could be decisive.[123] An instance of this is provided by the recently discovered decrees of the synod of Segovia in 1166, at a time when the kingdom of Castile stood in mortal peril. King Sancho III had died eight years before, leaving the crown to the two-year old Alfonso VIII. Competing regents fought for possession of the child while the king of León, Fernando II, threatened from the west and seized control of Toledo, and the Almohads were massing in the

[119] Truce of God: synod of Toulouges (1027): 'la primera vegada que apareix en la Història una treva general i periòdica': R. d'Abadal, *L'abat Oliba, bisbe de Vic i la seva època* (3 ed Barcelona 1962) pp 234–7; law and order: council of Palencia (1129): E. S. Procter, *Curia and Cortes in León and Castile 1072–1295* (Cambridge 1980) p 23; prohibition of Christians bearing arms against Christians: council of Valladolid (1155) c 17: ed C. Erdmann, *Das Papsttum und Portugal im ersten Jahrhundert der portugiesischen Geschichte, ADAW PhH Kl* (Berlin 1928) p 57; good money in Catalonia and Aragon from 1155: T. N. Bisson, *Conservation of Coinage. Monetary exploitation and its restraint in France, Catalonia, and Aragon (c. A.D. 1000–c. 1225)* (Oxford 1979) pp 78–83, 102–4.

[120] I. da Rosa Pereira, 'Les statuts synodaux d'Eudes de Sully au Portugal', *L'Année Canonique* 15 (Paris 1971) p 470 (Lisbon synod 1232x48), permitting a maximum of three godparents. Compare Linehan, 'Pedro de Albalat, arzobispo de Tarragona y su "Summa Septem Sacramentorum"', *Hispania Sacra* 22 (Madrid 1969) p 18 note m (Valencia 1258): limit of two.

[121] Early marriage is recommended in Partida 2, 20, 1, not only for its own sake but also because 'quando los homes casan temprano si fina alguno dellos, el que finca puede casar despues, asi que fará fijos con sazon, lo que non podrien tan bien facer los que tarde casasen': *Las Siete Partidas*, ed Real Academia de la Historia, 3 vols (Madrid 1807) 2 p 190. Inheritance patterns, however, tended to frustrate this effect: H. Dillard, 'Women in Reconquest Castile: the fueros of Sepúlveda and Cuenca', *Women in Medieval Society*, ed S. M. Stuard (Philadelphia 1976) pp 71–94, esp p 87. See also L. C. Kofman de Guarrochena and M. I. Carzolio de Rossi, 'Acerca de la demografía astur-leonesa y castellana en la Alta Edad Media', *CHE* 47–8 (1968) p 155.

[122] García de Cortazar p 344.

[123] For example, in the years after the death of Alfonso VI (1109): Valdeavellano 2, pp 392–423.

Religion and national identity in medieval Spain

south. In these circumstances it was the Castilian bishops—describing themselves as bishops 'of the kingdom of king Alfonso' not as bishops of the province of Toledo—who moved into the political void, employing ecclesiastical sanctions to oblige all holders of honours within the kingdom to swear the Castilian equivalent of the Oath of Salisbury to the king, requiring all Castilians to respond to the royal call to arms 'for the defence of his kingdom', excommunicating all the king's active enemies, and appropriating crusading indulgences to the cause—against the Christians of León as well as against the Almohads.[124] The interest of this testimony consists not least in its context. It is common enough in the thirteenth century, when the tide had turned decisively in favour of the Christians, to find bishops blessing the king's forces as they prepare for battle, or fighting alongside them. Here, however, in March 1166, churchmen seem to be acting as the last line of defence against national disaster.

Sixty years later all had changed. The thirteenth century, which began with the victory of Las Navas de Tolosa and before it had run half its course had seen the recovery of Córdoba, Valencia and Seville, has long been regarded by Spanish historians as 'the great medieval century'.[125] The whole triumphal process was recorded by two mitred contemporaries in Castile—Lucas of Túy and Rodrigo of Toledo. While numbers of nameless churchmen at a lower level provided the human sinews which helped to hold the newly won territories together, colonising Córdoba from Burgos or Jaén from Soria,[126] Lucas proudly proclaimed the more than peninsular significance of the success of the Spanish kings: *Pugnant Hispani reges pro fide et ubique vincunt.*[127] The regrettable fact of a plurality of kings was to a degree compensated for by the unity of faith. The beauty of unity was very apparent to Lucas and his contemporaries, and when the record failed to demonstrate this unity—as in the matter of the survival of Visigothic script—then Lucas adjusted the

[124] See Linehan, 'The synod of Segovia (1166)', *Bulletin of Medieval Canon Law* 10 (Berkeley 1980) pp 31–44. Note also the marked Visigothic content of the Burgo de Osma MS from which the text is derived.
[125] 'El siglo XIII es el gran siglo de la Edad Media, superior al siglo VI, equiparable en muchos conceptos al XVI'—and without the 'paganism' of the latter: Lafuente 4 p 6.
[126] Linehan, *La iglesia española [y el papado en el siglo XIII]* (Salamanca 1975) pp 104 n 81, 204–6.
[127] *Chronicon Mundi,* [ed A. Scottus], *Hispania Illustrata* 4 (Frankfurt 1608) p 113.

record.[128] Glossing Innocent III's *Venerabilem*, the canonist Vincentius Hispanus preached a similar message, in response to the claim to universal authority propounded for the Germans by Johannes Teutonicus, asserting that no such claim could encompass the Spaniards who, while the Germans were losing an empire by their folly, had successfully created one *virtute sua*—the equivalent of that quality of *strenuitas* recently attributed to the king of Portugal.[129]

Now was the time to orchestrate Isidore of Seville. Aggressive self-sufficiency is everywhere apparent. No longer was it a case of bargaining for foreign aid, as at Lisbon in 1147, but rather of rejoicing in the fact that those few foreigners who had come for the Las Navas campaign had found the weather too hot and had defected, leaving to Spaniards the salvation 'not only of Spain but of Rome and indeed of the whole of Europe too' in the words of a contemporary chronicler.[130] Appreciation of national characteristics is one of the many remarkable features of *Planeta*, the diatribe which Diego García, cleric and chancellor of the king of Castile, dedicated to archbishop Rodrigo in 1218. Diego ranges far and wide, from the Galicians and Castilians, notable for their loquaciousness and pugnacity respectively, to the *franci* whose *strenuitas* is remarked upon, the Scots and Irish for their studiousness and tall stories, as far afield as the pious Ethiopians and the charitable Indians.[131] Not that amidst all the euphoria there were not some elements of self-doubt. Indeed, Diego García is particularly remarkable for the magnificent and extravagant denunciation which his prologue contains of the Spanish episcopate and clergy— *quod verecunde assero, hispanus de hispanis*. They are idolators, no less, because they look to mammon rather than to God: a condition

[128] David, *Études historiques* pp 431–9, esp p 437: 'Luc de Tuy a bien vu que l'unité liturgique exigeait l'accord des écritures.' Compare A. M. Mundó, 'La datación de los códices liturgicos visigóticos toledanos', *Hispania Sacra* 18 (1965) pp 1–25, esp pp 20–21; Servatius pp 26–8. See also Linehan, *Spanish Church*, p 63 n 8, for another aspect of the same attitude.
[129] G. Post, 'Vincentius Hispanus and Spanish nationalism' in *Studies in Medieval Legal Thought* (Princeton 1964) pp 482–93. Compare above p 186.
[130] G. Cirot, ed, 'Chronique latine inédite des Rois de Castile (1236)', *Bulletin Hispanique* 14 (Bordeaux 1912) pp 357–8. (The author was almost certainly Bishop Juan of Osma: [D. W.] Lomax, 'The authorship of the *Chronique Latine des Rois de Castile,*' *Bulletin of Hispanic Studies* 40 (1936) pp 205–11). Compare M. Defourneaux, *Les Français en Espagne aux XIe et XIIe siècles* (Paris 1949) pp 182–93; Lomax, 'Rodrigo Jiménez de Rada [como historiador]', *Actas del Quinto Congreso Internacional de Hispanistas (Bordeaux 1974)* Bordeaux 1977) p 591.
[131] *Planeta*, ed M. Alonso (Madrid 1943) p 178.

Religion and national identity in medieval Spain

which the author attributes to a combination of the proximity of 'the gentiles, long-established custom, and papal connivance.'[132]

Book 7 of *Planeta* is entitled *De Pace*, and there Diego expatiates on the themes of *Deus pacis* and *pax vobis*.[133] What distinguished Spanish churchmen, however—lower clergy as well as bishops —was their *un*peaceful demeanour. A century later Alvarus Pelagius—who was in a position to know, being one himself —reminded them that even peninsular bishops were forbidden by canon law to shed blood. Yet his own writings reveal the inconsistency of his own position.[134] The collective experience went too deep. As Diego García was writing, the rural clergy of the diocese of Segovia were hunting their hapless bishop up hill and down dale because he had tried to discipline them; and only recently Innocent III had had to reprimand the bishop of Sigüenza for lashing out with his pastoral staff in his cathedral church and inflicting fatal wounds on one of his congregation.[135] *Presul probus dapsilis, mauris inhumanus* is the admiring description given of one of them in the mid-thirteenth century—and it was not only Moors to whom they show themselves inhuman or by whom they were themselves inhumanly treated. Lafuente's section entitled *asesinatos de varios obispos* refers to deeds done in the twelfth century by their coreligionists.[136]

In this respect then Spanish churchmen were totally identified with the militaristic aspect of the nationalist cause, despite the unease occasionally voiced. It was natural for them, and traditional of them, to regard the new cathedrals being built in the thirteenth century as physical testimony of Christian Spain's resurgence, as did Lucas of Túy, or Jaime I of Aragón in his expression of regret that the bishop of Huesca's see should be in a converted mosque and not in a proper Christian building.[137] In establishing the pre-

---

[132] *Ibid* pp 175–6, 183–93, esp p 185. †
[133] *Ibid* pp 452–7.
[134] Linehan, *Spanish Church*, pp 239–40.
[135] *Ibid* p 240; idem, 'Segovia: a "frontier" diocese in the thirteenth century', *EHR* 96 (1981) pp 482–6.
[136] Ed Catalán and Gil (above n 117) v 75; Lafuente 4 pp 197–9. For further instances see Hillgarth, *The Spanish Kingdoms*, 1 pp 109–11, 2 p 93.
[137] 'Episcopi, abbates et clerus ecclesias et monasteria construunt, et ruricolae absque formidine agros excolunt, animalia nutriunt, et non est qui exterreat eos': *Chronicon Mundi* p 113; R. I. Burns, 'The parish as frontier institution in thirteenth-century Valencia', *Speculum* 37 (1962) p 250. The attitude was deeprooted: Benito Ruano, 'La historiografía' pp 78–9.

Gothic historical past of Hispania, Lucas and Rodrigo figure as whole-hearted collaborators in the patriotic programme which is so marked a characteristic of this century.[138] There is, however, one important reservation to be made.

Lucas, Rodrigo and Diego García all wrote in Latin. It was not they, but the royal chancery and Alfonso X in his historical works who led the way in the establishment of the vernacular.[139] Churchmen were of course involved in the king's chancery and in his circle of translators, and churchmen in their historical works do not lag behind in their *expression* of nationalism—the monastic author of the *Gesta Comitum Barchinonensium*, for example, writing in the early 1300s felt it sufficient to describe Martin IV as *gallicus natione* to account for that pontiff's treatment of Pedro III after the Sicilian Vespers.[140] It was their expression of these sentiments in Latin that is at issue. The vernacular was the language of men of action, the language in which Jaime of Aragon's memoirs were written, thus establishing the tradition which was to last until Italian humanism made its impact.[141] When Pere Marsili came to translate king Jaime's work into Latin in 1314 he shamefacedly described the operation as being for the benefit of *clerici et claustrales*.[142] By then in Castile the change had come, with Jofré de Loiasa writing in Spanish too.[143] But half a century earlier the vernacular *Crónica de la población de Ávila* (1255/6) is an aggressively secular production, in which the local bishop appears only to be threatened with having his head broken for attempting to stop a fight between Christians.[144] In this crucial matter churchmen lagged behind.

[138] Maravall, *El concepto de España* pp 335–6; idem, *Estudios* pp 138, 151.
[139] See Lomax, 'La lengua oficial de Castilla', *Actele celui de-al XII-lea Congres Internaţional de Lingvistică şi Filologie Romanică* (Bucarest 1971) pp 411–17.
[140] *Cròniques Catalanes* 2, ed L. Barrau Dihigo and J. Massó Torrents (Barcelona 1925) p 77. Elsewhere he characterizes the *gallici*: 'ad vinum insuper anhelebant, in quo continue consueverant balneari'; attributes the victory of Las Navas de Tolosa to king Pedro II; and chides the *aragoneses* for failing to come to Pedro III's assistance against the *gallicos* (pp 87, 52, 90).
[141] Sánchez Alonso, 1 pp 235–45; R. B. Tate, 'Nebrija the historian', *Bulletin of Hispanic Studies* 34 (1957) p 144.
[142] Massó Torrents pp 517–19. The Latin text of pope Nicholas III's charges against Alfonso X in 1279 were translated into Spanish 'por que sopiessemos meior guardar al Rey e tractar en la corte algunas cosas a su servicio': Linehan, 'Spanish church revisited' p 141.
[143] Only the Latin translation of his chronicle has survived, ed. A. Morel-Fatio, 'Chronique des Rois de Castille (1248–1305)', *BEC* 59 (1898) pp 325–78.
[144] *Crónica de la población de Ávila*, ed A. Hernández Segura (Valencia 1966) p 31.

Religion and national identity in medieval Spain

At the same time it becomes possible to observe, as never before, churchmen gingerly parting company from the king and seeking to distinguish their best interests from those of the nation in so far as these were personified by the king. Whether the reasons for this distancing were primarily conscientious or primarily economic, or in individual cases were related to a shift in the balance of conscientious and economic considerations—as so eloquently (because so ingenuously) expressed by Alvarus Pelagius—it is striking that in the case of Castile these developments should have occurred so soon after all the heady euphoria of the 1230s and 1240s. The forty years after 1243 were critical. In that year Rodrigo of Toledo completed the *Historia Gothica*. Here was enshrined the neo-Gothic myth. An official history—the last such indeed prior to the assumption of the historicising function by the king himself —written at Fernando III's behest, it exclusively identified Fernando's Christian subjects with the Visigoths, the people who had once won and had then re-won Spain, and relegated those others who had had a hand in its history—Romans, Ostrogoths, Huns, Vandals etc and Arabs—to a series of appendices.[145] Yet Rodrigo's 'fundamental loyalty', it has been suggested, was not to the king or his kingdoms, the people or the nations, but to Toledo—*urbs regia* —and above all to the church of Toledo.[146] A generation later, after a number of false starts, Castilian churchmen came out into the open. In 1279 the bishops represented themselves to the pope as helpless victims of an infidel despot. Churches and churchmen had been subjected to wholesale persecution. Their income and property was at the king's mercy. They were forbidden to assemble together or to have contact with Rome. The pilgrimage to Santiago had been seriously disrupted by the king's vendetta against the archbishop of Compostela. Because the king preferred Jews to Christians the latter sought to curry favour with the former and allowed themselves to be corrupted by Jewish rites and traditions. King Alfonso himself was held in thrall by a naturalistic atheistic

Compare above n 119. For earlier, minor annalistic writings in Spanish see Sánchez Alonso, 1 pp 145–9; A. D. Deyermond, *A Literary History of Spain. The Middle Ages* (London New York 1971) pp 85–6.
[145] *De Rebus Hispaniae*, praefatio auctoris, ed Lorenzana pp 1–4; Sánchez Alonso, 1, pp 131–7.
[146] Lomax, 'Rodrigo Jiménez de Rada' pp 588–90.

philosophy, and surrounded by astronomers, augurers and sooth-sayers. *Claves ecclesie contempnantur.*[147]

It would be tempting, even it were not altogether too neat, to accept these charges on trust and to treat the episcopal *démarche*, together with episcopal involvement in the rebellion of the Infante Sancho against Alfonso X three years later, as marking the end of an era. But this was not so. Churchmen were soon whipped back into line by Sancho IV, and back into a posture of dutiful acquiescence to the royal will, so that when an era *did* end—when the kings of Aragón and Castile put an end in the next century to that peculiar institution, the practice of dating according to the *era hispanica* which went back to Hidacius—churchmen obediently executed the royal decrees of abolition.[148] But I must now end, by reviewing very summarily the most prominent of the fourteenth- and fifteenth-century themes which have a bearing on the subject and ought properly to receive fullscale treatment.

In 1390 the Cortes of Madrid ritualistically complained that no nation was more put upon by the papacy in the matter of provision of foreign clerics,[149] and in the following year the pogrom at Seville ushered in a period of Spanish history which it would be positively indecent to attempt to analyse in a hurry. How are we to interpret the fact that events there were incited by the archdeacon of Éjica, Ferrán Martínez? As the culmination of anti-Semitic tendencies which had been apparent for at least a century?[150] What fuelled the movement—racial hatred and political considerations, or religious zeal?[151] Should we suspect the existence of nationalistic sentiments? Hillgarth concedes that '1391 was a considerable step towards the

[147] Linehan, *Spanish Church*, cap 8; idem, 'Spanish Church revisited', pp 141–7.

[148] J. Villanueva, *Viage literario a las iglesias de España* 20 vols (Madrid 1803–52) 20 pp 3, 175–6; Lafuente 4 pp 384–5. Compare Benito Ruano, 'La historiografía' p 70.

[149] Sánchez-Albornoz, *España: un enigma histórico* 1 p 356; Hillgarth, *The Spanish Kingdoms* 2 p 92; Linehan, *Spanish Church* p 185.

[150] P. Wolff, 'The 1391 pogrom in Spain. Social crisis or not?', *PP* 50 (1971) pp 4–18, esp pp 8–10, 12, 16. For signs of these tendencies in 1279 and 1313 see Linehan, 'Spanish Church revisited' pp 135–6, 140. Note that in 1278 the standard text of anti-Jewish polemic, Raymundus Martini's *Pugio Fidei*, had been completed —compare I. Willi-Plein and T. Willi, *Glaubensdolch und Messiasbeweis. Die Begegnung von Judentum, Christentum and Islam im 13. Jahrhundert in Spanien* (Neukirchen 1980). For Rodrigo of Toledo's relationship with Jews see H. Grassoti, 'Don Rodrigo Ximénez de Rada, gran señor y hombre de negocios en la Castilla del siglo XIII', *CHE* 57–8 (1973) p 91.

[151] See B. Netanyahu, *The Marranos of Spain from the late XIVth to the early XVIth century according to contemporary sources* (2 ed New York 1973).

Religion and national identity in medieval Spain

spiritual "unification" of Spain', but though he adduces evidence of Catalan patriotism, Portuguese patriotism and Aragonese patriotism, he is no more willing to admit of the reality of Spanish nationalism in the fifteenth century than in the seventh.[152] In the course of making the case for the precedence of the Castilian delegation over the English at the council of Basle in 1434, the bishop of Burgos Alfonso de Cartagena stated that the king of Castile-León was *el principal e primero* of the peninsular monarchs. Because the critical acumen which Alfonso displayed in exploding the myth of the journey of Joseph of Arimathea to England was not applied to the legend of Saint James's to Spain, and despite the awkwardness involved in glossing over the murky passage of his country's Arian past, he succeeded in securing his primary objective on that occasion.[153] But what mattered more at a time when Castile was vying with Portugal for a title to the Canary Islands was his identification of the king of Castile as *rex Hispaniae*—though the objection may be made that this was an expression of a purely factitious nationalism equivalent to the nationalism of the national church for which 'royalism would be a more accurate term'.[154] Even more significant—apart from the threat to royal government in general which conciliarism represented—were the contemporary canonistic debates on the question of the possession of *dominium* by the natives of the Canaries (an enquiry potentially applicable to the case of the peninsular Moors), and—this not least—the failure of the Castilian attempt to nullify by amendment (*salvis remanentibus institutis et legibus regalibus*) the effect of the conciliar decree against clerical concubinage.[155] It would beg altogether too many questions to consider here whether it also mattered that the bishop of Burgos was of *converso* stock and the son of a former rabbi.[156]

---

[152] *The Spanish Kingdoms* 2 pp 141, 197–205.

[153] *Prosistas castellanos del siglo XV*, 1, ed M. Penna *BAE* 116 (Madrid 1959) pp 205–33, esp 210, 225–6, 229. See R. B. Tate, 'The *Anacephaleosis* of Alfonso García de Santa María, bishop of Burgos, 1435–1456', in *Hispanic Studies in honour of I. González Llubera* ed F. Pierce (Oxford 1959) pp 391–3; L. Suárez Fernández, *Castilla, el Cisma y la crisis conciliar (1378–1440)* (Madrid 1960) pp 115–20.

[154] Maravall, *El concepto de España* pp 324–5; Hillgarth, *The Spanish Kingdoms* 2 pp 395–6. Compare T. de Azcona, *La elección y reforma del episcopado español en tiempo de los Reyes Católicos* (Madrid 1960) esp chapter 12.

[155] A. J. Black, *Monarchy and Community: Political Ideas in the Later Conciliar Controversy 1430–1450* (Cambridge 1970) p 88; J. Muldoon, *Popes, Lawyers and Infidels. The Church and the Non-Christian World. 1250–1550* (Liverpool 1979) pp 120–130; Linehan, *Spanish Church* p 326.

[156] L. Serrano, *Los conversos D. Pablo de Santa María y D. Alfonso de Cartagena, obispos*

I

It is today still possible to make national catholicism (if not too
carefully defined) appear the formative influence in the history of
medieval Spain, to represent its society as being permanently
affected by the attitudes of the eleventh-century papal reformers:
Gregorianism without papalism, indeed, to match patriotism without nationalism.[157] Yet the abiding impression is one of churchmen
under the king's control and a church 'enclosed within itself', in
Lacarra's phrase.[158] From the seventh century to the twentieth a
continuing theme can be perceived which is more enduring than
any of the components mythical and real of which it is formed.
Historians may debate whether the period can be properly
described as 'the age of Reconquest'[159], but there can be no doubt
that when Cuba was lost in 1898 the bishop of Segovia called for a
crusade against the United States.[160] Only the language was un-
mistakably twentieth-century when Primo de Rivera in 1926
threatened to send the papal nuncio packing and to proceed to the
establishment of a national church if Rome would not cooperate in
the removal of a prelate suspected of being a Catalan nationalist; the
sentiments were those of Reccared.[161] What was remarkable about
cardinal Segura's pastoral letter five years later in May 1931 was not
the fond belief that the now fallen monarchy had as a rule respected
the rights of the church, nor the accompanying evocation of
Toledo's Visigothic councils, but its outspokenness at a time when,
as that authentically Gregorian prelate admitted, there could be no
question of his being rewarded for his pains.[162] The criteria of most

---

de Burgos, gobernantes, diplomáticos y escritores (Madrid 1942) esp pp 133–48.
Compare Castro, *The Spaniards* pp 188 n 30, 353, where (n 59) the bishop of
Burgos is made the author of *España en su historia!*

[157] V. Cantarino, *Entre monjes ỳ musulmanes. El conflicto que fue España* (Madrid 1978)
esp pp 121–2, 293–305.

[158] Above n 85.

[159] Barbero and Vigil, *La formación* p 235, and above p 167. Castro's objection to the
term was on different grounds. 'Let us imagine as a fantastic case', he suggested in
Structure of Spanish History p 376, 'that after a few centuries the Mexicans should
succeed in retaking California—Los Angeles and San Francisco—and let us ask
ourselves if this would be a reconquest. The retaking of Toledo, Cordova, Sevilla
and Granada must be thought of in the same way.' This passage was suppressed
in *The Spaniards*—wisely perhaps. Compare above n 114.

[160] L. de Granjel, *Panorama de la Generación de 98* (Madrid 1959) p 180.

[161] R. Muntanyola, *Vidal i Barraquer, El cardenal de la paz* (Barcelona 1971) p 146.

[162] J. Requejo San Román, *El Cardenal Segura* (2 ed Madrid 1932) p 139; R. Garriga[,
El Cardenal Segura y el nacional-catolicismo] (Barcelona 1977) pp 157–8.

Religion and national identity in medieval Spain

of his episcopal colleagues—though not his[163]—proved to be different when the civil war came, and, after it, the ecclesiastical historians weighed in with some serviceable history. It is not least for that reason that historians must probe these intricate matters with discretion and delicacy. For they are operating on live tissue.

University of Cambridge
St John's College

[163] Garriga pp 251–348.

II

The synod of Segovia (1166)*

In his *Historia de la insigne ciudad de Segovia* (1637), Diego de Colmenares made known a chance reference to an ecclesiastical assembly—a provincial council, he surmised, held at Segovia on the first Sunday of Lent (13 March) 1166, in the course of which a longstanding jurisdictional dispute involving the bishops of Segovia and Palencia received an airing. A second adventitious notice concerning the settlement of a case involving the bishop of Osma and the abbot of San Millán de la Cogolla 'in Concilio Segoviensi . . . in era MCCIV' has passed unobserved by historians of medieval councils and synods, and it has further been assumed that the *acta* of the Segovia assembly are lost.[1] The relevance of item 12 in Rojo Orcajo's description, published in 1929, of MS 8 of the cathedral library of Burgo de Osma, has not been appreciated. Item 12 ('excerpta ex synodo secoviensi') is there noted as treating of 'homenaje debido al Rey; de testimoniales, de prohibición de guerrear y de servir los sarracenos. Sínodo celebrado en Segovia por Juan, primado de las Españas y por todos los Obispos del reino de nuestro Señor Alfonso'.[2]

Rojo's description of MS 8 in inadequate. With regard to its text of Ivo of Chartres' *Panormia*, no mention is made of the substantial interpolation (fols. 105v-108r) not found in the admittedly defective edition of that work.[3] The identification of the fragmentary canonical collection (fols. 162v-182v) as part of the *Polycarpus* must be rejected. Rather it is an independent reworking of material from the collection of Burchard of Worms or Ivo himself (probably the latter), containing at least one item not found in either of the known recen-

---

* The author is grateful to John Crook, Antonio García and Walter Ullmann for their advice and assistance.

[1] D. de Colmenares, *Historia*, nueva ed. anotada (Segovia 1969) I 290-91; J. Loperráez Corvalán, *Descripción histórica del obispado de Osma* (Madrid 1788; repr. Madrid 1978) 137-40, III 558-9. Cf. G. Martínez Díez, 'Concilios españoles anteriores a Trento', *Repertorio de historia de las ciencias eclesiásticas en España* 5 (Salamanca 1976) 323. This is item 16 in appendix I below.

[2] T. Rojo Orcajo, 'Catálogo descriptivo de los códices que se conservan en la S. I. Catedral de Burgo de Osma', *Boletín de la R. Academia de la Historia* 94 (1929) 714.

[3] See below, 40. The deficiencies of the ed. repr. in PL 161 are exposed by J. Rambaud-Buhot, 'Les sommaires de la *Panormie* et l'édition de Melchior de Vosmédian', *Traditio* 23 (1967) 435-36; C. Munier, 'Pour une édition de la *Panormie* d'Ive de Chartres', *Revue des sciences religieuses* 44 (1970) 161.

32

sions of *Polycarpus*,[4] and apparently identical with the collection in Sigüenza Cathedral MS 5: a *Panormia* with the very same cluster of texts as occurs here.[5] Rojo Orcajo ascribed the manuscript to the thirteenth century,[6] although the hand of fols. 2v-192v looks mid- to late-twelfth, and he failed to identify or even to mention a number of the shorter items which it contains. But his account of item 12 is substantially correct. The appropriateness of its location in a manuscript the compilers of which exhibit concern for the liberties of churchmen and for the ecclesiastical primacy of the church of Toledo in particular, and a secondary interest in sacramental and liturgical matters, is considered in the the following paragraphs.

A double threat — to the liberties of churchmen and primacy of the church of Toledo — provided the setting for the Segovia synod of 1166. In that year the prospects for Castilian churchmen, as for Castilians generally, and for the rights of Toledo were distinctly unpropitious. King Sancho III had died in 1158 leaving

---

[4] Rojo Orcajo, 'Catálogo' 711 (whence Fournier-Le Bras, *Collections canoniques* 169 n. 5). Fols. 167v-8r and 177r-182r reproduce the sequence of canons *De homicidio* from lib. VI of Burchard's *Decretum* [PL 140.763-78] complete except for c.3-4, 6, 13, 20, 40-41, 43-5, or from Ivo's *Decretum*, X 130-76 [PL 161.730-42]. Other topics mentioned, in no discernible order, include simony, usury, 'De clericis monasterium appetentibus' (fol. 182v) [= Anselm of Lucca, *Collectio canonum* VII 169 (ed. Thaner, 432)], custody of vestments etc, excommunication, 'De accusatoribus', and correspond neither to Burchard/Ivo nor to the rubrics of *Polycarpus* publ. in A. Theiner, *Disquisitiones criticae in praecipuas canonum seu decretalium collectiones* (Rome 1836) 341-43. At fols. 180v-181r are the canons of Gregory VII's Roman Council of Nov. 1083 [JL 5299, 5260; Pflugk-Harttung II 125-7, no. 161], found in the MSS of neither of the recensions of *Polycarpus* studied by P. Fournier, 'Les deux recensions de la collection canonique romaine dite le *Polycarpus*', *Mélanges d'archéologie et d'histoire* 37 (1918-19) 71, 80ff. Cf. J. Gilchrist, 'The reception of Pope Gregory VII into canon law (1073-1141)', ZRG Kan. Abt. 59 (1973) 46. The contents of the canonical collection in MS 8 can now be checked against the material presented by U. Horst, *Die Kanonessammlung Polycarpus des Gregor von S. Grisogono*: Quellen und Tendenzen (Munich 1980) 103-269.

[5] A. García y García ,'Manuscritos jurídicos medievales de la Catedral de Sigüenza', *Xenia Medii Aevi historiam illustrantia oblata T. Kaeppeli O.P.* edd. R. Creytens and P. Künzle (Rome 1978) 39-40; MS 8 ends as MS 5 (PL 161.1338D) and has the same marginal note ('Ab hoc loco . . . decretis') at fol. 105v. The same collection (which is being studied by Prof. Fransen) occurs in Sigüenza MS 75 (García 48). For the cluster of texts see G. Fransen, 'Varia ex manuscriptis', *Traditio* 21 (1965) 517. The apparently close identity of the Sigüenza and Osma texts may suggest that MS 8 was subsequently brought to Osma from Sigüenza. If so, Bishop Pedro García of Osma (d. 1474) may have been responsible: see J. Frías Balsa, 'Don Pedro García Huete, arcediano de Sigüenza y obispo de Osma', *Wad-Al-Hayara* 5 (1978) 315-25.

[6] Rojo Orcajo, 'Catálogo' 710. But he is probably correct in suggesting (p. 711) that the *Catalogus romanorum pontificum* (with lengths of pontificates from Peter to Celestine II, thereafter with names only until 'Adrianus natione anglicus sed <it> a<nnos>') indicates 'de que entonces se escribía, o que allí terminaba el Códice del cual se tomaban los datos'. (The list is not in two hands, as Rojo implies).

the throne of Castile to his two-year old son Alfonso VIII. All the problems of a twelfth-century regency had ensued, fomented by Alfonso's uncle, Fernando II of León, and by the noble Castilian houses of Castro and Lara. From the south the Almohad forces threatened. The city of Toledo was controlled by Fernando Rodríguez de Castro acting for the king of León.[7] During the previous ten years Archbishop Juan of Toledo had secured rulings from two popes, Adrian IV and Alexander III, confirming Toledo's primatial authority over the church of Compostela.[8] Now, despite the temporary discomfiture of Martín of Compostela, who had been driven into exile by Fernando II and was thus prevented from pressing his advantage,[9] there was every prospect of the rights of Toledo, so recently secured by the efforts of Alfonso VII, suffering irreparable damage during the minority of his grandson, quite apart from whatever else might befall both Toledo and Castile at the hands of the Leonese and Almohads combined.[10]

We can only guess at the role played by the Castilian bishops during these difficult years: our sources — Rodrigo Ximémez de Rada and the author of the anonymous Latin chronicle, both writing in the following century — are silent on the subject. The presence of Archbishop Juan and four of his suffragans at the Leonese court in the spring of 1164 has been noted by Julio González,[11] but it is unlikely that they carried much weight there with a king who treated his own bishops with such scant respect.[12] Two years later at Segovia — where Juan was among friends — they seized the initiative, as the *acta* of their council reveal.[13]

---

[7] 'Crescentibus malis, usque adeo res processit, ut Regi Legionensi fere totius regni, et etiam Toleti per duodecim annos solverentur reditus et tributa': Rodrigo Ximénez de Rada, *De rebus Hispaniae*, VII 16 (ed. Lorenzana, *PP. Toletanorum quotquot extant Opera* [Madrid 1793; repr. Valencia 1968] 160b). 'Duodecim annos' cannot be correct: Sancho III died in August 1158. For the events of these years see J. González, *El reino de Castilla en la época de Alfonso VIII* (Madrid 1960) I 150ff.

[8] J. F. Rivera Recio, *La iglesia de Toledo en el siglo XII (1086-1208)* (Rome 1966) 342ff. Juan was archbishop of Toledo by September 1152: B. F. Reilly, 'On getting to be a bishop in León-Castile: The "Emperor" Alfonso VII and the post-Gregorian Church', *Studies in medieval and renaissance history*, n.s. 1 (1978) 65 n. 117.

[9] Rivera 374-75; R. A. Fletcher, 'Regalian right in twelfth-century Spain: The case of Archbishop Martín of Santiago de Compostella', JEH 28 (1977) 353-55.

[10] Rivera 344 n. 82; *Chronica Adefonsi Imperatoris*, c. 158 (ed. L. Sánchez Belda [Madrid 1950] 122-23).

[11] *El reino de Castilla* 168; idem, *Regesta de Fernando II* (Madrid 1943) 379-80. The silence of the anonymous Latin chronicle (completed between 1236 and 1239) is notable in view of D. W. Lomax's plausible identification of its author as Juan Díaz, bishop of Osma during those years: 'The authorship of the *Chronique latine des Rois de Castile*', *Bulletin of Hispanic studies* 40 (1963) 205-11.

[12] Fletcher, 'Regalian right' 358; idem, *The Episcopate in the Kingdom of León in the twelfth century* (Oxford 1978) 80-83.

[13] He was bishop of Segovia before his translation to Toledo and was possibly a native of the place: Colmenares, op. cit. 274-77; Rivera, *La iglesia de Toledo* 199.

The legislation of the Segovia council was of that mixed type which has occasioned so much debate about the nature of such assemblies, whether they should be regarded as church councils proper, as secular *cortes*, or as indefinable hybrid assemblies.[14] Formally, however, the meeting of March 1166 was an authentic ecclesiastical council; the sanctions that it invoked were excommunication, interdict and anathema (Indeed what *secular* sanctions could have been invoked in the circumstances?). But if the bishops of 1166 are to be regarded as the peninsular protagonists of *pax Dei* and *treuga Dei*, it must equally be observed that they described themselves not as suffragans of Toledo — however large the affairs of that church may have loomed in the minds of some of them — but as 'bishops of the kingdom of King Alfonso'.[15] The well-being of all their churches could only be secured in the shadow of a secular settlement, and it was this consideration that was to the fore. Despite Juan's attendance with two of his suffragans at the Council of Tours three years before,[16] and notwithstanding their expression of concern for *exaltatio domini pape*, the echo of recent papal legislation in the bishops' provisions is all but inaudible. Juan and his colleagues looked further back, to the Visigothic councils, employing the terminology of those assemblies (*conventus, decretum*), and reflecting perhaps on the happier conditions in which their predecessors had met five hundred years before.

For the history of Spanish feudalism cc. I-III are of special interest. The requirement (I.) 'ut quicumque honorem infra regnum regis Aldefonsi tenet sit eius uasallus et faciat ei hominium per se uel per alium usque ad octabas proxime Pasche [1 May 1166] uel dimittat ei honorem suum' was unprecedented. Never before, so far as is known, had the feudal obligations of holders of honours on a

---

[14] J. Maldonado y Fernández del Toro, 'Las relaciones entre el derecho canónico y el derecho secular en los concilios espanoles del siglo xı', AHDE 14 (1942-3) 227-381, esp. pp. 302ff, 318; A. García y García, 'Los concilios particulares en la Edad Media', *El Concilio de Braga y la función de la legislación particular en la Iglesia* (Braga 1975) 140-41, citing earlier literature.

[15] Cf. García y García, 'Los concilios', 174-75 (*pax Dei, treuga Dei*); and the texts of the Councils of Palencia, 1129: 'ego Raymundus Toletanus (*sic*) sedis archiepiscopus . . . una cum pontificibus quorum nomina scripta esse videntur', and Valladolid, 1143: 'residentibus R. Toletano et Petro Compostellano archiepiscopis eorumque suffraganeis P. Palentino' etc. in J. Tejada y Ramiro, *Colección de cánones y de todos los concilios de la Iglesia de España y de América* III (Madrid 1861) 257; C. Erdmann, *Papsturkunden in Portugal* (Berlin 1927) 199. Which of the bishops were present is not stated. However, a charter of Alfonso, dated Segovia 'in mense Marcii' 1166, was witnessed by Archbishop Juan, Pedro of Burgos, Raimundo of Palencia, Cerebrun of Sigüenza, Guillelmo of Segovia, Sancho of Ávila, Rodrigo of Calahorra and Juan of Osma (González, *El reino de Castilla* 133-34; cf. Loperráez, *Descripción histórica* III 559).

[16] R. Somerville, *Pope Alexander III and the Council of Tours (1163)* (Berkeley-London 1977) 28.

national scale been thus unequivocally stipulated.[17] Moreover, the effect of such an intervention was to override the instructions given on his deathbed by Sancho III, to the effect that the magnates should retain the feudal possessions which they held of him until Alfonso reached his fifteenth year (November 1169) — instructions which were taken at face value by interested parties in the 1160s.[18] In the enforcing of these measures the bishops seem to have regarded the authority of king and primate as equivalent and coterminous ('et nemini liceat eum uel terram eius absoluere sine consensu regis uel domini primatis'). It was not thought necessary or appropirate to mention the authority of Rome.

Of hardly less moment was the provision for a general call to arms in the event of an invasion of Castile, a call which was regalian in nature rather than feudal, addressed not just to the king's vassals but to 'omnes regni sui' whom the king might summon (c. II).[19] And since (as is implicit in c. III) they regarded the kingdom as threatened as much by Christian enemies as by the infidel, the promise of remission of 'tantum de injuncta sibi penitentia . . . quantum si Iherosolimam uisitaret' to whoever should volunteer his services in such circumstances, would seem to constitute the earliest known instance in Europe of the appropriation of crusading indulgences to the domestic scene, and the first stirrings of the 'political crusade'.[20] Similar disregard for the rules of canon law is envinced by the prohi-

---

[17] Cf. H. Grassotti, *Las instituciones feudo-vasalláticas en León y Castilla* (Spoleto 1969) 202-05, 121, 760, 961. Rodrigo of Toledo asserts (*De rebus Hispaniae* VII 16) that 'comes Amalricus [Manrique de Lara, the young king's guardian] ad tantae necessitatis articulum fuit ductus ut Regi Legionensi facere hominium cogeretur de dando Rege puero in vasallum' [ed. Lorenzana 160b-161a], and is our only source for the story of Alfonso's supporters insisting on keeping their promise to maintain his freedom and of the tearful child being spirited away from Soria, where the ceremony was to have been performed, hidden beneath the cloak of a loyal knight (?summer 1163). González doubts this account ('El punto del vasalaje y el de la promesa son algo fuertes de creer y no han dejado huella fidedigna', *El reino de Castilla* I 163-4 n. 102).

[18] The provision clearly caused difficulties for the regents, although the story told by Rodrigo of Toledo (VII 16) of the disinterment of the corpse of Gutierre Fernández de Castro, on the orders of Manrique de Lara, on account of his nephews' treasonable refusal to surrender family lands, is possibly apocryphal. The basis of the nephews' defense, however — 'responderunt se testamentali edicto regis Sancii terram sibi creditam usque ad annos quindecim retinere et tunc parati erant terram restituere regi suo' [ed. Lorenzana, 160b; González, *El reino de Castilla* I 172 n. 132] — underlines the significance of c.I.

[19] For this terminology cf. T. N. Bisson, 'The problem of feudal monarchy: Aragon, Catalonia and France', *Speculum* 53 (1978) 467-69.

[20] The Jerusalem indulgence had been extended to those fighting the peninsular Saracens by c.1 of the Council of Valladolid, 1155, ed. C. Erdmann, *Das Papsttum und Portugal im ersten Jahrh. der portugiesischen Geschichte* (Berlin 1928) 55, but here no restriction to non-Christians is specified. Cf. J. A. Brundage, *Medieval canon law and the crusader* (Madison-London 1969) 153-54; E.-D. Hehl, *Kirche und Krieg im 12. Jahrhundert*: Studien zu kanonischem Recht und politischer Wirklichkeit (Stuttgart 1980) 86-87, 141, 118, citing Peter the

bition of Christian service to the Saracen cause 'unless approved by the king' (cc. XI, XVII).[21]

In comparison with these provisions (of the effectiveness of which absolutely nothing is known), those relating to clerical matters comprise a relatively commonplace collection, artlessly compiled and unremarkable as to content, concerning lay excesses, diocesan and parochial integrity, clerical discipline and usury, culled from I and II Lateran, the Council of Tours (?), and from Gratian or, more likely, Gratian's sources. In c. IV the possibility of interdict imposed by the primate is introduced into the received canonical text, nicely balanced by a gratuitous reference to the authority of Rome.[22] Cattle-rustling was perhaps a peculiar hazard in contemporary Castile (c. VII).[23]

Yet despite the lesser interest to the historian of these canons it is probable that it was to these, containing as they do references to decrees of the Valladolid councils of 1143 and 1155 and other echoes of papal legislation,[24] rather than to cc. I-III that the late twelfth-century copyists (or abridgers) of MS 8 attached the greater importance.[25] Immediately following the conciliar *acta* two different hands have added the texts of two well-known papal letters (fols. 197v-199r) which related to matters treated at Segovia (cc. XV, XVI) — Leo's *Relatum est nobis* concerning payments due to their parishes from monastic recruits, and Adrian IV's *Nobis in*

Venerable, ep. 172: 'Non est, non est, vere minus defendendus consiliis, immo gladiis vestris, Christianus vim iniuste patiens a Christiano, quam esset defendendus eundem vim patiens a pagano' (*c.* 1150).

[21] The prohibition anticipates part of Conc. Lateranense III, c.26 (COD 223-4): X 5.6.5.

[22] See ed. below, n. 1. The possibility that papal interests were represented at Segovia should not however be excluded. The papal subdeacon 'P.' was present (Loperráez, loc. cit.) — doubtless the same P(etrus) whom Alexander III had sent 'ad partes illas' in December 1162 to summon the Aragonese prelates to Tours: P. Kehr, *Papsturkunden in Spanien*, I.2 (Berlin 1926) 381-82; R. Elze, 'Die päpstliche Kapelle im 12. und 13. Jahrhundert', ZRG Kan. Abt. 36 (1950) 162 n. 93.

[23] Cf. E. S. Procter, *Curia and Cortes in León and Castile 1072-1295* (Cambridge 1980) 23-24, 32, and references there cited.

[24] Noted in ed. below. The *acta* of Valladolid 1143 and 1155 are ed. in Erdmann, *Papsturkunden* 199-203, and *Das Papsttum* 55-58 respectively. Archbishop Juan and at least three of the bishops who may have been present in 1166 — those of Palencia, Calahorra and Osma — had attended the 1155 council. On the matter of papal influence, the treatment by R. Bidagor, *La 'iglesia propria' en España*: Estudio histórico-canónico (Rome 1933) 137-40, requires revision.

[25] The possibility that the original Segovia decrees were more extensive is suggested by the truncated appearance of what is preserved in MS 8. The laconic anonymity of the *praefatio* is especially striking when compared with the *acta* of Valladolid 1155 (Erdmann, *Das Papsttum* 55).

eminenti on the related theme of monastic payment of tithes.[26] Then on fols. 200v-201r, separated inconsequentially from the foregoing by the list of the contents of the *arca* of Oviedo, yet another hand has set down four *iudicia* which may be taken as representing something of what the churchmen had secured by the survival and triumph of Alfonso VIII. The first of these recalled the palmy days of Alfonso VII's reign, with the emperor defining for the benefit of Bishop Pedro, Juan's predecessor in the see of Segovia, those areas of ecclesiastical competence which the absence of a strong monarch put at such grave risk.[27] The second recorded the fate of those miscreants who had dishonored Archbishop Juan at Soria;[28] the third a similarly decisive royal judgment in favor of Bishop Pedro of Sigüenza against the inhabitants of Medinaceli (the scene of recurrent assaults

---

[26] See Appendix I, nos. 17, 18. On the latter cf. G. Constable, *Monastic tithes from their origins to the twelfth century* (Cambridge 1964) 280. For the topicality of the issue in the 1160s see Loperráez, *Descripción histórica* I 137-40; J. A. García de Cortazar y Ruiz de Aguirre, *El dominio del monasterio de San Millán de la Cogolla (siglos X a XIII)* (Salamanca 1969) esp. 315-16; *idem, La época medieval* (Historia de España Alfaguara 2; Madrid 1973) 349-51.

[27] 'Hoc est judicium quod judicauit dominus imperator apud Secoviam cum domino R. archiepiscopo Toletano et domino P. Palentino episcopo et domino B. Seguntino et E. [MS: S.] Abulensi et aliis multis nobilibus terre inter episcopum Secoviensem P. et populum civitatis. Quod de omnibus illis que ad ecclesiam pertinent scilicet de ecclesia uiolata uel de cimiterio deconuersato (?), de clerico uerberato, de omni sacrilegio, de decimis et primitiis, de ornamentis ecclesie, de oblationibus mortuorum et de hereditatibus quas ecclesia possidet uel possedit et per aliquam inuasionem amissa, et omnibus huiusmodi ad ecclesiam pertinentibus, dentur fideiussores episcopo uel archidiacono, et ecclesiastico iudicio in presentia episcopi determinentur. De debitis seu de hereditatibus quas ecclesia non tenet nec tenuit et de omnibus eiusmodi ad ecclesiam non pertinentibus, ad iudices secundum consuetudinem ciuitatis deferantur [MS : deferatur], et si alteri eorum non placuerit eorum iudicium ad imperatorem deferatur et eius iudicio terminetur. Imperator etiam iudicauit et mandauit quod clericus qui nullam habet possessionem preter ecclesiam non seruiat regi siue alicui principi nisi solo episcopo suo uel eius uicario' (fol. 200v) [1137 × 1152]. For the subsequent stormy history of the secular and ecclesiastical authorities of the region see my article 'Segovia: A "frontier" diocese in the thirteenth century', EHR (forthcoming).

[28] ' Iterum equidem apud Pinnamfidelem [Peñafiel] astante rege Sanctio et domino Gotierre et Garsie Garciez et Didago Fernandez de Boniel, Burgense merino, Martin Corrigia, multis etiam probis militibus et Secouie ciuibus ibi conuenientibus atque in presentia domini J. Toletani archiepiscopi et domini J. Oxomensis episcopi et domini Raimundi Palentini episcopi atque M. abbatis Sancti Domini (*sic*), Martini etiam Sancti Petri de Cardenia abbatis, Toletanis quoque et Secouiensibus archidiaconis et quamplurimis probis clericis ibidem astantibus, iudicauit dominus imperator quod illi qui inhonorauerant dominum archiepiscopum Toletanum apud Soriam .vi. m. solidos illius monete regionis persoluerent. Quod si minime complere potuissent cum omni possessione sua et omnibus hereditatibus suis in manibus archiepiscopi deuenirent' (fol. 200v) [1152 × 1155].

on churches and churchmen during the later twelfth century)[29]; and the fourth the restoration of ecclesiastical security in September 1170, a year after Alfonso VIII had assumed control of his kingdom, with the young king looking on as Archbishop Cerebrun — his *patrinus*, as he had described him in October 1166 — recalled the Medinaceli judgment and invoked the precedent of Alfonso VII, *piissimus imperator.*[30]

---

[29] 'Hoc est iudicium quod iudicauit dominus A. imperator in Sancto Stephano [San Esteban de Gormaz] inter dominum P. Seguntinum episcopum et uiros de Medina Chelim. Querebatur episcopus Seguntinus quod barones de Medina exhonorauerunt eum dirumpendo palatium suum se presente et equitaturas suas inde uiolenter abstrahendo. Querebatur etiam quod concilium de Medina assultum fecerant in ciuitatem suam et in aldeias suas et dirumperant domos et uiolenter abduxerunt boues, rapuerant suppellectilia et *ganado*'; all of which was denied by 'uiri de Medina'. 'Super hoc iudicauit imperator in arbitrio esse episcopi ut eligeret iudicium unum de duobus, scilicet quod eligeret episcopus XII. uiros de toto concilio de Medina qui iurarent sibi quod neque concilium de Medina neque uiri a concilio missi fecerant ea de quibus querebatur episcopus, uel daret episcopus duos quoslibet de canonicis suis excepto priore qui iurarent in manu episcopi sui quod concilium et homines de Medina fecerant omnia hec, et tunc concilium de Medina pro diruptione palatii et exhonoratione episcopi persoluerent episcopo .D. solidos monete ipsius regionis, et pro diruptione uniusquisque domus ciuitatis siue aldearum persoluerent eidem .CCC. solidos et quod omnes boues dupplatos restituerent dominis suis et cum singulis pectum .LX. solidorum, suppellectilia etiam et *ganado* dupplata restituerent' (fols. 200v-201r) [1152 × 1155]. During the period in which the Segovia synod met (1165-6) the church of San Nicolás at Medinaceli was set on fire, and three hundred men within perished. (González, *El reino de Castilla* I 171 n. 130). For subsequent events there, see T. Minguella y Arnedo, *Historia de la diocesis de Sigüenza y de sus obispos* I (Madrid 1910) 179ff.

[30] 'Hoc est iudicium quod iudicauit dominus C. Toletanus archiepiscopus et Yspaniarum primas in pleno concilio Oxome, presente A. illustri Yspaniarum rege et procurante assensu, presentibus etiam comite P. et Martino Gonzaluez et Petro Martino de Chouas aliisque multis nobilibus uiris iudicium archiepiscopi confirmantibus. Conquesti sunt G. sacrista et A. quod quidam homines de Oxoma contra illos commoti eos insecuti fuerant sic insequendo eos inhonorantes. Quibus hec negantibus iudicauit archiepiscopus quatinus predicti canonici iurarent sic esse ut dicebant et dato sacramento uiolenti insecutores utique illorum pro tali excessu soluerent .D. solidos iuxta constitucionem piissimi imperatoris A. quam apud Sanctum Stephanum constituit in causa que agitabatur inter P. Seguntinum episcopum et homines de Medina Celim. Era M.CC.VIII mense septembris' (fol. 201r). Cf Alfonso's important concession to the church of Osma (Soria, 17 Sept. 1170) in González, *El reino de Castilla* II 253-54. The reference in the king's will of December 1204 to the occasion, 'cum ego eram puer et a regibus Legionensis et Navarre, etiamque a Sarracenis, regnum meum acriter infestabatur, imo nitebantur ut me exheredarent' when D. Nunnus and Petrus de Arazuri, 'in quorum potestate eram et a quibus nutriebar', had accepted five thousand maravedis 'a quodam' for the vacant see of Osma (*ibid*. III 345-6) serves to highlight our ignorance of the ecclesiastical history of the 1160s since Bishop Juan of Osma is thought to have ruled his diocese undisturbed from 1148 to 1173 (Loperráez, *Descripción histórica* I 123ff). Alfonso's charter describing Cerebrun as 'patrinus meus' is publ. Minguella, *Historia* I 423-24. *Piissimus* recalls the Visigothic king Gundemar (Appendix I, no. 13), though Rodrigo of Toledo felt able to apply the epithet to Fernando II of León! *De rebus Hispaniae* VII 13 (ed. Lorenzana, 158a).

However little or much their action in March 1166 may actually have contributed to the restoration of royal authority, such was the prelates' reward for the initiative which they had displayed. Archbishop Juan's own reward came to him even sooner, when the city of Toledo was recovered by Castilian forces in August 1166.[31] Juan died one month later, doubtless well pleased with the outcome. He may even have had the satisfaction of knowing that Fernando Rodríguez de Castro had fled to the Almohad camp, thus incurring the plethora of penalties prescribed at Segovia.[32] In 1170 the influence and strength of the Castilian prelates seemed assured and impregnable. It is tempting now, as perhaps it was then for them, to discern in the decrees of the 1166 synod the foundations of that strength, and not to notice that those foundations were faulty, that by identifying themselves so completely with the secular power the bishops were condemning to eventual failure their own enactments aimed at limiting secular interference in ecclesiastical affairs. The limitations and the precarious nature of the position that they enjoyed at the pleasure of a strong king would be discovered by their episcopal successors at the hands of a succession of such monarchs over the following century.[33] The Leonese bishops who met at this very time to consider what feeble means of self-defence they possessed against Fernando II had made that discovery already;[34] and ironically MS 8 itself would be used in the late 1270s to record the chapter of Osma's protest against the cumulative effects of another century of royal repression.[35] Meanwhile, however, the Castilian bishops might enjoy the fruits of the timely action which they had taken at Segovia in March 1166.

St. John's College,
Cambridge.

APPENDIX I

Burgo de Osma, Biblioteca del Cabildo
MS 8

1. (fols. 1r-2r): 'Merito igitur patres constituerunt ut in ** sollempnitate beate uirginis Marie hoc euangelium "Intrauit Jhesus" legeretur — ipsa igitur optimam partem elegit que non aufertur ab ea. Intrauit Jhesus in quoddam castellum (Luke 10:38) — filium eius qui uiuat et regnat per omnia secula seculorum.'

---

[31] González, *El reino de Castilla* I 174.

[32] *Ibid.* 176. Juan died on 29 September 1166.

[33] Peter Linehan, *The Spanish church and the papacy in the thirteenth century* (Cambridge 1971) chaps. 6-8.

[34] Fletcher, 'Regalian right' 359-60.

[35] Linehan, 'The Spanish Church revisited: The episcopal *gravamina* of 1279', *Authority and power: Studies on medieval law and government presented to Walter Ullmann on his seventieth birthday*, edd. B. Tierney and P. Linehan (Cambridge 1980) 138.

2. (fols. 2v-5v): 'Incipit catalogus romanorum pontificum v. m. Dompnus Petrus natione galileus sedit annos xxv menses duos dies vii — Adrianus natione anglicus sedit annos.'

3. (fols. 6r-v): Catalogus romanorum imperatorum. Octauianus Augustus annis VI — Tiberius de hinc V agit annis v. m.'

4. (fols. 7v-162v): 'Canones Carnotensis episcopi est de armario Oxomensi. Si quis enim fuerit furatus uel alio modo de eo extraxerit sine licentia conuentus uel hunc librum (?) deleuerit anathema sit. Incipit prologus Panormie Iuonis uenerabilis Carnotensis episcopi de multimoda distinctione scripturarum sub una castorum eloquiorum fatie contentarum — ultimis suppliciis feriri. Expliciunt decreta Panormie Iuonis uenerabilis Carnotensis episcopi.'
Ed. PL 161.1041-1338. Inserted after lib. V, cap. 76 (PL col. 1228B) the following (cf. Fransen, *Traditio* 21 [1965] 517):
   (a) (fols. 105v-106r): Decrees of Council of Poitiers 1100 (Mansi 20.1123-4), lacking c.11, 12, 14; after c.15 fragments of Ivo, ep. 95, as Sigüenza, MS 5 (Fransen, *loc. cit.*)
   (b) (fols. 106r-v): Decrees of Council of Toulouse 1119, (misdated 1100), (Mansi 21.225-8); variants: cc.3 and 4 reversed; c.2 'Nullus in archiepiscopum, nullus in prepositum . . .'; c.3 *des.* 'dampnationis uinculo donec resipuerit innodamus'; c.7 'quartam decimarum et oblationum partem'; c.10 *des.* 'correxerit'.
   (c) (fol. 106v): 'Placuit ut si quis — neque prepositus perseueret ' (as Fransen, *loc. cit.*).
   (d) (fol. 106v-107r): 'De Priscillianistis qui se ab esu carnium subtrahunt. Ac primum — recipimus' (*Coll. Hisp.* c.1: PL 84.829-31).
   (e) (fol. 107r-108r): Letter of Ivo of Chartres to *Cadaricus*: 'In litteris tuis continetur — et auctoritate respondeo' (ep. 156, PL 162.160-62).

5. (fols. 162v-182v): 'Quisquis per pecuniam ordinatur — desiderium transire nituntur' (see above, note 4).

6. (fols. 182v-184r): 'Incipit relatio Aurelii Augustini de heresibus. Simoniaci a Simone — bonum Deum esse sed iustum': St Augustine, *De heresibus*: text closely related to that of MS M (S. Millan de la Cogolla MS 80, saec. ix, in R. Vander Plaetse and C. Benkers, edd. [Corpus Christianorum, ser. lat. 46; Turnhout 1969] 268, 290ff). Abbreviated account of *Menandriani* and *Saturniniani* (cap. ii and iii of ed.) attached to cap. i (*Simoniaci*); cap. ii-x here = cap. iv-xii of ed; cap. xiii of ed. (*Ptolomaeus*) lacking; cap. xi here (cf cap. xiv of ed.): 'Marcile carnis resurrectionem negant. Christum non uere sed putatiue passum asseuerant' cap. xv-xx of ed. lacking; cap. xii here = cap. xxi of ed. lines 1-3.

7. (fol. 184r): 'Gregorius papa in generali synodo. In die resurrectionis — antiquos imitantes patres.' De cons. D.5 c.15. Text, G. Morin, 'Règlements inédits du pape S. Grégoire VII pour les chanoines réguliers', RB 18 (1901) 179. Cf. C. Dereine, 'La prétendue règle de Grégoire VII pour chanoines réguliers', RB 71 (1961) 108-18.

8. (fols. 184r-188v): Constitutum Constantini: text is that of the so-called 'Nonantola-Gruppe' and is closely akin to that of MS N$_{PA}$, ed. H. Fuhrmann (Hanover 1968).

9. (fol. 188v): 'Iulius papa. Si qua mulier — synodus prorsus prohibuit.' C.27 q.2 c.15.

10. (fol. 188v): 'Item. Si quis desponsauerit — ullo unquam tempore.' C.35 q.10 c.5 fin (*recte* Innocentius).

11. (fol. 188v-189r): 'De celebritate festiuitatis dominice matris. Cum nichil fideli sinceritas — RECAREDI PRINCIPIS ERA DCLXXXXIIII.' Conc. Toledo X, c.1 (PL 84.441).

12. (fol. 189r-v): 'Exceptio de dignitate Toletane ecclesie. Notum est omnibus — sic loquitur dicens.' Ed. (from two Toledo Cathedral MSS) J. F. Rivero Recio, *La iglesia de Toledo en el siglo XII (1086-1208)* I (Rome 1966) 319-22.

13. (fol. 189v-192r): 'Incipit decretum piissimi atque gloriosissimi principis nostri Gundemari — Ego Venerius ecclesie Castolonensis episcopus ss'; 'In nomine domini nostri Jhesu Christi. Constitutio Cartaginensium sacerdotum in Toletana urbe — Sanabilis sancte ecclesie Elotane episcopus ss.' Conc. Toledo XII (PL 84.482-6).

14. (fol. 192r-v): 'Decreta domini Eugenii pape': decrees of Council of Rheims 1148 (Mansi 21.713-18), lacking c.4, 6, 7, 10-13.

15. (fols. 193r-195r): 'Gregorius papa de uerbis Andree apostoli. Agnus qui occisus est — et bibere sanguinem. Ambrosius. Omnia quecumque — corpus redisse' (De cons. D.2 c.74). 'Gregorius. Quotiens ei hostiam — hostia suffragatur. Augustinus. Hoc accipimus in pane — ex latere. Ambrosius. Quotiescumque accipimus mortem — medicinam. Isidorus. Accepta hoc — in nobis sit. De octabis sanctorum. Octabas celebrari — sollempnia celebramus.'

16. (fols. 195r-197v): 'Era M.CC.IIII. In nomine domini — sarracenorum ire presumant.' Decrees of Synod of Segovia 1166.

17. (fols. 197v-198v): 'Adrianus episcopus s. s. D. dilectis filiis priori et uniuersis monachis Ponticen. sal. et ap. ben. Nobis in eminenti — ultionem. Dat. Capue iii non. novembr.' JL 10444; ed. W. Holtzmann, 'Kanonistische Ergänzungen zur Italia Pontificia', QF 38 (1958) 88-89.

18. (fols. 198v-199r): 'Quod omnis qui conuerti uoluerit in monasterium ecclesie cuius parrochianus est medietatem sue substantie relinquerit, aliter non conuertatur. Unde Leo papa. Relatum est auribus — anathematis subiaceat.' JL 4269; ed. Holtzmann, 164-65.

19. (fols. 199r-200r): 'Dilectissimi fratres in Christo — annuente domino nostro Jhesu.' Account of relics in *arca* of Oviedo Cathedral (ed. from MS Valenciennes 99: D. de Bruyne, 'Le plus ancien catalogue des reliques d'Oviedo', *Analecta Bollandiana* 45 [1927] 93-6).

20. (fol. 200v): 'Hoc est iudicium quod iudicauit dominus imperator apud Secouiam — deuenirent.'

21. (fols. 200v-201r): 'Hoc est iudicium quod iudicauit dominus A. imperator in Sancto Stephano — restituerent.'

22. (fol. 201r): 'Hoc est iudicium quod iudicauit dominus C. Toletanus archiepiscopus — era M.CC.VIII mense septembris.'

23. (fol. 201v): (a) 'Dominus episcopus leuauit de armario V libros scilicet psalterium, epistolas, P. Matheum, sententias, summam teologie.' (b) 'Augustinus. Artifici Deo tam mundus est porcus quam agnus (*Enarr. in Ps.* CXLI, *Opera* X, 3, ed. E. Dekkers and I. Fraipont [Corpus Christianorum, ser. lat. 40. Turnhout

42

1956] p. 2046), et tam munda est caro quam sanguis. Satis enim delirat qui agnum dicit mundum et suem inmundam, uel qui carnem mundam et sanguinem inmundum diiudicat.' (c) Form of anathema and malediction. 'Canonica instituta et sanctorum patrum exempla sequentes — condignam penitenciam satisfecerint'. (d) 'Anno domini M.CC. septuagesimo nono — don Guillem Capellan mayor' (above, note 35).

APPENDIX II

Burgo de Osma, Biblioteca del Cabildo
MS 8, fols. 195r-197v.

Era M.CC.IIII. In nomine domini nostri Jhesu Christi celebrata est sinodus apud Secobiam a domino Johanne Toletano archiepiscopo et Hispaniarum primate et ab omnibus episcopis regni regis Aldefonsi, et quantum ad honorem Dei et exaltationem domini pape et ad pacem regni domini nostri Aldefonsi reformandam conuenimus.

I. Placet huic sacro conuentui in primis statuere ut quicumque honorem infra regnum regis Aldefonsi tenet sit eius uasallus et faciat ei hominium per se uel per alium usque ad octabas proxime Pasche uel dimittat ei honorem suum, et si alterum istorum infra predictum tempus distulerit extunc [fol. 195v] sit ipse excommunicatus et tota terra quam tenet interdicta, et nemini liceat eum uel terram eius absoluere sine consensu regis uel domini primatis, nisi urgente mortis periculo.

II. Preterea statuimus quod si aliquis inuaserit uel inuadere uoluerit terminos regni regis nostri uel in aliquam partem regni guerram mouerit omnes regni sui cum a domino rege uocati fuerint sine mora ueniant ad defendendum regnum eius, et qui hoc facere contempserit, principes et maiores ciuitatum siue uillarum, sint excommunicati, et ciuitates et uille interdicte donec de tanto excessu plenarie domino regi satisfaciant, et quicumque tunc uocatus ad seruicium eius uenerit tantum de iniuncta sibi penitentia remittimus quantum si Iherosolimam uisitaret.

III. Item generali capitulo de decreto addimus ut nullus decetero guerram in regno regis Aldefonsi facere presumat, quod si facere presumpserit et ammonitus ab episcopo suo desistere noluerit extunc sit excommunicatus et maledictus et sepultura [fol. 196r] Christianorum ei denegetur si in guerra illa mortuus fuerit.

IV. Item hec sancta sinodus sequens statuta Antioceni concilii statuit ut siquis presbiter uel diachonus uel subdiachonus excommunicatus uel interdictus a proprio episcopo uel a domino primate uel ex mandato episcopi ab eius uicario aliquid de ministerio sacro continere ausus fuerit uel in ecclesia prohibita scienter celebrauerit, sine spe restitutionis perpetuo careat officio et beneficio ecclesiastico nisi forte cui romana auctoritas spiritualiter indulpserit.[1]

---

[1] C.11 q.3 c.6. Cf. Valladolid (= Vall.) 1143 c.3,4; Vall. 1155 c.27.

V. Preterea hoc sacrum concilium decreuit iuxta[a] decretum Innocentii pape ut siquis uiolentas manus in clericum uel in quemlibet religionis habitum habentem iniecerit anathema sit et nullus possit eum absoluere nisi urgente mortis periculo quousque presentiam domini pape adeat et eius mandatum suscipiat[2]. **VI.** Si uero aliquis res eorum rapuerit uel bona eorum depredatus fuerit et sanctorum oratoria uisitancium seu peregrinorum uel mercatorum uel in requiem † euntium quousque uniuersa ablata restituat communione[b] careat Christiana [fol. 196v] secundum decretum Calixti pape.[3] **VII.** Preterea ad omnium utilitatem intendentes sub excommunicationis uinculo interdicimus ne quis boues rapere uel pignorare presumat.[4] **VIII.** Insuper sub eodem uinculo prohibemus ut nullus clericos uel religionis habitum habentes uel mercatores siue in requiem euntes pignoret nisi proprio debito.[5]

IX. Item pessimam et perniciosam consuetudinem ab ecclesia Dei erradicare cupientes iuxta capitulum Paschalis et Alexandri pape prohibemus[c] ut nullus clericus uel quilibet religiosus ecclesiam uel inuestituram ecclesie uel quamlibet ecclesiasticam dignitatem de manu laici accipiat. Qui uero ausu temerario contrafacere presumpserit gradus sui periculo subiaceat et communione priuetur.[6]

X. Preterea inherentes statutis Paschalis et Simachi pape interdicimus ut nullus laicorum ecclesias uel bona ecclesie occupet uel disponat nec statuendi aliquid in ecclesia aliquam habeat potestatem, ut sacrilegus iudicetur et excommunicationis sententiam substineat.[7]

XI. Item ut nullus stet in seruicium sarracenorum nisi permissu regis.

XII. Fratres ortamur christianitatem uestram iuxta[d] Calcedonensem concilium et aliorum sanctorum canonum [fol. 197r] statuta ut nullus episcopus clericum alienum sine comendaticiis litteris ordinare presumat. Si uero aliquis aliter ordinauerit placet huic sancte sinodo et eum qui[e] ordinauerit et qui ordinatus fuerit tandiu excommunicatos manere quandiu ipse clericus ad propriam reuertatur ecclesiam.[8]

XIII. Insuper generali capitulo prohibemus iuxta decretum Calixti pape ut presbiteri nec accipiant curam animarum nisi de manu illius episcopi cuius parrochiani sint uel ab eo cui ab episcopo hoc commissum fuerit. Si vero aliquis

---

ᵃ iusta   ᵇ comunione   ᶜ prohibemus *marg.*   ᵈ iusta   ᵉ quem

---

[2] Conc. Lateranense II c.15 (COD 200). Cf. Vall. 1143 c.14; Vall. 1155 c.24.

[3] Cf. Conc. Lateranense I c.14 (COD 193); Conc. Palencia 1129 (*Córtes de los antiguos reinos de León y de Castilla*, publicadas por la Real Academia de la Historia, I [Madrid 1861] 37); Vall. 1155 c.18 (on matters treated here in c.VI, VII).

[4] Cf. Conc. Oviedo 1115 (*Córtes* I 30); Conc. Palencia 1129 (ibid. 37).

[5] Cf. Conc. Turonense (1163) c.2 (X 5.19.1).

[6] C.16 q.7 c.17, 20. Cf. Conc. Lateranense II c.25 (COD 202); Vall. 1143 c.18; Vall. 1155 c.13, where *investitura* is not specifically mentioned.

[7] C.16 q.7 c.18, 23; Mansi 8.312 (cf. A. Thiel, *Epp. Romanorum Pontificum genuinae* I [Braunsberg 1867] 90-92; P. Hinschius, *Decretales Ps-Isidorianae* [Leipzig 1863] 657); Vall. 1155 c.13.

[8] D.71 c.8. Cf. Vall. 1143 c.22.

secus agere presumpserit ecclesie liminibus arceatur.[9] **XIV.** Presenti quoque decreto prohibemus ut nullus episcopus sepulture causa parrochianum alterius recipere presumat nisi forte aliquo casu in[f] eius episcopatu eum mori contigerit, ita tamen ut de omnibus que pro anima sua ei reliquerit uel eius ecclesie medietatem restituat illi ecclesie cuius parrochianus erat. **XV.** Si uero aliquis in uita siue in morte in monasterium conuerti uoluerit uel in aliquo religioso loco sepulturam sibi eligerit precipimus iuxta decretum Leonis pape ut medietatem omnium rerum et possessionum quas[g] dederit uel dare disposuit ecclesia apud quam [fol. 197v] fidei sacramenta uiuens suscepit, ecclesiastica censura sibi uendicet. Quicumque uero huius decreti nostri contradictor extiterit anathematis gladio feriatur.[10]

XVI. Ad hec inherentes decreto beatissimi Ambrosii et aliorum sanctorum patrum precipimus ut unusquisque integre decimas persoluat Deo et ecclesie de grano et uino aut de fructibus aut de peccoribus aut de negociatione sua. Si vero aliquis de omnibus supradictis integre decimas non dederit usque ad satisfactionem et emendationem congruam excommunicatum se sciat.[11] **XVII.** Item communi utilitati christianorum prouidentes ad destructionem inimicorum crucis Christi sub anathematis uinculo prohibemus ut nullus sine permissu regis Aldefonsi de regno eius deinceps in seruicium sarracenorum ire presumat.

---

[f] casui   [g] possessionum dederit

---

[9] Cf. Conc. Lateranense I c.16, 4 (COD 193, 190).
[10] X 3.28.2. See Appendix I no. 18.
[11] C.16 q.7 c.4,5. Cf. Vall. 1155 c.14, which is primarliy concerned with lay *possession* of tithes.

PEDRO DE ALBALAT,
ARZOBISPO DE TARRAGONA
Y SU
"SUMMA SEPTEM SACRAMENTORUM" *

Si bien hace ya sesenta años que Rudolf Beer llamó la atención sobre los grandes méritos de Pedro de Albalat, arzobispo de Tarragona de 1238 a 1251, éste aún espera su biógrafo [1]. Las pocas páginas que le dedica Morera apenas le hacen justicia [2]; pero hasta que no pueda consultarse el aparentemente rico archivo de la catedral de Lérida, de donde fue obispo de 1236 a 1238 [3], solamente se podrá dar de él una referencia parcial.

Con todo, se conoce ya lo suficiente para concluir que el juicio de Beer era correcto. En realidad no es que ocupara una distinguida posición solamente entre el clero catalán. La determinación con que se dedicó a complementar la legislación del Concilio IV Laterano de 1215 y a asegurar la *libertas ecclesiastica* contra la agresión secular le han hecho una de las relevantes personalidades de la Iglesia de Europa del siglo XIII. Mucho tiempo ha que Argáiz comentaba el

---

* Traducido del inglés por la Redacción.
[1] «Eine der bedeutendsten Gestalten des Katalanischen Klerus jener Zeit», *Die Handschriften des Klosters Santa Maria de Ripoll* (Sitzungsberichte d. phil.-hist. Kl. d. kais. Ak. d. Wissenschaften, Bd. CLVIII (Viena, 1909) 69. Cf. JAUME FEBRER, *Trobes ... en que tracta dels llinatges de la conquista de la ciutat de València e son regne*, ed. PASQUAL MARÍN (Valencia, 1796), p. 24; J. VILLANUEVA, *Viage literario*, XIX, pp. 183-85. Más información sobre su *curriculum vitae* se ofrecerá en mi libro en preparación sobre la historia de la Iglesia española en el siglo XIII. Véase entre tanto P. A. LINEHAN, *Councils and Synods in Thirteenth-Century Castile and Aragon*, en *Studies in Church History*, VII. ed. G. J. CUMING (Cambridge, 1970), en prensa.
[2] E. MORERA, *Tarragona cristiana*. II (Tarragona, 1899), pp. 274-89.
[3] VILLANUEVA, XVI, pp. 134-38.
[4] G. DE ARGÁIZ, *La soledad laureada por San Benito y sus hijos en España...* II (Madrid, 1675), f. 53 v.

gran número de concilios provinciales convocados por él — ocho, según sus cálculos, en el período de once o doce años: más de lo que hicieron los visigodos [4]. De hecho la realización del arzobispo superó este número. La serie de concilios provinciales sólo se interrumpió dos veces, en 1241 y 1245, cuando estuvo ausente de la diócesis para el fracasado concilio romano de Gregorio IX y el de Lyon, convocado por Inocencio IV [5]. La legislación de dichos concilios provinciales puede verse en la colección de Tejada [6]. Ella deja un largo vestigio. En diciembre de 1251, cinco meses después de la muerte del arzobispo Pedro, los cistercienses de Veruela basaban su recurso contra el concejo de Trasmos en la Constitución *Cum quidem* del concilio del arzobispo de 1245. En esta ocasión se trataba de un caso de propiedad de un predio rústico [7], pero no era éste el único beneficio eclesiástico que encontró protección en la actividad conciliar del arzobispo. La *libertas ecclesiastica* en general era así servida y más tarde, en la segunda década del siglo XIV, el cabildo de Valencia pensó por esto pedir a Tarragona copias autorizadas de la constitución *Cum quidem* y de la suplementaria del concilio de 1246 *Olim excommunicasse* [8].

Mentor de Pedro de Albalat fue el cardenal-obispo de Sabina y legado papal en la península ibérica en 1228-29, Jean d'Abbeville, teólogo parisino. El primer acto de Pedro en su primer concilio de 1239 fue el de adoptar *in toto* el programa de reforma del ex-legado [9]. Aunque fue Jean de Abbeville quien llevó a los reinos hispánicos el mensaje del IV Concilio Lateranense, no ha sido debidamente valo-

[5] Para sus experiencias, en estas ocasiones, véase J. L. A. HUILLARD-BRÉHOLLES, *Historia diplomatica Friderici Secundi*, V, 11 (París, 1859), pp. 1120-21; MATTHEW PARIS, *Chronica Maiora*, ed. H. R. LUARD (Rolls Ser., IV, Londres, 1877), p. 540.

[6] J. TEJADA, *Colección de cánones y de todos los concilios de la Iglesia de España y de América*, III (Madrid, 1849), pp. 349 ss. Cf. F. FITA, *Concilios tarraconenses en 1248, 1249 y 1250*, «Bol. R. Acad. Hist.» 40 (1902) 444-48, y para una breve descripción de los concilios: F. VALLS TABERNER, *Notes sobre la legislació eclesiàstica provincial que integra la compilació canònica tarraconense del Patriarca d'Alexandria*, «An. sacra Tarrac.» 11 (1935) 251-72.

[7] Archivo Histórico Nacional, Sección de clero, 3.767/14. El concilio de este año se tuvo en enero y no en la cuarta semana después de Pascua, como era costumbre: VALLS TABERNER, *Notes*, p. 258; TEJADA, l. c.

[8] Archivo de Valencia, perg. 8.987, reg. E. OLMOS CANALDA, *Inventario de los pergaminos del Archivo Catedral de Valencia* (Valencia, 1961), n.° 127, mal datado: «scriptis et registratis in registro domini archiepiscopi» (c 1309-15). Cf. TEJADA, VI, 40, 43.

[9] Ibid., VI, 30-31.

rada su contribución a la reforma de la Iglesia [10]. De momento, sea como sea, punto substancial es que en el año 1229 Pedro de Albalat era sacristán de Lérida, en donde el legado tuvo su concilio para la Iglesia de Aragón [11]. No está claro con evidencia si fue en esta ocasión que se encontraron, pero es ya cierta su íntima asociación en el año siguiente. En 1230 y 1231 el sacristán de Lérida debió informar al cardenal-obispo de Sabina acerca del curso de la elección episcopal para la Seo de Urgel, y al menos entonces hizo el viaje a Roma para tal información [12]. El cardenal murió en septiembre de 1237, cinco meses antes de la promoción de Pedro al arzobispado de Tarragona [13]. Pero su influencia sobre Pedro continuó igualmente desde la tumba. Es significativo que el arzobispo cuando cita la constitución del IV Concilio Lateranense, las palabras que usa no son aquéllas del año 1215, sino las del concilio de Lérida de 1229, presidido por Jean d'Abbeville [14].

El legado había manifestado una considerable devoción a la Orden dominicana. Mientras estuvo en España fue acompañado por Raimundo de Peñafort y dispensó su protección al convento de dominicos de Palencia [15]. Pedro compartió este entusiasmo tanto para la Orden en general como en particular para el santo dominico catalán. En el año 1248 había cinco obispos dominicos en la provincia eclesiástica tarraconense, uno de ellos, el de Valencia, Andrés, hermano de Pedro [16], y siete años antes él y el jurista catalán Raimundo pro-

---

[10] Valls Taberner, *Notes*, pp. 255-56, se refiere brevemente a la importancia de la legislación de Jean d'Abbeville y V. Beltrán de Heredia, *La formación intelectual del clero en España durante los siglos XII, XIII y XIV*, «Rev. esp. Teología» 6 (1946) 336 ss., se ocupa de sus reformas educativas, sobre las cuales, y como punto de vista contrario, podrá verse: P. A. Linehan, *Ecclesiae non mittentes: the Thirteenth-Century Background*, en *Studia albornotiona*, en preparación. La legación y sus efectos serán objeto de discusión en mi libro ya mencionado. Para los escritos teológicos de J. d'Abbeville, véase F. Stegmüller, *Repertorium biblicum Medii Aevi*, III (Madrid, 1951), pp. 340-44.

[11] Villanueva, XVI, 134.

[12] Archivo Catedral de Urgel, Documentos sin catalogar: Archivo Catedral de Lérida, caj. 202, n.° 569. Cf. Villanueva, XI, 74-75.

[13] P. Frizon, *Gallia Purpurata* (París, 1638), p. 213; *Les Registres de Grégoire IX (1227-41)*, ed. L. Auvray (París, 1890-1955), n.° 4.072.

[14] *Summa Septem Sacramentorum*, infra, nota 29.

[15] *Vita S. Raymundi*, ed. F. Balme y C. Paban, en *Raymundiana* (Mon. Ord. Frat. Praed. hist., VI) I (Roma-Stuttgart, 1900), p. 22; Archivo Histórico Nacional, sección de clero, 1724/15: publ. T. Ripoll, *Bullarium Ordinis Fratrum Praedicatorum*, I (Roma, 1729), n.° 47.

[16] En Barcelona, Vich, Gerona, Lérida y Valencia. Detalles en los volúmenes de Villanueva correspondientes a estas diócesis.

mulgaron una serie de instrucciones acerca el procedimiento a seguir en el trato de los herejes, que Dondaine considera como «le premier document digne du nom de manuel de procédure inquisitoriale», y a las que han prestado atención varios historiadores de la Inquisición [17].

La que ha sido totalmente ignorada de los historiadores es otra obra del mismo período del «manuel», es decir, un código de disciplina y descripción de los siete sacramentos, que publicó Pedro (quizá no por primera vez) en el sínodo *sede vacante* de Barcelona, de 1241: *Las escelentes constituciones sobre sacramentos, vida clerical,* etc., o *Tractatus Septem Sacramentorum,* según la llamaba el obispo Andrés de Albalat, conocidas por Villanueva y mencionadas en su *Viage* [18].

No fue sólo Barcelona que recibió esta atención. Otra versión de la *Summa* fue dirigida a su propia archidiócesis en un sínodo de data incierta, y su texto se ha conservado entre los papeles de Villanueva en la biblioteca de la Real Academia de la Historia de Madrid [19].

En Valencia, en octubre de 1258, su hermano Andrés, obispo, volvió a publicar la obra en un sínodo diocesano — aunque en la versión, publicada por Sáenz de Aguirre, la obra, por descuido, es atribuida no a Pedro de Albalat, sino a su antecesor [20].

Tres años más tarde todo el clero de Valencia era obligado a procurarse una copia de la *Summa* antes de la Navidad [21]. Los dos

[17] A. DONDAINE, *Le manuel de l'Inquisiteur (1230-1330),* «Arch. Fratrum Praedicatorum» 16 (1946) 96. El documento fue publicado por C. DOUAIS, *St. Raymond de Peñafort et les hérétiques,* «Moyen Age» 3 (1899) 315-35. Está datado de 1241-1242, pero la participación respectiva de los autores en su composición aún no está fijada. Para una visión de la literatura, cf. MAISONNEUVE, *Études sur les origines de l'Inquisition* (París, 1960), p. 287.

[18] VILLANUEVA, XVII, 212.

[19] Ms. $\frac{9\text{-}24\text{-}5}{4558}$, ff. 171 r-78 v.

[20] J. SÁENZ DE AGUIRRE, *Collectio Maxima Conciliorum...* V (Roma, 1755). pp. 197-202. En la pág. 197 Aguirre pone: «...de Tractatu septem Sacramentorum edito per venerabilem archiepiscopum *praedecessorum Domini* P. ... Tarraconensis Ecclesiae in Synodo Ilerdensi». El archivero de Valencia, don Ramón Robres, tuvo la amabilidad de informarme que las palabras subrayadas deberían ser: *patrem dominum.* El manuscrito es el n.° 163, cf. E. OLMOS CANALDA, *Códices de la Catedral de Valencia* (Valencia, 1943), p. 122.

[21] Ibid., p. 206. Para las variantes entre la versión de Valencia y su conocida fuente, la de Barcelona de octubre de 1241 (ib. p. 202), véase más abajo mi edición. De particular interés es la sustitución de tres por dos en el máximo de padrinos en la sección *De Baptismo:* una variación de la práctica normal probablemente para restringir el parentesco espiritual y favorecer los matrimonios cristianos en la región fronteriza conquistada. Cf. F. M. POWICKE y C. R. CHENEY, *Councils and Synods with other Documents relating to the English Church,* II (Oxford, 1964),

III

manuscritos de esta obra del Archivo Catedral de Barcelona, que hemos aprovechado en nuestra edición [22], son una nueva ulterior prueba de la utilización de la *Summa,* tanto en vida como después de la muerte de Pedro [23].

Una más detallada discusión sobre la influencia de la *Summa* se desarrollará en mi próximo libro. Aquí, empero, hay dos puntos que convendrá tratar referentes a sus fuentes. En primer lugar, si bien Raymundo de Peñafort vivía asociado a él y se han descubierto ciertas palabras paralelas en la *Summa* Raymundiana [24], no hay razón suficiente para suponer que el canonista fue en ninguna manera responsable de la composición de la *Summa* de Albalat, como lo fuera del llamado «manuel de procédure inquisitoriale», según queda dicho antes. Pero Pedro se dirigió a otra fuente para su material, al padre común de gran parte de esta clase de literatura de la época: a los Estatutos de París, atribuidos al obispo Eudes de Sully (1196-1208) [25]. Y la comparación con muchos préstamos de esta fuente (anotados más abajo) manifiesta que las ocasiones en que Pedro de Albalat deja su marca personal en la *Summa* son muy escasas [26].

El otro punto a notar es la referencia que en la versión de la

index a la palabra: *godparents;* R. I. BURNS, *The Crusader Kingdom of Valencia: Reconstruction on a Thirteenth-Century Frontier* (Cambridge, Mass. 1967), passim.

[22] *Constitutiones Synodales et Provinciales,* ff. 177 r-184 v; *Libro de la Cadena,* ff. 127 a-130 c.

[23] Sin embargo, cuando en 1296 otro obispo de Valencia, Ramón Despont, dominico, publicó un *Tractatus de sacramentis* propio, dice «de sacramentis ecclesiasticis in constitutionibus synodalibus ecclesiae Valentinae nihil fuerit constitutum», publ. por J. SANCHIS SIVERA, *Para la historia del Derecho eclesiástico valentino,* «An. sacra Tarrac.» 10 (1934) 123 ss. Pero setenta años después la sección eucarística de la *Summa* fue reavivada por el arzobispo Pedro de Clasquerí en un sínodo diocesano. Parece que entonces se olvidó su origen, ya que era descrita como «Constitutio sinodalis ecclesie Valentine», Archivo Catedral Barcelona, *Libro de la Cadena,* f. 184 r.

[24] Por ejemplo, la cita de san Jerónimo con que Pedro comienza la sección *De Penitentia.* Cf. *Summa de Poenitentia* (Roma, 1603), p. 1. Véase asimismo VALLS TABERNER, *San Ramón de Penyafort* (= *Obras selectas,* I, ii, Madrid-Barcelona, 1953), p. 290.

[25] Sobre la influencia de estos estatutos, cf. C. R. CHENEY, *English Synodalia of the Thirteenth Century* (Oxford 1941), pp. 55-56, 82-84 y su artículo *The Earliest English Diocesan Statutes,* «English historical Review» 75 (1960) 1-29. Ya bien pronto, en 1230, habían llegado al sud de Francia, y no mucho después ya eran conocidos en Portugal: L. DE LACGER, *Statuts synodaux inédits du diocèse d'Albi au XIII siècle,* «Rev. hist. de Droit français et étranger» 6 (1927) 434 ss.; I. DA ROSA PEREIRA, *Manuscritos de dereito canónico existentes em Portugal,* «Arquivo histórico da Madeira» 13 (1962-63) 36 ss.

[26] Uno de tales rasgos personales es la referencia en la sección *De Corpore et Sanguine Christi* a la limpieza de las vestiduras «ad morem Cistercii». Pedro es-

Summa por Andrés de Albalat se hace en 1258 a un sínodo de Lérida en el que el arzobispo, su hermano, la había presentado[27]. ¿Cuándo tuvo lugar este sínodo? ¿Entre los años 1236 y 1238, cuando él era obispo de esta diócesis (y en donde el mismo Andrés era un miembro del convento de dominicos en una data posterio)[28], o durante uno de los dos períodos *sede vacante,* cuando Pedro ya era arzobispo: en 1238 ó 1247-48? No es posible dar una solución evidente por ahora, si bien hay alguna razón para preferir el período 1236-38, y ésta se funda en que los estatutos sinodales del sucesor de Pedro en el obispado de Lérida, Raimundo de Ciscar (1238-47), tienen mucho de común con los atribuidos a Eudes de Sully, pero contienen también una serie de frases que se encuentran en la *Summa* según la tenemos, pero no en los Estatutos de París[29]. Posiblemente, pues, el obispo Ciscar tuvo acceso a una versión de la *Summa* anterior a la de octubre de 1241, que había publicado Pedro en un sínodo diocesano mientras era obispo de Lérida. Si esta hipótesis fuera correcta, veríamos que Pedro de Albalat fue tan activo en el gobierno pastoral de esta diócesis como lo había sido, según lo visto, en la organización temporal y espiritual del cabildo catedral allí mismo[30].

Pero hay que advertir que esto es sólo una hipótesis, que habrá que ser examinada a la luz de un estudio de otros manuscritos de la *Summa,* que seguramente deben existir en algunos de los archivos de la provincia tarraconense — especialmente en el de la catedral de Lérida —. Es con esta esperanza de que pueda suscitar interés que ofrecemos la presente seguramente imperfecta edición, basada en los manuscritos de Barcelona[31], en la copia de Villanueva y en la versión

taba íntimamente asociado a los Cistercienses, pero no era un miembro de esta Orden, como señaló J. Finestres y de Montalvo hace tiempo. Recientemente se ha repetido este error. Cf. *Historia del real monasterio de Poblet* II (Cervera, 1753, reeditado, Barcelona, 1948), p. 242. Cf. Burns, *The Crusader Kingdom,* p. 215.

[27] Sáenz de Aguirre, p. 197 (supra, nota 20).

[28] En septiembre de 1248: *Les Registres d'Innocent IV (1243-54),* ed. E. Berger (París, 1881-1921), n.° 4172. La data de la profesión de Andrés es desconocida, pero el convento de Lérida fue ciertamente fundado antes de 1230: F. de Diago, *Historia de la Provincia de Aragón de Predicadores* (Barcelona, 1599), f. 147 v.

[29] Estos estatutos fueron publicados en Villanueva, XVI, 297-308, sin indicación de data. P. Sáinz de Baranda, ES, XLVII (Madrid, 1850), p. 175, los atribuye al año 1240.

[30] Archivo Catedral Lérida, *Constitutiones Ecclesie Ilerdensis,* (caj. 218), ff. 2 v-5 r; Villanueva, XVI, 136.

[31] Parte de la sección eucarística fue publicada ya a base del manuscrito Sb

de Sáenz de Aguirre de los estatutos de Andrés de Albalat. Con todo, cualesquiera que sean los nuevos descubrimientos que quedan por hacer — y es de esperar sean muchos —, es improbable que la reputación de Pedro de Albalat sufra mucho detrimento. Ya que, con palabras de Artonne, la producción de un *liber sinodalis* como éste fue en la estimación de sus contemporáneos «l'oeuvre capitale d'un évèque» [83].

St. John's College. Cambridge.

He utilizado como base la copia de mediados del siglo XIV, contenida en el *Libro de la Cadena* del Archivo Catedral de Barcelona, ff. 127 a-130 c, señalada aquí con las siglas SB. La he colacionado con estas tres copias:

Sb: Barcelona, Archivo catedral, *Constitutiones Synodales et Provinciales,* ff. 177 r-184 v. Posiblemente es una copia anterior a SB pero contiene muchos errores por descuido.

ST: Madrid, Real Academia de la Historia ms. $\dfrac{9\text{-}24\text{-}5}{4558}$, ff. 171 r-178 v, copia hecha por Villanueva a últimos del s. XVIII, titulada: «Constitutiones domini P. Tarraconensis Archiepiscopi editae in synodo diocesana Tarraconensi (ex codice Barchinonensi apud Agustinianum)».

SV: SB, Según la versión del obispo Andrés de Albalat en el sínodo de Valencia de 1258. Publicado por J. Sáenz de Aguirre, *Collectio maxima Conciliorum,* V (Roma, 1755), pp. 197-202.

Se anotan solamente las variantes sustanciales de estas tres copias Sb, ST y SV.

Otras abreviaturas empleadas:

OS: Constituciones sinodales atribuidas a Odo de Sully, en MIGNE, PL 212, 57-68.

Lé: Estatutos de Jean d'Abbeville en el concilio de Lérida de 1229, en ES, XLVIII (Madrid, 1862), pp. 308-25.

RS: Constituciones sinodales de Ramón de Ciscar, obispo de Lérida (1240?), en VILLANUEVA, *Viage,* XVI (Madrid, 1851), pp. 297-308.

(ver Apéndice) en «Scrinium» 4-6 (1952) 73-75. Las muchas variantes entre este texto y el de SB las desatiende el editor anónimo, que las juzga «simples e insignificantes errores de transcripción». Pero ciertamente algunas representan diferencias sustanciales.

[83] A. ARTONNE, *Le Livre synodal de Lodève,* «Bibliothèque de l'Ecole des Chartes» 108 (1949-50) 71.

TEXTO DE LA *SUMMA* *

Anno domini millesimo CCXLI, die Sancti Luche, nos Petrus miseratione divina Tarrachonensis archiepiscopus in Barchinonensi sinodo, ad preces capituli Barchinonensis, vacante sede, mandamus constitutiones venerabilis Sabinensis bone memorie, apostolice sedis legati, inviolabiliter observari editas in concilio Illerdensi.

Item et eius ordinatio circa officium et alia in eadem ecclesia debeant observari; ad memoriam nichilominus reducentes illa capitula que per nos in Tarrachone et Valencie provincialibus consiliis fuere statuta; districte mandantes quod ad acolitatum nullus promoveatur ordinem nisi loqui sciat verbis latinis, et canonici qui non sunt in sacris compellantur per substractionem beneficiorum; firmiter statuentes quod nisi in primis quatuor temporibus se fecerint promoveri ad sacros, ex tunc sint privati voce capituli, nec admittantur ad omnes tractatus.

Item mandamus omnibus clericis habentibus curam sive locum qui residentiam requirant quod continuam decetero faciant residentiam in ecclesiis suis vel locis. Alioquin a kalendis januarii proximis in antea a beneficiis sint suspensi, salvis privilegiis apostolice sedis; adiungentes quod ad presbiteralem ordinem promoveantur. Aliter de locis et ecclesiis, cum iam multoties mandaverimus, ad collationes locorum et ecclesiarum auctore domino procedemus.

Et ideo si sunt aliqui qui causas habeant rationabiles hostendant coram nobis. Aliter non sit ei offensio cum nos processerimus ex post facto.

Mandamus nichilominus quod circa hereticos inquirendos sint clerici | vigiles et intenti, et in predicationibus | [Sb, f. 177 v | [SB, f. 127 rb suis moneant populum ne portent superfluitates in vestibus prout iam bone memorie B(erengarius) episcopus Barchinonensis mandaverat per diocesem Barchononensem.

De Ordinatione Sinodi [a], [1].

Item statuimus quod ad celebrandam sinodum omnes clerici cum mantellis vel cappis rotundis vel superpelliciis, jejuni, honeste conveniant prout decet et in sinodo audiant pacifice que leguntur. Et si aliqui

---

[a] ST empieza aquí.

* Quedo muy agradecido al Sr. J. A. Crook por sus valiosos comentarios al texto de la *Summa,* cuyas peculiaridades han sido retenidas en la edición que sigue.
[1] OS, II. 3-4; RS, 297.

habuerint dubium, ab episcopo [b] querant postmodum vel eius clericis, et eis de questionibus satisfiant. Nec tempore sinodi aliquid ab episcopo vel archidiaconis a clericis exhigatur, sed eis in suis dubitationibus respondeatur pacifice sine murmure, sinodo celebrata.

Item [2] dicimus quod clerici habentes curam animarum omnes veniant ad sinodum nisi in infirmitate aut aliqua necessitate canonica fuerint impediti, et tunc mittant suos capellanos aut clericos loco sui. Et [3] eundo et redeundo a sinodo honeste se habeant et ambulent bini et bini [c], et honesta querant hospitia in civitate et in via, ne status clericorum vertatur [d] in contemptum et opprobrium laicorum. Qua die si non venerint suspendantur et arbitrio episcopi puniantur. | | [ST, f. 171 v

De Sacramentis Ecclesie [e]

Item dicimus quod omnibus sacramentis a clericis et laycis magna exhibeatur reverentia; et hoc ab ipsis sacerdotibus populo predicetur.

De Baptismo et eius Forma [4]

Et quia baptismus janua est omnium sacramentorum mandamus quod cum magna celebratur cautela, maxime in distinctione verborum et prolatione, in quibus | tota virtus consistit sacramenti et salus | [Sb, f. 178 r puerorum.

Ista enim verba semper debet proferre sacerdos sine aliqua sincopatione: *Petre* | *vel Johannes* [f], *Ego te baptizo in nomine* | [SV, p. 198 a *Patris et Filii et Spiritus Sancti, Amen,* semper nominando puerum vel puellam.

Et [5] presbyteri moneant laycos quod in necessitate, cum timetur de morte puerorum, possunt pueros baptizare, dicentes: *Petre* [g], *ego te baptizo in nomine Patris et Filii et Spiritus Sancti, Amen.* Hoc idem possunt facere pater et mater cum de vita pueri dubitatur. Et si vixerit puer | taliter baptizatus ad ecclesiam apportetur et ibi catecu- | [SB, f. 127 va minetur et crismetur, sed non baptizetur [h] quia suppleri [i] debet caute quod ex necessitate fuerit pretermissum. Nec in alio liquore baptizetur [j] nisi

[b] ST: «archiepiscopus» por «episcopus» siempre.
[c] ST: «presbyteri» por «bini et bini».
[d] Sb omite «in civitate... vertatur»; ST omite «in civitate et in via».
[e] SV empieza aquí.

[f] SV: *Johannes vel Antoni;* RS: *Petre vel Arnalde.*
[g] SV: *Petre vel Antoni;* RS: Et in romantio dicant sacerdotes laycos posse et debere babtizare pueros ...
[h] SV: rebaptizetur.
[i] ST: repeti.
[j] ST: loco rebaptizetur.

[2] OS, II. 6; RS, 297.
[3] OS, II. 7; RS, 297.
[4] OS, III. 1; RS, 297.
[5] OS, III. 4; RS, 297.

III

in aqua. Et si verba predicta non essent prolata, ut superius dictum est, non dicatur aliquis baptizatus.

Et[6] si dubitaretur de aliquo utrum esset baptizatus baptizetur; sed sacerdos | dicat in prolatione verborum: *Si es baptizatus* | [ST, f. 172 r *non te baptizo, sed si non es baptizatus, Petre*[k], *ego te baptizo in nomine Patris et Filii et Spiritus Sancti, Amen;* quia non debet fieri iniuria sacramento.

Et[7] pro baptismo aliquid non queratur; sed si datum fuerit gratis, recipiatur.

Fontes[8] enim cum omni diligentia custodiantur, et aqua ad plus[l] de octo in octo diebus mutetur ne putrescat. Et caveant sacerdotes ne de aqua sortilegia fiant. Et[9] ultra tres[m] compatres ad levandum puerum de sacro fonte non admittantur, quia matrimonia impediuntur. Et illud presbiteri predicent populo, quia si maritus levet puerum de sacro fonte uxor que est in domo est commater, et e converso.

Illud autem non est pretermittendum, quod quando layci in necessitate baptizant pueros sacerdos debet querere diligenter qualiter dixerit verba. Si invenerit ut superius dictum est, bene quidem. Sin autem, baptizetur, vel si mortuus fuerit corpus non tradatur ecclesiastice sepulture[n].

Crisma[10] vero et oleum infirmorum et catecuminorum sub fideli custodia teneatur[o].

Quia semper | quolibet anno in Sancta die Jovis sancta | [Sb, f. 178 v ista sacramenta a solis episcopis benedicuntur, dicimus quod ultra diem illam crisma vetus et oleum penitus refutetur. Et ponatur in lampade et in aqua currenti ampulle laventur; et novum crisma et oleum apportetur[p]. Ee in Vigilia Pasche et Pentecostes in qualibet parrochiali ecclesia generalis[q] baptismus, si baptizandi fuerint pueri, celebretur[r].

De confirmatione

De confirmatione, que fit in fronte[s], precipimus[11] quod fit ab episcopis, quod sacerdotes moneant populum ad confirmationem, quia post

[k] ST omite *Petre*.
[l] ST: «opus fontium» por «plus».
[m] SV: duo.
[n] SV: sin autem baptizet, vel si mortuum fuerit corpus quod baptizatum non reperietur, nullatenus tradatur ecclesiasticae sepulturae.
[o] SV: tenentur.

[p] Por «apportetur» ST tiene «recipiatur in locis consuetis, et mittant honestas personas pro crismate».
[q] ST: generaliter.
[r] SV: celebretur, et mittantur personae honestae pro crismate.
[s] SV: fonte.

[6] RS, 298.
[7] OS, III. 2; RS, 297, 307.
[8] OS, III. 3; RS, 297-98, 304.
[9] OS, III. 5; RS, 298.
[10] RS, 298.
[11] OS, IV. 1-2. RS, 298.

baptismum debent confirmationis | sus|ci- | [ST, f. 172 v | [SB, f. 127 vb
pere sacramentum. Et [12] adulti confirmandi confiteantur, et postea con-
firmentur. Et quia in sacramento confirmationis continetur robur et gratia, et debilitatur penitus inimicus, dicatur [13] laycis ne expectent diu ad
confirmandum adventum |, episcopi, sed ducant pueros ad | [SV, p. 198b
eum vel vadant ubi adesse audierint prope; et quod possint mutari nomina in confirmatione. Et est sciendum quod soli episcopi possunt con-
firmare [14], consecrare virgines, ecclesias dedicare, clericos ordinare, cruces, vestimenta, calices et corporalia benedicere, litteras ordinationis
dare, indulgentias facere [t] secundum canonica instituta.

Illud autem est sciendum quod sacramenta baptismi et confirmationis
nunquam iterantur; etiam si confirmatus et baptizatus faceret se judeum
vel sarracenum et postea vellet redire ad fidem catholicam non baptiza-
retur nec confirmaretur, quia sufficit contritio in hac parte cum reconciliatione episcopi [u].

De Penitentia

Item quia penitentia est secunda tabula post naufragium, precipimus
quod sacerdotes moneant populum quod si quis | deliquerit | [Sb, f. 179 r
mortaliter recipiat penitentiam a proprio confessore vel a predicatoribus
vel minoribus [v] quibus data est licentia audiendi confessiones. Et [15] circa
confessionem curam adhibeant et cautelam, scilicet ut diligenter inquirant
peccata usitata sigillatim; inusitata non nisi a longe per circumstantias
aliquas, sic tamen ut expertis [va] detur materia confitendi.

Et [16] sacerdotes cum debent audire confessiones locum sibi in ecclesia eli-
gant convenientem ut communiter ab omnibus videantur. Extra ecclesiam
vero nullus audiat confessiones nisi in necessitate magna aut infirmitate.

Preterea [17] sacerdos in confessione audienda semper vultum habeat hu-
milem et oculos ad terram, nec facies respiciat confitentium, | [ST, f. 173 r
maxime mulierum, causa debite honestatis. Et patienter audiant que
dixerint in spiritu lenitatis [w], eis compatiendo. Nec admirentur de com-
missis quantumcumque | turpibus, sed eis pro posse per- | [SB, f. 128 ra
suadeant et pluribus modis ut confiteantur integre. Aliter enim dicant
eis nichil valere ad vitam eternam.

[t] ST omite «indulgentias facere».
[u] ST omite «cum reconciliatione episcopi».

[v] SV: majoribus.
[va] OS: ex peccatis.
[w] levitatis (!) in MS.

[12] OS, IV. 3.
[13] OS, IV. 4.
[14] OS, IV. 5; RS, 298.
[15] OS, VI. 1; RS, 299.
[16] OS, VI. 2; RS, 299-300.
[17] OS, VI. 3; RS, 300.

Audita [18] autem confessione semper confessor interroget confitentem si velit abstinere ab omni peccato. Aliter autem non absolvat, nec penitentiam iniungat, nec inde confidat [x] ; et moneat enim [y] ut interim agat quicquid boni potest, quia nisi proponat confitens decetero non peccare non est ei penitentia iniungenda. Et [19] in iniungendis penitentiis caveant sacerdotes quod secundum qualitatem culpe et possibilitatem confitentium eis iniungant, quia secundum qualitatem culpe debet esse quantitas penitentie. Alioquin quod minus est requiretur ab eis, quia facilitas venie incentivum tribuit delinquendi.

Debent [20] enim iniungere jejunium, elemosinas, venias, orationes, peregrinationes et huiusmodi. Et moneant quod jejunent Adventum et Quadragesimam, et dies veneris et in sabbatis non comedant carnes, nisi in infirmitate, et statuta jejunia observent, et festivitates colendas colant, et decimas et | primitias donent, et ad ecclesiam libenter | [Sb, f. 179 v veniant, et jura dominis | suis integre persolvant, aliter | [SV, p. 199 a graviter peccarent; ut sic paulatim ad id quod facere debent inducantur.

Item [21] dicimus sacerdotibus quod majora peccata reservent majoribus et discretioribus in confessione, sicut homicidia, sacrilegia, peccata contra naturam, incestus, stupra monialium, vota fracta, injectiones manuum in parentes, stupra [z] et huiusmodi. Provisio, tamen, quod si peccata enormia fuerint publica transmittantur huiusmodi penitentes penitentiario episcopi; et in Die Cineris ab ecclesia expellantur, et in Die Sancto Jovis introducantur, secundum quod in ecclesiis cathedralibus dinoscitur observari [aa].

Item [22] incendiarios, verberatores cleri|corum vel reli- | [ST, f. 173 v giosorum, simoniacos, et illos qui portant arma sarracenis, vel aliquod suffragium contra christianos eis faciunt [ab], hereticos, credentes, fautores, | receptatores, defensores eorundem, fractores ecclesia- | [SB, f. 128 rb rum qui Deum vel sanctos et precipue qui Beatam Virginem blasfemant vel maledicunt [ac]: omnes episcopo transmittantur. Item parentes qui inveniunt pueros mortuos iuxta se penitentiario episcopi transmittantur [ad]. In [23] dubiis tamen sacerdotes semper consulant episcopum aut viros sapientes, quorum consilio certificati, secure solvant vel ligent.

[x] SV: contingat.
[y] SV: tamen; ST: tantum.
[z] Laguna en SV, ST.
[aa] Por «secundum... observari» ST tiene «ut in predicta ecclesia dinoscitur observari».

[ab] SV, ST omiten «vel... faciunt».
[ac] SV, ST omiten «qui Deum... maledicunt».
[ad] Sentencia que falta en SV.

[18] OS, VI. 8; RS, 300.
[19] OS, VI. 9; RS, 300.
[20] RS, 300.
[21] OS, VI. 5. RS, 300.
[22] OS, VI. 6; RS, 300.
[23] OS, VI. 7.

Item [24] in furto, usura, rapina valde [ae] sibi caveant sacerdotes ne penitentiam iniungant nisi prius restituerint quibus debent, quia non remittitur peccatum nisi prius restituatur ablatum.

Nec [25] sacerdos missas aliquas quas iniunxerit celebrandas celebret, causa debite honestatis [af].

Item [26] in confessione sibi caveant sacerdotes ne inquirant nomina personarum cum quibus peccaverint confitentes, sed circumstantias tantummodo et qualitates

Et [27] nullus sacerdos ira vel odio vel metu mortis audeat relevare confessionem generaliter vel specialiter. Quod si fecerit deponatur.

Item quando sacerdos audit confessionem infirmi sibi penitentiam innotescat sed non iniungat nisi in peccato restitutionis, sed dicat | ei quod cum sanus fuerit ad ipsum revertatur. Si vero | [Sb, f. 180 r obierit roget Deum pro eodem ne sibi paretur laqueus transmigrandi [ag].

Item [28] provideat sacerdos quod quilibet parrochianus confiteatur generaliter semel in anno, scilicet in Quadragesima, ita quod non expectent finem Quadragesime, et postea communicent in festo Pasche. Alioquin procedat in pena secundum formam concilii generalis, que talis est: *Vivens arcebitur ab introitu ecclesie et moriens carebit ecclesiastica sepultura* [29]. Et hoc ut melius valeat observari, precipimus quod rectores

---

[ae] «Fraude» por «valde» en ST.

[af] SV añade: «quod pro illis tricennaria vel annualia celebrentur». ST: «nec pro viris tricennarium vel annuale celebretur»; ambos hacen mayor uso de OS que SB.

[ag] «Transmigranti» por «transmigrandi» en SV, ST. Después SV omite lo restante de la sección *De Penitentia*. ST continúa: «Item quoniam nonnulli in ecclesiis cathedralibus et alii conventicula illicita presumunt contrahere contra jura, sacramentis et pactionibus se ad invicem colligantes, ut ratione majoris numeri in ecclesia beneficium valeant obtinere, et conspirationes contrarias equitati tam contra socios quam (f. 174 r) contra majorem suum temere facientes, propter quod ecclesiae Dei grave imminet detrimentum, sacro approbante concilio statuimus, regimine utentes officii pastoralis, ut morbo huiusmodi utiliter succurratur, quod quicumque talia fece-

rit usque ad xv dies ex quo notitia constitutionis ad eum pervenerit vinculum colligationis dissolvat. Alioquin si in malitia sua perseverare presumpserit ipso facto suspensionis sententiam se noverit incurrisse. Et qui talia facere presumpserit in futurum penam suspensionis se noverit incurrisse. Item cum aliqui quaerentes quae sua sunt, non quae Jesu Christi, cum beneficia ecclesiastica in ecclesia Dei vaccent socios sibi atrahunt et pactionibus illicitis eos sibi alligant, ut propter majorem numerum pravitatis obtinere valeant quae intendunt, in offensam Dei et scandalum populi christiani, ut propriae ambitioni dampnabiliter satisfaciant. Ideoque statuimus, sancto concilio approbante, quod quicumque decetero talia presumpserit attentare, omnino beneficio careat sic obtento, ita quod numquam in eadem ecclesia beneficium valeat adipisci».

---

[24] OS, VI. 11; RS, 300.

[25] OS, VI. 12; RS, 300.

[26] OS, VI. 14; RS, 300.

[27] OS, VI. 15; RS, 300.

[28] OS, VI. 13.

[29] Lé, 314: «et vivens ab ingressu ecclesiae arceatur, et moriens ecclesiastica

ecclesiarum per se audiant confessiones parrochianorum suorum et non per conducticios nisi forte in necessitate, vel sit certus de predicatoribus vel minoribus qui eas audiverint a predictis parrochianis, ne ipsa parrochianorum fraude vel malitia ecclesie illudatur. Et ut de parrochianis confitentibus possit esse certus, omnia parrochianorum nomina in uno memoriali constabat.

Et quia clerici parrochiales predicare debent non solum verbo sed etiam exemplo, | statuimus quod predicti clerici ad minus | [SB, f. 128 va semel in anno confiteantur generaliter de peccatis suis nobis vel penitentiario nostro vel alicui fratri predicatori vel minori qui nos de sua confessione certificet secundum formam quam super hiis certificandis tam in clericis quam in laycis duxerimus ordinandam.

De Extrema Unctione

Quia de unctione extrema que datur in extremis laborantibus, nichil in ecclesiis ovservabatur, dicimus quod decetero omnibus in egritudine constitutis tradatur, et a sacerdotibus in ecclesiis publice predicetur. Et in Die Sancto Jovis quilibet sacerdos parrochialis mittat pro oleo infirmorum, catecuminorum et crismate sancto tres ampullas. Et [30] cum omni reverentia oleum sanctum ad infirmos deferatur. Et eos ungant | [Sb, f. 180 v sacerdotes cum magno honore et orationum celebritate que ad hoc sunt institute. Et nichil inde penitus exhigatur sive | a paupere | [ST, f. 174 v sive a divite; sed si quid gratis datum fuerit accipiatur.

Illud [31] tamen est notandum, quod istud sacramentum tantum prestatur adultis et sicut penitentia iteratur; ita [32] et istud sacramentum nec obligat aliquem, qui si convaluerit post unctionem accedere debeat ad uxorem.

Item [33] dicimus quod sacerdotes parrochiales omnes librum habeant in quo continetur ordo extreme unctionis, catecismi [ah], baptismi et huiusmodi, qui dicitur | *Manuale,* et [34] ordinarium officiorum | [SV, p. 199 b ecclesie secundum usum et modum qui observatur in ecclesia majori.

De Corpore et Sanguine Christi

Quia Corpus Christi consuevit dari infirmis, dicimus quod cum reverentia deferatur cum lumine et campanella. Et sacerdos qui portaverit

[ah] ST: catecumini.

careat sepultura. «Cf. el canon 21 del IV Concilio Laterano al referirse a la *christiana sepultura.*
[30] OS, VIII. 1; RS, 301-02.
[31] OS, VIII. 2; RS, 302.
[32] OS, VIII. 3; RS, 302.
[33] OS, VIII. 4; RS, 302.
[34] OS, VIII. 5. RS, 302.

induat superpellicium et stolam [ai], et det infirmo. Et si infirmus facit forte vomitum recognoscat corpus et non det ei. Et si [aj] revertitur ad ecclesiam campanella non pulsetur nisi corpus portaret [ak]. Et [35] admoneant populum sacerdotes quod cum viderint corpus vel audierint campanellam omnes se inclinent vel genua flectant ob reverentiam Jesu Christi. Nec presbiteri [36] permittant diaconos deferre Corpus Christi infirmis nisi in necessitate, cum absens fuerit sacerdos. | Sed | [SB, f. 128 vb semper deferant sacerdotes cum magna reverentia et maturitate, in calice vel in pixide multum honeste, et dicant psalmos [al] penitentiales cum letania pro infirmo in eundo et redeundo et alias orationes secrete. Sic enim debitum solvant pro infirmo.

Item [37] dicimus quod honor maximus exhibeatur altaribus, et maxime ubi Corpus Christi reservatur et missa celebratur. Et [38] in media parte altaris cum summa diligentia et honestate, sub clave si fieri po- | test, corpus domini custodiatur. | [ST, f. 175 r

Item [39] nulli clericorum [am] permittatur servire altari nisi cum superpellicio | vel cappa rotunda. Nec [40] aliquis sit ausus bis in | [Sb, f. 181 r die celebrare missam nisi ex magna necessitate, et tunc non recipiat in prima missa post communionem vinum.

Item [41] nec aliquis presumat missam celebrare nisi prius matutinas dixerit canonicas et primam, aliqua necessitate [an].

Et [42] lintheamina altaris et indumenta sacerdotalia sepe abluantur ob reverentiam et presentiam Jesu Christi et totius curie celestis que cum eo presens est quotiens missa celebratur.

Calices [43] etiam unde infirmi communicant decenter et munde [ao] custodiantur ut devotius communicent infirmi. Ampulle [44] quoque vini et aque in ministerio altaris munde et integre habeantur, et una ab altera cognoscatur.

Item [45] prohibemus sacerdotibus ne habeant secum prolem ad servitium altaris propter scandalum. Et [46] de octo in octo diebus renovetur

[ai] ST omite «et stolam».
[aj] SV, ST: cum.
[ak] SV, ST: portaretur.
[al] SV, ST: septem psalmos.

[am] SV, ST: clerico.
[an] ST: nisi ex aliqua necessitate.
[ao] Por «decenter et munde» ST tiene «mundi».

[35] OS, V. 6.
[36] OS, V. 5; RS, 298-99.
[37] OS, V. 1; RS, 298.
[38] OS, V. 7; RS, 299.
[39] OS, V. 8.
[40] OS, V. 9; RS,299.
[41] OS, V. 10; R. S, 299.
[42] OS, V. 2; RS, 298.
[43] OS, V. 3. RS, 298.
[44] OS, V. 4.
[45] OS, C(ommunia) P(raecepta) 29; RS, 306.
[46] OS, CP 21; RS, 304.

Corpus Christi ne sui vetustate aliquid a Dei devotione removeantur.

Et dicimus quod in primo *Memento* [ap] de sacra sacerdotes habeant memoriam pro benefactoribus vivis; in secundo pro mortuis. Et [47] cum inceperint *Qui Pridie* non statim elevent manus alte, sed ante pectus teneant donec dixerint: *Hoc est enim Corpus Meum.* | Et | [SB, f. 129 ra tunc elevent caute ita ut possit videri ab omnibus quia tunc est Corpus Christi ibi. Et predicetur populo quod tunc omnes flectant genua et adorent Corpus Christi.

Et licet totum canonem debeant dicere cum diligentia et maturitate, ab illo loco *Qui Pridie* usque *Unde et memores Domine* [aq] cum majori devotione et sollicitudine precipimus | observari quia om- | [SV, p. 200 a nia illa verba fere sunt de substantia sacramenti.

Item [48] dicimus quod vinum rubeum potius quam | [ST, f. 175 v album ministretur in calice propter aque similitudinem, et purum et bonum et non ineptum [ar] ad reverentiam Jesu Christi.

Item corporalia munda et nitida teneantur et ad morem Cistercii [as] fiant decetero | ac etiam incidantur. Et [49] si quid de san- | [Sb, f. 181 v guine Domini ceciderit super corporale rescindendum est ipsum corporale et in locum reliquiarum honorifice reponendum.

Si super pallas vel super casulla vel vestimentum abluantur in aqua, et partes ille postea comburantur; et cinis in sacrario ponatur [at].

Et [50] si musca vel aranea enim [au] contingente super calicem ceciderit, si viva fuerit vel mortua, caute extrahatur et [av] comburatur; et cinis in sacrario reponatur. Si [51] autem infirmus recepto corpore vomitum fecerit, in vase aliquo recipiatur; vel si vas habere non poterit et in terra vomitum fecerit, locus radatur et totum in aqua prohiciatur. Tamen caveat sacerdos cum dat corpus quod querat utrum infirmus consueverit facere vomitum, ut servet quod superius est dictum. Et etiam moneat quod si contingerit infirmus [aw] vomitum facere in vase recipiatur.

Item dicimus quod Corpus Christi non tradatur illis qui suspenduntur vel debent justitiari, nisi impunitas promittatur [ax] usque ad quatuor [ay]

[ap] SV, ST: momento.
[aq] *«Supra quae propitio»* por *«Unde et memores Domine»* en SV, ST.
[ar] Por «ineptum ad» ST tiene «emptum ob».
[as] SV: ad modem vel morem Cisterciensium.
[at] ST añade: «Si vero in terra vel in lapide ceciderit locus radatur et in sacrario rasura ponatur». Cf. OS, CP 25.
[au] SV, Sb: casu. ST omite «enim contingente».
[av] Sb omite «extrahatur et».
[aw] «Infirmum» en MSS.
[ax] ST: impuniti permittantur.
[ay] ST: tres.

[47] OS, CP 28; RS, 315-16.
[48] OS, CP 28; RS, 306.
[49] OS, CP 23; RS, 305.
[50] OS, CP 24; RS, 305.
[51] RS, 305.

dies post susceptionem sacramenti, ob scandalum laycorum. Sed si adorare voluerint, adorent ac recognoscant.

Tradi autem possunt ecclesiastice sepulture si fuerit de principis voluntate.

Missam vero ultra meridiem nullus cantet nisi in vigilia Pasche, nec de nocte nisi in Nativitate Domini.

De Matrimonio | | [SB, f. 129 rb

Item [52] quia matrimonium est apud omnes gentes dic- | [ST, f. 176 r imus quod cum honore et reverentia celebretur, et in facie ecclesie non in risu vel in joco ne condempnatur [az]. Et per octo dies antea [ba] dicat sacerdos in ecclesia sub pena excommunicationis quod talis vult talem ducere in uxorem et si sciunt impedimentum consanguinitatis vel adulterii vel affinitatis carnalis vel spiritualis veniant coram eo; aliter peccarent mortaliter. Et non audirentur nisi infra illos octo [bb] dies dixerint que sciunt. Et sacerdotes querant | ad hostium ecclesie si | [Sb, f. 182 r est aliquis qui sciat impedimentum, et si dicatur *Non* desponset eos per verba de presenti, recipiendo anulum primo de manu mariti, et dicat: *Ego Petrus recipio te Bertam* [bc] *in uxorem et trado meipsum in legalem virum.* Et ita ponat anulum in quarto digito mulieris, dicendo: *In nomine Patris et Filii et Spiritus Sancti, Amen* [bd]. Eodem modo faciat uxor ut dicitur de marito [be]. Et sic est matrimonium confirmatum [bf].

Et prohibeant sacerdotes ne fiant clandestina matrimonia. Nec dent sibi ad invicem fidem de contrahendo matrimonio nisi coram sacerdote et coram pluribus hominibus, quia ex hoc multa mala consueverunt venire.

Item [53] dicimus sub pena excomuni|cationis ne sor- | [SV, p. 200 b tilegia fiant nec maleficia nec ligationes que fiunt per malificas mulieres.

Et qui sciunt impedimentum matrimonii dicant sicut est, votum, ordinem, consanguinitatem, affinitatem, disparem cultum, compaternitatem et huiusmodi. Nec [54] in casu dubio sacerdotes audeant perficere matrimonio, episcopo inconsulto, sed ad eum referant semper omnes matrimonii questiones.

Item [55] dicimus sacerdotibus ne aliquid exhigant ante benedictionem nuptialem nec ante sepulturam, sive pro matrimonio celebrando. Sed cele-

[az] SV, ST: contemnatur.
[ba] Por «octo dies antea» ST tiene aliquot diei ante».
[bb] ST omite «octo».
[bc] ST: *Ego P. accipio te Berengariam.*

[bd] ST omite «*Sancti, Amen*».
[be] ST: Eodem modo fiat uxori ut dicitur.
[bf] SV: consummatum.

[52] OS, VII. 1; RS, 301.
[53] OS, VII. 2; RS, 301.
[54] OS, VII. 3; RS, 301.
[55] OS, VII. 4. CP 55; RS, 301.

bratis nuptiis exhigant | fercula sua ^{bg}, si necesse fuerit, | [ST, f. 176 v vel mortuarium, quia post licite facere possunt consuetudine celebrante ^{bh}.

Item [56] dicimus quod aliquis conjugum non intret religionem vel recipiatur, episcopo inconsulto.

Dicimus [57] sacerdotibus ut cum aliquis confitetur eis se fidem dedisse alicui mulieri de matrimonio contrahendo cum ea et, fide data, cognovit eam, non det ei licentiam contrahendi cum alia, quia carnalis copula | cum illa cui fidem dedit, matrimonium consummavit. | [SB, f. 129 va Nec intersint clandestinis matrimoniis nisi in multorum presentia, facta denuntiatione, ut supra dicitur.

Et [58] sciant sacerdotes et clerici parrochiales quod si circa ista matrimonia prohibenda necligentes extiterint et denuntiationes, ut factum est, facere non curaverint, | vel talibus clandestinis matrimoniis | [Sb, f. 182 v interfuerint, iuxta generale concilium per triennium ab officio suspendantur. Et aliter nichilominus gravius puniantur ^{bi}, quia qui male agit odit lucem.

Item dicimus sacerdotibus ne faciant nuptias ab Adventu Domini usque ad festum Beati Ilarii, et tunc faciant usque ad Dominicam ^{bj} Septuagessime; et ex tunc cessent usque ad Dominicam de Quasimodo; et tunc fiant usque ad Dominicam de Voce Jocunditatis que precedit festum Ascensionis Domini. Et tunc cessent continue per tres septimanas usque ad Dominicam de Trinitate ^{bk}. Et ex tunc celebrent nuptias usque ad Dominicam de Adventu ^{bl}; hoc proviso, quod prima Dominica Adventus que inducit prohibitionem intelligatur prohibita, et festum Sancti Ilarii quod inducit permissionem intelligatur concessa, et sic de aliis.

Item [59] dicimus quod mulieres votum non faciant nisi cum magna deliberatione animi, et tunc faciant virorum assensu et consilio sacerdotum | | [ST, f. 177 r

De Ordinibus Clericorum

Item quia in ordinibus recipiendis multa veniunt pericula, dicimus quod quarta feria quatuor temporum ^{bm} omnes ordinandi archidiaconibus se presentent ut tam de vita quam de moribus quam scientia possit fieri

^{bg} Por «fercula sua» ST tiene «quod consuetum est».

^{bh} SV: «tolerante» por «celebrante»; ST: possunt velante consuetudine tolerante.

^{bi} «Et sciant... puniantur» omiten SV, ST.

^{bj} ST: septimanam.

^{bk} Sb: Adventu.

^{bl} Sb omite «Et... Adventu».

^{bm} ST omite «quarta... temporum».

[56] OS, VII. 5.
[57] OS, CP 46; RS, 307.
[58] OS, CP 47-48; RS, 306-07.
[59] OS, CP 11; RS, 302.

III

scrutinium diligenter, utrum cantent vel legant vel sint legitimi [bn] vel loqui sciant latinis verbis, sic quod cum diligentia sint examinati et probati die Veneris, qualiter in domo Domini conversari debeant. Et dicimus clericis et precipimus quod ad ordines suscipiendos et sinodum honeste veniant tam in vestibus quam in coronis. Nec aliquid dent vel permittant [bo] archidiaconibus vel eorum clericis vel episcopo vel clericis episcopi ut ordinentur, quia simoniacum esset.

Item quod aliquis non recipiat ordines nisi fuerit nomen eius scriptum in matricula archidiaconi de conscientia episcoporum, quia excomminicati essent.

Item dicimus archidiaconibus ne presentent | clericos | [Sb, f. 183 r aliorum episcopatuum sine litteris episcoporum | proprio- | [SB, f. 129 v rum quas tradant episcopo | cum sigillo pendenti. Et no- | [SV, p. 201 a mina omnium clericorum qui fuerint ordinandi [bp] tradantur episcopo et apud ipsum in matricula reponantur.

Item dicimus quod religiose persone que habitum recipiant aliorum episcopatuum vel nostri non se presentent sine litteris sui majoris.

Item dicimus quod nullus presentet ad quartum gradum nisi loqui sciat latinis verbis [bq], et ut possint habere doctorum copiam, sicut statutum est, semper in cathedrali ecclesia detur portio magistris [br].

Item [60] dicimus quod nullus sacerdos habeat in domo sua aliqua occasione mulierem nisi sit mater aut soror, nisi esset persona de qua nulla suspitio possit haberi.

Item [bs] dicimus clericis habentibus ecclesias quod portionarios non ponant in ecclesiis, episcopo inconsulto. Nec [61] aliquis clericus sit ausus recipere decimas nisi per episcopum.

Item [62] dicimus quod nullus faciat pactum aliquod patronis super facto ecclesiarum antequam sit | episcopo presentatus, vel etiam | [ST, f. 177 v post sine conscientia episcopi [bt]. Nec [63] admittatur aliquis ad predicandum nisi sit autentica persona, vel ab epicopo missa vel licentiata.

Qualiter Christiani Orare Debent

Exortentur [64] sepe presbiteri populum [bu] ad dicendum *Orationem Dominicam* [bv] et *Credo in Deum* et *Beate Virginis Salutationem,* et quod

[bn] SV omite «vel sint legitimi».
[bo] ST: promittant.
[bp] ST: ordinati.
[bq] Por «latinis verbis» ST tiene «latinum», y omite lo restante de la sección.

[br] SV: magistro grammaticae.
[bs] ST omite esta sección.
[bt] SV, ST omite «vel... episcopi».
[bu] SV: Exhortamur ut saepe; ST: Excitent semper populum presbyteri.
[bv] ST: scilicet *Pater Noster.*

[60] OS, CP 12; RS, 302.
[61] OS, CP 14; RS, 302.
[62] OS, CP 17. RS, 302.
[63] OS, CP 16; RS, 303.
[64] OS, CP 10; RS, 302.

doceant filios *Oracionem Dominicam* et *Credo in Deum* et *Salutationes*. Et [65] in aliqua parte sermonis aliquando exponant fideliter populo [bw] simbolum fidei, et eis diligenter distingant articulos fidei et confirment auctoritatibus et rationibus sacre scripture pro posse et scientia sua, propter laycos instruendos [bx] et hereticos et corruptores fidei confunden- dos. | | [Sb, f. 183 v

De Vita et Honestate Clericorum

Item [66] prohibemus universis clericis ludere cum taxillis vel interesse spectaculis et coreis mulierum, vel intrare tabernas causa potandi, vel sine socio intrare domos mulierum suspectarum, aut discurrere per vicos et plateas, vel ire cotidie ad mercata cum non subesset causa, nec sus- pensioni latronum nec combustioni hominum aliquorum nec sanguinis effusioni intersint.

Item | moneant populum quod illi qui veniunt ad | [SB, f. 130 ra vigilias ecclesiarum caute et honeste se habeant, nec [67] permittant coreas facere in cimiteriis vel ecclesiis vel turpes cantilenas cantare [by]. Nec in ecclesia fiant conjurationes aque ferventis vel ferri candentis vel aque frigide conjurate, quia omnia ista superstitiosa sunt penitus et contra Deum.

Item [68] nullus clericus fidejubeat judeo vel feneratori; nec obliget calicem vel vestimenta vel pallas altaris vel libros judeis vel aliis, nisi in casibus licitis et de licentia episcopi [bz].

Item dicimus clericis quod immobilia | non alienent | [ST, f. 178 r aliquo casu, episcopo inconsulto. Et [69] fiat inventarium de omnibus pos- sessionibus ecclesie et scribant omnia in missali, ut cum episcopus vel archidiaconus videre voluerint meliorata inveniant. Nec aliquis faciat mutuum super ecclesias, episcopo inconsulto, quia satis est quod clerici hab|eant redditus ecclesiarum. Nec obligent sine causa | [SV, p. 201 b quam episcopus debet scire.

Item [70] dicimus sacerdotibus vel habentibus curam quod nullus renun- tiet nisi in manu episcopi. Et [71] cum venerint ad sinodum perquirant parrochiam et visitent infirmos et dent penitentiam eisdem, exponendo

---

[bw] Por «fideliter populo» ST tiene «populo fideli».
[bx] Sb: instituendos.

[by] SV, ST omiten «vel... cantare».
[bz] SV, ST omiten «vel... episcopi».

[65] OS, CP 32; RS, 306.
[66] OS, CP 13; RS, 302.
[67] OS, CP 36; RS, 307.
[68] OS, CP 15; RS, 302-03.
[69] OS, CP 1; RS, 303.
[70] OS, CP 8; RS, 304.
[71] OS, CP 20; RS, 304.

eis qualiter tenentur ire ad sinodum, ut si interim morerentur sine penitentia non decederent. A qua sinodo cum revenerint non requisiti visitent infirmos et faciant quod saluti animarum videbitur expedire.

Item [72] dicimus quod questores, quantumcumque portent litteras domini pape vel archiepiscopi vel aliorum episcoporum, non admittantur ad predicationem nisi expressas litteras habuerint ab episcopo; sed ipsi sacerdotes legant litteras indulgentiarum et exponant in populo, quia in predicatione huiusmodi questorum hereses intelleximus predicari. Quomodo enim predicabunt | nisi mittantur. | [Sb, f. 184 r

Item dicimus quod fratres predicatores et minores honorifice a clericis recipiantur et eis in necessitatibus subveniatur. Hoc idem populo exponatur [ca].

Item dicimus quod si festum fuerit die Lune que habeat jejunium | precedenti Sabbato jejunetur. Festivitates autem Beati | [SB, f. 130 rb Francisci, Beati Dominici ac Sancti Antonii, quas sanctorum catalogo novimus ascriptas, festivari precipimus, et novem inde fieri lectiones.

Item [73] dicimus quod clerici pannos lisatos [cb] non portent, nec manicas sutas [cc], nec sotulares rostratos [cd], et maxime presbiteri.

Item dicimus quod in Quadragesima dicantur semper novem lectiones pro defunctis, exceptis festivitatibus novem lectionum, diebus aliis feriatis tres vel secundum quod erit de consuetudine [ce].

Et ad horas Beate Virginis non sedeant, neque ad *Magnificat,* neque ad *Nunc dimittis* et *Benedictus* et *Quicumque Vult.* Semper assurgant ad *Gloriam Patri.* Et ubi plures clerici fuerint semper unus levet psalmos, et punctantes [cf] sine sincopa legant psalmos ac etiam lectiones.

In festivitatibus vero cantent honorifice et decenter. Et semper cantetur *Gloria in Excelsis Deo* in dominicis diebus et festivis, exceptis diebus dominicis Quadragesime et Adventus. *Credo,* autem, *in Unum Deum* numquam cantetur nisi dominicis diebus et festivitatibus apostolorum et duplicibus festis; causa tamen reverentie Domine nostre in Sabbato cantari potest.

Item dicimus quod quilibet sacerdos cum audierit mortem sui parrochiani roget Deum pro eo. Et [74] quilibet portet ad sinodum nomen sive nomina clericorum qui decesserint in anno in sua parrochia, et ibi quilibet absolvat eos. Processiones autem pro defunctis fiant semper diebus Lune nisi festivitas occurrerit novem lectionum.

[ca] SV omite «et... exponatur».
[cb] SV, Sb: listatos; ST: virgatos.
[ce] SV: sutitias; ST: consutitias.
[cd] ST: rotartos.

[ce] SV, ST omiten «vel consuetudine».
[cf] SV: punctatis; ST: puntatim.

[72] OS, CP 9, 41; RS, 304.
[73] RS, 307.
[74] OS, CP 57.

Item dicimus quod quilibet sacerdos caute et diligenter inquirat in sua parrochia quis male vivat, et si invenerit eum corrigat ter vel quater monendo; et nisi resipuerit interdicatur persona, ad majorem penam de consilio episcopi nichilominus processurus.

Item [75] dicimus quod quatuor tempora mandentur semper jejunari: quorum jejunium est primum in Adventu; secundum in Quadragesima; tertium in festo Pentecostes; quartum in mense Septembris. Et pos-|sunt scribi [cg] per hos versus: | [SV, p. 202 a | [SB, f. 130 va | [Sb, f. 184 v

Vult crux, lucia, cinis et Carismata [ch] dia,

Ut det vota-[ci] pia, quarta sequens feria [cj],

Et jejunent in cibo quadragesimali.

In diebus autem letaniarum possunt comedere caseum et ova, Ascensionis vigilia excepta [ck].

[cg] ST: sciri.

[ch] SV: Verismata.

[ci] SV: «devota» por «det vota».

[cj] Villanueva (ST) enmienda la línea así: «Ut sit in angaria IIII sequens ferias».

[ck] SV, ST continúan: «Item sacerdotes moneant populum quod quilibet parrochianus addiscat *Salutationes Beate Marie, Pater Noster* et *Credo in Deum*» (explicit ST). SV concluye: «Ista mandavit Dominus Archiepiscopus Tarraconensis observari in Synodo per eum celebrata in Sede Barchinonensi, sede vacante, anno domini 1241, in die Sancti Lucae Evangelistae».

[75] OS, VI. 16; RS, 301.

IV

LA CARRERA DEL OBISPO ABRIL DE URGEL: LA IGLESIA ESPAÑOLA EN EL SIGLO XIII*

Cuando llegue el momento en que algún historiador futuro quiera † proporcionar una información completa sobre la iglesia española en el siglo XIII, tendrá motivos para quejarse, como el Dr. Waley, de que primero tiene que cocer sus propios ladrillos y mezclar su propia argamasa [1]. Hay una deplorable falta de monografías, y particularmente de monografías dedicadas al episcopado. Apenas hay estudios biográficos de los eclesiásticos más destacados [2]. Por ejemplo, la preeminente figura del arzobispo Rodrigo de Toledo, escritor y guerrero, espera aún un estudio crítico basado en la extensa documentación existente en Toledo y en otros lugares. Hace cuarenta años se le dedicaron simultáneamente dos biografías: una, un trabajo esencialmente hagiográfico, celebraba la memoria del gran abanderado de una reforma

* Deseo hacer constar mi gratitud al profesor Walter Ullmann por su liberal dirección y al profesor Antonio García y García por las muchas amabilidades que tuvo conmigo durante mis investigaciones en España, particularmente en Salamanca. Apenas necesito añadir que a no ser por la tolerancia de cierto número de archiveros catedralicios este trabajo no se habría escrito. El Dr. Derek Lomax leyó amablemente un primer borrador de este artículo e hizo sugerencias muy valiosas.

Se han utilizado las abreviaturas siguientes:

AC = Archivo de la Catedral.
ACS = Archivo de la Catedral de Salamanca (Cuando se cita un documento de Salamanca se acompaña el número que tiene asignado en F. MARCOS RODRÍGUEZ, *Catálogo de Documentos del Archivo Catedralicio de Salamanca, siglos XII-XV*, Salamanca, 1962).
ACSC = Archivo de la Catedral de Santiago de Compostela.
ACU = Archivo de la Catedral de Seo de Urgel.
AD = Archivo Diocesano.
AE = Archivo Episcopal.
ACA = Archivo de la Corona de Aragón, Barcelona.
AHN = Archivo Histórico Nacional, Madrid.
AHA = Archivo Histórico Archidiocesano (Tarragona).
ASV = Archivio Segreto Vaticano.
RV = Registros del Vaticano.
CP = Collecció Plandolit (cf. n. 13).

[1] D. WALEY, *The Papal State in the Thirteenth Century*, Londres, 1961, pág. XIII.

[2] D. W. LOMAX, *Don Ramón, bishop of Palencia, 1148-84*, «Homenaje a Jaime Vicens Vives», I (Barcelona, 1965), págs. 279-291. Entre un pequeño número de estudios que son importantes, deben señalarse en particular los siguientes: L. SERRANO, *Don Mauricio, obispo de Burgos y fundador de su catedral*, Madrid, 1922; J. GOÑI GAZTAMBIDE, *Los obispos de Pamplona del siglo XIII*, «Príncipe de Viana», 66 (1957), págs. 41-237; D. MANSILLA, *El Cardenal hispano Pelayo Gaitán*, «Anthologica Annua», I (1953), págs. 11-66; E. JUNYENT, *Diplomatari de Sant Bernat Calvó abat de Santes Creus, bisbe de Vich*, Reus, 1956.

de cuyos resultados demostraba que era imposible descubrir huella alguna [3]; la otra, una obra más crítica, resultaba incompleta porque al autor le fue negado por su competidor, el archivero de la catedral de Toledo, el acceso a los documentos de este archivo [4]. Como historiador, Estella no se propuso otra meta que la del memorialista Gil González Dávila tres siglos antes: demostrar que el objeto de sus estudios había sido un hombre «meritorio». Después de todo, ¿podía haber algo más importante en un obispo? [5]. Tratada así, la historia eclesiástica tiende a degenerar en una forma de piedad, en una clase de literatura en la que pueden encontrarse las virtudes que se recomiendan a la juventud, y cuya forma ideal son las vidas de hombres no grandes, sino santos (o al menos irreprochables), tales como las que Yepes solía consultar en sus años jóvenes [6].

Los eclesiásticos españoles se han librado del escrutinio que han sufrido sus contemporáneos de otros países y han escapado a la clase de investigación que pretende diagnosticar la enfermedad pasajera de un arzobispo muerto hace ocho siglos [7]. Ni Rodrigo de Toledo ni Pedro de Albalat, arzobispo de Tarragona en la misma época, y quizá el mayor reformador de la iglesia española en este siglo, han sufrido semejante tratamiento. Por tanto, no puede sorprendernos que los obispos de segunda fila, que jugaron poco o ningún papel en la vida pública, hayan pasado inadvertidos. Sin embargo merecen atención por el propio hecho de ser de segunda fila, porque la historia de la Iglesia, diremos parafraseando a Thomas Carlyle, no es sólo la biografía de los grandes eclesiásticos —de papas del calibre de Gregorio VII e Inocencio III— o de prelados de la eminencia de Becket o del propio Rodrigo de Toledo. Para conseguir un sentido de la proporción es necesario mirar detrás de los gigantes [8], a pesar de

---

[3] E. ESTELLA ZALAYA, *El fundador de la Catedral de Toledo. Estudio histórico del pontificado de D. Rodrigo Ximénez de Rada*, Toledo, 1926, págs. V y 92.

[4] J. GOROSTERRATZU, *Don Rodrigo Jiménez de Rada, gran estadista, escritor y prelado*, Pamplona, 1925. Su relato del caso está incluido en la introducción. Estella, después de afirmar que el silencio era la única reacción adecuada a las acusaciones de Gorosterratzu, se dedica a disculparse a sí mismo (*op. cit.*, pág. VII).

[5] Gil GONZÁLEZ DÁVILA, *Historia de las antigüedades de Salamanca*, Salamanca, 1606, lib. III, pág. 240: «Con una palabra que dixera bastava y con ella se avia dicho todo lo que compone y adorna la vida de un buen obispo. Fue digno del nombre de Prelado. ¿Qué más se pudo dezir?» Del obispo Pedro Pérez, tan sumariamente despachado, se trata más adelante.

[6] A. de YEPES, *Corónica de la Orden de San Benito*, I, Valladolid, 1609-1621, dedicatoria: «En mis primeros años y estudios, Padres Reverendísimos, fui inclinado a leer historias eclesiásticas y hallaba en ellas singular gusto y consuelo».

[7] M. D. KNOWLES, *Archbishop Thomas Becket: a character study*, «Proceedings of the British Academy», 35 (1949), págs. 177-205, en n. 53.

[8] Cf. las observaciones de J. GAUDEMET en *Recherches sur l'épiscopat médiéval en France*, «Proceedings of the Second International Congress of Medieval Canon Law. Monumenta Iuris Canonici», ser. C, subsidia, vol. I,

la observación del Sr. E. H. Carr de que la historia «es inevitable-
mente una historia del éxito». Porque, siguiendo la analogía de la
historia del cricket que él propone, la suerte del segundo equipo
tiene interés, —y no sólo por la razón de que ocasionalmente un miembro de este equipo pueda ganar sus colores y obtener la promoción— [9].

I

Abril, obispo de la sede pirenáica de Urgel de 1257 a 1269, difícilmente hubiera recibido la absolución del Sr. Carr. Lo poco que
sabemos de él con certeza —y algo más sin ella— puede encontrarse
en el *Dictionnaire d'histoire et de géographie ecclésiastiques*[10]. En el siglo
pasado, Villanueva, cuyos viajes por los archivos de Cataluña pre-
pararon el camino para un renacimiento del estudio serio de la historia eclesiástica de la región, descubrió en Urgel cierto número de
cartas enviadas por Abril a sus amigos y relaciones en las distantes
Galicia y Salamanca[11]. Ahora nos es posible añadir bastante a la
historia narrada por Villanueva y repetida por el autor del artículo
dedicado a Abril en el *Dictionnaire*, y proporcionar alguna información
sobre la carrera del obispo tanto antes como después de su promoción.
Pero queda aún mucha incertidumbre. Como sucedía con el gorrión
de Beda, se sabe mucho menos de sus comienzos y de su fin que de
otros aspectos de su carrera. Su lugar de origen y la fecha de su naci-
miento se prestan a la conjetura; la época y localización de su muerte
y sepultura son objeto de discusión. Y Villanueva añadió la confusión
a la ignorancia al poner en duda que su nombre fuera Abril siquiera.

La creencia de Villanueva de que su nombre era en realidad
Alfonsus Aprilis se basa en lo que parece haber sido una lectura defec-
tuosa de la correspondencia de Abril en el archivo de la catedral de
Urgel. Villanueva menciona las cartas enviadas por la madre del

Ciudad del Vaticano, 1965, págs. 139-154, en la pág. 139: «Si la vie de certains prélats illustres est bien connue,
et si, à travers ces exemples peut-être exceptionnels, on s'est souvent fait une image de cet épiscopat, il n'est
pas sans intérêt d'étudier des cas plus nombreux et par là même plus communs, à fin de corriger parfois les
touches d'un tableau trop haut en couleurs».

[9] E. H. CARR, *What is History?*, Londres, 1961, págs. 120-121.

[10] Ed. A. BAUDRILLART y otros, París, 1912, III, col. 1070, artículo por A. LAMBERT; cf. también J. VINCKE,
Staat und Kirche in Katalonien und Aragon während des Mittelalers, Münster, 1931, pág. 278.

[11] J. VILLANUEVA, *Viage literario a las iglesias de España*, 11, Madrid, 1850, págs. 94-101 y 237-239. Sobre
la importancia de las investigaciones de Villanueva, véase F. MATEU I LLOPIS, *El viaje literario del P. Villanueva
y las iglesias de Cataluña*, Barcelona, 1947.

obispo, Auroana Pérez, por su hermana Sancha Peláez y por tres canónigos de Compostela —Alfonso Pérez, su tío, y M. Abril y P. Abril, tesorero de la iglesia— que según Villanueva eran sus hermanos [12]. Villanueva no publicó las cartas en las que se basaba esta afirción, y la pérdida de gran parte de los fondos del archivo de Urgel durante la guerra de 1936-1939, en que fueron enviados a Barcelona, complica más aún la tarea de averiguar la verdad sobre este punto. Sin embargo, las pérdidas de la guerra están hasta cierto punto subsanadas por la supervivencia de una colección de transcripciones de documentos originales realizadas a fines del siglo pasado por el entonces archivero Don Joaquín Plandolit [13], y la cita por Villanueva de una frase de la carta de M. Abril, identifica esta carta con una copia hecha por Plandolit. Ni M. Abril ni P. Abril se llaman a sí mismos hermanos del obispo [14], parentesco que, de haber existido, difícilmente hubieran dejado de mencionar en el curso de un par de cartas de súplica. El tío del obispo no dejó de recordar a su sobrino la voz de la sangre [15]. Además, cuando en mayo de 1232 Pelayo Sebastiánez, arcediano de Orense, redacta su testamento antes de emprender peregrinación a Jerusalén, no hace mención alguna del futuro obispo de Urgel, mientras que tanto Martín Abril como Pedro Abril, sobrinos del arcediano (y según Villanueva hermanos de Abril) aparecen como beneficiarios [16]. Aún en el caso de que Abril de Urgel hubiera sido excluido por despecho por su tío Pelayo Sebastiánez, podríamos esperar que se le mencionase de todos modos. Los testamentos del siglo XIII no dejaban nada por decir [17]. Pero el futuro obispo de Urgel parece haber tenido alguna relación con Pelayo Sebastiánez, la cual es posible descubrir examinando los testamentos de dos miembros del cabildo de Compostela, el tesorero Pedro Abril y el canónigo Alfonso Pérez.

[12] VILLANUEVA, op. cit., págs. 97-99.

[13] El archivo de Urgel está, en septiembre de 1966, sin catalogar en absoluto, y ni el gran número de documentos que datan de la Edad Media ni las hojas sueltas de papel que contienen las copias de Plandolit tienen ningún sistema de referencia. Sin embargo, el actual archivero, D. Lluis Serdà —a cuya generosísima cooperación estoy enormemente agradecido— ha comenzado la inmensa tarea de ponerlo todo en orden. La fidelidad de las copias de Plandolit, excepto en una o dos palabras escasas, está fuera de duda, porque en un considerable número de casos fue posible comparar sus versiones con los originales.

[14] VILLANUEVA, op. cit., pág. 97. Cf. el Apéndice 1 y más adelante (pág. 158).

[15] Cf. el Apéndice 2.

[16] ACSC, Tumbo C, fol. XV v. Legó todo, 'domino Aprili fratri meo', y después a los hijos del dicho hermano, Pedro Abril, Pelayo Abril y Martín Abril. Dice A. LÓPEZ FERREIRO, Historia de la santa iglesia de Santiago de Compostela, Santiago de Compostela, 1902, págs. 5, 362, que Abril Sebastiánez era «cambiador y noble burgués compostelano».

[17] Por ejemplo, Fernando Alfonso, canónigo de Salamanca y de León, especificaba en su testamento de 1294 que sus hermanos Martín y Alfonso «no ayan de lo mio ninguna cossa» (ACS, 20/2/25—2 = Marcos, 432).

En su testamento, fechado en 1279, Pedro Abril cita a Pelayo Sebastiánez como su tío paterno«patruus meus donnus Pelagius Sebastiani, quondam archidiaconus auriensis»[18]; y cuatro años más tarde, Alfonso Pérez menciona a otro tío de Pedro Abril, Juan Sebastiánez, como hermano suyo[19]. Solamente en la suposición de que Alfonso Pérez, tío del obispo Abril, con «hermano» quería decir «cuñado», en el sentido de que una hermana suya se había casado con el hermano menor del arcediano de Orense, Abril Sebastiánez, sería posible explicar el porqué Pedro Abril y su hermano Martín pudieron reivindicar algún parentesco con Abril, el sobrino de Alfonso Pérez, después de su elevación al episcopado de Urgel[20]. En este caso fue a la hermana de Pedro Abril, Auroana Abril, que Auroana Pérez, la madre del obispo, menciona como su «sobrina»[21]. Nada se sabe acerca del padre del obispo Abril, excepto que su nombre debió haber sido Pelayo[22]. No hay fundamentos para identificarle con el peregrino arcediano de Orense, cuya aparente falta de interés por el hijo de la hermana de la mujer de su hermano no es ni despreciable ni significativa. Pero la frialdad del arcediano de Orense hacia la familia de la hermana de su cuñada como se evidencia en las cláusulas de su testamento de 1232, quizá explique, en parte, el escaso afecto en que el obispo de Urgel parece haber tenido a sus parientes, tanto a los de la rica familia con la que había casado su tía, como a sus consanguíneos.

Con la única base de los documentos de Urgel, ni Villanueva ni Pujol[23] pudieron identificar las relaciones de Abril; el primero se apoyó en la conjetura de que Pedro Abril era hermano de Abril, sugiriendo que el nombre del obispo no era en manera alguna Abril, sino Alfonso Abril[24]. López Ferreiro, habiendo tenido acceso a los documentos de Santiago, ha podido corregir a Villanueva[25]. Incluso estos trabajos hipotéticos están llenos de dificultades y, por confu-

---

[18] *Galicia histórica : colección diplomática*, ed. A. LÓPEZ FERREIRO, Santiago de Compostela, 1901, I, pág. 239.
[19] *Ibidem*, I, pág. 251.
[20] De hecho, ninguno de los hermanos reivindicó parentesco directo con Abril. Pedro, al recomendarle a un anónimo «lator presentium», se dirigió a él «cum famulatu tam debito quam devoto» (CP). Cf. Apéndice 1. Para Alfonso Pérez, véase Apéndice 2.
[21] *Galicia histórica*, I, pág. 241; VILLANUEVA, *op. cit.*, pág. 239.
[22] Cf. Apéndice 3: «...vuestro ermano el arcidiagono Johan *Paiz*».
[23] P. PUJOL, *Documents en vulgar dels segles XI, XII i XIII procedents del bisbat de la Seu de Urgell*, Barcelona, 1913, págs. 27-30.
[24] *Op. cit.*, págs. 98-99; G. ARGÁIZ, *La soledad laureada*, II, Madrid, 1675, fol. 156 v., presenta el misterioso alegato de que el «verdadero nombre (de Abril)» era D. Jayme de Eril».
[25] *Historia de ... Santiago de Compostela*, V, pág. 362.

sión de las dos Auroanas, el investigador Beltrán de Heredia se ha visto obligado a concluir que el obispo Abril de Urgel fue sobrino de Pedro Abril [26].

Sin embargo, su correspondencia ciertamente sugiere que procedía de Compostela, aunque su nombre no aparece entre las listas de testigos de ninguna de las actas transcritas en los diversos cartularios de la iglesia [27]. El único testimonio documental sobre él en la parte occidental de la Península data del año 1243, cuando en marzo y julio fue testigo de documentos redactados en Salamanca, donde era ya arcediano [28]. Cuánto tiempo disfrutó de esta dignidad es cuestión que no puede determinarse. Pero era uno más entre los muchos gallegos que se habían establecido allí durante el siglo anterior y sobre

[26] *Cartulario de la Universidad de Salamanca (1218-1600)*, ed. V. BELTRÁN DE HEREDIA, Salamanca, 1970, I, pág. 81, n. 58.

La identificación que hace Beltrán de Alfonso Pérez, tío de Abril, con el arcediano de Salamanca de este nombre, es también dudosa. El tío del obispo se define invariablemente a sí mismo como canónigo de Compostela «tout court» y, aunque en su testamento de 1264 (AHN, Sección Clero, pergaminos, 1884/5), el arcediano de Salamanca hizo un modesto legado a Juan Peláez, hermano de Abril, no le define como su sobrino. (Publ., en parte, por BELTRÁN, pág. 610, de una copia tardía).

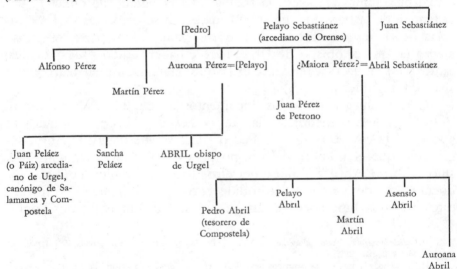

Fuentes. Véanse las notas 16-22; *Galicia histórica: colección diplomática*, I, págs. 179-182, 239-243 y 248-254. Es posible que Mayora Pérez hubiera casado con Juan Sebastiánez, no con Abril Sebastiánez. Esto explicaría mejor la designación de Juan Sebastiánez como hermano de Alfonso Pérez, pero limitaría el sentido de «sobrina» usado por Auroana Pérez (n. 21).

[27] Para una descripción de estos cartularios, véase A. LÓPEZ FERREIRO y F. FITA, *Monumentos antiguos de la Iglesia Compostelana*, Madrid, 1882, págs. 45-53.

[28] ACS, 20/2/32 = Marcos 207; AHN, Sección de Clero, pergaminos, 1882/14 = Marcos 208. Según la *Memoria de los aniversarios que haze el cabildo de la iglesia mayor de Salamanca* del siglo XV, fol. 33 v, su arcedianato

cuya importancia se ha llamado recientemente la atención[29]. Emigrados de su región nativa, constituían una minoría étnica *in partibus* y actuaban conjuntamente en defensa de los intereses comunes, manteniendo contacto con sus lugares de origen[30].

La ausencia de Abril de los registros capitulares después de 1243 sugiere que era una especie de petrel de las tormentas. Si no estaba en Salamanca ni en Compostela ¿donde estuvo durante estos años? † Si se encontraba en el extranjero estudiando, es extraño que no volviese una vez, como hacían los demás, para descansar durante los meses de verano[31]. No sería imposible que Abril estuviera ya en la curia romana defendiendo los intereses de la iglesia de Salamanca, porque las condiciones de esta iglesia no favorecían el absentismo prolongado, que producía el agotamiento de los recursos. Como recalcaban las constituciones de la iglesia, que recibieron confirmación papal en 1245, no era justo que los menos celosos disfrutasen así de una vida fácil[32]. Las provisiones de estas constituciones se preocupan sobre todo de la reducción de gastos: los *extranei* no debían ocupar prebendas ni canonjías vacantes «dum ibidem idonei poterint reperiri». Parecidas restricciones se aplicaban a los principales cargos capitulares, cuya elección compartían el obispo y el capítulo, así como a los cuatro arcedianatos —una prerrogativa episcopal— a no ser que, en el último caso, se creyera que podría resultar provechosa

era el de Ledesma: «Por Don Abril obispo de Urgel y arcediano de Ledesma (sobre una palabra borrada ¿Salamanca?) que jaze cerca del altar de Santo Cristo se haze aniversario este día (el 22 de octubre) y parten setenta y dos maravedís que a de pagar el que fuere arcediano de Ledesma de unas casas en que al presente vive el que fuere arcediano de Ledesma. Son a la calle de los leones».

[29] V. BELTRÁN DE HEREDIA, *Los orígenes de la universidad de Salamanca*, «Ciencia Tomista», 81 (1954), páginas 69-116, en pág. 79; J. GONZÁLEZ, *Alfonso IX*, I, Madrid, 1944, págs. 265-268; BELTRÁN DE HEREDIA, *op. cit.*, pags. 59 y ss.

[30] Cf. Apéndice 3: «... yo quantos Galegos son en Salamanca assí clérigos quomo legos ...», y la carta del deán de Salamanca a Abril quejándose de que el obispo había partido hacia la Curia «irrequisito consilio Gallecorum», de la que se trata más adelante.

[31] La ausencia a causa de los estudios podría explicar el hecho de que Johannes Lombardus, canónigo de Lugo, figure como testigo de los asuntos capitulares únicamente en los meses del verano [AHN, Sección de clero, pergaminos, 1327B/14 (septiembre 1223); 1327C/16 (mayo de 1228); 1327D/10 (septiembre de 1229); 1327E/6 (julio de 1230); 1327E/24 (abril de 1232); 1327G/3 (junio de 1234); 1327G/7 (agosto de 1234); 1327G/19 (junio de 1235)].

[32] D. MANSILLA, *Iglesia Castellano-Leonesa y Curia Romana en los tiempos del rey San Fernando*, Madrid, 1945, reedita estas constituciones del registro de Inocencio IV en las págs. 321-330. Véanse especialmente en la pág. 327, las medidas contra el absentismo «cum ... indignum sit ut qui altario non serviunt luxurientur ex ipso». La bula original de Inocencio IV confirmando las constituciones está ahora en el ACS,3/3/55 = Marcos 227, y de ella deriva la edición de las mismas en V. BELTRÁN DE HEREDIA, *Bulario de la Universidad de Salamanca, 1219-1549*, Salamanca, 1966, I, págs. 310-317. El autor de las constituciones fue el cardenal Gil Torres, de cuyas actividades se trata más adelante, en la pág. 157.

para la iglesia la introducción de algún extraño distinguido [33]. Pero, aunque el arcediano Abril fuera un modelo, importado para añadir tono al capítulo de Salamanca, él y otros gallegos eran objeto de la crítica de los nativos ilustres que, habiendo soportado el peso y el calor del día, se veían continuamente desplazados de la fila de los que esperaban beneficios por recién llegados a los que consideraban con resentimiento como oportunistas ignorantes [34]. Se tomaban también nuevas medidas para impedir que los canónigos estudiantes permanecieran ausentes durante largos períodos de tiempo [35].

Las quejas de este tipo no eran exclusivas de Salamanca. Otras iglesias españolas pasaban los mismos apuros: en mayo de 1233 el obispo Martín había enviado a Gregorio IX un relato de las calamidades de su iglesia de Zamora, donde, durante los pontificados de Honorio III y Gregorio se habían impuesto a la iglesia trece clérigos extraños, con el resultado de que era imposible encontrar beneficios para el clero local que los merecía [36]. Ni tampoco en Salamanca era su desconcierto una experiencia nueva en ningún sentido. Veinte años antes, el capítulo de Salamanca había asegurado aparentemente su posición como intentaba hacer ahora. En diciembre de 1224 había obtenido de Honorio III una sentencia favorable sobre su negativa a aceptar como canónigo a un tal *D. presbyter*, basándose en que debía respetarse el estatuto que restringía su número [37], y dos meses después había tenido éxito en su solicitud de confirmación papal de otra costumbre de la iglesia que excluía de un beneficio a cualquier clérigo cuya residencia personal estuviera en otra localidad [38]. Pero estos resultados quedaron anulados cuando a la muerte del obispo Gonzalvo el capítulo se dividió para la elección de su sucesor y Ho-

[33] «nisi pensatis ecclesie utilitate et necessitate propter litteralis scientie eminentiam et morum prerrogativam aliunde alii assumantur» (*ibid.*, pág. 324).

[34] «filii nobilium seu potentium ac civium aliorum, qui laudabiliter a pueritie primariis rudimentis tam litteris quam moribus in ejusdem ecclesie sinu maternis usibus alebantur, cogerentur ad habitum laicum retransire desperando de beneficiis matris sue, que, ipsis penitus derelictis, extraneos et incognitos preferebat vel forsitan id agebat, ut contra canonum sanctiones, imperit magistris, novi antiquis, rudes eminentibus viris, ordine perturbato, sine respectu modestie preferentur» (*ibid.*, pág. 323).

[35] *Ibid.*, pág. 327. BELTRÁN DE HEREDIA, *Cartulario*, págs. 61-63.

[36] Reg. Greg. IX (ed. Auvray), 1318.

[37] Reg. Hon. III (ed. Pressutti), 5237; ed. D. MANSILLA, *La documentación pontificia de Honorio III (1216-1227)*, Roma, 1965, núm. 530. El decretal se introdujo en el Derecho Canónico: decr. Greg. IX lib. 2, tit. 28, de apell. c. 63, en E. FRIEDBERG, *Corpus Juris Canonici, editio Lipsiesis secunda*, Leipzig, 1879-1881, II, pág. 439. En cualquier caso, *D* se había retirado ya voluntariamente de la competición «aserens quod super receptione sua potius volebat implorare gratiam episcopi et capituli quam contra eos per sententiam obtinere». La mayoría de los candidatos estaban hechos de un material mucho más duro que el de *D*.

[38] Reg. Hon. III, 530 = ed. MANSILLA núm. 539.

norio III intervino nombrando al obispo de Ludd, en Palestina, que estaba en aquél momento en España recolectando la décima de cruzada [39]. Aunque el obispo Pelayo pudo haber sido español y además no sobrevivió mucho tiempo a su promoción, la batalla contra los intrusos estaba ya perdida de todos modos [40]. Durante estos años debió ser nombrado arcediano Abril, y hacia 1245 la iglesia de Salamanca estaba más abierta a las interferencias de lo que había estado en 1224.

Entre los que tenían sus planes sobre los beneficios de Salamanca —y de Zamora— se destacaba ámpliamente el arzobispo metropolitano Juan de Compostela. Juan Arias estaba decidido a excluir de su propia iglesia toda influencia exterior, incluso la papal, y a seguir al mismo tiempo una política de expansión y colonización a expensas de las diócesis vecinas, dentro y fuera de su provincia. Su predecesor, el arzobispo Bernardo, había tenido éxito al obligar al obispo de Oviedo —una sede exenta— a reconocer su hegemonía y a prometer que pagaría un tributo anual a Compostela, y antes de Bernardo la sede de Porto había llegado a un acuerdo semejante con el arzobispo Pedro. Juan, sin embargo, operaba en un campo mucho más amplio: en 1260 el arzobispo de Sevilla tuvo que prevenirle para que no pasease su cruz a través de toda esta provincia [41]. Sin embargo, él mismo había sido el primero en conseguir el arzobispado en defensa de su propia iglesia contra las influencias externas. Había surgido como campeón de los mismos principios de autonomía capitular que, a través de los veintinueve años que gobernó la provincia, iba a socavar constantemente en todas las demás. A la muerte del arzobispo Bernardo en 1238, el capítulo entero había delegado todos sus poderes electivos en siete de su número. Pero dos canónigos —Juan Pérez y M. Pérez— habían estipulado que la elección debería restringirse

[39] Reg. Hon. III, 569 = ed. Mansilla, núm. 584; Reg. Hon. III, 5888 = ed. Mansilla, núm. 598; Reg. Greg. IX, 101.

[40] Al ser elegido para la sede de Ludd en 1223 se le había permitido retener las rentas que había disfrutado previamente en la iglesia de Orense: Reg. Hon. III, 4197. Martín, su sucesor, fue «electus» hacia julio de 1229; ACS 3/3/59 = Marcos 181. En 1239 se permitió a Bóvalo, arcediano de Coria, tener una prebenda en Salamanca, siempre que compensase su ausencia «per vicarium», clara negación de lo dispuesto por Honorio III en febrero de 1225 (Reg. Greg. IX, 4831).

[41] ACSC, Tumbillo de Tablas, de privilegios y constituciones, fol. 100 v.-103 v.; AC Oviedo, B/4/15-16, registrado por S. García Larragueta, Catálogo de los pergaminos de la Catedral de Oviedo, Oviedo, 1957, núms. 266 y 281. Censual do Cabildo da Sé do Porto, Oporto, 1924, págs. 377-380. A. Ballesteros, Sevilla en el siglo XIII, Madrid 1913, págs. CX-CXI. Cf. Peter Linehan, The Spanish Church and the Papacy in the Thirteenth Century, Cambridge, 1971, págs. 265-267.

a los miembros de la iglesia de Compostela, y cuando a pesar de esta condición los electores escogieron al obispo Lorenzo de Orense, celebrado canonista que había actuado como adjunto de la iglesia desde la dimisión de Bernardo a principios del año anterior, los dos partidarios de la autonomía apelaron a Gregorio IX, y su apelación fue mantenida «eo quod multi in eadem ecclesia reperiebantur idonei». Además el papa, en vez de proveer la sede por sí mismo, remitió libremente la elección al capítulo, que dentro de los cuarenta días de plazo eligió a Juan Arias, que había llevado a Roma la apelación contra Lorenzo. Pero el arzobispo no se corrigió en lo más mínimo ante el estrecho escape que él mismo y su iglesia habían experimentado, ni resultó afectada en absoluto la confianza colectiva que Compostela tenía en sí misma [42].

Juan Arias era aficionado a buscar beneficios para su clero en otras iglesias. En octubre de 1255 recomendó con éxito que se admitiera en Orense a su *consanguineus* Pedro Yáñez. La iglesia de León se vio obligada a acomodar a su procurador en Roma, Martín Yáñez, en un momento en que apenas podía permitirse sostener a su propio beneficiado Pedro Pérez [43]. Los más antiguos miembros del capítulo siguieron la pauta marcada por el arzobispo, y amontonaron sobre sí mismos innumerables beneficios. Fernando Alfonso, hijo bastardo del rey de León Alfonso IX y deán de Compostela durante cuarenta y cinco años [44], era arcediano de Salamanca antes de la muerte de

---

[42] Reg. Greg. IX, 4177; 4488; A. García y García, *Laurentius Hispanus*, Madrid-Roma, 1956, págs. 16-17. El breve relato de la elección que contiene el *Tumbillo de Tablas*, fol. 83 r. 83 v., manifiesta simplemente que Juan Arias fue elegido «per viam spiritus sancti», omitiendo el resto de la historia. López Ferreiro, *Historia*, pág. 151, basa su relato de la elección en esta única fuente.

[43] Linehan, *op. cit.*, pág. 266.

[44] S. Portela Pazos, *Decanologio de la S. A. M. Iglesia de Santiago de Compostela*, Santiago, 1944, páginas 99-102. En mayo de 1245, Inocencio IV dispensó su ilegitimidad, y la dispensa estableció su parentesco con Alfonso IX (Reg. Inn. IV, 1275. Esto se corrobora en ACS, 28/2/1 = Marcos 370). La *Memoria de los Aniversarios* de Salamanca le describe erróneamente como «fijo del rey Don Fernando que ganó a Córdoba y a Sevilla», fol. 17 v.; el Marqués de Mondéjar, *Memorias históricas del rei D. Alonso el Sabio*, Madrid, 1777, pág. 490, creía que era hijo de Alfonso X. Cf. González, *Alfonso IX*, I, págs. 314 y 459, y para más detalles de su carrera, Id., *El deán de Santiago Don Fernando Alfonso y su hijo Don Juan*, «Correo erudito», 3 (1942), páginas 194-204. Debe observarse que «el arcediano Fernando Alfonso» al que se hace referencia en este último artículo, pág. 194, n. 3, no es, como afirma González, el hijo de Alfonso IX que figura como testigo en el mismo documento como deán de Santiago. El juez firma como *F. Alfonsi*, no *Fernando Alfonso*, y no es arcediano. El pasaje dice: «... presentibus domino archiepiscopo, domino *F. decano*, P. cantore, P. Martini et G. Roderici archidiaconis, *F. Alfonsi* et magistro Vitali judicibus ... et pluribus aliis canonicis compostellanis» (ACS, 14/2/8 = Marcos, 185). Además, la fecha de 1240 que da González al documento está equivocada, como lo está la escrita por el notario Oduarius Johannis, «era MCCLXVIII», 1230. Por los nombres de los prelados asistentes hay que llegar a la conclusión de que los acontecimientos descritos tuvieron lugar entre 1253 y 1261.

su padre en 1230 [45]. Vivió hasta 1286 [46], constituyendo un obstáculo inamovible para una distribución más equitativa de las rentas entre los cuatro arcedianatos, tal como se proyectaba en las constituciones de 1245 [47]. Además recibía, por lo menos hasta 1250, una elevada pensión del obispado de Ávila [48]. Otro acumulador de beneficios, con miras bastante más amplias, era el arcediano de Trastamar [49], uno de los nuncios de Alfonso X de Castilla en la corte papal [50], y beneficiario en el testamento del arzobispo Juan Arias [51], que en agosto de 1264 aseguró la confirmación por el papa de sus arcedianatos de Compostela y Astorga, del deanato de Lugo, de la abadía secular de Santa María de Arbas (Oviedo) y de otros beneficios en Orense y León, así como su promoción a una dignidad más elevada en León, puesto que, como proclamaba, sus rentas anuales de todo el resto sólo sumaban cuarenta marcos de plata [52]. A la muerte del arzobispo, su señor, estaba decidido a sucederle en la sede. Y esto fue su perdición, porque en noviembre de 1267 la parte del capítulo que se oponía a sus ambiciones demostró que el indulto inicial de Inocencio IV, que había permitido al arcediano embarcarse en su carrera de acumulación de beneficios, había sido obtenida con falsos pretextos, y entonces todo el edificio en el que se basaba su éxito se vino abajo al reservar Clemente IV todos sus beneficios [53]. Pero el arcediano poseía una sorprendente capacidad de recuperación, y con su característica pertinacia reapareció como candidato a la inmediata vacante arzobispal, siendo una vez más arcediano. Pero esta vez intervino la muerte para desbaratar sus proyectos [54]. Al final, también el arzobispo se

[45] AHN, sección de clero, pergaminos, 1881/19; ACS, 17/6 = Marcos 156, 158. Ninguno de estos documentos está fechado. El primero ha sido publicado por GONZÁLEZ, *Alfonso XI*, II, pág. 737, donde se le sitúa en el año 1230; en el artículo citado en la nota anterio_, pág. 194, González lo fechaba en el año 1217, y afirmaba que el destinatario no era Fernando Alfonso. En cualquier caso, para diciembre de 1223 era con seguridad canónigo en Salamanca (AHN, Sección de clero, pergaminos, 1221/17 = Marcos, 154).

[46] PORTELA PAZOS, *op. cit.*, pág. 102; cf. GONZÁLEZ, *art. cit.*, págs. 199-200.

[47] MANSILLA, *Iglesia*, pág. 325: «De archidiaconatu Salamantino qui ceteris plus habundat, cui nichil in prestimoniis, nunc addendum decernimus, taliter providemus, ut cum vacaverit, pars illa archidiaconatus ... archidiaconatui de Ledesma per episcopum perpetuo applicetur». Abril, arcediano de Ledesma, era por tanto el principal perjudicado.

[48] AC Ávila, núm. 14: «... taxationem ducentorum et triginta morabotinorum et decem marcharum quas debet habere decanus Compostellanus». Véase también C. M. AJO Y SÁINZ DE ZÚÑIGA, *Avila I: Fuentes y Archivos*, Madrid, 1962, pág. 102.

[49] Juan Alfonso: véase también LINEHAN, *op. cit.*, pág. 260.

[50] Marqués de MONDÉJAR, *op. cit.*, págs. 173-174; D. MANSILLA, *La documentación eclesiástica española del archivo Castel S. Angelo*, «Anthologica Annua», 6 (1958), págs. 285-448, en la pág. 323.

[51] ACSC, *Tumbo C*, 1, fol. 4 v.

[52] Reg. Urbano IV (ed. GUIRAUD) 2080, 2093.

[53] Reg. Clem. IV (ed. Jordan), 545.

[54] Reg. Greg. X (ed. GUIRAUD), 110. Véase también LÓPEZ FERREIRO, *Historia*, V, págs. 277 y ss.

sobrepasó a sí mismo. En agosto de 1257 recibió una suave reprimenda de Alejandro IV, el cual había oído a cierto número de iglesias de la diócesis de Compostela que procuraba beneficios a sus clérigos en la jurisdicción de otros apoyándose en mandatos papales que en realidad no le concedían en absoluto semejante autoridad [55]. En septiembre de 1260, bajo su dirección, el capítulo juró solemnemente oponerse a las provisiones papales, pero poco después de esta muestra de independencia cometió un grave error y atrajo sobre su cabeza las iras de Roma [56]. Tuvo la temeridad de entrometerse en la elección para proveer la sede de Ávila mientras el caso estaba sometido a la consideración de la Curia, con el resultado de que Urbano IV le privase del derecho de confirmar y consagrar a los obispos de su provincia —palpablemente un duro golpe [57]. El arzobispo respondió declarando que no era ningún secreto que la iglesia romana tenía sus miras sobre los derechos de su iglesia [58].

Abril, el arcediano de Salamanca, no figuraba entre los protegidos del arzobispo Juan Arias. Su popularidad no era mucha en Compostela, como averiguó para desilusión suya su agente Alfonso Pérez cuando intentó asegurarle una prebenda vacante allí. Alfonso Pérez escribió a Abril muy alarmado [59]. La carta no lleva fecha [60], pero fue escrita antes de 1257 (en que Abril fue designado para Urgel), durante su estancia en la Curia [61]. En estos años no hay evidencia directa de

---

[55] ACSC, *Tumbillo de Tablas*, fols. 85 v.-86 r.

[56] Reg. Urbano IV, 331, 2826.

[57] RV 26-194-108 + Reg. Urbano IV, 331; RV 29A-330 = Reg. Urbano IV, 2826.

[58] «Cum Ecclesia Compostellana fuerit in ista quasi possessione a tempore quo non extat memoria ut providere possit de pastore iure metropolitico ecclesie sue suffraganie viduate non solum in casu negligentie set in quocunque alio sive propter formam sive propter vicium persone cassetur electio per canonicos eiusdem ecclesie celebrata, et Romana Ecclesia, ut publice asseritur, eamdem hoc iure privare intendat, remedium est necessarium adhibendum» (ACSC, *Libro I de Constituciones*, fols. 9 v.-11 r., y *Constituciones sinodales y capitulares* † *antiguas*, fols. 18 v.- 20 r.). El concilio (que esta última fuente atribuye al arzobispo Juan Arias), no está fechado, pero López Ferreiro (*op. cit.*, V, pág. 186 y apéndice 29) lo atribuye a la década 1245-1255. Sin embargo, a la luz de la elección de Ávila y de sus consecuencias, el principio de los 1260 parece ser una fecha más adecuada. Es característico del arzobispo que, en el curso de una sola frase, «quasi possessio» se convierta en «ius».

[59] Apéndice 4. Alfonso Pérez, el informador de Abril, sobrevivió por lo menos hasta 1291, presenciando los negocios capitulares en Compostela a intervalos regulares (ACSC, *Constituciones sinodales y capitulares antiguas*, fols. 16 r., 20 r., 56 v., 60 r.-v., 61 v., 63 r.). Si éste es entonces el mismo hombre que escribió la carta del Apéndice 2, el tío sobrevivió al sobrino durante veinticuatro años por lo menos. Pero en el año 1283 era «eger corpore» (López Ferreiro, *Galicia histórica: colección diplomática*, pág. 248). En 1272 vivía un canónigo de Compostela llamado *Alfonso Pérez* (J. González, *Alfonso IX*, I, pág. 461).

[60] Fernando Álvarez, el arcediano de Palencia, cuya muerte creó la vacante de Compostela, ha escapado a mis investigaciones tanto en Palencia como en Compostela. Tampoco figura en los registros papales. Por ello no es posible fechar la carta con más exactitud.

[61] Está dirigida: «Magistro Aprili Salmanticensi archidiacono et summi pontificis capellano in romana curia detur».

las actividades de Abril, a no ser que se identifique con el *Magister Aprilis* que era procurador en Perugia en 1252, actuando en representación del obispo de Segovia [62]. Como representante de la iglesia de Salamanca (si lo era) no era el único; en agosto de 1254 *Johannes de Pinello* [63] y en enero anterior *Martinus* eran procuradores a los que se encomendaban los asuntos referentes a Salamanca [64]. Pero podemos suponer que Abril estuvo implicado en la obtención del escrito que instaba al rey de Castilla a devolver la «villa que Almenara dicitur» al obispo y capítulo de Salamanca, de quienes la había tomado [65]. Almenara está en el arcedianato de Ledesma, que era el de Abril.

Aunque la evidencia directa sea escasa para estos años, lo cierto es, sin embargo, que Abril era considerado por sus colegas de Salamanca como un valioso abogado en la Curia [66]. Esto se hace patente en una carta dirigida a él después de haberse convertido en obispo por el deán de Salamanca, Domingo Martínez [67]. El deán estaba muy preocupado y escribía para pedir a Abril que hiciese lo posible y que utilizara toda la influencia que tuviera en la Curia en apoyo de su antigua iglesia. Explicaba que el obispo había partido a Roma y que entre los canonigos, los gallegos estaban seriamente preocupados, porque aunque no sabían con certeza cuales eran las intenciones del obispo, sospechaban que pretendía renunciar a la sede —paso que casi con seguridad conduciría a que se les impusiera a algún intruso. El deán instaba a Abril a que impidiese que esto sucediera, y, evidentemente nervioso, concluía pidiendo al obispo que destruyera la carta una vez leída —petición que, afortunadamente para su historiador, Abril no cumplió [68].

Tras las circunstancias descritas por el deán yace la desdichada historia de la iglesia de Salamanca a mediados del siglo XIII —esto es, desdichada desde el punto de vista de los que pensaban como el

[62] AC Segovia, 32 (olim C/2/14): su nombre aparece al dorso del rescripto.
[63] ACS, 23/28 = Marcos 259, dorso. Cf. AC Burgos, vol. 46, fol. 423 dorso: copia de la misma bula emitida el mismo día. *Johannes* era el agente del arzobispo de Braga João (Arquivo Distrital de Braga) *Livro I dos testamentos*, fol. 10 r.
[64] ACS, 23/69 = Marcos 248, dorso. La indistinta escritura del dorso de otra bula de Salamanca de mayo de 1253 (ACS, 23/57 = Marcos, 243) podría también posiblemente representar al mismo *Martinus*.
[65] AHN, Sección de clero, pergaminos, 1883/8 = Marcos 234.
[66] No se sabe la fecha en que se le hizo capellán apostólico.
[67] VILLANUEVA, *op. cit.*, 11, pág. 238. La carta no está datada; los párrafos siguientes intentan situarla en su contexto. Domingo Martínez era deán de Salamanca desde enero de 1243 (AHN, Sección de clero, pergaminos, 1882/12 = Marcos, 205) ¿Sería tal vez el *Domingo Martín Salmantino* que actuaba como «scriptor» en la corte leonesa en septiembre de 1211, cuando Juan Arias —el futuro arzobispo— era canciller? (Cf. GONZÁLEZ, *Alfonso IX*, pág. 487).
[68] *Ibíd.*: «... Paternitati vestre presentibus intimetur quod Episcopus noster irrequisito consilio Galle-

156

deán y compartían la esperanza de que se permitiese a la iglesia ocuparse de sus propios asuntos, según el espíritu de las constituciones de 1245. Resulta un tanto extraño que este partido estuviera acaudillado por un intruso, y que éste pidiera ayuda a otro: Domingo Martínez era gallego, lo mismo que Abril [69]. Desde 1245 habían sufrido una serie de reveses. En agosto de 1245, el obispo Martín, que en 1240 había estado demasiado enfermo para atender a sus ocupaciones [70], renunció a la sede, y ante la negativa del deán de Compostela —Fernando Alfonso— a aceptar su elección, en diciembre de 1246, Inocencio IV nombró a Mateo, arcediano de Palenzuela (Burgos) [71]. Aunque ignorado por diversos historiadores de la iglesia, el obispo Mateo constituyó una responsabilidad sobradamente real para Salamanca [72]. Sus beneficios en Burgos no enriquecieron a la iglesia para la que había sido nombrado, sino a su hermano Juan [73]. No parece que llegara a visitar su sede, pero cuando fue trasladado a Cuenca al año siguiente, la iglesia de Salamanca se vio obligada a pagar las deudas que había contraído en la Curia durante su episcopado de un año [74]. En febrero de 1248 la iglesia tenía un nuevo obispo llamado Pedro Pérez [75]. Es difícil deducir cual fue su postura en la lucha a muerte en que la iglesia se hallaba engolfada. Tal vez fuera un sobrino del obispo Gonzalvo, cuya muerte en 1226 había proclamado el fin del orden [76]. Había estado en la Curia junto con el deán y otros varios canónigos de la iglesia en diciembre de 1246,

corum proponit romanam curiam visitare, et apud nos causa penitus ignoratur. Verum quia malum habuit principium, sicut scitis, credimus ipsum proponere resignare. Quapropter, vobis significo quod mihi et vestris amicis videtur quod vobis cedat in commodum et honorem, ut in curia romana detis opem et operam cum vestris amicis, ne aliquis extraneus nobis in nostra ecclesia supplantetur... Lecta littera rumpatur. Cf. BELTRÁN DE HEREDIA, *Cartulario*, pág. 76: «Excusado es advertir que la palabra *extraneus* empleada por el deán es con relación a los gallegos».

[69] En su testamento dejaba 200 maravedís «a todos los nietos de nostras ermanas que moran en Galiça» (ACS, 20/1/33 = Marcos, 315).

[70] Reg. Inn. IV, 1439. En noviembre de 1240 se excusó de asistir a la audiencia de la agria disputa entre el arzobispo de Toledo y la orden de Calatrava, en la que era juez-delegado, «propter egritudinem et debilitatem nostram» (AHN, Sección de clero, pergaminos, 3020/4).

[71] Reg. Inn. IV 2317, publicado por MANSILLA, *op. cit.*, pág. 335. La última aparición del obispo Martín en los negocios capitulares tuvo lugar en abril de 1245 (ACS, 3/3/47-1 = Marcos, 216).

[72] Gil GONZÁLEZ DÁVILA, *Historia de las antigüedades de Salamanca*, Salamanca, 1606, lib. III, pág. 239; ID., *Teatro eclesiástico de las iglesias de España*, Madrid, 1650, III, págs. 271 y ss., contiene una lista totalmente equivocada de los obispos del siglo XIII, y Mateo no figura entre ellos. Tampoco aparece en M. VILLAR Y MACIAS, *Historia de Salamanca*, I, Madrid, 1887, pág. 385.

[73] AC Burgos, vol. 71, n. 98, registrado por D. MANSILLA, *La diócesis de Burgos vista a través de la documentación del archivo capitular en los siglos XIII y XIV*, «Anthologica Annua», 9 (1961), págs. 417-473, n. 12.

[74] Ascendían a 190 marcos: RV 21/142/454 = Reg. Inn. IV, 3191.

[75] AHN, Sección de clero, pergaminos, 1883/3 = Marcos 224.

[76] En junio de 1220 el obispo Gonzalvo hizo diversas donaciones al cabildo, pero especificó un interés

cuando se había nombrado obispo a Mateo [77]. Algunas autoridades le describen como dominico [78], pero no hay evidencia que apoye esta afirmación en los documentos de Salamanca. Puesto que el traslado del obispo Mateo a Cuenca se efectuó en la Curia, puede suponerse que su promoción se arregló allí, o que *de iure* debería haberse arreglado, pero no lo fue, y de ahí la preocupación del deán al enterarse de que pensaba ir a la Curia, «quia malum habuit principium» [79].

Fue un mal principio para un gobierno peor. Sus enemigos informaron a Alejandro IV de que estaba a las puertas de la muerte y el papa, probablemente basándose en que había resultado perjudicado por la promoción del obispo, reservó la elección inmediata —medida que canceló Urbano IV en 1261 [80]. El capítulo estaba dividido en lo referente a los derechos de enterramiento en la catedral, con el deán y los dignatarios de un lado y los canónigos del otro, hasta que en enero de 1260 intervino el obispo Pedro [81]. De las constituciones otorgadas por el cardenal Gil se hacía caso omiso: en febrero de 1253 se permitió al arcediano de León, Adán, retener sus prebendas en Salamanca violando los principios establecidos en 1224 y 1245 [82] —principios que el propio Adán sostendría diez años más tarde para su iglesia de León [83]. El cardenal Gil fue uno de los primeros en retirar lo que había concedido. En diciembre de 1253 había asegurado la reserva de tres beneficios vacantes [84], y de ello se aprovecharon los clérigos de su Zamora natal: en julio de 1254 se ordenó al deán de Salamanca que proporcionase una canonjía a *Elias, alumpnus* de Zamora, a petición del obispo y capítulo de Zamora [85]. En enero de 1264 las constituciones del cardenal fueron anuladas expresamente *hac vice* en favor del *magister scolarum* de Zamora —un pariente del

---

vitalicio en su propiedad de Miranda para «Petrus Petri canonicus nepos meus» (AHN, Sección de clero pergaminos, 1881/13 = Marcos 146).

[77] Reg. Inn. IV, 2317. En esta época era arcediano de Medina, Salamanca: ACS, 202/32=Marcos, 207.

[78] Gil GONZÁLEZ DÁVILA, *Teatro*, pág. 277, de quien lo toma ARGÁIZ, *Soledad Laureada*, III, Madrid, 1675, fol. 201; J. A. VICENTE BAJO, *Episcopologio Salmantino*, Salamanca, 1901, pág. 59.

[79] Véase más arriba, n. 68.

[80] ACS, 23/33 = Marcos 295; publicado por Gil GONZÁLEZ DÁVILA, *Historia*, lib. III, pág. 236-237, que lo atribuye al episcopado de Gonzalvo, y por VILLAR Y MACIAS, *op. cit.*, pág. 400. El pretexto de Urbano para cancelar la reserva fue que Alejandro había sido mal informado «per falsam suggestionem quorundam quod venerabilis frater noster Salamantinus episcopus adeo erat gravatus senio quod de morte dubitabatur ipsius».

[81] ACS, 28/1/53 = Marcos, 283.

[82] RV 22-429-328 = Reg. Inn. IV, 6286.

[83] RV 29-61-144 = Reg. Urbano IV, 1095.

[84] RV 23-466-60 = Reg. Inn. IV, 7302.

[85] RV 23-810-116 = Reg. Inn. IV. 7675.

158

cardenal [86]— a quien se proporcionó una canonjía en Salamanca [87]. Constituye una señal de la presión a que toda la diócesis estaba sometida el hecho de que, aunque la defensa proporcionada por las constituciones fuese evidentemente una ficción, otras iglesias de la diócesis se agruparan en oposición al obispo [88], consiguieran acceso al sello del cardenal Gil y con él falsificaran cartas que les concedían frente a la iglesia catedral la misma protección que la propia iglesia catedral había conseguido para sí misma en 1245 [89].

Una diócesis así dividida constituía una abierta invitación para el codicioso arzobispo de Compostela. No desperdició la oportunidad. Utilizando su acostumbrada habilidad para interpretar los mandatos papales en su propio beneficio, consiguió introducir a parte de su clero en los beneficios de Salamanca. Cuando Alejandro IV ordenó que se proporcionaran canonjías a Gonzalvo Peláez y a otros racioneros de Salamanca, especificando que hasta que se hallaran prebendas para ellos deberían retener sus raciones, el arzobispo, con los más especiosos pretextos, hizo caso omiso de la garantía papal y procedió a adjudicar las raciones a clérigos de Compostela y Salamanca [90].

La ansiedad del deán de Salamanca, Domingo Martínez, era por lo tanto bien fundada, y parece que no en vano recurrió al obispo de Urgel, porque en marzo de 1264 también él se había convertido en obispo [91]. La suerte que corrió Pedro Pérez, a quien sustituyó, es incierta; no se conocen los acontecimientos que se desarrollaron en la Curia a su llegada allí. Es posible sin embargo que Domingo Martínez y él se limitaran a intercambiar sus respectivos puestos, y que el Pedro Pérez que sucedió a Domingo como deán de Salamanca no fuera otro, en efecto, que el ex-obispo del mismo nombre. Ciertamente entre los dirigentes del capítulo en los años inmediatamente anteriores a 1263 no había ningún otro canónigo llamado Pedro Pérez, y existe algún fundamento —que reconocemos muy ligero— para

---

[86] RV 29-188-881 = Reg. Urbano IV, 1831.

[87] RV 29-92-253 = Reg. Urbano IV, 1205. Aparentemente había sido recibido en Salamanca para agosto siguiente: RV 29-213-1096 = Reg. Urbano IV, 2046.

[88] J. GONZÁLEZ, *La clerecía de Salamanca durante la Edad Media*, «Hispania», 3 (1943), págs. 409-430, especialmente págs. 427-430; BELTRÁN DE HEREDIA, *Cartulario*, pág. 63.

[89] El obispo Pedro había apelado con éxito contra estas constituciones (RV 24-596-90 = / Alex. IV, 747). La pugna entre la catedral y la diócesis seguía candente en 1291 cuando el entonces obispo pidió a la Curia una copia de la sentencia emitida contra el clero en 1257: RV 46-129-638 = Reg. Nich. IV (ed. Langlois), 6365.

[90] «... asserens portiones ipsas eo pretextu quod dicti portionarii in predicta ecclesia in canonicos sunt recepti tanto tempore vacavisse quod ad eum erat ipsarum collatio secundum Lateranensis statuta concilii legitime devoluta» (ACS, 23/31 = Marcos 293 y ACS, 23/66 = Marcos 294).

[91] AHN, Sección de clero, pergaminos, 1884/5. Domingo Martínez ha escapado a la atención de todos

esta suposición [92]. El nuevo deán sobrevivió al obispo unos veinte años [93], y subsiguientemente disfrutó de una carrera al servicio real [94].

Seguramente no es mera coincidencia que durante los últimos seis meses de 1263, cuando debían ir progresando las negociaciones referentes a la sede de Salamanca, estuviese en la Curia Abril de Urgel [95]. Al menos debe ofrecer cierta garantía por el ascenso del deán. Un gallego apoyó a otro. Pero una válvula de escape tan pobre fue casi con seguridad la causa de que la iglesia de Salamanca contratase los servicios de una persona de posición en la Curia que pudiera defender allí sus intereses sobre una base permanente —el cardenal Huberto de S. Eustaquio [96].

Durante el agitado gobierno del obispo Pedro de Salamanca, el arcediano Abril se encontraba en la Curia. Los últimos años del pontificado de Inocencio IV presenciaron en ella una explosión de actividad por parte de los españoles, y la mayor parte de esta actividad estuvo relacionada con el español Gil Torres, cardenal-diacono del título de los Santos Cosme y Damián, que actuaba como cónsul permanente para los clérigos españoles que visitaron la Curia [97]. Además de Salamanca, las iglesias de Burgos, Calahorra, Segovia, Plasencia

los historiadores precedentes hasta BELTRÁN. Gil GONZÁLEZ DÁVILA, ARGAIZ, VILLAR, VICENTE BAJO, *op. cit.* y C. EUBEL, *Hierarchia catholica medii aevi...*, I, Munich, 1923, pág. 428, mencionan todos en esta etapa a un obispo Domingo Domínguez. Este inexistente prelado era identificado como el autor de un formulario de la época: L. ROCKINGER, *Briefsteller und Formelbücher des eilften bis vierzehnten Jahrhunderts*, «Quellen und Erörter ungen zur Bayerischen und Deutschen Geschichte», 9-II (1864), págs. 515-592, en pág. 524.

[92] Su última aparición como obispo tuvo lugar en febrero de 1263: ACS, 3/3/494=Marcos 300; la primera † señal del deán Pedro Pérez aparece en junio de 1271 (ACS, 3/1/49-5 = Marcos 325). Pero pudo permanecer en la Curia durante estos años representando los intereses de Alfonso X (véase más adelante, n. 94). Estando allí consiguió una dignidad para Aparicio, canónigo de la iglesia, en agosto de 1264 (RV 27-129-1 = Reg. Urbano IV, 454). Aparicio era un estrecho aliado de Pedro Pérez el obispo y de Pedro Pérez el deán: al hacer una donación de ciertas casas al cabildo en 1257, el obispo le reservó un interés vitalicio (ACS 3/1/48 = Marcos 266), y cuando Aparicio hizo testamento como chantre en febrero de 1273, el deán estaba presente, a pesar de que fue hecho «media nocte» (ACS, 20/33/4 = Marcos 334). Cf. BELTRÁN, pág. 79.

[93] Era el albacea principal del obispo Domingo (ACS, 20/1/53 = Marcos 715).

[94] Era uno de los procuradores de Alfonso X que, en su viaje a la Curia en 1268, fue atacado por unos † rufianes en Toscana Reg. Clem. IV, 696).

[95] El 6 de junio estaba en la casa del cardenal Jaime Savelli: RV 29-37-76 = Reg. Urbano IV, 1027. El 20 de noviembre se había trasladado ya a la casa del cardenal Esteban de Palestrina y allí permaneció por lo menos hasta el 12 de enero de 1264 [RV 29-5-3; 29-7-6; 29-36-21; 29-20-17 = Reg. Urbano IV, 957, 959, 988 y (fechado erróneamente por Guiraud en 1263) 978]. Los demás motivos de Abril para estar allí se discuten más adelante.

[96] La carta del cardenal Huberto al obispo, deán y capítulo en noviembre de 1265 prometiéndole su protección subrayaba sus sentimientos de benevolencia hacia la iglesia (ACS, 40/43-1 = Marcos 311). Pero las asociaciones de este tipo no se alimentaban sólo de la buena voluntad: el obispo Domingo Martínez en su testamento legó, «al cardenal don Uberto de Cucu Nato CL morabotinos pora .I. mulo que le enviamos prometer per † nostra carta e mandamos que lo aixi pelo pora de los otros feleros del bispado». Esta cláusula se añadió en un codicilo después de haber sido datado el testamento en 21 de enero de 1267 (ACS, 20/1/33 = Marcos 315).

[97] Sobre él, véase L. SERRANO, *Don Mauricio, obispo de Burgos y fundador de su catedral*, Madrid, 1922, págs.

y Ávila recibieron todas constituciones que habían sido preparadas por el cardenal Gil. Organizó préstamos para los españoles necesitados en la Curia —arzobispos, obispos y arcedianos [98]. Cuando el obispo Rodrigo de Palencia murió en la Curia, se encargó a Gil la tarea de sustentar a su *familia* —clero, legos y médicos [99]. Cuando suavizó el rigor de las sentencias que el legado Juan de Abbeville había impuesto a los clérigos mujeriegos, lo hizo en compañía de «los prelados y otros españoles ilustres de la Curia» [100]. Es probable que en algún momento de su carrera Abril se contase entre estos hombres, y cuando murió el cardenal en 1254, él, lo mismo que otros españoles [101], se vieron obligados a ponerse al servicio de otro señor. El cardenal al que se volvieron Abril y otros muchos fue el obispo de Palestrina, Esteban.

Esteban era húngaro, y había llamado por primera vez la atención de la Curia romana cuando, siendo obispo de Vácz, fue enviado por el rey Bela IV en 1241 para buscar ayuda contra los invasores mogoles. Habiendo consultado con el emperador Federico II, pasó a la Curia [102]. Ganó la estimación de Inocencio IV, y en 1252 fue elevado al cardenalato-episcopado de Palestrina mientras se encargaba de la sede primada de Gran [103]. No parece haber representado ningún papel en los movidos acontecimientos políticos que comprometieron al papado en los años siguientes [104], y en junio de 1253 se le permitió volver a su tierra natal bajo pretexto de que el clima romano no le probaba [105]. Pero para octubre de 1254 había vuelto a la Curia [106]. Le preocupaba grandemente mantener intachable su reputación: cuando en sep-

---

70-74; LINEHAN, *op. cit.*, cap. 12. No hizo visita a Salamanca, como supone BELTRÁN, *op. cit.*, pág. 61.

[98] AC Toledo, A-7-C-2-13; AC Zamora, 13 (D-3) 46; AC León, 1569.

[99] RV 23-249-179 = Reg. Inn. IV, 8079.

[100] Su suavización de las normas del legado tuvo amplia influencia y se aplicó en Orense (RV 23-71-154 = Reg. Inn. IV, 7885), Compostela (RV 24-322-47 = Reg. Alex. IV, 389), Tortosa (VILLANUEVA, *op. cit.*, 5, 1806, págs. 284-286), Vich (AC Vich, códice 220, fols. 28 r., 43 v. y códice 147, fol. 6 r. y v.) y Barcelona (AC Barcelona, *Libro de la Cadena*, fol. 72).

[101] Otro era el sobrino de Gil Torres, Esteban, al que se había permitido acumular beneficios en Compostela, Palencia, Oviedo, Salamanca, Ávila, Calahorra, Chartres, Châlons, Verdun, Douai y Praga (RV 22-187-213 = Reg. Inn. IV, 6044). Cuando, tras la muerte de su tío, incurrió en el desagrado de Alfonso X, el cardenal Esteban intervino en su favor (AC Toledo, E-7-D-2-4).

[102] A. F. GOMBOS, *Catalogus fontium historiae hungaricae*, II, Budapest, 1937, núms. 959 y 1583. Cf. también *Monumenta ecclesiae Strigoniensis ... illustravit Ferdinandus* KNAUZ (Stryj, 1874), I, págs. 349-350, y Janos KARACSONYI, *A magyar nemzetségek a XIV szdzad közepéig*, I, Budapest, 1900, págs. 197-198. (Debo estas últimas referencias al señor C. A. Macartney y al profesor G. Györffy).

[103] RV 22-308-226 = Reg. Inn. IV, 6165.

[104] No figura en E. JORDAN, *Les origines de la domination angevine en Italie*, París, 1909.

[105] RV 22-940-curiales 33-309 = Reg. Inn. IV, 6800.

[106] Véase más adelante, n. 167.

tiembre de 1263 fue delegado por Urbano IV para considerar los méritos de la petición presentada por el preboste y capítulo de Zagreb reclamando a su sobrino Esteban le causó gran ansiedad la posibilidad de un escándalo producido por sospechas de nepotismo y entregó la sede a otro —el arcediano Timoteo de Pécs [107]. Pero sus escrúpulos disminuían cuando estaba lejos del escrutinio público, y su aparente desinterés resulta menos admirable cuando se recuerda que no vaciló en escribir a Abril después de su nombramiento para Urgel, instándole a entregar uno de sus pocos beneficios en la diócesis, el arcedianato de Tremp, a su capellán, al mismo Timoteo, y ofreciendo a Abril, a cambio de su consentimiento, el incentivo de un cargo más alto [108]. Además, cuando Timoteo fue elevado a la sede de Zagreb, todos sus beneficios fueron entregados por el cardenal a clérigos húngaros [109].

Las relaciones entre españoles y húngaros no eran nada nuevo [110]. Durante el pontificado de Honorio III, el cardenal español Pelayo Gaitán había sido auditor en cierto número de disputas referentes a la iglesia húngara [111]. Sin embargo, la asociación de Esteban con la iglesia y los eclesiásticos españoles era de carácter mucho más íntimo, y es interesante señalar que se preocupaba particularmente de las iglesias que habían estado más estrechamente relacionadas con el cardenal Gil —Burgos y Zamora. En julio de 1260 estaba encargado de la provisión de todos los beneficios y dignidades vacantes en Burgos [112], y entre sus capellanes se encontraba el abad de Salas (Burgos), Fernando Velázquez [113]. Martín Gómez, deán de Burgos, que estaba presente en la casa del cardenal en enero de 1264, había sido anteriormente huésped del cardenal Gil en Lyon en 1249 [114]. En junio de

---

[107] «... nolens ad carnem et sanguinem habere respectum» (RV 28-3-10 = Reg. Urbano IV, 407); publicado por A. Theiner, *Vetera monumenta historica Hungariam sacram illustrantia maximam partem nondum edita*, I, Roma, 1859, pág. 245.

[108] Apéndices 5 y 9. Abril había conocido a Timoteo en la Curia. Timoteo estaba presente cuando el cardenal Esteban suspendió al obispo Ponce de Urgel en octubre de 1254 (Archivo Histórico Archidiocesano, Tarragona, *Cartoral A B*, fol. 16 r.). De este incidente se trata más adelante. Y ambos compartieron de nuevo el mismo techo en 1263-1264, en cuya época Timoteo era obispo de Zagreb [Reg. Urbano IV, 959, 978, 988 (como arriba, n. 95)].

[109] Knauz, *op. cit.*, I, pág. 396.

[110] Jaime I de Aragón estaba casado con Yolanda, hija de Andrés II de Hungría. Véase también Flóris Holik, *Saint Jacques de Compostelle et Saint Ladislas de Hongrie*, «Revue des Études Hongroises et Fino-Ougriennes», I (1923), págs. 36-55, especialmente págs. 49-52.

[111] Referencias en D. Mansilla, *El cardenal hispano Pelayo Gaitán*, «Anthologica Annua», 1 (1953), páginas 1-66, en la pág. 63.

[112] RV 25-250-82 = Reg. Alex. IV, 3142.

[113] *Ibid.* En 1265 se convirtió en obispo de Segovia [AC Segovia, 21 (*olim* C/2/17)].

[114] RV 29-36-21 = Reg. Urbano IV, 959; AC Gerona, bula de Inocencio IV, sin clasificar, «dilectis filiis

1264 se designó a Esteban como árbitro de una discusión referente a una prebenda vacante en Zamora entre el deán, Martín Vicente y Esteban Domínguez [115], y antes, en octubre, se le había dirigido la apelación del obispo de Zamora contra el nombramiento de Martín Vicente [116].

Las relaciones del cardenal con Abril, Salamanca y Urgel, están suficientemente atestiguadas. Abril permaneció con él en 1263-1264 [117]. El proceso de divorcio del conde Álvaro de Urgel tuvo lugar ante él y por él fue sentenciado en Viterbo en abril de 1267 [118]. Diez años antes había sido auditor de un caso en que se disputaba el derecho a la iglesia de Colono, en la diócesis de Urgel [119]. Juan Peláez, canónigo de Salamanca y de Urgel, y hermano aliado de Abril, era su capellán [120]. El maestro Diego, arcediano de Salamanca, estaba con él en la Curia en junio de 1264 [121]. Y fue a otro clérigo de Salamanca, Alfonso Vidal, a quien se dirigió en agosto de 1263, cuando Urbano IV [122] le ordenó conferir el deanato de Ávila a uno de sus capellanes, dignidad y responsabilidad que no impidieron al que las recibía pasar gran parte de su futura carrera como procurador de varias iglesias castellanas, especialmente de la de Salamanca, en la curia [123]. Pero, y esto es más importante, Esteban fue el responsable de la elevación de Abril a la sede de Urgel.

II

La carrera del predecesor de Abril, el obispo Ponce de Urgel, fue bastante más agitada que la del obispo Pedro de Salamanca, y sus dificultades parecen deberse en gran parte a su propia culpa. Ponce

duodecim presbiteris ecclesie Gerundensis: Ea que iudicio ... *Lugdunii* non. julii pontificatus nostri anno septimo», confirmando la sentencia de Gil del año anterior, que Martín había presenciado.

[115] RV 29-44-96 = Reg. Urbano IV, 1047.

[116] AC Zamora, 11-D-5: 2.ª parte. Véase LINEHAN, *op. cit.*, págs. 301-303.

[117] Véase arriba, n. 95.

[118] ACA, Cancillería real, letras pontificias, leg. XV, núm. 5, registrado por F. J. MIQUEL ROSELL, *Regesta de letras pontificias del Archivo de la Corona de Aragón*, Madrid, 1948, núm. 191; D. MONFAR Y SORS, *Historia de los Condes de Urgel* (ed. P. Bofarull y Mascaró, Barcelona, 1853), I, págs. 556-558.

[119] AHA Tarragona, *Cartoral AB*, fol. 35 r. RV 24-794-119 = Reg. Alex IV, 986.

[120] Véase A. RAVICINI BAGLIANI, *Un frammento del testamento del cardinale Stephanus Hungarus (†1270)*, «Rivista di Storia della Chiesa in Italia», 25 (1971), págs. 168-182; más adelante, n. 183.

[121] RV 29-44-96 = Reg. Urbano IV, 1047.

[122] RV 29-264-1398 = Reg. Urbano IV, 2349. El arcediano Timoteo de *Pécs* tomó posesión formal del deanato en representación de Alfonso.

[123] ACS 39/1/19; 43/3/35 & 43/3/29 = Marcos 383-4-5. A su vuelta a Salamanca recibió el arcedianato

de Vilamur se convirtió en obispo al retirarse Pedro de Puigvert en abril de 1230 [124]. Para la iglesia de Urgel, su gobierno hizo época en el peor sentido de la palabra [125]. Fue perseguido por cierto número de sus canónigos —que también habían importunado a su predecesor [126]— y finalmente causaron su caída. Para ello contaron materialmente con la ayuda del propio Ponce, que no hacía ningún secreto de sus compromisos. La embajada de Juan de Abbeville a los reinos españoles en 1228-1229 [127] había iniciado un período de lucha por la reforma en ciertos medios, con los que Ponce se enfrentó con gran determinación. Su porfía, sin embargo, no pasó inadvertida, porque el legado y su heredero espiritual, Pedro de Albalat, obispo de Lérida y arzobispo de Tarragona [128], manifestaron especial interés por su diócesis. Juan de Abbeville escribió al recién elegido Ponce instándole a emprender una lucha justa [129], pero el obispo prefirió ignorar la advertencia que contenía la carta, traída desde Roma por Pedro de Albalat [130]. Pedro seguía con gran atención la carrera de Ponce. Estuvo presente en su elección y prestó su apoyo a la causa de Ponce, que era sobrino del obispo de Lérida y hasta su elección para Urgel había desempeñado el puesto de sacristán en la iglesia de su tío, dignidad en la que le sucedió Pedro [131]. El sacristán de Urgel, que capitaneaba las fuerzas opuestas a la elección de Ponce, le consideraba como un enemigo: era de todos sabido que había matado a una de las mulas de Pedro y herido a otra [132]. El papel de Pedro en la elección fue el de un observador distinguido, comisionado tal vez por Roma para presenciarla: al final de la contienda, que se resolvió con la elección

de Alba-Salvatierra: ACS, 3/2/16-2 = Marcos 406. Retuvo esta dignidad hasta su muerte en 1286 (AHN, Sección de códices, 914 B, fol. 98 v.), en cuya época ya había recibido también la tesorería de Braga (RV 44-16-60 = Reg. Nich. IV, 111). Fue enterrado en Salamanca (ACS, *Memoria de los aniversarios*, fols. 18 v. y 65 v).

[124] VILLANUEVA, *op. cit.*, 11, págs. 71-74.

[125] *Ibid.*, pág. 76.

[126] RV 10-189-763 = Reg. Hon. III, 2466, editado por D. MANSILLA, *Documentación,* núm. 286.

[127] Véase LINEHAN, *op. cit* , págs. 20-34.

[128] *Ibid.*, págs. 54-82; ID., *Pedro de Albalat, arzobispo de Tarragona y su «Summa Septem Sacramentorum»,* «Hispania Sacra», 22 (1969), págs. 9-30.

[129] ACU: «Venerabili in Christo patri ... Dei gratia episcopo J. eiusdem permissione Sabinensis episcopus salutem in Domino. Cum sitis promotus ad ecclesiam Urgellensem, paternitatem vestram requirimus et rogamus quatinus operam detis ut sic in cura suscepti regiminis vos geratis quod acceptus sitis minister Deo et populum vestrum pascatis sana doctrina pariter et exemplo. Cetera vobis exprimere poterit viva voce dilectus noster lator presentium sacrista Ilerdensis comissorum sacri negotiorum fidelis et sollicitus procurator ... Dat. Roma in crastina cinerum».

[130] Pedro estaba en Roma en diciembre de 1230 (AC Lérida, cajón 202, núm. 569).

[131] La información que sigue deriva de un relato *verbatim* de la audiencia de una encuesta, efectuada con posterioridad a la elección de Ponce, que se conserva parcialmente en Urgel. Véase también VILLANUEVA, *op. cit.*, 11, pág. 74 n.

[132] «Item dixit (Gombaldus de Acuta) quod fama publica est in ecclesia Urgellensi quod sacrista fecit in-

de Ponce, fue él quien recitó la oración final[133]. El sacristán de Urgel y su partido no habían ahorrado ningún esfuerzo en su ansiedad por excluir a Ponce: sus métodos fueron desde el soborno a la emboscada[134]. En favor de Ponce se alegaba que sus poderosas relaciones cooperarían a la tarea de librar a la diócesis de la herejía en lo espiritual y de las incursiones del conde de Foix en lo temporal[135]. Pero para el sacristán era más importante excluir al intruso —sentimiento que era compartido por los canónigos de Salamanca y Compostela en sus iglesias respectivas. Finalmente, a pesar de las violentas tácticas de los adversarios de Ponce, que empujaban a su candidato, el sacristán, hacia el trono episcopal[136], Ponce resultó elegido. Quedaba por ver si las recomendaciones de sus abogados significaban algo.

No fue así. En lugar de hacer las paces con sus enemigos, Ponce se las arregló para engrosar sus filas. No se consiguió ningún progreso en las tareas paralelas de extirpar la herejía y de enfrentarse con el conde de Foix[137] y en 1243 el conde apeló a Roma. Sus motivos de queja eran de naturaleza puramente feudal[138], y seguían siéndolo cuando los reiteró en 1252, aunque en esta segunda ocasión procuró buscar más salidas alegando que el obispo, *utinam pius*, le había atacado con ambas espadas, y obtener ventaja recordando al papa que ambos descendían de un linaje común[139]. Pero las futuras dificultades de Ponce nacieron menos de las quejas del conde que de las de cierto número de sus canónigos que llegaron a la corte papal a primeros de noviembre de 1251 e informaron al papa de que el obispo era culpable de simonía, adulterio, incesto y de otros crímenes que el procurador

terfeci unam mulam et alteram vulnerari magistri P. de Albalato». Este testimonio fue corroborado por Bertrandus Gay.

[133] «... et finito Te Deum Laudamus dicta fuit oratio per sacristam Ilerdensem».

[134] Berenguer de Meyá había sido testigo de los intentos de apartar a B. de Muro de la lealtad a Ponce «cum si hoc faceret magnum commodum esset ipsius B. de Muro et posset semper facere quicquid vellet in ecclesia Urgellensi». Cuando G. Vidal estaba en camino para la elección, «venit quidam homo currendo et dixit eis quod nullo modo deberent accedere ad ecclesiam. Sacrista enim Urgellensis fecerat poni insidias scilicet pedites qui Poncium predictum de Villamur et dictum testem deberent capere».

[135] G. Vidal intentó disuadir al sacristán de que se opusiera a Ponce «nam per eum et avunculum suum episcopum Ilerdensem poterat episcopatui consuli tam in temporalibus quam in spiritualibus, et poterat recuperari ecclesie Urgellensi eorum potencia mediante ea que comes Fuxensis de bonis ecclesie iniuste detinebat. Item episcopatus erat heretica pravitate infectus et per ipsos poterat ab huiusmodi labe et crimine expiari».

[136] Ante el anuncio de la elección de Ponce, P. de Timor, uno de los partidarios del sacristán (según G. Vidal), «accepit sacristam per capam et duxit eum ad cathedram que est iuxta altare S. Marie et posuit eum super cathedram et dictus testis non intellexit quod sacrista fuisset electus verbo».

[137] F. VALLS TABERNER, *Obras Selectas*, I, Madrid-Barcelona, 1953, págs. 291 y ss. relata algo de esta disputa; M. MENÉNDEZ PELAYO, *Historia de los heterodoxos españoles*, ed. BAC, Madrid, 1956, I, págs. 525-528; J. MIRET Y SANS, *Investigación histórica sobre el vizcondado de Castellbó*, Barcelona, 1900, págs. 207-212.

[138] VILLANUEVA, *op. cit.*, 11, págs. 220-221.

[139] *Ibid.*, págs. 87 y 226-228. Véase también la bula de Inocencio IV de junio de 1247 registrada por J.

de Ponce, al informarle, prefirió no especificar [140]. Era, dijeron a Inocencio IV, mucho más dañino que el conde [141]. Sus actividades habían conseguido que los canónigos olvidaran sus diferencias personales y se unieran contra él. El arcediano Ricardo y Ramón de Piera, que nueve años antes habían estado enzarzados en fiera disputa, actuaban ahora al unísono en su determinación de librarse del obispo [142]. El primero se quejaba de que, aunque Ponce había estado aceptando procuraciones de su iglesia durante veinte años, todavía no se había dignado visitarla [143], y el clero de Lilia recibía tan mal trato de su preboste, a quien sostenía el obispo, que había pasado una Cuaresma excesivamente frugal [144].

Los malos antecedentes de Ponce le privaron, en el momento en que más lo necesitaba, del valioso apoyo que había puesto a su disposición Pedro de Albalat. En vez de ayudarle, el arzobispo, a cuyos concilios reformistas [145] Ponce había dejado de acudir, añadió leña al fuego con un memorial a Inocencio IV recomendando que la iglesia de Urgel fuera reformada en su cabeza y en sus miembros [146]. Ponce había roto con la reforma y los reformistas, a su vez, estaban decididos a destruirle. El hermano del arzobispo, el dominico Andrés, obispo de Valencia, se encontraba en la Curia, y atizó las llamas que habían de consumir al acusado [147]. El sacristán de Gerona añadió

PAZ, *Documentos relativos a España existentes en los Archivos nacionales de París*, Madrid, 1934, núm. 64.

[140] VILLANUEVA, *op. cit.*, 11, págs. 84 y 228.

[141] Su procurador informó: «E an dit al Apostoli que maior mal a feit en P. de Vilamur a la sgleia que no avie lo Comte de Foix» (VILLANUEVA, *op. cit.*, 11, pág. 223).

[142] CP Véase más adelante. Los otros demandantes eran Arnaldo de Mur, Bernardo de Fluviano y Arnaldo de Querol (RV 22-156-135 = Reg. Inn. IV, 5592). El último mencionado pudo posiblemente estar relacionado con la familia Queralt, en decadencia en este período: véase P. BOFILL Y BOIX, *Lo castell de Gurb y la família Gurb en lo segle XIII*, «Congrès d'història de la Corona d'Aragó», segona part, Barcelona, 1913, páginas 695-743, 715 y ss. El procurador de Ponce pidió que los detalles del caso en que el arcediano había sido la figura principal fueran enviados a la Curia, sin duda con la esperanza de desacreditar a Ricardo (VILLANUEVA, *loc. cit.*, pág. 223).

[143] La procuración resultaba costosa: se exigía de Ricardo que sostuviese treinta hombres de a caballo. Su queja está fechada en 23 de agosto de 1251 (ACU).

[144] CP: «Scitis enim quod non fuit in ecclesia nostra nisi unus sacerdos qui vix pane et aqua vivebat per totam quadragesimam et postquam in possessionem reduxistis cum, olla et quicquid potuit extrahit inde et honores alienavit et vendidit et fecit ad dilapidacionem domus que non sunt scribenda»; habiendo saqueado el lugar, el preboste se aseguró la inmunidad tomando la cruz.

[145] VILLANUEVA, *loc. cit.*, pág. 79. En su primer concilio provincial en 1239, Pedro había acentuado la obligación de sus sufragáneos de asistir en el futuro; todas las «excusationes frivolas» fueron suprimidas (E. MARTENE y U. DURAND, *Thesaurus novus anecdotorum*, París, 1717, IV, pág. 287).

[146] Su memorandum fue presentado en la Curia después de su muerte por los canónigos de Urgel, como relata el procurador de Ponce: «elsque aduxeren letres del fals archebisbe que è mort, que deien que la sgleia Durgel ere en gran mal per faliment de pastor, è que iavie obs corretio en lo cap, en los membres ...» (VILLANUEVA, *op. cit.*, pág. 221).

[147] Villanueva niega que el obispo de Valencia estuviese en la Curia en esta época: «No sé de qué Valencia sería este obispo; pero es cierto que no era de la del Cid», pág. 83 n. En realidad Andrés estaba allí en aquel

su prestigio a la acusación, por carta[148] y en persona[149]. Lo mismo
† hizo el sobrino de Ponce, procurador del obispo de Zaragoza, aunque
el agente de Ponce no estaba seguro de que el obispo no le hubiera
dado instrucciones para adoptar esta postura. Puede suponerse
que era así, porque Arnaldo, obispo de Zaragoza, era un reformista
que había cooperado con todas sus fuerzas con el arzobispo Pedro[150],
y en aquel preciso momento estaba luchando en la retaguardia, junto
con los obispos de Valencia y Lérida, contra la sucesión a la sede de
Tarragona de un hombre que representaba exactamente todo aquello
que Pedro de Albalat se había lanzado a destruir, Benito de Rocaberti[151] —la única figura de cierta posición que podía prestar alguna
ayuda a Ponce de Urgel, y cuyo nombramiento para Tarragona
puso allí fin inmediatamente a la causa de la reforma[152].

La investigación de los asuntos del obispo Ponce constituía por
tanto una piedra de toque —un duelo de fortaleza entre los ideales
de Benito de Rocaberti, que logró su ascenso en el período en que
fue decidida, y los del arzobispo difunto y sus correligionarios super-
vivientes. Los cargos levantados contra él eran ciertamente graves:
que era un asesino y *deflorator virginum*, que era padre de diez hijos
a los que había entregado propiedades de la iglesia, que había falsi-

---

preciso momento (febrero de 1252) por asuntos del rey de Aragón (ACA, Cancillería real, letras pontificias, leg.
XII, núm. 65; Reg. F. MIQUEL ROSELL, *op. cit.*, núm. 174).

[148] *Ibid.*, pág. 221. El sacristán de Gerona era Guillermo de Montgrí que, mientras existió la vacante de
Tarragona, antes del nombramiento de Pedro, fue guardián de la iglesia (MORERA Y LLAURADÓ, *Tarragona cristiana*, Tarragona, 1899, II, pág. 272; RV 18-145-36 = Reg. Greg. IX, 3099). Como tal fue delegado para actuar
contra la herejía que infestaba la diócesis de Ponce (ACU, *Dotium sive dotaliarum ecclesie Urgellensis liber secundus*,
fol. 71 v.). Era amigo del arzobispo Pedro, que fue testigo de su testamento en enero de 1248 (AHA, Tarragona,
Cartoral AB, fol. 4 r.). de Jaime de Aragón, que le asignó una generosa pensión en enero de 1259 (ACA, Cancillería real, reg. 6, fol. 129 v.) y de una serie de pontífices, de Gregorio IX a Urbano IV, que en julio de 1264 le
nombró ayuda de campo del legado Sinitus (Reg. Urbano IV, C473). Su testimonio contra Ponce fue en consecuencia un fuerte golpe para la causa del obispo.

[149] RV 27-387-129 = Reg. Inn. IV, 5825.

[150] VILLANUEVA, *op. cit.*, pág. 222. Había sido trasladado a Zaragoza desde Valencia (donde fue sustituido
por el obispo Andrés) en 1248 (J. SANCHIS SIVERA, *El obispo de Valencia, Arnaldo de Peralta*, «Boletín de la
Real Academia de la Historia», 82 [1923], págs. 40-64 y 104-121). Ciertamente en Zaragoza era necesaria la
energía que había desplegado en Valencia, a juzgar por los hallazgos del arzobispo en marzo de 1241 (Archivo
arzobispal de Zaragoza, 152).

[151] En abril de 1252, Inocencio IV desoyó las acusaciones lanzadas contra Benito por estos tres obispos
es decir «duplicis adulterii crimen, super quo dicebaris infamatus, et quedam alia objecta», y aprobó su elección
(RV 22-239-149 = Reg. Inn. IV, 5675).

[152] No hay ningún estudio sobre Benito, pero véase MORERA Y LLAURADÓ, *op. cit.*, II, págs. 289 y ss.,
y VILLANUEVA, *op. cit.*, 19, págs. 185-188. Había pasado varios años en la Curia durante el gobierno de Pedro
de Albalat, con el que había entablado una fiera controversia sobre ciertas posesiones pertenecientes a la came-
raria de Tarragona, en la que había cesado al advenimiento de Pedro. Para octubre de 1248 la amistad de Inocencio IV le había valido la reinstalación. Véase LINEHAN, *op. cit.*, pág. 85. Sus posteriores ausencias en la Curia como
arzobispo, se tratan en S. CAPDEVILA, *Els Franciscans i l'arquebisbe de Tarragona Benet de Rocaberti*, «Franciscalia»
(Barcelona, 1928), págs. 39-45.

ficado moneda y malbaratado la mitad de la diócesis, que había dormido con su hermana y con su prima carnal, «e moltes altres coses»[153]. Pero tenía en la Curia amigos contra cuyas represalias buscaron protección sus acusadores[154], y cuando éstos presentaron por primera vez su caso, fueron arrojados de la presencia del papa en desgracia[155]. Raimundo de Liriis, procurador del obispo[156], no escatimó esfuerzos en beneficio de su cliente; contrató los servicios de *Magister Andreas* y de una plantilla de seis abogados[157], a pesar de que el obispo no le había enviado fondos, y sobornó a un sobrino del papa prometiéndole un par de buenos caballos[158]. Todo esto costaba dinero, y Ramón tuvo que pedir un préstamo incluso antes de que empezara el proceso[159]. Y a pesar de todo fracasó en conseguir un auditor que le fuera favorable; el obispo de Valencia obtuvo en esto la preferencia[160]. De este modo se fue prolongando la encuesta hasta que en marzo de 1252 Inocencio IV comisionó a Ramón de Peñafort y al ministro de la orden franciscana para que investigasen en Urgel[161]. Aunque el arzobispo Benito hizo todo lo posible para diferir su tarea[162], los comisionados se las arreglaron para terminar su trabajo[163] y trasladar el caso a la Curia para la sentencia. Al llegar a este punto se designó al cardenal Esteban de Palestrina para emitir el fallo y en octubre de 1254 suspendió al obispo Ponce[164]. Una de las primeras

---

[153] VILLANUEVA, *op. cit.*, 11, págs. 221-222.

[154] *Ibid.*, «è soplicaren ... que·ls asseguràs que no peressen mal per les vostres amicos de cort».

[155] *Ibid.*, «è no.ls volgeren oir, ans los negitan del palau a ontadament».

[156] No B. de Liriis, como dice VILLANUEVA, *op. cit.*, pág. 221. Había estado relacionado con Urgel por lo menos desde 1215, y en enero de 1249 había hecho las paces con Ponce, tras una disputa que los había dividido (ACU, *Dotium ... liber secundus*, fol. 34 v. y CP).

[157] No he conseguido identificar a *Magister Andreas*. En enero y marzo *Petrus Ademarii clericus* defendía los intereses del obispo en la *audientia contradictorum* (ACU y CP).

[158] *Ibid.*, pág. 223. Es curioso que Raimundo especifique los caballos que han de enviarse en vez de su precio. †

[159] En Lyon, en mayo de 1250 tomó en préstamo de los mercaderes romanos Petrus Cinthii de la Turre y sus sobrinos Paulus Bonifacii y Jacobus, la suma de 110 marcos pagaderos en la próxima fiesta de San Miguel, bien en la Curia, «si fuerit citra montes», o alternativamente en Tours (CP).

[160] VILLANUEVA, *op. cit.*, pág. 222: «Puis procura lo bisbe de València que agessen oidor enpatraren en P. Caporixo lo Cardenal». Este era el cardenal Pedro Capocci de S. Georgius ad Velum Aureum que antes de marzo de 1246 había sido comisionado para la audiencia de un caso referente al obispo de Pamplona (Reg. Inn. IV, 1783).

[161] Reg. Inn. IV, 5592.

[162] VILLANUEVA, *op. cit.*, págs. 230-236.

[163] VILLANUEVA, *op. cit.*, pág. 85, sostiene que la comisión de Inocencio de marzo de 1252 fue posteriormente revocada, y que las investigaciones no se llevaron a cabo. Sin embargo, en noviembre de 1255 fueron reembolsados a Arnaldo de Cornellá y Juan de Cascalis, arcedianos, y a Bernardo de Garrigosa y Bernardo de Tost, canónigos, por el prior y capítulo de Urgel, todos los gastos «quas nos feceramus racione illius contumacie quam incurristis propter adventum et moram quam contraxit apud sedem Urgellensem et castrum civitatis frater Raymundus de Penaforti et alii sibi adherentes et prosequentes factum inquisicionis impetrate a sede apostolica contra D. Poncium episcopum Urgellensem ...» (CP. VALLS TABERNER, *op. cit.*, págs. 292-293, reitera la opinión de Villanueva).

[164] AHA, Tarragona, *Cartoral AB*, fol. 16 r.

providencias de Alejandro IV fue confirmar esta sentencia y declarar depuesto a Ponce[165]. Durante casi dos años la sede de Urgel permaneció vacante, hasta que en 11 de agosto de 1257 el papa designó a «magistrum Aprilem ... tunc archidiaconum Salamanticensem et capellanum nostrum»[166], ascenso que probablemente se debió casi por completo a la asociación entre Abril y el juez que decidió el caso contra Ponce —Esteban de Palestrina.

La nueva sede de Abril no era ninguna sinecura. Aparte de todo lo demás, heredó las deudas que Ponce había contraído durante sus últimos años en la Curia y se vio obligado a pagar una pensión al ex-obispo[167]. Su promoción representaba una pérdida de influencia para el arzobispo Benito, que había actuado como guardián de la sede mientras ésta estuvo vacante, y parece que este puntilloso personaje no se lo perdonó nunca, porque, al igual que el arzobispo Juan de Compostela, era un expansionista, y no acostumbraba a sufrir reveses con el ánimo sereno[168]. Tampoco la iglesia de Salamanca tenía muchos motivos de regocijo por la promoción de Abril. Al ganar un *alumpnus* distinguido había perdido los servicios de un representante influyente. El tesorero de la iglesia parecía creer que Abril había partido al destierro: desde su punto de vista Urgel estaba mucho más lejos que Roma, y manifestaba la esperanza de que el

[165] Reg. Alex. IV, 93.

[166] Reg. Alex. IV, 2149. VILLANUEVA, *op. cit.*, pág. 94, que cita esta bula de AGUIRRE, *op. cit.*, llama la atención sobre la existencia en el archivo de Urgel de un documento que se refiere a un obispo. A. en febrero de 1257, y deduce que Aguirre equivocó la fecha de la bula de Alejandro. Sin embargo, tanto el Registro Vaticano como la bula original al cabildo de Urgel, que he visto en ese archivo, están fechados «tertio idus augusti ... anno tertio» tal como figura en Aguirre. He visto también en CP el documento de febrero de 1257 al que se refiere Villanueva, y que publica (*op. cit.*), págs. 236-237. Por tanto debe suponerse que se fechó mal. No he encontrado rastros de ningún obispo Bernardo como el que menciona MONFAR Y SORS, *Historia*, en n. 117, página 537. El historiador de los Condes de Urgel parece haber cometido un error: cf. MIQUEL ROSELL, *Regesta* número 182.

[167] Alejandro IV había otorgado a Ponce una pensión anual de la diócesis de 100 libras *turonenses* (RV 24-83-11 = Reg. Alex. IV, 93). Ponce, que estaba en la Curia en octubre de 1253, había conseguido dos préstamos con la garantía de los bienes de su sede, de 800 libras *lucenses* y 300 libras *pruvinienses* respectivamente (RV 23-222-26, 23-240-28 = Reg. Inn. IV, 7044, 7062). En octubre de 1258 Abril había pagado a B. de Vilamur, sobrino de Ponce y heredero del difunto ex-obispo, la suma de 2.000 *solidi malgurienses*, «quos dominus papa dari mandavit et solvi quondam predecesori vestro a domino Tarraconensi archiepiscopo procuratore pro ipso in ecclesia et diocesi Urgellensi racione provisionis sue ut ex illis vivere posset et causam suam duceret in curia romana» (ACU).

[168] La personalidad de Benito destaca vívidamente en el relato de su intervención en la elección para la sede de Tortosa, cuando intentó forzar a los canónigos de esta iglesia a que aceptasen a su candidato. Cuando encontró resistencia, se negó a admitir la elección, como ellos le recordaron: «Vos provocatus et valde commotus dixistis, asseruistis et affirmastis stricto repente cum quodam impetu calcaribus mulo quem equitabatis, vultu valde turbato, provocatus et commotus jurastis per Deum et per sanctam ecclesiam votum etiam emittendo et alia verba turpissima dicendo que reservamus suo loco et tempore probare coram judice competenti» (AC Tortosa, cajón *Arcediano maior*, II, núm. 29). Véase LINEHAN, *op. cit.*, págs. 90-92.

vagabundo pudiese volver como obispo de Salamanca o incluso arzobispo de Compostela. Pero su mayor preocupación la constituía el destino de las propiedades de Abril, de las que el nuevo obispo había dispuesto en una forma que desagradó considerablemente al capítulo de Salamanca [169]. Tal vez hubieran servido para arreglar las cuentas de Abril y como *douceurs* distribuídos antes de que abandonase la escena de sus recientes triunfos, del mismo modo que Viviano que fue nombrado para la sede de Calahorra en 1264, cedió sus beneficios de Toledo a un sobrino del cardenal Huberto de San Eustaquio [170].

De todas formas, Abril era ahora para sus amigos y relaciones de Compostela y Salamanca un hombre de recursos, y le escribían esperanzados y confiando en obtener fáciles ventajas. Martín Abril, canónigo de Compostela, pedía un beneficio para el portador de la carta, pariente suyo, y compartía la esperanza del tesorero de Salamanca de que Abril pudiese volver para ocupar una sede en aquella zona [171]. El *magister scolarum* de Compostela recomendaba a Pedro Rodríguez [172], y el tesorero de la misma iglesia escribía en beneficio de un candidato innominado [173]. Sancha Peláez, hermana de Abril, que en su pobreza había vendido su casa prácticamente por nada, preguntaba si no podía solicitar algunas de las limosnas que tenía a su disposición para socorro de los pobres, y proyectaba aligerar su carga encargándole el cuidado de uno de sus hijos [174]. Su tío Alfonso Pérez, cargado de deudas y de parientes pobres, expresaba la esperanza de que hubieran llegado tiempos mejores [175]. Algunos de sus apurados compañeros enumeraban sus pesares poniéndolos en versos leoninos que, en parte, daban preferencia al estilo sobre el significado [176]. La carta más conmovedora procedía de su madre: llena de deudas, sumida en la duda y en la desesperación ¿no era preferible que le pidiese limosna a él y no a otros? ¿Y tendría la bondad de elegir él mismo

---

[169] La carta del tesorero está publicada en VILLANUEVA, *op. cit.*, págs. 237-238. Añade: «De rebus autem vestris Garsias, quando recesserit, vobis totam certitudinem reportabit». Garsias era el *hombre* de Abril. Cf. Apéndice 3.

[170] Véase P. A. LINEHAN, *The «Gravamina» of the Castilian Church in 1262-1263*, «English Historical Review», 85 (1970), págs. 730-754

[171] Véase Apéndice 1 y n. 68, arriba.

[172] CP.

[173] CP.

[174] Véase Apéndice 6.

[175] Véase Apéndice 4.

[176] Véase Apéndice 7.

entre los diversos pretendientes que pedían la mano de su prima, ahora que era un pariente que valía la pena tener? [177].

Si estos buitres suponían que había beneficios en Urgel para cualquiera que los pidiese, iban a sufrir una desilusión. El estado de la diócesis obligó a Abril a hacer oídos sordos incluso ante las súplicas de su tío [178]. Un estudio de las listas de testigos de los canónigos de Urgel en los años siguientes a 1257 sugiere que pocos de estos gritos del alma consiguieron la respuesta deseada. Con un par de excepciones, no hay huella alguna de los clérigos que estaban en Salamanca y Compostela inmediatamente antes. Sin embargo, es natural que Abril llevara con él al «destierro» a uno o dos de sus antiguos colegas, y dos de ellos por lo menos hicieron una brillante carrera en su nuevo ambiente. Su hermano, Juan Peláez, canónigo de Salamanca, estaba con él en Urgel en 1258, como observó Villanueva [179]. Había sido *clericus chori* en Salamanca cuando el futuro obispo había acudido al capítulo en 1243 [180], y para agosto de 1257 Alejandro IV le había proporcionado una canonjía, aunque, a causa de las difíciles circunstancias de la iglesia, exacerbadas por la interferencia del arzobispo de Compostela [181], hasta enero de 1264, en que Urbano IV intervino en su favor, no se le asignó ninguna renta [182]. Para entonces era capellán del cardenal Esteban, que en marzo siguiente le consiguió una canonjía en Compostela [183]. Por tanto había ascendido a la sombra del obispo Abril, en cuya *familia* disfrutaba de una importante situación. En febrero de 1262 era arcediano de Urgel, y representó al capítulo cuando se entregaron ciertos diezmos a Ramón Vidal de Puigcerdá [184]. Se había adaptado a su nuevo ambiente con notable rapidez, y en diciembre de 1265 era ya deán [185]. Incluso después de la muerte de Abril continuó su éxito. Retuvo el cargo de sacristán, al que había ascendido en marzo de 1268, hasta su propia muerte, que tuvo lugar poco después de 1286 [186]. El segundo clérigo que llegó a Urgel con Abril era Juan

---

[177] VILLANUEVA, *op. cit.*, págs. 228-229. La palabra que falta en la transcripción de Villanueva es, según CP, *nutrivi*.

[178] Alfonso Pérez no había sabido nada de Abril durante un año o más: Apéndice 4. Véase también la queja de Juan Domínguez en Apéndice 8.

[179] *Op. cit.*, págs. 96-97. Puede haber sido hermano de Abril: véase Apéndice 3 y n. 18, arriba.

[180] AHN, Sección de clero, pergaminos, 1881/14 = Marcos, 208.

[181] Véase arriba, n. 90.

[182] AHN, Sección de clero, pergaminos, 1881/11 = Marcos, 267; RV 29-112-365 = Reg. Urbano IV, 1315.

[183] RV 29-300-1561 = Reg Urbano IV, 2509.

[184] CP.

[185] CP. Como tal fue testigo de una donación de tierras a Ferrer de Guardiola.

[186] ACU, *Dotium ... liber secundus*, fol. 124 v.; CP y ACU, *passim*.

Domínguez, quizá un hermano del obispo Domingo de Salamanca [187]. †
Testigo de diversos documentos en Salamanca desde 1240 lo más
tarde [188], y en mayo de 1256 capellán del tesorero corresponsal de
Abril [189], en la época de la promoción de Abril no había conseguido
aún una canonjía allí [190]. Por ello no puede sorprendernos que fuera
uno de aquellos clérigos que intentaron extender el embargo de 1245
a otras iglesias de la diócesis [191]. Cuando escribió su carta felicitando
al nuevo obispo de Urgel no era más que «suus clericus humilis et
alumpnus» y agente en Compostela [192]. En julio de 1258 estaba tra-
bajando como notario de Abril [193], y durante los cuarenta y cinco
años siguientes su ortografía característica figuró regularmente entre
los documentos de Urgel. Como hombre de confianza del arzobispo
de Compostela sabía enseñar los métodos de una burocracia avanza-
da [194]. En marzo anterior era ya canónigo [195] y en enero siguiente
procurador general del capítulo, encargado de las negociaciones con
el vicario del rey de Aragón en Cardona [196]. En abril de 1260, Abril
le nombró su procurador en la corte papal [197]. Su promoción dentro
de la iglesia fue más lenta que la de Juan Peláez, pero en abril de
1279 estaba en posesión de la capellanía de S. Odón y de la *preposi-
tura mensis januarii* [198], beneficios ambos que iban unidos a la *scribanía*
capitular [199]. Por tanto había echado raíces en Urgel más como oficial
del capítulo que como amanuense personal de su primitivo señor.
Vivía aún en el siglo siguiente, sobreviviendo a su patrón más de

[187] BELTRÁN DE HEREDIA, *Cartulario*, pág. 77, n. 38.

[188] ACS, 14/1/16 = Marcos, 199. No era —puede suponerse— el mismo hombre que obtuvo el beneficio de Compostela con preferencia a Abril: véase Apéndice 4.

[189] AHN, Sección de clero, pergaminos, 1881/14 = Marcos 263.

[190] AHN, Sección de clero, pergaminos, 1881/11 = Marcos, 267.

[191] Reg. Nich. IV, 6365. Véase arriba, n. 89.

[192] Véase Apéndice 8. A juzgar por la escritura, el documento en Apéndice 4 podía haber sido escrito por él. Seguramente era hecho por una mano distinta de la otra carta de Alfonso Pérez (Apéndice 2), que es muy tosca y de dificilísima lectura.

[193] CP.

[194] «Noscat vestra paternitas quod sum cum achiepiscopo et teneo segellum suum et est mihi bonus cum † ipso ...» (Apéndice 8).

[195] ACU, siendo testigo de un documento referente a las reparaciones efectuadas en el castillo de Alas.

[196] CP.

[197] ASV, *Collectorie* 397, fol. 53 r. (Apéndice 9).

[198] ACU, *Dotium ... liber secundus*, fols. 33 v.-34 r.

[199] La reorganización de la estructura capitular efectuada por el obispo Guillermo en agosto de 1299 separó la *scribania*, que conservaba aún Juan Domínguez, de la capellanía de S. Odón, y la unió a la *mensa episcopalis*. Además se obligaba al *notarius* a pagar en lo sucesivo sus propias materiales de escribir. Pero estas reformas no habían de efectuarse antes de la muerte o retiro de Juan Domínguez (ACU).

treinta años, y al final de una vida que debió ser larga, delegó sus obligaciones en manos más jóvenes [200].

El peligroso estado de la diócesis impidió que Abril proporcionase puestos a otros. Su primera tarea fue la de proponer economías. Pero hacerlo inmediatamente le planteó dificultades y le obligó a elegir entre las nuevas responsabilidades en que él había incurrido y el deber de gratitud que estaba obligado a pagar. El preciso resultado se relacionó con el decanato o arcedianato rural de Tremp que estaba en el territorio de su dotación.

Cuando Abril llegó a Urgel, el arcediano de Tremp, Guillem de Moncada, había sido recientemente elevado a la sede de Lérida [201], y, con el asentimiento de su cabildo, el obispo ordenó, en enero de 1258, su supresión y la vinculación de sus rentas a la «mensa episcopal», en parte por razones de economía, ya que sus ingresos episcopales ascendían a 80 marcos al año [202], en parte en consideración al comportamiento tradicionalmente enojoso de los arcedianos [203]. Incluso había evidentemente alguna sospecha de que alguien había pretendido la posesión del arcedianato: la medida únicamente se haría efectiva «quam cito vaccaverit». En junio de 1259, o quizás antes, la identidad de tal demandante fue conocida por Abril, cuando su viejo patrón, el cardenal Esteban de Palestrina, le escribió como amigo suyo, diciéndole que Alejandro IV lo había otorgado a su sobrino y capellán, Timoteo, rogándole su cooperación y sugiriéndole, que a cambio, Abril podría cuidar de obtenerle una dignidad superior [204]. Sin embargo, Abril se hizo sordo a los ruegos del cardenal, con el resultado de que en octubre de 1259, el caso fue discutido en la curia, estando Abril allí para defender sus intereses, no sólo contra Timoteo, sino también contra otro demandante —el abad Sancho de Valladolid, hijo del rey Jaime de Aragón [205].

---

† [200] Suscribió un documento de abril de 1302 escrito por *Jacobus Moxela*, notario público «vice Johannis Dominici»; en junio siguiente Guillermo de Alb, párroco de Hix, era *notarius episcopi*.

[201] VILLANUEVA, *op. cit.*, 16, pág. 146. Guillem se había opuesto a la elección de su predecesor, Berenguer de Peralta, y la disputa fue aducida en la curia papal en septiembre de 1256 (AHA, Cartoral AB, fol. 17 r.).

[202] «Attendentes quod mensa episcopalis Urgellensis sit adeo tenuis et exilis et pluribus debitis aggravata quod non possit sufficere ad episcopatus honera supportanda...» (ACU, *Dotium ... liber secundus*, fol. 23 r.).

[203] *Ibid*: «propter rebelliones quas vidimus et sensimus de archidiaconis seu decanis predicti loci et inobedientias contra episcopum et capitulum Urgellense». El obispo Ponce había sido arcediano de Tremp hasta su elección (VILLANUEVA, *op. cit.*, 11, pág. 74 n.) y había sido sucedido por Bernardo de Mur (AC Vich, cax. 6, núms. 77 y 84), a quien se recompensó de este modo por haber resistido a los esfuerzos que se hicieron para apartarle de la amistad de Ponce en 1230 (véase nota 134, arriba).

[204] Véase Apéndice 5.

[205] ASV, *Collectorie* 397, fol. 52 r.

El 28 de noviembre la audiencia fue prorrogada[206] y antes de su reasunción, Abril llevó a cabo un considerable «coup», asegurándose la confirmación papal del documento de enero de 1258, el cual había autorizado la supresión del mismo arcedianato que entonces estaba para proveerse: un excelente ejemplo de la confusión que reinaba en la curia[207]. Diez días más tarde fue concedida una nueva prórroga hasta marzo de 1260, y subsiguientemente hasta el 6 de mayo y el siguiente noviembre[208]. El 26 de mayo, la confirmación de Alejandro IV fue copiada en el cartulario de Urgel[209].

Desgraciadamente, el resultado de este incidente es desconocido. No hay ninguna otra referencia del caso en el registro del cardenal Ottaviano Ubaldini, ante quien había sido disputado[210]. Sin embargo, por lo que éste nos dice sobre Abril de Urgel, lo poco que sabemos es muy valioso. Abril estaba dispuesto a todo en su propia defensa —incluso hasta el límite de indisponerse con el hijo de su rey y con el sobrino de su patrono. En el caso la disputa tuvo escasas consecuencias. Sancho de Aragón guardó para sí un precio mucho mayor, el arzobispado de Toledo; Timoteo fue nombrado obispo de Zagreb[211]; y, finalmente, en invierno de 1263-1264, Abril y Esteban se reconciliaron[212]. Pero Abril había manifestado al menos que él estaba dispuesto a mejorar las finanzas de su sede, recurriendo precisamente a los sistemas de anexión de los que quince años antes había sido víctima su propio arcedianato de Ledesma[213]. Como *quid pro quo* en favor de los empobrecidos canónigos, Abril dispuso que, durante un año después de su muerte, la renta de los beneficios que habían disfrutado continuase siendo pagada para cancelar sus deudas y establecer aniversarios por ellos[214]. El obispo tenía que proceder con gran cuidado. Era extranjero y estaba por ello mucho más preocupado de no perturbar a los canónigos, que habían probado el sabor de la sangre tan recien-

---

[206] *Ibidem.*

[207] ACU, *Dotium ... liber secundus*, fols. 22 v.-23 v.: *Petitio vestra* (8 diciembre 1259).

[208] ASV, *Collectorie 397*, fols. 53 r.-v.

[209] ACU, *Dotium ... liber secundus*, fols. 23 v.-24 r.

[210] Para una descripción de la *Collectorie* 397, véase U. BERLIÈRE, *Causes belges en cour de Rome (1259-1263)*, «Bulletin de la Commission Royale d'Histoire», 74 (1905), págs. 1-26 y para este cardenal, LINEHAN, *op. cit*, pág. 300. El manuscrito ha sido hasta ahora olvidado por los historiadores de España.

[211] El arcediano de Tremp rendía veinte marcos anuales (*Dotium ... liber secundus*, fol. 23 r.), pero los gastos reclamados por Timoteo en abril de 1260 alcanzaban la suma de cuarenta libras *turonenses* (ASV, *Collectorie* 397, fol. 52 v.).

[212] Véase arriba, n. 95.

[213] Véase arriba, n. 47.

[214] *Dotium ... liber secundus*, fols. 20 v.-22 r. (marzo de 1258).

temente. El recuerdo de Ponce no podía por menos de influir en sus actos. En tan delicada situación, se vio obligado a deshacer virtualmente todo lo que Ponce había hecho y a hacer todo lo que había omitido. Ramón de Peñafort había recordado al arzobispo Benito que el mal ejemplo de Ponce había sido el responsable de todos los males acaecidos [215]. Había que intentar reformas, pero la reforma espiritual dependía de la solidez económica —una verdad evidente tal vez, pero no menos vital por eso [216].

Desgraciadamente para Abril, sus esfuerzos por proporcionar una base más sólida a la diócesis chocaron con los intereses de uno de sus más duros e influyentes eclesiásticos —el arcediano Ricardo de Aristot [217]. Ricardo formaba parte del partido anti-Ponce en los primeros años de la segunda mitad del siglo, y en lo que se refiere a los beneficios, era un pluralista aficionado al litigio, un antiguo maestro en el arte de las apelaciones y las excepciones. En 1243 había capeado con éxito el intento de varios miembros del capítulo, dirigidos por Ramon de Piera, de privarle de su arcedianato, demostrando que sus detractores estaban excomulgados y que, en cualquier caso, él poseía un indulto apostólico que le permitía conservar cierto número de beneficios [218]. Al principio Abril contemporizó con él: en mayo de 1258 consiguió imponer un compromiso en la disputa que mantenía el arcediano y el deán sobre la iglesia de Adrall. Durante los años inmediatamente siguientes Ricardo se mantuvo tranquilo. Respetando sólo su propia ley, vivía en un semi-retiro, rehusando cumplir la obligación de residencia que, en opinión de Abril le imponía su arcedianato, y declinando la ordenación. Pero finalmente se entabló la batalla por estos dos motivos. En diciembre de 1266 el obispo le había recordado sus deberes y Ricardo había respondido ásperamente, achacando esta nueva interferencia a la mala voluntad de Abril y de otras personas oficiosas que tenían designios sobre sus beneficios, y volviendo a las tácticas que hasta entonces le habían proporcionado el éxito —desenterrando el privilegio de Gregorio IX y colocándose

---

[215] «Si dicatur: fecit ille quod potuit; respondeo: non. Quia ut nec verbis audatia detur, nec exemplo praedicavit sufficienter, nec verbo. Et ideo ibi, sicut in aliquibus locis, secuta est corruptela» (VILLANUEVA, *op. cit.*, pág. 236).

[216] «Ceterum cum spiritualia sine temporalibus diu esse non possint», según palabras del testamento del obispo Jazpert de Valencia en 1287 (AC Valencia, perg. 5565).

[217] La totalidad del presente párrafo se basa en ACU y CP.

[218] Véase n 142, más arriba. Era el párroco de Balaguer. Su indulto fue concedido n marzo de 1241 (RV 20-40-242 = Reg. Greg. IX, 5931).

bajo la protección papal[219]. En la Pascua siguiente, Abril hizo otro infructuoso intento a través de su procurador, el párroco de Tartareu[220]. En la época de la cosecha estalló la tormenta. Una mañana temprano, a fines de julio, Bartolomé, párroco de Tartareu y procurador de Abril, llegó a la iglesia de El Pedrís para recoger la porción acostumbrada que correspondía al obispo de la *primicia* del lugar[221]. Pronto se le unió Ricardo, llevando consigo tres documentos que, según proclamó, contenían una sentencia del arzobispo Benito concediendo al arcediano el derecho a la *primicia*[222]. Bartolomé, que evidentemente no estaba convencido de que los documentos aportados por Ricardo fueran genuínos, se dispuso a asegurar la porción de la cosecha para el obispo. Pero Ricardo no era hombre capaz de depender exclusivamente de prescripciones legales. Había llegado acompañado por hombres armados de Balaguer y valiéndose de su presencia procedió a desarmar a Bartolomé y a despedirle[223]. Al día siguiente, el obispo excomulgó al arcediano[224]. Claro que esto no desanimó a Ricardo, porque contaba con un pronto aliado en el arzobispo, el cual ordenó a Abril concluir con lo que se había presentado como una venganza personal dirigida contra la persona del arcediano. Sin embargo, Abril, después de haber estado diez años tratando tanto con el arcediano como con el arzobispo, se había

[219] «... me ordinem ad recipiendum presbiteratus compellere non poterat (scil. episcopus) nec deberat nec etiam ad faciendum residenciam in ecclesia kathedrali propter inimicias quas ibidem non mea culpa habeo capitales».

[220] La negativa de Ricardo, fechada en 1 de abril: «... me monuit perhemtorie die sabbati scilicet quinto idus aprilis nulla alia monicione premissa quod in sabbato sancto paschali proximo venturo me facerem promoveri ad ordinem sacerdotis quem requirit cura ecclesie de Balagario. Item quod usque ad diem lune proximum post octabas pasche proxime venture venirem ad ecclesiam Urgellensem facturus ibi residenciam debitam et continuam sicut onus beneficii postulat in ea me obtinere assero postulat et requirit».

[221] La información que sigue está basada en el memorandum *ex parte* hecho a requerimiento del procurador del obispo por el capellán de El Pedrís. Bartolomé había llegado «summo mane ... ad dividendum mecum et percipiendum medietatem primiciarum ecclesie des Pedriz nomine domini episcopi Urgellensis sicut recipere consueverat et habere».

[222] El primer documento, pretendidamente del arzobispo, en el que se citaba a Abril «perhemtorie» a una audiencia relacionada con la *primicia*, era «de papiro sine sigillo»; el segundo, que se pretendía contenía la sentencia de P. Andrés (en quien el arzobispo había delegado el caso) concediendo las *primicias* a Ricardo, era «de pergameno sine sigillo aliquo et publica subscripcione»; el tercero, una carta del arzobispo —de papiro cum sigillo de cera— instruía a ciertos ejecutores nombrados para poner a Ricardo en posesión de la *primicia* «et omnium redditum quos dominus episcopus Urgellensis percepit in Balagario». Bartolomé puso objeciones «cum non esset scriptura authentica nec per publicam manum conscripta».

[223] «Et cum ipse Bartholomeus inciperet aperire cigias cum lingone volens inde bladum abstraere et percipere partem ipsius bladi nomine domini episcopi accessit ad eum dominus archidiaconus supradictus et abstulit ei lingonem quem tenebat presentibus et assistentibus illis probis hominibus de Balagario qui cum eo venerant et pluribus hominibus des Pedriz ...».

[224] «... pro violencia quam mihi (scil. Bartholomeo) intulit Ricardus ... per se et suos homines auferendo mihi violenter lingonem cum ego personaliter aperiebam cigias in quibus erat bladum domini episcopi quod habuerat cum fratribus milicie Templi ...».

vuelto más atrevido. Llevó su sentencia a la práctica y privó a Ricardo de sus beneficios [225]. No sabemos cual fue el resultado final, pero cuando murió Abril dos años más tarde, Ricardo estuvo presente en la reunión del capítulo en la que se eligió a un personaje local, el arcediano Pedro de Urg, para ser el siguiente obispo de Urgel. De todas formas, incluso aunque Abril no consiguiera imponer su voluntad, el arcedianato de Ricardo no sobrevivió mucho tiempo, porque en la reorganización de la diócesis en 1299 se desmembró el pequeño imperio que había construído, y el arcedianato, junto con la iglesia de Balaguer, pasó a formar parte del nuevo arcedianato de Urgel, al que se unió de forma permanente el deanato [226].

La resistencia del arcediano Ricardo no fue el único obstáculo que encontró Abril en sus esfuerzos de reorganización de la diócesis, tanto espiritual como temporalmente, Urgel, lo mismo que otras iglesias, tenía que soportar la pesada carga de las tasas papales, y aunque los reinos españoles no contaban con un Mateo Paris que relacionase sus quejas, existe amplia evidencia de que fue durante estos años de mediados de siglo cuando se sintió más agudamente la irritación motivada por las exigencias papales y se las criticó con más libertad. Ciertamente hay pocas señales de que «el objetivo consciente y el mérito real» del pontificado de Alejandro IV «fuese renovar la organización normal y aceptada cuyo funcionamiento había impedido Inocencio (IV)», conclusión a la que, según el Sr. Barraclough «no podemos escapar» [227]. Ciertamente la iglesia de Salamanca no opinaba así pues, debía mucho más a Urbano IV, que revocó varias decisiones de Alejandro que le habían resultado extremadamente penosas [228]. Más aún, la responsabilidad de Alejandro en la intolerable carga de las provisiones fue señalada y recibió especial condena por parte del obispo de Cuenca en enero de 1262 [229], en cuyo año los

---

[225] En diciembre de 1267 los procuradores de Ricardo recordaron a Abril las órdenes del arzobispo «ut gravaminibus et molestiis suis penitus desisteretis et cessaretis. Vosque spreta appellacione et monitione predictis eidem archidiacono contra justiciam subtracxistis et subtrahi fecistis proventus archidiaconatus sui ac suam canonicam portionem quam recepit et recipere consuevit per plures annos in sua absentia in ecclesia Urgellensi». Dos meses después el arcediano de Aristot era Bernat Guinard (J. SERRA VILARÓ, *Baronies de Pinós i Mataplana*, Barcelona, 1930, pág. 55).

[226] ACU.

[227] G. BARRACLOUGH, *The constitution 'Execrabilis' of Alexander IV*, «English Historical Review», 49 (1934), págs. 193-218, en la pág. 212.

[228] Véase más arriba, n. 57, 80 y 90.

[229] La apelación del obispo, junto con la del cabildo de Toledo, se dirigía contra las exacciones del Maestro Raimundo, un capellán del cardenal Esteban de Palestrina y *collector* en la provincia de Toledo. Véase LINEHAN, «English Historical Review», 85 (1970), págs. 730-754.

obispos de Castilla se decidieron unánimemente a escribir a Urbano IV pidiendo alguna medida que aliviase la contribución al fondo para el Imperio de Oriente, ese elefante blanco por el que apenas disimulaban su desprecio, en un momento en que Castilla sufría una gran hambre y el clero se veía obligado a cultivar el suelo para ir malviviendo, al mismo tiempo que se ocupaba de gran número de iglesias que no tenían pastor [230]. Se mostraron especialmente contrarios a la costumbre de Alejandro de convertir a los exiliados de las guerras italianas en carga para sus iglesias [231], pero que Urgel tuvo que soportar cuando en 1259 los jueces delegados para buscar pensiones dentro de la provincia de Tarragona para Balduino y Mateo de Messina, y ocho servidores suyos, eligieron la diócesis de Abril [232]. Se hacía una gran excepción con las demandas de los nuncios papales de que el pago se efectuase en oro puro [233] —una comodidad que no tenía precio— tanto en Castilla, donde las ambiciones imperiales de Alfonso X constituían una sangría permanente de los recursos nacionales, como en Aragón, donde, aunque el estado de la economía era aparentemente mucho más satisfactorio, la iglesia de Urgel fue incapaz de encontrar oro para el legado en 1274 [234]. Poco debió quedar para el obispo Arnaldo de Comminges, que escribió a Abril en 1258, pidiendo autorización para realizar una colecta de fondos en la diócesis de Urgel con destino a la restauración del hospital de San Beltrán, en Comminges [235].

A pesar de todas estas dificultades, Abril consiguió hasta cierto punto mejorar el estado de la diócesis. Villanueva observó que había convocado sínodos, pero que no se habían conservado sus constituciones [236]. Cualquiera que fuese el contenido de esta legislación sinodal, está claro que Abril siguió el ejemplo de Pedro de Albalat al insistir en la asistencia del clero diocesano. Cuando R. de

[230] E. BENITO RUANO, *La Iglesia española ante la caída del Imperio Latino de Constantinopla*, «Hispania Sacra», 11 (1958), págs. 5-20, en las págs. 12-17.

[231] *Ibid.*, «... ipse dominus Alexander fecit ibi exulibus eiusdem regni Apulie provideri, et Vos Pater fecistis similiter, exulibus eiusdem regni provideri» (BENITO RUANO, pág. 17).

[232] CP. La suma anual debida era de 15 sueldos *turonenses seu malgurienses*. Para la posterior carrera de Balduino, véase Steven RUNCIMAN, *The Sicilian Vespers*, Cambridge, 1958, págs. 218, 224 y 229.

[233] E. BENITO RUANO, *op. cit.*, pág. 15.

[234] ACU: El *census* que debía la iglesia de Urgel fue pagado al legado Adegario de Parma en moneda de Tours «cum aurum in hac terra non inveniatur nunc ad vendendum».

[235] CP, fechado «apud Sanctum Gaudentium in festo Pentecostes, anno Domini 1258».

[236] *Op. cit.*, pág. 99: «Incipiunt constitutiones sinodales editae per dominos Aprilem et Petrum bonae memoriae episcopos Urgellenses. Sed est verum quod nulla constitutio reperitur dicti domini Aprilis» (Ms. de Ripoll, 164).

Balaguer se hirió en una pierna tan seriamente que no pudo montar a caballo para acudir al sínodo, se tomó el trabajo de hacer que el guardián de los franciscanos de Lérida escribiese a Abril y ocupase su puesto, cosa que Fr. Benito hizo complacido «quia est amicus nostri ordinis» [237].

El aparente triunfo de Abril al inculcar el hábito de la obediencia a su diócesis, tuvo algo que ver seguramente con la práctica de llevar registros —un procedimiento nuevo en Urgel. Algunos fragmentos de un registro de actas episcopales se han conservado sin haber sido descubiertos hasta ahora, en el archivo capitular, dentro de un volumen referente al año 1298. Los roedores y la humedad han cobrado su tributo a estas pocas páginas y las han hecho ilegibles en gran parte, pero aún es posible descifrar lo suficiente para sugerir que la mayoría de las entradas registraban dispensas concedidas por el obispo a individuos que habían transgredido la constitución sinodal que obligaba a los miembros del clero a abandonar a sus mujeres, y que se concedió al deanato de Urgel un privilegio general en el mismo sentido. Junto con estas páginas han sobrevivido los restos de una memoria de cuentas. Algunas están escritas de mano de Juan Domínguez, el notario de Abril procedente de Compostela, quien debe ofrecernos al menos una parte de garantía por esta medida de organización —desconocida en las demás iglesias catalanas hasta un par de décadas más tarde [238]. Sería interesante saber si la práctica de llevar los registros episcopales, que se supone sin precedentes en los reinos españoles en este período, tuvo algo que ver con la estancia de Abril en la Curia romana, y si fue continuada por los sucesores de Abril en Urgel. El obispo Ponce no había sido ciertamente un modelo de orden, y había hecho aún más difícil la tarea de su procurador en la Curia enviándole cartas de procuración insuficientemente autorizadas [239]. Abril al menos estaba mejor preparado para rechazar las acusaciones que se hicieran contra él y las reclamaciones contra sus intereses.

Y éstas no faltaron. En 1267 disputaba con el rey de Aragón y

[237] CP. Se describe a *R* como *capellanus de Portella*, Lérida, y pudo haber sido el fastidioso arcediano Ricardo, párroco de Balaguer. Sufría «grave vulnus ... in tibia, ita quod non valet etiam equitare. Quare, prudentem paternitatem vestram in Domino exoramus ut eum quia non potuit ad sinodum vestrum accedere vel etiam suis adversariis coram vestra presentia respondere».

[238] La supervivencia de los registros episcopales del siglo XIII merece tratarse aparte, y no podemos ocuparnos de ella aquí. Sobre este tipo de registro en Inglaterra en el mismo período, véase C. R. CHENEY, *English Bishop of Chanceries 1100-1250*, Manchester, 1950, cap. IV.

[239] VILLANUEVA, *op. cit.*, 11, pág. 228.

con los recursos de su burocracia, altamente desarrollada, y se veía envuelto en un conflicto jurisdiccional motivado por una «ricxa» entre los habitantes de Montelian —«qui sunt homines ecclesie Urgellensis»— y los de Bexeb [240]. La pugna con el conde de Urgel, siempre latente, se encendió otra vez, y Abril asestó un fuerte golpe colocando las tierras del conde bajo entredicho. Roger IV respondió buscando la protección papal y sometiendo la cuestión a Roma, pero no se sabe si la disputa se solventó allí por delegación: «une lacune regrettable». Sin embargo puede suponerse que este asunto proporcionó a Abril uno de los motivos para visitar la Curia en 1263 [241]. Y tenía otros. Estaba la disputa relativa a la jurisdicción sobre los prioratos de la abadía de San Saturnino de Tavernoles, que se discutió extensamente en la Curia antes de solucionarse allí en marzo de 1268 [242], y también la cuestión del diezmo contra el convento de San Miguel de Cuixà [243]. La presencia en la Curia del preboste de San Miguel en mayo de 1264, sugiere un examen definitivo del caso, realizado en un momento en que tanto el obispo como el preboste se hallaban presentes [244]. Ciertamente las razones de Abril para visitar la Curia en el invierno de 1263-1264, no eran exclusivamente altruístas.

En 1269, época de la muerte de Abril, se habían conseguido ya algunos progresos hacia la recuperación económica de la diócesis. En enero de 1266 el obispo había podido comprar castillos a los albaceas de Bernardo de Bescheran y los había pagado en el plazo de un mes. Se habían manejado fuertes sumas de dinero [245]. Pero su muerte causó poca o ninguna conmoción en la iglesia catalana. Su partida, como su llegada allí, fue un acontecimiento sobre el que disponemos de poca información, y esa poca es contradictoria. Porque, mientras el relato de la elección de su sucesor afirma que fue enterrado en Urgel el 22 de octubre de 1269 [246], la *Memoria de Aniversarios* de Salamanca, —una fuente tardía y poco digna de crédito— proclama que fue

---

[240] La cuestión quedó resuelta con el arbitraje de Pedro de Urg, arcediano (y futuro obispo) de Urgel, y R. Vidal, «iurisperitus», en septiembre (ACA, Cartas reales diplomáticas, Jaime I, caja 1, núm. 104). Véase también *ibid*, núms. 34 y 102.

[241] Ch BAUDON DE MONY, *Les relations politiques des comtes de Foix avec la Catalogne jusqu'au commencement* † *du 14eme siècle*, II, París, 1896, págs. 33, 201.

[242] ACU, *Dotium ... liber secundus*, fols. 120 v.-123 v.: «in curia romana fuisset diucius questio ventilata...».

[243] *Ibid.*, fols. 37 v.-42 v., publicado por F. VALLS-TABERNER, *Diplomatari de San Ramón de Penyafort*, «Analecta Sacra Tarraconensia», 5 (1929), págs. 249-304, en págs. 291-296. Ramón de *Liriis* había consultado al obispo Ponce sobre esta disputa en una carta que no publicó Villanueva. Está en CP.

[244] RV 29-49-109, 29-74-175 = Reg. Urbano IV, 1060, 1126.

[245] CP: Abril pagó 5.250 *solidi malgurienses*, 440 *solidi barchinonensis* y 910 *solidi 'accenses*.

[246] ACU.

IV

sepultado allí, de cuyo error han derivado los escritores posteriores la equivocada creencia de que Abril fue trasladado vivo a Salamanca, como obispo, aquél mismo año [247], acontecimiento que, de haber sido cierto, hubiera causado gran satisfacción al tesorero de aquella iglesia.

Esta incertidumbre sobre el fin de Abril es típica de toda la historia de su carrera. A cada paso la tarea se complica por la falta de evidencia concreta. De haberse conservado su testamento, por ejemplo, podría haber proporcionado respuesta a cierto número de cuestiones que de otra forma permanecen insolubles —acerca de sus relaciones familiares y especialmente de sus intereses intelectuales, tal como nos hubiera reflejado el contenido de su biblioteca. ¿Poseía instrucción legal? El *maestro* Abril debió ir a la universidad, muy probablemente siendo arcediano, después de 1243. Ciertamente tenía conciencia del valor de una educación legal: mientras fue obispo la diócesis de Urgel envió a Bolonia a cierto número de canónigos como estudiantes [248]. Sin embargo, hay una falta total de evidencia acerca de estos importantes aspectos de la carrera de Abril.

Las líneas generales son confusas, en el mejor de los casos, y tal vez fuera esta persistente permanencia en el anónimo de su poco agradecido personaje la que indujo al autor del párrafo dedicado a Abril, en el *Dictionnaire d'histoire et de géographie ecclésiastiques,* a aventurar la afirmación de que el obispo de Urgel era el autor de un diálogo en verso de la época, conocido desde tiempo atrás por los historiadores, que describía la moral y costumbres de la corte papal a una luz que nos permitiría profundizar en el carácter del obispo Abril mucho más que la utilización de toda la evidencia examinada hasta aquí —esto es, si pudiera demostrarse que es correcta la identificación del obispo con el poetastro.

III

Los versos —unos diez centenares de líneas de longitud— fueron publicados varias veces antes de que en 1912 H. Grauert presentara

[247] Véase arriba, n. 28. Gil GONZÁLEZ DÁVILA, *Historia de las antigüedades de Salamanca*, III, pág. 224; IDEM, *Teatro eclesiástico de las iglesias de España*, III, pág. 278 y de ahí ARGÁIZ, *Soledad laureada*, II, Madrid, 1675, fol. 156 v. [En febrero de 1968, después que este artículo estuvo terminado, recibí noticias del canónigo-archivero de Seo de Urgel del descubrimiento de la tumba del obispo Abril en aquella catedral: PAL].

[248] «Chartularium Studii Bononiensis», VII (1923), págs. 99, 209; VIII (1927), págs. 48, 216; X (1936), páginas 34, 49.

una edición provista de un comentario exhaustivo [249]. Mabillon los había titulado *Veteris Poetae Carmen Apologeticum Interlocutoribus Gaufrido et Aprile*, pero Grauert probó que su autor era el poeta alemán Enrique de Würzburg —«Magister Heinricus poeta de Swevia oriundus»— basándose en una adición del siglo XIV a un manuscrito de Würzburg que contenía la obra [250]. Sin embargo, a pesar de lo concienzudo de su estudio, Grauert manejó solamente ciertos manuscritos alemanes, y no hizo caso de la sugerencia, hecha por primera vez, según parece, por Pedro de Marca en 1688 [251], de que el Abril del verso «hispana gente profectus» estaba inspirado en realidad en el Abril que fue obispo de Urgel. Villanueva reiteró esta conjetura, mientras que en 1924 A. Lambert fue mucho más lejos, afirmando pura y simplemente que Abril de Urgel era el autor de la obra —sugerencia para la que no ofrecía una sóla muestra de evidencia. Lambert ignoraba la edición de Grauert, como Grauert había ignorado la identificación sugerida por Marca y Villanueva. A la vista de estos tratamientos independientes y sin relación entre sí que ha recibido el poema, sería conveniente para el presente estudio examinar, aunque sea brevemente, el peso de la evidencia interna que contiene el poema.

El poema adopta la forma de un diálogo sobre la vida en la Curia, que se desarrolla entre Gaufredo, hombre muy versado en sus costumbres, y el español Abril, un recién llegado ansioso de saber cuántas son cinco:

> Nuper apostolica Gaufredus sede relicta
> In patriam rediit, cuncta peracta tenens.
> Obviat Aprilis Hyspana gente profectus,
> Obviat, inque vicem verba salutis agunt.
> Iste locum nondum Romane viderat Urbis
> Alter erat tota cognitus Urbe diu [252].

Grauert se tomó pocas molestias para identificar a Abril, contentándose †

---

[249] Hermann GRAUERT, *Magister Heinrich der Poet in Würzburg und die römische Kurie*, «Abhandlungen der Wiss. Phil.-phil. und Hist. Klasse», 27 (München, 1912).

[250] J. MABILLON, *Veterum Anelectorum*, IV, París, 1685, págs. 535-565; GRAUERT, *op. cit.*, pág. 65, nota, y págs. 149-161.

[251] P. DE MARCA, *Marca Hispanica sive limes hispanicus, hec est geografica descriptio Cataloniae ...*, París, 1688, col. 534, refiriéndose al nombramiento de Abril para Urgel por Alejandro IV, «Patet autem enim fuisse virum literarum ac, nisi conjectura falit, Romanae curiae sequacem. Quo fit ut facile mihi persuadem de eo agi in dialogo ...». *Dictionnaire d'histoire et de geographie ecclésiastiques*, III, col. 1070: «il faut sûrement reconnaître en lui l'un des interlocuteurs et sans doute aussi l'auteur»; Cf. VILLANUEVA, *op. cit.*, 11, pág. 95, y, siguiéndole, LÓPEZ FERREIRO, *Historia*, 5, págs. 361-363; BELTRÁN DE HEREDIA, *Cartulario*, pág. 88.

[252] El poema se cita de aquí en adelante como *Carmen*, el Abril del poema como *Abril* y el obispo de Urgel como Abril. La edición de Grauert se encuentra en las págs. 65-106. Las líneas citadas arriba son las 49-54.

IV

182

con observar la existencia de Fernando Abril, clérigo del cardenal Gil y canónigo de León[253]. Pero hay otros candidatos españoles llamados Abril, que se encontraban en Roma en los años cincuenta y sesenta del siglo XIII. Entre ellos estaban el procurador del obispo de Segovia[254]; Abril Rodríguez, procurador del obispo de Astorga en 1250[255], que en 1257 era capellán del cardenal Octaviano de Santa María in Via Lata y protegido del infante Enrique de Castilla[256], y por supuesto Abril Peláez, arcediano de Salamanca, luego obispo de Urgel. Habría sido perfectamente lógico describirle a él, gallego, † como *hispanus*[257]. Y las dificultades que llevaron a Abril a la Curia en busca de una promoción sería ciertamente aplicable a Salamanca:

> Studui lustris ter quinque nec ulla
> Respondit meritis philosophia meis.
> Papa meos solus poterit relevare labores
> Et removere sitim fonte perhennis aque.
> Hunc peto, si forsan nostri miserebitur, et si
> Paupertatis hyemps tanta movebit eum.
> Ampla tenent alii stipendia divitis agri.
> Hic tribus, hic senis, dives at ille decem.
> Sed mihi sufficeret prebendula pauperis orti
> Quinque talenta valens, quinque parumve magis.
> Credo, quod Urbis apex sanctissimus ille virorum,
> Si me cognoscat, non neget ista michi.
> Ditat eos, qui pauca sciunt, vir sanctus et a me
> Forsitan excutiet pulveris istud onus[258].

† Las circunstancias de Abril eran las de los naturales de Salamanca que se encontraban aprisionados entre las piedras de molino de un arzobispo avaricioso y de una serie de provisiones papales que les hacían desesperar de conseguir algún ascenso dentro de su propia iglesia. Pero estas condiciones se daban lo mismo en otros lugares; Salamanca no era la única a este respecto. Por tanto, si ha de sostenerse la identificación del obispo Abril, deberá apoyarse en bases más sólidas que estas. Tal vez la aproximación más provechosa pueda realizarse considerando las figuras notables de la Curia que se mencionan en el *Carmen*.

† Abril expresa sus dudas acerca de la confianza que merecen los

[253] GRAUERT, *op. cit.*, pág. 208; Reg. Inn. IV, 7861, 7909, 7980.
[254] Véase n. 62, más arriba.
[255] AD Astorga, 3-62 (RV 22-1-1 = Reg. Inn. IV, 4751), dorso; 363, dorso.
[256] RV 25-754-102 = Reg. Alex. IV, 2372; AHN, Sección de clero, pergaminos, 1883/20 = Marcos, 289.
[257] N. IUNG, *Un franciscain théologien du pouvoir pontifical au XIVe siècle: Alvaro Pelayo, évêque et pénitencier de Jean XXII*, París, 1931, pág. 7 nota.
[258] *Carmen*, líneas 58-71.

procuradores de la Curia y menciona algunos de los bajos trucos a los que, según se le ha dicho, están dispuestos a recurrir:

> Estne fides aliqua procuratoribus illis?
> Qui se credit eis, non bene tutus erit.
> Audivi quod dant adversis partibus arma,
> Et sic occulte munus utrimque petunt ...   [259]

Gaufredo intenta calmar los temores del otro describiendo a los procuradores como un cuerpo de hombres sobresalientes en todas las virtudes, y sus deliberaciones y procedimientos como ordenados y equitativos: un cuadro totalmente incompatible con lo que se conoce acerca del desbarajuste que reinaba entre ellos frecuentemente[260]. Tal como Gaufredo los describe, constituían una casta celosa de su elevada reputación, y para ilustrar este punto cita el caso de uno a quien el fracaso en la observación del código le valió el ostracismo:

> Petrus ab Assisio subitam quia nuper in iram
> Surrexit solito litigiosa movens
> Turpiter eiectus fuit et locus ille
> Non potuit strepitum dissimulare viri [261].

Petrus ab Assisio era un procurador de la Curia, y Grauert relata algunas de sus actividades entre 1241 y 1265, en cuyo año actuó en representación del Würzburg Neumünster[262]. Más recientemente se ha demostrado que era un abad cisterciense empleado como procurador por cierto número de casas de su orden en Baviera, entre los pontificados de Inocencio IV y Gregorio X[263]. Pedro actuó también en representación de las casas cistercienses españolas desde el octavo año de Inocencio IV en adelante[264]. En el sexto año de Bonifacio VIII, él —o un homónimo— representaban aún a la gran casa de Poblet, para la cual, desde 1255 por lo menos, había ido adquiriendo copias de los privilegios que se emitían en favor de toda la orden[265].

---

[259] *Carmen*, líneas 143-146.

[260] R. J. Brentano, *York Metropolitan Jurisdiction and Papal Judges Delegate, 1279-1296*, Berkeley, 1959, pág. 212; Emmy Heller, *Der Kuriale Gescheftsgang in den Briefen des Thomas von Capua*, «Archiv für Urkundenforschung», 13 (1933-1935), págs. 197-318, en pág. 262.

[261] *Carmen*, líneas 171-174. En la línea 145 se refiere de nuevo a Pedro, «Cuius nequiciam publica fama refert».

[262] Grauert, *op. cit.*, págs. 255-256.

[263] P. Herde, *Beiträge zum päpstlichen Kanzlei und Urkundenwesen im 13 Jahrhundert*, Kallmünz, 1961, páginas 86 y 92. Véase también W. Stelzer, *Beiträge zur Geschichte der Kurienprokuratoren im 13 Jahrhundert*, «Archivum Historicum Pontificiae», 8 (1970), págs. 113-138, en las págs. 129-135.

[264] Esta afirmación se basa en el estudio de gran cantidad de bulas de estas casas que se conservan ahora en el Archivo Histórico Nacional de Madrid. Véase Linehan, *op. cit.*, pág. 281.

[265] AHN, Sección de clero, pergaminos, 563/17; 2232/5.

184

† Más adelante en el poema, Gaufredo describe a Abril cómo había sido introducido en la corte papal:

> Ille tamen qui me promovit et ante tribunal
> Duxit et adiecit: Flecta poeta genu!
> Gaietanus erat, qui cardinis instar habendo
> Crescit et in postis edificatur opus [266].

Grauert, siguiendo a Mabillon, identificó a *Gaietanus* con el cardenal-diácono de S. Nicolás, Johannes Gaietanus Orsini, que en 1277 se convirtió en el papa Nicolás III [267]. Ascendido por Inocencio IV en 1244 [268], tenía cierto número de relaciones con las iglesias de España y Portugal. A él fue sometida inicialmente la reclamación del tesorero de Braga, Tomás, que decía haber sido despojado de los beneficios que poseía allí por el arzobispo [269]. En noviembre de 1254, cuando estalló de nuevo la vieja disputa de límites entre las diócesis de Coimbra y Guarda, se le nombró auditor, y en su casa estuvieron presentes, aparte de los obispos de ambas sedes y de los canónigos de las dos iglesias, que actuaban en representación de sus capítulos, otros dos españoles, canónigos de Orense [270]. Durante el pontificado de Alejandro IV, el maestro Gonzalo, canónigo de Astorga, figuraba entre sus capellanes [271]. En diciembre de 1263 su *medicus* era un canónigo de León, el maestro Domingo [272], y fue a él y a su sobrino el cardenal Mateo de Sta. María in Porticu, a quienes Clemente IV pidió opinión en su incertidumbre sobre la persona a quien debería elevar a la sede vacante de Toledo [273]. Él proporcionó al procurador de la iglesia de León 24 marcos de plata del legado que el cardenal español Pelayo había dejado para que fuese dedicado a su capilla de la catedral de León [274]. Parece, por el testamento de Rodrigo Pérez, arcediano de León, que el cardenal Gil le había cargado con la responsabilidad de recaudar lo que se le debía [275]. En el alojamiento de su pariente el

---

[266] *Carmen*, líneas 745-748.
[267] Grauert, *op. cit.*, págs. 47-49 y 141.
[268] J. Maubach, *Die Kardinäle und ihre Politik um Mitte des 13 Jahrhunderts*, Bonn, 1902, pág. 22.
[269] RV 23-420-53 = Reg. Inn. IV, 7250. Tomás era un protegido del arzobispo Juan Arias de Compostela: RV 23-90-157 = Reg. Inn. IV, 7907.
[270] RV 24-764-110/12 = Reg. Alex. IV, 947.
[271] RV 25-104-13 = Reg. Alex. IV, 1683.
[272] RV 29-92-254 = Reg. Urbano IV, 1206.
[273] RV 30-42 = Reg. Clem. IV, 1108.
[274] AC León, 1603.
[275] AC León, 1569.

cardenal Jaime Savelli de Sta. María in Cosmedin permaneció Abril de Urgel antes de trasladarse al del cardenal Esteban de Palestrina [276].

Sin embargo, el futuro papa no era el único *Gaietanus* cuyas relaciones con las iglesias españolas se extienden a lo largo del período. Aunque a juzgar por el contexto en que se le menciona, parece altamente probable que fuese el cardenal quien estaba en la mente del poeta [277], había de todos modos otro *Gaietanus* a quien Grauert ignoró: *Petrus Gaietanus*. Antes de su elevación a la sede de Todi, recibía pensiones de las iglesias de Segovia y Toledo [278], y en 1267 actuaba en la Curia en representación de la casa cisterciense de Armenteira (Galicia) [279].

Tanto los dos *Gaietani* como Pedro de Asís tenían por tanto relaciones con la iglesia española y con los eclesiásticos españoles. Pero incluso aunque pudiera demostrarse que estaban estrechamente relacionados con Abril de Urgel, de ello no debe seguirse necesariamente que Abril hubiera servido de modelo para el ingenuo interrogador del *Carmen*. Es posible que pudiera arrojarse una luz más clara sobre el problema si pudiera consultarse el manuscrito de la obra que utilizó Villanueva (pero no Grauert) —es decir, la copia que en la época del *Viage* de Villanueva se encontraba en la biblioteca del monasterio de Ripoll. Pero desapareció a principios del siglo xix, y no figura entre los manuscritos de Ripoll que se conservan ahora en el Archivo de la Corona de Aragón de Barcelona [280]. Por otra parte, el arcediano de Salamanca pudo estar en la mente del autor como uno de los muchos clérigos españoles de este nombre que se encontraban entonces en la Curia. Sin embargo, para la afirmación de que el propio Abril compusiera los versos no hay ni un átomo de justificación.

IV

Despojado de todo derecho a la fama como autor y siendo una figura que aún cuando parece más próxima tiende a moverse en

---

[276] RV 29-37-76 = Reg. Urbano IV, 1027.

[277] S. KUTTNER, *Cardinalis: The History of a Canonical Concept*, «Traditio», 3 (1945), págs. 129-214, especialmente págs. 145-146.

[278] RV 22-757-278; 22-769-281 = Reg. Inn. IV, 6617, 6629. De Toledo recibió 200 mor. anuales entre 1248 y su nombramiento para Todi en 1252, «tam propter probitatem vestram quam propter obsequium quod ex persona vestra ecclesie nostre proventurus expectamus». Véase también HERDE, *op. cit.*, págs. 4-5.

[279] AHN, Sección de clero, pergaminos, 1767/2.

[280] No está claro el método de Villanueva al referirse a los manuscritos de Ripoll. Por ejemplo, describe las constituciones sinodales de Urgel (cf. n. 236) como 164. Pero este número no guarda relación con ninguno

una zona entre dos luces, en la que la mirada del historiador no puede penetrar demasiado lejos, podría argumentarse que Abril no destaca como individuo de extraordinaria significación en la historia de la iglesia española en su siglo. No obstante, su carrera merece atención, porque se desarrolló en dos zonas periféricas de la península, el noroeste y el nordeste —los dos reinos de Castilla-León y Aragón— y en la Curia papal durante un período de crisis en las relaciones de la iglesia romana con las iglesias provinciales, cuando, al mismo tiempo que aumentaba el número de clérigos españoles establecidos en la Curia, al servicio de los cardenales, como procuradores, o esperando la ocasión de un ascenso, en la propia España se hacía aún más pronunciada la reacción contra las demandas fiscales del papa. Los temores del deán de Salamanca por el futuro de su iglesia cuando el obispo partió hacia Roma —temor que le indujo a solicitar de Abril la destrucción de la carta cuando la hubiera leído— reflejan este estado de ánimo, como lo hace la reacción del concilio de Compostela ante la creencia de que la iglesia de Roma estaba decidida a destruir su libertad. En algunos casos parece haber existido una obsesión casi patológica. Llegó a considerarse a la Madre Iglesia como una madrastra. Podía hacerse responsable a Roma del fracaso nacional: quizá inconscientemente, quizá no, el cronista de Fernando IV asoció por yuxtaposición los gastos de enviar nuncios a la corte de Bonifacio VIII con la pobreza y hambre del campo castellano [281]. En 1262 los obispos castellanos habían sido más específicos [282]. Y sin embargo, tanto los obispos como el clero acudían en gran número a Roma, porque Roma era el manantial:

---

de los tres sistemas de numeración —«actual», «moderno» y «antiguo»— enumerados por Próspero de Bofarull cuando los manuscritos de Ripoll fueron trasladados al Archivo de la Corona de Aragón en octubre de 1823, (ed. F. VALLS TABERNER, *Códices manuscritos de Ripoll*, «Revista de Archivos, Bibliotecas y Museos», 52 [1931], págs. 5-16 y 139-175, en la pág. 149). Del mismo modo en el caso del manuscrito del *Carmen*, que cita como 169, no aparece rastro de la obra ni en R. BEER, *Die Handschriften des Klosters Santa Maria de Ripoll*, «Sitzungsberichte der phil.- hist. Kl. der Kaiserlichen Ak. der Wissenschaften», 158 (Viena, 1908) ni en Z. GARCÍA VILLADA *Biblioteca Patrum Latinorum Hispaniensis*, II, Viena, 1915. Tampoco figura en los primeros catálogos de la biblioteca de Ripoll: ni en 1381 (A. RUBIÓ I LLUCH, *Documents per la història de la cultura catalana mitgeval*, II, Barcelona, 1921, pág. 237) ni en 1751 (Real Academia de la Historia, *Col. Abad y Lasierra*, vol. 19, n. 40: 12-21-3/40). Suponiendo que Villanueva viese efectivamente el poema en un manuscrito de Ripoll, debió formar parte de un volumen designado de otra forma y desaparecido desde el *Viage* de Villanueva, quizá destruido en el incendio que consumió Ripoll en 1835 (véase F. UDINA MARTORELL, *Los fondos benedictinos custodiados en el Archivo de la Corona de Aragón*, «Analecta Montserratensia», 8 [1954-1955], págs. 397-420, en la pág. 404).

[281] *Memorias de D. Fernando IV de Castilla*, anotadas por D. Antonio BENAVIDES, I, Madrid, 1860, página 81. Éste parece ser un relato casi contemporáneo: véase J. PUYOL, *El presunto cronista Fernán Sánchez de Valladolid*, «Bol. Acad. de la Hist.», 77 (1920), págs. 507-533.

[282] Cf. arriba, págs. 174-175.

Ecclesias alias rivus ab urbe rigat [283].

Acudían como moscas a la miel, y algunos en cambio sufrían la suerte de la mariposa atraída por la luz. Para pagar las deudas que había contraído en Roma, el obispo de Vich se vio obligado a empeñar su capilla [284]. Más serio fue el caso de las iglesias de León y Palencia, que cayeron en la bancarrota en los años 1250 y 1260, y veinte años más tarde el arzobispo de Toledo era prisionero de sus acreedores franceses, que no le permitían salir de su custodia para visitar su provincia [285]. Sin embargo, la culpa era en gran parte suya. La bancarrota no era inevitable: la iglesia de Silves llegó a un acuerdo para repartir equitativamente los gastos del litigio en la Curia entre el obispo y el capítulo [286]. No iban como ovejas inocentes al matadero. Ni tampoco estaban los españoles peor dotados que los italianos o los franceses para ejercitar las artes de la supervivencia adecuadas al enrarecido ambiente de la Curia. La conmovedora suposición, expuesta aún en ocasiones por algunos historiadores españoles [287], de que las virtudes hispanas —especialmente las castellanas— no eran compatibles con la vida en Roma y explicaban los reveses sufridos a manos de los intrigantes italianos, fue enunciada en la época por hombres defraudados en sus ambiciones. Cuando en 1280 Nicolás III se negó a confirmar la elección para Toledo del abad de Covarrubias, Fernán Rodríguez de Cabañas, de quien se sospechaba que había sobornado a los canónigos, el fracasado abad escribió al capítulo de Covarrubias presentándose a sí mismo como alguien tratado injustamente: «e no le perdi por mal fazer, mas por bien fazer» [288]. Sin embargo, no le habían

[283] *Carmen*, línea 250.

[284] AC Vich, cax. 6, II, núm. 66, fechado en enero de 1243. Véase también E. JUNYENT, *Diplomatari de Sant Bernat Calvó, abat de Santes Creus, bisbe de Vich*, Reus, 1956, pág. 238.

[285] LINEHAN, *op. cit.*, págs. 128-151, 177.

[286] En 1273: J. B. da SILVA LOPES, *Memórias para a história eclesiástica do bispado do Algarve*, Lisboa, 1848, página 563.

[287] D. MANSILLA, *El cardenal Petrus Hispanus obispo de Burgos 1300-1303*, «Hispania Sacra», 9 (1956), páginas 244-280, explica la facilidad con que Napoleone Orsini indujo al cardenal Pedro que apoyase la candidatura del futuro Clemente V, señalando que «el antiguo obispo de Burgos *como buen castellano* (el subrayado es mío) no entendía ni de dobleces ni de intrigas». Pero el español, festivo compañero de Bonifacio VIII, estaba perfectamente habituado a las costumbres de la Curia, y la forma en que decidió anunciar su cambio de opinión sugiere un certero instinto para las más delicadas situaciones de la política clandestina: según el agente del rey de Aragón, «Dominus Yspanus respondebat quod placebat sibi, set quod volebat loqui cum domino Napoleone, sic quod iverunt ad latrinam, quia alibi loqui non poterant ita secrete» (T. S. R. BOASE, *Boniface VIII*, Londres, 1933, págs. 284 y 346-348, y H. FINKE, *Aus den Tagen Bonifaz VIII*, Munster-i-W, 1902, pág. LXIV. Para la actitud similar de los historiadores españoles del siglo XVI, véase R. P. MORTIER, *Histoire des Maîtres Généraux de l'Ordre des Frères Prêcheurs*, II, París, 1905, pág. 252.

[288] L. SERRANO, *Cartulario del Infantado de Covarrubias*, Valladolid, 1907, pág. LXVII.

IV

188

faltado aliados en la Curia[289]. Resultaba tentador atribuir un revés temporal a las imaginarias maquinaciones de una camarilla anti-española que en realidad no existía. A pesar de todo, es asombroso que tan gran número de clérigos se apresurasen a acudir a Roma, y que una vez llegados se negaran a marchar: en 1263 fue necesario exigir a Pedro Yspano una garantía de que, tan pronto como se le proporcionase el beneficio de Mondoñedo al que aspiraba, abandonaría la ciudad[290]. El propio Gaufredo, tan satisfecho de sí mismo, pudo muy bien haber sido español.

El atractivo de la Curia resultaba irresistible por dos razones: era el centro de la justicia y la inextinguible fuente de la generosidad. La confianza de Abril en que no había de irse con las manos vacías, era la típica de muchos clérigos españoles que acudían allí en busca de recompensas no siempre merecidas. El hecho de que los efectos de la escandalosa desigualdad en el valor de los beneficios, castigada en Astorga en septiembre de 1228 por el legado Juan de Abbeville[291], les llevasen allí con la esperanza de adelantarse en la fila, arroja sobre ellos tanto descrédito como sobre el sistema que permitió al arcediano de Trastamar pasar por «pauper clericus» durante muchos años[292]. Se hacían esfuerzos ocasionales para disuadirles por completo de emprender el camino: Fernando Alfonso, canónigo de Salamanca, que en su testamento de 1294 dejó propiedades para la provisión de canónigos estudiantes, especificaba que los que eligiesen Roma no habían de beneficiarse en forma alguna de su legado[293], y en 1262 Alfonso X escribió al arzobispo electo de Toledo, Domingo Pascual, para desanimarle a fin de que no emprendiese el viaje a la Curia[294]. Con el mismo espíritu, el deán y capítulo de Calahorra tenían la mirada fija en su obispo por miedo de que, si no conseguía cubrir los beneficios vacantes, su provisión recayese en la iglesia de Roma[295]. Sin embargo, esta cautela sólo derivaba en rebelión cuando se reclamaba de

---

[289] IDEM, loc. cit.: «... fablaron conmigo quatro cardenales, mios amigos ...»; véase también D. CASTEJÓN Y FONSECA, Primacía de la iglesia de Toledo, II, Madrid, 1645, pág. 770, y España Sagrada, XXIII, pág. 415.
[290] RV 26-116-215 = Reg. Urbano IV, 353. Sin embargo, siete meses más tarde estaba todavía allí, en compañía del cardenal Esteban de Palestrina (RV 29-35-72 = Reg. Urbano IV, 1023).
[291] «Cum autem in ecclesia Astoricensi clamor esset, et scandalum et animarum non modica turbatio super eo quod alii in bonis ejusdem ecclesiae superabundare viderentur, alii gravem penuriam pati ...» (P. RODRÍGUEZ LÓPEZ, Episcopologio Asturicense, II, Astorga, 1907, pág. 593).
[292] Véase más arriba, pág. 153.
[293] ACS 20/2/25-3 = Marcos, 432 («e a los que estodieren enna corte de Roma que les non den ende nada»).
[294] AC Toledo, A. 7. D. 1. 1.; Biblioteca Nacional, Madrid, 13023 (olim Dd 42), fols. 9-11, y de ahí Memorial Histórico Español, Madrid, 1811, págs. 191-192.
[295] En marzo de 1301 (AC Calahorra, 492).

los eclesiásticos alguna contribución para el sistema del que se estaban aprovechando. En diciembre de 1255 las iglesias castellanas se negaron a proporcionar pensiones a altos oficiales de la Curia. Pero su resistencia no sobrevivió mucho tiempo a la eficaz represalia de Alejandro IV, que les privó de las facilidades sin las que no podían sostenerse frente a sus rivales —el acceso a la Curia «ad impetrandum vel contradicendum ... pro ipsis vel eorum ecclesiis» [296]. Y, observadas las cosas más atentamente, los extranjeros no se caracterizaban invariablemente por ese vicio de la rapacidad que tradicionalmente se les ha atribuído: Tadeo de Montealto, por ejemplo, invirtió en la iglesia de Calahorra las ganancias que había obtenido de ella como deán [297].

La inevitable realidad era, sobre todo, que España no pagaba su parte correspondiente en la financiación de la iglesia de Roma, aquel Estado de bienes tan espiritual, cuyos beneficios pretendía disfrutar pero siempre sin contribuir a sus fondos centrales. «Hispania sibi non sufficit» se quejaba Clemente IV a Carlos de Sicilia [298]. Y en 1292 Nicolás IV, al describir a Eduardo I de Inglaterra la empobrecida situación de la iglesia romana, señalaba que de la *decima* recaudada en el reino de Castilla, no llegaba nada a las arcas papales [299].

¿Cuál era, pues, la importancia de todo esto para la iglesia en España? Queda la impresión de que los eclesiásticos cedían demasiado fácilmente a la tentación de evitar las asperezas temporales, perdiendo terreno en lo que se refiere a sus recursos de crédito espiritual. Este punto no puede tratarse aquí con amplitud. Bastará un ejemplo. En 1324 el arzobispo Gonsalvo de Mondoñedo —a fin de salvar a su iglesia de sus acreedores romanos— buscó la ayuda del clero de su diócesis, ofreciéndoles el cebo de una recompensa financiera; a saber, una ampliación del período durante el cual, después de su muerte, disfrutaban de la renta de sus beneficios [300]. El sínodo diocesano se convirtió así en una reunión de negocios, convocada para equilibrar el presupuesto: no se permitía que se interpusieran las cuestiones de

[296] RV 24-125-8 = Reg. Alex. IV, 1014.

[297] En abril de 1309 (AC Calahorra, 521 bis), los ingresos conseguidos deberían distribuirse entre aquellos canónigos que asistieran a maitines «in tempore messium vel vindimiarum». Era «capellanus familiaris et continuus commensalis» del cardenal Napoleone Orsini, y en julio de 1309 estaba con su patrón en la Curia (AC Calahorra, 529).

[298] En agosto de 1265 Reg. Clem. IV, 923).

[299] RV 46-184-88 = Reg Nich. IV, 6857.

[300] AC Mondoñedo, *Kalendario Antiguo*, I, fols. 151 v.-152 r.: hacían falta 20.000 mor. Véase R. SANJURJO Y PARDO, *Los obispos de Mondoñedo*, Lugo, 1854, pág. 50. La donación hecha a los miembros del clero catedralicio

reforma moral. Quedaba por ver qué daño real —mucho más grave para su prestigio que una bancarrota pasajera— había padecido la iglesia. Ya el laicado estaba proclamando su disconformidad con las actividades de sus pastores [301], y Álvaro Pelayo, convencido de que el día del Juicio estaba cerca, predicaba que el episcopado español se había hundido en el pecado mucho más que el de ninguna otra nación [302], juicio que encontraba elocuente confirmación en la práctica de la Curia papal en el siglo XIV de admitir para los beneficios españoles a clérigos claramente menos competentes de lo que se toleraba en los demás países [303].

Abril de Urgel no representó ningún papel importante en estos acontecimientos. Era un producto del sistema, y éste le trató bastante bien. Pero como ejemplo de un tipo de prelado que no era bajo ningún concepto corriente en su época [304], su carrera sirve para ilustrar algunos aspectos de la historia eclesiástica que todavía precisan investigación. Y es más digno de atención ahora, precisamente porque no fue la figura más notable entonces.

St. John's College
Cambridge (England)

---

por el obispo Juan en 1251 había sido concedida precisamente a causa de su pobreza (Biblioteca Nacional, Madrid, 5928, fol. 59). Los obispos de Mondoñedo se encontraban con frecuencia en la Curia durante estos años, como agentes de la corona de Castilla, y estaban constantemente retrasados en sus pagos de los *servitia communia* [BN, 5928, fol. 65 v., AC Toledo, I. 5. C. 1. 69; RV 49-12-45; 49-58-245 = Reg. Bon. VIII (ed, Digard et al.) 2437, 2637; E. GÖLLER, *Die Einnahmen der Apostolischen Kammer unter Johann XXII*, Paderborn, 1910, págs. 239, 259, 266].

[301] Las calamidades padecidas en Salamanca antes de 1245 habían producido este mismo efecto: «non levis instantia et contemptus gravis tam adversus episcopum quam clerum in populo consurgebant» (MANSILLA, *Iglesia*, pág. 323). Los amotinamientos sediciosos se habían percibido allí en fecha tan temprana como 1219. Reg. Hon. III, 2272 = MANSILLA, *Documentación*, núm. 252; Cf. *Fueros leoneses*, ed. Américo CASTRO, y F. de ONÍS, Madrid, 1916, págs. 167 y 192-193).

[302] Alvarus PELAGII, *De Planctu Ecclesiae*, Lyon, 1517, fol. 122. Para otra triste descripción del estado de la iglesia castellana, véase J. GOÑI GAZTAMBIDE, *Una bula de Juan XXII sobre reforma del episcopado castellano*, «Hispania Sacra», 8 (1955), págs. 409-413.

[303] M. TANGL, *Die Päpstlichen Kanzleiordnungen von 1200-1500*, Innsbruck, 1894, pág. 48.

[304] El servicio del rey, la administración diocesana o la universidad (eran) los campos de entrenamiento normales de los obispos en el siglo XIII»; D. LOMAX, *art. cit.*, en nota 2, pág. 279.

APÉNDICE

1

M. Abril, canónigo de Compostela, escribe al obispo Abril de Urgel con la petición de un beneficio por su parentesco (no especificado), y expresa el deseo de que Abril vuelva a su lugar de origen como obispo o arzobispo.

AC Urgel, sin numerar

Reverendo patri ac domino Aprili, Dei gratia Urgellensi episcopo, M. Aprilis cano- †
nicus Compostellanus manuum osculamen. Pro latore presentium consanguineo meo paternitati vestre humiliter supplico, quatinus, si dignetur benefacere intuitu pietatis cum potius
ad eam quam ad aliquem alium intendat habere recursum. Comitto me gratie vestre, et
utinam in terra vestra assumamini in episcopum vel archiepiscopum.

2

Alfonso Pérez, canónigo de Compostela, tío del obispo Abril, le escribe para felicitarle por su nombramiento como obispo de Urgel. Le recuerda su gran pobreza y la del resto de la familia. Espera recibir una respuesta de Abril quien no le ha escrito desde hace un año o más.

AC Urgel, s. n.

Reverendo patri ac domino A. divina miseracione Urgellensi episcopo, Alfonsus †
Petri canonicus Compostellanus, eius avunculus, manuum osculam et se ipsum. Laudans
invocabo Dominum et ad Deum meum preces porrigam incessantes et merito, quia quod
desideravit animus meus et quod oculus concupivit audivit auris mea, videlicet, pro-
motionem vestram in episcopum Urgellensem. Nam modo spero per vos sublevari a
fluctibus paupertatis in quibus diu et intollerabiliter fluctuavi. Spero etiam exhonerari
a matre vestra et eiusdem nepotibus qui me usque ad intima cor reserant. Non possum
etenim illis succurrere neque neque (*sic*) mihi, et portio per quam aliquantulum suble-
vabar est atenuata, taliter quod ego de ipsa non possum solummodo gubernari. Sum insuper multis debitis irretitus, ita quod nisi vos manum porrexeritis adiutricem cruciabor
in manibus debitorum. Unde paternitatem vestram exoro precibus quibus possum quatinus me et matrem vestram et paupertatem nepotum et parentum vestrorum ad memoriam reducatis et mihi expectanti gratiam recondatis. Supplico etiam quod me vellitis
vestris litteris visitare quod non fecistis annus et amplius est elapsus. Valete.

3

Juan Domínguez, repostero del obispo de Salamanca, escribe al obispo Abril, enviándole la relación de un pleito sobre un cabrillo y un préstamo, entre él y otros gallegos de Salamanca de una parte, y Juan Mateo, hombre del obispo Abril, de la otra.

AC Urgel, s. n. [1]

Al mucho ornado padre e sennor don Abril, por la gracia de Dios obispo de Rogel, yo Johan Domínguez, repostero del obispo de Salamanca e vuestro compadre salut, con besamiento de pies e de manos. Fago vos saber ela quexumne que ei del vuestro ome Johan Mathes, yo e quantos galegos son en Salamanca assi clérigos quomo legos, de XVIIII morabetinos, que me ha de dar de un cavallo que vendie que era mio e so, e de III morabetinos que le emprestei. E sobre esto lamelo ante los alcaldes, ca non los podía del aver. E allí ante los alcaldes me conoció quomo me devía estos morabetinos e demande le casa con penos ante los alcaldes. E non pudo aver casa con penos, e elos alcaldes quesieron travar del. Et Diego Moniz criado del obispo don Martín e del dayan de Salamanca e vuestro dévolo sobre si, e el fizo le pleito e omenage que non salisse de Salamanca ata que estos maravedís non me pagasse. Ca recelava se que se quería venir pora vos, quomo selo fizo. Et esto fue ante los alcaldes que eran entonze Migael Martín e Fernán Sánchez e Johan Thome, e ante otros cavaleros Alfonso (Johannis) primo del obispo de Salamanca, e ante Pedro Froez e Fernán Froez e ante otros omes bonos a San Çolecz, hu an elos plazos. Et en este comedianedo, fino se Diego Moniz, e yo con los alcaldes testei le quanto avía, e tenemos ielo testado así que nenguna cosa dela manda es por él pagada. Et el chantre e el dayan de Salamanca e el thesorero e el arcidiagano don Alfonso me rogaron que vos enuia sse carta de tal pleito quomo fizo Johan Mathes que lo sobiéssedes e que lo fiziéssedes meyorar. Ca bien creen elos que quando lo vos sobierdes que luego lo faredes meyorar. Et de esto vuestro ermano el arcidiagano Johan Paiz bien sabe la verdade, e García vuestro ome. Et beso vos elos pies e elas manos que me enviedes dezir per vuestra letra quomo faga.

(En el dorso aparece escrito: Domino Rouilen episcopo detur).

4

Alfonso Pérez, canónigo de Compostela, escribe al Maestro Abril, archidiacono de Salamanca (que está viviendo en la corte papal), y le dice que ha fracasado en asegurarle el beneficio que recientemente había quedado vacante en Compostela por la muerte de Fernando Álvarez, archidiacono de Palencia. Añade que Abril es impopular en Compostela y que el arzobispo Juan Arias está decidido a que no reciba ningún beneficio allí.

AC Urgel, s. n.

† Discreto viro et provido magistro Aprili archidiacono Salamantino, Alfonsus Petri, canonicus Compostellanus, salutem et de bono in melius proficisci. Scire vos volo quod Fernandus Alvari, archidiaconus Palentinus, viam universe carnis est ingressus, et quamcito inde noticiam ad me venit, incontinenti, misi ad dominum archiepiscopum nun-

---

[1] Estoy en deuda con el Dr. Paul Russell-Gebbett, de la Universidad de Manchester, por su ayuda para descifrar este documento.

cium specialem ut vobis assignaret fructus prebende ipsius, qui sub quadam convenientia permisit eos recipere Johanni Dominici stimulo carnis vestre, qui non solum eos percipit in vestrum preiudicium, verum etiam famam vestram nititur denigrare. Unde consulo quod in hoc exibeatis vos viriliter virum fortem. Alioquin posponendi preponentur et preponendi ad nichilum redigentur. Sciatis preterea quod nullus est in capitulo compostellano qui, ut mihi videtur, vos diligat puro corde, et si forte quispiam vos diligat mutire in capitulo non est ausus. Insuper, sciatis quod libenter ad vos mitterem Bartholameum consanguineum vestrum qui vobis serviret fideliter et devote et assisteret etiam iuxta posse, si quod vobis placeret aliquatenus certus essem. Quid autem circa hec omnia et singula duxeritis faciendum, rogo si placet quod me velitis vestris litteris reddere certiorem. Item sciatis quod quando dominus Alfonsus appellavit supcr hoc dominus archiepiscopus respondit quod non conferebat sibi canoniam; sed dominus papa sibi per suas litteras conferebat. [*Al dorso:* magistro Aprili Salmanticensi archidiacono et summi pontificis capellano in romana curia detur].

5

Esteban, cardenal obispo de Palestrina, escribe a Abril de Urgel pidiéndole que confirme en el archidiaconato de Tremp (Urgel) a su camarlengo Timoteo, archidiacono de Pécs (Hungría). Recuerda a Abril su anterior asociación y le promete ayudarle para posteriores ascensos. Anagni, 31 de mayo (no consta el año, pero probablemente esta carta debió de escribirse en 1259, ya que en esta fecha la corte papal estaba en aquella ciudad).

AC Urgel, s. n.

Venerabili in Christo patri amico suo A. Dei gratia, episcopo Urgellensi, Ste. † (*sic* = Stephanus?) divine miseratione episcopus Penestrinus, salutem et sinceram in domino caritatem. Probata quam habemus ad personam vestram affectio indubitatam nobis fiduciam tribuit quod vota nostra et presertim que infra mentis claustrum consistunt, totis debeatis amplecti affectibus, et per subsequentem operis effectum in illis velitis nostri memoriam in secretioribus vestri cordis reconditam munifica comprobari. Quantum, igitur, Tymotei dilecti camerarii nostri promocio nos urgere debeat vos non latet. Hic enim familiaris oneris assiduus supportator magis nostre quam proprie dinoscitur zelator salutis, propter quod non immerito in ipsum oculum fructuosi dirigentes favoris archidiaconatum de Trempo vacantem in ecclesia vestra sibi studuimus per dominum papam conferri. Pro cuius possessione pacifica et quieta nanciscenda, paternitatem vestram rogamus et petimus pro munere speciali quatenus ad hoc sic adhibeatis opem et operam efficaces ut nullius difficultatis obstaculum ab aliquo valeat in hoc facto interponi, sed plene quod auctoritate apostolica est collatum eidem Tymoteo ymmo nobis in ipso ad effectum liberaliter perducatur, ita ut pro vobis et vestris ad sollempnioris culminis titulum obtinendum reddamur promptiores. Valete, et quicquid inde feceritis, nobis per latorem presencium rescribatis. Dat. Anagnie, ultimo die maii.

6

Sancha Peláez escribe a su hermano, el obispo Abril de Urgel, explicándole su gran pobreza, pidiéndole limosna y rogándole que acomode uno de sus hijos en su casa.

AC Urgel, s. n.

Reverendo patri ac domino A. Dei gratia, Urgellensi episcopo, Sancia Pelagii, quamvis non digna soror vestra, manuum oscula adque pedum. Sciatis me esse in magnis

IV

194

angustiis et in magna pauperie posita, taliter quod iam vendidi domum meam pro paucis
nummis, quos dedi in debitis meis et modo non possum vivere cum filialibus meis. Unde,
paternitatem vestram exoro, si placet vobis, quod de mercede quam vos daretis aliis pauperibus, detis inde mihi amore Dei et bonitatis vestre. Et si videritis quod esset bonum,
mitterem vobis unum scolarem, filium parvum meum, quia non valeo manutenere illum
et faciatis ibi de vestra mercede. Valete.

7

*Verso leonino, dirigido al obispo Abril de Urgel, probablemente por un clérigo o clérigos de San-
tiago, con la esperanza de recibir limosna del obispo.*

AC Urgel, s. n. [2]

Pontifici claro, casto, justo quoque, naro
A, se deflentes B. Jacobus ere carentes.
Nos ignoramus, Pater inclite, quid faciamus
Posquam securi sumus ullo, nil habituri.
Vos exoramus, cum consilio careamus
Sic, ut discamus, quidquam per vos habeamus
Maxima namque viget gravitas in partibus istis
Nos nimis unde piget, iam sumpto quod tribuistis.
Saltem si vobis constat, nil mittere nobis
Se placeat, gratis nos ibimus, aut faveatis.

8

*Juan Domínguez escribe al obispo Abril poniendo bajo su protección a dos hermanos, definiendo su
propio servicio con respecto al arzobispo de Compostela y lamentando la conducta del siervo
de Abril, Pelayo.*

AC Urgel, s. n.

Reverendo patri ac domino ac singulari refugio domino magistro Aprili, divina providencia Urgellensi episcopo, Johannes Dominici suus clericus humilis et alumpnus manus
ac pedes humiliter osculari. Quia divina providencia vos ad tante dignitatis culmen voluit
promovere omnes parentes vestri amici et clientuli in parte letamur et in parte con-
tristamur quamplurimum cum speraremus in terra nostra inter nostros indigenas per
vos cito et feliciter sublimari. Hinc est quod cum Bartolameus Johannis et frater suus
Jacobus Johannis clientuli vestri licet remoti a vobis existerent vestrum consilium et ausilium non valentes excusare comode ad vestram paternitatem recurrant, licet indignus
clericus vester pro ipsis donacioni vestre preces porrigo cum affectu, quod cum sciant
bene cantare, legere, notare et apti ad omne bonum existant, necessitati eorum dignemini subvenire. De statu autem meo noscat vestra paternitas quod sum cum archiepiscopo et teneo sigillum suum et est mihi bonum cum ipso sicut latores presencium vobis
enarrare poterunt, et quidquid boni mihi adcreverit semper erit in omnibus ad vestrum
et vestrorum servicium et honorem, sed quamplurimum doleo quod intantum a vestra pater-
nitate disto et quod ex quo a vobis recessi nunquam vestram litteram nec mandatum recepi,
licet per Pelagium vestrum servientem semper et per alios plures euntes ad curiam sepe
ac sepius paternitati vestre litteratorie nunciassem qualiter vestra negocia procurabantur

[2] Estoy agradecido al Sr. A. G. Lee del St. John's College, Cambridge, por sus valiosas observaciones
sobre estas líneas.

seu etiam tractabantur. Sed suspicor quod cum Pelagius vester serviens valde remissus et negligens in vestris negociis procurandis existeret et ego in littera quam paternitati vestre dirigebam per eum diem in qua veniebat et recedebat et moram quam conterebat insererem, credens ipse quod per hoc possetis ipsius negligenciam sive nequiciam perpendere, paternitati vestre meas cartulas ocultavit. Qualiter autem me habuerim et habeo in vestris et vestrorum negociis procurandis et in prebendo consilium et ausilium eidem Pelagio et in mutuando sibi pecuniam quam sibi fuit necesse, quam nondum habeo, pro vestro negocio procurando, latores presencium tamquam experti in facto paternitati vestre verbotenus poterunt enarrare.

9

Causa Episcopi Urgellensis

Archivio Segreto Vaticano, Collectorie 397, fols. 52 r.-53 r.

l. 52 r.   In nomine Domini Amen. Anno Domini MCCLVIIII die sabbati VII exeunte octubris, pontificatus domini Alexandri pape quarti anno V [25 oct. 1259]. Mandavit dominus S(tephanus) episcopus Penestrinus per magistrum Bartholomeum capellanum suum, ex parte domini pape domino O(ctaviano) Sancte Marie etc. quod ipse audiat et decidat causam sive causas quam vel quas dictus dominus Aprilis episcopus Urgellensis movet vel intendit movere contra magistrum Tymoteum canonicum Quinquecclesiensem, camerarium ipsius domini Penestrini, et dompnum Sancium abbatem Vallis Oleti, filium illustris regis Aragonum, super archidiaconatu de Trempo.

Item causam que est inter predictum dominum S(ancium) et Tymoteum, que est super eodem archidiaconatu.

Item causam que est inter episcopum et capitulum Urgellense, ex una parte, et nobilem iuvenem (?) comitem F(oi)x, ex altera.

Die mercurii XVIIII novembris intrante [19 nov.] representavit se dominus P. Guillelmi canonicus Tirasonensis pro domino Sancio filio illustris regis Aragonum.

Eodem die domino episcopo Urgellensi oblatus fuit libellus per dominum Timotheum canonicum Quinquecclesiensem et mandatum fuit per dominum cardinalem eidem episcopo ut super ipso libello die veneris sequenti respondere deberet.

Die veneris III novembris exeunti [28 nov.] comparentibus domino episcopo Urgellensi et (*sic*) pro domino Sancio assignatum est terminum ad diem martis proximum ad comparendum in causa.

Die jovis XVIII decembris tertie indictionis [18 dec.] comparentibus venerabili patri domino Urgellensi episcopo et discreto viro domino Petro Guillelmi canonico Thirasonensi coram venerabili patre domino O(ctaviano) cardinali, idem dominus de speciali domini pape mandato ordinavit quod causa que vertitur inter ipsum episcopum et dominus (*sic*) Sancium filium illustris regis Aragonum commissa ad audiendum eidem domino cardinali sit in suspenso usque ad sequentem diem post dominicam de Laetare Jerusalem [15 marzo 1260], dicens et ordinans quod si in dicto termino non compareret dictus dominus S(ancius) vel procurator ipsius quod ex tunc procedatur in causa sicut presens esset, non obstante absentia sua, et quod citatio aliqua postea de ipso non fiat.

. 52 v.   Die veneris XXVII (*sic*) martii [26 marzo] comparuerunt partes coram domino cardinali et cum ex parte domini episcopi allegaretur quod procuratorium exhibitum a procuratori domini Sancii esset minus sufficiens dominus cardinalis pronunciavit procuratorium ipsum esse sufficiens et supplevit defectum si quis esset in eo. Et sic datus est terminus peremptorius partibus ut in crastino post octabas pasce [12 abril] pareant coram ipso ad procedendum prout de iure fuerit procedendum.

Die lunis XII aprilis [12 abril] dominus episcopus comparuit coram domino cardinali.

Die martis XIII aprilis [13 abril] presentibus partibus coram domino cardinali idem dominus commisit prescriptam causam audiendam loco sui magistro Gerardo de Parma.

Qui magister Girardus statuit terminum partibus ipsis ut die jovis primo venturo [15 abril] post nonam compareant coram ipso ad procedendum in ea sicut de iure fuerit [*suppl.:* procedendum].

Die jovis XV aprilis [15 abril] comparuerunt partes predicte coram magistro Gerardo predicto et dominus episcopus Urgellensis seu nomine ipsius exhibuit quoddam instrumentum appellationis in iudicio, partibus ipsis presentibus, et dictus magister G(erardus) ordinabat id porrigi alteri parti et statuit ei terminum peremptorium ad recipiendum dictam copiam et ad deliberandum super ipso instrumento et dicendum quicquid voluerit die sabbati proximum (*sic*).

Coram nobis reverendo patre domino O(ctavianus) Sancte Marie in Via Lata diacono cardinali, partibus auditori concesso, dicit et proponit Tymoteus canonicus Quinquecclesiensis, camerarius venerabilis patris domini S(tephani) dei gratia episcopi Penestrini, contra venerabilem patrem dominum A(prilem) episcopum Urgellensem quod licet dominus papa archidiaconatum ruralem de Trempo, qui decanatus a plerisque nuncupatur, et canonicatum et prebendam vacantes quos venerabilis pater .. episcopus Ylerdensis in ecclesia Urgellensi tempore sue promotionis obtinebat duxerit conferendos sibique de illis auctoritate apostolica providerit, nichilominus tamen predictus episcopus collationi et provisioni predictis contra iusticiam se opposuit ac ipsum impedivit quominus possit predictorum archidiaconatus sive decanatus et canonicatus pacifica possessione gaudere. Quare petit predictus (Tymoteus) dictum archidiaconatum sive decanatum cum omnibus iuribus et pertinentiis suis ad ipsum T(ymoteum) sententialiter declarari et sibi adiudicari, ac prefatum episcopum ab oppositione et impedimento premissis compesci et prohiberi sibique super hiis perpetuum silentium imponi ipsumque ut dictum T(ymoteum) permittat pacifica possessione dictorumque archidiaconatus sive decanatus et canonicatus gaudere sententialiter condempnari. Haec omnia petit cum dampnis et expensis legitime factis que et quas extimat XL libras turonenses et de futuris protestatur usque ad finem litis, salvo iure addendi vel minuendi.

Die jovis XV aprilis [15 abril] predictus dominus .. episcopus litem contestando negat narrata vera esse prout narrantur et dicit petita fieri non deberent, salvis exceptionibus iuribus et defensionibus suis.

Coram venerabili domino Octaviano dei gratia Sancte Marie in Via Lata diacono cardinali a domino papa partibus auditori concesso proponit in iure (?) Urgellensis episcopus quod Timoteus canonicus Quinquecclesiensis et domini S(tephani) dei gratia Penestrini episcopi camerarius decanatum seu archipresbiteratum (*sic*) ruralem de Trempo diocesis Urgellensis assignari seu conferri sibi per sedem apostolicam, ut asseritur, contra iusticiam procuravit in ipsius episcopi et ecclesie Urgellensis non modicum preiudicium et gravamen, propter quae idem episcopus quamcito id ad eius noticiam pervenit sedem apostolicam appellavit in scriptis. Quare petit idem episcopus nomine suo et ecclesie Urgellensis per vos (?) huius appellationem ab eodem episcopo factam iustam pronunciari et provisionem, assignationem seu collationem huius iniuste factam cassari, irritari et cassam seu irritam nunciari, et quicquid post ipsam appellationem vel occasione collationis huius attemptatum est seu contigerit attemptari, et predictum Timoteum conpesci

fol. 53 r. et conpescendum decerni ne ipsum episcopum vel ecclesiam Urgellensem molestet decetero super eo et ipsum Timoteum ad dampna et interesse condempnari et ad expensas factas et faciendas in lite que suo loco et tempore taxabuntur. Salvo etc.

Item eodem die jovis predictus Timoteus litem contestando negat narrata vera esse prout narrantur et dicit petita fieri non deberent, salvis exceptionibus, iuribus et defensionibus suis.

[Desde aquí con otra mano] Die sabbati XVII mensis aprilis intrante [17 abril] venerabilis dominus episcopus Urgellensis fecit et constituit procuratorem suum apud acta Johannem Dominici canonicum Urgellensem.

Die sabbati XVII aprilis [17 abril] dictus magister Gerardus statuit terminum domino Raimundo procuratori predicto ad proponendum omnes exceptiones dilatorias et dandum in scriptis quas proponere voluerint in causis quas movent contra ipsum et contra dictum dominum Sancium, cuius procurator existit, dominus episcopus Urgellensis et dominus Thimotteus camerarius domini episcopi Penestrini. Hinc ad diem mercurii proximam et ad recipiendum interrogationes quas predicti dominus episcopus et Thimotteus facere voluerint, et precepit ei quod non recederet de curia nisi dictis interrogationibus responderet.

Die mercurii XXI mensis aprilis [21 abril] partes comparuerunt et partis (sic) domini Sancii dedit dilatorias suas et dominus episcopus dedit quasdam interrogationes suas super quibus petebat interrogari procuratorem dicti domini Sancii, et eadem die dominus Gerardus, datus auditor per dominum O(ctavianum) c(ardinalem), terminum prefixit partibus peremptorium ut proxima die sabbati compareant ad procedendum in causa quantum de iure fuerit procedendum.

Die jovis VI madii instrante tercie indictionis [6 mayo 1260] prorogatus est terminus de voluntate domini episcopi Urgellensis et procuratoris·sui et magistri Thimotei camerarii venerabilis patris episcopi Penestrini et magistri Raimundi de Uliola (?) et Gregorii de Piperno, procuratorum domini Sancii supradicti, in causa quam predictos (sic) dominus episcopus movebat contra dominum S(ancium) predictum et contra magistrum Thimoteum et quam magister Thimoteus movebat contra predictos episcopum et S(ancium) super ecclesiam seu archidiaconatum de Trempo Urgellensis diocesis usque ad festum proximum Omnium Sanctorum [1 nov. 1260].

NOTA DE LA REDACCIÓN. - El Rev. P. Cebrià Baraut, del Monasterio de Montserrat, ha tenido la gentileza de corregir los documentos de este Apéndice sobre los originales urgelitanos, a excepción del n.º 3, que no le ha sido posible encontrar. Le manifestamos, desde aquí, nuestro agradecimiento.

V

Segovia: a 'frontier' diocese in the thirteenth century *

CENTURIES after The Cid and Columbus – and a century almost after F. J. Turner – the medieval Spanish frontier continues to exert influence and attract settlers. But now it is not the preachers and warriors who are drawn thither; it is the historians, many of whom, unlike their predecessors, are sufficiently self-critical to feel unsure about precisely where they are going and just when they should stop. Recent work by MacKay, Ruiz and Glick has amply demonstrated the extent of the area of debate regarding the frontier's nature and chronology, geography and *mentalités*.[1] It is from this uncertainty, of course, that the interest and conceptual value derive; but from its implications the sceptics are apt to recoil, not least when devotees particularize about such constructs as 'the religion of the frontier' – the belief that religious life on the frontier exhibited a 'frontier spirit' with all its attendant Turnerian connotations, as advocated by R. I. Burns the historian of the thirteenth-century kingdom of Valencia, but less readily accepted by some other historians.[2] We may look for laymen and ecclesiastics liberated by distance and environment from the constraints of authority, but, limited as we are by the nature of the evidence – conciliar and synodal primarily, and not much of that –

* The author wishes to express his gratitude to the British Library Board for permission to publish the document printed in the Appendix and to D. Hilario Sanz y Sanz, archivist of Segovia cathedral, for allowing him to consult documents there.

1. Angus MacKay, *Spain in the Middle Ages, From Frontier to Empire, 1000–1500* (London, 1977); T. F. Ruiz, 'Expansion et changement: la conquête de Séville et la société castillane (1248–1350)', *Annales-Économies-Sociétés-Civilisations*, xxxiv (1979), 458–65; Thomas F. Glick, *Islamic and Christian Spain in the Early Middle Ages: Comparative Perspectives on Social and Cultural Formation* (Princeton, 1979).

2. *The Crusader Kingdom of Valencia: Reconstruction on a thirteenth-century Frontier* (Cambridge, Mass., 1967), p. 59 (parish network as frontier's 'major single unifying factor'); *idem*, 'The Parish as Frontier Institution in thirteenth-century Valencia', *Speculum*, xxxvii (1962), 244–51. I have questioned the appropriateness of the frontier terminology employed by Professor Burns in 'The Religion of the Frontier in Medieval Spain' (forthcoming in the Proceedings of the Second International Colloquium in Ecclesiastical History, Oxford 1974). J. N. Hillgarth takes issue with Burns regarding his use of the terms 'crusaders' and 'colonialism' in his review of *Islam under the Crusaders. Colonial Survival in the thirteenth-century Kingdom of Valencia* (Princeton, 1973) in *Catholic Historical Review*, lxiii (1977), 129. *Cf.* my own review of this work in *Times Literary Supplement*, 17 Jan. 1975, and E. Costa y Belda, 'Las constituciones de Don Raimundo de Losaña para el cabildo de Sevilla (1261)', *Historia. Instituciones. Documentos*, v (1978), 195, 216, n. 83.

† we find an ecclesiastical society whose thirteenth-century pastors
described it in conventional post-Lateran IV terms, and who thereby
convey the impression of difficulties hardly distinguishable from those
experienced by their episcopal brethren in Italy, France and England.
All too rarely are we afforded a glimpse of parochial conditions with
which to compare what was so regularly, and so ineffectually, denounced by popes, councils and synods. Clerical ignorance there
certainly was, and clerical concubinage; but because the clergy's
failings were orthodox (or were thought to be so) we have no Spanish
Montaillou.

If then there is an elusive quality about the religion *of* the frontier,
we are not much better informed (except in the kingdom of Valencia)
about religion *on* the frontier. For all that has been written about the
contest of cathedral bell and muezzin's call, or the missionary prepara-
tions of the evangelizing mendicants, we have too little information
for the Castilian area about the Christians' attitude to the mosques, or
the preaching done in the marketplace.[1]

The same uncertainty shrouds our knowledge of conditions in the
Christian hinterland, at some distance from the front-line. The
records left by the cathedral chapters are predominantly formal and
institutional. True, contemporary wills can be revealing of fashions in
piety – where they have survived in any number. But so self-regarding
and inward-looking in general are these records that an issue as
central as that of the endowment and financing of the great cathedral
churches still remains an enigma.[2]

Because any record of the relationship of bishop and chapter on the
one hand and the usually muted diocesan churches on the other is so
precious, Professor García's recent account of the disputes between
Bishop Giraldo of Segovia and his clergy in and after 1216 is particularly valuable.[3] As related by García, the indiscipline of Giraldo's
diocesan subjects in matters both moral and pecuniary eventually
cost him both his see and, apparently, his reason. The spectacle of a
reforming prelate struggling for survival and sanity in an area only

---

1. Burns, 'The Parish', p. 247; *Islam*, pp. 187–9 (muezzin). *Cf.* J. M. Coll, 'Escuelas
de lenguas orientales en los siglos XIII–XIV', *Analecta Sacra Tarraconensia*, xvii
(1944), 115–38; R. I. Burns, 'Christian-Islamic Confrontation in the West: the
thirteenth-century Dream of Conversion', *American Historical Review*, lxxvi (1971),
1403–4; *idem*, 'Journey from Islam: Incipient Cultural Transition in the Conquered
Kingdom of Valencia (1240–1280), *Speculum* xxxv (1960), 352–3 (preaching). In
1274 King James of Aragon urged the church of Huesca to replace its converted
mosque with a cathedral 'ecclesiarum more christiano constructarum', whereas
eleven years earlier Alfonso X of Castile had retained the Moorish craftsmen of
Córdoba to work for two days a year (with all meals found) on the cathedral there:
Burns, 'The Parish', 250, n. 35; Córdoba, Biblioteca del Cabildo, Libro de las Tablas
(MS 125), fo. 16ᵛ.

2. P. A. Linehan, 'La iglesia de León a mediados del siglo XIII', *León y su historia*,
III (León, 1975), p. 31.

3. A. García y García, 'Primeros reflejos del Concilio IV Lateranense en Castilla,
I. Vazquez (ed.) *Studia Historico-Ecclesiastica: Festgabe für Prof. Luchesius G. Spätling
O.F.M.* (Rome, 1977), pp. 249–82.

recently wrested from the wild, the local *fueros* of which have made it synonymous with independence and lawlessness, and this on the very morrow of the Fourth Lateran Council, may seem to constitute a prime example of 'frontier religion' in near-laboratory conditions.[1] The purpose of this article is to consider the context of this conflict, and by tracing the course and the nature of developments there during the following decades, to discover what can be learnt from it about that shadowy subject as it concerns this region of Castile.

Bishop Giraldo had attended the 1215 Council and it is likely that it was his conciliar experiences that prompted him on his return to Segovia to summon the synod which led to trouble. But there is a distinction to be made between that presumption and the unqualified inference that IV Lateran provided the *fons et origo* of the dispute.[2] For there was nothing new about either the bishop's problems or his attempts to overcome them. His predecessor, Gonzalo, had been beset both by an obstructive minority within his chapter, against whom he invoked papal assistance,[3] and by the diocesan clergy. What was at issue between Giraldo and his clergy in 1216–17 – episcopal procurations and provision to vacant churches, the interdict of entire parishes, exaction of *cathedraticum* on the one hand; clerical *confratarias illicitas* and wholesale defiance of episcopal authority on the other – had no less engaged Gonzalo and *his* clergy ten years before. On that occasion, however, the matter of clerical concubinage and Gonzalo's attempt to suppress it had been to the fore: an issue which, interestingly, did not figure in Giraldo's decrees of 1216–17. This should not suggest either that Giraldo was less of a 'reformer' than his predecessor or that concubinage was no longer a problem; only that for the diocese – and the bishop – of Segovia, IV Lateran may have constituted rather less of a watershed than has been assumed.

Diego de Colmenares, writing in the early seventeenth century, provided a summary account of the conflict of Bishop Gonzalo and his clergy, and was inclined to blame the trouble on the mob.[4] Prompted by certain reforming decrees of Archbishop Martín López of Toledo, Gonzalo ordered the clergy to put away their women.

1. Ibid. pp. 258–9. In May 1107 Alfonso VI had described the restored diocese of Segovia as 'terram de ursorum et aprorum diversique generis ferarum ereptam', converted by his efforts 'de heremo in agriculturam': C. Sánchez-Albornoz, *Despoblación y repoblación del Valle del Duero* (Buenos Aires, 1966), p. 388. *Cf.* E. Sáez et al., *Los Fueros de Sepúlveda* (Segovia, 1953); M. del Carmen Carlé, *Del concejo medieval castellano-leonés* (Buenos Aires, 1968).

2. 'Llena su mente de ideas lateranenses, celebra un sínodo diocesano en la capital de su diócesis (fines de 1216), por el que trata de introducir algunas reformas del Concilio General.... El rechazo de tales constituciones fue instantáneo y fulminante': García, 'Primeros reflejos', p. 259.

3. D. Mansilla, *La documentación pontificia hasta Inocencio III (965–1216)* (Rome, 1955), no. 159 (June 1198).

4. *Historia de la insigne ciudad de Segovia y compendio de las historias de Castilla* (Segovia, 1637; nueva ed. anotada, Segovia, 1969, cited here), 327: '. . . o animados, como suele ser, de la muchedumbre'.

They countered by accusing the bishop of having acquired the see unlawfully, being under the canonical age at the time, imposing unjust taxation upon them, and devoting himself to the pleasures of the chase. The case was referred by Innocent III on 2 May 1206 to Bishop Rodrigo of Sigüenza and the archdeacons of Almazán and Molina (Sigüenza), whose judgment (16 May 1207) struck a middle position, supporting the bishop in his disciplinary measures, and ordering him to make good his unjust exactions from the clergy.[1]

What Colmenares did not mention (though surely not because it provided no support for his view that la muchedumbre was responsible for this unedifying encounter, if anything the contrary) was a document in the archive of Segovia Cathedral which, although undated, unquestionably belongs to this context. This[2] contains part of the evidence presented to the judges ex parte episcopi by the archpriests of Coca, Pedraza, Sepúlveda and Cuéllar and by sundry clerics and laymen of those places. There had indeed been two issues, as Colmenares stated – morals and money, but it is the detailed and circumstantial nature of the testimony, rather than the substance, that is arresting. All too rarely at this date can we hear ordinary people talking.[3]

The core of the problem was described by one witness, the abbot of San Tomé de Sepúlveda, and confirmed by dozens more.

He stated on oath that he knows that the majority of the clergy of Sepúlveda, both in the town and the villages, had concubines before the beginning of this process, and in many cases have them still. He heard from various of them that the bishop of Segovia had ordered them by letter to put away their women by St John's day, or they would incur sentences of interdict and their women excommunication; and that none of them had appealed against the bishop's letters. He heard from the bishop that after St John's day he had sent further letters, excommunicating the clergy, and from Juan Guillélmez that he had delivered these and that they were read in the chapter of Sepúlveda, whereupon the cleric Migael entered an appeal. Regarding the matter of conspiracy, he stated that he heard from various of them that most of the clergy of Sepúlveda went to the church of S. Pedro and there swore to assist and defend one another and their churches against the bishop and to take the case to Rome.[4]

1. Colmenares, loc. cit. Doubts had also been expressed (by Archbishop Martín) about Gonzalo's immediate predecessor, Bishop Gutierre, who had not looked old enough to be a bishop when elected in 1195, but they had proved unfounded: J. F. Rivera Recio, La iglesia de Toledo en el siglo XII (1086–1208), (Rome, 1966), i. 281–2.
2. A[rchivo de la] C[atedral] S[egovia], doc. 16, undated but containing inter alia the text of a letter from the abbots J. of Sacrameña and B. of Sotos Albos to Bishop R(odrigo) of Sigüenza and the archdeacons P. of Almazán and G. of Molina. Cf. Colmenares, loc. cit.
3. For example, nothing of the kind has survived in the Salamanca documentation of the period, recently published: Documentos de los archivos catedralicio y diocesano de Salamanca (siglos XII–XIII), ed. J. L. Martín Martín et al. (Salamanca, 1977).
4. ACS, doc. 16: 'Iuratus dixit quod scit quod clerici Septempublicenses de villa et de aldeis pro maiori parte tenebant concubinas ante inicium istius cause et multi eorum adhuc tenent, et audivit a quibusdam illorum quod episcopus Secobiensis mandavit eis per litteras suas quod abicerent eas usque ad festum Sancti Johannis

Evidently the conspirators were litigious. They were also organized. Petrus Petri clèric of S. Tomé provided corroborative detail of how almost all the clergy of Sepúlveda, of both the town and the villages, met in a church and, joining hands, swore to assist one another against the bishop, anyone breaking the oath to be ostracised and fined fifty *aureos*. And then they summoned the officials to their chapter and made them swear to withhold the bishop's procurations.[1]

Although there was some conflict of evidence regarding the level of the penalty prescribed against backsliders – Dominicus Garsie *presbiter* of Cuéllar maintaining that it had first been set at five aureos and then raised to sixty – none of the witnesses denied that formal declaration of economic war had been made both at Sepúlveda and elsewhere. Petrus Gasco *presbiter* had been present 'apud Coylar in capitulo' both when the bishop's letters 'de continencia servanda' had been received, and at the assembly after St John's Day when the sanctions clause was, he said, sworn 'ante alcaldos laycos'. Confederation followed. When the bishop reiterated his demands at Sotos Albos 'ubi clerici sex capitulorum usque ad octo eo amplius erant' the clerics renewed their opposition. Petrus Roiz *sacerdos de La Alameda* was there 'et vidit eos ambulantes per aldeas et petentes auxilium a conciliis aldearum'. At Sepúlveda lay support was sought and obtained: Sancius Johannis *laycus* 'dixit quod ipse interfuit concilio ubi clerici rogaverunt concilium ut iuvarent eos contra episcopum et maior pars concilii promiserunt eis ut iuvarent illos'.

As witnesses to his entitlement to an annual payment of one *aureus* from each priest and half that sum from each deacon (in addition to *procurationes*, vacant *portiones*, *primicie* and *mensure* in kind – *unam de tritico, aliam de siligine, aliam de ordeo*), Bishop Gonzalo was able to produce a string of aged authorities – 'valetudinarii et senes' – whose collective memory stretched back to the 1150s. J. dean of Segovia testified that during the reigns of bishops Guillelmo, Gonzalo, Gutierre 'et huius episcopi usque nunc' the clergy had always paid these sums, unless excused on grounds of poverty; and that 'a tempore primi episcopi Petri' – Pedro de Agen, the first bishop of reconquered

---

sinautem essent ipsi interdicti et ille excommunicate. Et audivit ab eis quod nullus appellaverat ab illis litteris. Audivit etiam ab ipso episcopo quod miserat eis post festum Sancti Johannis alias litteras de excommunicatione clericorum et audivit a Johanne Guillelmi quod ipse attulit litteras illas et fuerunt lecte in capitulo Septempublicensi et Michael clericus appellavit. Interrogatus de conspiracione dixit quod audivit a quibusdam illorum quod omnes clerici Septempublicenses exceptis paucis intraverunt ecclesiam Sancti Petri et ibi iuraverunt quod adiuvarent se et defenderent se et ecclesias suas contra episcopum et mitterent Romam pro causa ista.'

1. *Ibid.*: 'Clerici Septempublicenses de villa et de audeis (*sic*) fere omnes convenerunt in quadam ecclesia et posuerunt manus suas inter manus aliorum ad invicem iurantes quod iuvarent se in causa ista contra episcopum et quicumque de illis iuramentum illud non servaret exiret de societate illorum et pectaret. L. aureos et postea vocaverunt sesmarios ad capitulum suum et fecerunt eos iurare quod non darent episcopo procurationes.'

Segovia – it had been episcopal practice to bestow the contested *portiones* on canons, monks and other clerics. Two papal legates had confirmed the bishop's rights therein.[1] Archdeacon G. confirmed the dean's account. He had been sixty years in his archdeaconry and his memory reached back one bishop further than the dean's, to Vicente (d. *ante* 1158). Regarding recent events he claimed that the conspirators had sought to influence not only the people but the king, Alfonso VIII, too: 'populum et regem concitaverunt adversus episcopum.' A different version of the bishop's entitlement came from Michael Petri *laycus* of Sepúlveda. According to him, it derived from a payment previously owed by the clergy to the king, from which bishop Gonzalo had succeeded in liberating them.[2]

Whatever may be the limitations of this partial testimony, it is clear that the diocesan clergy were fully accustomed to defending their interests. The fact that Bishop Giraldo did not raise the issue of concubinage in 1216–17 ought not to imply that they had accepted meekly the prohibition of the bishop of Sigüenza and his colleagues ten years before. That the other issue – the *aureus* and *half-aureus* obligation – remained live is proved by the *allegationes ex parte clericorum*, the work of a competent canonist, which García has published. The date of these as we have them must be post-1215; they may have been directed at the hapless Bishop Giraldo.[3]

1. 'et . . . quidam qui moverunt questionem super huiusmodi portionibus condempnati fuerunt a legato domini pape Jacinto tempore quo fungebatur legatione in Yspania, et quidam sacerdos ruralis propter consimilem questionem condempnatus fuit a domino Gregorio cardinali et legato domini pape.' *Cf.* García, *art. cit.* p. 279. For the legations of Cardinal Jacintus of S. Maria in Cosmedin (1172–5) and Cardinal Gregory of S. Angelo (1191–4, 1196–7), see G. Säbekow, *Die päpstlichen Legationen nach Spanien und Portugal bis zum Ausgang des XII Jahrhunderts* (Berlin, 1931), pp. 53–60; J. González, *El reino de Castilla en la época de Alfonso VIII*, i (Madrid, 1960), 378–83.

2. 'et ipse solus laycus cum alio nobili interfuit sinodo facta tempore Gondisalvi episcopi quando ipsi clerici qui more laycorum etiam si decem (?) haberent aureos regi pectare solebant; quod episcopus eos [ab] solvi faceret a pecta regis et concederet eis vitam quam cum suis predecessoribus habuerunt, dando scilicet ei singulos aureos et diachoni medios': the meaning of this is far from clear. At another council (*concilium*) of Bishop Gutierre, 'patruus et antecessor episcopi huius', according to P. Bela *vicarius* of Coca, the clergy had undertaken to pay the annual *aureus* 'sicut solvere consueverant'. *Cf* González, *El reino*, ii. 583, 599–600 (*anno* 1180).

3. 'Primeros reflejos', pp. 278–81. García (p. 259) states that the piece is 'ciertamente posterior al *Liber Extra* de 1234, que aparece citado varias veces'; but, with a single exception (p. 281, n. 17, which indicates a date post-1215), all of the *Liber Extra* material might equally well have been found in *Compilationes Antiquae* I–III or in other collections of decretals. The *allegationes* may therefore date from *c.* 1216 or earlier, and have been subsequently updated by the addition of the chapter references to *Extra*. The allusion (p. 280) to the dispute of the bishop of Sigüenza and the inhabitants of Medinaceli – 'nec valet confirmatio quam impetravit dominus Segontinus contra Meditenses, quia ibi directe agebatur pro cathedratico' – may suggest a date soon after November 1212 when Innocent III confirmed an earlier settlement of that controversy (T. Mingüella y Arnedo, *Historia de la diocesis de Sigüenza y de sus obispos*, i (Madrid, 1910), 524), although there had been other abortive settlements over the previous sixteen years. Bishop Rodrigo had encountered clerical hostility akin to that alleged at Segovia (where he would have been an expert

In 1216 and thereafter Bishop Giraldo had the support of his chapter (formally at least) in his battles with the diocesan clergy. Economic interests held them together. With the passage of time, however, these same interests worked to force them apart, a process hastened doubtless by the widespread depredations suffered by them at the hands of King Fernando III and the laity while the diocese was in the custody of Archbishop Rodrigo of Toledo.[1] As elsewhere in Castile, declining rents at Segovia impelled the canons to seek income from other churches. By 1234, when Giraldo's successor Bernardo was authorized by Pope Gregory IX to deprive non-resident canons, the pastoral consequences of these economic developments were fully apparent.[2] Ten years later a remedy was overdue. In 1215 Giraldo's enemies had appealed against him to the pope while the bishop was at the pope's council. In the summer of 1245 likewise, when Bernardo was at Lyons for Innocent IV's council, the clamours of the chapter reached the ears of the pope, and their complaints were referred by him to the Castilian cardinal Gil Torres.

Cardinal Gil was no stranger to the type of problems that beset the church of Segovia. Indeed he came to the case fresh from the investigation which he had just conducted into the affairs of the church of Salamanca, for which he had issued a set of constitutions in the previous April.[3] The principles common to these and to other sets of constitutions which Gil issued for other Castilian churches during the next seven years have been described elsewhere. They were, briefly, to provide the material basis for moral reform, by assigning to each member and associate of the chapter fixed income and specified duties. The text of the complaints from Segovia has not survived, but to judge by the cardinal's response in October 1245 they

judge in 1206–7), and the two anti-episcopal movements display many similar features – conspiracy, confederation, lay complicity, etc. (*ibid.* pp. 181, 494–6, 499). The very same methods used at Sepúlveda to terrorise Gonzalo of Segovia's supporters in 1206 had been employed at Medinaceli ten years before (*ibid.* pp. 482–4).

1. García, 'Primeros reflejos', pp. 252–8; Peter Linehan, *The Spanish Church and the Papacy in the Thirteenth Century* (Cambridge, 1971), p. 11. On 4 Sept. 1218 Rodrigo imposed a settlement of the dispute regarding payment of *cathedraticum* at Pedraza: ACS, caj. A, no. 8. The *political* role played by the *concejos* of the region at this time, in the matter of the succession to the throne on the death of Enrique I of Castile (1217), is noted by J. González, 'La Extremadura castellana al mediar el siglo XIII', *Hispania*, xxxiv (1974), 368: 'se movilizaron políticamente con aires de hermandad.' His source, presumably, is Rodrigo Jiménez de Rada, *De rebus Hispaniae*, IX. v (ed. F. Lorenzana, *PP Toletanorum quotquot extant Opera*, III (Madrid, 1793), 196–7). For the part played by churchmen, see C. Sánchez-Albornoz, 'La sucesión al trono en los reinos de León y Castilla', in *Estudios sobre las instituciones medievales españolas* (Mexico, 1965), pp. 676–7.

2. *Les Registres de Grégoire IX (1227–41)*, ed. L. Auvray (Paris, 1890–1955), no. 2006.

3. Ed. D. Mansilla, *Iglesia castellano-leonesa y curia romana en los tiempos del rey San Fernando* (Madrid, 1945), pp. 321–30; A. Riesco Terrero, 'Constitución pontificia de Inocencio IV dada a la iglesia de Salamanca el año 1245. Estudio histórico-diplomático', *Ius Canonicum*, xvii.i (1977), 244–50.

appear to have been of an exclusively economic nature. It seems that it was Innocent IV who grasped the opportunity to widen the terms of Gil's investigations to include other aspects of reform.[1]

We have no information regarding the remuneration of members of the chapter prior to 1245, but it seems clear that, in this as in other financial matters, the bishop enjoyed a large – and often resented – measure of discretion.[2] Since 1123 the *vita communis* had gradually declined; in 1258 all that remained of it was a symbolic vestige. The effect of Gil's action was to accelerate this natural process by dividing the *communis mensa*. To each dignitary, canon and *socius* – from the dean to the lesser portionaries – *prestimonia* of a specified value were to be assigned. In October 1245 Cardinal Gil stated what these values should be. Presumably he had received representations from the bishop and chapter as well as advice from Segovians resident at the curia (including the archdeacon of Cuéllar, Nicolás, to whom the pope had recently made a provision of rents worth 500 maravedís: a vast sum in the context of Segovia incomes).[3] Nevertheless the dis-

---

1. 'Hinc est, dilecti filii capitulum, quod clamoribus vestris quia tenuitate proventuum intolerabili ut asseritis pressi, subveniri vobis de prestimoniis ecclesie vestre supplicastis, dominus papa . . . curam et sollicitudinem ecclesie vestre nobis committere voluit super quibusdam articulis seu capitulis, videlicet beneficiorum ordinationibus seu collationibus, prestimoniorum distributionibus et super aliis que correctionis seu reformationis remedium in vestra ecclesia requirebant': ACS, doc. 37 (Cardinal Gil to dean and chapter of Segovia, 3 Oct. 1245). On the following day the cardinal wrote in identical terms to the bishop, dean and chapter jointly (ACS, doc. 241). For Cardinal Gil's work see Mansilla, *Iglesia castellano-leonesa*, pp. 195–221; Linehan, *Spanish Church*, pp. 269–75. Gil Torres worked from the curia; there is no support for the view, recently restated by Costa y Belda, *art. cit.* p. 196, that he came to Castile to carry out investigations. *Cf.* Linehan, *op. cit.* p. 276.

2. Royal endowments were formally made 'Deo et ecclesie S. Marie Secobie et . . . eiusdem ecclesie presenti episcopo et omnibus successoribus vestris', as in the case of Sancho III's grant of Alcazarén (July 1158), but the exchange of Alcazarén for other property in May 1181 was authorized by Bishop Gonzalo alone (González, *El reino de Castilla*, ii. 87–88, 639–40). In October 1196 Gonzalo himself argued that the alienation of the *villa* of Navares by his predecessor Guillelmo was void since capitular approval had been lacking: *ibid.* iii. 767.

3. *Ibid.*: 'Volumus itaque et mandamus ut salva provisione sive gratia 500 mor(abitinorum) quam dominus papa Magistro N. subdiacono suo archidiacono Collarensi in prestimoniis predecessoris sui vel equivalentibus ecclesie vestre sibi voluit et mandavit, decanus preter vestiarium et portiones et distributiones cotidianas, hiis que annexa sunt decanatui et 80 mor. sibi tanquam canonico assignandis et hiis que modo habet in prestimoniis in hac summa provisionis reddituum computandis, 400 habet mor.' The archdeacons, *cantor*, treasurer and *magister scolarum* were assigned 300, 250, 250, and 200 mor. respectively, *preter vestiarium*, 'portiones et distributiones cotidianas' and 80 mor. each in respect of their canonries; 'quilibet canonicus integer' 80 mor, 'quilibet canonicus qui dicitur dimidius integram portionem habens' 60 mor, 'quilibet canonicus qui dicitur dimidius dimidiam portionem habens' 40 mor, in each case 'preter vestiarium et portiones et distributiones cotidianas'; *portionarii* and *dimidii portionarii* 40 and 20 mor. respectively, 'preter portionem et distributiones cotidianas'. Some idea of the real value of these sums is provided in Cardinal Gil's constitutions for Burgos Cathedral (1252) which give as the equivalents of one maravedí 'duo almudes de tritico et tres de alio blado', or ten sheep, on the basis of which and of the value of livestock in Spain in the early 1940s Mansilla estimated the value of the maravedí to be 40 pesetas (*Iglesia castellano-leonesa*, p. 212).

V

positions made in October 1245 – of 400 maravedís to the dean, down to 20 to each *porcionarius dimidius* – were provisional, it having been alleged that a combination of *sterilitas possessionum* and *raritas inhabitancium* had so reduced the rent income of the church that payment of these sums might not be possible. Accordingly Gil directed the dean and archdeacons of Segovia and Sepúlveda to make a survey of available resources – 'inquisitio prestimoniorum que in ecclesia vestra vel extra ecclesiam consueverunt conferri' – on the basis of which *inquisitio* (or *taxatio*) the bishop was within fifteen days to proceed to the assignment of *prestimonia* to each member of the chapter.[1]

The text of this *inquisitio* has not survived, but we know that its findings were not sufficiently extensive to provide all the information that was needed.[2] What it did reveal however was that the root of the trouble at Segovia lay in delay in conferring benefices 'ultra tempus a canone diffinitum' and in an inequitable division of *prestimonia*.[3] Sometime probably in the year 1246 Cardinal Gil accepted the chapter's major allegation against the bishop, and authorized the payment to each member of a *supplementum* 'tum de prestimoniis que tunc temporis habebantur tum de porcionibus ecclesiarum parrochialium que prestimoniales dicuntur'. Settlement of the issue, however, was frustrated by the inadequacy of the *inquisitio* of the dean and his colleagues. So Gil ordered a second survey to be done – 'super quantitate proventuum predictorum . . . inquisitio et extimatio.' At the suggestion of the bishop's proctors the composition of the team of investigators was changed, by the substitution for the dean of the abbot of Sotos Albos (possibly on the grounds that he was a neutral

In so far as this method of calculation has any validity, reference to the *Anuario Estadístico de España* would suggest a value thirty times as great in 1979.

1. *Ibid.*: 'Ceterum quia propter sterilitatem possessionum [MS possessionem] et raritatem inhabitancium occasione quorum redditus ecclesie vestre diminuti dicantur plenam certitudinem non habemus an vacancia prestimonia ad complementum dicte provisionis in presenti sufficiant.' If any surplus should be discovered, the details were to be reported 'statim' to the cardinal 'ut intellecta proventuum quantitate cerciorari possimus qualiter eadem oporteat dispensari'. This testimony suggests that the demographic effects of Christian expansion were already being felt in the decade before the capture of Seville. *Cf.* Ruiz, 'Expansion et changement', pp. 548–9; Linehan, *Spanish Church*, ch. 6.

2. ACS, doc. 36 (Cardinal Gil to bishop, dean and chapter, 14 Sept. 1247): 'Quia de summa proventuum villarum, cellariorum et possessionum episcopi et capituli inquisitio diligens et extimatio non fuerat habita, ordinatio quam provideramus in eadem ecclesia faciendam tunc non potuit finaliter terminari.'

3. 'Intelleximus quod prefati scandali radix et seminarium origo ac fomes ex eo potissime pullarat quod beneficia vacantia ultra tempus a canone diffinitum detenta non suo tempore contingebat conferri, et in prestimoniis dividendis que vel extra ecclesiam concedi solebant pro beneplacito conferentis nimium inequalis distributio procedebat, dum in extraneos prestimoniis largiter dispensatis filiorum ipsius ecclesie ratio minus quam equitas distributionis exigeret habebatur. Unde de facili sequebatur adversum patremfamilias non levis occasio murmurandi et mortalis infirmitas cui molestum est per inopiam affici et indigentiam perpeti difficulter scrupuloso corde commota videbatur sibi iustam habere materiam conquerendi' (*ibid.*).

figure). At the same time bishop and chapter were asked for their
opinion on the question of the *porciones prestimoniales* in the parish
churches: could these continue to be enjoyed without damaging
pastoral consequences being incurred?

The intention was that, armed with the commissioners' findings,
Gil would finally settle the issue – unless the parties were able to reach
an agreement sooner, which in the event bishop and chapter did
achieve on 30 April 1247 – presumably on the basis of evidence
assembled by the second *inquisitio*. The episcopal *mensa* was formally
endowed with an annual income of 5000 *aurei* (comprising 2700m.
from 'cellaria ville et possessiones alie[1] . . . cum cathedratico' and
2300m. from *prestimonia* of the bishop's choosing). To each canon
was assigned 50 maravedís 'in prestimoniis seu portionibus prestimonialibus'. This was 30 maravedís less than in Gil's provisional
assignment, and the same reduction was made in the allowances to
the dignitaries: 370 to the dean, 270 to each of the archdeacons, 220
to the cantor and treasurer, 170 to the *magister scolarum*. These sums
(which excluded the *vestiarium* and *distributiones cotidianas*) represented
the total values which were to be achieved by the award to each, as
necessary, of *supplementum*. What remained after these supplementary
payments had been made was reserved to the bishop's discretion (*ad
gratificationem*), to be assigned by him 'infra tempus a iure statutum'.
Bishop and chapter were agreed that no obligation of residence should
attach to those deserving, literate and useful individuals who were to
benefit thus from episcopal favour, but this point alone Cardinal Gil
declined to confirm: the literate would have to content themselves
with the resources of Segovia, and make themselves useful there. It
was further agreed that the bishop should retain rents worth 400
maravedís from this residue as recompense for the loss of those –
assigned presumably to individual dignitaries[2] – which he had
formerly controlled; and also that those rents reserved *ad gratificationem* should provide a reserve fund to protect bishop and chapter
against the effects of inflation. Finally, bishop and chapter recorded in
a nicely weighed neutral phrase their opinion that their income from
the parishes should be left intact, unless the clergy would greatly
suffer thereby. The decision regarding the conflicting interests of
cathedral and diocese was left for the cardinal to make, and those of
the latter were not reflected in his confirmation of the settlement of
bishop and chapter, approving all but one of its clauses and dated
Lyons 14 September 1247.[3]

1. 'quorum nomina in alia cedula sub sigillis nostris vobis mittimus interclusa':
ACS, doc. 31 (bishop and chapter to Cardinal Gil, 30 Apr. 1247; text transcribed in
ACS, doc. 36).
    2. See below.
    3. 'Alia vero prestimonia que remanent censuimus donationi et gratificationi
episcopi reservanda, de quibus infra tempus a iure statutum gratificari valeat et bene
meritos *tam extravagantes quam mansionarios socios* honorare et litteratas ac utiles

Before then, on 1 June 1247 – a date which suggests that they regarded the cardinal's agreement as a foregone conclusion – bishop and chapter had settled the details and recorded their agreement in a document listing the specific revenues assigned to each of the seven dignitaries, twenty-three full canons, five half-canons with full portions, thirteen half-canons with half-portions, seven full portionaries and nineteen half-portionaries.[1] Their total agreed income was to be 3865 maravedìs, to achieve which – as the preamble to the list describes – the bishop had disbursed rents worth 1680m. from the fund *ad gratificationem*. So, although some of the dignitaries were found to have been over-endowed in terms of the recent (and still provisional) award,[2] the average amount by which, in Cardinal Gil's view, each beneficiary was *under*-endowed was as much as 43.5 per cent.[3] This striking revelation would appear to justify the capitular grievances. No less remarkable is the fact that the bishop's receipts

---

personas dum tamen ecclesia patrocinium in suis necessitatibus possit reddere obligatos. Insuper de prestimoniis ad gratificationem deputatis quadringentos morabitinos liceat episcopo retinere in recompensationem domorum et villarum quas iuxta consuetudinem Segobiensis ecclesie diucius observatam sibi licuit usque ad hec tempora in prestimoniis sociis ecclesie et aliis assignare quousque ad mensam redeant casu quolibet contingente. . . . Statuimus insuper quod si aliqua vel aliquid de prestimoniis tam mense episcopi quam provisioni personarum et canonicorum deputatis minuatur enormiter vel ad nichilum penitus redigatur, de prestimoniis gratificationi deputatis debeat resarciri. De portionibus autem quas prestimoniales iuxta consuetudinem nuncupamus super quibus vestra paternitas nos requirere dignum duxit an remanere eas expediat vel extingui, respondemus plurimum utilitati ecclesie expedire ut remanere debeant que remanere possunt sine grandi gravamine clericorum. Alioquin non leve in earum remotione pateretur ecclesia detrimentum': ACS, doc. 36 (the words in italics are those not confirmed by Cardinal Gil).

1. ACS, doc. 17; ed. González, 'La Extremadura castellana', pp. 403–15.

2. No *supplementum* was paid to the dean or to the archdeacons of Segovia, Sepúlveda and Cuéllar. *Cf.* González, 'La Extremadura castellana', pp. 395–7, whose calculations are confused by his conflation of the rents assigned to the archdeaconry of Cuéllar and those assigned to Nicolas archdeacon of Cuéllar *in propria persona* by papal provision. Innocent IV had awarded Nicolás the revenues of his predecessor Gutierre at Tres Casas, Escobar (de Rio Milanos), Eglesias Albas, Modua, Buhones [Buforico in papal register], Cuevas de Provanco, Binbibre, Moral ('cum domibus que idem archidiaconus ibi prope consuevit habere'), La Nava, S. Trinidat (Coca), Oter de Rebollo, S. María de las Vegas, S. Juannes de Pedraza, and 'quindecim morabitini annuatim in portatico et omnia prestimonia seu beneficia que idem archidiaconus G. habebat in civitate Segobiensi et diocesi sive in portatico sive alibi', in the belief that they were worth 50 marks of silver. But – doubtless in the course of the second *inquisitio* – their value was found to be not more than 40 marks [268m. 14s. according to the 1247 valuation]. The bishop was accordingly instructed to assign further revenue to make up the difference, and specified those of S. Pedro del Val, S. Salvador de Maderuelo, S. Salvador de Fuentidueña, S. Estevan de Sepúlveda, Aldea de Estevan Yuannes, Sancho Fruela, Val de Avellano, Vaziaodres [valued at 85m. 14s. in 1247] 'et quedam alia'; the settlement was recorded by Cardinal Gil and received papal approval in June 1247: Reg. Vat. 21, fo. 408^{r-v} (*Les Registres d' Innocent IV (1243–54)*, ed. E. Berger (Paris, 1881–1921), no. 2863). *Cf.* Gonzalez, p. 415. Nicolás was a man of substance and possessed his own seal: A. Guglieri Navarro, *Catálogo de sellos de la Colección de Sigilografía del Archivo Histórico Nacional*, ii (Madrid, 1974), 609.

3. No account is taken here of the archdeacon of Cuéllar's papal provision.

greatly exceeded the total of those enjoyed by the seventy-four
members of the chapter. Moreover, the bishop's fund stood to gain
at the demise or resignation of those fortunate few who had been
found to be better provided for than they deserved.[1]

The interest of this document is considerable, providing as it does
quantifiable evidence relating to a subject and period long bedevilled
by general theories. But it has its shortcomings: it is a Domesday
without the *terre regis*. The bishop's rents (those of the *alia cedula*) are
not listed; nor those of the reserve fund (*ad gratificationem*); nor those
retained for communal purposes (*de refitor*). No text of the *inquisitio et
extimatio* by the abbot of Sotos Albos and the two archdeacons – upon
which the June distribution must have been based – is known to be
extant at Segovia.

The gaps in the Segovia evidence can, however, be made good
from the Segovia manuscript acquired by the British Museum from
Bossange and Company of Paris in 1841, and now BL MS Egerton
910. Possibly identifiable with the 'quaderno de 4°' of the cathedral
archive to which Colmenares referred in his working notes, this
manuscript contains the text of the lost *inquisitio* – written up between
1258 and 1265, it would seem, from a copy made slightly prior to
June 1247. Its interest and importance to historians and topographers
were obscured by the summary description provided in the nineteenth
century by Pascual de Gayangos.[2] An edition and description have
been printed elsewhere, together with some estimate of its value as a
means of discovering 'lost' villages and of calculating the agricultural
value of the region in the mid-thirteenth century.[3]

The bishop's property is listed first: (i) 'ville et cellaria et possessiones' to the value of 2700m. both *ultra serram* and *citra serram*, in
the outright ownership of the episcopal *mensa*[4] and thus distinguished
from (ii) the rents of 2300m. newly assigned to him in the archdeaconry of Segovia and the *archipresbiteratus* of Sepúlveda, Pedraza,
Frexno, Maderuelo, Cuéllar, Fuentidueña, Coca and Iscar. There
follow lists of (iii) 'prestimonia . . . cum annexis personatibus et cum
porcionibus prestimonialibus' (generally 30 per cent of the tithe
revenue of the parishes specified) assigned to members of the chapter
in 1247; (iv) the revenue from certain *prestimonia*, tithes, 'tercias

---

1. 'Quicquid autem persone, canonici seu socii tenent vel tenuerint in prestimoniis
seu portionibus ultra summas iuxta provisionem domini Egidii cardinalis superius
pretaxatas integrationi mense episcopalis vel gratificationi cum vacaverit totum
cedat': ACS, doc. 36.

2. *Catalogue of the Manuscripts in the Spanish Language in the British Museum* (London,
1875), i. 363.

3. P. A. Linehan, 'A Survey of the Diocese of Segovia (1246–7)', *Revista Española
de Teologia*, xli (1981).

4. 'Alia vero que per industriam vel diligenciam domini episcopi fuerunt vel
fuerint acquisita ordinationi eiusdem episcopi sunt commissa' (fo. 4ᵛ), in addition to
the rest, and were left to his free disposal. *Cf.* the similar wording of the Ávila
ordinance (July 1250), ed. González, 'La Extremadura castellana', pp. 416–17.

solidorum' and *redecime*[1] annexed to the dignities; (v) 'porciones prestimoniales' comprising an additional charge of (generally) 16·66 per cent on the tithe revenue of certain parishes: the inflation-proof income which bishop and chapter were particularly anxious to retain;[2] (vi) *prestimonia* reserved *gratificationi episcopi* for distribution amongst the *socii* of the church; (vii) *prestamos de refitor* (= *refectorium*) by which the communal purposes of the church – *vestiario, missada, matinada, vesperada, huebra* (building and repairs) – were funded; and (viii) those associated with the anniversaries for the parents of Bishop Gonzalo II (d. 1211).

The total value of iii–vi is calculated by the compiler (fos. 12ᵛ, 15ᵛ) at 4855m. 6s. 3d. But of this sum only 3600m. was in fact distributed, the remainder (some 1250m.) apparently being retained by the bishop rather than being referred, as had been stipulated, to Cardinal Gil's discretion: more than adequate compensation for the traditionally episcopal rents worth 400m. which had been transferred to others in June 1247.[3] As to the seventy-four members of the chapter to whom assignments were made, only three were significantly over-endowed, and therefore permitted to retain a life interest in their surplus income: the archdeacon of Segovia (by 75m.); Pedro Ferrández, canon (by 32m.); and Petrus Gaetanus (by 16½m.)[4] All the indications are that, by achieving the reduction of the canons' portion from 80m. to 50m., by deploying arguments of general economic recession, and otherwise, the bishop had succeeded in retaining effective control of the economy of the church of Segovia. Provision for the canons and lesser clergy, though not for the dignitaries, was markedly less generous than that accorded by Cardinal Gil to those of Salamanca two years earlier.[5]

1. Linehan, 'A Survey'.

2. Above, p. 490, n. 3. In only three places was the value of these *porciones* expressed in fixed money terms; whence Bishop Bernardo's anxiety (Aug. 1247) regarding laymen who, abandoning their own parish churches, 'ad alienas accedant ecclesias divina officia inibi audituri': Reg. Vat. 21, fo. 454ʳ (Berger, no. 3186).

3. 'in recompensationem domorum et villarum que iuxta consuetudinem Segobiensis ecclesie diucius observatam sibi licuit usque ad hec tempora in prestimoniis sociis ecclesie et aliis assignare': ACS, doc. 36.

4. Petrus Gaetanus (Pietro Caetani, chaplain of the cardinal bishop of Alba, Pietro da Collemezzo) had received from the dean and chapter of Segovia a promise of rents worth eight marks 'bonorum novorum et legalium sterlingorum' payable annually to Nicolas of Cuéllar 'vel alio certo nuncio si maluerit', doubtless for services rendered. The agreement, dated 20 June 1246, was sealed by Bishop Bernardo and Cardinal Gil: A. Paravicini Bagliani, *Cardinali di curia e 'familiae' cardinalizie dal 1227 al 1254*, i (Padua, 1972), 183; Reg. Vat. 22, fo. 281ᵛ (Berger, no. 6629). His rents of 66½m. represent a less favourable rate of exchange than that secured by the archdeacon of Cuéllar (above, p. 491, n. 2). He was also in the pay of the archbishop of Toledo: Linehan, *Spanish Church*, 286; AC Toledo, O.9.B.2.73.

5. *Cf.* González, 'La Extremadura castellana', pp. 398-9, for comparative data. The poverty of the church of Coria in Extremadura is revealed in the constitutions of 1315 which assigned two-thirds of the goods of the *communis mensa* to the bishop: publ. J. L. Martín Martín, 'Las constituciones de la iglesia de Coria de 1315', *Miscelánea Cacereña* (Cáceres, 1980), pp. 68-69, 76.

As between bishop and chapter, it is unlikely that proceedings before the commissioners were altogether cordial. Both parties, doubtless, had designs on particular *prestimonia*, reflected in the incomplete state of the June 1247 distribution and in references therein to 'controversie et questiones'.[1] Which these *prestimonia* were, however, how such disputes were resolved, and to what extent the distribution reflected existing arrangements,[2] are questions to which the evidence provides no certain answers. All that is clear is that the economic burden of supporting bishop and chapter was not distributed equally in each archdeaconry or rural deanery: in Fuentidueña, for example, the bishop took the lion's share; in Pedraza the chapter; and reference to the earliest detailed map available[3] reveals that within these territorial divisions no concentration of interests was attempted – or, if attempted, was successful. The conjoint burden which bishop and chapter represented for the parishes is, however, unequivocally stated on fo. 32ᵛ of MS Egerton 910. There an anonymous calculator – not all of whose computations tally with the evidence of the survey – states that the clergy of the 544 parish churches listed enjoyed a total tithe revenue (*i.e.* the third part of the tithe) of 8942m. – an average annual income of less than 16½ maravedís.[4] On this evidence the economic supremacy of bishop and chapter can be readily appreciated.

The survey of diocesan resources, and the use made of it, were only two elements of Cardinal Gil's strategy. On the day on which he ratified the agreement of bishop and chapter, 14 September 1247, he sent them two more communications regarding other matters. The first of these, though it had pastoral consequences, touched their pockets; the second was directed squarely at their consciences. Firstly, the cardinal confirmed Bishop Gonzalo II's constitution of October 1204, the subject matter of which provides further evidence of pre-Lateran IV attempts by that beleagured prelate to regulate the affairs of his church.[5] The recently completed survey had revealed

1. González, 403; Linehan, 'A Survey'.
2. *Cf.* González, p. 392.
3. That of T. López Vargas Machuca (Madrid, 1773).
4. Linehan, 'A Survey'. *Cf.* G. Constable, *Monastic Tithes from their Origins to the Twelfth Century* (Cambridge, 1964), pp. 43–44, 54; R. Bidagor, *La 'iglesia propria' en España. Estudio histórico-canónico* (Rome, 1933), pp. 112–22, 137–40; A. García Sanz, 'Los diezmos del obispado de Segovia del siglo XV al XIX', *Estudios Segovianos*, xxv (1973), 14.
5. ACS, doc. 229. It treated of four matters: (i) its *testamentary provisions* were elaborate. The current year's income of a canon who died between Christmas and All Saints was to be devoted to the payment of any debts outstanding at the time of death, any residue to be divided three ways, between the *refectorium* for capital purposes ('non ad comedendum nec ad dividendum inter canonicos sed ad aliquas possessiones ad opus refectorii emendas'), the poor, and the *capellani ecclesie*. The year's income of a deceased canon who left no debts unpaid was also to be divided three ways, in this case between the *refectorium*, the canon's servants and chaplains (with the ambiguously phrased restriction 'non concubinis nec parentibus nisi sint servientes') and the bishop – unless the canon had bequeathed to the bishop silver, horseflesh or the like, in which case the bishop's share should pass to the

V

that numbers had lapsed from the levels set in 1204: to thirty or thirty-one canons, six portionaries, and hybrid sub-groups – five or six 'integri portionarii et dimidii canonici', thirteen 'dimidii canonici et dimidii portionarii' and nineteen 'dimidii portionarii'. This was doubtless a response to benefice inflation, and it produced an establishment of seventy-five which, while three over strength, was actually maintained at a small saving.[1] Yet although the survey had also shown that funds existed for a return to, or beyond, the 1204 levels, Gil Torres did not press this. His policy was to hold numbers at a level at which they could certainly be afforded, and to allow himself to be guided in this by the interested parties themselves. Thus, the one clause of the agreement of bishop and chapter which he declined to confirm was that which would have enabled the bishop to devote surplus funds to the support of non-residents, and when in August 1250 he received the view of bishop and chapter on the matter he readily accepted it, fixing the numbers of resident canons, prebendaries and minor prebendaries at forty, ten and twenty respectively, and leaving the question of the future of the *canonici extravagantes* to be resolved by them.[2]

Cardinal Gil appears no more masterful in his other rather lapidary communication of 14 September 1247. Whether or not this should be described as a set of statutes or constitutions (since what it comprised was no more than a series of responses to issues raised by the bishop and chapter), the general effect was certainly more bitty and less comprehensive than the constitutions which he issued for the other Castilian churches. It is perhaps hardly surprising that no trace of them is to be found either in the archive of Segovia Cathedral or in the papal registers. Colmenares does not mention them. But their text is

---

canon's servants and chaplains. 'Et hec omnia suprascripta secundum arbitrium episcopi fiant'; (ii) the annual value of *vestiarium* of each resident canon was fixed at 20m., with a sliding scale of penalties for unauthorized absence; (iii) in the year after the death of a canon the income of his prebend was to be distributed amongst the *capellani* attending his grave and choir daily throughout the year; (iv) the numbers of resident canons, resident portionaries, and *canonici extravagantes* were fixed at 40, 20 and 12 respectively. Expectancies were not to be conceded 'nisi per suspensionem officii et beneficii vel excommunicationem domini pape vel eius precepto in virtute obedientie'. Cardinal Gil confirmed all of these provisions, with the single exception of that clause which had sought to bind future bishops to observe the statute *de numero canonicorum* ('utpote iuri et eorum [decani et capitulorum] iuramento contraria').

1. The cost in 1247 of an establishment as envisaged in 1204, even without the twelve *canonici extravagantes* would have been 2500m. The actual cost was 2487½m.

2. Above, p. 490, n. 3. 'Numerum vero canoniarum extravagantium tollendum omnino, augendum vel minuendum et ipsarum collationem omnino vestre ordinationi committimus, iuramento quod olim super hac re prestitum fuisse dicitur non obstante'; ACS, doc. 224 (10 Aug. 1250). The bishop and chapter's representative in discussions with the cardinal had been Nicolás of Cuéllar. (The matter was resolved in Oct. 1258 when the chapter set the number of *canonici extravagantes* at fifteen: MS Egerton 910, fo. 26ᵛ; H. Sanz y Sanz, 'Don Raimundo de Losana', *Estudios Segovianos*, xviii (1966), 53.)

preserved in the British Library MS, roughly copied at the end. Their casual survival there (without the illuminated capitals which adorn the earlier folios) is appropriate, reflecting perhaps the minor importance attached to the matters of which they treat, in comparison with the economic issues which loomed so large. They do nevertheless provide a view of life at Segovia which those other documents do not, nor were intended to, afford.

Gil's priority was to recapitulate his beneficial strategy before passing to the theme of capitular discipline. The church of Segovia seems to have been markedly more rustic-mannered than the other Castilian cathedrals: nowhere else did it prove necessary to banish the pigs whose claustral grazing was deterring the faithful from attendance at divine service. Less surprising, in view of events of the previous forty years, is the revelation that women and *conspiratores* as well as pigs lurked there. Duties were neglected and the proper ecclesiastical vestments not worn.[1] There was the risk of alienation of the church's property to the canons' families. The bishop interfered in matters which were the province of the dean and archdeacons. Under-age boys not in orders – *clericelli* – were introduced into the choir without authority. The affairs of the diocese receive some attention though less than those of the cathedral, in the form of the concluding diatribe against the archpriests. The list of charges against them is formidable; they grant letters of commendation to clerics of other dioceses; they take cognizance of marriage cases, uncanonically 'maxime cum periciam iuris non habeant que requiritur in causis matrimonialibus decidendis';[2] they usurp episcopal and archidiaconal rights in matters of benefices and presentation thereto; they admit candidates for ordination without reference to the archdeacons; they tolerate *clerici concubinarii* and collude at their offences; they are

1. Appendix, below. At Burgos cathedral pigs had wings: in Nov. 1463 the *campanero* was reported to be keeping his animals in the church tower – 'e había grand suçiedad' (N. López Martínez, 'Don Luis de Acuña, el cabildo de Burgos y la reforma (1456–1495)', *Burgense*, ii (1961), 292, n. 437); while at Jaén, in the south, dogs were the problem, necessitating the establishment of a *perrero*, an officer charged with the task of preventing *benefiçiados* bringing them in and removing the traces of those which succeeded in eluding him (J. Rodríguez Molina, 'Estatutos de la catedral de Jaén de 1368. Recopilación de 1478', *Boletín del Instituto de Estudios Giennenses*, xxi, no. 85–86 (1975), 53, 119–20). The regulation regarding 'decent capes' for Segovia dignitaries was totally disregarded. On 4 Aug. 1250 Cardinal Gil made their provision a charge on the heirs and beneficiaries of members of the chapter who had failed to equip themselves (ACS, doc. 265). This was evidently the origin of the Seville requirement, established by Archbishop Raimundo in 1261, and mistakenly described by Costa y Belda, 'Las constituciones', p. 206, as 'unknown in the Castilian constitutions': *ibid.* p. 228, lines 304–6.

2. *Cf.* A. Hamilton Thompson, 'Diocesan Organization in the Middle Ages: Archdeacons and Rural Deans', *Proc. Brit. Academy* (1943), p. 188 [Treves, 1310]; J. Sánchez Herrero, *Concilios provinciales y sínodos toledanos de los siglos XIV y XV* (La Laguna, 1976), 176 [Toledo, 1323]; F. J. Fernández Conde, *D. Gutierre de Toledo, obispo de Oviedo (1377–1389). Reforma eclesiástica de la Asturias bajomedieval* (Oviedo, 1978), p. 183 [Oviedo, 1382].

V

extortionate. So apparently circumstantial an account of the arch-priests' failings might suggest that Gil Torres had probed deeply into their case – except that he had denounced the archpriests of Salamanca in almost identical terms two years before, and was similarly to excoriate those of Ávila three years later.[1] The charge-sheet was a stereotype. Although the archpriests of Segovia were probably no better than they ought to have been, on this evidence it cannot be proved that they were certainly any worse.

In his constitutions for Salamanca and Ávila the cardinal followed the denunciation of the archpriests with an injunction to the bishop and archdeacons to take vigorous and regular action to root out concubinage.[2] There is no such passage in the Segovia 'constitutions' which, as we have them, end at this point. The cardinal, the bishop and the chapter appear to have been willing to accept the *status quo* in this respect (as Bishop Giraldo appears to have been thirty years before).[3] And in general the perfunctory review of the affairs of the church and diocese of Segovia compares very unfavourably with Gil's constitutions for Salamanca, Ávila, Burgos and Calahorra. There is, for example, no provision made for studious canons.[4] The overall impression is of a church little concerned with the affairs of the diocese, except in their financial aspects, and of a cardinal as little inclined to force the issue.

There was, however, another side to cathedral life. Although the cloister may have had the aspect of a farmyard, nearby was the refectory, and there a measure of charity was dispensed to laymen as well as to canons. In November 1258 Bishop Raimundo, Bernardo's successor but one, regulated the scale of daily payments made to canons and *socii* for attendance at divine service in the cathedral. These constitutions mark the extinguishing of the last vestiges of the *vita communis* there. Formerly the income from the *prestimonia* of Val de Lobingos[5] had been expended on provisions for the common table on the great ecclesiastical feastdays of the year, Easter, Pentecost, the Assumption and Christmas; but now most of it was attached to the fund from which payments were made to canons and others in respect of their attendance at cathedral services. For old times sake,

1. Mansilla, *Iglesia castellano-leonesa*, pp. 328, 355. In the 1180s the clergy of Alba (Salamanca) had claimed to be entitled to choose their own archpriests 'de suo capitulo' without reference to the bishop: *Documentos de Salamanca*, ed. Martín Martín, no. 95.

2. *Ibid.* pp. 329, 354, where the discipline of annual synods is assumed.

3. Above. p. 483.

4. *Cf.* Mansilla, pp. 327 (Salamanca), 353 (Ávila), 362 (Burgos), 376 (Calahorra-La Calzada).

5. MS Egerton 910, fo. 20ᵛ. The *prestimonia* are identified as the five grouped together at fo. 17ʳ, from Sant Yuanes (Las Fuentes) to Sant Peydro dela Defesa, which realized 78m. To these Raimundo added 'medietatem reddituum fabrice ecclesie nostre assignatorum qui secundum taxacionem eiusdem ecclesie sunt in numero cxxx morabitinorum positi' (ed. Linehan, 'A Survey').

however, and in order to preserve the memory of a relationship which bishop and chapter fondly chose to remember as having been a cordial one, the tradition was kept alive. Once a year, at Easter, bishop and chapter were to eat together.[1] On the other three feasts, the meals were henceforth to be consumed by the chaplains of the church and forty paupers, the former receiving payment for the privilege of playing host at a good but not excessive repast of pork and beef done in different ways.[2] The symbolism of the poor eating at the bishop's table, at his behest and in his absence, is striking. But the practical benefit is not to be denied, however small the numbers involved. In 1258, after a run of bad harvests and a period of sharply rising prices, 120 hot dinners counted for something.[3]

The year 1258 also witnessed the reaction of the Castilian Church generally to the burden of royal taxation for the reconquest of Andalucia. Corporate loyalty to the crown wavered temporarily. The diocese of Segovia had borne this burden with the rest, notably in the form of the *tercias* appropriated by Fernando III and Alfonso X.[4] But Bishop Raimundo had fared better than many of his episcopal colleagues, and although his palace collapsed in that year, with him and the king inside, both emerged unscathed, Raimundo soon to pursue his ecclesiastical career as archbishop of Seville.[5] He had already profited from the reconquest of Seville, and some of his profits passed to the chapter of Segovia. *La vesperada* – the fund from which those attending vespers were rewarded – was augmented by the episcopal revenue from the capitation tax on the Jews of Sepúlveda and Cuéllar, and by the rents of part of the property which he had received in the *repartimiento* of Seville: a nice example of the new frontier redressing the balance of the old.[6] In other ways too, Raimundo – very much a king's man, confessor to Fernando III and confidant of Alfonso X –

1. 'Verum ne supradictis prandiis memoria penitus extinguatur in quibus paternalis affectio erga filios et filialis devocio erga patrem videbatur per caritatis insignia mutue designari. . . .' *Ibid.* fos. 22ᵛ–23ʳ. *Cf.* Colmenares, *Historia*, p. 401.
2. 'Ne vero ebdomadarius et dispensator ac capellani predicti gule inservitores pocius videantur quam participes beneficii Jhesu Christi in preparandis sibi cibariis hunc modum duximus observandum ut ex porcinis arietinis seu vaccinis due genere carnium preparentur, unum duobus modis, reliquum uno modo.' Annual expenditure of 9m. was authorized for this, and of 19m. for the bishop and chapter eating elsewhere: fo. 23ʳ⁻ᵛ.
3. Colmenares, *Historia*, pp. 397–9. *Cf.* Linehan, *Spanish Church*, pp. 162–5.
4. Linehan, *op. cit.* pp. 111 ff.
5. *Ibid.* p. 163; J. Alonso Morgado, *Prelados sevillanos* (Seville, 1904), pp. 252–72; A. Ballesteros y Beretta, 'Don Remondo de Losana, obispo de Segovia', *Correo Erudito*, i (1940–1), 313–18.
6. 'Horum autem denariorum redditus quos ad vesperos distribuendos decrevimus in hiis locis specialiter assignamus, videlicet in possessionibus in Ispalensi territorio constitutis, in Axaraf, in Turre de AvenZophar prope Gadiambar cui loco illustrissimus rex Alfonsus felicissime recordationis quondam regis Fernandi filius nomen imposuit Segoviola, quarum possessionum medietatem nos supradictus episcopus Segobiensis ecclesie donavimus, assignamus sexaginta morabitinos': MS Egerton 910, fo. 22ᵛ. *Cf.* J. González, *Repartimiento de Sevilla* (Madrid, 1951), ii. 309, 314, 315–16; Colmenares, *Historia*, p. 401.

V

was able to ease the way for Segovians, promoting the interest of individuals in the royal service and securing exemption of his cathedral clergy from payment of royal tribute.[1] The latter, in turn, acknowledged the 'many and immense benefits' which they had received from him.[2]

Episcopal-capitular concord on this scale, and the replacement of 'occasio murmurandi adversus patremfamilias' by expressions of 'paternalis affectio erga filios et filialis devocio erga patrem'[3] might suggest that one at least of Cardinal Gil's objectives had been achieved. But the achievement was fragile and was to prove all too temporary. In different hands the bishop's formidable powers, as confirmed by the cardinal,[4] would wreak fresh havoc. In July 1259, on Raimundo's translation to the see of Seville, the election of Fr Martín O.P. ushered in a period of renewed conflict.[5] It is appropriate that it should have been a Dominican whose arrival occasioned this turn of events, for in a period of rising prices the economic consequences of the new orders were more than ever bitterly resented by the ecclesiastical establishment.[6] Faction and conspiracy again prospered and on Martín's death dean and chapter, made wiser (so they said) by recent experience, entered into a solemn compact, to which in perpetuity all canons and *socii* were to be obliged to subscribe, against future bishops, hitting them where it most hurt – in the pocket.[7]

1. Colmenares, pp. 398–9; Ballesteros, 'Don Remondo de Losana'.
2. 'A cuius benignitate nos decanus et capitulum profitemur multa et inmensa beneficia recepisse': MS Egerton 910, fo. 21ᵛ.
3. See above p. 489, n. 3; p. 498, n. 1.
4. To cite but one example, in 1258 Bishop Raimundo assigned the *prestimonia* of Arconada de Yuso to the archpriest of Segovia. Eleven years earlier this had been associated with the archdeaconry of Segovia: MS Egerton 910, fos. 9ʳ, 20ᵛ.
5. AC Toledo, X.2.B.2.1 (a).
6. Between 1247 and 1258 – a decade of severe inflation and widespread hardship (Linehan, *Spanish Church*, pp. 162–3) – the money values attached to Segovia *prestimonia* remained unchanged: MS Egerton 910, fos. 17ʳ, 24ʳ (above, p. 497 n. 5). T. F. Ruiz has noted the sharp decline in activity of the cathedral chapter of Burgos in land transactions there (67·7 per cent of the total recorded, 1200–49; 4·3 per cent, 1250–99): 'The Transformation of the Castilian Municipalities: the Case of Burgos 1248–1350', *Past & Present*, lxxvii (1977), 14–15. Similar conclusions emerge from a study which I am preparing on the conflicts between the cathedral chapter and the Dominicans both at Burgos and elsewhere in the kingdom of Castile-León in the same period. See also R. Gonzálvez, 'El arcediano Joffre de Loaysa y las parroquias urbanas de Toledo en 1300', *Historia Mozárabe* [I Congrego Internacional de Estudios Mozarabes 1975] (Toledo, 1978), p. 145, for Archbishop Gonzalo's substantial reduction of the number of parishes in response to complaints regarding the inadequacy of parochial income. *Cf.* Ruiz, 'Expansion et changement', pp. 552–3.
7. 'Ex preteriti calicis gustacione amara circa ventura in posterum effecti.' The bishop having laid claim to rents assigned by Raimundo to *matutinare*, *missare* and *vesperare*, the dean and chapter – 'consilium et auxilium nobis prebentes ad invicem (note the recurrence of the collaborative adverb: *cf.* above, p. 485 n. 1) facto pariter atque verbo' – decreed 'ut episcopis qui pro tempore fuerint decimarius a canonicis nunquam detur' (25 Jan. 1265): MS Egerton 910, fos. 27ᵛ–28ʳ (ed. Linehan, 'A Survey'). On the following day they elected one of their own number – Fernando Blázquez, canon, *magister scolarum* of Toledo – as next bishop: Colmenares, *Historia*, i. 407–8.

Thus locked in conflict, bishop and chapter turned their backs on the diocese and neglected pastoral matters. For a period of sixty years there is no trace of diocesan synods,[1] and when – at Cuéllar in June 1325 – Bishop Pedro did address himself to the accumulated problems of government and discipline, what he discovered, unsurprisingly, was that things were not as they ought to have been, that 'en nuestro obispado algunas cosas non se husan bien, que son contra derecho e contra razon'.[2] Nothing had changed there, it would seem, in the century that had elapsed since Gonzalo and Giraldo had confronted their belligerent clergy. Illicit *cabildos* and *cofradias* abounded, to the great *perjuyzio* of Pedro 'e de los otros prelados'.[3] Forever engaged in litigation, the clergy conspired to strip the churches of their assets.[4] Tithe-collection provided ample opportunity for abuse and speculation, with which the bishop was especially concerned.[5] On the four great feastdays of the year, while the poor were being regaled in the cathedral refectory, the faithful in the parishes were to be solemnly reminded of their duty to pay the tithe in full.[6] Secular encroachments were not limited to the material sphere however. Laymen and women were reported to be involving themselves in the celebration of divine office.[7] Meanwhile all the familiar evils remained rife – clerical concubinage, pluralism, and the celebration of 'malos casamientos . . . en grado devedado'.[8] Bishop Pedro sought to remedy these various abuses by providing his diocesan clergy with the *Catechism* which he issued on this occasion. Clerical deficiencies – their 'grand sinpliçitat' – are noted. There is much emphasis on the sexual failings of both clergy and laity alike – but the instruction offered is laconic to a degree and, in marked contrast to the very specific material provided in contemporary mendicant manuals for confessors elsewhere, strikingly jejune.[9] The roast pork served to the poor at Pentecost hardly compensated for the spiritual dilapidation recorded in 1325. The pigs rootling around the foundations of the nascent, and costly, cathedral church in 1247[10] provided altogether more appropriate symbolism.

1. J. M. Ochoa Martínez de Soria, 'El Centro de Estudios Medievales del Seminario de Vitoria en el Archivo Catedral de Segovia', *Scriptorium Victoriense*, vi (1959), 332.

2. J-L. Martín, 'El sínodo diocesano de Cuéllar (1325)', *Homenaje a J. Pérez de Urbel*, II (Silos, 1977), 165.

3. *Ibid.*, pp. 161, n. 29 ('conjuraçiones entre si, e mayormente contra su prelado'), 165.

4. '. . . tener pleitos e ser procuradores e abogados en las cosas que non deven': *ibid.* p. 166.

5. *Ibid.* pp. 169 ff.   6. *Ibid.* p. 171.

7. *Ibid.* p. 168.   8. *Ibid.* pp. 164, 168–9, 166.

9. *Ibid.* pp. 146, n. 5 (Professor Martín is preparing an edition of the *Catechism*), 153–4: 'Ay adulterio e inçesto, e es mayor inçesto que adulterio'. *Cf.* the *Tractatus de Sacramentis* of Ramón Despont O.P. bishop of Valencia (d. 1312), ed. J. Sanchis Sivera, 'Para la historia del derecho eclesiástico valentino', *Analecta Sacra Tarraconensia*, x (1934), 123 ff.

10. Consecrated by the papal legate Jean d'Abbeville in July 1228, the cathedral

Wherever he looked Bishop Pedro saw evidence of individuals trespassing upon the rights of others. Cupidity was the besetting sin of Castilian society, and neither bishops nor kings were without guilt.[1] Events in his diocese during the previous century certainly support this view, rather than a Turnerian analysis of a Christian frontier ridding the Segovia hinterland of potentially destructive excess energy. For the churchmen of Segovia, both the acquisitive and the hard-pressed, the celebrated 'safety valve' was no more than what has been described as 'at best a whistle on a peanut roaster'.[2] Their horizons were narrow, and their attention fixed on finite rents and interminable litigation. (Nor, to judge by the incomes assigned to the members of the chapter of Seville, were the rewards and opportunities markedly better on the physical frontier itself.)[3] If those clerics who defended their interests so resolutely against successive bishops were frontiersmen, in the sense of 'combative men who were willing to live dangerously and uncomfortably rather than submit to established hierarchies', the scrabbling for sustenance in which they engaged mark them out as unheroic inhabitants of the Closing Frontier.[4] The clergy of Cuéllar, whose archives have survived in such revealing quantity, were certainly not men unsubmissive to 'established hierarchies'. Indeed much of their energy was spent in despatching proctors and petitions to the court of the most sublime (and distant) of hierarchs, remaining deaf only to directives emanating from that

---

attracted no bull of indulgence until July 1250 (ACS, doc. 199), Bishop Bernardo contenting himself with reissuing three provided by the legate in 1228 (ACS, doc. 177 = docs. 144, 184, 311). In Aug. 1247 he appealed to the diocese for funds since although 'los calonges an hy dado grandes alimonias de lo suyo e la huebra de la eglesia . . . todo non lo cumple' (H. Sanz y Sanz, 'Bosquejo histórico de dos catedrales', *Estudios Segovianos*, xix (1967), 182). Thereafter three more papal indulgences were secured, in Oct. 1257, May 1266 and March 1291 (ACS, docs. 188/189, 186, 195 (= *Les Registres de Nicolas IV (1288–1292)*, ed. E. Langlois (Paris, 1886–1905), no. 4664), and a collection of apparently spurious relics 'de Romania' secured † (Linehan, 'La iglesia de León', p. 31, n. 108). Sanz produces evidence (*loc. cit.* p. 181) that the church was reconsecrated in 1257 'por motivos que hoy por hoy desconocemos': had sacrilege been committed there during the recent stormy period? The presumably problematic financing of the construction of the cathedral has yet to be studied. Note however that there was an 'organista' Magister Martinus on the capitular strength in 1247 (ACS, doc. 17).

1. The former 'poco a poco tiran sus derechos a los clérigos parrochiales e a las fábricas', the latter threatened 'sus derechos a los clerigos': J-L. Martín, 'El sínodo', pp. 155–6.

2. F. J. Turner, *The Frontier in American History* (New York, 1921); *Turner and the Sociology of the Frontier*, ed. R. Hofstadter and S. M. Lipset (New York, 1968), p. 191.

3. The annual capitular income at Seville in 1261 was calculated to be 25,870m. – three and half times that of the chapter of Segovia – but this advantage was not reflected in the incomes assigned to its members – 400m. to the dean, 60m. rising to 100m. 'si escreverint facultates' to a resident canon: sums not significantly greater than those paid at Segovia: Costa y Belda, 'Las constituciones', 220–7. In all 22.7 per cent of capitular income at Seville was assigned to members of the chapter.

4. G. Jackson, *The Making of Medieval Spain* (London, 1972), pp. 36–37 on the subject of 'early medieval Spain' as 'a miniature "wild west"'; A. R. Lewis, 'The Closing of the Medieval Frontier, 1250–1350', *Speculum*, xxxiii (1958), 475–83.

source regarding their own behaviour.[1] Their well organized assemblies were the clerical equivalent of the secular *hermandades* which emerged in these years as counterweight to the excess or deficiencies of royal power, operating within the ecclesiastical eternal triangle with the sole purpose of maintaining their own peculiar institutions.[2]

Yet if political expression was distinctive in the frontier environment, the underlying motives of the clergy of Segovia were scarcely distinguishable from those of the clergy of Rouen or of Lincoln. If these patterns of behaviour be treated, as Burns has treated various expressions of lay control exercised in the kingdom of Valencia, as 'a mark and effect of the frontier', remaining 'in the social and economic structure of the kingdom of Valencia, just as they remained in the structure of the older provinces, as a permanent souvenir of former frontier status', what normative value does the concept of 'frontier religion' eventually have?[3] Of course, a frontier environment does not imply the actual presence of the physical frontier; at Segovia, as elsewhere, the one survived the removal of the other.[4] But are not those features characterized as 'a permanent souvenir of former frontier status' encountered to a greater or lesser degree in every diocese of medieval Europe?

Professor Burns insists that 'each juncture of time and place in Spanish medieval history was so unique that its measure of contact and conflict was qualitatively different from that of conditions a generation before or a province away'.[5] What distinguished Segovia from Valencia was the absence of a Moorish majority, the lack of any sense of Christians living in an alien milieu, or seeking 'to stamp it with a new personality'. This was no Turnerian frontier, serving 'the ambitious, the restricted, the inventive, the acute, the restless, the

---

1. A. Ubieto Arteta, *Colección Diplomática de Cuéllar* (Segovia, 1961), esp. pp. 39–40; B. Velasco Bayón, *Historia de Cuéllar* (Segovia, 1974), pp. 148–50.

2. T. F. Ruiz sees in the *hermandades* of the late-thirteenth and early fourteenth centuries an alliance of the urban oligarchies (*caballeros villanos*) and crown against the landed nobility, and describes the period 1250–1350 in terms of 'une relation triangulaire' between these three parties ('Expansion et changement', pp. 558–9). Ruiz's generalizations depend on evidence from Burgos and will need to be tested elsewhere. The description of the genesis of the crown's allegedly anti-aristocratic policy is unconvincing: in 1252, it is suggested (*ibid.* pp. 556, 557), Alfonso X was both forced to indulge the nobility with large land-grants, and able to undermine their position by means of sumptuary legislation – an analysis accepted by Glick, *Islamic and Christian Spain*, 159. On the *hermandades*, see L. Suárez Fernández, 'Evolución histórica de las hermandades castellanas', *Cuadernos de Historia de España*, xvi (1951), 5–78; Linehan, *Spanish Church*, pp. 165–6; on the 'ecclesiastical triangle', *ibid.* pp. 103.

3. *Crusader Kingdom*, p. 72.

4. At Medinaceli, for example (above, p. 486, n. 3), well after the place had ceased to be on the geographical frontier which the Arab geographers had formerly located there (Glick, *Islamic and Christian Spain*, 59); or at Cuenca where, as late as the 1260s, justified fears were expressed about its exposed position (Linehan, 'The *Gravamina* of the Castilian Church in 1262–1263', *ante*, lxxxv (1970), 749).

5. 'Muslim-Christian Conflict and Contact in Medieval Spain: Context and Methodology', *Thought*, liv (1979), 244.

younger son, the rural rebel, the entrepreneur'. The 'clerical short-comings' evident there were possibly, as has been urged of those at Valencia, little more than 'the faults which shadowed medieval times, exacerbated perhaps . . . by the circumstances of a frontier environment'.[1] However, it is the familiar complex of faults which shadowed medieval times north of the Pyrenees – rather than any frontier-related peculiarity – and their economic dimension in the decades preceding the Black Death, that distinguishes the activities of the clergy of Segovia, for example in the opposition to the Franciscans manifested at Cuéllar in the 1240s.[2] The tithe, as Burns has indicated elsewhere, 'would seem to have been . . . a not unimportant aspect of the history of the medieval frontier',[3] but then, where was it *not* important? What the 'religion of the frontier' amounted to was a dimension of the spirit of self-help which had established and maintained Christian settlement from the very beginning,[4] only rarely challenged by prelates more intent (there as elsewhere) upon preserving their own privileged position than upon making their dioceses conform to the spiritual standards prescribed by distant authority.

Bishop Pedro mentioned the cupidity of kings – something which had been experienced at Segovia more than once, not least in the 1230s, at the hands of a king with a reputation for sanctity. To church-men lower down the line, kings posed a greater threat than the bishops whom the kings controlled. In a frontier area this control was virtually unlimited, and it remained so when with the passage of time the frontier had become hinterland. It was the king who had tamed the region of Segovia in the twelfth century, and established the church there. Canon law had not helped him, and Pedro of Aragón had spoken for all peninsular kings of the period when he had protested to Urban II in 1095 about the activity of meddlesome reforming bishops 'modernis temporibus meis' intent on securing control of his own frontier chapels and on dismantling the proprietary church system in his kingdom. Pedro asked to be relieved of this 'episcopal oppression'. It was 'new and unheard of', and a stab in the back of Christian warriors, 'milites nocte dieque cum gente pagana dimicantes'.

1. *Crusader Kingdom*, pp. 8–9, 111.
2. The complaints were the customary ones, encountered all over Europe, but the clergy's fear for their incomes and the implication of their own pastoral inadequacy are striking. 'Procurant etiam [*scil*. fratres minores] in clericorum ipsorum preiudicium ut laici disponant ultimas voluntates constituendo fratres eosdem testamentorum suorum executores, propter quod parrochiales ecclesie debita iustitia defraudantur. Nec hiis contenti asserunt publice quod in predicando verbum Dei in secularibus ecclesiis ac aliis locis ubi clerici prefati conveniunt sint ecclesiarum ipsarum clericis paratis verbum huiusmodi proponere preferendi' (May 1247): Cuéllar, Archivo Parroquial, doc. 11.q (ed. Ubieto Arteta, *op. cit.* pp. 35–36). To judge by the extensive endorsements (many of them illegible) on the letter, the charges were fiercely contested at the papal curia. *Cf.* p. 493, n. 2 above.
3. 'A Medieval Income Tax: the Tithe in the thirteenth-century Kingdom of Valencia', *Speculum*, xli (1966), 452.
4. *Cf.* Glick, *Islamic and Christian Spain*, p. 89.

Deprived of income from their churches, they would be reduced to mendicancy, and 'milicia . . . absque pecunia exerceri non potest'.[1]

Pedro of Aragón's sense of outrage seems unfeigned. It sprang from the assumptions of pre-Gregorian society which recent research has revealed in greater clarity,[2] and which the conditions of inter-mittent Holy War kept alive in the peninsular kingdoms in the post-Gregorian centuries. Twelfth-century bishops shared these assump-tions. They were the king's natural allies not merely because the king was God's champion, *athleta Christi*, but because by the eclipse of royal authority they stood to suffer even more harshly at the hands of the magnates. They could manipulate the eternal triangle formed by pope, king and themselves. A quadrilateral which included the nobility, even temporarily, was unmanageable in comparison, if not perilous. In 1166 therefore the Castilian bishops threw all their weight behind the child-king Alfonso VIII, appropriating crusading indulgences to the cause and readily allowing the king to determine the limits of ecclesiastical jurisdiction, irrespective of papal decisions to the contrary.[3] They were warriors themselves, muscular bishops not afraid to belabour the faithful with their pastoral staffs – as Rodrigo of Sigüenza, the judge of the Segovia imbroglio, once did, with fatal consequences which earned him a letter of reproof from Innocent III.[4] With such ministers at the helm, the religion of the frontier would be a pale reflection indeed of that envisaged by Innocent III's Council, with the reconquest of souls – in Pierre Chaunu's arresting phrase – destined to lag far behind the movement that the historians can chart and measure, the reconquest of lands.[5]

St John's College, Cambridge

---

1. 'Capellas quoque meas episcopi nostri . . . inquietare impugnando non differunt, que in confinio utriusque terre paganorum et christianorum site sunt, quibus in locis frequencius quam alibi immoror propter assuiditatem belli, quod inter nos atque paganos exercetur': P. Kehr, *Das Papsttum und die Königreiche Navarra und Aragon bis zur Mitte des XII Jahrhunderts* (Berlin, 1929), pp. 55–57.

2. E. Magnou-Nortier, *La société laique et l'église dans la province ecclésiastique de Narbonne (zone cispyrénéenne) de la fin du VIIIe à la fin du XIe siècle* (Toulouse, 1974), pp. 512 ff. *Cf.* P. Bonnassie, *La Catalogne du milieu du Xe à la fin du XIe siècle* (Toulouse, 1975), ii. 550–4.

3. Linehan, 'The Synod of Segovia (1166)', *Bulletin of Medieval Canon Law*, x (1980), pp. 31–44.

4. *Idem, Spanish Church*, p. 240.

5. 'La *Reconquista* s'est historiquement opérée sur des terres non sur des âmes': 'Jansenisme et frontière de catholicité (XVIIe et XVIIIe siècles): à propos du Jansenisme lorrain', *Revue Historique*, ccxxvii (1962), 137. Archbishop Raimundo's provision of funds at Seville for two *magistri*, of theology or law – 'cum Ispalensis ecclesia sit plantula tenera et de novo redata cultui cristiano et indigeat clericis literatis' – exhibits some consciousness of the need to bridge the gap (Costa y Belda, 'Las constituciones', pp. 224–5).

APPENDIX

Statutes of Cardinal Gil Torres for the church of Segovia. Lyons, 14 September 1247.
British Library, MS Egerton 910, fos. 30^v–32^r.

Venerabili in Christo patri et amico karissimo B. dei gratia episcopo, dilectis in Deo decano et capitulo Segobiensibus, Egidius divina paciencia Sanctorum Cosme et Damiani diaconus cardinalis salutem et optatum beatitudinis incrementum. Quoniam petitiones que nobis ex parte vestra fuerint proposite utpote diversas condiciones habentes idem iudicium sortiri minime potuerunt idcirco eas non similibus sed diversis cedulis vobis duximus transmittendas. Ille cause que in subditis continentur tamquam rationabiles iuri, equitati et honestate consone comprobationem prima facie requirebant. Nos igitur utpote divini numinis honorem Segobiensis ecclesie, honestatem domus domini servitorum, reformacionem morum et vite mundiciam continentes eas ampliandas duximus et inposterum servari volumus et mandamus.

Haec sunt peticiones.

⟨1⟩ Volumus et mandamus quod nullus introducatur de novo in Segobiensi ecclesia donec numerositas personarum per integrationem earum faciendam secundum canonicas sanctiones ad statutum in ecclesia vestra numerum reducatur, ita quod integrationi eorum quos nominatim successive per ordinem integrari mandavimus et mandamus per hoc minime derogetur, proviso ut canonia seu portio vacans integra conferatur et integrandi de hiis que vocantur dimidie integrentur,[1] non obstante finali clausula constitutionis tempore bone memorie G. secundi Segobiensis episcopi de consensu capituli sui edite qua canoniarum et porcionum sectionem faciendam decrevit, quam tamquam iuri contrariam et iuramento prestito repugnationem quantum ad hoc merito reprobamus, constitutionem eandem in ceteris capitulis approbando, quam sub sigillo nostro vobis duximus transmittendam.

⟨2⟩ Quod thesaurarius vel qui eius locum tenet thesaurum ecclesie episcopo et capitulo in communi hostendat et de manu ipsorum sub inventario recipiat et teneat, eisdem de ipso redditurus debitam rationem. Ita ut siquid culpa vel negligentia ipsius diminutum fuerit vel deperditum resarcire cogatur.

⟨3⟩ Quod nulla mulier cohabitet canonicis[2] seu sociis ecclesie intra vel extra claustrum, illis dum [fo. 31^r] taxat exceptis in quibus naturale phedus nichil permittit leve[3] crimen suspicari.

---

1. MS: ut canonica seu portio vacans integra conferatur et integrandi de hiis que vocadi (sic) dimidie integretur.
2. MS: canonicus.   3. MS: levi.

⟨4⟩ Quod layci uxorati, vidue vel alie mulieres separatim non habitent infra claustrum.

⟨5⟩ Quod in tonsura, habitu et armis circa personas, presbiteros et alios socios et omnes ecclesie servitores statuta generalis concilii observentur.

⟨6⟩ Quod in choro, capitulo, processione, refectorio, lectionibus, loquicionibus, subscriptionibus et aliis communibus quisque locum sibi teneat deputatum, nichil prerogative alterius seu iuris usurpans.

⟨7⟩ Quod coniuratorum temeritas sine personarum delectu pena debita castigetur.

⟨8⟩ Quod porci intra claustrum nullatenus nutriantur.

⟨9⟩ Quod claustrum nec sorde nec immundicia polluatur, presertim propter quam populus a frequentacione ecclesie maxime in diebus sollempnibus retrahatur.

⟨10⟩ Quod circa coniuratores et conspiratores serventur canonice sanctiones.

⟨11⟩ Quod generales arrendationes rerum capituli non fiant nisi in capitulo generali et ad id comuniter statutis diebus.

⟨12⟩ Quod socii ecclesie pileos, capucia et alia capitum operimenta deponant quando legerint [vel] cantaverint in publico ad hoc deputati, et in hoc ipso domino episcopo reverenter honorem debitum exhibentes.

⟨13⟩ Quod decanus et alii in dignitatibus et personatibus constituti exequantur et impleantur ea ad que tenentur in ecclesia ratione officiorum suorum tam in hiis que sunt honeris quam honoris.

⟨14⟩ Quod quilibet constitutus in dignitate vel personatu teneatur emere decentem capam xericam de xamito vel alio bono panno infra annum. Alioquin duo vel plures socii suspicione carentes deputati ab episcopo et capitulo tantum de redditibus prestimoniorum suorum accipiant unde dicta capa valeat comparari.

⟨15⟩ Quod tres canonici simplices seu portionarii mansionarii de familia episcopi quamdiu fuerint in ipsius comitatu, ipso etiam extra civitatem existente, cotidianas percipiant porciones. Ipso vero episcopo in civitate manente omnes mansionarii de ipsius familia qui presentes fuerint similiter cotidianas porciones recipiant et in ipsis percipiendis et serviciis ecclesie exhibendis aliorum mansionariorum lege utantur.

⟨16⟩ Quod canonicus seu socius de bonis ecclesie non possit relinquere personis infamatis nec de bonis per ecclesiam acquisitis contra iura condere testamentum.

⟨17⟩ [fo. 31ᵛ] Quod sententias quas decanus et archidiaconus in hiis qui ad eorum officium pertinent rite tulerint necnon et processus iudiciorum coram eis habitos episcopus sine cause cognitione ac satisfactione debita nec revocet nec retractet.

⟨18⟩ Quod cum ad cantoris officium spectare dicatur introducere

clericellos in coro, canonicos et alios socios installare, nemini
liceat ipsius officium usurpare, et quod nullus installetur in
stallo quod dicitur super forma nisi sit pubes et in sacris ordinibus
constitutus.

In premissis omnibus exequitioni mandandis unicuique sua
iurisdictio reservetur.

⟨19⟩ Ad reprimendam archipresbiterorum insolenciam superest
aliquid[1] adiungendum de qua gravis et multiplex pestilencia in
perniciem animarum exoritur, ex eo maxime quod ab eis pro
clericis ordinandis presumptione temeraria plerumque littere
commendacicie ad extraneos episcopos conceduntur, per quas
sine licencia episcopi[2] vel eius vicarii seu decani et capituli[3] cum
ecclesiam vacare contingit[4] clerici a non suis episcopis ordi-
nantur. Item cause matrimoniales coram eis tractantur perperam
contra canonicas sanctiones maxime cum periciam iuris non
habeant que requiritur in causis matrimonialibus decidendis.
Temeritate quoque propria parrochiales ecclesias vacantes[5]
conferunt et plerumque commendant necnon in eisdem
assignant pro suo libito porciones sine licencia episcopi vel
archidiaconi.[6] Presentant etiam clericos ordinandos episcopo[7],
inconsultis archidiaconis quibus subsunt, usurpantes sibi per
hoc officium archidiaconi,[8] ecclesias et clericos talliis et exactionibus indebitis gravant et opprimunt supra modum, con-
cubinarios clericos in suis sordibus computrescere permittentes
et eorum interitum premio seu gracia dissimulatione dampnabili
procurantes dum excessus talium tolerant, nec ipsi cum possint
arguunt nec episcopo vel archidiaconis[9] denunciant corrigendos.
Unde contra huius pestilencie corruptelam per antidotum
necessarium quantum industria humana sufficit, ita duximus
obviandum[10] ut quicquid deinceps in matrimonialibus causis, in
presentationibus clericorum ad ordines, in litteris concedendis
ad extraneos episcopos, in clericis ordinandis per dictas litteras[11]
in conferendis ecclesiis seu etiam commendandis, in [fo. 32r][12]
portionibus quibuslibet[13] assignandis vel clericis de beneficio
ad beneficium transferendis absque licencia episcopi vel archidiaconi seu decani et capituli cum ecclesiam vacare contingat[14]

1. aliquid] *om* A.   2. episcopi Abulensis A; Salamantini episcopi S.
3. capituli] canonicorum A.   4. contingit] contigerit A.
5. vacantes] *om* A.   6. vel archidiaconi] *om* A.
7. clericos ordinandos episcopo] episcopo clericos ordinandos A, S.
8. archidiaconi] archidiaconorum A, S.
9. archidiaconis] archidiacono A, S.   10. obviandum] ordinandum A.
11. ordinandis per dictas litteras] ordinatis per litteras predictas A; ordinatis per
dictas litteras S.
12. diff. hand here   13. quibuslibet] cuilibet A.
14. vel archidiaconi seu decani et capituli cum ecclesiam vacare contingat] seu decani
et canonicorum quando sedes vacaverit A; vel archidiaconorum seu decani et
capituli quando sedes vacaverit S.

per eosdem archipresbiteros fuerit attemptatum ipso iure cassum prorsus et irritum habeatur, nullo umquam tempore valiturum, non obstante consuetudine contraria que pocius dicenda est corruptela.[1] Quicquid etiam de talliis et exactionibus per eosdem exactum fuerit vel extortum per diligenciam episcopi vel archidiaconi[2] eidem[3] persone quam leserint duplicatum restituere compellantur, et in hoc nullam eis gratiam[4] permittimus faciendam. Si quis autem ex eis convictus fuerit a quocumque clerico presertim concubinario seu layco simoniace quippiam[5] accepisse sine spe venie cum ignominie nota ab archipresbiteratus officio repellatur. Datum Lugduni xviii kal. octobris anno domini MCCXLVII pontificatus domini pape Innocentii iiii anno quinto.

A = Constitutions of Ávila. Reg. Vat. 22, fo. 13^{r-v}: ed. with minor errors in Mansilla, *Iglesia castellano-leonesa*, 355–6. S = Constitutions of Salamanca. Orig. AC Salamanca, 15/2/51: ed. Riesco Terrero, *Ius Canonicum*, xvii.i, 248–9 (collated with Reg. Vat. 21, fo. 186^{r-v}).

1. consuetudine contraria que pocius dicenda est corruptela] contraria consuetudine que dicenda est pocius corruptela A, S.
2. archidiaconi] archidiaconorum A, S.
3. eidem] ecclesie seu A, S.
4. eis gratiam] *tr* A.
5. quippiam] quidpiam A.

A survey of the Diocese of Segovia
(1246-7)

In May 1841 the British Museum purchased from the Paris firm †
of Bossange and Company the manuscript which is now British
Library, MS Egerton 910. That its original provenance was the capitular library of Segovia Cathedral is indicated by the fact that its
subject matter is concerned exclusively with the affairs of the bishops
and chapter of Segovia in the middle years of the thirteenth century — but it has proved impossible to discover whether it left
Segovia during Mendizabal's *desamortización* of the late 1830s, or
earlier. It is reasonable to assume that, had it been accessible, it
would have been used by Diego de Colmenares for his *Historia de
la insigne ciudad de Segovia y compendio de las historias de Castilla* (Segovia, 1637), and indeed it may have been to this that he
referred in his working notes as 'quaderno de 4' (1). But Colmenares does not mention the survey of the possessions of the bishop
and chapter, which is its most striking feature. Nor was this part
of its contents revealed by Pascual de Gayangos in his published
catalogue of 1875 (2). Thus, a document which, within its limitations,
is of an importance comparable with that of the *repartimientos* of
the period has remained neglected to this day.

The circumstances which occasioned the composition of the survey have been described elsewhere (3) and may be resumed here

(1) Nueva ed. anotada (Segovia, 1969), i. 418 ff., notes 33, 40, 74.
(2) *Catalogue of the Manuscripts in the Spanish Language in the British Museum* (London, 1875), i. 363. The information regarding the acquisition of the MS
is written on the flyleaf. I am grateful to the British Library Board for permission
to publish this material.
(3) D. Mansilla Reoyo, *Iglesia castellano-leonesa y curia romana en los tiempos
del rey San Fernando* (Madrid, 1945), cap. VII; J. González, 'La Extremadura castellana al mediar el siglo XIII', *Hispania*, xxxiv (1974), 394-7; P. Linehan, *La Iglesia
española y el papado en el siglo XIII* (Salamanca, 1975) 236-42; idem, 'Segovia: a
"frontier" diocese in the thirteenth century', *English Historical Review*, xcvi (1981),
481-508.

only briefly. Throughout the 1240s the Castilian cardinal, Gil Torres, devoted himself, at the behest of Pope Innocent IV, to the moral reform of the dioceses of his native country, by means of economic measures which defined the episcopal and capitular *mensae* within the cathedral churches and allotted specified revenue to the dignitaries, canons and other members of the chapters. There is evidence of his activity at Ávila, Burgos, Calahorra-La Calzada, Ciudad Rodrigo, Córdoba, Cuenca, Plasencia and Salamanca, as well as at Segovia. Clearly such operations must have necessitated much preliminary investigation and valuation of resources. Yet hitherto very little of the material thus generated has been brought to light (4).

Since at least the beginning of the century the diocese of Segovia had stood in grave need of reform. There, as elsewhere, the message promulgated at the Lateran Council of 1215 had fallen on deaf ears. The local clergy offered fierce and organised resistance to episcopal attempts to improve their manner of life, notably in the matter of clerical concubinage, and reacted by witholding payment of the tithe and other renders due to the bishop and chapter (5). Bishop and chapter too were at odds regarding the former's control of the income of the *communis mensa* at a time when, in addition to the burden represented by rapid inflation and royal taxation of the churches for the *reconquista*, the cost of building their new cathedral fell heavily upon them (6).

In October 1245 Cardinal Gil specified the value of income which was to be assigned to each member of the chapter of Segovia, provisional upon the findings of a survey of the resources of the *communis mensa* to be undertaken by the dean and the archdeacons of Segovia and Sepúlveda, since it had been represented to him that the rent income of the church had been diminished by the combined effects of *sterilitas possessionum* and *raritas inhabitancium* (7). This 'inquisitio prestimoniorum que in ecclesia vestra vel extra ecclesiam consueverunt conferri' proved insufficient, however, and a second and fuller survey was commissioned from the two archdeacons and the Cistercian abbot of Sotos Albos. By 30 April 1247 the three ecclesiastics had completed their work, for on that day Bishop Bernardo and the chapter reached agreement, on the basis of their findings, regarding the level of revenue to be assigned

---

(4) Cf. A. Ubieto Arteta, 'Un mapa de la diócesis de Calahorra en 1257', *Revista de Archivos, Bibliotecas y Museos*, lx (1954) 375-94 (which contains very little information regarding rental values); González, op. cit. (Segovia and, pp. 416-24, Ávila).

(5) A. García y García, 'Primeros reflejos del Concilio IV Lateranense en Castilla', in I. Vázquez (ed.), *Studia Historico-Ecclesiastica: Festgabe L. G. Spätling O. F. M.* (Rome, 1977) 249-82.

(6) Linehan, *La Iglesia española*, cap. 6; Colmenares, *Historia*, i. 367; Linehan, 'Segovia', 500; H. Sanz y Sanz, 'Bosquejo histórico de dos catedrales', *Estudios Segovianos*, xix (1967) 161-204, esp. p. 182.

(7) A[rchivo de la] C[atedral,] S[egovia], doc. 37, 241.

to each (8). On 14 September Cardinal Gil approved their agreement in all its essentials. The cardinal's letter of confirmation is the first of the documents transcribed in MS Egerton 910 (fos. 1r-3v) (9).

Meanwhile, on 1 June 1247, bishop and chapter had settled most of the details of the agreement whereby specific rents were assigned to each of the 74 members of the chapter. The record survives in the archive of Segovia Cathedral (doc. 17) and has recently been published by Professor Julio González (10). But valuable though this is in identifying the members of the chapter at this date, it does not reveal in full the resources of the *communis mensa* of Segovia. It does not list the *prestimonia* and other properties assigned to the *mensa episcopalis*, worth 5000 maravedís and thus more valuable in total than those acquired by the dignitaries and canons, nor those reserved 'donationi et gratificationi episcopi... de quibus infra tempus a iure statutum gratificari valeat et bene meritos honorare et litteratas ac utiles personas dum tamen ecclesie patrocinium in suis necessitatibus possit reddere obligatos' (11), nor those *prestamos de refitor* retained for the communal purposes of the church. For this information we must turn to the text of the second *inquisitio* in MS Egerton 910.

The bishop's property is listed first: 'ville et cellaria et possessiones' to the value of 2700 maravedís 'ad mensam episcopi pertinentia' both *ultra serram* and *citra serram*, and distinguishable by long usage from the rents of 2300 maravedís newly assigned to him in the archdeaconry of Segovia and the *archipresbiteratus* of Sepúlveda, Pedraza, Frexno, Maderuelo, Cuéllar, Fuentidueña, Coca and Iscar (fos. 4r-6v). It will be observed that the running totals of value provided by the scribe are incorrect in all cases but one (the *archipresbiteratus* of Frexno), but that the grand total stated on fo. 6v ('summa omnium prestimoniorum superius adnotato[rum]') is very nearly the exact sum of all the items listed (2299 mor. 5 sol. 6 den.). The explanation of this discrepancy would seem to be that in adding up the totals for each *archipresbiteratus* the scribe excluded from his calculations those *prestamos* which he knew —and which

---

(8) ACS, doc. 31.
(9) ACS, doc. 36; copy in MS Egerton 910, fos. 1r-3v.
(10) Op. cit., 403-15. González's calculations (pp. 395-7) are confused by his inclusion of the archdeacon of Cuéllar amongst those to whom additional revenue —*supplementum*— was assigned in June 1247, notwithstanding the statement in ACS, doc. 17 'Colarensi archidiacon(o)... nihil contulimus de prestimoniis seu portionibus'. The sums assigned to Nicolás archdeacon of Cuéllar, in accordance with the provision of benefices to him by Innocent IV (Reg. Vat. 21, fo. 408r-v : E. Berger, *Les Registres d'Innocent IV (1243-1254)* (Paris, 1881-1921), no. 2863), were additional to those assigned to the archdeacon of Cuéllar *ex officio*. Nor were the numbers of canons, portionaries etc to whom revenues were assigned in June 1247 those which González uses in his calculations (p. 396), as reference to the text of ACS, doc. 17 shows.
(11) ACS, doc. 36. The background to these events is more fully described in Linehan, 'Segovia', 487-96.

reference to the settlement of 1 June 1247 shows— to have been awarded not to the bishop, as stated here, but to others: Moral, Cuevas de Provanco and Benbinbre (fo. 6r) to Nicolás archdeacon of Cuéllar, and S. Estevan and S. Migael de Cuéllar to 'P. cantor'. Indeed, the sum total of Torre Eglesia (fo. 5r) and these is 356 mor. 7 sol. —almost precisely the amount by which the true total of the figures for the various *archipresbiteratus* (1942 mor. 13 sol. 6 den.) falls short of the figure of 2300 maravedís.

What this suggests is that the text of the survey in MS Egerton 910 was compiled during the final stages of the negotiations prior to the settlement of 1 June 1247. The discrepancies facilitate identification of those *prestimonia* over which bishop and chapter were wrangling. And the wrangling —'controversie et questiones' (fo. 10v)— had not finished either when the survey was written up, for there are other *prestimonia* which the scribe includes in his calculations but which were assigned elsewhere in June: Oter de Cavalleros (fo. 4v) to 'R. decanus', Aldea Nueva and El Collado de Sotos Alvos (fo. 5v) to 'P. Roderici nepos episcopi', and Castiel de Tierra (fo. 5v) to 'Petrus Ferrandi' canon —or indeed by 1 June (12). These four *prestimonia* are valued at 49 mor. 14 sol. 3 den. Taken with the group reckoned to be worth 356 mor. 7 sol., they produce a figure which strongly suggests identification with the 400 maravedís which Cardinal Gil permitted the bishop to recover 'de prestimoniis ad gratificationem deputatis... in recompensationem domorum et villarum que iuxta consuetudinem Segobiensis ecclesie diucius observatam sibi licuit usque ad hec tempora in prestimoniis sociis ecclesie et aliis assignare' (13).

There follow lists of (i) 'prestimonia... cum annexis personatibus et cum porcionibus prestimonialibus' assigned to members of the chapter in June 1247 (fos. 6v-10r); (ii) the revenue from specified *prestimonia*, tithes, 'tercias V solidorum' and *redecime* (14) annexed to the dignities of the church (fo. 10v); (iii) 'porciones prestimoniales', identifiable in the settlement of June 1247 as an additional charge on the tithe income of certain churches, generally a half or a third of the *tercias* (fos. 11r-12v): inflation-proof revenue which, because it maintained its value as that of money declined, bishop and chapter were particularly anxious to retain (15); (iv) *presti-*

---

(12) Thus, 'thesaurarius... In aliis debet habere C et XXXV mr. minus tercia' (González, 405).

(13) ACS, doc. 36. 'Consuetudo Segobiensis ecclesie diucius observata' suggests the existence of established valuations, and this is confirmed by the note in ACS, doc. 17: 'Hec tria prestimonia (Finoiosa, Moliniella, Fuente Rebollo) consueverunt arrendari cum domo Sancte Marie de la Foz pro XXIIII mrs...' (González, 404). Specific *prestimonia vestiarii* had been assigned in 1204 (ibid., 392); the commissioners' main task in 1246-7 may have been to revise the valuations of these and others.

(14) 'Tercias V solidorum' suggests a fixed render, previously commuted for money and thus insensitive to falling money values. For *redecime,* see below, notes 29-30.

(15) 'De portionibus autem quas prestimoniales iuxta consuetudinem nuncupa-

monia reserved *gratificationi episcopi* for distribution amongst the
socii of the church (fos. 12v-15v); (v) *prestamos de refitor* (= *refectorium*), from the income of which funds for the communal purposes of the church, including *vestiario, matinada* and *huebra* (building and repairs) were financed (fos. 17r-19v); and (vi) those associated with the anniversaries for the parents of Bishop Gonzalo II,
d. 1211 (fo. 20r).

At this point the survey ends, though the fact that what follows
it —the episcopal-capitular statutes of October and November 1258
(fos. 20v-27r)— is written in the same hand as fos. 4r-20r, whereas
the capitular ultimatum to the bishop in January 1265 (fos. 27v-28r)
is not (16), indicates that the text as we have it in MS Egerton 910
was copied sometime between 1258 and 1265 from a text prepared
prior to June 1247, and —to judge from the fineness of the calli-
graphy of this part of the manuscript and its illuminated capitals—
that it was intended to serve as a permanent record of a period of
concord which had recently ended (17). The recurrent controversies
between bishop and chapter have been considered elsewhere (18).
Here it must suffice to treat the survey in its own immediate context.

Its interest is twofold. Its topographical value will need to be
judged by students interested in subjecting it to the sort of treatment accorded by Dr Esther Jimeno to the 'Padrón que mandó
hacer Alfonso X de los vezinos de Soria' in 1270 (19). There is
material here for the study of depopulation in late medieval Castile: for example, comparison with the earliest detailed map of the
province of Segovia available to the writer of this article —that
of T. López Vargas Machuca (Madrid, 1773)— reveals as 'lost' by
the later date thirteen of the twenty nine places listed as lying
within the *archipresbiteratus* of Fuentidueña (20).

To the economic historian it is potentially hardly less valuable.
It has recently been said of this period that 'los datos sobre el valor económico de los diezmos son escasos e indirectos' and that

---

mus super quibus vestra paternitas nos requirere dignum duxit an remanere eas
expediat vel extingui, respondemus plurimum utilitati ecclesie expedire ut remanere
debeant que remanere possunt sin grandi gravamine clericorum. Alioquin non leve in
earum remotione pateretur ecclesia detrimentum' : ACS, doc. 36 (bishop and chapter
to Cardinal Gil). In three places only —Torreziella, Coçuelos and El Aldea de Don
Sancho— were these *porciones* fixed money renders (González, 405, 407, 414).

(16) See Appendix II and III. For the statutes of 1 October 1258, see Colmenares,
Historia, i. 400.

(17) The remaining contents of the MS are as follows : fo. 28v, calculations for
the date of Easter; fos. 29r-30r, repetition of fos. 24v-25v ('Esto es de la vesperada');
fos. 30v-32r, Statutes of Cardinal Gil for the church of Segovia, Lyons 14 Sept. 1247
(ed. Linehan, 'Segovia', 505-8); fol. 32v, 'Suma de todos los préstamos' (below).

(18) Linehan, 'Segovia', 499-500.

(19) 'La población de Soria y su término en 1270', in *Boletín de la Academia de
la Historia*, cxlii (1958) 207-74, 365-494.

(20) Cf. González, 344 : 'Con frecuencia en mapas y en autores modernos se con-
sideran despoblados los que nunca han pasado del caserío propio de una finca'.
However, not all the 'lost' settlements in this case were of such modest proportions.

'en ningún caso es posible conocer con exactitud el valor de los ingresos decimales' (21). Yet from the valuations of *préstamos* in this survey (fos. 11r-12r), supplemented by the information in the settlement of 1 June 1247 identifying these sums as fractions of the *tercias*, it should prove possible to calculate the total agricultural value of each place listed.

Three cases in the June settlement in which the values of both 'el préstamo' and 'la ración' (i. e. 'ración prestamera': 'porcio prestimonialis') are stated provide the basis for calculation:

	el préstamo	la ración =	% of tercias
Villivela (Segovia)	18 m.	10 m.	50 %
El Castro (Fuentidueña)	15 m. 4 $^1/_2$ s.	8 $^1/_2$ m.	50 %
Valseca (Segovia)	12 m.	6 m. 10 s.	50 % (22)

In each case 'el préstamo' represents 30 % and 'la ración' 16.66 % of tithe values of 60, 51 and 40 maravedís respectively. And the same relationship is found to obtain in most of 43 instances where the value of the *ración* as a proportion of the tithe value as given in the June settlement can be checked against the valuation of the *préstamo* in the survey (23). (Of course, where the value of the *racion* is less than a half of the *tercias* its relationship to the tithe value is proportionately less than 16.66 %.) In most cases, then, the value of the *préstamo* is that share of the tithe which A. García Sanz has shown to have been represented at a later period by the 'mesa capitular' or 'mesa episcopal': 30 % which, together with the *rediezmos* of the archdeacon and the archpriest or archpriests (2 % and 1 % respectively), made up that third part of the tithe accorded to the bishop in the 'Spanish' system of tripartition between bishop, clergy, and fabric (24). In ten of these 43 cases, however, the value

---

(21) J. L. Martín, 'Diezmos eclesiásticos. Notas sobre la economía de la sede zamorana (s. XII-XIII)', *Actas de las I Jornadas de Metodología Aplicada de las Ciencias Históricas*, II (Santiago de Compostela, 1975), 69, 70 n. 7.

(22) González, 406, 408; Appendix I, below.

(23) Comparison of ACS, doc. 17 and MS Egerton 910 reveals that 19 of the 62 *raciones* listed in the survey were not distributed in 1247, and that the June settlement contains mention of nine more not listed in the survey: Ienego Munnoz, S. Johann de Baguilafuente, Coçuelos, Valseca, Sotosalvos, S. Johann de Moiados, Carrascal, S. Maria de Moiados, El Aldea de Don Sancho.

(24) A. García Sanz, 'Los diezmos del obispado de Segovia del siglo xv al xix', *Estudios Segovianos*, xxv (1973), 14. Cf. Giles Constable, *Monastic Tithes from their Origins to the Twelfth Century* (Cambridge, 1964) 43-4, 54; M. L. Guadalupe, 'Relaciones entre Derecho canónico y secular sobre diezmos en Castilla', in S. Kuttner and K. Pennington (eds.), *Proceedings of the Fifth International Congress of Medieval Canon Law* (Città del Vaticano, 1980) 510 ff.; Martín, 'Diezmos', 76.

of the préstamo is either more or less than 30 % (25), so that although it is possible to calculate the estimated agricultural value of many particular parishes from the evidence of the survey, the total agricultural value of the whole diocese cannot be discovered by this means. There is, moreover, the further objection that the total of 542 listed in the survey does not necessarily include all the parishes of the diocese (26). Additional allowance may need to be made for an unknown number of parishes not included in the survey since they provided bishop and chapter with no revenue, because either their rents had been the subject of royal grants in the past (27), or their tithes were in monastic or other possession in 1246-7 (28).

The existence of this uncertainty also hampers any attempt to use the figures given in the survey for *rediezmo* (fo. 10v) as a means

(25)

	tithe	préstamo	%
Segovia			
Migael Hannez	90 m.	$22 \frac{1}{2} + 11$ m.	36.6
Carvonero	65 m. 6 s.	?	—
Sepúlveda			
Bociguiellas	43 m. 3 s.	16 m. 3 s.	37.5
Oter de Rebollo	37 m.	$31 \frac{1}{2}$ m.	117.5 (!)
Pradana	90 m.	19 m. 12 s.	22.2
Maderuelo			
Quintana Cidiello	156 m.	54 m.	34.6
Val de Vernes	64 m.	28 m. 12 s.	45
Fuentideña			
Torre Adrada	99 m.	26 m. $1 \frac{1}{2}$ s.	26.4
Fuentelolmo	90 m.	32 m. 6 s.	36
El Bivar	54 m.	24 m. $4 \frac{1}{2}$ s.	45

(26) The 542 listed are distributed thus :

archidiaconatus/ *archipresbiteratus*	i	ii	iii	iv	v	totals
Segovia	17	50	35	105	6	213
Sepúlveda	12	41	29	3	2	87
Pedraza	6	17	5	2	—	30
Frexno	7	10	4	—	—	21
Maderuelo	7	12	6	—	—	25
Cuéllar	13	16	17	33	—	79
Fuentidueña	14	16	4	1	—	35
Coca	—	—	1	2	18	21
Iscar	5	1	—	—	13	19
Moncejo	—	12	—	—	—	12
Totals	81	175	101	146	39	542

(i: bishop; *ii:* chapter; *iii: gratificationi; iv : refitor, vestiario, huebra, matinada, anniversarios; v:* shared between more than one of *i-iv).*

(27) Cf. González, 389-90.
(28) *Decretales Gregorii IX,* 3. 30. 34. See, for example, the case of the monastery of S. María de los Huertos : MS Egerton 910, fo. 22v (below, Appendix II); González, 384. Cf. Martín, 'Diezmos', 73-4.

VI

of arriving at a total agricultural value. Moreover, whatever may have been the precise significance of the term at a later date (29), its meaning in the mid-thirteenth century is far from clear (30). Comparison of the *rediezmo* figures for the archdeaconries of Segovia, Sepúlveda and Cuéllar with the totals of the figures given in the survey for the *prestamos* in these archdeaconries reveals no discernible relationship which would be of use for our purposes (31).

MS Egerton 910 does, however, contain a further piece of evidence which, according to the interpretation that is given to it, may be of relevance here. On fo. 32v, written in a hand different from that of the scribe of the survey, there appear the following undated calculations:

> Suma de todos los prestamos e de todas las raciones prestameras e de todas las eglesias que ha el obispo e los calonges e todos los otros que han prestamos en el obispado de Segovia. Nuef mil. syetecientos e quareynta e ocho moravedis e XI sol. e III d.

> Otro tanto tienen los clerigos parrochiales del obispado. sacados ochocientos e VII mor. menos quarta que montan las raciones prestameras. E monta lo que tienen los clerigos ocho mil e IX cientos e quareynta e dos moravedis menos VI dineros.

> El cabildo e los otros que han prestamos en el obispado tienen por todo siete mil e quatrocientos e quareynta e ocho moravedis e XI sueldos e tres dineros.

> El obispo tiene por todo de prestamos e de eglesias en todo el obispado dos mil e trescientos moravedis.

> Suma de todas rentas que tienen en las eglesias del obispado de Segovia el obispo e los calonges e los otros que han prestamos e los otros clerigos parrochiales del obispado diez e nuef mil e quatrocientos e novienta e siete moravedis e medio.

> Sacados dos mil e trescientos del obispo tienen los calonigos e los clerigos diez e sete mil e ciento e novienta e siete moravedis e medio. Suma de todas las eglesias deste nustro obispado. DXLIIII. fallo...

(29) García Sanz, loc. cit.
(30) The meaning of *redecima* —tithe of the tithe; 'second tithe'; or tithe of goods not liable to tithe— has been contested by scholars. Non-Spanish evidence is reviewed by Constable, *Monastic Tithes*, 104. What González refers to as *rediezmo* in the case of Cardinal Gil's constitutions for Salamanca and Ávila ('La Extremadura castellana', 394, 397-8) seems rather to have been the parochial *raciones* —'redditus sive proventus portionum quas in parrochialibus ecclesiis civitatis vel diocesis... vacare contigerit', which were in these places suppressed (Mansilla, *Iglesia castellano-leonesa*, 329, 356) but which the bishop and chapter of Segovia managed to retain (above, n. 15).
(31)

	préstamos	rediezmo
Segovia	2220 m.	171 m.
Sepúlveda	1097 m.	171 m.
Cuéllar	1073 m.	186 m.

Note also that the value of the *rediezmo* received by the *archipresbiter* of Cuéllar was 30 m. —not a half, but less than a sixth of that of the archdeacon: González, 406. Cf. García Sanz, loc. cit.

The number given of parish churches 'deste nuestro obispado' is so close to that of those listed in the survey that it must be supposed that the calculations are based upon the evidence of the survey alone. But does the calculator assume —and correctly assume— when he refers to 'los clerigos parrochiales del obispado' that all the parish clergy —and thus all the parishes— of the diocese are under consideration here? For if that is indeed the proper inference to draw, then the total agricultural value could be approximately calculated, disregarding (or equalising) the préstamos of untypical value, and treating the sum total of all préstamos listed in the survey (c. 7500 maravedís) as 30 % of the tithe value and 3 % of the total agricultural value of the whole diocese —25,000 and $^1/_4$ million maravedís respectively.

Regardless of these considerations, these calculations have the merit of focussing upon the disparity between the wealth of bishop and chapter on the one hand and that of the average parish priest, with an annual income from his church of less than 17 maravedís, on the other (32). On this evidence alone, the bishop possessed three hundred times the wealth of the local rector. And, in reality, the gulf was probably even greater, for not all the revenues estimated as being worth 4855 maravedís (fos. 12v, 15v) had been assigned to the canons and others in 1247. For example, all prestimonia in the archipresbiteratus of Moncejo had been retained (fo. 14r-v). The settlement of June 1247 had disposed of revenue valued at 3600 maravedís. The remaining 1250 maravedís was at the bishop's disposal, and would later prove a source of bitter strife between his successors and the chapter.

In comparison with the local clergy, the canons and dignitaries of Segovia were well provided for, and Cardinal Gil's award had increased their average income significantly though by less than they had initially been promised. On consideration of the information assembled by the commissioners —and on the advice doubtless of Bishop Bernardo— the cardinal had reduced, by 30 maravedís, in each case, the size of all payments provisionally assigned to members of the chapter, so that, in addition to 50 maravedís in respect of their canonries, the dean, archdeacons, cantor, treasurer and magisterscolarum were to receive 370, 270, 220, 220 and 170 maravedís respectively; the canons 50; and the lesser members of the

---

(32) The calculator appears to have failed to add the value of the raciones prestameras (807 m.) to the total assets of the bishop and canons —although he has subtracted it from the parochial clergy's share of diocesan revenues. The bishop and chapter's total figure ought therefore to be not 9748 m. but 10555 m. This figure is considerably in excess of the total of all rents listed in the survey : bishop 2300 m., chapter 2367 m.; 'adnexa dignitatibus' 770 m.; porciones prestimoniales 807 m.; 'gratificationi' 912 m.; refitor, vestiario, etc., 2000 m. : total 9156 m. The difference cannot be explained by including the bishop's other revenues worth 2700 m.

172

chapter those sums shown below in the key to Appendix I (33). *Vestiarium* and certain daily distributions were in all cases payable. Members of the chapter of Segovia were thus considerably better provided for than those of Plasencia, for example —though less generously treated than those of Burgos or Salamanca (34). Yet in a period when the fortunes of others were of particular interest to the Castilian clergy (35), and in the very year in which Pope Innocent IV fatally committed ecclesiastical revenue to the king (36), the settlement of 1247 was doomed to be of only temporary duration. Human nature, quite apart from *sterilitas possessionum* and *raritas inhabitancium*, would ensure that within twenty years the old divisions between bishop and chapter would be reopened, thus perhaps providing the occasion for the writing of MS Egerton 910 (37).

APPENDIX I

Survey of diocesan possessions of bishop and chapter of Segovia, c. 1246-1247.

British Library, MS Egerton 910, fos. 4r-20r.

The individuals to whom particular rents were assigned (ACS, doc. 17) are identified below by number in accordance with the following key:

1. R. decanus
2. J. archidiaconus Segobiensis
3. W. archidiaconus Septempublicensis

---

(33) Further details in Linehan, 'Segovia', 490-92.

(34) Cf. González, 398-9. In this connexion Professor González calculates the tercias of 'la Extremadura castellana' 'en más de 16.000 maravedís'; but this calculation contains an underestimate for the diocese of Segovia for which he has allowed only *c.* 400 *aldeas* (p. 345). The total provided by the survey is 542 churches, 90 of which were located *in villa* (Segovia 27; Sepúlveda 13; Pedraza 4; Frexno 4; Maderuelo 9; Cuéllar 18; Fuentidueña 6; Coca 5; Iscar 3; Moncejo 1) rather than *in termino*. Cf. J. M. Lacarra, 'Les villes-frontières dans l'Espagne des XIe et XIIe siècles', *Moyen Age*, lxix (1963), 205-22.

(35) Cf. the terms of the objection of Bishop Pedro Lorenzo of Cuenca in August 1263 to the distribution of the cost of papal provision within the province of Toledo for the Italian refugee Paolo di Sulmona : 'quod non fecit taxationem prefatis facultatibus ecclesiarum sicut debuerat, cum ecclesie Conchensi imposuerit... ducentos et quinquaginta morabitinos et quadrigentos ecclesie Tholetane que est ricior in quadruplum et ultra. Item cum ecclesia Segontina sit ricior in duplo quam ecclesia Conchensis et taxatio utriusque imposita sit equalis' : Linehan, 'The *Gravamina* of the Castilian Church in 1262-3', *English Historical Review*, lxxxv (1970) 754. On this occasion Segovia was charged 250 m. and Córdoba 100 m. (ibid., 753), although the value of canons' portions at Córdoba was the same as at Segovia, 50 maravedis (J. Gómez Bravo, *Catálogo de los obispos de Córdoba* (Córdoba, 1778), i. 262-3). At Baeza in 1241 bishop and chapter had agreed to divide all present and future resources equally (J. Rodríguez Molina, 'Patrimonio eclesiástico del obispado de Baeza-Jaén (siglos XIII al XVI', *Boletín del Instituto de Estudios Giennenses*, xx, no. 82 (1974) 15). Comparison of such arrangements with their own position may have made the frontier churches appear attractive to clergy further north. But cf. Linehan, 'Segovia'. 493, and E. Costa y Belda, 'Las constituciones de Don Raimundo de Losaña para el cabildo de Sevilla (1261)', *Historia. Instituciones. Documentos*, v (1978) 220-27.

(36) Linehan, *La Iglesia española*, 99-100.

(37) Appendix III, below.

4. N. archidiaconus Collarensis
5. P. cantor
6. Thesaurarius
7. R. magister scolarum
   Isti sunt canonici integri et habet eorum quilibet. L. mor.
8. Pascasius Iusti
9. Petrus Rotundus
10. Petrus Ferrandi
11. R. Didaci
12. Dominicus Gentilis
13. M. archipresbiter Collarensis
14. P. Guillelmi
15. P. Gaetanus
16. Lazarus
17. Peregrinus maior
18. M. Xemeni
19. M. Ricardi
20. Petrus Roderici
21. Petrus Alvari
22. Rodericus Burg(ensis)
23. Petrus Garsie
24. Bartholomeus maior
25. Didacus
26. Gundissalvus
27. Dominicus Blasi
28. Bricius
29. Dominicus Johannis
30. Michael Dominici
30a. (blank)
   Isti sunt integri portionarii et dimidii canonici et habet eorum quilibet
   .XXXVII. et dimidium
31. Ferrandus Blasii
32. D. Dominici episcopi
33. Bartholomeus episcopi
34. J. Dominici capellanus
35. P. Ferrandi minor
   Isti sunt dimidii canonici et dimidii portionarii et habet quilibet eorum
   .XXV.
36. Petrus Gundisalvi
37. B. de Calataut
38. M. Petri regine
39. Mag. S. Johannis
40. Petrus Martini
41. Sancius de Altare
42. Petrus Quirici
43. Laurencius episcopi
44. R. Xemeni
45. Vincencius
46. Egidius Munionis
47. Paschasius Sancii
48. Nunius
   Isti sunt integri portionarii et habet quilibet eorum .XXV. mor
49. Sancius Dominici
50. Mag. Garsias
51. G. Xemeni

52. Arnaldus Poncii
53. P. Roderici nepos episcopi
54. G. Petri nepos episcopi
55. Salvator
    Isti sunt dimidii portionarii tantum et habet quilibet eorum .XII. et dimidium
56. D. Petri archidiaconus Modiensis
57. Dominicus Garsie
58. Martinus scriptor
59. Clemens
60. Peregrinus minor
61. Garsias Sancti Andree
62. M. Petri decani
63. J. Petri decani
64. Nicolas Lazari
65. Nicolas Sancii
66. Mag. Martinus organista
67. G. de Altari
68. M. de Almendro
69. Michael canciller
70. Alfonsus Roderici
71. Sancius Gomicii
72. Gunterius
73. Ramirus
74. Garsias Roberti
75. D. Munionis
76. Prestimonia Mag. Nicolai archidiaconi Collarensis

(fo. 4r) Hec sunt ville et cellaria et possessiones ad mensam episcopi pertinentia.

Ultra serram

Gerindot cum p[ertinentiis] s[uis] et d[ominio] v[assallorum]
Bovadiella cum p. s. et d. v.
Meprada cum p. s. et d. v.
Del Monte cum p. s. et d. v.
In loco qui dicitur El Corral viginti iuga boum

Citra serram

Turuegano cum p. s. et d. v.
Cavallar cum p. s. et d. v.
Fuente Pelayo cum p. s. et d. v.
Moiados cum p. s. et d. v.
In Alcaçren viginti arençade vinearum
Luguiellas cum p. s. et d. v.
Domus de Coxezes cum p. s.
Domus de Iscar cum p. s.
Domus de Cuellar cum p. s.
Laguniellas cum p. s. et d. v.
Cellarium de Fuente Duenna cum p. s. et cum hereditate Sancti Mametis
Nabares de Las Cuevas cum p. s. et d. v. et cum hereditate de Nava Frida et de Sancto Vincencio
Domus Sancte Marie de La Foz cum p. s.
In Baruolla duo iuga boum

Cellarium de Frexno cum p. s.
Domus de Pedraza cum p. s.
(fo. 4v) Palacium de Sotos Alvos cum p. s.
Villa qui dicitur Rio Daça cum d. v.
Domus de Albades cum ecclesia et p. s.
La Serna de Rio Milanos
Et omnia alia que sunt prope civitatem
Cathedraticum clericorum
Hec supradicta cellaria, ville et possessiones episcopi cum cathedratico cleri-
corum sunt taxata in 2700 mor. et sunt mense specialiter deputata.
Alia * vero que per industriam vel diligenciam domini episcopi fuerunt vel
fuerint acquisita ordinationi eiusdem episcopi sunt comissa ut sine capitulo
pro anniversario suo vel pro exequiis suis vel pro festis sive pauperibus vel
capitulis ecclesie aliquod legare voluerit possit inde canonice condere testamentum.

Hec sunt prestimonia que dominus episcopus providit   episcopali mense de
consensu capituli specialiter assignanda.

---

* Cf the similar provision in the Ávila survey, ed. González, 416-17.

In archidiaconatu Segobiensi

In civitate:					
Sant Migeal	45 mor.				
Sancta Trinidat	22 mor.	9 sol.			
Sancta Olalia	33 mor.	4 ¹/₂ sol.			menos 3 sol.
In termino:					
Oter de Cavalleros	20 mor.				
Domingo Garcia	18 mor.				
Migael Hanez	22 ¹/₂ mor.				menos 3 ¹/₂ sol.
Sarçuela	27 mor.				
(fo. 5r) La Sirviença	12 mor.				menos 3 ¹/₂ sol.
Sancta Maria del Campo	18 mor.				
Torre Eglesia	57 mor.				
Los Otones	13 ¹/₂ mor.				
Escalona	27 mor.				menos 4 ¹/₂ sol.
In termino de Turuegano:					
Santi Yague	21 mor.				
Sant Migael	26 mor.		18 den.		
Vega de Infançones	14 mor.	6 sol.			
Cavallar	34 mor.	3 sol.			
In Fuente Pelayo:					
Sancta Maria	59 mor.	6 sol.			
Sant Salvador	21 mor.	9 sol.			
Summa:	435 mor.	10 sol. menos 3 den.			

In archipresbiteratu de Sepulvega

In villa:				
Sant Millan	19 mor.	3 sol.		
Santi Yague	16 mor.	3 sol.		
Sancta Maria	19 mor.			menos 18 den.
In termino:				
Pradana	20 mor.			menos 3 sol.
Vallarivela	32 mor.			menos 3 sol.

		mor.	sol.	den.	
	Frexneda	21	9		
	Cereso de Suso	23	6		
	Oter Ruviolo	23	9		
	Oter de Rebollo	31½			
	Nabares de Medio	31½			
	Nabares de Yuso, Sancta Maria	21	9		
	Ferniello	21			
	Huruelo	22½			
	(fo. 5v) Pradaniella	5	6		
	Summa:	307	6		menos 4½ sol.

In archipresbiteratu de Pedraza

In termino:

		mor.	sol.	den.	
	Vallarivela	22½	6		
	Archones	26	9½		
	El Cubiello	13			
	Mannuveros	28			
53	Aldea Nueva	3	2	3	
53	El Collado de Sotos				
	Alvos	9	8	9	
	Summa:	102	8		menos 18 den.

In archipresbiteratu de Frexno

In villa:

		mor.	sol.	
	Sant Nicholas	16	3	

In termino:

		mor.	sol.	
	Rio Daça	53		
	Sequera	27		
	Corporalio	20		
	Cascaiar	23	6	
10	Castiel de Tierra	18		
	Rio Frio	12	9	
	Summa:	170		menos 3 sol.

In archipresbiteratu de Maderuelo

In villa:			
Sancta Coloma	21 mor.		menos 4 ½ sol.
In termino:			
Ventosiella	13 ½ mor.		
Val de Vernes	29 mor.		menos 3 sol.
Rio Daguas	18 mor.		
Sancta Maria del Campo	30 mor.	9 sol.	
(fo. 6r) Cilleruelo	30 mor.		menos 4 ½ sol.
76 Moral	63 mor.		
Summa:	141 mor.	4 sol.	

In archipresbiteratu de Cuellar

In villa:			
Sancta Maria	12 mor.		menos 4 ½ sol.
Sant Savastian	19 mor		menos 18 den.
Sancta Trinidat	25 mor.	3 sol.	
Sant Andres	31 ½ mor.		
5 Sant Estevan	54 mor.		
5 Sant Migael	29 mor.		menos 3 sol.
In termino:			
Dominguela	36 mor.		
Casarejos	18 mor.		
Campaspero	16 mor.	3 sol.	
Forambrada	23 mor.	6 sol.	
Sant Peydro del Val	17 mor.		18 den.
El Canon	15 mor.		menos 4 ½ sol.
Torre Escartel	23 mor.		menos 9 den.
Summa:	235 mor.	10 sol. menos 3 den.	

In archipresbiteratu de Fuente Duenna

In villa:					
76 (part) Sant Martin	21	mor.	9	sol.	
76 (part) Sant Estevan	15	mor.	4 ¹/₂	sol.	menos 4 ¹/₂ sol.
In termino:					
Cuevas de Provanco	111	mor.			
Benbinbre	40 ¹/₂	mor.			
Aldea Senna	34	mor.	3	sol.	
Fuente Soto	28	mor.			
Pradecha Roman	41	mor.	6	sol.	
Torre Adrada	26	mor.		18 den.	menos 18 den.
(fo. 6v) **Tejares**	16	mor.	3	sol.	
Torreziela	30	mor.	2	sol.	
Fuente Sauco	52	mor.	3	sol.	
El Bivar	24	mor.	4 ¹/₂	sol.	3 den.
Sant Martin de Sagramenna	39	mor.			menos 3 ¹/₂ sol.
Santa Maria	23	mor.			menos 9 den.
Summa:	341	mor.			

In archipresbiteratu de Coca

In villa:					
Sancta Maria	35	mor.			menos 3 sol.
Santi Yuste	13	mor.	3	sol.	
Sant Adrian	16	mor.			menos quarta
In termino:					
Santi Yuste	30	mor.			
Summa:	90	mor.	menos quarta		

In archipresbiteratu de Iscar

In termino:		
Coxezes	25	mor.

	Mexezes	19 mor.		menos 18 den.
	En Mojados Sancta Maria	25 mor.	3 sol.	
	Sant Yuannes	17 mor.	6 sol.	et 18 den.
	Santi Yague de Alcacren	32 mor.	9 sol.	
	Summa:	119 mor.		

Summa omnium prestimoniorum superius adnotato (*sic*) 2300 mor.

Hec prestimonia inferius adnotata cum annexis personatibus et cum porcionibus prestimonialibus que subsequuntur provisioni seu ordinationi canonicorum de consensu episcopi et capituli specialiter assignantur

(fo. 7r) *In archidiaconatu Segobiensi*

In civitate:

5	Sant Fagunt	13 ½ mor.		
7	Sant Gil	14 mor.	6 sol.	
	Santi Yuste	18 mor.		
	Sant Salvador	12 mor.		menos sexma

In termino:

22	Nieva	15 mor.		menos 3 sol. 3 den.
22	Migael Yuannes	11 mor.		menos 3 sol.
47	Piniellos de Prestanno (*sic*)	10 mor.		menos 18 den.
17	Sant Migael de Parraçes	8 mor.		
44	Villoslada	7 mor.	10 sol.	menos 3 den.
18	Las Lastras de Blasco Garcia	7 mor.	3 sol.	
18	Naval Pino	10 mor.		menos 18 den.
35	Sanquiello	18 mor.		menos 18 den.
	El Aldea de Yuan Pasqual	10 mor.		
8	Cani de Palos	16 mor.	3 sol.	menos 18 den.
19	Pedraquela	10 mor.		
	Yanguas	8 mor.		18 den.
5	El Aldea Sancto Domingo	20 mor.	6 sol.	
61	Adrada de Piron	14 mor.	6 sol.	
	Madrona	12 mor.		menos 2 sol. 3 den.
	Tavanera	7 mor.	3 sol.	

60	Sant Cristoval	7 mor.	3 sol.		
45	Vela Diaz	8 mor.		18 den.	
35	Pasquales / Penniella Ambroz}	15 mor.		18 den.	
	Ortigosa	8 mor.		18 den.	
	Losana	9 mor.			
	Pinar Negriello	10 mor.			menos 7 sol. 2 den.
27	(fo. 7v) Valseca	12 mor.			
34	Sant Meder	8 mor.			menos 5 sol. 3 den.
9	Maraçuela	24 mor.			
11	El Maello	16 mor.			
10	Villivela	18 mor.			menos 18 den.
10	Palaciolos	16 mor.			
10	Riofrio	10 mor.	3 sol.	3 den.	
12	Val Verde / Val Verdeio}	14 mor.	5 sol.		
14	Nido del Aguila	7 mor.	2 sol.		menos 3 den.
14	Tavanera	9 mor.	10 sol.		
31	El Espino	11 1/4 mor.		3 den.	
38	Ochando	9 mor.	8 sol.		
38	Melque	15 mor.	4 1/2 sol.		
58	Yenego Munnoz	14 mor.	6 sol.		
15	El Quadron	8 mor.		18 den.	
15	Salvador	8 mor.	8 sol.		menos 3 den.
34	Xuharros de Boltoya	9 mor.	7 sol.		menos 3 den.
15	Spiritu de Riviales	6 mor.	9 sol.		
76	Fontanares	6 mor.			
76	Tres casas casas (sic)	14 mor.			
76	Escobar	13 mor.			
7	Eglesias Alvas	10 mor.			
	Modua	8 1/2 mor.			
	Summa:	568 1/2 mor.			

In archidiaconatu de Sepulvega

		mor.	sol.	den.
	In villa:			
76	Sant Estevan	8 mor.	8 sol.	
75	Sant Andres	7½ mor.		
	In termino:			
45	Bociguiellas	16 mor.	3 sol.	
20	(fo. 8r) Sant Cristoval de Baruolla	7 mor.	3 sol.	
26	Gragera	13½ mor.		
54	Paiares	9 mor.		
76	Aldea Esteva Yuannes	**13½ mor.**		
	Sant Peydro de Gasiellos	25 mor.	3 sol.	
7	Carrascal	13½ mor.		
	Yruennas	15 mor.	4½ sol.	
54	Villa Veses	13½ mor.		
33	Villa Seca	9 mor.		
	Sancta Maria del Olmo	22½ mor.		
	Bassamos	12 mor.	9 sol.	
7	Val de Avellano	18 mor.		
76	Sant Martin de la Varga	13½ mor.		
53	Cereso de Yuso	14 mor.	6 sol.	7 den.
1	Mansiella	15 mor.	4½ sol.	
1	Castro Larna de Yuso	14 mor.	6 sol.	
1	Sancta Maria de Duracon	28 mor.	5 sol.	
1	Aldea Nueva	9 mor.	9 sol.	
1	Verzanivel (? Vezenruel)	15 mor.	4½ sol.	
1	Peydro Nunó	18 mor.		
1	Castiel Xemeno	12 mor.	9 sol.	18 den.
1	Val de Symeon	8 mor.		
27	Cereso de Medio	8 mor.	6 sol.	
7	Sancta Agnes	10 mor.		18 den.
12	La Serna	8 mor.		
7	Castellejo	12 mor.		menos 18 den.
29	El Soto	10 mor.		menos 18 den.

		mor.	sol.	den.	menos
	Cantalejo	20 mor.			menos 3 sol.
	La Cabaçuela	7 mor.			menos 2 den.
	Casula	13½ mor.		3 den.	
(fo. 8v)	El Rahuetes	8 mor.	8 sol.		
	Sotiello	15 mor.	4½ sol.		
20	Sonna	12 mor.	9 sol.		
51	Las Aldevelas	8 mor.	9 sol.		
23	Tejadiella	10 mor.			
	Ciruelos	13 mor.	9 sol.		
15	Catsiel Serrazin	24 mor.	4½ sol.		
76	Espioja	14 mor.	6 sol.		
?74	Las eglesias de Nabares	22 mor.			
	Summa:	572 mor.			

In archipresbiteratu de Pedraza

In villa:

		mor.	sol.	den.	menos
27	Sancto Domingo	13 mor.	9 sol.	3 den.	
23	Sant Migael	11 mor.		18 den.	
76	Sant Johan	15 mor.			menos 4½ sol.
	In termino:				
67	Sancta Yusta	8 mor.		18 den.	
71	Sant Nicholas	7 mor.	10 sol.		menos 3 den.
	Orejana	17 mor.		18 den.	
	Sant Cristoval de Cannicosa	17 mor.			menos 22 den.
55	Sant Johan de Otero	10 mor.			
76	Sant Peydro del Val	14 mor.			menos 4 sol. 1 den.
	Milcaranos	17 mor.			
	El Aldenela	11 mor.	4 sol.	3 den.	
17	Yerrega	16 mor.	3 sol.		
17	La Puebla	15 mor.			menos 4½ sol.
	Val de Vacas	18 mor.	9 sol.		
30	Arevaliello	14 mor.			menos 4 sol. 2 den.
76	Oter de Rebollo	25 mor.	3 sol.		
76	Sancta Maria de las Vegas	10 mor.			menos 18 den.
	Summa:	240½ mor.			

(fo. 9r) *In archipresbiteratu de Frexno*

In villa:

		mor.	sol.	den.	menos
26	Sancta Maria	10½ mor.			

In termino:

		mor.	sol.	den.	menos
18	Barahona	10 mor.			
32	Mezquitiellas	9 mor.			
30a	Gallinera	9 mor.			
62	Rio Seco	7 mor.	8 sol.		menos 18 den.
70	Cinco Villas } Gomez Naharro	8 mor.	5 sol.	5 den.	
5	Aldea Nueva	13 mor.	3 sol.	9 den.	
28	Pajares	12 mor.			
22	Aldea Yennego	9 mor.			menos 4½ sol.
	Summa:	87¼ mor.			

In archipresbiteratu de Maderuelo

In villa:

		mor.	sol.	den.	menos
5	Sancto Domingo	11 mor.			
30	Sancta Cruz	10 mor.			menos 3 sol.
28	Sant Johan	8 mor.		18 den.	menos 18 den.
76	Sant Salvador	8 mor.		18 den.	

In termino:

		mor.	sol.	den.	menos
31	Fuente Miçarra	18 mor.			
	Aldea Luenga	23 mor.	6 sol.		
2	Quintana Cidiello	54 mor.			
7	Caravias	12 mor.	9 sol.		
5	Val de Conejos	9 mor.			
2	Archonada de Suso	22½ mor.	4½ sol.		
2	Archonada de Yuso	24 mor.			
20	Linares	18 mor.	10½ sol.		
	Summa:	208 mor.			

In archidiaconatu Collarensi

		mor.	sol.	den.	menos
	In villa:				
33	(fo. 9v) Sant Salvador	13 ¹/₂ mor.			
51	Sant Gil	8 mor.	8 sol.	3 den.	
	Sant Peydro	31 ¹/₂ mor.			
	In termino:				
34	Gomez Serrazin	20 mor.	10 ¹/₂ sol.		
32	Aviença	7 mor.	3 sol.		
49	Channe	9 mor.			
5	Moriel	11 mor.			menos 3 sol.
29	Bahabon	12 mor.			
5 (part)	Fuent Alviella del Pinar	24 mqr.	4 ¹/₂ sol.		
19	Las Villorias	24 mor.	4 ¹/₂ sol.		
13	Poz Yague el Mayor	9 mor.			
11	Sancto Thome de Val Elado	10 mor.			menos 18 den.
11	Sant Yuanes de Val Corva	16 mor.	5 sol.	3 den.	
	Traspinedo	28 mor.	5 sol.	3 den.	
	Pedrosiello	12 mor.	9 sol.		
35	Pinarejos	22 ¹/₂ mor.			
	Summa:	260 ¹/₂ mor.			

In archipresbiteratu de Fuente Duenna

		mor.	sol.	den.	menos
	In villa:				
76	Sant Salvador	12 mor.			
30	Sant Juannes	11 mor.			
48	Sant Miguel	15 mor.	4 ¹/₂ sol.	18 den.	menos 4 ¹/₂ sol.
48	Sancta Maria	12 mor.	e sexma		
	In termino:				
68	Cuevas de Baço	8 mor.			
25	El Castro	15 mor.	4 ¹/₂ sol.	18 den.	
7	Habuba	10 mor.			
7	Sant Migael de Bernuy	21 mor.	e sexma		menos 18 den.

		mor.	sol.	menos
21	Vega Fria	11 mor.		
16	(fo. 10r) Fuente Pelliel	21 mor.	9 sol.	menos 3 sol.
	Castriello	66 mor.		menos 4 ½ sol.
56	Villiellas	7 mor.	3 sol.	
	Fuentelolmo	32 mor.	6 sol.	
	Aldea Falcon	27 mor.		
	Calabaças	25 mor.	3 sol.	
?21	Coçuellos	25 mor.	3 sol.	
	Summa:	320 mor.		

In archipresbiteratu de Coca

In termino:

		mor.	sol.	menos
76	Lanava	11 mor.		menos 3 sol.
25	El Aldea de la Fuent	9 ¼ mor.		
	Summa:	20 mor.		

In archipresbiteratu de Iscar

In villa:

		mor.	sol.	menos
	Sant Peydro	7 mor.		menos quarta
	Sancta Maria	9 mor.	6 sol.	
43	Sant Migael	11 mor.		menos 3 sol.

In termino:

		mor.	sol.	menos
43	Las Pedrajas	12 mor.	9 sol.	
66	Sant Yuanes de la Vega	7 ½ mor.		
	Sant Peydro de Alcaçren	22 ½ mor.		
76	Vazia Odres	10 mor.	3 sol.	
	Summa:	80 mor. menos quarta		

Summa prestimoniorum provisioni seu ordinationi canonicorum deputatorum 2367 mor. 3 sol.

Adnexa sunt ista *Decanatui.*

In Segobia:

(fo. 10v) Sant Savastian   7 mor. 3 sol.   Sant Cebrian   1 mor.
Septem modii annone qui dantur a capitulo et sunt taxati in .xv. mor. minus i sol. Tamen sunt in contraversia et questione.

Archidiaconatui Segobiensi

Redecime archidiaconi de Segovia sunt taxate preter terciam partem archipresbiteri in 171 mor. et 14 * den.

* ACS, 17: 18 den.

Tercie quinque solidorum quas recipit archidiaconus a clericis sui archidiaconatus sunt taxate in 62 * mor. et tercia.

* ACS, 17: 6 den.

Archidiaconatui Septempublicensi

Redecime archidiaconi de Sepulvega sunt taxate preter terciam partem archipresbiterorum in 170 mor. et 12 sol. et 4 den.

Santi Yuste de Sepulvega   22   mor. 3 sol.   Medietas pech de Rio de Aça 12 ¹/₂ mor.

Archidiaconatui Collarensi

Redecime archidiaconi de Cuellar sunt taxate preter terciam partem archipresbiterorum in 187 mor.   minus 3 sol. et 3 den.

Precentorie

Sancto Domingo   7 ¹/₂ mor.   Hereditas et vinee de Mal Baruados et de Abbades   7   mor.

Tesaurarie

Decime episcopi que ponuntur in 50 mor. cum domibus (fo. 11r) conducticiis dignitate annexis.
Sant Quilze de Segovia   20 mor.   5 * den.   Sancta Maria de Pedraza   15 mor. 4 ¹/₂ sol.

Magisterioscolarum

In portatico de Segovia   20 mor.
Summa: 769 mor. 10 sol. 2 den.

Hec sunt porciones prestimoniales.

In Segovia

$^1/_3$ tercie cler. 16	Torre eglesia	21 mor.
$^1/_2$ tercie cler. 28	Escalona	15 mor.
	Sauquiello	10 mor.
$^1/_2$ tercie cler. 24	Camdepalos	9 mor.
$^1/_2$ tercie cler. 32	Migael Hannez	15 mor.
$^1/_2$ tercie cler. 33	Paradinas	15 mor.
	Revenga	11 mor. e sexma
$^1/_2$ tercie cler. 69	Vega de Infançones	8 mor.
	El Aldea de Don Garcia	12 mor.
	Sompsoto	8 mor.
	Villacastin	25 mor.
	Villivela	10 mor.
$^1/_2$ tercie cler. 10	Adrada del Otero	12 $^1/_2$ mor.
$^1/_2$ tercie cler. 14	Eglesia Gandul (? Guendul)	21 $^1/_2$ mor.
$^1/_2$ tercie cler. 14	Nieva	9 mor.
$^1/_2$ tercie cler. 19	Carvonero	12 mor. 8 $^1/_2$ sol.
$^1/_2$ tercie cler. 26	(fo. 11v) Palacios de la Sierra	9 mor.
$^1/_2$ tercie cler. 12	Valisa	23 $^1/_2$ mor.
	Adrada de Piron	8 mor.
	Summa:	255 mor. e quarta

In Sepulvega

$^1/_2$ tercie cler. 50	Pradana	15 mor.
$^1/_2$ tercie cler. 65	Bociguiellas	7 mor. 3 sol.
	Cantalejo	11 mor.
$^1/_2$ tercie cler. 17	Frexniello	11 $^1/_2$ mor.
$^1/_2$ tercie cler. 40	Vallariola (? Vallorivela)	18 mor.
$^1/_2$ tercie cler. 40	Oter de Rebollo	12 $^1/_3$ mor.
	Summa:	75 mor.

In Pedraza

$^1/_2$ tercie cler. 55	Mannuveros	15 $^1/_2$ mor.
	Oter de Rebollo	14 mor.
$^1/_2$ tercie cler. 10	Arcones	15 mor.
$^1/_2$ tercie cler. 8	Orejana	9 $^1/_2$ mor.
	Rabinat	7 mor.
	Summa:	66 mor.

In Frexno

$^1/_2$ tercie cler. 10	Castiel de Terra	10 mor.
$^1/_2$ tercie cler. 49	Corporalio	11 mor.
$^1/_2$ tercie cler. 41	Cascajar	13 mor.
	Summa:	34 mor.

In Maderuelo

	Aldea Luenga	7 mor. 6 sol.
$^1/_2$ tercie cler. 9	Archonada de Yuso	13 $^1/_2$ mor.
$^1/_3$ tercie cler. 47	Sancta Maria del Campo	11 $^1/_3$ mor.
$^1/_2$ tercie cler. 30a	Quintana Cidiello	13 mor.

$^1/_4$ tercie cler. 22	Moral	17 $^1/_2$ mor.
$^1/_2$ tercie cler. 46	Val de Vernes	11 mor. menos tercia
$^1/_2$ tercie cler. 39	Rio de Aguas	10 mor.
	Summa:	33 mor. 6 sol.

In Cuellar

	(fo. 12r) Fuent Alviella del Mont	8 mor.
	Sant Johan de Val Corva	9 $^1/_4$ mor.
$^1/_2$ tercie cler. 29	Dominguela	20 mor.
	Los Fuentes	13 $^1/_2$ mor.
	Traspinedo	16 mor. menos quarta
$^1/_2$ tercie cler. 21	Forambrada	13 mor.
$^1/_2$ tercie cler. 59	Pinarejos (? Pinarcios)	12 $^1/_2$ mor.
	Fuent Alviella del Pinar	13 $^1/_2$ mor.
	Summa:	100 $^1/_3$ mor.

In Fuente Duenna

$^1/_2$ tercie cler. 35	Fuente Soto	15 $^1/_2$ mor.
$^1/_5$ tercie cler. 74	Sant Martin de Sagramenna	8 $^1/_2$ mor.
$^1/_2$ tercie cler. 42	Torre Adrada	16 $^1/_2$ mor.
$^1/_3$ tercie cler. 30	Fuentel Olmo	10 mor.
$^1/_4$ tercie cler. 60	Sant Migael de Bernuy	5 $^1/_4$ mor.
$^1/_2$ tercie cler. 57	El Bivar	9 mor.
$^1/_3$ tercie cler. 21	Fuente Sauco	19 mor.
$^1/_2$ tercie cler. 25	El Castro	8 $^1/_2$ mor.
7	Torreziela	7 mor. fixos
$^1/_2$ tercie cler. 56	Calabaças	14 mor.
	Sonna	19 mor.
	Summa:	132 $^1/_4$ mor.

In Coca

	In villa:	
$^1/_3$ tercie cler. 52	Sancta Maria	16 mor. 8 $^1/_2$ sol.
	In termino:	
$^1/_2$ tercie cler. 23	Santi Yuste	25 mor.
	Summa:	41 mor. 8 $^1/_2$ sol.

In Iscar

| | Coxezes | 9 mor. |
| | *Summa:* | 9 mor. |

(fo. 12v) Summa porcionum prestimonialum 807 mor. menos quarta.

Summa praestimoniorum annexorum porcionum prestimonialium que provisioni seu ordinationi canonicorum sunt deputata 3944 mor. menos quarta.

Hec prestimonia inferius adnotata de consensu episcopi et capituli gratificationi specialiter deputantur per provisionem episcopi sociis ecclesie canonice conferenda.

In archidiaconatu Segobiensi

In civitate:

50	Sant Johan	5 mor. menos 9 den.
44	Sant Nicholas	3 mor. 9 sol.
14	Sant Peydro	1 mor.

In termino:

	Sant Illan	4 mor. menos 18 den.
44	Ortigosiella	3 mor. menos 4 ½ sol.
22	Amacara	3 mor. 2 sol. 3 den.
64	Maniel	7 mor. 3 sol.
23	El Alamada	1 ½ mor.
39	La Mata	4 mor. 9 den.
71	Palomar	5 mor. menos 2 sol. 1 den.
72	Huerta de Cercos	5 mor. 6 sol.
63	Monnico	6 mor. 4 ½ sol.
57	Cristovales	3 mor. 9 sol.
50	La Matiella	3 mor. 2 sol. 3 den.
49	Caldas	21 sol. 3 den.
62	(fol. 13r) Cabanniellas de Piron	5 mor. menos 9 den.
49	Palacios de Bernuy	4 mor. menos 6 sol.
39	Bernuy de Rio Milanos	5 mor. 4 sol. 2 den.
44	Quintanas	4 ½ mor.
44	Fuentes de Covos	5 mor. 6 den.
73	Gumer e Carrascal	3 mor. 9 sol.
50	Caldiellas	2 mor. menos 18 den.
42	Tormejon	2 mor. menos 3 sol.
18	Valverde	2 mor. menos 9 den.
64	Piniellas de Polendos	6 mor. 9 sol.
8	Tel Tellez	7 mor. 3 sol.
	Las Cuevas de Piron	4 ½ mor.
46	Cabaniellas del Monte	6 mor. menos 2 sol. 3 den.
47	Castellaniellos	2 mor. 7 den.
9	Munno Bivas	4 mor. menos 3 sol. 3 den.
11	Gallegos	6 mor. menos 2 sol. 3 den.
11	Monte Negro	5 mor. menos 3 sol.
13	El Almunnuela	4 mor. 3 sol.
13	Hanne	3 mor.
13	Donnez	
13	Migael Hannez ⎫	6 mor.
13	Annaya ⎭	
31	Tabladiello	6 mor. menos 11 den.
(part) 15, 76	El Portadgo	160 mor.
76	Buhones	4 ½ mor.
	Grajal	40 mor.
	Summa:	354 mor. menos 6 ½ sol.

In archipresbiteratu Septempublicensi

In villa:

25	Sant Peydro	5 mor. menos 9 den.
67	(fol. 13v) Sant Savastian	4 1/2 mor.
51	Sant Bartholome	4 mor. menos 18 den.
26	Sant Gil	3 mor. 9 sol.
24	Sant Martin	1 mor.
4	Sancto Domingo ⎫	
4	Sant Salvador ⎬	30 mor.
4	Sant Yuanes ⎭	

In termino:

18	Mata Espedos	10 mor. 3 sol.
30a	Quiscannera	4 mor. menos 7 den.
	Sant Martin de Figuero	4 mor. 10 sol. 3 den.
29	Sancta Maria de Figuero	3 mor. 2 sol. 3 den.
24	El Sepulcro	6 mor.
39	Castro Sarna de Suso	6 mor. 4 1/2 sol.
65	Fradres	5 mor. 6 sol.
32	Sant Nicholas de Neguera	6 mor. 4 1/2 sol.
24	Val de Salze	4 mor. 9 den.
	Sant Yuanes de Nabares	4 1/2 mor.
37	Sant Peydro de Murera	8 mor. 18 den.
28	Enzinas Cavalleras	6 mor. menos quarta
76	Sancho Fruela	3 mor. menos 4 1/2 sol.
	El Alameda	2 mor.
36	Sant Cristoval de Enebral	11 mor. menos 3 sol.
36	El Villar	11 mor. 10 1/2 sol.
1	Finojosa	5 mor. menos 9 den.
1	Moliniella	3 mor. menos 4 1/2 sol.
1	Fuente Rebollo	3 mor. 9 sol.
	Tabladiello ⎫	8 mor. 8 sol. 3 den.
	Pajares ⎭	
24	En el portadgo	30 mor.
	Summa:	187 mor. 3 sol.

(fol. 14r) *In archipresbiteratu de Pedraza*

In villa:

8	Sant Peydro	3 mor. 2 sol. 3 den.

In termino:

26	El Collado	6 mor. 2 sol. 3 den.
51	Rosueros	4 mor. 3 sol. 1 den.
28	Robrediello	4 1/2 mor.
	Bannuelos	nichil
	Summa:	18 mor.

In archipresbiteratu de Frexno

In villa:

41	Sant Johan	6 mor. 4 ¹/₂ sol.
14	Sancto Domingo	2 mor. menos 3 den.
20	En el portadgo	12 mor.

In termino:

52	Aldea Cervigal	4 ¹/₂ mor.
	Rio Aguelas	14 mor. 6 sol.
	Summa:	39 mor. 2 sol. 3 den.

In archipresbiteratu de Maderuelo

In villa:

16	Sant Migael	3 mor. 9 sol.
41	Sant Millan	5 mor. 8 sol. 3 den.
5	Sant Martin	4 ¹/₂ mor.
12	Sant Andres	4 ¹/₂ mor.

In termino:

	Villamayor	7 mor. 3 sol.
	Val de Perales	3 mor. 9 sol.
	Summa:	29 mor. menos 1 sol.

In archipresbiteratu de Moncejo

In villa:

| | Sant Andres | 11 mor. menos 3 den. |

In termino:

	Miraglos	8 mor. menos 5 sol. 4 den.
	(fol. 14v) Pardiella	7 mor. menos quarta
	Pradales	6 mor. 4 ¹/₂ sol.
	Penniella de Archos	3 mor. 9 sol.
	Val de Ferreros	8 mor. 18 den.
	Tamaron	3 mor. 9 sol.
	Val de Vacas	12 mor. 9 sol.
	Villaverde	19 mor. menos 18 den.
	Fuente Cespet	11 mor. menos 3 sol.
	Fuente Ruvia	14 mor. 6 sol.
	Santa Cruz	14 mor. 6 sol.
	Summa:	117 ¹/₂ mor.

In archipresbiteratu de Cuéllar

In villa:

8	Sant Bartholome	21 sol. 7 den.
3	Sant Cristoval	6 mor. menos 4 sol.
3	Sant Johan	7 mor. 3 sol.

In termino:

30a	Garcy Sancho ⎫	
30a	Los Hannes ⎬	4 1/2 mor.
46	Gallegos	2 1/4 mor.
34	Torre	6 mor. 4 1/2 sol.
44	Cardedar	2 mor. 10 1/2 sol.
68	Tor Don Gutierre	4 1/2 mor.
69	Ovilo	6 mor. 4 sol. 3 den.
66	Val Harro	5 mor. 6 sol.
42	La Piquera	6 mor. 9 sol.
8	Sancta Maria del Henar	4 1/2 mor.
61	Sancho Munno	5 mor. 6 sol.
13	Alcuerna	4 1/2 mor.
30a	La Perra	13 1/2 sol.
13	La Lastra	5 mor.
25	(fol. 15r) El portadgo	5 mor.
	Suma:	83 mor.

In archipresbiteratu de Fuenteduenna

In termino:

30	Los Valles	5 mor. 18 den.
29	Poz Pedrazo	4 1/2 mor.
21	Sarasona	3 mor. menos 4 1/2 sol.
70	Munno Roso	5 mor. 18 den.
	Suma:	17 1/2 mor.

In archipresbiteratu de Coca

In villa:

28	Sant Nicholas	4 mor. menos tercia

In termino:

16	Vellaguiello	7 mor. menos 6 sol.
46	Bernuy	6 mor. 3 sol.
27	Sanchon	5 mor. menos 3 sol.
52	Ciruelos	4 mor. menos 18 den.
27	Castriello	1 1/2 mor.
27	Bernaldos	1 1/2 mor.
28	El Lomo	18 sol.
23	Negullan	16 sol.
76	Sancta Trinidat	5 mor menos quarta
9	Moraleja	3 mor. 4 1/2 sol.
9	Villagonçalvo	5 mor. 9 sol.
8	Las Heras	1 1/2 mor.
		45 1/2 mor.

In archipresbiteratu de Iscar

In termino:

25	Fuentel Olmo	5 mor. 11 sol.
43	Aldea Nueva	2 mor.

194

26	Villanueva ⎫	
26	Echamartin ⎬	7 mor. 6 sol.
30	(fol. 15v) Sancho Sesgudo ⎫	
30	Remondo ⎬	5 mor. 3 sol.
23	Castrejon	1 1/2 mor.
		21 1/2 mor.

Summa prestimoniorum gratificationi deputatorum 912 mor. menos sexma.

Estos prestamos son de refitor.

In archipresbiteratu Segobiensi

In civitate:

Sant Martin	14 mor.
Sant Estevan	18 mor
Sant Andres	11 mor. menos 3 sol.
Sant Bartholome	nichil
Sancto Thome	7 mor. menos 3 den.
Sant Climent	25 mor. menos quarta
Sant Loreynt	13 1/2 mor.
Sant Mames	2 mor. 10 1/2 sol.
Santi Yague	25 mor. menos quarta
Sant Marchos	5 mor. 6 sol.
Sant Sepulcro	14 mor. 6 sol.
Sant Antolin	nichil

In termino:

Carvonero de Agosin	8 mor. 18 den.
Carbonero de Liedos	27 mor.
(fol. 16r) Moçonciello	13 1/2 mor.
El Aldea del Rey	10 mor. menos 18 den.
Olmediello Santi Yuste	2 mor. 10 1/2 sol.
Escaravajosa	5 mor. menos 9 den.
Sancta Maria de los Huertos	7 1/2 mor.
Lobones ⎫	
Maçuelos ⎬	6 mor. 4 1/2 sol.
Palacios del Rey	1 mor. 5 sol. 3 den.
Paradinas	27 mor.
Oter Redondo ⎫	
Sagramenna ⎬	5 mor. 6 sol.
Villafria	5 mor. 6 sol.
Sant Esidro	15 mor. 4 1/2 sol.
Huerta de Parrades	2 mor. 10 1/2 sol.
Redonda	7 1/2 mor.
Abbat Don Blanco (?)	6 mor. 4 1/2 sol.
Castellaniella	2 mor. 7 sol.
Peydro Domingo	6 mor. menos 9 den.
Blasco Peydro	7 mor. menos 18 den.
Fontoria	3 mor. 9 sol.
Sagramenna de Rio Viejas	6 mor. 9 sol.
Frexneda	2 mor. 10 1/2 sol.
Las Vegas	9 mor. 7 sol. menos 3 den.
Matut	7 mor. 3 sol.

Ferreros	8 mor. 8 sol. 3 den.
Adrada del Mont	22 ¹/₂ mor.
Revenga	20 mor. 18 den.
Fontoria	7 mor. menos 18 den.
Yuharriellos	27 ¹/₂ sol.
Sant Peydro de la Losa	12 mor. 9 sol.
(fol. 16v) Sompsoto	14 mor. 9 sol.
Spiritu de Cuchareros	12 mor.
La Figuera	14 mor.
Brieva	9 mor.
Adradiella	7 mor. 3 sol.
Val Sardiella	14 mor. 6 sol.
Atençuela	7 mor. 3 sol.
Eglesia Guendul	38 mor. 10 ¹/₂ sol.
Quintanar	4 ¹/₂ mor.
Fajejas	1 mor. menos 2 den.
Escobar de Polendos	7 ¹/₂ mor.
El Parral	6 mor. menos 18 den.
Pennas Ruvias	3 mor. menos 16 den.
Las Covatiellas	27 sol.
Fuente Milanos	5 mor. 18 den.
Mojadiellos	3 mor.
Xuharros de Rio Moros	4 ¹/₂ mor.
Sanchaznar de Rio Moros	3 mor. 3 sol. menos 1 den.
Roda	11 mor. menos 3 sol.
El Aldea de la Fuent ⎫ Enziniellas ⎭	·4 mor. 2 sol. 1 den.
El Aldea de Domingo Martin	1 mor. 5 sol. 3 den.
Oter Moroso	5 mor. 6 sol.
Las Lastras del Pozo	12 mor. menos 4 ¹/₂ sol.
Macoaleja ⎫ Sancta Maria del Pollo ⎭	9 mor.
(fol. 17r) Sotos Alvos	45 mor.
Pelayos	18 mor.

Estos prestamos son del refitor.

In archipresbiteratu de Cuéllar

In villa:

Sancta Martina (?)	21 mor. 9 sol.
Sant Martin	42 mor. 9 sol.
Sant Nicholas	nichil.
Santi Yague	23 mor. 6 sol.
Sancto Thome	19 mor. menos 18 den.
Sancto Domingo	3 mor. 10 ¹/₂ sol.

In termino:

Adrados	11 mor. menos 3 sol.
Fuente Tariego	8 mor. 18 den.
Frumales	14 mor. 6 sol.
El Aldeyuela	7 mor.
Sant Yuanes	36 mor.
Sant Estevan	18 mor.

Sancta Maria del Otero ⎫ Sant Migael ⎰	11 mor. menos 3 sol.
Sant Peydro de la Defesa	13 ¹/₂ mor.
Sancta Coloma	[nichil]
Poz Yague el Menor	4 ¹/₂ mor.
La Piliella	12 mor. 9 sol.
Sant Estevan del Arroyo	3 ¹/₂ mor.
Sant Cristoval del Val	9 mor.
(fol. 17v) Navalmaçano	8 mor. 18 den.
Trasfuentes	5 mor. 6 sol.
La Matha	20 mor. 10 ¹/₂ sol.
Frexneda	6 mor. 4 ¹/₂ sol.
Navasdolfo	9 mor.
El Aldea del Caron	11 ¹/₄ mor.
Chatun	8 mor. menos 9 den.
Malerado	3 mor. 2 sol. 3 den.
Ventosiela	nichil

In archipresbiteratu de Coca

Estos prestamos son de refitor en cada eglesia.

In villa:

Sancta Maria	18 mor. 6 sol.
Sant Adrian	8 mor. menos 3 sol.
Sant Sadornin	nichil
Sant Nicholas	2 mor. menos tercia
Sant Yuste	6 mor. 9 sol.

In termino:

Santi Yuste	15 mor.
La Nava	5 mor. 6 sol.
El Lomo	9 sol.
Sancta Trinidat	2 mor. 12 sol. 8 den.
Sanchon	2 mor. 6 sol.
Negullera	8 sol. 3 den.
Bernuy	3 mor. 18 den.
El Aldea de la Fuente	4 mor. 9 sol. 4 den.
Ciruelos	2 mor. menos 9 den.
(fol. 18r) Vellaguiello	3 mor. 4 ¹/₂ sol.
Bernaldos	11 sol. 3 den.
Castiella	11 sol. 3 den.
Navasdolfo	8 mor. menos 5 sol. 9 den.
Villafonçalvo	3 mor. menos 3 sol.
Las Heras	tres quartas
Moraleja	1 mor, 9 sol. 8 den.

In archipresbiteratu de Iscar

Estos prestamos son del refitor en cada eglesia.

In villa:

Sant Peydro	3 mor. 5 sol. 7 den.
Sancta Maria	4 mor. 10 ¹/₂ sol.

?7
?7

| Sant Migael | 5 mor. 6 sol. |

In termino:

Las Pedrajas	6 mor. 4 ½ sol.
Sancho Sesgudo	2 mor. 6 sol.
Villanueva	2 mor. menos 3 sol.
Echa Martin	1 ½ mor.
Aldea Nueva	1 mor.
Vazia Odres	5 mor. 18 den.
Fuentel Olmo	3 mor. menos 1 sol.
Castrajon	11 sol. 3 den.
Remondo	3 sol.
Sant Yuanes de la Vega	4 mor. menos quarta

(fol. 18v)   Estos son los prestamos del vestiario.

In archidiaconatu Segobiensi

In termino:

Villa Castin	38 mor. menos 3 sol.
Quexigar	8 mor. 18 den.
Sanchaznar de Parrazes	11 ¼ mor.
Lavajos	19 ½ mor.
Matamaçano	9 mor.
Vela Gomez	10 mor. 4 sol. menos 1 den.
Lumbreras	10 mor. menos 18 den.
Martin Migael	15 mor. 11 den.
Aragoneses	15 mor. 4 ½ sol.
Fermoro	14 mor. 6 sol.
Valisa	42 mor. 4 ½ sol.
Bernaldos	6 mor. 3 sol.
Sotedrado	9 ½ sol.
Cabannas	6 mor. 4 ½ sol.

In archipresbiteratu Septempublicensi

Estos prestamos son del vestiario.

In termino:

El Aldea de Don Sancho	18 mor.
Sancta Martha	8 mor. 18 den.
Heguera	2 mor. menos 3 sol.

(fol. 19r)   Estos prestamos son del vestiario.

In archipresbiteratu de Pedraza

In termino:

| Rabinat | 36 mor. |
| Navafria | 16 mor. 3 sol. |

Estos prestamos son del vestiario.

In archipresbiteratu de Cuéllar

In termino:

Moraleja	16 mor. 3 sol.
Fuent Alviella del Mont	38 mor. menos 3 sol.
Mari Feles	16 mor. 3 sol.
Sant Martin de Cam Redondo	10 mor. menos 18 den.

Estos prestamos son del vestiario.

In archipresbiteratu de Fuente Duenna

In termino:

Covos	14 mor. 6 sol.

Estos prestamos son dela huebra.

In Segovia

In la villa:

Sant Millan	8 mor. 18 den.
Sancta Coloma	8 mor. 18 den.
Sant Benito	1 mor. 9 sol.
(fol. 19v) Sant Roman	16 mor. 3 sol.
Sant Polo	4 1/2 mor.

In termino:

Foyuellas	9 mor.
Laguna Rodrigo	11 mor. menos 3 sol.
Ribiella	6 mor.
Sancta Onenna	14 mor. menos 9 den.
Matha Mala	3 mor. 2 sol. 3 den.
Valseca	9 mor. 4 1/2 sol.
Xemen Nunno	4 1/2 mor
Tel Domingo	2 mor. 10 1/2 sol.
Azedos	11 1/4 mor.
Garci Yllan	14 mor. menos 4 sol. 5 den.

Estos prestamos son de la matinada.

In Baguila Fuent

Sancta Maria	40 1/2 mor.
Sant Johan	18 mor. menos quarta
En Sancta Maria una racion pres-tamera	10 mor.

In termino de Segovia

En Sarçuela

Una racion prestamera · · · · · 18 mor.

(fol. 20r) Estos prestamos son por los anniversarios del padre e de la madre del obispo don Gonçalvo segundo.

In termino de Segovia

Cardenna	5 mor. 6 sol.
Ferrandos ⎫	
El Collado ⎭	8 mor. 18 den.

APPENDIX II

(i) *Statutes of Bishop Remondo and the chapter of Segovia regarding distribution of* missada, vesperada *and provision of meals for the poor in the* refectory. Segovia, 29 Nov. 1258.

British Library, MS Egerton 910, fols. 20v-23v.

Noverint universi quod nos Reymundus dei gracia episcopus Segobiensis una cum decano et capitulo eiusdem considerantes quod reditus illorum prestimoniorum de Val de Lobingos, videlicet Sancte Marie, Sancti Michaelis. Fuentes, Sancti Stephani de Lobingos, Sancti Petri de la Defesa qui expendi consueverant in prandiis ab episcopo et capitulo in quatuor festivitatibus, videlicet Resurrectionis domini, Pentecostes, Assumptionis beate Marie atque Nathalis domini poterant melius dispensari, et ut melius ac honorificencius divinum officium expleretur, statuimus ut iidem reditus distribuantur cotidie inter illos personas, canonicos, portionarios mansionarios qui interfuerint celebrationi maioris misse in ecclesia nostra iuxta modum inferius annotatum. Huic etiam distributioni adicimus medietatem reditum fabrice ecclesie nostre assignatorum qui secundum taxacionem eiusdem ecclesie sunt in numero centum triginta morabotinorum positi ita videlicet ut si summa illa morabotinorum excrescat vel diminuatur semper accipitur medietas ad distribucionem faciendam superius nominatam.

Insuper adicimus statuentes ut archipresbiteratus Segobiensis numquam nisi canonico mansionario Segobiensis ecclesie conferatur, ita quod quinquaginta morabotini qui secundum ordinationem eiusdem ecclesie illum canonicum cui archipresbiteratus predictus collatus fuerit contingebant, in distributionis dicte superius usus cedant. Istos autem quinquaginta morabotinos in prestimonio de Arconada de Yuso et in prestimonio de Traspinedo specialiter assignamus.

Statuimus etiam ut arrendacio predictorum prestimoniorum de Val de Lobingos necnon prestimoniorum que sunt fabrice (fol. 21r) deputata et illorum etiam prestimoniorum que habebit canonicus ille cui collatus fuerit archipresbiteratus predictus, in canonicorum capitulo semper fiat. Receptio autem ac distributio supradictorum redituum ad illum socium seu illos socios pertineat cui vel quibus capitulum duxerit comittendum.

Statuimus etiam ut computatio fiat cotidie a computatoribus deputatis a capitulo in hunc modum. Cotidie distribuatur dimidius morabotinus inter illos socios qui interfuerint celebracioni misse maioris, exceptis diebus festivis annotatis inferius quibus unus morabotinus debet distribui secundum modum in sequentibus designatum, ita quod nulli detur porcio nisi chorum intraverit antequam lectio epistole perlegatur et choro intersit quando Sanctus Sanctus decantantur. Distribucio autem denariorum fiat postquam Sanctus Sanctus fuerint decantata. Item in diebus festivis in quorum festivitatibus sit distribucio denariorum in quibus sunt reditus perpetuo assignati nichil de supradictis reditibus misse assignatis inter socios dividatur. Iterum in quolibet die dominico et in qualibet festivitatum Beati Stephani prothomartiris, Beati Laurentii, Beati Martini confessoris et pontificis, Beate Marie Magdalene distribuatur unus morabotinus integer inter socios qui interfuerint celebracioni misse maioris iuxta modum superius annotatum. Distribucio autem denariorum supradictorum inter personas, canonicos et porcionarios tam maiora quam habentes beneficia sit equalis, illis vero qui sub forma sunt porcionis quam illos qui super formam sunt contingerit medietas conferatur. Iterum in qualibet quatuor festivitatum beate Virginis, videlicet Assumpcionis, Nativitatis, Annunciacionis que celebra- (fol. 21v) tur marçio, et Annunciacionis que celebratur in mense decembris, et in festo Epiphanie domini et in festo Circumcisionis domini et in festis Duodecim apostolorum, in qualibet unus morabotinus integer dividatur.

Insuper in perpetuam memoriam venerabilis patris nostri Raymundi supradicti episcopi, a cuius benignitate nos decanus et capitulum profitemur multa et inmensa beneficia recepisse, volumus ut in festo Ascencionis domini inter socios quatuor morabotini distribuantur iuxta morem qui in distribucionibus factis in aliis festivitatis perpetuis in nostra ecclesia observatur, et in vigilia eiusdem festi unus morabotinus ad vesperos dividatur.

Horum autem distribuciones redituum prout temporis qualitas exegerit circa predictorum augmentacionem vel diminucionem redituum et diminuendam providimus seu etiam ampliandam.

Circa predicta statuimus ut sociis qui non interfuerint processioni diebus dominicis et aliis in quibus processio celebratur, de denariis qui distribuentur inter socios qui misse interfuerint nichil detur.

Statuimus etiam ut nullus socius de denariis ad missam distribuendis percipiat nisi chorum intraverit in hora superius pretaxata, et si causam habuerit necessariam recedendi tunc licenciatus ab episcopo vel decano si interfuerint, quibus absentibus petita licencia a presbitero ebdomadario vel ab eo qui pro eo missam celebraverit, recedat et de denariis porcio detur ei. Hanc autem licenciam dari nolumus nisi tantummodo in hiis casibus, videlicet si socium oporteat propinqui vel consanguinei sepulture seu exequiis interesse vel comitetur lectum defuncti socii convicini. Volumus (fol. 22r) autem quod socii qui dominum episcopum conduxerint seu comitati fuerint cum a Segobiensi recesserit civitate vel eidem obviam exiverint in adventu eiusdem ad civitatem eandem licet celebrationi misse non intersint suam percipiant porcionem.

Quum autem nichil melius expenditur quam quod in laudibus divini nominis dispensatur, hanc ordinationem inferius annotatam decrevimus faciendam ut vesperorum officium sollempnius expleatur. Statuimus siquidem ut quinque solidi pipionum inter illos personas, canonicos, portionarios mansionarios qui vesperorum celebrationi interfuerint equaliter cotidie dividantur iuxta modum inferius annotatum.

Volumus et statuimus ut nulli socio de dictis quinque solidis distribuendis ad vesperos detur porcio nisi chorum intraverit antequam primus psalmus finiatur cum eadem die in honore beate Virginis vesperi celebrantur. In diebus vero in quibus non consueverunt de beata Virgine vesperi celebrari socius cui danda erit porcio antequam secundus psalmus finiatur totaliter intret chorum. Fit etiam conputatio cotidie a computatoribus a capitulo deputatis. Distribucio autem denariorum fiat psalmorum recitacione totaliter iam expleta. Volumus etiam ut in diebus festivis in quibus denariorum inter socios distribuendorum sunt reditus perpetuo assignati, de denariis quos nunc dividendos ad vesperos ordinamus nichil inter socios dividatur.

Statuimus insuper ut tempore quo maioris ieiunium quadragesime celebratur denarii superius pretaxati qui inter socios qui interfuerint celebrationi maioris misse distribuendi fuerint, ad vesperos dividantur iuxta modum in vesperis superius annotatum. Denarii vero qui (fol. 22v) erant ad vesperos inter socios dividendi ad completorium dividantur. Nulli autem sociorum detur porcio qui non interfuerit vesperis aut completorio nisi in casibus qui in ordinacione misse superius annotantur.

Horum autem denariorum reditus quos ad vesperos distribuendos decrevimus in hiis locis specialiter assignamus, videlicet in possessionibus in Ispalensi territorio constitutis, in Axaraf, in Turre de Avenzophar prope Gadiambar cui loco illustrissimus rex Alfonsus felicissime recordationis quondam regis Fernandi filius nomen imposuit Segoviola, quarum possessionum medietatem nos supradictus episcopus Segobiensis ecclesie donavimus, assignamus sexaginta morabotinos; in portione de Laguniellis sexdecim morabotinos; in portione Sancti Jacobi de Torogano octo morabotinos; in judeis Septempublicensis et Collarensis morabotinos quos consueverunt dare quilibet judeus pro capite suo, videlicet duos solidos et dimidium annuatim; in terciis deputatis clericis, videlicet de Torre Eglesia sex morabotinos in denariis, in Las Pedrajas sex morabotinos in denariis; et in decimis a monasterio Sancte Marie de Ortis de possessionibus suis dandis, ut ex proventibus ex hiis omnibus supradictis locis provenientibus accipiantur denarii inter socios ad vesperos dividendi ut est superius constitutum.

Verum ne supradictis prandiis memoria penitus extinguatur in quibus paternalis affectio erga filios et filialis devocio erga patrem videbatur per caritatis insignia mutue designari duximus statuendum ut in festo Resurrectionis dominice, dumtaxat in die exclusa vigilia, (fol. 23r) episcopus et capitulum insimile, absente vero episcopo per se capitulum, caritative in refectorio comedant annuatim. Ne vero loca illa que in tribus festivitatibus, videlicet Pentecostes, Assumpcionis beate Marie virginis, Natalis domini remaneant destituta que presencia episcopi et canonicorum hiis diebus consueverant decorari, huic statuto adicimus ut quadraginta pauperes in qualibet trium festivitatum reficiantur in eodem refectorio aut plures vel pauciores secundum quod creverint vel decreverint reditus ad id inferius assignati. Item statuimus quod ebdomadarius, cui officium misse maioris celebrande in maiori altari per ebdomadam comissum fuerit, necnon socius qui pauperum refectorii curam gesserit, et omnes capellani nostre ecclesie sedentes ad mensam maiorem ubi consuevit episcopus residere cum caritate refectiones eisdem diebus in eodem refectorio suscipiant epularum, ita quod cura tam capellanorum quam pauperum reficiendorum totaliter competat ebdomadario ac dispensatori pauperum supradictis. Ad hec adicimus ut decem solidi pipionum inter ebdomadarium, dispensatorem ac capellanos memoratos in quolibet prandiorum in predictis tribus festivitatibus celebratorum dividantur, ita quod ebdomadarius ac dispensator supradicti eorum quilibet de hiis decem solidis duplicem percipiat porcionem, singuli vero capellanorum singulas percipiant porciones. Ne vero ebdomadarius et dispensator ac capellani predicti gule inservitores pocius videantur quam participes beneficii Jhesu Christi in preparandis sibi cibariis hunc modum duximus observandum, ut ex porcinis arietinis seu vaccinis duo (fol. 23v) genera carnium preparentur, unum duobus modis, reliquum uno modo.

Ad hec autem ordinata superius adimplenda porcionem Sancte Marie de Fuente Pelayo et porcionem de Cavallar que taxate sunt in triginta et octo morabotinis specialiter assignamus, ita quod medietas horum redituum in prandium supradicti episcopi et capituli dispensatur, reliqua vero medietas in refeccione pauperum ebdomadarii, dispensatoris et capellanorum et in decem solidis inter hos distribuendis ut superius statuimus expendatur. Volumus autem ut omnium supradictorum prestimoniorum ac porcionum arrendatio fiat in capitulo et ad hec arrendanda dies statuatur et capitulum convocetur. Ut hec autem superius salubriter ordinata perhennitate irrefragabili roborentur nos supradicti episcopus et capitulum hanc nostre ordinationis cartam sigillorum munimine duximus roborandam. Acta sunt hec in vigilia Sancti Andree anno domini millesimo.CC.L.octavo *.

(ii) *Disposition of revenues of the church of Segovia giving effect to the foregoing (1258).*

British Library, MS Egerton 910, fols. 23v-25v.

Estos dias manda el privilegio dela missada que partan un maravedi a missa alos compañeros.

Todos los domingos. Sant Estevan prothomartiris. Sant Loreynt. Sant Martin. Sancta Maria Magdalena. Assumpcio Sancte Marie. Nativitas Sancte Marie. Annunciacio Sancte Marie de março. Anunciacio Sancte Merie de deziembre. Eppihanie *(sic)* domini. Circumcisionis domini. Las fiestas de los xij apostolos.

(fol. 24r) El dia de Ascension .iiij. maravedis por la fiesta del Obispo. Et destos .iiij. maravedis que partan el uno la vigilia de Ascension a viesperas.

Estos prestamos son dela missada

In termino de Cuellar

Santa Maria ⎱
Sant Migael ⎰ 11 mor. menos 3 sol.
Las fuentes Sant Johannes 36 mor.
Sant Estevan 18 mor.
Sant Peydro dela Defesa 13 mor. e medio

Dela huebra

---

* Cf. Colmenares, ed. cit., i. 401, 419, and the statement, referring to these statutes, 'esto esta todo en el quaderno de 4.°' (n. 40). In the margin of Colmenares' MS are the words 'poterant melius dispensari' : words which are underlined in MS Egerton 910, fo. 20v. Also underlined in MS Egerton 910 (fos. 26r, 26v-27r) are the passages in the statutes of October 1258 (not here transcribed) which Colmenares noted in his own MS : ed. cit., 418, n. 34, 35. These coincidences, and that noted in Appendix III (below), suggest that Colmenares may have used (and marked) MS Egerton 910; but in that case it is surprising that he made no reference to the statutes of Cardinal Gil which are there transcribed (for which see Linehan, 'Segovia').

La meatat de todos los prestamos dela huebra de la villa e del termino 65 mor.

In termino de Cuellar

El prestamo de Traspinedo 28 mor. e 5 sol. e 3 den.

In termino de Maderuelo

El prestamo de Archonada de Yuso 24 mor. e 4 sol. e medio (fol. 24 v)

Esto es dela vesperada

In termino de Sevilia

En la Torre de Aven Zophar cerca Gadiambar heredat que es del Obispo Don Remondo 60 mor.
In la eglesia de Laguniellas una racion 16 mor.
In la eglesia de Sancti Jague de Turuegano una racion prestamera 8 mor.

In Sepulvega e en Cuellar

El pecho delos judios que pecha cada uno .ij. sol. e medio por su cabeça quanto montare cada anno.

In termino de Segovia

In Torre Eglesia. En la racion del clerigo 6 mor. en dineros

In termino de Iscar

In Las Pedrajas. En la racion del clerigo 6 mor. en dineros

In Segobia

In civitate. El diezmo delas possessiones de Sancta Maria delos Huertos quanto montare

(fol. 25r) En Fuente Pelayo

In Sancta Maria. Una racion prestamera 19 mor. menos sexma
In Cavallar. Otra racion prestamera 19 mor.

La meatad dela renda destas dos raciones sobredichas es pora el dia de Pascua dela Resurrecion que coman cada anno en uno el obispo e los canonigos e los companeros en refitor como es ordenado e establecido.
Et la otra meatad dela renda destas mismas dos raciones de susodichas es pora el dia de Cinquesma e el dia de Assumpcio Sancte Marie e el dia de Navidat que coman estos tres dias en uno cada anno en refitor el semanno cuya fuere es dia la missa del altar mayor e el companero que toviere el refitor q diere alos pobres a comer e todos como es ordenado e establecido e que coman con ellos cada anno en estas tres fiestas XL pobres cada fiesta.

(fol. 25v) Estas raciones don delos moços que sirven el chor

In termino de Maderuelo

Val de Vernes del un tercio delos clerigos el tercio 11 mor. menos tercia
Moral del tercio delos clerigos el quarto 17 mor. e medio
Quintana Cidiello dela meatad el tercio 10 mor.

APPENDIX III

Declaration of resistance by dean and chapter of Segovia against the bishop or any other seeking to vary the terms of the ordinatio of Cardinal Gil Torres. Segovia, 25 Jan. 1265.

British Library, MS Egerton 910, fols. 27v-28r.

Licet ex debito necessitatis honeste ac necessarie honestatis iura ecclesie sue illibata servare ac manutenere illesa quilibet teneatur nemo sane mentis ignorat, ad hoc multomagis unumquemque teneri cum super hoc expresse certa constitutio editur, presertim si iuramenti vinculo indissolubiliter confirmetur. Hinc est quod nos decanus totumque Segobiense capitulum ex preteriti calicis gustatione amara circa ventura in posterum cauciores effecti (1) ad conservacionem iurium ecclesie nostre firmam et firmitatem eorum perempniter habituram duximus irrefragabiliter statuendum quod si episcopus qui pro tempore fuerit vel alius quicumque ad ea que iuris nostre esse noscuntur et in quorum possessionem esse dinoscimur manum quod absit duxerit apponendam, nos omnes et singuli de capitulo ei resistere ac opponere manifeste viriliter et absque palliatione qualibet teneamur, consilium et auxilium nobis prebentes adinvicem facto pariter atque verbo; presertim si super villis de Vaguila Ffuent, de Sotos Alvos et de Pelayos et rebus et redditibus earundem; vel si super prestimoniis et proventibus Matutinare, Missare seu etiam Vesperare; vel si super possessionibus et aliis bonis ecclesie nostre iusto titulo acquisitis nobis questio moveatur; vel si super ordinatione facta in Segobiensi ecclesia per venerabilem patrem Egidium cardinalem ab episcopis qui pro tempore fuerint innovari quicquam contingat in preiudicium nostrum seu etiam innovari. Item statuimus firmiter et irrevocabiliter ut episcopis qui pro tempore fuerint decimarius a canonicis numquam detur, immo eis si exigantur penitus denegatur. Statuentes etiam ut cum aliquis in canonicum vel in (fol. 28r) socium fuerit de novo receptus promitat prestito iuramento premissa omnia se perpetuo servaturum, quod si forte adimplere renuerit pro non canonico seu socio non obstante sua receptione ab omnibus habeatur. Adicimus insuper quod si episcopus qui pro tempore fuerit aliquem de capitulo occasione premissorum aut alias indebite vel maliciose attemptaverit molestare omnes alii de capitulo consilio et auxilio ipsum deffendere ac in expensis iuvare si opus fuerit teneantur. Et ne premissa omnia ullo umquam tempore occasione qualibet ab aliquo vel ab aliquibus valeant retractari, nos supradicti decanus et capitulum Segobienses omnes et singuli iuramus ad sancta Dei evangelia omnia et singula statuta predicta firmiter et inviolabiliter observare. Actum hoc in pleno capitulo Segobiense, die dominica .VIII. kalendis februarii. Anno nativitatis domini millesimo. CC.L.X quinto. In cuius rey testimonium presenti littere sigillum nostrum duximus apponendum.

---

(1) 'ex preteriti... circa' underlined. Cf Colmenares, ed. cit., 407 and 421, n. 74 : 'esta este estatuto en el quaderno de 4. Sigue "donde dice *ex praeteriti calicis gustatione amara circa ventura in posterum cautiores effcti"* '.

NOTA

It was only after the proofs of this article had been passed for press that the recent joint study by A. García Sanz, J.-L. Martín, J. A. Pascual and V. Pérez Moreda, *Propiedades del cabildo segoviano, sistemas de cultivo y modos de explotación de la tierra a fines del siglo XIII* (Salamanca, 1981), came to my attention. This work contains various studies and an edition of the text of the *Registro antiguo de heredamiento de los señores deán e cabildo de la yglesia de Segovia*, a compilation of information collected in the 1290s concerning the chapter's possessions (or some of them) within the diocese. Had I known of it earlier I might have wished to reconsider some of what appears above. Though the *Registro* is not a source strictly comparable with the Survey, since it deals (in detail) with territorial *arrendamientos* and not with ecclesiastical tithe-based revenues, there are nevertheless sufficient points of contact between the two sources (e. g. regarding the possession by *el chantre* of 'una arençada de viña en Abades': *Propiedades*, p. 120; cf. above, p. 25) to suggest that further study of the issues raised in *Propiedades* and here is likely to prove fruitful.—P. L.

SUMMARY

Although acquired by the British Museum 140 years ago, Ms. Egerton 910 has not hitherto been studied or its contents published or evaluated. The manuscript, formerly the property of the church of Segovia, constains a topographical survey of the possessions of the bishop and chapter of that church in the years 1246-7, which is unusually detailed for that age, together with related documents (some of which are published here) concerned with the division of the *communis mensa* between bishop and chapter according to the direction of the Castilian Cardinal Gil Torres. The subject was studied in the seventeenth Century by Diego de Colmenares, who may have used this manuscript. Consideration of its contents, together with that of other documents of the archive of Segovia Cathedral, provides material for some hypotheses concerning the economic condition of a sector of the Castilian Church on the eve of the reconquest of Seville.

RESUMEN

Documentación sobre bienes de la iglesia de Segovia (1246-7)

El Ms. Egerton 910, adquirido por el Museo Británico hace ciento cuarenta años, no ha sido estudiado aún, y su contenido no ha sido publicado ni evaluado. Este manuscrito, antes propiedad de la iglesia de Segovia, contiene una visión topográfica, extraordinariamen-

206

te detallada, de las posesiones diocesanas del obispo y del cabildo en el año 1246-7, junto con varios documentos, algunos de ellos aqui publicados, relacionados con el tema de la distribución de la *communis mensa* entre el obispo y el cabildo, de acuerdo con las normas del cardenal castellano Gil Torres. En el siglo XVII trató este tema el historiador Diego de Colmenares, y quizá utilizó el citado manuscrito Egerton 910. De su contenido y del de otros documentos conservados en el Archivo Catedralicio de Segovia pueden deducirse algunas hipótesis sobre la situación económica de un sector de la iglesia castellana en vísperas de la reconquista de Sevilla.

LA IGLESIA DE LEON A MEDIADOS DEL SIGLO XIII

En una obra publicada hace cuatro años sugerí que a mediados del si- †
glo XIII las iglesias de Castilla y León experimentaron una aguda crisis económica. Cargadas de impuestos destinados a los ejércitos de la Reconquista —que a cambio les proporcionó menos provecho del que se suele
atribuirlas— padecieron tales dificultades que, a finales del año 1250, ini-
ciaron un movimiento de resistencia al gobierno del rey Alfonso X [1]. Tal
afirmación da pie para formular varias preguntas, o al menos ésta: ¿si era
esa la situación, cómo pudieron las empobrecidas iglesias sufragar los gastos ocasionados por la construcción de las diversas catedrales que perpe-
túan tan magníficamente el recuerdo del siglo XIII español? Creo que no
falten los datos necesarios para el estudio de un tema tan importante de
la historia socioeconómica de España. De momento, no pretendo hacer
otra cosa que resaltar algunas de las condiciones económicas que necesariamente afectaron a los miembros eclesiásticos de una de estas iglesias, la
de León [2]. Ojalá me sigan otros.

En cuanto a la situación económica de la iglesia de León en el siglo XIII, no era distinta ni de las otras iglesias de los reinos españoles, ni
de las del resto de Occidente. Como comunidad corporativa estaba constantemente expuesta a las apetencias de ambiciosos individuos, que busca-
ban los beneficios que le pertenecieron. Normalmente, estos *alieni* —ya de

---

[1] Peter Linehan, *The Spanish Church and the Papacy in the Thirteenth Century*, Cambridge 1971, 101-187 (hay una edición española revisada, publicada en
Salamanca, 1975); véase también mi *The Gravamina of the Castillian Church in
1262-63:* English Historical Review, 85 (1970) 730-754.

[2] Quiero agradecer muy cordialmente al canónigo archivero de la catedral de
León, don Agapito Fernández Alonso, y a don José María Fernández Catón, director
del Archivo Histórico Diocesano de León, su amabilidad enviándome xerocopias de
varios documentos del archivo de la catedral.

Astorga, ya de Asti— habrían obtenido un mandato papal de provisión. Así, impulsados por los invasores, los obispos de León y sus cabildos a veces pelearon juntos, a veces lucharon entre sí. Por eso habrá que estudiar las relaciones internas de las iglesias de la época —lo que no pude hacer en mi libro—, en el que sólo intenté delinear unos rasgos de la historia eclesiástica de la península. Del contenido de los archivos de León y del Vaticano, entre otros, es posible reconstruir algo que pueda interesar a la historia leonesa.

Por toda la Península Ibérica había más clérigos sin beneficio, que beneficios sin clérigo: prevaleció un estado de inflación beneficial, para la cual el único remedio efectivo hubiera sido el equilibrio entre la oferta y la demanda según las reglas del *ius canonicum*[3], mas para los cabildos era esencial que no se redujese más el valor de los beneficios por el procedimiento de subdivisión de los mismos. Tal subdivisión produjo una serie de beneficios incapaces de sustentar a un beneficiado cualquiera, con las consecuencias de pluralismo y absentismo que de ello se siguen. Por eso fijaron límites numéricos para las canonjías y beneficios menores, *statuta de numero,* obligándose formal y solemnemente a que nunca sobrepasarían tal límite. Muy pronto descubrieron las desventajas de sus estatutos. Quedándose sin los medios suficientes para mantener a quienes pidieron su apoyo, aunque otorgarlos era su unánime voluntad, suplicaron al papa que les permitiera hacer subdivisión *statuto de numero non obstante.* Cartas suplicatorias de esta índole existen en todas partes de la península, desde Guarda hasta Vich[4].

En el caso de León partimos del año 1224, cuando las constituciones del cardenal leonés (y quizá ex obispo de León[5]), Pelayo Gaitán, redujeron el número de canónigos a cincuenta y el de porcionarios a veinticinco. El estado de la iglesia, según la descripción lacónica del cardenal, era bastante malo. Los capitulares, más interesados en sus ingresos financieros que en sus deberes religiosos, se marchaban de la misa después del evangelio —*consuetudo detestabilis*—, según el cardenal, quien para suprimirla

---

[3] Véase el decreto *Episcopus si aliquem* del con. Lat. III (1179) c. 5 (c. 4. *X.* III 5).

[4] Véase LINEHAN, *The Spanish Church,* 45n, 296.

[5] Según la *Chronique latine inédite des Rois de Castille (1236),* ed. G. Cirot: Bulletin Hispanique, 15 (1913) 278. Cf. D. MANSILLA, *El cardenal hispano Pelayo Gaitán (1206-1230):* Anthologica Annua, 1 (1953) 11-66; J. Mª FERNÁNDEZ CATÓN, *El cardenal leonés Pelayo Albanense (1206-1230):* Archivos Leoneses, 7 (1953) 103-105; LINEHAN, *The Spanish Church,* 279n. Para las constituciones, véase *Reg. Hon. III,* 5017 (publ. en D. MANSILLA, *La documentación pontificia de Honorio III (1216-*

invocó censuras económicas, pero sin éxito, a juzgar por lo que sucedió[6]. Debe notarse el énfasis de estas constituciones. Su motivo principal no era la reforma de la vida canonical (que caracteriza las del cardenal Gil Torres en 1240[7]), sino el arreglo de los presupuestos de los canónigos y porcionarios que se discutían con bastante ardor durante el pontificado del obispo Rodrigo Alvarez (1209-32). El cardenal hizo varias cosas que no se mencionan en sus constituciones: resalta la transferencia de unas propiedades de la *mensa episcopalis* a la *mensa capitularis*. No se olvidaría pronto[8]. Otra consecuencia llena de problemas para el futuro era la formación de una serie de porcionarios sin beneficios[9].

Contribuyeron muy poco al buen orden de la iglesia de León las constituciones del cardenal Pelayo. Continuaban en el cabildo la discordia y el rencor, entre otras causas, porque los beneficios mayores se reservaron para los parientes del citado cardenal. Las dos elecciones episcopales en 1232 y 1235 produjeron un partidismo que reflejaba la división del clero catedralicio. En la diócesis, entre tanto, se propagó la herejía, favorecida por la falta de ejemplo de la clerecía. En junio de 1240 el papa Gregorio IX permitió al obispo Martín Arias enriquecer su *mensa episcopalis* con unas rentas de la iglesia, recibiendo los canónigos su *quid pro quo* siete meses después, cuando se adoptó la práctica de pagar las rentas a los ejecutores testamentarios de un canónigo fallecido. en el año después de su muerte: una verdadera hipoteca sobre el futuro[10]. Al fin, en octubre de 1245, se puso en peligro el objeto central de las constituciones de veinte años antes, cuando el obispo Nuño Alvarez recibió autorización papal para instituir cuatro prebendados *extra numerum,* con las consecuencias para el cabildo que se pueden suponer. Es de notar que el obispo no se sirvió

1227), Roma 1965, núm. 504); ID., *ib.:* Anthologica Annua, 1, 53 ff. Recientemente termina de aparecer una extensa y documentada obra que estudia ampliamente la vida del cabildo de León, véase T. VILLACORTA RODRÍGUEZ, *El cabildo catedral de León. Estudio histórico-jurídico, siglos XII-XIX,* León 1974, 688 pp. (Colección «Fuentes y Estudios de Historia Leonesa», núm. 12).

[6] MANSILLA, *La documentación,* loc. cit. Cf. ES, clviii, para la misma práctica en el año 1259.

[7] LINEHAN, *The Spanish Church,* 268-275.

[8] ACL, doc. 6.322 (apéndice 12).

[9] Estipulan las constituciones pelagianas: «Quia vero plures portionarii residentes in eadem ecclesia reperiuntur ad presens, irrefragabiliter duximus statuendum ut nullus de cetero in socium et fratrem recipiatur de novo quousque portionarii nunc residentes ad predictum numerum (*scil.* 25) redigatur...»: MANSILLA, *La documentación,* loc. cit.

[10] LINEHAN, *The Spanish Church,* 291-292; *Reg. Greg. IX,* 920, 3591, 5231; ES, 35, 295 ff. 307.

de este indulto, sin duda a causa de la resistencia capitular, y que uno de los beneficiados hubiera sido un clérigo romano, Nicolás de Urbe[11].

Antes de marzo de 1247 había descendido la situación económica de la iglesia a tan bajo nivel, que el papa ordenó al obispo Nuño que se presentase a la Curia Romana (a la sazón en Lyon), y puso al frente de los negocios de la iglesia a dos miembros del cabildo[12]. En Lyon no lo hizo el obispo mejor que en León. Su estancia allí no produjo novedad alguna.

Desde 1224, cuando el obispo Rodrigo Alvarez había sido citado a Roma, varios canónigos y dignidades habían visitado la corte papal —principalmente a causa de las elecciones episcopales de 1232, 1238 y 1244[13]. Pero después de 1247 lo que era un hilo de agua se convierte en torrente. Las luchas del cabildo de León se libraron en Lyon y, más tarde, en Italia. Los individuos que vinieron en busca de letras papales de provisión se agregaron a las familias cardenalicias, y no se marcharon.

No conocemos la duración de la estancia del obispo Nuño en Lyon, ni las circunstancias en que se reincorporó al gobierno de su sede. Sin embargo, murió en abril de 1252 y quedó vacante la sede de León durante dos años y medio, hasta que en agosto de 1254 hizo Inocencio IV la promoción de Martín Fernández, arcediano de Saldaña y notario del rey Fernando III[14].

No se saben tampoco las causas de esta larga demora. En agosto de 1254 se supo cómo Martín Fernández había gozado del apoyo de más de dos tercios del cabildo, cómo la minoría dio preferencia a Rodrigo, y cómo se opusieron a Martín Fernández solamente dos individuos —el canónigo Lope Suárez y el porcionario Alfonso Gómez—, cuyos reparos sobre sus cualidades personales exigieron la consulta de la colección de deposiciones en España y una investigación de la Curia, presidida por el cardenal Ottobono de S. Adriano en presencia de testigos[15]. Este proceso podría haber exigido la demora mencionada. ¿Pero, en tal caso, cómo se explicaría el

---

[11] *Reg. Inn. IV*, 1735; ACL, doc. 5.779 (16 febrero 1250: publ. en apéndice 1). En abril de 1249 Nicolás se quejó de que no hubiese recibido nada de León, «nisi labores et expensas»: *Reg. Inn. IV*, 4573. Para otro clérigo romano, *Stephanus dictus Surdus*, sobrino del cardenal Riccardo Annibaldi, que recibió ciertas rentas leonesas del obispo Nuño, véase *Reg. Inn. IV*, 5113 (apéndice 2).

[12] *Reg. Inn. IV*, 2499-2500.

[13] *Reg. Hon. III*, 5017; *Reg. Greg. IX*, 920, 4594; *Reg Inn. IV*, 412.

[14] ES, 35, 313; *Reg. Inn. IV*, 7919. Se instruyó al arzobispo de Compostela para que ordenase a Martín Fernández al diaconato, etc., y que le consagrase obispo. Es de suponer que el nuevo obispo se hallase con la corte castellana.

[15] *Reg. Inn. IV*, 7919 (apéndice 7).

LA IGLESIA DE LEÓN A MEDIADOS DEL SIGLO XIII

hecho de que en febrero de 1253 y en abril del mismo año cartas papales se dirigieran al *episcopo Legionensi,* y no al *electo* —tales cartas eran enviadas por parte del vicecanciller de la Iglesia Romana y del maestre Fernando de Compostela, deán de Orense, que tuvieron la pericia suficiente de no consentir en el nombramiento de un ejecutor ficticio? [16].

Entretanto se continuó la lucha por los beneficios. Al frente se halló Nuño Velázquez, maestrescuela de Astorga y figura importante en los asuntos de la iglesia de León desde el año 1238, al menos, habiendo sido uno de los emisarios del cabildo que fueron a Roma para pedir la confirmación de la elección del obispo Martín Arias [17]. En abril de 1247 se le cargaba con la responsabilidad de las deudas de la iglesia, y en octubre del mismo año representó los intereses del obispo y del cabildo en la disputa con la iglesia de Lugo sobre el arcedianato de Triacastela [18]. Parece haber pertenecido más a León que a Astorga —el procurador de Astorga en la corte papal en 1250 era Abril Rodríguez [19]—, aunque tuvo beneficios en Palencia y Oviedo también. En noviembre de 1252, por intervención de Esteban de Husillos (el sobrino del citado cardenal español Gil Torres), obtuvo un beneficio en León. Ya tenía los *prestimonia* del fallecido arcediano de Valderas, Pedro Yáñez. En enero de 1253 consolidó la tenencia de sus beneficios en León, porque sospechó que les había recibido del obispo Nuño en forma irregular. Probablemente dos motivos le impulsaron a actuar así: el hecho de que los *prestimonia* de Pedro Yáñez habían sido concedidos igualmente por el cardenal Gil al vicecanciller de la Iglesia Romana, Guillermo de Parma; y la apetencia que causó la desmembración de los *prestimonia* de la chantría, cuando murió Pedro Yáñez, de modo que unas rentas de valor de 50 maravedís se reservaron para Pelayo Fernández y otra suma para Guillermo de Parma [20].

No todos los que buscaron beneficios en León eran oriundos de allí. En noviembre de 1252 se dio al clérigo Juan, hijo de Rodrigo Yáñez y pariente del cardenal Gil, a quien la iglesia de Astorga había rehusado admitir, una renta anual de diez marcos de plata [21]; y en febrero de 1253

---

[16] *Reg. Inn. IV,* 6620, 6485-6486.

[17] LINEHAN, *The Spanish Church,* 284-285; ACL, doc. 1.294 (= *Reg. Greg. IX,* 4594).

[18] *Reg. Inn. IV,* 2500; A. C. Lugo, doc. 21/3/19. Cf. B. CAÑIZARES, *Los grandes pleitos de la iglesia de Lugo: la iglesia de Lugo y la iglesia de León:* Boletín de la Comisión de Monumentos de Lugo, 2 (1946) 151.

[19] Archivo diocesano, Astorga, docs. 3-62, 3-63.

[20] *Reg. Inn. IV,* 6701, 6631, 7860 (apéndice 4).

[21] *Reg. Inn. IV,* 6696.

se hizo provisión de una dignidad prebendada en favor de Martín Yáñez, hermano del ilustre canonista Bernardus Compostellanus [22]. Así pasó a Bernardus, bastante bien provisto de beneficios en Compostela, Palencia, Tuy y Lisboa, el arcedianato leonés del nuevo obispo de León, el de Saldaña: una promoción ordenada por el papa Inocencio IV ordenó que se diese preferencia a Bernardus sobre cualquier otro pretendiente —aunque el papa se interesó particularmente en la pensión de veinticinco marcos reservada para su *familiaris* Bontempus [23].

La pensión prometida a Bontempus no era la única concesión a un extranjero. De la misma índole fueron las pensiones concedidas en favor de Guillermo de Parma y de su sobrino Hugolino, lo mismo en León (donde aumentaban *sede vacante* mientras que se reducían en Astorga) que en otras iglesias españolas [24]. Varias veces trataron los dos curiales obtener su pago, que en el caso de Guillermo se dijo haber sido prometido por el obispo de León (probablemente Nuño) [25]. En febrero de 1253, por mediación del cardenal Gil, fueron asignadas a Hugolino la prebenda y la canonjía de Giraldo Diego, *quondam* prior de León, y los *prestimonia* de Giraldo Diego y Pedro Yáñez, *quondam* cantor, a Guillermo de Parma [26]. Pero ellos no recibieron nada de lo que se les debía (veinte y ocho marcos anuales, respectivamente) hasta agosto de 1254, cuando los procuradores del nuevo obispo de León —Pedro Núñez, arcediano de Benamariel, y Fernán Abril, el tesorero— fueron autorizados para pedir prestada una suma de 76 marcos, añadidos a los 451 de que hubieron menester para pagar sus deudas a la curia papal. Sus acreedores fueron Bonifacio Buenaventura y sus compañeros, mercaderes de Siena, y el obispo Martín Fer-

---

[22] *Reg. Inn. IV*, 6317. Obtuvo el arcedianato de Cea, no obstante su reserva para un leonés (*Reg. Alex. IV*, 825).

[23] *Reg. Inn. IV*, 8300 (apéndice 5). Está una de las seis cartas (núms. 8300-05) del año 12 de dicho pontífice, puesta al final del registro del año 10 (Reg. Vat. 22). Dice Berger (*Reg Inn. IV*, iii, 555): «nous ignorons les raisons pour lesquelles elles ont été mises à part». Nos es lícito sospechar la intervención de altos personajes de la curia: las cartas 8300-02 tienen relación con Bernardus Compostellanus; 8303, con el frustrado candidato para la sede leonesa, el arcediano Rodrigo; y 8304 y 8305, con mandatos de provisión en favor de un capellán papal y de un capellán del cardenal Ottobono Fieschi, respectivamente.

[24] *Reg. Inn. IV*, 6615, 6619.

[25] *Reg. Inn. IV*, 7861 (apéndice 6).

[26] *Reg. Inn. IV*, 6628 (apéndice 3), 6631: «Magistro Roderico archidiacono Legionensi. Olim in Legionensi ecclesia per decessum Girardi Didaci eiusdem ecclesie prioris canonicatu, prebenda et prestimoniis ac postmodum in eadem ecclesia prestimoniis per obitum Petri Johannis ipsius ecclesie cantoris vacantibus, dilectus filius noster (*sic*) Egidius Sanctorum Cosme et Damiani diaconus cardinalis tam littera-

nández tuvo que devolverlos antes de enero del año siguiente (1255)[27]. Esto representó una carga más que se unió a las que había heredado Martín Fernández de su predecesor. En el mismo mes —20 de agosto de 1254— se le envió un indulto limitando su responsabilidad sobre las deudas causadas en la curia papal[28].

Las deudas financieras provenientes del pontificado del obispo Nuño representaron una parte solamente de los problemas de Martín Fernández. Fue muy favorecido por el rey Alfonso X y, a instancias de Alfonso, también por el papa, recibiendo en agosto de 1254 varios indultos: uno contra las provisiones papales (que sirvió de bien poco, como se verá después); otro protegiéndole de sus acreedores en caso de que no pudieran probar que su dinero había sido utilizado en favor de la iglesia de León; y otros dándole los ingresos de un año de las iglesias de su diócesis que habían quedado vacantes durante tres años, la cuarta parte de las tercias diocesanas por dos años, y la colación de los beneficios diocesanos que pertenecieron a Roma[29]. Pero, a pesar de todo eso (repetido por Alejandro IV dos años después), la iglesia a que volvió a finales de 1254 le presentó muchos problemas apremiantes[30]. Su paz y tranquilidad habían desaparecido bajo el tráfico beneficial, como informó al papa Inocencio en agosto de 1254, cuando se le autorizó a no hacer caso de los pretendientes en su diócesis «nisi tibi mandatum super hoc apostolicum ostendatur»[31]. El indulto sirvió de poco, porque casi todos los pretendientes ya gozaban de tales mandatos apostólicos. Lo peor era que en el futuro los derechos normales de colación tendrían un valor nulo y que, en efecto, todo el tráfico beneficial habría de pasar por Roma.

Murió el papa Inocencio a finales de 1254, sucediéndole Alejandro IV. Se dice que los registros del nuevo papa contienen una cantidad importante

---

rum quam specialis mandati nostri auctoritate redditus et proventus prestimoniorum huiusmodi dilecto filio Guillelmo magistro scolarum Parmensi vice nostro et canonicatum et prebendam predictos Hugolino alumpno et capellano suo ipsius vice nepoti contulit ac de ipsis eosdem per suum anulum investivit...» (Reg. Vat. 22, núm. 771, ff. 281v, 283v).

[27] *Reg. Inn. IV*, 7861, 1909, 1980.

[28] *Reg. Inn. IV*, 7957: «... concedimus ut super huiusmodi debitis a creditoribus italicis non nisi apud sedem apostolicam valeas conveniri».

[29] *Reg. Inn. IV*, 7922-23, 7957, 7959-61; ACL, doc. 1.299 (Alejandro IV a Martín Fernández, *Tuis et karissimi*, disculpándole las deudas de su predecesor, «nisi probatum fuerit legitime debita ipsa in utilitatem ipsius (Legionensis) ecclesie fore versa», Anagni, 20-X-1255; al dorso: Rex Castelle); LINEHAN, *The Spanish Church*, 145.

[30] *Reg. Alex IV*, 1637-38, 1641-43, 1645-46, 1648; ACL, doc. 6.321; ES, 35, 314.

[31] *Reg. Inn. IV*, 7958.

de cartas beneficiales [32]; pero no es así en el caso de León, que se registraron tres solamente: en octubre de 1255 la próxima canonjía era reservada para Marco Domínguez, que había visto frustrada su ambición de adquirir el arcedianato de Cea [33]; y en octubre de 1256 dos cartas en favor de Pedro Fernández, chantre de Astorga y capellán de Alfonso X, y de Martín Yáñez, un clérigo leonés del obispo Martín Fernández, a la sazón en la corte papal en nombre del rey [34]. En la última carta afirma el papa que había creído que el cabildo leonés querría complacerle «etiam si eas [cartas] pro extraneis dirigamus»: vana esperanza, que ya Guillermo de Parma y Hugolino habían comprobado. Antes de un año, en efecto, Alejandro había tomado medidas para forzar a las iglesias españolas que no habían querido pagar las rentas debidas a los dos curiales, negándolas todo acceso a su corte mientras no pagasen [35]. Por supuesto, las dos constituciones del papa Alejandro, de abril de 1255 —Discrimen, que anuló todas las expectativas inocencianas para los beneficios mayores y menores que nombraban a una persona particular para un beneficio concreto, y Execrabilis, que redujo a cuatro el número de expectativas de canonjías en cualquier iglesia [36]— proporcionaron algo de tranquilidad, aunque (como el papa informó a dos porcionarios de León, Martín Pérez y Alfonso Pérez, en abril de 1256 [37]) Execrabilis no afectó a los derechos de porcionarios en expectación. Pero la calma no era más que temporal: en León, como en otros sitios, se obtuvieron nuevas cartas apostólicas y se formó de nuevo una cola [38].

En diciembre de 1263 León necesitó el mismo remedio, esta vez aplicado por el papa Urbano IV, que era conocedor en relación con León de que «ad multam, ut credimus, importunitatem petentium, pro duodecim personis vel amplius et felicis recordationis Alexander papa predecessor noster pro pluribus aliis, diversimodo beneficiandis... tam super dignitatibus vel personatibus, tam super prebendis vel portionibus aut prestimoniis, tam etiam super commutatione dignitatis... vel personatus ejusdem ecclesie...

---

[32] EDITH PÁSZTOR, Contributo alla storia dei Registri Pontifici del secolo XIII: Bullettino dell'«Archivio Paleografico Italiano», ser. 3, 1 (1962) 78-79.
[33] Reg. Alex. IV, 825. Cf. Reg. Inn. IV, 6317.
[34] Reg. Alex. IV, 1644, 1648.
[35] Reg. Alex. IV, 1014.
[36] G. BARRACLOUGH, The Constitution «Execrabilis» of Alexander IV: English Historical Review, 49 (1934) 193 ff.
[37] Reg. Alex. IV, 1339.
[38] BARRACLOUGH, ut supra, 198-199.

LA IGLESIA DE LEÓN A MEDIADOS DEL SIGLO XIII

dicimur litteras direxisse»[39]. Aunque los registros de Alejandro IV contengan tan pocos detalles para la historia eclesiástica de León en estos años, podemos llenar la laguna utilizando la información de los dos documentos contenidos en el manuscrito vaticano *Collectoriae* 397, que publicamos en el apéndice.

Claro es que las circuntancias de la elección de Martín Fernández habían contribuido poco a la restauración de la paz en el cabildo de León. Los dos líderes de la facción opuesta al nuevo obispo consiguieron salvarse[40], pero dada una situación en que, como informó Martín Fernández al papa Urbano, la colación de las prebendas perteneció al obispo sólo y la de las porciones al obispo y cabildo juntos[41], era natural que se levantasen contiendas, sea lo que sea del estado general de la oferta y la demanda de los beneficios eclesiásticos. Dada también la presencia de un obispo que buscaba la ayuda papal para anular los derechos de su cabildo en materia de colaciones para poder infiltrar a sus mismas creaturas[42], y que se dedicó a sanear las finanzas de su sede, motivo con el que volvió a

---

[39] *Reg. Urban. IV*, 1206.

[40] *Reg. Alex. IV*, 292. Relata la carta de que Lope Suárez y Alfonso Gómez se habían opuesto a Martín Fernández, «inter alias exceptiones propositas contra ipsum specialiter excipiendo proponere curavistis quod cum idem electus duos archidiaconatus curam animarum habentes... absque dispensatione sedis apostolice retineret prefici post altercationes diutinas et fere lapsum biennii dispensatio super hoc fuisset ostensa eidem ecclesie de iure non poterat nec debebat. Unde cum ex parte electi iamdicti idem predecessor (Inocencio IV) exceptionibus aliis quampluribus non admissis electionem confirmavit eandem». Su petición era «ut... providere vobis adversus penam constitutionis *Statuimus* misericorditer curaremus». El significado del verbo *Statuimus* no queda claro en el texto publicado por Bourel de la Roncière, etc. (*Les Registres d'Alexandre IV*, loc. cit.). Trata de la constitución 4 (*De electione*) del concilio de Lyon I (año 1245), *Statuimus ut si quis:* «... Adicimus etiam ut qui non plene probaverit quod in forma opponit, ad expensas quas propter hoc pars altera fecisse docuerit, condemnetur. Qui vero in probatione defecerit eius, quod in personam obicit, a beneficiis ecclesiasticis triennio noverit se suspensum...». Véase *Conciliorum Oecumenicorum Decreta...* curantibus J. Alberigo, etc., ed. altera (Basilea, etc., 1962) 260-261; H. WOLTER & H. HOLSTEIN, *Lyon I et Lyon II* (París, 1966) 81.

[41] *Reg. Urban. IV*, 1938: «... in eadem ecclesia in qua prebendarum ad te solum et portionum ad te et ipsius ecclesie capitulo collatio sicut asseritur pertinet»; 1939: «... in qua prebendarum ad te solum et ad te ac ipsius ecclesie capitulum communiter portionum collatio pertinere dicitur» (Reg. Vat. 29, núms. ⁰88-989, fol. 200r).

[42] *Ibíd.* Le dieron el nombramiento de tres canónigos «ac totidem ex eisdem in eiusdem ecclesie portionarios... non obstante... quod direximus, ut asseris, in ipsa ecclesia scripta nostra pro quatuor canonicandis et tribus beneficiandis recipiendis in portionarios quorum tribus iam, ut dicitur, per ipsa scripta receptis in canonicos» (1938); la promoción de cinco porcionarios de la iglesia «in canonicos» (1939) 14-VII-1264.

plantear cuestiones que habían sido decididas por el cardenal Pelayo cuarenta años antes [43], era inevitable un choque.

El informe incompleto de litigación en *Collectoriae* 397 intitulado *Causa Magistri Gondasalvi cum archidiacono Astoricensi* ilustra algunos de los problemas padecidos por la iglesia de León en estas circunstancias y, sobre todo, las enemistades capitulares.

El pleito tocó al arcedianato de Benamariel, por reclamación de Melendo Pérez, arcediano (y futuro obispo) de Astorga, apoyándose en mandatos apostólicos de Inocencio IV y Alejandro IV. A la muerte de Pedro Núñez, en febrero de 1261, ya llevaba siete años, por lo menos, esperando. Pero entonces, y muy rápidamente, en el curso de pocos días, y pasando por alto sus derechos, se promovió ilícitamente al dicho arcedianato a Maestre Gonzalvo, a instancias del obispo, «dicti Petri Nuni corpore nondum tradito sepulture» [44]. Por supuesto, no tenía la iglesia leonesa ningún motivo corporativo para dar la bienvenida a Melendo Pérez.

En abril de 1247 el procurador leonés, Fernán Abril, se había opuesto a su nombramiento como *receptor* de testimonios en la disputa con la iglesia de Lugo sobre el arcedianato de Triacastela, porque Melendo Pérez emparentó con el obispo de Lugo, «et quia etiam idem dominus Lucensis erat executor predicti domini Melendi in quadam provisione quam a sede apostolica impetraverat, et quia etiam contra ecclesiam Legionensem super sua provisione litteras apostolicas impetraverat» [45]. Su carrera siguiente se había desarrollado en la corte papal y en Sicilia, con su protector el

---

[43]   ACL, doc. 6.322 (apéndice 12).

[44]   A. S. V., *Collectoriae*, 397, ff. 114v, 126v (apéndice 10). Para una descripción del *Coll.* 397 véase J. DE LOYE, *Les archives de la Chambre Apostolique au XIV siècle: inventaire*, París 1899, 163; U. BERLIÈRE, *Causes belges en cour de Rome (1259-63): Bulletin de la Commission Royale d'Histoire*, 74 (1905) 1-26, donde se reproducen varios extractos; P. A. LINEHAN, *La carrera del obispo Abril de Urgel:* Anuario de Estudios Medievales, 8 (1972-1973) 195-197, para otros extractos de interés español. Se intitula «Regestum causarum per Alexandrum papam IV Ottaviano S. Marie in Vialata diacono cardinali commissarum necnon acta quedam earumdem causarum, 1257-1263», pero claro es que lo que nos queda no representa más que una parte de una colección de registros de los pleitos oídos por el cardenal Ottaviano Ubaldini: al fol. 94r, dentro de la relación de la *Causa Vicensis episcopi,* se halla la nota: «Que quidem acta registrata fuerant in alio quaterno de mandato mei notarii Johannis cum in isto registro competens non habetur spatium registrandi». Dos consideraciones tocantes al presente pleito sugieren que el manuscrito fuese un borrador de los notarios del dicho cardenal: la pieza suelta (fol. 153) que reproduce la información dada al fol. 118r; y la escritura de la sección de repregunta que parece marcadamente peor (y que contiene muchas más inserciones) que la de las deposiciones de los procuradores, etc. Merece un estudio atento este manuscrito.

[45]   AHN, cód. 267B (*Tumbo Nuevo de Lugo*), fol. 278v.

cardenal Guglielmo Fieschi [46]. Sin embargo, tenía sus amigos en León en 1261: Pelayo Fernández, canónigo (el receptor de la concesión de los *prestimonia* de la chantría en 1253 [47]); Maestre Domingo, canónigo, y Alfonso Gómez, el adversario del obispo de hace siete años, y que solamente es todavía *socius* de la iglesia [48]. Así (aunque no es siempre fácil identificarlos con certeza [49]), tenía enemigos y amigos el obispo. Entre los primeros es razonable incluir a aquellos que él había privado de sùs beneficios: Pelayo Fernández y el chantre Julián, promovido por Inocencio IV, quien en julio de 1255, tal vez refugiándose, se hallaba en la corte papal entre la *familia* del protector de Melendo Pérez, el cardenal Guglielmo Fieschi [50].

Cada obispo tiene sus amigos. Entre los de Martín Fernández se contaba el canónigo Jaime Yáñez, quien, según el procurador de Melendo Pérez, había incurrido en pena de excomunión por su participación en la campaña contra el chantre Julián, y que fue encargado de instituir a Maestre Gonzalvo en el arcedianato de Benamariel en 1261 [51]. Cinco más habían sido nombrados por él para las canonjías que el papa Alejandro le permitió proveer, anulando los derechos capitulares para hacerlo [52]. Con todo, la situación a que alude nuestro documento es bastante distante de la de una vida capitular templada y pacífica. Los *adherentes* de cada grupo se mencionan muchas veces. La iglesia de León en los años de 1250 era un campo dividido en grupos y partidas.

Falta en el documento la defensa del Maestre Gonzalvo. Falta también la decisión del cardenal Ottaviano Ubaldini, pero sabemos que era favorable a Gonzalvo, porque en junio de 1264 los dos pretendientes se presentaron en Orvieto, como testigos de un pleito tocante a la iglesia de Saintes (Francia) presidido por el cardenal de San Marco, Guillaume de Bray : Melendo Pérez, arcediano de Astorga, y Maestre Gonzalvo, arcediano de León [53]. No sabemos nada de la carrera posterior del afortunado Maestre Gonzalvo. Su triunfo y la vindicación de la táctica brusca del obispo —brusca según Melendo Pérez—, pueden sorprendernos en vista de la fuerza evidente de la causa opuesta, pero corresponde bien a lo ocurrido

---

[46] A. S. V. *Collectoriae* 397, fol. 126r. No se menciona en A. PARAVICINI BAGLIANI, *Cardinali di Curia e «familiae» cardinalizie dal 1227 al 1254*, I (Padova 1972) 334 ff.

[47] *Reg. Inn. IV*, 7860 (apéndice 4).

[48] A. S. V. *Collectoriae* 397, fol. 114v; arriba, notas 15, 40.

[49] Por ejemplo, «Maestre Miguel hermano que fu del otro Maestre Miguel que fu canoligo»: ACL, doc. 1.564 (apéndice 13).

[50] A. S. V. *Collectoriae* 397, fol. 127v; *Reg. Inn. IV*, 7860; *Reg. Alex. IV*, 657.

[51] *Ibíd., ff.* 127v, 114v.

[52] *Ibíd.*, fol. 127v.

[53] *Reg. Urban. IV*, 1111.

varias veces en la Península Ibérica durante el siglo XIII, cuando las personalidades locales se mostraron mucho más efectivas que los mandatos papales [54]. En León en esta época el obispo Martín Fernández empleó los mismos métodos cuando impuso al sobrino del cardenal Pelayo, Miguel Sánchez, a la chantría después de Julián, con poca atención a los derechos del cabildo que —en las personas de los arcedianos Rodrigo Pérez (quizá el competidor de Martín Fernández para la sede de León), Adán y Pedro Domínguez, del tesorero Fernán Abril y de otros— hizo la objeción pertinente de que no era apto para el puesto de chantre «cum nesciret canere», observando, además, que a la sazón el obispo «apostolico esset auctoritate suspensus»; pero todo sin fortuna [55].

La historia de Melendo Pérez se vio poco afectada por su revés. Curialesco consumado, fue promovido a la sede de Astorga en 1272-73, y la gobernó con éxito [56]. De las demás personalidades complicadas en este asunto, es de suponer que el procurador de Maestre Gonzalvo y del obispo era hombre de habilidad comparable en los asuntos de la curia romana. †Fernán Patino demostró gran maestría en los engaños procesales del sistema judicial, y en la táctica de la dilación sobre todo —hasta el punto de negar la autoridad del notario público de León, Alfonso Pérez, un personaje que debía serle perfectamente conocido [57]—. Fernán Patino perteneció a una dinastía establecida en el cabildo de León, y fue sobrino del *magister scolarum* Fernán Guillélmez, que en 1247 había sido encargado de los asuntos de la iglesia [58]. Vivió hasta los últimos años del siglo, un hombre de negocios que se presentó en Burgos en mayo de 1286 atestiguando la elección del abad de Husillos, Juan Alvarez, para la sede de Osma, ya hacía dos años nombrado juez eclesiástico de León [59]. Según su testamento de

---

[54] LINEHAN, *The Spanish Church*, 183-184, 304-305.

[55] *Reg. Urban. IV*, 1095 (apéndice 11). Miguel Sánchez se presentó en la corte romana en marzo 1253 y marzo 1263 (*Reg. Inn. IV*, 6485; *Reg. Urban. IV*, 1100). Fue sobrino del cardenal Pelayo Gaitán (*Reg. Inn. IV*, 6731).

[56] ES, 243-245; P. RODRÍGUEZ LÓPEZ, *Episcopologio asturicense*, II, Astorga 1907, 287; T. MINGUELLA Y ARNEDO, *Historia de la diócesis de Sigüenza y de sus obispos*, I, Madrid 1901, 590. Para su asociación con el cardenal Ottobono Fieschi, véase A. S. V. *Collectoriae* 397, fol. 126r.

[57] A. S. V. *Collectoriae* 397, fol. 116r. Existen en ACL muchos documentos escritos por él.

[58] ACL, doc. 1.672; *Reg. Inn. IV*, 2500. Fernán Guillélmez tuvo también algunas posesiones en la diócesis de Zamora: A. C. Zamora, doc. 17 (E-1) 43.

[59] BN, 13.035, ff. 238r-243r: «in parrochia S. Laurentii in domibus episcopi Burgensis ubi tunc dictus episcopus (el arzobispo Gonzalo de Toledo) hospitabat in camera». Entre sus clérigos en el año 1292 hubo un cierto Nuño Patino, canónigo de Osma: ACL, doc. 1.672; ES, 35, 323. Véase también ACL, doc. 1.603 (apéndice 15).

1295, era una persona acaudalada, de la misma índole de su predecesor como procurador episcopal, Nuño Velázquez. Sus «libros de física» pueden sugerir horizontes intelectuales más amplios que los del limitado abogado, pero es evidente que para él la ocupación eclesiástica era un complemento de la profesión legal [60].

El número de los procuradores españoles empleados en esta causa era notable; solamente un procurador italiano se menciona [61]. Pero no es de suponer que fuesen todos hombres de tal condición, como Nuño Velázquez o Fernán Patino. Hay una carta elocuente de un procurador turolense de c. 1290 que registra las dificultades de hallarse en la curia romana sin los recursos necesarios [62]. En el caso de León, el procurador episcopal en octubre de 1263, Pedro Pérez, no recibió (según él) más que tres marcos de plata por año, y tal era la poca esperanza de ser promovido a beneficio de León, que en agosto de 1264 Urbano IV le promovió a una canonjía con prebenda en Santiago de Compostela [63]. Si los compostelanos le admitieron, resultó, en efecto, que el obispo Martín Fernández había podido trasladar la cuenta de su sirviente a otra iglesia, pero, a juzgar por el otro pleito leonés en *Collectoriae* 397 (intitulado *Causa archiepiscopi Compostellani*), parece poco probable que lo hicieran sin lucha. La causa demuestra tanto la resistencia con que tropezó el mandato apostólico en favor de Fernán Patino en Compostela, como el ensayo de cada iglesia de trasladar el *onus provisionis* a cualquier otra (en este caso a la desafortunada iglesia palentina [64]), y la confusión que reinó en un sistema central que no tuvo registros suficientes de sus transacciones. No tuvo nada que ver con el papa que el rescripto de provisión que se expidió no fuese discordante con otro rescripto anterior. Y en este caso admitió Alejandro IV que no se acordaba de las circunstancias particulares: «dominus papa dixit se non recordari...» [65]. Por eso —y sobre todo cuando se trató de la iglesia compostelana, que había adquirido cierta reputación de agresión en materia de provisio-

---

[60] ACL, 1.630 (apéndice 16).

[61] Antonio de Narni: A. S. V. *Collectoriae* 397, fol. 113v.

[62] LINEHAN, *The Spanish Church*, 289-290.

[63] *Reg. Urban. IV*, 906, 2025: «intellecto... quod eadem ecclesia (*scil.* Legionensis) per nostras (*scil.* litteras) et felicis recordationis Alexandri pape predecessoris nostri super receptione et provisione multorum gravata fuerat».

[64] A. S. V. *Collectoriae* 397, ff. 85v-87v (apéndice 9). Para las dificultades de la iglesia palentina en esta época, véase LINEHAN, *The Spanish Church*, 177-178; ID., *The «Gravamina» of the Castilian Church in 1262-63*: English Historical Review, 85 (1970) 730-754.

[65] *Ibíd.*, fol. 86v. Cf. G. BARRACLOUGH, *Papal Provisions* (Oxford 1935) 97.

nes [66]—, no es difícil explicar el siempre creciente volumen de litigación beneficial. Ignoramos el resultado de este pleito, así como si Fernán Patino o Alfonso Pérez consiguieron el beneficio vacante [67]. Pero no hay duda de que fueron muchos tales pleitos en esta época y que muchas personalidades leonesas frecuentaron la corte papal.

Continuaba la tensión entre obispo y cabildo: en agosto de 1264 se dio a Martín Fernández en Orvieto el nombramiento de tres y cinco canónigos entre los porcionarios de su iglesia, y de dos dignidades [68]. Durante el invierno de 1263-64 se encontraron allí tres arcedianos —Pedro de Triacastela, Adán y Gonzalo— con el chantre [69], y cuando eventualmente, en septiembre de 1263, obtuvo Alfonso Peláez un beneficio leonés, se atribuyó su éxito en parte a «quedam persone Legionensis ecclesie apud sedem apostolicam existentes» [70] que le habían recomendado al auditor, cardenal Ottobono Fieschi. Había estado ocupado en la litigación desde el pontificado de Alejandro IV, como igualmente Domingo González, *diaconus chori*, a quien la frustración de fracaso continuado había impelido a la corte papal [71].

Era suya la suerte de «Aprilis hispana gente profectus» en los versos del poeta contemporáneo que vio a los otros acumulando muchos beneficios y él mismo ninguno:

> *Ampla tenent alii stipendia divitis agri.*
> *Hic tribus, hic senis, dives at ille decem.*
> *Sed mihi sufficeret prebendula pauperis orti*
> *Quinque talenta valens, quinque parumve magis.*
> *Credo quod urbis apex sanctissimus ille virorum,*
> *Si me cognoscat, non neget ista michi.*
> *Ditat eos, qui pauca sciunt, vir sanctus et a me*
> *Forsitan excutiet pulveris istud onus* [72].

Pues, como queda dicho, el objeto de *Execrabilis* había sido el proporcionar un descanso pasajero, nada más, y cuando en diciembre de 1263

---

[66] LINEHAN, *The Spanish Church*, 267.

[67] La identidad de Alfonso Pérez no es fácil fijarla con certeza. Véase mi artículo *La carrera del obispo Abril de Urgel: La iglesia española en el siglo XIII:* Anuario de Estudios Medievales, 8 (1972-1973) 147, 169.

[68] Vid. *supra*, nota 42; *Reg. Urban. IV*, 1946.

[69] *Ibíd.*, 233, 1100, 1111.

[70] *Ibíd.*, 2201.

[71] *Ibíd.*, 2216.

[72] Ed. H. GRAUERT, *Magister Heinrich der Poet in Würzburg und die römische Kurie* [Abhandlungen der Wiss. Phil.-phil. u. Hist. Klasse, 27] (München 1912) líneas 64-71.

LA IGLESIA DE LEÓN A MEDIADOS DEL SIGLO XIII

el papa tomó nuevas medidas quirúrgicas en León, los que menos padecieron y cuyos intereses más propiciamente se defendieron fueron los curialescos: Maestre Domingo, *physicus et capellanus* del cardenal Giovanni Gaetano Orsini; Rodrigo Sánchez, sobrino del canonista Bernardus Compostellanus; Pedro Pérez, el procurador episcopal; Pedro Domínguez, arcediano de Triacastela y capellán del cardenal Giacomo Savelli; Rainerio, sobrino del cardenal Uberto Coconato [73]. Ellos —y otros de su índole, como el arcediano de Trastámara [74]— tenían sus amigos influyentes. Las posibilidades de un Alfonso Pérez de Arvis, *pauper clericus* de Oviedo, sin recursos para litigar, fueron mínimas; pero se fue también a la curia [75].

Se conocieron perfectamente los españoles curiales: el sello del deán de Zamora fue muy conocido allí, según nuestra información [76]. Hasta su muerte, en el año 1255, el cardenal español Gil Torres formó un foco natural [77]. Después, los españoles se encomendaron a nuevos patronos: los clérigos leoneses se encontraron en las familias de los cardenales Gullielmo Fieschi, Giacomo Savelli, Guillaulme de San Marco y Giovanni Gaetano Orsini [78]. Contra uno de estos clérigos, el arcediano de Triacastela y capellán doméstico del cardenal Giacomo Savelli, objetó el cabildo, con el fin de que no se le atribuyesen sus rentas leonesas cuando viviese *in curia romana*. Se siguió el pleito al mismo tiempo que el de Benamariel, y fracasó [79].

Había uno, quizá el más distinguido español de la época, que se entrometió frecuentemente en los asuntos de la iglesia de León durante los años 1250 y 1260: el canonista Bernardus Compostellanus [80]. Cuando se le transfirió en 1254 el arcedianato de Saldaña (antes poseído por el nuevo obispo de León, Martín Fernández) era ya una figura importante en la corte romana y muy amigo del papa Inocencio [81]. A su hermano Martín Yáñez, canónigo de Compostela, se cedió por provisión papal el arcedia-

---

[73] *Reg. Urban. IV*, 1206; LINEHAN, *The Spanish Church*, 299.

[74] *Reg. Urban. IV*, 2080, 2093; LINEHAN, *The Spanish Church*, 204.

[75] *Ibíd.*, 2683.

[76] A. S. V. *Collectoriae* 397, fol. 127r.

[77] LINEHAN, *The Spanish Church*, 276 ff.

[78] El chantre Julián (*Reg. Alex. IV*, 657); el arcediano de Triacastela (*Reg. Urban. IV*, 233, 1206); Maestro Gonzalo (*ibíd.*, 1111); Maestro Domingo (*ibíd.*, 1206). Este último fue *physicus* de su cardenal.

[79] *Ibíd.*, 2360.

[80] Véase G. BARRACLOUGH, *Bernard of Compostella:* English Historical Review, 49 (1934) 487-494.

[81] *Reg. Inn. IV*, 8300 (apéndice 5).

nato de Cea en octubre de 1255, prefiriéndole sobre Marco Domínguez, clérigo leonés, a quien se lo había prometido el cardenal Gil en febrero de 1253 a la muerte del arcediano Abril Abril[82]. Parece que Martín Yáñez vivió en la curia con su hermano[83]. Entre los restantes familiares del canonista se mencionan Pelayo Fernández, su clérigo y el adversario del obispo Martín Fernández[84]; el arcediano Adán; el chantre Miguel Sánchez[85]; su sobrino Rodrigo Sánchez[86]. Como uno de los *auditores sacri palatii*, estuvo Bernardo muy ocupado en los asuntos de la colación de beneficios. De él escribe Geoffrey Barraclough en un artículo importante: «"Beneficial" law was avowedly Compostellanus' speciality: it was in this branch of jurisprudence that he added most to Innocent IV's conclusions... The elucidation of the legal operation of provisions was his special contribution to canonistic knowledge... Among the officials of the Curia who were conspicuously active in transforming the practice of papal provisions into a system, though many must have had a share in the work, there is none whose influence is more apparent at the decisive, formative period»[87]. Muy inocenciano en su punto de vista jurisprudencial, desaprobó la quebrantadora influencia de la constitución alejandrina *Execrabilis*. Para él, «it was», como escribe Barraclough, «an interference with the normal running of the accepted machinery of ecclesiastical organization, and as such was bound to give rise to a certain number of disorders»[88]: «Dicam dictam constitutionem esse odiosam et contra iuris rationem», opinó en la sección sobre varios problemas prácticos de materia beneficial que insertó en su Comentario a las *Decretales* de Gregorio IX[89]. Escribió esta sección porque conoció las dificultades que surgieron en la interpretación del *ius canonicum*: «Quia questiones de beneficiis frequentes sunt et involute ita quod periti et exercitati in causis sepe falluntur, ideo de ipsis quedam utilia per dominum papam in diversis notata capitulis et quedam alia que in curia vidi determinari in facto hic inserere credidi expedire...»[90].

---

[82]   *Ibíd.*, 6317; *Reg. Alex. IV*, 825.

[83]   *Reg. Inn. IV*, 8300.

[84]   *Ibíd.*, 5759, 7860.

[85]   *Reg. Urban. IV*, 1100.

[86]   *Ibíd.*, 1206.

[87]   BARRACLOUGH, *ob. cit.*: English Historical Review, 49, 494.

[88]   ID., *ibíd.*: English Historical Review, 210.

[89]   Esta sección de *Notabilia* ocurre después de sus glosas sobre c. 30 X 1, 3. Cf. BARRACLOUGH, *ut supra*, 207-208, 210, 488. He utilizado dos manuscritos de Cambridge: Peterhouse, MS 80, ff. 263va-7ra; University Library, MS Ii-II-30, ff. 199r-204r. La cita en el texto es del Peterhouse MS 80, fol. 264vb.

[90]   *Ibíd.*, fol. 263 va.

VII

LA IGLESIA DE LEÓN A MEDIADOS DEL SIGLO XIII

Su maestría y su conocimiento de las circunstancias españolas[91] le hicieron persona ideal para resolver los varios asuntos que surgieron de la emisión de *Execrabilis*, cuando los pretendientes suplicaron nuevas cartas apostólicas. Se mencionó en uno de los pleitos en *Collectoriae* 397. Fue, para terminar, uno de los sucesores del cardenal Gil como *chargé d'affaires espagnoles* en la curia papal [92].

Esta visión del estado de la iglesia de León a mediados del siglo XIII, aunque limitada a sus aspectos económicos, debe sugerir varias preguntas bastante fundamentales. Las largas demoras experimentadas por los clérigos que litigaron en la curia romana nos hacen maravillarnos ante la prontitud con que se emprendieron tantos pleitos. La *Causa archiepiscopi Compostellani* duró no menos de dieciséis meses, incluida una pausa de un año, entre enero de 1260 y enero de 1261; dos pleitos pendientes durante el pontificado de Urbano IV habían sido planteados en vida de su predecesor [93]. Dada la ineficacia de los mandatos apostólicos, y aunque la intervención de los reyes, los cardenales y otros curiales pudiera discriminar entre pobres y ricos (cosa que, evidentemente, no pudo hacer el sistema como tal [94]), para la mayoría no valía la pena, y no son escasos los indicios en los documentos contemporáneos de un deseo de evitar estos procesos judiciales. Por eso, Maestre Pedro, el *magister scolarum* de Lugo, en contienda con el obispo y cabildo de Orense sobre el arcedianato de Benevento «per plures annos... expensis et laboribus fatigato» sometió su pleito al arbitraje de Bernardus Compostellanus en 1263, «strepitu judiciali postpo-

---

[91] Barraclough cita su discusión en su Comentario *Ad*. c. 1 in VI° I, 6, *v*. Canoniis: «Sed quid de prestimoniis, que in Yspania in ecclesia Legionensi et aliis pluribus, licet non sub nomine prestimoniorum, personis vel canonicis conferuntur?» (*ut supra*, 491), mientras que en nuestros MSS (Peterhouse 80, fol. 296vb; Cambridge University Library, Ii-II-30, fol. 243vb) se lea no *Legionensi* pero *Lugdunensis:* una confusión de algún interés filológico. En las *Notabilia* (fol. 264r) se refiere al deanato de Orense (cf. *Reg. Inn. IV*, 6485; *Reg. Alex. IV*, 410), pero no específicamente a la iglesia de León, aunque discute varios aspectos del sujeto que sirven para ilustrar a la *Causa Magistri Gondasalvi:* la cuestión de precedencia entre dos o más pretendientes (fol. 263vb); las tácticas evasivas adoptadas por los obispos y cabildos frente al ejecutor de un mandato de provisión (*ibíd.*).

[92] A. S. V. *Collectoriae* 397, fol. 87r. En julio de 1260 se confirmaron las sentencias del cardenal húngaro Esteban de Palestrina, «cui ordinandi de quibusdam dignitatibus, personatibus, beneficiis et prestimoniis in... Burgensi ecclesia vacantibus plenariam contulimus potestatem»: *Reg. Alex. IV*, 3142.

[93] *Reg. Urban. IV*, 2201, 2216

[94] Bernardus Compostellanus, *Notabilia:* «... quia pluralitas beneficiorum magna tolleratur in sublimibus et litteratis personis qui maioribus debent beneficiis habundare quam in aliis, i. de preb. de multa» [c. 28 X. 3. 5] (Peterhouse, MS 80, fol. 266vb). Cf. abajo, págs. 35-36.

29

sito», prefiriendo no fatigarse más en una serie interminable de apelaciones, etc. [95]. Y lo mismo hicieron el obispo Martín Fernández, el deán y el cabildo de León en cuanto a su disputa sobre varias propiedades que los capitulares alegaron haber sido enajenadas injustamente por el obispo, nombrando al arcediano de Benamariel, Maestre Fernando, como árbitro [96].

Otros remedios dentro del sistema vigente enconaron las relaciones entre obispo y cabildo. Del muy interesante informe de las deposiciones hechas en la investigación del año 1267 [97] podemos ver que los obispos modernos, tanto Nuño como Martín Fernández, habían intentado transferir parte de los costos de la litigación de la iglesia al cabildo. Y hasta 1284 continuaron las disputas sobre cantidades concretas de dinero [98]. Las disputas que se levantaron anularon las relaciones familiares: el deán Alfonso Yáñez, que dirigió la campaña capitular en su contienda con el obispo sobre las posesiones disputadas, era sobrino del mismo Martín Fernández y su ejecutor testamentario [99]. Las tensiones causadas por una falta de recursos en toda la península y que en otros sitios (en Burgos, por ejemplo) se manifestaron en forma de ataques contra las órdenes mendicantes [100], se acrecentaron en León dentro de la misma iglesia.

Entre los testigos de un documento de febrero de 1261, citado por Melendo Pérez en el curso de su litigación, encontramos a Maestre Simón, «operis eiusdem [Legionensis] ecclesie magister» [101]. Maestre Simón sirve para recordarnos que la construcción de la catedral leonesa durante estos años representa una hazaña aún más formidable que su belleza, y para volvernos a la pregunta del principio de este ensayo. ¿De dónde se proveyó para sufragar los gastos de construcción? La concesión de las tercias «reales» hecha por Alfonso X en 1258 no pudo representar mucho, y si

---

[95] *Reg. Urban. IV*, 1100.

[96] En el año 1290 lo prorrogaron el obispo Fernando —«velut bonus pater et dominus cupiens gregem sibi commissum in tranquillitate regere et caritate fovere, lites et iurgia execrando similiter»— y el cabildo —«cum per lites et causas non sit dubium partes expensis et laboribus in dampnum ecclesie fatigari»— queriendo todos proceder «sine strepitu judicii»: ACL, doc. 1.619.

[97] ACL, doc. 1.564 (apéndice 13).

[98] ACL, doc. 1.603 (apéndice 15).

[99] ACL, doc. 1.619; ES, 36, clviii.

[100] LINEHAN, *The Spanish Church*, 317.

[101] A. S. V. *Collectoriae* 397, fol. 115r. Hubo un arquitecto de este nombre en León a mediados o finales del siglo XIV, según J. M. QUADRADO, *España: sus monumentos y artes, su naturaleza e historia: Asturias y León* (Barcelona 1885) 441. Cf. las noticias dadas por E. LAMBERT, *L'art gothique en Espagne aus XIIe et XIIIe siècles* (París 1931) 229, 240-242.

hubiera valido algo, habría estado hecha a cuenta de las demás iglesias de la diócesis [102]. Una ojeada por varios testamentos de canónigos y dignidades leonesas de la segunda mitad del siglo indica, *pace* Risco, la insignificancia de sus legados *ad opus cathedralis ecclesie*. Ninguno legó más de veinte maravedís [103]. Las indulgencias otorgadas por los papas [104] y otros prelados [105] pudieron aportar algo, pero sin saber a quién correspondió la última responsabilidad de los gastos, o si hubo algunas donaciones reales y nobiliarias, es imposible descubrir lo que pasó realmente. Se admitió a la sazón lo que la construcción de la catedral debe a las contribuciones de los fieles [106]. Pero no tenemos para León los detalles que han iluminado el mismo proceso en Reims o en Milán [107]. Y no sabemos si los fieles se animaron a contribuir por un importante hallazgo —o, como sucedió en Segovia en esta época, por una compra— de las reliquias [108]. A lo menos, es importante que se distinga entre la pobreza de la iglesia de León en los aspectos discutidos más arriba y la riqueza de algunos de sus canónigos y obispos [109]. Y es de notar que entre los canónigos y la iglesia a la que pertenecían había una importante distinción, tanto teórica como práctica:

---

[102] ES, 36, clvi; *Reg. Inn. IV*, 7960; *Reg. Alex. IV*, 246; LINEHAN, *The Spanish Church*, 112, 244.

[103] ES, 35, 325-326. Lo que se dice arriba se apoya en el estudio de unos veinte testamentos de canónigos y dignidades de entre 1254 y 1321, y, por supuesto, queda mucho menos que definitivo. Un testamento típico de la época (ACL, doc. 1.569) se publica en apéndice 14.

[104] *Reg. Alex. IV*, 160 (feb. 1255); *Reg. Urban. IV*, 2060 (julio 1264).

[105] ES, 35, 268-270.

[106] *Ibíd.*, 269.

[107] R. BRANNER, *Historical Aspects of the Reconstruction of Reims Cathedral 1210-1241:* Speculum, 36 (1961) 23-37; E. BISHOP, *Liturgica Historica* (Oxford 1918) 411-421.

[108] A. C. Segovia, doc. 181 (Reliquias, 4-38; sin fecha) relata la donación «ad opus Segobiensis ecclesie» por Maestre P. Martínez, canónigo, de varias reliquias «de Romania» de los santos Pablo, Andrés, Esteban el protomártir, Laurencio, Sebastián, y de santa Cristina *virginis,* las cuales P. Martínez había recibido de su «socius in scolis» Maestre Melior, deán de Atenas. Fueron garantizadas por un desconocido arzobispo de Atenas, Crescencius. La primera piedra de la catedral segoviana se puso en 1228: D. DE COLMENARES, *Historia de la insigne ciudad de Segovia* (Segovia 1637) 192. Dichas reliquias fueron bastante corrientes, excepto las de san Sebastián (raras) y de santa Cristina (únicas): Véase COMTE DE RIANT, *Exuviae Sacrae Constantinopolitanae,* II (Ginebra 1878). Véase también C. R. CHENEY, *Churchbuilding in the Middle Ages:* Bulletin of the John Rylands Library, 24 (1951-52) 20-36.

[109] Véase las listas de deudas del obispo Martín Fernández (31.000 maravedíes en suma) y de sus donaciones al cabildo de León: ES, 36, clviii-xii.

las constituciones del cardenal Pelayo les permitieron legar a sus parientes su propiedad patrimonial, de modo que no es inverosímil que perdiera la iglesia de León algo de lo que la pertenecía [110].

Cambridge, Inglaterra

---

[110] «Bona vero ab intestato decedentium sive mobilia, que de bonis ecclesie constiterint acquisita, inter episcopum et capitulum dividantur salvis tam episcopo quam capitulo quibusdam, que precipua consueverunt habere. Si vero patrimonialia fuerint, vel alio iusto titulo ad eos pervenire constiterit, ab eorum successione nolumus legitimos heredes excludi»: vid. más arriba, nota 5.

APENDICE DOCUMENTAL

SIGLAS

— palabra o palabras entre [y] interlineada(s) en el manuscrito.

— [...] : palabra ilegible.

Y las siguientes abreviaturas:

ACL = Archivo de la catedral, León.

AHN = Archivo Histórico Nacional, Madrid.

ASV = Archivio Segreto Vaticano.

BN = Biblioteca Nacional, Madrid.

ES = España Sagrada.

Reg. Alex. IV = Les Registres d'Alexandre IV (1254-61), ed. C. Bourel de la Roncière, etc. (París 1902-59).

Reg. Greg. IX = Les Registres de Grégoire IX (1227-41), ed. L. Auvray (París 1890-1955).

Reg. Hon. III = Regesta Honorii papae III (1216-27), ed. P. Pressutti (Roma 1888-95).

Reg. Inn. IV. = Les Registres d'Innocent IV (1243-54), ed. E. Berger (París 1881-1921).

Reg. Urban. IV = Les Registres d'Urbain IV (1261-64), ed. J. Guiraud (París 1892-1906).

1

1250, febrero, 17. Lyon.

Inocencio IV manda al obispo Nuño de León que promueva al clérigo
romano Nicolás a un beneficio en la iglesia de León.

León, ACL, doc. 5.779.

Innocentius episcopus servus servorum Dei. Venerabili fratri... episcopo Legionensi salutem et apostolicam benedictionem. Exposuit nobis dilectus filius Nicolaus
clericus natus quondam Crescentii Nicolatri de Urbe civis Romani quod cum nos
tibi per nostras litteras duxerimus concedendum ut quatuor clericis quos moribus
et scientia nosceres adiuvari totidem prebendas cum canoniis seu portiones in Legio-
† nensi ecclesia ultra numerum canonicorum prebendarum seu portionum in illa statum,
non obstante eodem numero iuramento seu quacumque alia firmitate vallato, et
quod in ipsa prebendarum et portionum collatio ad episcopum Legionensem qui est
pro tempore una cum ipsius ecclesie capitulo pertinere dinoscitur conferre valeres,
tu auctoritate concessionis huiusmodi eidem clerico prebendam cum canonia seu
portione in prefata ecclesia ultra predictum canonicorum numerum et prebendarum
seu portionum in ipsa statutum prout in tuis litteris inde confectis contineri dicitur
contulisti. Quare idem clericus nobis humiliter supplicavit ut cum tu in capitulo
Legionensi litteris renuntiaris eisdem propter quod ex facta in hac parte sibi gratia
nullum ut asserit est commodum consecutus providere super hoc ei de benignitate
sedis apostolice curaremus. Nos igitur ipsius clerici supplicationibus inclinati faciendi
ipsum si tibi placuerit recipi de novo in eadem ecclesia in canonicum et in fratrem
ac eidem providendi de portione vel prebenda cum prestimoniis ibidem cum ad id
obtulerit se facultas necnon et compescendi per censuram ecclesiasticam appellatione
postposita contradictores et rebelles auctoritate presentium fraternitati tue liberam
concedimus facultatem. Non obstantibus certo ipsius ecclesie canonicorum numero
iuramento confirmatione sedis apostolice seu quacumque firmitate alia roborato sive
si personis ipsius a sede sit indultum eadem quod ad provisionem alicuius minime
teneantur, aut quod per litteras apostolicas interdici suspendi vel excommunicari non
possint nisi in eis de indulgentia huiusmodi expressa mentio habeatur sive qualibet
alia per quam huiusmodi gratia impediri valeat vel differri et de qua in nostris
litteris specialem oporteat fieri mentionem. Dat. Lugduni .XIII. kal. martii pontificatus
nostri anno septimo.

Al dorso: N. clericus de Urbe.

2

1251, febrero, 7. Lyon.

Inocencio IV ratifica la donación de ciertas rentas leonesas hecha por el obispo Nuño de León a «Stephanus dictus Surdus», sobrino del cardenal Riccardo Annibaldi di San Angelo.

Archivio Segreto Vaticano, Reg. Vat. 22, núm. 379, fol. 51v (reg. BERGER, *Registres d'Innocent IV*, núm. 5113).

Stephano dicto Surdo, canonico Legionensi. Attendens tua merita probitatis libenter petitionibus tuis benignum accommodamus auditum easque liberaliter quantum cum Deo possumus exaudimus. Cum itaque sicut asseris venerabilis frater noster... Legionensis episcopus prestimonia de Capiolas, de Castro Vau, de Fontes, de Caruyr de Comelas, de Gosendas et de Bergianos de Camino que quondam P. Arie decanus Legionensis obtinuit, tibi auctoritate nostra canonice duxerit concedenda, prout in ipsius litteris inde confectis plenius continetur, nos tuis supplicationibus inclinati concessimus... gratam et ratam habentes eam auctoritate apostolica confirmamus... tenor litterarum ipsarum de verbo ad verbum presentibus inseri facientes, qui talis est: Noverint universi presentes litteras inspecturi quod nos M[unio] dei gratia Legionensis episcopus damus et concedimus... auctoritate domini pape dilecto filio nostro Stephano Surdo Legionensi canonico et nepoti venerabilis patris domini R[icardi] Sancti Angeli diaconi cardinalis prestimonia de Capiolas, de Castro Vau, etc., ut supra usque de Camino integre cum omnibus iuribus ac pertinentiis suis sicut olim dicta prestimonia bone memorie P. Arie Legionensis decanus habuit vel habere debuit usque modo ut ea cum prestimonio Sancti Petri de Ocos de Re quod alias sibi concessimus habeat in vita sua pacifice et quiete. In cuius rei testimonium et perpetuam firmitatem presentibus litteris sigillum nostrum duximus apponendum.

Dat. Lugduni .vii. id. februarii anno .x.

3

1252, octubre, 18. Perugia.

El cardenal Gil Torres asigna a Hugolino, sobrino del vicecanciller de la Iglesia Romana, el canonicato y la prebenda leonesas del fallecido prior de León, Giraldo Diego.

Archivio Segreto Vaticano, Reg. Vat. 22, núm. 768, ff. 281r-v (conf. 25, II, 1253; reg. BERGER, *Registres d'Innocent IV*, núm. 6628).

Egidius... Cum dudum recepissemus apostolicis litteris in mandatis ut Hugolinum dilectum clericum et alumpnum nostrum, dilecti nostri Guillelmi magistri scolarum Parmensis, Sacrosancte Romane Ecclesie vicecancellarii tunc auditoris contradictarum

domini pape nepotem, in aliqua ecclesiarum Yspanie cathedrali vel alia recipi face-
remus in canonicum et in fratrem et sibi de prebenda etiam provideri quodque tam
in ecclesia ipsa quam alibi expedire videremus de prestimoniis provideremus eidem,
et nuper in ecclesia Legionensi canonia et prebenda quas quondam Girardus Didaci
ipsius ecclesie prior obtinuit in eadem per illius obitum vacasse noscantur, nos ar-
bitrantes in ipso Hugolino non minus eidem provideri ecclesie quam persone cum
per se ac suos ei esse valeat multipliciter fructuosus earundem litterarum auctoritate
ac de ipsius domini speciali mandato canoniam et prebendam predictas nominato
vice nomine ipsius Hugolini cum plenitudine iuris canonici conferimus et eum de
illis vice ipsius Hugolini per nostrum anulum presentialiter investimus, ab eis de-
tentorem quemlibet ammoventes. Decernimus insuper irritum et inane siquid contra
collationem et investituram huius a quoque contingerit attemptari et ex nunc in
contra(*fol. 281v*)dictores et rebelles... Perusii .xv. kal. novembris pontificatus domini
Innocentii pape IIII anno X.

4

1253, marzo, 29. Perugia.

*Inocencio IV confirma la decisión del cardenal Gil Torres en cuanto
a las rentas tocantes a la cantoría de la iglesia de León.*

Archivio Segreto Vaticano, Reg. Vat. 23, núm. 53, iii, ff. 151v-152r (reg. BERGER,
Registres d'Innocent IV, núm. 7860).

Magistro Juliano cantori Legionensi, capellano dilecti filii nostri G[uillelmi]
Sancti Eustachii diaconi cardinalis. Cum a nobis petitur, etc., usque effectum. Sane
licet dilecto filio nostro E[gidio] Sanctorum Cosme et Damiani diacono cardinali
nostris dederimus litteris in mandatis ut tibi de personatu vel dignitate cum prestimoniis cedentis vel decedentis illius qui personatum vel dignitatum (*sic*) huiusmodi
obtineret in Legionensi ecclesia si tunc vacabat ibidem vel quamprimum ad id opor-
tunitas se offeret, auctoritate nostra, curaret per se vel per alium providere, nichilominus tamen idem cardinalis, vacante cantoria in dicta ecclesia per mortem Petri
Johannis cantoris ipsius et ea tibi cum omnibus iuribus ac suis pertinentiis assignata,
de prestimoniis dicti P. cantoris retinuit L marabutinos pro Pellagio Fernandi Legionensi canonico quos sibi per te solvi annuatim mandavit donec esset ei provisum
aliter de eisdem, ac etiam tot et tanta de prestimoniis que fuerunt dicti cantoris
idem cardinalis dilecto filio G[uillelmo] magistro scolarum Parmensi vicecancellario
nostro assignavit et contulit quot et quanta ad supplementum .xx. marcarum plenarie satisfacerent (*sic*) computatis prestimoniis que quondam Giraldus Didaci ipsius
ecclesie prior obtinuit in eadem, que quidem prestimonia per cardinalem prefatum
assignata fuerunt dicto vicecancellario et collata. Verum postmodum, ne per sub-
tractionem huiusmodi factae tibi a nobis gratie huiusmodi commodo frauderetis, idem
cardinalis dilecto filio Lupo Suggerii ecclesie supradicte canonico, auctoritate nostra
districte precipiendo per litteras suas, mandat ut de prestimoniis primo in prefata

LA IGLESIA DE LEÓN A MEDIADOS DEL SIGLO XIII

ecclesia vacaturis tibi compensationem congruam ad extimationem communem per se vel per alium faciat de predictis et te vel aliquem tuo nomine in ipsorum possessionem inducat et inductum auctoritate apostolica tueatur, decernendo eadem auctoritate irritum et inane siquid contra mandatum et provisionem huiusmodi contigerit attemptari, prout in eiusdem cardinalis litteris exinde confectis plenius continetur. Nos itaque tuis precibus inclinati quod ab eodem cardinale super hoc factum est ratum et gratum habentes, illud auctoritate apostolica confirmamus, etc., usque continentur, litterarum ipsarum tenorem de verbo ad verbum presentibus inseri facientes qui talis est:

Egidius divina patientia Sanctorum Cosme et Damiani diaconus cardinalis dilecto in Christo Lupo Suggerii canonico Legionensi salutem et gratiam. Cum dominus papa suis nobis litteris et viva voce dederit in mandatis ut magistro Juliano nunc cantori Legionensi capellano venerabilis fratris nostri domini Guillelmi Sancti Eustachii diaconi cardinalis de personatu (fol. 152r) vel dignitate cum prestimoniis cedentis vel decedentis illius qui personatum vel dignitatem huiusmodi obtineret in Legionensi ecclesia si vacabat ibidem ad presens vel quamprimum ad id offeret se facultas auctoritate apostolica procuraremus per nos vel per alium providere, et nos collata sibi cantoria que per mortem Petri Johannis olim cantoris in Legionensi vacabat ecclesia, de prestimoniis eiusdem tenuimus .L. morabutinos pro Pelagio Fernandi canonico eiusdem, quos eidem per ipsum cantorem solvi mandavimus annuatim donec eidem esset provisum aliter de eisdem, et tot et tanta de prestimoniis qui fuerunt eiusdem cantoris magistro G[uillelmo] domini pape vicecancellario auctoritate apostolica assignavimus et contulimus quot et quanta ad supplementum .xx. marcarum plenarie sufficiunt computatis prestimoniis que quondam Giraldus Didaci ipsius ecclesie prior obtinuit in eadem discretioni tue auctoritate apostolica qua fungimur in hac parte districte precipiendo mandamus quatenus in prestimoniis que primo in prenominata ecclesia vacare contigerit dicto cantori compensationem congruam ad communem extimationem per te vel per alium facias de predictis et eundem vel aliquem nomine suo in possessione eorum inducas et inductum auctoritate apostolica tuearis, decernendo eadem auctoritate irritum et inane siquid contra nostrum mandatum et provisionem tuam fuerit attemptatum, contra impedientes et rebelles per censuram ecclesiasticam conpescendo. Dat. Perusii .vi. non. martii pontificatus domini Innocentii pape iiii anno .x.

Dat. Perusii .iiii. kal. aprilis anno .x.

5

1254, julio, 28. Anagni.

Inocencio IV confirma la donación del arcedianato de Saldaña a maestre Bernardo, deán de Lisboa (el canonista Bernardus Compostellanus).

> Archivio Segreto Vaticano. Reg. Vat. 22, núm. 960, fol. 313r (reg. BERGER, *Registres d'Innocent IV*, núm. 8300).

Magistro Bernardo capellano nostro, decano Ulixbonensi. Nota est probitatis opinio et experta bonitatis integritas quibus in nostris et fratrum nostrorum oculis

persone tue merita comprobantur. Sane apostolice sedis providentia singulorum merita diligentes attendens maioribus remunerat premiis quos considerationis examine
potiora diffinit eosque uberiori retributione prosequitur qui digniori virtute precel-
lunt. Nuper equidem dilectus filius noster Ottobonus Sancti Adriani diaconus cardinalis archidiaconatum de Sandanya, canoniam et prebendam quos dilectus filius Martinus Fernandi electus, tunc archidiaconus Legionensis, in Legionensi ecclesia obtinebat,
tibi prout ei viva voce mandavimus cum omnibus iuribus et pertinentiis suis contulit
teque de ipsis per suum anulum investivit, non obstante quod tempus nondum
effluxerat de episcopis consecrandis seu gratia quam super provisione tua in Compostellana ecclesia de personatu seu dignitate cum prestimoniis cedentis vel decedentis tibi hactenus feceramus, quam ratam et integram permanere de nostro mandato decrevit, vel quod in Compostellana et aliis cathedralibus ecclesiis prebendas et
prestimonia consueta canonicis dictarum ecclesiarum conferri quorum unum curam
animarum annexam habere dicitur et pensionem quamdam in Ulixbonensi ecclesia
nosceris obtinere, seu quod in eadem Legionensi ecclesia super simili provisione pro
aliis direximus scripta nostra, aut presentationibus, reservationibus et inhibitionibus
per eadem scripta seu alias auctoritate vel mandato nostro a quocumque factis, seu
quibuscumque processibus pro aliis habitis quibus quoad assecutionem archidiaconatus, canonie ac prebende predictorum, cardinalis ipse te voluit, et nos etiam volumus
anteferri, sive si in dicta Legionensi ecclesia certus sit canonicorum numerus iuramento confirmatus sede apostolica vel alia qualibet firmitate vallatus aut quavis apostolica indulgentia cuicumque persone vel loco concessa cuiuscumque tenoris existat
de qua specialem seu de verbo ad verbum oporteret fieri mentionem. Idem preterea
cardinalis de mandato nostro irritum et inane decrevit quicquid contra collationem
suam a quoque fuerit attemptatum prout in litteris ipsius cardinalis inde confectis
et sigillo munitis ipsius plenius continetur. Nos igitur tuis supplicationibus inclinati
quod per eundem cardinalem in hac parte factum est ratum habentes et gratum id
auctoritate apostolica confirmamus, etc., usque communis, supplentes defectum siquid
in premissis existit de plena potestate ac tenorem litterarum ipsarum de verbo ad
verbum presentibus inseri facientes. Qui talis est:

Ottobonus miseratione divina Sancti Adriani diaconus cardinalis dilecto in Christo
suo Magistro Bernardo domini pape capellano et Ulixbonensi decano in vera salu-
tari salutem. Cum dominus papa vos ob vestri merita et devotum obsequium quod
sibi diu et fideliter impendistis dono favoris et gratie prosequi libenter intendat, nos
auctoritate et speciali mandato eiusdem domini pape viva voce nobis iniuncto archidiaconatum de Saldanya in ecclesia Legionensis, canoniam et prebendam quas venerabilis vir Martinus Fernandi Legionensis electus in ecclesia ipsa obtinet vobis
cum omnibus iuribus et pertinentiis suis conferimus et vos de ipsis per nostrum
anulum investimus, non obstante quod tempus de consecrandis episcopis nondum sit
decursum, seu gratia qua dominus papa in Compostellana ecclesia de personatu seu
dignitate cum prestimoniis cedentis vel decedentis persone personatum obtinentis eundem fieri, vobis decanatum Ulixbonensem resignare paratis, mandavit, cui gratie per
collationem predictam nec idem dominus nec nos intendimus preiudicium generari,
gratiam ipsam ratam manere ac integram de mandato eiusdem domini decernentes,
vel quod in Compostellana, Palentina et Tudensi ecclesiis prebendas et quedam prestimonia consueta canonicis dictarum ecclesiarum conferri quorum unum curam animarum habere dicitur et pensionem quamdam in Ulixbonensi ecclesia obtineatis, vel
quod dominus papa pro aliis in Legionensi ecclesia super consimilibus beneficiis litte-

LA IGLESIA DE LEÓN A MEDIADOS DEL SIGLO XIII

ras suas direxerit, seu presentationibus aut inhibitionibus per easdem litteras vel auctoritate seu mandato eiusdem domini pape a quocumque factis vel quibuscumque processibus pro aliis habitis quibus quoad assecutionem archidiaconatus, prebende et canonie predictorum idem dominus papa et nos de ipsius mandato vos volumus anteferri, vel quod in Legionensi ecclesia certus sit canonicorum numerus iuramento confirmatus sede apostolica vel quacumque alia firmitate vallatus aut indulgentia sedis eiusdem cuicumque persone vel loco concessa cuiuscumque tenoris existat de qua specialem seu de verbo ad verbum oporteat fieri mentionem; decernentes de ipsius domini pape mandato irritum et inane quicquid contra collationem nostram a quocumque fuerit attemptatum; presentibus Petro Nunni archidiacono Legionensi, Fernando Aprilis thesaurario Legionensi, Petro Petri canonico Zamorensi, Martino Johannis et magistro Fernando capellano nostro. In cuius rei testimonium has litteras fieri fecimus et signari nostra manu.

Dat. Anagnie anno a nativitate domini .M.CC.L.IIII. IX kal. augusti, pontificatus domini Innocentii pape IIII anno XII.

Nolumus autem quod... filio Bontempi familiaris nostri cui in dicta Legionensi ecclesia de prestimoniis usque ad valorem annuam XXV marcarum argenti provideri mandavimus per collationem seu confirmationem predictas aliquod preiudicium generetur. Nulli, etc., nostre confirmationis et superius, etc. Dat. Anagnie .V. kal. augusti anno .XII.

6

1254, agosto, 3. Anagni.

Inocencio IV autoriza a Pedro Núñez y Fernán Abril, procuradores del obispo-electo de León, Martín Fernández, para tomar prestado de una suma de 76 marcas esterlinas, y estipula las penas en que incurrirán los deudores si no liquidasen dentro del período fijado.

Archivio Segreto Vaticano, Reg. Vat. 23, núm. 53, iv, fol. 152r (reg. BERGER, *Registres d'Innocent IV*, núm. 7861).

Petro Nuni archidiacono et Fernando Aprilis thesaurario Legionensibus, procuratoribus dilecti filii M[artini] electi Legionensis. Ut dilecto filio Guillelmo magistro scholarum Parmensi vicecancellario nostro pro annua provisione .XX. marcarum sterlingorum sibi ab.. episcopo Legionensi qui pro tempore fuerit, et H[ugolino] nepoti eius canonico Legionensi ab eadem ecclesia pro prestimoniis annuis octo marcarum sterlingorum pro duobus annis preteritis et presenti ipsi vicecancellario et pro duobus annis preteritis videlicet ac presenti ipsi H. debitis satisfacere, quod carum plurimum et acceptum gerimus, valeatis contrahendi mutuum usque ad summam septuaginta sex marcarum sterlingorum nomine dilecti filii.. electi Legionensis ipsumque ac Legionensem ecclesiam et eorum bona mercatoribus cum quibus contraxeritis obligandi et renunciandi constitutioni de duabus dietis edite in concilio generali et bona restituendi in integrum necnon et conventioni iudicum si apostolicas litteras cuiuscumque tenoris super hoc creditorum ipsorum nomine contra dictos electum et ecclesiam vel eiusdem electi successores contigerit impetrari ac etiam omnibus litteris et indulgentiis apostolicis impetratis et impetrandis vobis concedimus auctoritate presenti plenariam facultatem. Ita tamen quod electus et successores sui ac eadem ecclesia dictis creditoribus ipsam pecuniam solvere necnon et ad dampna expensas et interesse si in termino statuendo eamdem pecuniam non solverint super quibus simplici verbo sine sacramento vel probatione alia credi volumus teneantur et prefatis creditoribus pretextu alicuius constitutionis canonice vel civilis aut cuiuscumque privilegii vel indulgentiae de quibus in nostris litteris plenam et expressam de verbo ad verbum oporteat fieri mentionem et per quas prefati electus et successores aliquatenus valeant se tueri dictam pecuniam in utilitatem prefate ecclesie versam esse probandi necessitas non incumbat. Dat. Anagniae .III. non. augusti anno XII.

7

1254, agosto, 6. Anagni.

Inocencio IV confirma la elección del arcediano Martín Fernández para la sede legionense.

Archivio Segreto Vaticano, Reg. Vat. 23, núm. 102, fol. 160r (reg. BERGER, *Registres d'Innocent IV*, núm. 7919).

Decano et capitulo Legionensibus. Ecclesia vestra pastoris solatio destituta et congregatis die ad eligendum prefixa qui debuerunt voluerunt et potuerunt comode interesse ac premisso iuxta formam concilii generalis scrutinio, plusquam due partes de vobis dilectum filium Martinum Fernandi notarium carissimi in Christo filii nostri.. illustris regis Castelle, ac reliqui Rodericum ipsius ecclesie archidiaconos in Legionensem episcopum elegerunt. Procuratoribus igitur partium apud Sedem Apostolicam constitutis cum ex parte illorum qui predictum Martinum elegerunt electionis facte de ipso Martino, quam asserebant esse canonicam, confirmatio peteretur, procuratoi Lupi Suggerii canonici et Alfonsi Gometii portionarii eiusdem ecclesie habens speciale mandatum ab eis de obiciendo in personam ipsius Martini defectum natalium et scientie ac pluralitatem beneficiorum cum cura et dationem quorumdam archipresbiteratum sub annuo censu contra suspensionis sententiam latam a bone memorie J. episcopo Sabinensi tunc in partibus Ispanie legato Sedis Apostolice obiecit eidem, ex parte illorum qui prefatum Martinum elegerant in personam dicti Roderici criminibus quibusdam obiectis. Cum autem testes ab utraque parte producendos super ooiectis huiusmodi quod de illis apud Sedem eandem plene liquere non poterat in illis partibus recipi mandassemus, tandem partibus cum eorundem attestationibus publicatis de assensu partium iuxta formam mandati apostolici ad Sedem accedentibus supradictam nos eis dilectum filium nostrum Ottobonum Sancti Adriani diaconum cardinalem concessimus auditorem. Examinatis itaque utriusque partis attestationibus diligenter et hiis qui coram ipso cardinali fuerunt hinc in proposita nobis per eum fideliter recitatis, nos quod de obiectis in personam iamdicti Martini nichil inventum est esse probatum cum immo ipsum Martinum de legitimo natum matrimonio et competentis esse scientie constitit evidenter electionem celebratam de ipso Martino utpote canonicam reliqua rite cassata de fratrum nostrorum consilio duximus confirmandam, spe nobis proposita quod cum predicto Martino de scientia, munditia vite ac honestate morum testimonium perhibeatur laudabile auctore illo qui... gratiam gratie superaddit per eiusdem industriam et diligentie studium dicta ecclesia grata in spiritualibus et temporalibus suscipiet incrementa. Quocirca... usque observari. Dat. Anagniae .VIII. id. augusti anno .XII.

8

1259, marzo, 17. León.

Testamento de Nuño Velázquez, arcediano de Cea.

León, ACL, doc. 1.538.

In dei Nomine Amen. Sub era .M.CC.XC.VII. xvii. dias andados del mes de Marzo. Connozuda cosa sea atodos pora queste escripto que yo don Monio velasquez Arcidiano de leon en Çea. he Maestre escola de Astorga, sanno mio seso e contodo mi entendemiento e de Mia clara Voluntat. ffago mio testamiento, enna primeramientre Mando a sancta Maria de Leon. ela yglessia de villa meriel con quantas conpras yo hy ffiz. e con quanto que yo hy he. que me lexo mia hermana donna Sancha Velasquez. he todo escobar. he Mandoye elas mias Casas que yo he en Maorga. yela parte delas Casas que me leyxo mia hermana que son hy en Maorga. Salvo mios derechos delos ffruchos que levaron mios hermanos e mios sobrinos desde trinta annos aca. que me deven aentregar. Mando helas yglessias que yo he en Senabria. e en Caruayeda. e sancta Maria de Astorga. he todo elo otro padremunio que yo he entoda Senabria enna Villa de quintaniella e enna de lobanes. he en Riavaniellos he en toda Caruayeda. he ennas villas con vien asalar. de villar de Ciervos. e de san Pelao de valde arcos. he de Mazanal dela Ynfante. he en villa nova de val roxo he en todos los otros lugares que ami pertenezen ennas tierras sobredichas. de Senabria e de Caruayeda. do he otorgo Al Monesterio de san martin de Castanera. por mia alma e en Rremession de mios peccados. e por alma de mio Padre e de mia madre. e de mia hermana donna Sancha velasquez. todo aquesto. Do. he otorgo commo de suso ye dicho. alos lugares sobredichos. tanbien que ami perteneze. commo elo de mia hermana donna Sancha velasquez. Salvo me ffinque entoda mia vida que Reciba yo elos ffruchos pora mi. de todos estos lugares sobredichos. he por que esto non venga endubda he sea mas ffirme por iamas. seelle este mio testamento de mio seyello pendiente. he por meior ffirmedunme Rogue a Maestre rodrigo dean de plazençia e canoligo de Leon. he a don Fernan abril Tessorero dela Yglessia de Leon. que pussiessen eneste testamento soz seyellos pendientes. he nos devandichos Maestre rodrigo. e don Fernan abril. a Ruego del devandicho don Monio velasquez. seellemos este testamento de nuestro seyellos pendientes. he todas estas cosas sobredichas fueron fechas he otorgadas en Casa del devandicho arciano (sic) don Monio velasquez. sub la era desta carta. Qui pressentes ffuerunt: Johan Martinez escriva. Esydro so criado. Frey Ruy perez prior. Frey Domingo. anbos del monesterio de san martin de castanera. Pedro garcia ffiyo de Garcia navarro. Domingo perez clerigo de reveo. Pedro moro. Pedro garcia escudero. Pedro domingo. todos .V. criados del arcidiano devandicho. Pedro martinez tendero. don Ramos de mansiella. Alffonso fiyo de Domingo iohannis alfarice heyo Maria gutierrez escrivi este testamento per mandado de alvar garcia escrivan del Rey e notario de leon: he fiz enella esta sinal:

9

1259-1261.

Causa archiepiscopi Compostellani.

Archivio Segreto Vaticano, *Collectoriae,* 397. Para información sobre las vías judiciales de la corte pontificia en esta época, véase la *Summa Introductoria super officio Advocationis in Foro Ecclesiae* de Bonaguida de Arezzo, tratado escrito hacia diez años antes, y esp. part. IV, tít. 2 (ed. A. WUNDERLICH, *Anecdota quae processum civilem spectant* [Göttingen 1841] 311-318). Para la fecha, véase G. BARRACLOUGH, en *Dictionnaire de Droit Canonique,* ed. R. Naz, ii, París 1937, col. 938.

(*fol. 85v*) MCCLVIIII indictione tertia III kal. decembris [29-XI-1259] denunciatum fuit venerabili patri domino O[ctaviano] Sancte Marie in Vialata diacono cardinali ex parte domini pape per Petrum de Alatro familiarem Nicholay hostiarii ipsius domini ut audiat [MS. adiat] causam a (*sic*) tam appellationis quam principalem que vertitur vel verti speratur inter reverendum patrem archiepiscopum, capitulum et Alfonsum Petri canonicum Compostellanum ex parte una et Fernandum Patinum canonicum Legionensem ex altera super canonicatu ecclesie Compostellane et prebenda cum prestimoniis que magister P. Johannis [olim d: *borrado*] canonicus Compostellanus in eadem ecclesia obtinuit et debita fine decidat.

[Die mercurii III decembris intrantis [3-XII-1259] comparentibus [Johanne Johannis pro archiepiscopo et capitulo] partibus assignatus est terminus ad diem veneris proximo sequentem ad comparendum: *todo borrado*].

Die mercurii III decembris intrante comparentibus Johanne Johannis canonico Compostellano pro archiepiscopo et capitulo Compostellanis et Anfonso Petri qui se dicit canonicum Compostellanum et Martino Petri clerico pro Fernando Pattino canonico Compostellano, ut asserit, mandatum fuit per dominum cardinalem ut die veneris proximo sequenti [peremptorie] comparare debent cum sufficienti mandato hinc inde.

Die veneris id. (*sic: recte* non.) decembris [5-XII-1259] comparuit Fernandus (?) Martini procurator Fernandi Pattini canonici Compostellani et dedit mihi notario procuratorium suum.

Die [ ] martis VIIII decembris [9-XII-1259] comparentibus partibus Johannes Johannis procurator archiepiscopi et capituli Compostellani dedit procuratorium suum mihi notario et assignatus est terminus ad diem veneris proximam ad comparendum et procedendum in causa.

LA IGLESIA DE LEÓN A MEDIADOS DEL SIGLO XIII

Die lune viiii februarii intrante [9-II-1260] comparentibus partibus assignatus est terminus Petro de Deo ad diem mercurii proximam ad faciendum declarationes super libellis oblatis sicut de iure fuerint declarande.

(fol. 86r)   Januar in Anagnia

Die veneris viiii eiusdem [9-I-1260] Fernandus Patinus canonicus Compostellanus comparuit pro se in causa que vertitur vel verti speratur inter ipsum et Alfonsum Petri.

In eodem die Johannes Johannis procurator archiepiscopi et capituli Compostellani comparuit pro eisdem quibus datus est terminus ut in crastinum compareant.

Die lune xii [12-I-1260] comparuerunt partes coram domino cardinali cum quibus comparuit Petrus de Deo canonicus Compostellanus qui dixit se habere procuratorium pro Alfonso Petri canonico Compostellano, quod procuratorium obtulit se exhibiturum in iudicio die mercurii proximo [MS. primo] venturo.

Die veneris iii decembris iiii *(sic)* indictione [3-XII-1259] in Urbe, magister Johannes de Sancto Germano domini pape notarius misit domino cardinali subscriptam cedulam sigillatam sigillo suo, et idem dominus cardinalis mandavit cedulam ipsam registrari et dari in copiam Fernando Patino canonico Legionensi, et datus est terminus eidem Fernando et Martino Johannis procuratori archiepiscopi et capituli Compostellani et Petro de Deo procuratori Afonsi Petri ut die veneris proximo venturo compareant coram domino cardinali ad procedendum in causa prout de iure fuerit.

Tenor cuius cedule talis est:

Significant sanctitati vestre archiepiscopus et capitulum Compostellani quod licet ipsi diu litigaverint cum magistro B. coram domino J[ohanne] Gaietano et adhuc litigent etiam coram domino Ricardo cum F[ernando] Johannis magistroscolarum Auriensi et canonico Legionensi qui competentia beneficia obtinens se petivit admitti ad canonicatum Compostellanum set tamdiu litigaverint donec inviti et compulsi a vobis nuper eum in canonic[at]um receperunt, nichilominus tamen Fernandus Patinus canonicus Legionensis ad Compostellanam ecclesiam vestras litteras impetravit ut admitteretur ibidem ad canonicatum et prebendam cum prestimoniis qui quondam magister P[etrus] ipsius ecclesie canonicus habuit in eadem qui apud Urbem viam fuerat universe carnis ingressus. Sed ipsi videntes hominem indignum et quod ecclesia per eius receptionem merito scandalizari poterat ad vestram audientiam appellarunt et causam appellationis sue obtinuerunt comitti domino Ottaviano Sancte Marie in Vialata cardinali. Sed idem Fernandus pendente causa huiusmodi a vobis alias obtinuit litteras ad ecclesiam Palentinam. Unde cum dictus Fernandus in dicta Palentina ecclesia [predicta] auctoritate seu occasione litterarum huiusmodi sit receptus et ecclesia Compostellana in huiusmodi litigiis multipliciter affligatur, sanctitati vestre supplicant quatinus eos a gravamine ipsius Fernandi de speciali gratia relevantes domino cardinali mandare dignemini ut si ei constiterit quod memoratus Fernandus auctoritate seu occasione litterarum huiusmodi in Palentinam ecclesiam est receptus ipsum Palentina et Legionensi ecclesiis in quibus est sibi de mandato vestro provisum faciat manere contentum, ei super receptione et provisione in Compostellana ecclesia perpetuum silentium imponendo.

Ego magister Johannes de Sancto Germano legi hanc petitionem domino nostro et idem dominus mandavit vobis quod si innoveritis sic esse provisum Fernando Patino prout in petitione continetur imponatis ei perpetuum silentium super receptione et provisione huiusmodi in ecclesia Compostellana.

fol. 86v) Die veneris xiiii januarii [14-I-1260] magister Benedictus clericus magistri Jordani vicecancellarii presentavit coram domino cardinali cedulam infrascriptam sıgillatam sigillo ipsius magistri Jordani patentem, qui dominus cardinalis mandavit ipsam cedulam registrari et fieri in copiam Fernando Patino.

Cuius cedule tenor talis est:

Significant sanctitati vestre... perpetuum silentium imponendo (*ut supra*).

Ego magister Jordanus dixi sanctissimo in Christo patri et domino domino pape quod mandatum fuerat vobis ex parte sua super peticione predicta quod si innoveritis sic esse provisum Fernando Patino prout in ipsa peticione continetur imponeritis ei silentium super canonicatu et prebenda Compostellanis. Super quo idem dominus papa dixit se non recordari sed vult quod non obstante mandato huiusmodi sıquid fuit fiat iustitia dicto Fernando Patino et si de iure privari debet canonicatu et prebenda predictis privetur eisdem et imponatis ei silentium super hiis. Alioquin non.

Die martis xviii (*sic*) januarii [18-I-1261] comparuerunt coram domino cardinali et pluribus allegatis hinc inde. Idem dominus cardinalis statuit eis terminum ut die veneris post nonam compareant coram eo.

(*fol. 87r*) Die mercurii xxiii februarii, iiii^a indictione [23-II-1261] in Urbe, Fernandus Patinus exhibuit et representavit domino cardinali ex parte magistri Jordani vicecancellarii cedulam patentem infrascriptam sigillatam sigillo ipsius magistri Jordani, cuius tenor talis est:

Ostensis domino pape per me magistrum Jordanum litteris apostolicis super collatione canonicatus et prebende Compostellane facta per eundem dominum papam et eıus auctoritate Fernando Patino canonico Legionensi, et quia in eisdem litteris de canonia Legionensi mentio plena fiebat, vult et mandat idem dominus papa vobis reverendo patri domino Octaviano Sancte Marie in Vialata diacono cardinali quod idem Fernandus habeat provisionem sibi factam in ecclesia Compostellana cum provisione quam obtinet in ecclesia Legionensi et quod renuntiet receptioni facte de ipso in ecclesia Palentina et omnibus aliis beneficiis siqua habet, non obstantibus quibuscumque mandatis ab eodem domino papa in causa huiusmodi vobis factis.

Die veneris iiii intrante martii [4-III-1261] presentibus coram domino cardinalı Fernando Patino et procuratoribus supradictis dictus cardinalis dixit quod dominus papa mandaverat sibi heri presente predicto Fernando Patino quod si idem Fernandus renuntiare vellet iuri quod competit sibi occasione receptionis sue in ecclesia Palentina et ipsius receptioni, dictus dominus cardinalis audiat eum in iure suo super negotio ecclesie Compostellane, non obstante si dictus Fernandus in Legionensi ecclesıa sit receptus. Et sic assignatus est utraque parti terminus ut die veneris proximo venturo compareant coram domino cardinali predicto.

Die lune xxi martii [21-III-1261] comparentibus partibus coram domino cardinali datus est per eum terminus peremptorius adversariis Fernandi Patini ut in crastinum compareant ad videndum resignationem ipsius Fernandi de receptione sua in ecclesia Palentina.

Die martis sequenti comparuerunt partes coram domino cardinali et predictus Fernandus obtulit se paratum resignare ius quod habet in ecclesia Palentina et cum ex parte adversariorum allegarentur plura dominus cardinalis dixit quod omnia essent in eo statu quo sunt usque in crastinum ad horam none. Et ex parte procuratoris archiepiscopi exhibita est protestatio infrascripta:

LA IGLESIA DE LEÓN A MEDIADOS DEL SIGLO XIII

Protestatur procurator archiepiscopi et capituli Compostellanorum contra renuntiationem quam Fernandus Patinus facere intendit quod non fiat eis aliquod preiudicium per eam cum paratus sit prosequi gratiam eis factam et ius sibi per eandem acquisitum nec usque hoc petierunt a domino papa, et quod hoc fieri non debeat paratus est persuadere vobis de facto et de iure et domino pape et fratribus in consistorio, et petit se ad hoc admitti antequam ad alia procedatur.

Die mercurii xxiii martii [23-III-1261] comparentibus partibus coram domino cardinali Fernandus Patinus renuntiavit in manibus ipsius domini cardinalis [*palabra borrada*] receptioni sue [dicta: *subrayada*] ecclesia Palentina quam dixit se nunquam acceptasse nec acceptare [litteris] et omni iure sibi per receptionem ipsam seu per collationem aliquorum prestimoniorum vel quorumlibet (aliorum?) in eadem ecclesia acquisito (*sic*), quam renuntiationem dixit se facere de mandato domini pape ne ius suum super provisione Compostellane ecclesie non conservetur. Et sic dominus cardinalis renuntiationem ipsam recepit, presentibus magistro Uberto de Cochenato, magistro Bernardo Ispano, magistro Frederico de Monticulo et aliis. Et sic procurator Petrus Alfonsi exhibuit petitionem seu protestationem subscriptam:

Petrus procurator Alfonsi Petri canonici Compostellani nomine ipsius Alfonsi tamen salvo iure archiepiscopi et capituli Compostellanorum eis acquisito per gratiam sibi factam a domino papa per (*fol. 87v*) magistrum Johannem de Sancto Germano et per processum vestrum, Reverende patri, et salva appellatione interposita ab (?) antiquo processu magistri Uberti domini pape capellani, petit litis contestationem fieri super libellis oblatis et exceptionibus propositis contra Fernandum Patinum, et hoc ei mandari peremptorie.

Et sic dominus cardinalis statuit partibus ipsis terminum ut in die sabbati proxima [26-III-1261] compareant coram eo.

Die sabbati xxvi [martii] comparuerunt partes coram domino cardinali.

10

Causa magistri Gondasalvi cum archidiacono Astoricensi.

Archivo Segreto Vaticano, *Collectoriae*, 397.

(*fol. 113v*) Mandat venerabilis pater dominus Octavianus Sancte Marie in Vialata diaconus cardinalis a domino papa datus auditor partibus infrascriptis citari in audientia publica magistrum Gundisalvum canonicum Legionensem vel eius legitimum procuratorem si quis est in curia pro eodem ut proximo die mercurii post nonam compareat coram eo processurus quoniam de iure fuerit in causa tam super appellatione quam super archidiaconatu de Valdemeriel in ecclesia Legionensi et quibusdam prestimoniis ex altera. Dat. Viterbii vi kal. octobris pontificatus domini Urbani pape iiii anno primo [26-IX-1261].

Adveniente vero die mercurii supradicto [28-IX-1261] procuratores utriusque partis comparuerunt, et datus est eis terminus a domino cardinali ut in diem veneris proximum compareant.

Die veneris ultimo septembris [30-IX-1261] dicti procuratores comparuerunt in curia domini cardinalis, et quia non potuerunt adire presenciam eius de communi consensu receperunt terminum in diem lune proximum ad exhibendum procuratoria hinc inde.

Exhibitum [procuratorium infrascriptum] die lune III intrante octubris [3-X-1261] a procuratori archidiaconi Astoricensis domini Menendi, et mandatum est Fernando procuratori magistri Gundisalvi ut in crastinum exhibeat procuratorium suum. Alioquin dominus cardinalis procedet in negocio. Et sic datus est terminus ut utraque pars compareat die mercurii proximo.

Tenor cuius procuratorii talis est:

Pateat universis presentem litteram inspecturis quod anno domini MCCLX, scilicet VIII id. martii [8-III-1261], ego Menendus Petri archidiaconus Astoricensis et Legionensis facio, constituo atque ordino Fernandum Garsie canonicum Zamorensem et magistrum Dominicum clericum chori ecclesie Legionensis et Antonium Narniensem procuratores meos in Curia Romana, videlicet quemlibet eorum in solidum ad impetrandum, contradicendum et judices seu judicem petendum vel etiam eligendum, et agendum, respondendum in causa sive causis, littibus et controversiis quas habeo vel habere spero super archidiaconatu de Valdemeriel ecclesie Legionensis mihi auctoritate apostolica collato, contra venerabilem patrem Legionensem episcopum et magistrum Gundisalvum canonicum Legionensem, cui magistro dictus episcopus eundem archidiaconatum sicut dicitur conferre presumpsit. Concedo etiam predictis procuratoribus et cuilibet eorum in solidum constituendi alium vel alios procuratores quotiens viderint expedire, dans eis potestatem iurandi in animam meam et confaciendi quicquid potest facere legitime procurator, ratum et firmum quicquid super premissis † per ipsos vel eorum alterum, suos substitutum ab ipsis vel eorum altero gestum fuerit procurat or is officio habiturus. Et ne hoc in dubium venire possit presentem litteram procuravi sigilli capituli Astoricensis et mei predicti archidiaconi munimine roborari. Actum apud Astoricam anno, mense et die superius nominatis.

Die martis IIII octubris [4-X-1261] magister Fernandus Patinus canonicus Legionensis exhibuit procuratoria infrascripta quorum tenor talis est:

Noverint universi presentem litteram inspecturi quod nos M[artinus] divina permissione Legionensis episcopus constituimus et ordinamus procuratorem nostrum Fernandum Patinum canonicum nostrum in causa seu causis que vertuntur vel verti sperantur inter nos ex una parte et Melendum Petri archidiaconum Astoricensem ex altera super archidiaconatu de Meriel et quibusdam prestimoniis que a Legionensi ecclesia P[etrus] Nuni quondam archidiaconus obtinebat et specialiter ad appellaciones prosequendas (fol. 114r) contra eundem per nos et per quemcumque nostro nomine interiectas, dantes eidem liberam et plenariam facultatem agendi, respondendi, excipiendi, replicandi et ad oppenanda iniuria (?) et defectus contra ipsum et prestandi in anima nostra iuramentum de calumpnia et de veritate dicenda et cuiuslibet alterius generis sacramentum et ad omnia et singula facienda que legitime facere potest procurator, necnon substituendi alium vel alios procuratores loco sui ad singula et omnia supradicta et revocandi eosdem cum sibi vel predicte cause viderit expedire, ratum et firmum quicquid super premissis per ipsum vel eius substitutum seu substitutos actum fuerit habituri. Et ne hoc in dubium evenire valeat presentem procuratorium sigilli nostri fecimus communiri. Dat. apud Banedum VI id. junii anno domini MCCLXI [10-VI-1261].

LA IGLESIA DE LEÓN A MEDIADOS DEL SIGLO XIII

Aliud:

Noverint universi quod ego magister Gundisalvus archidiaconus de Valdemeriel constituo et ordino nomine meo et clericorum meorum in archidiaconatu meo de Valdemeriel commemoratum procuratorem meum Fernandum Patinum concanonicum meum in causa seu causis que vertuntur vel verti sperantur inter nos ex una parte et Melendum Petri archidiaconum Astoricensem ex altera super archidiaconatu de Valdemeriel, et specialiter ad prosequendas appellationes nomine meo et predictorum clericorum meorum interpositas a Nicolao Martini Legionensis ecclesie factas contra eundem archidiaconum et contra executionem dompni Carasci thesaurarii Zamorensis qui se ipsius Melendi super predictis asserit executorem factam super archidiaconatu supradicto. Do etiam eidem procuratori super premissis liberam et plenariam potestatem agendi, respondendi, excipiendi, replicandi et prestandi animam meam iuramentum de calumpnia et de veritate dicenda et cuiuslibet alterius generis sacramentum et omnia et singula faciendi que legitime procurator facere potest, necnon substituendi alium vel alios procuratores loco sui ad omnia et singula supradicta et revocandi eosdem cum sibi vel predicte cause viderit expedire, ratum et firmum quicquid super premissis per ipsum procuratorem vel eius substitutum vel substitutos actum fuerit habiturus. Et ne hoc in dubium veniat, quia sigillum proprium quod alibi sit notum non habeo, presenti procuratorio sigillum domini Legionensis episcopi rogavi apponi. Et nos M[artinus] dei gratia Legionensis episcopus ad preces domini archidiaconi sigillum nostrum facimus huic procuratorio apponi. Dat. apud Mansiellam XI kal. martii anno domini MCCLX [20-II-1261].

Die mercurii comparuerunt partes et exhibito mandato a Fernando Patino mandatum est quod fiat copia hinc inde et quod die veneris compareant.

Die veneris comparentibus partibus dominus cardinalis mandavit domino Ottoni vicecomiti quod causam ipsam audiat loco sui.

(fol. 114v) Die martis XI octubris [11-X-1261] exhibita est coram domino Ottoni a Fernando Patino protestatio infrascripta; et ipsam eandem protestationem fecit cum exhibuit procuratoria:

Protestatus est Fernandus Patinus canonicus Legionensis quod non offert se ad defensionem domini episcopi nec magistri Gundisalvi archidiaconi Legionensis super causa archidiaconatus de Valdemeriel nisi predicti dominus episcopus et archidiaconus probentur super ista causa citari ad curiam ab homine vel a iure, et sub ista protestatione obtulit et offert procuratoria pro eisdem, et sic datus est terminus procuratoribus domini Menendi ad docendum quod causa sit in curia in diem jovis proximam. Salvo tamen iure dicti Fernandi tam super impugnatione procurationis quam super aliis.

Die veneris XIIII octubris [14-X-1261] procuratores domini Menendi exhibuerunt coram domino Ottoni instrumenta infrascripta: Noverint universi per hoc scriptum quod cum dominus papa venerabilibus viris .. decano et .. thesaurario Zamorensibus per apostolica scripta dederit in mandatis ut mihi Melendo Petri archidiacono Astoricensi et canonico Legionensi in ecclesia Legionensi de personatu vel dignitate si vacabat ibidem vel quamprimum vacare contingeret, archidiaconatu de Triacastella dumtaxat excepto, cum prestimoniis competentibus cedentis vel decedentis, auctoritate apostolica providerent vel facerent per alium provideri, et predicti executores auctoritate sibi commissa dignitatem vel personatum cum prestimoniis competentibus cedentis vel decedentis si in ecclesia Legionensi vacabat vel quamprimum vacare contingeret donationi sue auctoritate apostolica reservassent mihi predicto archidiacono per ipso vel per alium conferenda, ac predicti executores .. episcopo, decano totique capitulo Legionensi adhibuissent ne circa premissa in preiudicium mei Melendi Petri archidiaconi Astoricensis et canonci Legionensis aliquid attemptarent, decernendo irritum et inane siquid contra predictum mandatum super premissis a quoque contingeret attemptari, et Jacobus Johannis canonicus Legionensis in elusionem mandati apostolici et contra reservationem et inhibitionem predictorum executorum archidiaconatum de Valdemeriel per mortem P. Nuni vacantem post protestationem et appellationem a Pelagio Fernandi et magistro Dominico canonicis Legionensibus et ab Alfonso Gometii socio eiusdem ecclesie factam, petentibus copiam illius rescripti sibi fieri quam nec ipsi nec ego archidiaconus Melendus Petri habueramus, cuius auctoritate dictum archidiaconatum attemptabat conferre [ne: *borrado*] in mei preiudicium et contra reservationem et inhibitionem dictorum executorum, immo domini pape, dictus Jacobus aliquid attemptaret. nichilominus contempta appellatione idem Jacobus die jovis post festum Purificationis [3-II-1261] dictum archidiaconatum magistro Gundissalvo canonico Legionensi, ut dicitur de facto cum de iure non possit, auctoritate episcopi ut dicebat non erubuit assignare, dicti P. Nuni corpore nondum tradito sepulture. Verum die sabbati sequenti [5-II-1261] ego supradictus archidiaconus existens in capitulo Legionensi ratam habens protestationem et appellationem ab ipsis sociis factam, petii a dicto Jacobo ut mihi faceret copiam auctoritatis qua asserebat se archidiaconatum predictum contulisse ex hiis omnibus et singulis supradictis, et quia copiam predicte auctoritatis quam dicebat se habere mihi noluit exhibere, viva voce sedem apostolicam appello, et die veneris sequenti [11-II-1261] in capitulo Legionensi coram Alfonso Johannis publico notario civitatis Legionensis in scriptis appellavi et predictas appellationes innovavi et apostolatus petii et iterum cum instantia petii, et me et mea tam spiritualia quam mundana et sociorum meorum sub protectioni domini pape posui. Acta sunt hec in capitulo Legionensi III id februarii anno domini MCC sexagesimo [11-II-1261]. Et ego Alfonsus Johannis notarius iamdictus huic (*fol. 115r*) appellationi in scriptis facte interfui et rogatus a supradicto domino Melendo Petri archidiacono hanc appellationem in publicam redegi et hoc instumentum inde feci et signum meum in eodem apposui. Qui presentes fuerunt: magister Johannes decanus, Gundissalvus Fernandi prior, Ysidorus Michaelis, M. Sancii, R. Petri, Sancius Ysidori, Thomas Petri, Jacobus Johannis, magister Petrus, magister Dominicus, dompnus Albertus, J. Paci, Mattheus Ysidori, dompnus Hugolinus, J. Petri, canonici; A. Gomecii, Dominicus Johannis, M. Alvari, Nicholas Martini, Alfonsus Petri, P. Ovetii, socii ecclesie Legionensis; dompnus Carascus thesaurarius Zamorensis; Alfonsus Johannis qui notavit.

Noverint universi quod cum Legionensis episcopus Jacobo Legionensi canonico in elusionem mandati apostolici et preiudicium mei Melendi Petri Astoricensis et Legionensis archidiaconi conferendi archidiaconatum de Valdemeriel magistro Gundissalvo canonico Legionensi tenenti in diocesi Astoricensi ecclesiam de Toreñ curam animarum habentem cuius rectorem se asserit, sicut dicitur, dederit potestatem, vel ipsemet eundem ardidiaconatum dicto magistro presumptorie duxerit conferendum, ego predictus archidiaconus ponens me et mea tam spiritualia quam mundana sub protectioni sedis apostolice ad eiusdem sedis presidium in scriptis appello. Appello etiam quia prefatus episcopus prestimonia per mortem P. Nuni quondam archidiaconi Legionensis in Legionensi ecclesia vacantia mihi auctoritate apostolica collata de facto cum de iure non posset aliis conferre presumpsit. Insuper appello ne prefatus episcopus contra me pendente appellatione aliquid attemptare presumat in mei preiudicium vel gravamen. Et ne hoc in dubium evenire possit rogavi Alfonsum Johannis publicum notarium concilii Legionensis ut presentem appellationem in formam publicam redigeret. Et ego Alfonsus Johannis notarius iamdictus huic appellationi interfui et rogatus a predicto archidiacono eam in formam publicam redegi et hoc instrumentum propria manu scripsi et in eodem signum meum feci. Acta sunt hec in capitulo Legionensi et extra capitulum in predicta ecclesia cathedrali vi kal. marcii anno domini MCCLX [24-II-1261] (presentibus) Gundissalvo Fernandi priore, magistro Dominico, Johanne Paci, dompno Hugolino, canonicis; Gomecio socio; Petro Johannis presbitero; Andrea Dominici, Dominico Thomash, clericis chori Legionensibus; magistro Symone operis eiusdem ecclesie magistro; Petro Tonto, Petro Jacobi, Alfonso Johannis qui notavit.

Noverint universi per hoc scriptum quod cum papa venerabilibus viris .. decano et .. thesaurario Zamorensibus per apostolica scripta dederit in mandatis ut mihi Melendo Petri archidiacono Astoricensi et canonico Legionensi in ecclesia Legionensi de personatu vel dignitate si vacabat ibidem vel quamprimum vacare contingeret, archidiaconatu de Triacastella dumtaxat excepto, cum prestimoniis competentibus cedentis vel decedentis auctoritate apostolica providerent vel facerent provideri per alium, et predicti executores auctoritate sibi commissa dignitatem vel personatum cum prestimoniis competentibus cedentis vel decedentis si in ecclesia Legionensi vacabat vel quamprimum vacare contingeret donationi sue auctoritate apostolica reservassent mihi predicto archidiacono per ipsos vel per alium conferenda, ac predicti executores .. episcopo, decano totique capitulo Legionensi inhibuissent ne circa premissa in preiudicium mei Melendi Petri archidiaconi Astoricensis et canonici Legionensis aliquid attemptarent, decernendo irritum et inane siquid contra predictum mandatum super premissis a quoque contingeret attemptari, et Jacobus Johannis canonicus Legionensis in elusionem mandati apostolici et contra reservationem et inhibitionem predictorum executorum archidiaconatum de Valdemeriel per mortem P. Nuni vacantem post protestationem iuris mei et appellationem a Pelagio Fernandi et magistro Dominico canonicis Legionensibus et ab Alfonso Gometii socio (fol. 115v) eiusdem ecclesie factam, petentibus copiam illius rescripti sibi fieri quam nec ipsi nec ego archidiaconus Melendus Petri habueramus, cuius auctoritate dictum archidiaconatum attemptabat conferre ne in mei preiudicium et contra reservacionem et inhibitionem dictorum executorum, immo domini pape, dictus Jacobus aliquid attemptaret, nichilominus contempta appellatione, idem Jacobus die jovis post festum Purificationis [3-II-1261] dictum archidiaconatum magistro Gundissalvo canonico Legionensi, ut dicitur, de facto cum de iure non posset, auctoritate episcopi ut dicebat non erubuit assignare, dicti P. Nuni corpore nondum tradito sepulture. Verum die veneris iii id. februarii [11-II-1261] ego supradictus archidiaconus existens in capitulo Legionensi ratam habens protestationem et appellationem ab ipsis sociis factam petii a dicto Jacobo ut mihi faceret copiam auctoritatis qua asserebat se archidiaconatum predictum contulisse ex hiis omnibus et singulis supradictis, et quia copiam predicte auctoritatis quam dicebat se habere mihi noluit exhibere, in scriptis sedem apostolicam appello et predictas appellationes innovo et apostolatus peto et iterum cum instancia peto et me et mea tam spiritualia quam mundana et sociorum predictorum et aliorum canonicorum et sociorum Legionensium mihi adherentium sub protectioni domini pape pono. Et ne hoc in dubium valeat revocari rogavi Alfonsum Johannis publicum notarium civitatis Legionensis ut hanc appellationem redigeret in formam publicam. Et ego Alfonsus Johannis notarius iamdictus huic appellationi in scriptis facte interfui, et rogatus a supradicto domino Melendo Petri archidiacono hanc appellationem in publicam formam redegi. Et hoc instrumentum inde feci et signum meum in eodem apposui. Acta sunt hec in capitulo Legionensi III id. februarii anno domini MCCLX. Qui presentes fuerunt: magister Johannes decanus, Gundissalvus Fernandi prior, Ysidorus Michaelis, M. Sancii, Sancius Ysidori, R. Petri, Thomas Petri, Jacobus Johannis, magister Petrus, magister Dominicus, dompnus Albertus, J. Paci, Mattheus Ysidori, dompnus Ugolinus, J. Petri, canonici; A. Gomecii, Dominicus Johannis, M. Alvari, Nicolas Martini, Alfonsus Petri, M. Petri, P. Ovetii, socii ecclesie Legionensis; dompnus Carrascus thesaurarius Zamorensis; Alfonsus Johannis qui notavit.

Anno domini MCC sexagesimo, VII id. marcii [9-III-1261]. Noverint universi quod ego Alfonsus Johannis notarius publicus et iuratus concilii Legionensis vidi Dominicum Gundissalvi clericum chori ecclesie Legionensis et procuratorem domini Melendi Petri archidiaconum Astoricensem iter arripuisse ab Astorica ad curiam romanam ad prosequendum negotium predicti archidiaconi. In cuius rei testimonium ego supradictus Alfonsus Johannis notarius, rogatus a predicto archidiacono, hoc instrumentum scripsi et publicavi, et in eodem hoc signum meum faci. Presentibus domino Petro Dominici archidiacono Legionensi, Johanne Parisii prebitero, Dominico Johannis clerico, Martino de Paradella et Martino Sancti Facundi servientibus predicti P. archidiaconi; Alfonso Petri qui notavit.

Die mercurii XVIIII octubris [19-X-1261] comparuerunt partes coram domino Ottoni et datus est terminus Fernando Patino ad impugnandum instrumenta exhibita a parte adversa per que intendit probare pars ipsa quod causa est in curia in diem sabbati proximam.

(fol. 116r) Die sabbati XXII octubris [22-X-1261] comparentibus partibus coram domino Ottoni, Fernandus Patinus exhibuit protestationem subscriptam:

Fernandus Patinus, protestans quod salve essent sibi rationes omnes et iura per que instrumenta producta per partem adversam ad probandum quod causa erat in curia quibuscumque modis alias poterunt impugnari, negavit tabellionem subscriptum in instrumentis ipsis esse tabellionem publicum et habere auctoritatem conficiendi publica instrumenta.

Cui Fernando datus est terminus peremptorius ad dicendum et proponendum quicquid voluerit contra instrumenta exhibita in diem martis proximam.

Die martis XXV [25-X-1261] comparentibus partibus, prorogatus est dictus terminus eidem Fernando in crastinum ut compareat cum advocatis suis et dicat contra instrumenta prescripta quod voluerit.

Die jovis XXVII [27-X-1261] comparuerunt partes et prorogatus est dictus terminus eidem Fernando in diem sabbati proximam.

Die sabbati XXVIIII eiusdem [29-X-1261] comparuerunt partes cum advocatis et [prorogatus: borrado] datus est dictus terminus eidem Fernando peremptorius ad dandum in scriptis quicquid voluerit dicere contra instrumenta exhibita a parte adversa in diem jovis proximo venturam.

Die jovis III intrante novembris [3-XI-1261] Fernandus Patinus exhibuit coram domino Ottoni rationes suas, de quibus mandatum est fieri copiam adversariis eius, et sic datus est utraque parti terminus ad comparendum in diem lune proximam.

Die mercurii XI januarii [11-I-1262] exhibitum est procuratorium infrascriptum ab archidiacono Astoricensi, presente Fernando Patino adversario suo:

Pateat universis presentem litteram inspecturis quod anno domini MCCLX, videlicet VIII id. marcii [8-III-1261] ego Menendus Petri archidiaconus Astoricensis et Legionensis constituo et ordino Fernandum Garsie canonicum Zamorensem et Dominicum Gundisalvi clericum chori ecclesie Legionensis et Antonium Narniensem procuratores meos in Curia Romana, videlicet quemlibet eorum in solidum in causa seu causis que vertuntur vel verti sperantur inter me ex una parte et magistrum Gundisalvum canonicum Legionensem ex altera super archidiaconatu de Valdemeriel et quibusdam prestimoniis que P. Nuni quondam archidiaconus Legionensis in ecclesia Legionensis obtinebat, et specialiter ad appellationes prosequendas super dictis archidiaconatu et prestimoniis nomine meo et quorundam canonicorum michi adherentium interiectas, dans eisdem liberam facultatem agendi et respondendi et defendendi, excipiendi et replicandi et prestandi in anima mea iuramentum de calumpnia et de veritate dicenda et cuiuslibet alterius generis sacramentum et ad omnia et singula que legitime potest facere procurator, necnon substituendi alium vel alios procuratores loco sui ad singula et ad omnia supradicta et revocandi eosdem cum sibi vel predicte cause viderit expedire, ratum et firmum quicquid super premissis per ipsos procuratores vel eorum alterum vel substitutum seu substitutos ab eis actum fuerit habiturus. Et ne hoc in dubium valeat evenire capitulum Astoricensem rogavi ut presens procuratorium sigilli sui proprii munime roborarent. Et nos capitulum Astoricense ad preces archidiaconi supradicti presens procuratorium sigilli nostri fecimus communiri. Et ego Melendus Petri archidiaconus supradictus presens procuratorium communivi. Dat. Astorice, anno, die, mense superius notatis.

(fol. 116v) Die jovis VIIII intrante februarii [9-II-1261], Vª indictione. Presentibus fratre Ruffino, domino Ottoni vicecomite, magistro Thoma rectore ecclesie Sancti Medardi Suessionensis diocesis, et Oddoni familiari domini cardinalis, idem dominus cardinalis interloquendo pronunciavit causam que vertitur inter dominum episcopum Legionensem et magistrum Gondisalvum canonicum Legionensem ex parte una et dominum Melendum archidiaconum Astoricensem ex altera super archidiaconatu de Valdemerel in ecclesia Legionensi et quibusdam prestimoniis esse devolutam in curia decetero agitari.

Die sabbati XXV eiusdem [25-II-1261] archidiaconus Astoricensis exhibuit coram domino cardinali libellum infrascriptum de quo mandatum est fieri copiam adversario suo, et datus est ei terminus ad respondendum ipsi libello in diem mercurii proximam. Tenor autem libelli talis est:

Coram vobis venerabili patre domino Octaviano Sancte Marie in Vialata diacono cardinali partibus auditore concesso dicit et proponit Menendus archidiaconus Astoricensis contra magistrum Gundissalvum canonicum Legionensem quod cum archidiaconatus de Vallemeriel in ecclesia Legionensi per mortem Petri Nuni vacasset fuit de ipso archidiacono cum iuribus et pertinentiis suis et de prestimoniis que vacaverunt per mortem ipsius P. quondam archidiaconi eidem Melendo auctoritate apostolica provisus et de predictis collatio sibi facta fuit etiam, idem Melendus de ipso archidiaconatu et de prestimoniis investitur et in eorum possessionem inductus ac stallum in choro et locus in capitulo pertinentes ad archidiaconatum predictum sibi assignati fuerunt et ipsorum stalli et loci aliquamdiu possessione usus fuit. Dictus vero Gundissalvus predictum archidiaconatum et quedam prestimonia de illis que vacaverunt per obitum dicti Petri dicto archidiacono assignatis illicite occupavit et contra iustitiam detinet occupata in ipsius Melendi preiudicium et gravamen. Unde petit per vos, reverende patre, dictum archidiaconatum cum iuribus et pertinentiis suis et dicta prestimonia que idem detinet occupata sibi adiudicari et ad eum spectare de iure finaliter declarari et predictum Gundissalvum ab ipso archidiaconatu et prestimoniis que detinet penitus amoveri ac ipsum Gundissalvum ad restituendum et dimittendum ei premissa cum fructibus medio tempore perceptis vel eorum estimatione que ascendit ad CCC libras turonenses compelli et condempnari et super hiis predicto Gundissalvo perpetuum silentium imponi cum nullum ius habet in eisdem. Et hec omnia petit cum dampnis et expensis legitimis que et quod extimat CCC marchis sterlingorum; et protestatur factas expensas salvo iure addendi vel minuendi.

Die mercurii kal. martii [1-III-1261], Vᵃ indictione. Comparuerunt partes coram domino cardinali, et cum a Fernando Patino non responderetur libello dominus cardinalis dedit ei terminum peremptorium ad proponendum omnes dilatorias et diulinatorias (?) exceptiones in scriptis in diem veneris proximam.

Die martis VII martii [7-III-1261] comparuerunt partes coram domino cardinali et mandatum est Fernando Patino ut die veneris proximam peremptorie compareat ad respondendum libello.

Die veneris X intrante martii [10-III-1261], presentibus partibus coram domino cardinali, Fernandus Patinus litem contestando negavit narrata prout narrantur in libello vera esse et dixit petita fieri non debere. Et sic prestitum est ab utraque parte iuramentum de veritate dicenda.

(fol. 117r) Ab utraque parti dati sunt articuli in termino peremptorio, videlicet die martis post Ephifaniam (?) domini in LXII [anno], indictione [VII]*, et renuntiatum est ab utraque parte omnibus articulis famosis tam in ista causa quam in causa cantorie. Ante vero articulorum assignationem protestatus fuit magister Dominicus procurator Melendi archidiaconi Astoracensis (sic) quod offert predictos articulos, et quod liceat sibi non obstante termino peremptoria prefixione ad dandos articulos facto (?) liceat ei si contingat aliam partem dare aliquas indulgentias sive litteras apostolicas vel alia quelibet instrumenta vel alios articulos novos, et quod liceat ei circa hec probare tam per instrumenta quam per testes et super hiis articulos producere et offere, et protestatur quod non astringitur se ad probandum omnia que in suis articulis continentur set ad ea tantum que sibi sufficiunt ad victoriam cause sue.

Item protestatur quod liceat sibi renuntiare articulis quibus voluerit. Ista eidem fuit adversa pars protestata.

Item assignatus fuit terminus de consensu partium die jovis sequenti ad procedendum in causa prout de iure fuerit.

Item de consensu partium assignatus fuit terminus ad diem lune sequentem ad disputandum super impertinentia articulorum. [resto del fol. 117r en bianco].

(fol. 117v) Die sabbati XX maii [20-V-1262], Vᵃ indictione, comparuerunt coram domino cardinali dominus Melendus archidiaconus Astoricensis pro se et Fernandus Patinus canonicus Legionensis procuratorio nomine pro episcopo Legionensi et magistro Gondisalvo supradictis, et de voluntate et consensu ipsorum assignatus est terminus peremptorius partibus ipsis ut in octava die post festum beati Michaelis proximo ventura [6-X-1262], vel in prima die que proximo feriata ipsius fuerit si dies illa forsitan occurerit feriata, per se vel per procuratores legitimos in Curia Romana compareant coram eo in causa que vertitur inter ipsos super archidiaconatu et prestimoniis que vacaverunt in ecclesia Legionensi per mortem Petri Nuni legitime processuri, ita quod causa remaneat in eo statu in quo nunc est. Et nullum preiudicium

---

* Fecha equivocada.

LA IGLESIA DE LEÓN A MEDIADOS DEL SIGLO XIII

genereteur partibus quoad archidiaconatum et omnia prestimonia que per mortem predicti Petri Nuni in dicta Legionensi ecclesia vacaverunt per prorogationem huiusmodi.

Item dictus archidiaconus protestatus est coram dicto domino cardinali quod non stabat per eum quoniam procederetur super prestimoniis super quibus nondum est libellus oblatus. Et tunc dictus dominus cardinalis et Fernandus prefatus protestationi huiusmodi admiserunt et acceptaverunt eodem archidiaconi, promittentes quod super ipsis prestimoniis non procedetur usque ad terminum supradictum.

Die mercurii XVII januarii [17-I-1263] apud Urbemveterem presentibus partibus dominus cardinalis mandavit quod archiepiscopus (sic) Sancte Severine audiat quolibet die de mane et sero audiat disputationes partium super articulis datis.

Die mercurii XXII martii [22-III-1262], Vᵃ indictione, exhibite sunt positiones infrascripte:

Ponit Dominicus Gundisalvi procurator domini Melendi archidiaconi Astoricensis quod felicis recordationis dominus papa Innocentius IIII mandavit per suas litteras decano et thesaurario Zamorensibus quod personatum vel dignitatem si vacabat in ecclesia Legionensi, vel quamprimum ibi vacaret, cum prestimoniis competentibus cedentis, archidiaconatu de Triacastella dumtaxat excepto, per se vel per alios dicto archidiacono Astoricensi [conferrent], etc., prout in litteris apostolicis continetur.

Item ponit quod mandavit eisdem ut eundem archidiaconum vel procuratorem in corporalem possessionem dignitatis vel personatus et prestimoniorum de quibus ei providerent inducerent et inductum defenderent, etc., et supra.

Item quod predicte littere domini Innocentii pape IIII fuerunt talis tenoris: Innocentius, etc., etc.

Item quod littere fuerunt eisdem decano et thesaurario Zamorensibus presentate ante mortem mandatoris.

Item quod pervenerunt ad ipsos ut supra proximo.

Item ponit quod dictus dominus papa decrevit in eisdem litteris irritum et inane [MS: in anane] siquid de dignitate vel personatu et prestimoniis predictis [in eisdem litteris continetur: borrado] contra reservationem suam quod quidquam contingeret attemptari, etc., ut supra proximo.

Item ponit quod fuerunt dicte littere domini Innocentii et domini Alexandri presentate antedictis decano et thesaurario eodem anno quo mortuus fuit dominus Innocentius. C *, post mortem Innocentii. (fol. 118r) Item ponit quod [idem] decanus et thesaurarius easdem litteras habuerunt et receperunt ut supra proximo.

Item ponit quod predictus dominus papa Innocentius reservavit donationi apostolice in eisdem litteris personatum vel dignitatem [si] in ecclesia Legionensi tunc vacabat vel quamprimo vacare contingerit cum prestimoniis competentibus cedentis vel decedentis eidem archidiacono conferendum preter archidiaconatum de Triacastella, etc., prout [in eisdem litteris continetur].

Item ponit quod dominus Alexander papa IIII mandavit per suas litteras decano et thesaurario Zamorensibus ut eidem archidiacono Astoricensi providerent iusta (sic) continentia litterarum domini Innocentii predecessoris sui ad eosdem decanum et thesaurarium compromissarum. C, prout in eisdem litteris apostolicis continetur.

Item ponit quod in eisdem litteris continebatur ut ipsi decanus et thesaurarius eidem archidiacono de dignitate vel personatu in Legionensi sine qualibet difficultate per se

---

* C: creditur o contestatur. Véase BONAGUIDA DE ARREZO, Summa, ed. WUN-DERLICH, ut supra, 319.

53

vel per alium providerent cum prestimoniis competentibus cedentis vel decedentis exepto (sic) archidiaconatu de Tria Castelle (sic). C, prout in eisdem litteris continetur.

Item ponit quod in eisdem litteris continebatur quod ipsi decanus et thesaurarius procederent ad provisionem dictam faciendam quamquam littere domini Innocentii pape IIII ante obitum ipsius eisdem non fuerunt presentate. C, prout in eisdem litteris continetur.

Item ponit quod predicte littere domini Innocentii et domini Alexandri fuerunt predictis decano et thesaurario ante obitum domini Alexandri presentate, dividendo si negaverit coniunctim (?). C [mortem Innocentii: *borrado*].

Item ponit quod primo anno pontificatus domini Alexandri fuerunt littere domini Innocentii pape IIII iamdictis decano et thesaurario presentate . C, post mortem domini Innocentii.

Item ponit quod littere domini Alexandri IIII fuerunt anno primo sui pontificatus iamdictis decano et thesaurario presentate. C, ut supra proximo.

Item quod dicti decanus et thesaurarius auctoritate apostolica eis commissa dignitatem vel personatum cum prestimoniis competentibus cedentis vel decedentis donationi sue reservaverunt dicto archidiacono conferendam. C, quod de facto tantum cum [non] haberent auctoritatem super hoc.

Item quod inhibuerunt episcopo et capitulo Legionensibus ne de predictis dignitate et personatu et prestimoniis supradictis aliud attemptarent. C, ut supra proximo.

Item quod decreverunt irritum et in anane (sic) siquid contra mandati sui tenorem a quocumque contingerit attemptari. C, ut supra proximum.

Item quod predicte littere inhibitionis executorum ad episcopum et capitulum Legionenses pervenerunt. C.

Item ponit quod ille qui presentavit litteras sibi ex parte decani et thesaurarii fecit sibi copiam de litteris supradictis. C.

Item quod pervenerunt ad eosdem ante mortem domini Alexandri. C.

Item quod pervenerunt ad eosdem pontificatus domini Alexandri anno primo. C.

Item quod pervenerunt ad eos ante mortem P. archidiaconi Nunii. C.

Item quod dicti episcopus et capitulum certificati fuerunt de litteris predictis domini Innocentii IIII et de litteris domini Alexandri. C.

Item quod habuerunt copiam de omnibus litteris supradictis. C.

Item quod postmodum [vacavit] in ecclesia Legionensi archidiaconatus de Valle Meriel per mortem P. Nunii archidiaconi eiusdem ecclesie cum prestimoniis quos idem P. in eadem ecclesia optinebat.

Item quod auctoritate predictarum litterarum videlicet domini Innocentii et domini Alexandri archidiaconatus de Valle Meriel cum prestimoniis quas idem P. Nunii in eadem ecclesia optinebat fuit predicto M[elendo] archidiacono Astoricensi collatus. Non C. quod auctoritate predictarum litterarum.

Item quod ipse M. de eodem fuit investitus per thesaurarium Zamorensem. C. de facto cum de iure eum non potuit investire.

Item quod fuit in possessionem inductus. Non C.

Item quod dictus thesaurarius excommunicavit contradictores et rebelles et dictum archidiaconatum impendentes. C. quod excommunicavit de facto cum non haberet iurisdictionem in eas (sic).

LA IGLESIA DE LEÓN A MEDIADOS DEL SIGLO XIII

Die sabbati primo aprilis [1-IV-1262] comparuerunt partes coram domino Oddoni et responsum est posicionibus istis; et datus est alteri parti terminus ad dandas posiciones ad primam diem post festum Resurrectionis [10-IV-1262] qua tenebuntur cause in curia.

Die lune XVII aprilis [17-IV-1262] exhibite sunt posiciones iste per dominum... archidiaconum... et datus est terminus partibus ad respondendum in diem jovis proximam post Dormitionem [17-VIII-1262].

(*fol. 153*) Die sabbati primo aprilis comparuerunt partes coram domini Oddoni et responsum est quibusdam positionibus ipsius domini archidiaconi per magistrum Fernandum; et datus est terminus parti alteri ad dandas positiones diem post festum Resurrectionis qua tenebuntur cause in curia.

Die lune XVII aprilis comparuerunt partes coram dicto domino Ottoni (*sic*) et exhibuerunt quasdam positiones quibus datus est terminus ad respondendum ipsis positionibus in diem jovis proximo venturam post Dormitionem.

Item ponit quod littere bone memorie domini Alexandri pape IIII fuerunt huius tenoris:

Alexander episcopus servus servorum Dei dilectis filiis decano et thesaurario Zamorensibus salutem et apostolicam benedictionem. Olim pro dilecto filio Melendo Petri [archidiacono] ecclesie Astoricensis et canonico Legionensi capellano dilecti filii nostri Guillelmi Sancti Eustachii diaconi cardinalis felicis recordationis Innocentius papa predecessor noster vobis sub certa forma suis dedit litteris in mandatis ut eidem archidiacono de personatu vel dignitate aç prestimoniis in ecclesia Legionensi providere per vos vel per alios curaretis. Eandem itaque gratiam intuitu (?) cardinalis predicti ad debitum effectum perduci volentes, discretioni [vestre] per apostolica scripta (*fol. 118v*) mandamus quatenus in executione provisionis ipsius per vos vel per alios seu alium sine difficultate qualibet procedatis iuxta directarum ad vos eiusdem predecessoris nostri continentiam [litterarum] directarum (*sic*) quamquam ipse ante obitum predecessoris eiusdem vobis non fuerint presentate, non obstante quod ipse quedam ecclesiastica beneficia quibus animarum cura non est annexa in Ovetensi, Legionensi et Astoricensi ecclesiis dignoscitur obtinere que quedam quadraginta marcarum argenti valentia, ut asseritur, non excedant. Dat. Neapoli II id. januarii pontificatus nostri anno primo [12-I-1255].

Item quod reservatio et inhibitio quas predicti decanus et thesaurarius fecerunt de dignitate vel personatu in ecclesia Legionensi fuerunt facte vivente domino papa Alexandro. Non C. quod omnes inhibitiones vel reservationes quas dicti decanus et thesaurarius fecisse dicuntur fuerunt facte ante mortem predicti domini Alexandri.

Item quod episcopus et capitulum Legionenses sciverunt de omnibus reservationibus et inhibitionibus quas ipsi fecerunt. Non C.

Item quod de earum (*sic*) sciverunt et notitiam habuerunt antequam archidiaconatus de quo agitur vacaret per mortem quondam P. Nunii archidiaconi Legionensis. Dependent.

Item quod magister Gondissalvus canonicus Legionensis scivit et notiam (*sic*) habuit de predictis litteris domini Innocentii et domini Alexandri optentis super provisione dicti Melendi Petri archidiaconi Astoracensis (*sic*). C.

Item quod scivit et notitiam habuit de reservacione et inhibicione predictis factis auctoritate aliarum litterarum. Non C.

Item quod de eis scivit et notitiam habuit vivente domino papa Alexandro. Dependent.

[Item quod dictus Gondissalvus erat canonicus Legionensis et unus de capitulo Legionensi eo tempore quo predicte littere domini Innocentii et domini Alexandri pervenerunt ad decanum et capitulum Legionenses: *borrado*].

[Item quod erat canonicus Legionensis eo tempore quo premisse reservatio et inhibitio pervenerunt ad episcopum et capitulum Legionenses: *borrado*].

Item quod quando facte fuerunt predicte inhibitiones [erat] apud ecclesiam Legionensem cum domino episcopo. Non *C*.

Item quod fuit presens cum aliis de capitulo quando predicte littere domini Innocentii et domini Alexandri pervenerunt ad episcopum et capitulum et fuerunt eis presentante. Non *C*.

Item quod erat cum eis presens quando predicte reservatio et inhibitio pervenerunt ad eos. Non *C*.

Item quod quondam predictus P. Nuni archidiaconus Legionensis decessit iam sunt xiiii menses descendendo. *C*.

Item quod decessit in mense februarii fuit [...] vel in fine januarii circa principatum huius februarii ultima die januarii. *C*.

[*margen* + Item quod decessit in civitate Legionensi. *C*].

Item quod fuit sepultus apud ecclesiam Legionensem. *C*.

Item quod magister Gundissalvus erat absens ab ecclesia Legionensi tempore mortis predicti P. Nuni. *C*.

Item quod erat absens ipse sepulture ipsius ab eadem ecclesia. *C*.

Item quod tunc distabat ab ecclesia Legionensi per VIII dietas descendendo si negaverit. *C*.

Item quod predictus archidiaconatus vacavit postquam predicte littere domini Innocentii et domini Alexandri fuerunt presentate episcopo et capitulo supradictis. *C*.

Item quod vacavit postquam constitit eis de reservatione et inhibitione predictis. Dependent.

Item quod postea vacavit per mortem eiusdem cum prestimoniis que ipse P. obtinebat in ecclesia Legionensi. Dependent.

Item quod predictus archidiaconatus de quo agitur collatus predicto Melendo archidiacono Astoricensi. *C* quod fuit sibi collatus de facto tantum cum non potuerit nec debuerit conferri sibi.

[*margen:* Item quod fuit ei collatus cum prestimoniis que dictus P. Nuni optinebat in ecclesia Legionensi. *C* ut supra proximum].

Item quod fuit ei collatus cum iuribus et pertinenciis suis. [Non] ut [*C*] [ut supra proximum: *borrado*]

Item quod fuit ei collatus per thesaurarium Zamorensem. *C*. de facto ut supra confessus est.

Item quod fuit ei collatus auctoritate domini pape. Non *C*. (*fol. 119r*) Item quod thesaurarius dixit in collatione quam fecit quod conferebat auctoritate domini pape et potestate college sui eii translata. Non *C*.

Item quod fuit ei collatus per dictum thesaurarium post mortem dicti P. Nuni et postquam corpus eius fuit traditum sepulture ecclesiastice. *C*. de ea collatione de qua supra confessus est.

Item quod post ipsius Petri sepulturam non fuit facta aliqua collatio de ipso archidiaconatu alicui alio nisi predicto Melendo archidiacono Astoricensi. *C*. contrarium.

Item quod eidem Melendo fuit facta assignatio stalli in choro pertinentis ad ipsum archidiaconatum de quo agitur. *C.* de facto tantum cum non potuerit nec debuerit sibi de iure fieri.

Item quod fuit facta assignatio loci in capitulo pertinentis ad eundem archidiaconatum. *C.* ut in supra proximum.

Item quod huius[modi] assignatio fuit facta per thesaurarium supradictum. *C.* ut supra proximum.

Item quod idem thesaurarius in assignatione huius faciende fungebatur vice decani Zamorensis college sui. Non *C.*

Item quod idem thesaurarius [fungebatur] vice eiusdem college in collatione quam fecit eidem Melendo de archidiaconatu supradicto. Non *C.*

Item quod fungebatur vice eiusdem college in investitura quam fecit eidem Melendo de archidiaconatu supradicto. Non *C.*

Item quod fungebatur vice eiusdem college in investitura quam fecit eidem Melendo de archidiaconatu predicto. Non *C.*

Item quod ipse decanus excusavit se eidem thesaurario tempore collationis premisse super provisione quam debebat fieri per ipsos eidem Melendo auctoritate apostolica. Non *C.*

Item quod comisit ei vices suas. Non *C.*

Item quod illas vices comisit ei super provisione facienda eidem Melendo prout in litteris apostolicis continebatur. Dependet.

Item quod decanus tempore illius commissionis erat aliis negotiis impeditus et corporis debilitate detentus. Dependent.

Item quod ipse decanus fecit huius commissionem ante collationem factam eidem Melendo de predicto archidiaconatu per predictum thesaurarium. Dependet.

Item quod illa comissio pervenit ad prefatum thesaurarium. Dependet.

Item quod pervenit ad eum antequam procederet ad collationem et investituram quas fecit eidem Melendo de archidiaconatu predicto et de illis pertinentiis. Dependet.

Item quod predictus Gundissalvus detinet archidiaconatum predictum. *C.* quod ipsum possidet et detinet sicut debet.

Item quod detinet quedam prestimonia de illis que vacaverunt per mortem dicti Petri. Dependet.

Item quod detinet illum archidiaconatum cum dictis prestimoniis, dividendo si negaverit. Dependet.

Item quod incepit detinere illum archidiaconatum post collationem et investituram predictas factas predicto archidiacono. Non *C.*

Item quod (*sic*). Item quod incepit detinere eundem post assignationem factam eidem Melendo de stallo in choro et loco in capitulo spectantibus ad eundem archidiaconatum. Assignacionem non *C.* nec de facto, et *C.* quod ante tempus illud dictus magister Gundissalvus possidebat archidiaconatum huius vel alius ipsius nomine.

Item quod percepit et habuit fructus et proventus de predictis archidiaconatu et prestimoniis, dividendo si negaverit. Dependet.

Item quod habuit et percepit eos a tempore detentionis premisse. Dependet.

Item quod fructus et proventus archidiaconatus et prestimoniorum valent annuatim communi extimatione cc libras turonenses, descendendo si negaverit. Dependet.

Item quod prefatus Gundissalvus gerit se pro archidiacono Legionensis ecclesie in archidiaconatu predicto. *C.* quod est et quod gerit se pro archidiacono in eodem archidiaconatu.

Item quod opposuit et opponit se eidem Melendo super eodem archidiaconatu et predictis prestimoniis. Dependet.

Item quod impedit eum quod minus possit gaudere pacifica possessione eiusdem archidiaconatus. *C.* quod impedit eum prout debet, aliter non *C.*

(*fol. 119v*) Item quod idem Melendus incurrit dampna plura et fecit expensas occasione oppositionis et contradictionis dicti Gundissalvi.

Item quod incurrit dampna et fecit expensas occasione impedimenti quod ei prestat super optentatione et possessione predicti archidiaconatus.

Item quod propter hoc incurrit dampna et fecit expensas usque ad valorem CCC marcarum, descendendo si negaverit. [Resto del fol. en blanco].

(*fol. 126r*) seu alium sine difficultate qualibet procedatis iuxta directarum ad vos eiusdem predecessoris nostri continentiam litterarum quamquam ipse ante obitum predecessoris eiusdem vobis non fuerint presentate, non obstante quod ipse quedam ecclesiastica beneficia quibus animarum cura non est annexa in Ovetensi, Legionensi et Astoricensi ecclesiis dingnoscitur (*sic*) obtinere que quedam quadraginta marcarum argenti valentia, ut asseritur, non excedunt. Dat. Neapoli II id, januarii pontificatus nostri anno primo [12-I-1255: *ut supra*]. Quarum auctoritate percipiendo (?) sibi quatinus de personatu vel dingnitate (*sic*) cum prestimoniis competentibus cedentis vel decedentis que alicui de iure non debentur si in ecclesia vestra vacant ad presens vel quamprimum vacere contigerit dicto archidiaconatu iuxta mandatum apostolicum providere curetis. Alioquin auctoritate predicta personatum vel dignitatem et prestimonia huiusmodi apostolice donationi reservamus per nos vel per alium dicto archidiacono conferenda, decernentes nichilominus ex nunc irritum et inane siquid contra mandatum [...] apostolicum super premissis a quoque contigerit attentari. Dat. Çamore v id. maii anno domini MCCLV [11--V-1255].

Item noveritis nos recepisse litteras a sede apostolica sub hac forma:

Alexander episcopus servus servorum Dei dilectis filiis decano et thesaurario Zamorensibus salutem et apostolicam benedictionem. Dilectus filius Melendus Petri archidiaconus Astoricensis dilecti filii O[ttoboni] Sancti A[driani] diaconi cardinalis capellanus in nostra proposuit presentia constitutus quod felicis recordationis Innocentius papa predecessor noster vobis dedit litteris in mandatis ut eidem archidiacono provideatis in Legionensi ecclesia in qua existit canonicus de personatu vel dignitate si tunc vacaret in ipsa vel quamprimum ad id opportunitas se offeret [...]. Nos postmodum ad instantiam bone memorie G[uillelmi] Sancti Eustachii diaconi cardinalis cuius insistens obsequiis in negotio regni Sicilie cum eo fideliter laboravit, vobis meminimus per nostras litteras iniunxisse ut ad provisionem procederetis ipsius iuxta prefati predecessoris continentiam litterarum. Set quia venerabili fratri nostro episcopo et dilectis filiis capitulo Legionensibus dicuntur indulsisse ut ad receptionem seu provisionem alicuius minime teneantur per nostras litteras impetratas per quas non sit ius alicui adquisitum (vel impetrandas?) non facientes plenam et expressam de indulto huiusmodi mentionem dictus capellanus non inmerito dubitat quod eius (propter?) hoc posset provis[i]o impediri. Nos igitur predicti cardinalis precibus inclinati, volentes ei super hoc salubri remedio providere [...] per apostolica scripta mandamus quatinus indulto huiusmodi et generis alia indulgentia sedis apostolice impetrata vel impetranda de qua plenam et expressam oporteat in presentibus fieri mentionem cuiuscumque tenoris existat per quam huiusmodi gratia impediri seu etiam retardari nequaquam obstantibus ad provisionem procedatis ipsius per vos vel per [al]ios iuxta dictarum continentiam litterarum. Dat. Lateran v kal. februarii pontificatus nostri anno tertio [28-I-1257]. Quo[circa] auctoritate nobis comissa dignitatem vel personatum cum prestimoniis competentibus cedentis vel decedentis que alicui alteri de iure [non] debentur si in ecclesia vestra vacet ad presens vel quamprimum vacare contigerit donationi nostre reservamus archidiacono per nos vel per alium coferende (sic) inhibentes vobis auctoritate qua fungimur ne circa premissa in preiudicium d[icti] [archid]iac[oni] aliquid attemptetis, decernentes irritum et inane siquid contra mandati nostri tenorem super premissis a quoque [conti]ger[it] attemptari, forma supra proxime [...] quam super hac executione vobis direcximus non obstante. Dat. Çamore (?) kal. magii sub anno domini MCCLVII [?-IV-1257]

Item quod in presentia decani et [canoni]corum et dicti thesaurarii existentium (? in dicto) capitulo lecta fuit littera missa a decano et thesaurario (fol. 126v) Çamorensibus episcopo et capitulo Legionensibus supradictam provisionem facienda et super inhibitionibus et reservationibus in licteris (sic) apostolicis contemptis (sic) et ab ipsis decano et thesaurario factis cuius tenor talis est: [palabra borrada] Reverende

Item quod decanus Çamorensis dicto thesaurario college sue totaliter vices suas comisit super provisione facienda dicto Melendo archidiacono de archidiaconatu de Valle Moriel et prestimoniis vacantibus per mortem P. Nuni in ecclesia Legionensi.

Item quod dictus decanus comisit vices suas eidem thesaurario eo quod dicte provisioni dicto Melendo faciende archidiaconatus propter debilitatem corporis et quia aliis negotiis occupatus non poterat commode interesse.

Item quod super huius excusatione et commissione fuerunt confecte littere ex parte ipsius decani que erant sigillate sigillo ipsius, quarum tenor talis erat et est:

Noverint universi presentes licteras (sic) inspecturi quod cum ego J. decanus et [...] thesaurarius Çamorenses a sede apostolica recepimus in mandatis prout in licteris (sic) apostolicis plenius continetur ut ambo vel alter nostrum provideremus domino Menendo archidiacono Astoricensi de personatu vel dignitate si tunc vaccabat in ecclesia Legionensi vel quamprimum ad id opportunitas se offeret, et nunc relatione quorundam didicerimus quod per mortem bone memorie P. Nuni vacat archidiaconatus in eadem ecclesia, quia ego J. decanus aliis negotiis impeditus et etiam corporis debilitate detentus dicte provisioni non possum commode interesse prefato thesaurario college mer totaliter vices meas comicto (sic) et ne hoc venire possit in dubium presentem licteram (sic) sigilli mei feci munime roborari. Dat. Çamore VII id. februarii aub anno domini millesimo CCLX [7-II-1261].

Item quod ille littere super huius commissione fuerunt confecte et sigillo domini decani sigillata post vacationem dicti archidiaconatus et dictarum prestimoniorum et antequam fieret de hiis aliqua collatio predicto archidiacono per thesaurarium supradictum.

Item quod littere ille super huius commissione pervenerunt ad dictum thesaurarium post vacationem predicti archidiaconatus et antequam ipse provideret ad aliquam collationem sive investituram faciendam etidem Menendo de predicto archidiaconatu et predictis prestimoniis.

Item quod anno domini MCCLX videlicet IIII yd. februarii [10-II-1261] pulsata campana prout moris est et decano et canonicis Legionensibus congregatis in capitulo et in presentia dictorum decani et canonicorum et dicti thesaurarii Çamorensis lecta fuit predicta littera decani Çamorensis.

Item quod fuit lecta post vacationem dictorum archidiaconatus et prestimoniorum et antequam fieret aliqua collatio de eis per thesaurarium supradictum.

Item quod in sigillo apposito in illis litteris dicti decani confectis super commissione huius est et erat sculta [et] singnata (*sic*) ymago beate (?) Marie Virginis cum flore in manu cum filio suo et ad pedes ipsius quedam ymago flexis genibus et circumcirci (?) erant sculpte et descripte littere: Sigillum J. Johannis decani Çamorensis.

Item quod in sigillo apposito in illis litteris dicti decani et erat tempore predicte commissionis et etiam ante illud tempus.

Item quod dictus decanus utebatur tunc temporis et antea et postea illo sigillo tamquam suo in sigillando litteras et s[cripturas] quas sigillari faciebat.

(*fol. 127r*) Item quod illum sigillum est notum et autenticum in partibus illis et adhibetur ei fides circa sigillatione quam facit fieri dictus decanus in scripturis suis et litteris.

Item quod illud sigillum est notum in curia domini pape apud multas personas qui noverunt et viderunt illud sigillum.

Item quod anno domini millesimo CCLX, IIII id. februarii [10-II-1261] in presentia decani et canonicorum Legionensium et dicti thesaurarii Çamorensis existentium in capitulo supradicto post vacationem archidiaconatus de Valle Moriel et prestimoniorum que quondam P. Nuni archidiaconus in Legionensi ecclesia optinebat et antequam dictus thesaurarius procederet ad collationem de archidiaconatu et prestimoniis antedictis faciendam dicto Menendo littera domini Innocentii et omnes littere domini Alexandri misse decanis (*sic*) et thesaurario Çamorensibus supradicta provisione facienda dicto Menendo archidiacono Astoricensi lecte fuerunt.

Item quod perlectis litteris omnibus supradictis dictus thesaurarius Çamorensis anno domini millesimo CCLX, IIII id. februarii existens in capitulo Legionensi, pulsata campana Legionensis ecclesie prout moris est, et decano et canonicis Legionensibus in dicto capitulo existentibus, et lectis et recitatis omnibus litteris supradictis contulit dicto Menendo archidiaconatum de Valle Meriel et prestimonium de Cephinos et prestimonium de Monesteruelo vacantia per mortem domini P. Nuni [in Legionensi ecclesia: *borrado*] optinebat (*sic*) cum omnibus aliis prestimoniis que dictus P. Nuni in Legionensi ecclesia optinebat.

Item quod thesaurarius Çamorensis usus fuit hiis litteris in collatione quam fecit archidiacono supradicto de archidiaconatu et prestimoniis predictis que conferebat auctoritate qua fungebatur et potestate sui college in eo translata dicto Menendo archidiaconatum et prestimonia supradicta.

Item quod facta collatione de archidiaconatu et prestimoniis supradictis incontinenti dictum Menendum per pileum suum dictus thesaurarius investivit de archidiaconatu et prestimoniis supradictis.

Item quod assignavit sibi locum in capitulo et stallum in choro pertinentia ad archidiaconatum dicti archidiaconatus.

Item quod per duas dies horis consuetis sedit in capitulo dictus M. tamquam archidiaconus in dicto loco sibi per thesaurarium assignato in prima et missa et vesperis.

[Item quod stetit et sedit in stallo chori per duas dies sibi per dictum thesaurarium assignato in prima et missa (et vesperis)].

Item quod per illas duas dies sedit et stetit in stallo chori in prima et missa et vesperis.

Item quod lecta fuit quedam littera confecta nomine domini Alexandri pape quarti in capitulo Legionensi in presentia episcopi Legionensis in qua continebatur quod dictus dominus Alexander ad preces et instantiam dicti episcopi dabat ei potestatem conferendi quinque ca[nonias].

Item quod dicte littere fuerunt concesse ad preces et instantiam dicti episcopi.

Item quod in littera illa continebatur quod non obstante certo canonicorum numero faceret illos quibus item debeat providere de dictis canoniis recipi in canonicos et in fratres, contradictores per censuram ecclesiasticam compescendo.

(fol. 127v) Item quod ista littera predicti domini Alexandri pape quarti fuit lecta in capitulo Legionensi anno tertio predicti domini Alexandri.

Item quod fuit lecta (? eodem anno) inter festum Natalis Domini et festum Purificationis Beate Marie [25-XII-1256 - 2-II-1257].

Item quod ista littera lecta in capitulo Legionensi in presentia dicti episcopi recepit dictus episcopus incontinenti Egidium Gometii, magistrum Petrum maiordomum suum, magistrum Pelagium Gallecum, Petrum Fernandi cantorem Astoricensem et Petrum Fernandi de Laguna in canonicos et in fratres, nulla prebenda vel canonia in dictas Legionensi ecclesia vacantibus.

Item quod postquam dicte quinque canonie et quinque prebende in dicta Legionensi ecclesia vacaverunt eas per se vel per p[rocuratores] dictus dominus contulit auctoritate litterarum illarum.

Item quod decem anni sunt et ultra quod dictus Menendus Petri fuit canonicus ecclesie Legionensis.

Item quod Jacobus Johannis canonicus Legionensis fuit specialiter excommunicatus pro eo quod impedivit magistrum Julianum super cantoria sibi assignata auctoritate apostolica per Pelagium Fernandi canonicum Legionensem executorem super provisione dicti cantoris deputati.

Item quod dominus Egidius auctoritate apostolica excommunicavit omnes qui dictum magistrum Julianum super dicta cantoria et prestimoniis sibi auctoritate apostolica assignatis impedirent.

Item quod episcopus Legionensis qui nunc est dictum cantorem impedivit et impediri procuravit.

Item quod de hoc est fama publica in civitate Legionensi.

Item quod prestimonia sibi auctoritate apostolica assignata aliis duxit conferenda.

Item quod episcopus Legionensis existens impedimentis excommunicationis [...] se [...].

Item quod post dictam sententiam excommunicationis et post sententiam suspensionis [...] celebravit divina et contulit beneficia ecclesiastica.

Item quod propter hoc incurrit irregularitatem.

Item intendit probare predictus procurator quod dominus Alexander quartus mandavit per suas litteras domino Martino episcopo Legionensi qui nunc est ut magistrum Julianum cantorem Legionensem, Petrum Roderici archidiaconum Salmantinum capellanum domini pape, magistrum Pelagium, Pelagium Fernandi, Johannem Roderici canonicos Legionensis ecclesie, Johannem Fernandi portionarium ipsius ecclesie et quosdam alios clericos ecclesie quod destiteret eos suis beneficiis quibus eos spoliaverat [...].

Item quod si hoc infra unum mensem post receptionem litterarum (dictarum?) negligerit adimplere dictus dominus Alexander dominum episcopum volebat extunc suspensionis sententie subiacere.

Item quod in illis continebatur quod non obstante si episcopo vel aliis a sede apostolica esset indultum quod excommunicari, suspendi vel interdici per apostolicas litteras non possent seu qualibet alia indulgentia dicte sedis sub quacumque forma [...] concessa per quam dicta restitutio impediri valeret vel differri.

Item quod littera ista presentata fuit et lecta dicto episcopo Legionensi anno domini millesimo CCLV, VI kal. (? septembris: MS: *optumbris*) [? 27-VIII-1255].

Item quod post duos menses ex quo predicta littera domino episcopo fuit lecta mortuus fuit magister Julianus cantor Legionensis... [termina el *fol. 127v*].

fol. 153. Die jovis XX eiusdem [*scil.* mensis aprilis: 20-IV-1262] dictus dominus archidiaconus [*scil.* Melendus Petri] comparuit coram dicto domino O[ddoni] ad respondendum posicionibus datis, alia parte non comparente.

Die sabbati XXII aprilis comparuerunt partes coram dicto domino Ottoni (*sic*) et responsum est quibusdam posicionibus ipsius domini archidiaconi et datus est eis terminus [...] ad dandas alias posiciones in diem mercurii proximo venturam.

Die jovis XXVII eiusdem comparuerunt partes coram dicto domino O. et responsum est quibusdam posicionibus per dictum dominum archidiaconum et datis per magistrum Fernandum, et datus est utraque parti [...] terminus peremptorius diem martis proximo venturam ad dandas omnes positiones.

11

1263, agosto, 8. Orvieto.

La sentencia del cardenal Uberto di Coconatu sobre la cantoría de la iglesia legionense.

Archivio Segreto Vaticano, Reg. Vat. 29 (*Litt. ben. et aliarum gratiarum*), núm. 144, ff. 61v-62r (reg. GUIRAUD, *Registres d Urbain IV*, núm. 1095).

Sane vacante dudum in Legionensi ecclesia per mortem quondam magistri Juliani cantoris ipsius ecclesie cantoria, et capitulo ipsius ecclesie, ad quod de antiqua et approbata et hactenus pacifice observata consuetudine cantoris electio pertinet, vocatis omnibus eiusdem ecclesie canonicis qui debuerunt voluerunt et potuerunt comode interesse, die ad eligendum prefixa, more solito congregato, maior pars canonicorum ibidem presentium Michaelem Sancii eiusdem ecclesie canonicum in ipsum consentiendo ac eundem nominando in cantorem ipsius elegerunt ecclesie. Insuper discretus vir Martinus Johannis domini pape, capellanus, prefate ecclesie archidiaconus, tam apostolica quam ordinaria potestate quam ex commissione venerabilis patris Legionensis episcopi ad quem ipsius cantoris confirmatio et institutio pertinet obtinebat, cantoriam ipsam canonico contulit memorato, ipsum investiens per suum pileum de eadem. Verum R[oderico] Petri archidiacono et quibusdam canonicis Legionensibus pro se et sibi adherentibus se electioni, collationi et investiture opponentibus antedictis eisque propter hoc ad dominum papam appellantibus, idem dominus papa nos Ubertum Sancti Eustachii diaconum cardinalem concessit partibus auditorem, dicto itaque Michaele pro se et Jacobo Juvenalis procuratore predicti archidiaconi et adherentium sibi canonicorum nomine libellum obtulit in hunc modum:

Coram vobis reverendo patre domino Uberto Sancti Eustachii diacono cardinale

LA IGLESIA DE LEÓN A MEDIADOS DEL SIGLO XIII

a domino papa partibus auditore concesso proponit Jacobus Juvenalis procurator domini Ade et Petri Dominici archidiaconorum, Fernandi thesaurarii, Menendi archidiaconi Legionensium et aliorum quorum habet ad hoc speciale mandatum contra
Michaelem Sancii qui se gerit pro cantore Legionensi, quod cum vacaret cantoria in
eadem ecclesia que consuevit illi per electionem capituli conferri in quem ipsum capitulum vel maior et sanior pars consentiret ipsius, et Martinus Johannis archidiaconus
in eadem ecclesia asserens se potestatem habere a venerabile patre Legionensi episcopo
cantoriam predictam Michaeli Sancii conferendi, ipsam cantoriam tam auctoritate
apostolica quam dictum episcopum habere dicebat, quam etiam ordinaria eiusdem
episcopi dicto Michaeli conferre intenderet, ex parte predictorum petitum extitit ab
eisdem quod auctoritatem apostolicam siquam idem vel dictus episcopus habebat eis
ostenderet et copiam eiusdem eis similiter exhiberet. Fuit etiam petitum coram eo
quod auctoritate ordinaria potestatem conferendi eandem non habebat cum predicta
cantoria conferri non possit nisi illi in quem capitulum vel ipsius capituli maior pars
et sanior consentiret, quod in persona dicti Michaelis non extare dicebant. Fuit etiam
propositum coram eo quod dictus Michaelis non erat sufficiens et ydoneus ad dictam
dignitatem adipiscendam et eius officium exercendum cum nesciret canere prout pertinet ad officium cantoris, ne dictus archidiaconus dictam cantoriam dicto Michaeli
conferret, et quia auctoritatis apostolice supradictam siquam habebat eiusdem exhibere
iustitiam denegavit ex parte ipsorum extitit ad Sedem (fol. 62r) Apostolicam legitime
appellatum. Sed dictus archidiaconus propter appellationes predictas, licet idem episcopus auctoritate cuius in collatione huius se fungi dicebat tunc apostolica esset auctoritate suspensus, ipsis etiam appellationibus vilipensis, de facto cum de iure non
posset dicto Michaeli cantoriam contulit supradictam et de eadem investivit et installa-
vit eundem non sine Apostolice Sedis iniuria et contemptu et ipsius illusione ecclesie
et in scandalum plurimorum. A qua collatione dictus thesaurarius et magister Ascensius
portionarius, quorum consensus erat de iure et consuetudine requirendus, quia con-
tempti et irrequisiti fuerunt, ac etiam ipsi duo et alii supradicti quia per eum qui de
iure non poterat collata extiterat et dicto Michaeli persone minus ydonee, sicut superius est expressum, ad Sedem Apostolicam appellarunt. Unde petit dictam collationem et processum dicti archidiaconi et quicquid ex eo vel ob id secutum est per vos
cassari et irritari, cassa seu nulla et irrita nuntiari, et quatinus de facto processit
totaliter revocari, et dictas appellationes et earum quamlibet legitimas esse decerni,
et ipsum ab eadem cantoria sententialiter amoveri ac ipsi Michaeli super ea silentium
imponi cum nullum ius habeat in eadem. Petit etiam condempnari sibi nomine predictorum et fructus quos percepit et quos percipere potuit, quos extimat viginti marcas
argenti. Petit etiam expensas factas et protestatur faciendas. Salvo iure, etc.
    Lite autem super eodem libello legitime contestata et de veritate dicenda prestito
a partibus iuramento factisque positionibus et responsionibus ad easdem ac datis articulis hinc et inde, diligenter audivimus ea que partes ipse tam super dictis articulis
quam super toto negotio proponere voluerunt, et tandem in causa ipsa (?) concluso
ac iurisperitorum consilio requisito pluribus ex eis rationabiliter videbatur quod licet
predicti articuli probarentur non tamen propter hoc collatio et investitura cantoris
predicti essent aliquatenus infirmande, quas si etiam per eosdem articulos infirmari
contingeret ius quod dicto cantori per electionem capituli seu maioris partis eiusdem
ad quod ipsius cantoris electio pertinet, ut superius est expressum, nullatenus adimeretur
eidem, sed igitur salvum et integrum remaneret, et articuli qui ad impugnandum collationem et investituram predictas dabantur, si etiam probarentur, essent inutiles et inanes

cum eis probatis et collatione ac investitura predictis irritatis per eos prefata electio
esset de iure per superioris officium confirmanda. Nos igitur relatione super hiis fideliter domino pape predicto facta et prenominato Michaele in cantandi officio in quo
eum pati defectum pars altera proponebat per diligentem examinationem ydoneo com-
probato de speciali eiusdem domini pape mandato eiusdem providentia volentis ut
earundem partium parcatur laboribus et expensis predictos articulos minime admitten-
tes sepedictum Michaelem Sancii ab impeticione dicti archidiaconi et sibi adherencium
canonicorum sententialiter absolvimus eisque ac predicto procuratori ipsorum nomine
super oppositione huius perpetuum imponentes silentium, electionem predictam auctoritate nobis super hoc tradita confirmamus et nominatum Michaelem de cantoria ipsa
presentialiter per nostrum anulum investimus. Tulimus autem hanc sententiam et acta
fuerunt predicta apud Urbemveterem in camera nostra, presentibus testibus ad hoc
vocatis venerabili patre A. Humanate episcopo, magistro Bernardo Yspano, et domino
Jacobo de Thonerga domini pape capellanis, magistro Fernando magistro scolarum
Auriensi et domino Pepone de Senis Romane Curie advocatis, Subgerio Gundisalvi
Auriensi et Tudensi canonico, Pelagio de Cana et Fernando Fructuosi canonicis Compostellanis, Pelagio Fernandi canonico Palentino, Johanne Fernandi canonico Salmanticensi, Petro Petri clerico predicti cantoris, et ipso cantore, ac prefato Jacobo Juvenalis procuratore. In cuius rei testimonium... sub anno domini .M.CC.LXIII. die VIII
intrante Augusti, Indictione sexta, pontificatus domini Urbani pape IIII anno secundo.
Ego Paris de Spoleto notarius publicus predictis omnibus interfui et mandato predicti
domini cardinalis ut supra legitur scripsi, publicavi et meo signo signavi.

12

1264, agosto, 1. Orvieto.

*Urbano IV dirige carta al deán y cabildo de León, mandándoles que
satisfagan al obispo Martín Fernández, sobre ciertas propiedades que el
cardenal Pelayo Gaitán había donado en 1224, según sus constituciones,
a la dicha iglesia.*

León, ACL, doc. 6.322.

Urbanus episcopus servus servorum Dei. Dilectis filiis .. decano et capitulo Legionensibus salutem et apostolicam benedictionem. Venerabilis frater noster .. Legionensis episcopus nobis significare curavit quod cum olim bone memorie P. Albanensis
episcopo fuerit ab apostolica sede commissum ut in ecclesia Legionensis divideret seu
distribueret prestimonia et beneficia proportionaliter inter canonicos et alias personas
ecclesie supradicte, idem episcopus nonnullas villas et ecclesias, decimas ac alias
possessiones et quedam alia bona ad mensam ipsius episcopi spectantia inter prefatos
canonicos et personas huiusmodi commissionis pretextu pro sua distribuit voluntate,
cuius distributionis occasione mensa eiusdem episcopi est non modicum diminuta,
super quo provideri a nobis dictus episcopus humiliter supplicavit. Quia vero pietatis
credimus esse consilium inter vos et eundem episcopum spiritualem patrem vestrum

provida industria iurgiorum cohibere materiam ne in turbationem pacis mutue per dissensionem membrorum et capitis convalescat, universitatem vestram rogamus, monemus et hortamur attente sano vobis consilio suadentes quatinus eidem episcopo tanquam patri animarum vestrarum in hiis pro bono pacis precipue deferentes super bonis eiusdem mense inter vos sic divisis cum ipso componere sibique de hiis satisfacere taliter studeatis quod nulla propter hoc ad eandem sedem iterata querela percurrat et nos devotionem vestram exinde merito commendantes super hiis providere aliter non cogamur. Dat. apud Urbemveterem kal. augusti pontificatus nostri anno tertio.

13

1267, agosto, 25. León.

Los testimonios de algunos personajes leoneses sobre la responsabilidad financiera para las deudas de litigación contraídas por la iglesia de León.

León, ACL, doc. 1.564.

Esto ye elo Don Miguiel (*sic*) Sanchez chantre, e el arcidiano don Rodrigo, e Don Pedrannes chantre de Orens, e Don Fernant Abril thesorero, dados comunalmientre del bispo e del cabildo deven saber se el cabildo usa de dar costas ennos pleytos que acayaron enna yglesia de Leon sobre pessonadgos e canongias e raciones e prestamos e sobre los otros derechos dela yglesia, ho selos bispos que furon fezieron estas costas o que non las fizo.

Era M.CCC.V. siete dias por andar del mes de agosto.

Don Mestre Iohan dean de Leon iurado e preguntado dixo que el primo anno que el fu canoligo de Leon Mestre Rodrigo de Villalobos, que fu depues dean de Plazencia, se fizo dar a Mestre Florenz que estuencia yera dean de Zamora e per su companno el chantre desse lugar Religos por LXXX maravedis en oro de provision per auctoridat del bispo de Sabina que fura legado de Roma en Espanna, e este testigo morava con lo bispo Don Rodrigo Alvarez bispo de Leon, e perso mandado deste bispo el appello de tal provision al Apostoligo, e depues fu rennovar esta appellacion a Zamora ante Mestre Florenz dean e antal chantre de suso dichos, e depues fu a Roma per mandado desse bispo procurador deste pleyto e fizo denunciar enna corte de Roma esse processu non valer nada per auctoridat del papa, e diz que a la yda de Roma sobre este pleyto le fizo dar al obispo Don Rodrigo per mano de Gutier Rodriguez so despensero e so omme XL livras de torneses, e otro nenguno non pago hy dinero que el saba nen el crea se non ala venida que vino de Roma. Elos que eligiron al arcediano Don Martin Alfonso le rogaron que tornas a Roma por aquella eleycion que fazieran e ellos entregaronle por las costas que faziera delas bonas del bispado segundo como el cree XVII livras de torneses. Preguntado quanto tiempo ha que esto fu dixo que el anno que morio Don Fernan Alfonso. Otrossi dixo que Martin Dominguez de Quintaniella demandava al bispo Don Rodrigo per antel obispo Don Nuno de Astorga per auctoridat de Roma provision e el dean de Leon devandicho permandado del bispo Don Rodrigo fu Astorga per costa del obispo de Leon. Otrossi dixo que Abril Perez clerigo del choro se fizo dar el prestamo de Santiago de Maliellos per auctoridat del papa e el dean devandicho per mandado del bispo Don Rodrigo appello e seguio la appellacion perlas despesas de suso dichas que recebio como dicho ye. Otrossi dixo quel bispo Don Munio Alvarez lo envio a Cacaviellos sobrel pleyto del arcediaganadgo de Tria Castiella contra la yglesia de Lugo per suas costas del bispo segundo como el cree. Fu conel Don Fernan Abril thesorero e Don Fernan Rogel. Preguntado se el cabillo diera dalquen enestas costas dixo que nolo sabe nelo cree e dixo que Iohan Perez so escrivan del bispo fu conellos, e fazia estas costas per mandado del bispo. Otrossi dixo que este bispo Don Martin Fernandez que agora ye lo envio a Cacaviellos sobrel arcedianado de Tria Castiella con Mestre Bernaldo e el so omme del bispo fizo yelas costas. Otrossi dixo quel bispo Don Martin Rodriguez lo envio al conceyo que papa Gregorio queria fazer con sua procuracion por si e el dean Don Pedro Arias he el cabillo de Leon con sua procuracion por si, he el bispo le dio elas costas convienes assaber XIIII marcos de esterlines he letras de enprestido, e el cabillo non le dio nada. He quando elos otros furon pressos enna mar del emperador echo aquellas letras del emprestido enno mar, e dixo que quando el torno de aquella prision a Leon que demando al bispo Don Monio seyendo el eleyto de Leon los danos elas costas que el feziera por razon de aquella carrera. He fu fecha avenencia entrellos ambos quele entregas XL marcos por ello, he diolle pollos XXV marcos IIII mulas de sua casa, he elos otros XV furon por pagar. He dixo quel arcediano Don Lope Arnaldo recebio el arcediaganado de Tria Castiella de mano del bispo Don Rodrigo, he esse arcidiano salio por fazer todas las cosas que salissen al arcedianado, e dixo que assi lo conplio. Otrossi dixo que el ovo pleyto grande e gran discordia conno bispo Don Tello de Palencia sobre muchas yglesias de (?) Pernia e de Lievana que dezia el bispo de Palencia que yeran suas he el que yera arcidiano del lugar dezia que yeran suas por razon dela yglesia de Leon lo spiritual he cree verdaderamientre que costo este pleyto al obispo Don Tello bien XII mil maravedis e ael costo mas poco, e delas costas que hy fizo non le dio el bispo ne el cabillo nenguna cosa ne el noyelas pedio. Otrossi dixo que quantos pieytos ovo el arcidiano Don Fernan Garcia por razon del arcediano conno bispo de Palencia e connos clerigos deste arcediagado que elle lo seguio aiudando al arcidiano e el arcediano fazia todas las costas. Otrossi dixo que delos pleytos que los arcedianos avian sobrellos arcediaganados que nunqua viu que el cavillo hy pagas ren ata que vino este bispo que agora ye.

Don Gonzalvo Fernandez prior iurado e enpreguntado dixo que en tiempo del bispo Don Rodrigo e del arcediano Ruy Gutierrez que yera arcediano de Tria Castiella movio ela yglesia de Lugo pleyto contra ela yglesia de Leon sobrel arcediaganado de Tria Castiella, e vio que esse arcidiano seguia esse pleto con conseyo e con mandado del bispo, e diz quelas despesas non sabe como selas pagavan mas cree quelas pagava el arcediano e el obispo e nunqua viu ne odio al cabillo demandar nenguna cosa por aquestas despesas, nen cree que hy pagava ren. Preguntado del tiempo diz que ha bien XL annos e mas. E diz que depoys deste arcidiano Ruy Gotierrez fu arcidiano de Tria Castiella el arcidiano Lope Arnaldo, e quando se pleyto movia sobre esse arcediaganado esse Lope Arnaldo fazia las despesas e non sabe se con aiudorio del bispo se per si, mas nunqua vio nen odio que el cabildo enestas costas pagasse nada nelo cree, e esto mismo diz del arcidiano Don Abril, fueras que diz que el bispo Don Monio pagava lo mas delas costas. Et otrossi dixo que vio quando el arcidiano Don Fernan Garcia yera arcidiano de Saldanna he alzaron seye elos clerigos del arcidiaganado una pieza dellos conna yglesia de Palencia e esse mismo arcidiano Don Fernando fazia elas despesas e cree que el cabillo non dava hy nada. Depoys desto fu este dean Mestre Johan arcidiano de Saldanna he ovo pleyto connos clerigos del arcidiaganado e conno bispo de Palencia he el seguio el pleyto e non sabe nen cree que el cabildo hy pagasse nada. Otrossi dixo que Martin Dominguez de Quintaniella e Martin Bernaldo demandavan per letra de Roma raciones enna yglesia de Leon e el bispo Don Rodrigo opusoseyes e seguio el pleyto e non sabe nen cree que cabildo hy pagasse nada nen le fusse demandado. Otrossi dixo quel legado bispo de Sabina dio el prestamo de Religos a Mestre Rodrigo canoligo que fu de Leon e dean de Plazencia he el bispo Don Rodrigo opuseye he seguio el pleyto e non sabe nen cree quel cabildo hy pagasse nada nen cree quele fusse demandado. Otrossi dixo que Maestre Julian chantre que fu de Leon demandava en tiempo del bispo Don Rodrigo racion e calongia he arcidiaganado ena yglesia de Leon, he el bispo Don Rodrigo opusoseye e seguio el pleyto e non sabe nen cree que el cabildo hy pagasse nada nen cree quele fusse demandado. Otrossi dixo que contienda fu levantada entrel bispo Don Martin Rodriguez dela una parte he el conceyo de Leon dela otra sobre iantar e sobre otras cosas muchas que el conceyo demandava alos vassalos quela yglesia ha enno alfoz, he el obispo Don Martino seguio este pleyto ante el rey Don Fernando en Burgos e en otros lugares hu fu perso corpo mismo, he fizo las despesas e non vio nen cree que el cabildo hy pagasse nada, nen le fusse demandado. Otrossi dixo que entiempo del bispo Don Rodrigo vio e delos otros bispos que furon ante del, assi como el cree. el bispo helas pessonas se aiuntavan en casa del bispo e traytavan delos fechos grandes de la yglesia e de como se seguirien elos pleytos he non davan ende traballo ne enxeco al cabildo mas ellos selo fazian persi, ne demandavan ren al cabildo. Otrossi dixo que se dalgun omme ho dalgun conceyo fazia dalguna demanda al canoligo sobre so prestamo el canoligo selo seguia per sua costa he el bispo lo aiudava en sua sentencia he en suas letras mas non en costas, he el cabillo non paga hy nada ni yelo demandan.

El arcidiano Don Rodrigo iurado e preguntado dixo assi: yo vi e se por verdat que entrel bispo Don Martin Rodriguez he el conceyo de Leon fu pleyto antel rey Don Fernando sobre muchas cosas que demandava el conceyo alos vassalos dela yglesia que moran en Vernasga he en Torio he en Sobreriba, e vi e fuy en ello que el rey devandicho cito al bispo he al cabildo de Leon e mando que los vassallos del bispo que moran en Vernasga enviassen dos pessoneros he elos de Torio otros dos elos de Sobreriba otros dos e el bispo fu por si e por lo cabildo a Burgos ala corte del rey, he yua conel el arcidiano Don Monio he el arcidiano Maestre Fagunde he el arcidiano Don Pedro Iohan he el chantre Monio Rodriguez e el maestre scola Martin Perez he yo Ruy Perez arcidiano e canoligos muchos dela yglesia e otras grandes compannas, e fumos a Burgos e moremos hy bien tres selmanas sobrelas cosas que demandavan el conceyo ala yglesia e Iohan Abrianes canoligo que yera despensero del bispo fazia cada dia todas las despesas delos dineros del bispo perso mandado. Preguntado como lo sabia dixo quelo vio elo oyu e despendia el bispo cadal dia bien cxx maravedis he alas vegadas mucho mas, he depues vinosse pora Leon e yendo e veniendo e estando enna corte sobrel pleyto siempre el bispo fizo todas elas despesas muy bien e mucho ondradamientre. He despues otras duas vezes envio el bispo por si e pollo cabillo e por sos vassallos el arcidiano Don Munio Alvarez he ami sobrestos pleytos mismos ala corte del rey he dionos mil maravedis pora despender e yo mandelos dar a Ruy Sanchez mio clerigo e mio pariente quelos despendisse e fumos a Burgos, he estodiemos hy hotras tres selmanas segundo como yo cuydo e despendiemos siempre de aquellos mil maravedis. Et depues otra vegada elas pessonas dela yglesia posioron entressi que non fusse hy nenguno he el bispo envio ami e a Maestre Rodrigo comigo e dionos todas elas despesas muy bien e muy ondradamientre, e fumos antel rey nos e los personeros del conceyo de Leon, he el rey dio la sentencia contra el conceyo sobre quantas cosas demandavan. He desta sentencia a carta del rey seellada enno tesoro. He en aquel tiempo avia el dean Don Pedro Arias aprestamos en Sobreriba, Tollanos he Martine (?), he el arcidiano Don Adam Paradiella, e Domingo de Cangas Villavente e el cabildo connellos que ha oy dia. He avia el cabildo otras heredades he otros vassallos en Sobreriba que ha oy dia; he en Vernesga avia el prior Giraldo Diez Sancta Olaya por prestamo; he otrossi en Torio avian canoligos aprestamos; he empero el bispo fazia todas las despesas, e nunqua odi nen vi quel cabillo diesse en estas despesas nen que ren le fusse demandado de parte del bispo. Otrossi sey por verdat quel rey Don Fernando gano del papa que las yglesias del regno de Leon e del regno de Castiella le diessen LX mil maravedis, segundo como yo creo por tres annos; he gano por executor al chanceller Don Iohan bispo de Burgos, he el chanceller en puso gran quantidat al bispo he al cabildo he ala yglesia del bispado de Leon; he ellos appellaron e enviaron ami al chanceller a Burgos sobresto pleito. He el bispo Don Martino me dio todas elas despesas a hyr e avenir he aestar hy. He el ianceller tollio de aquella quantidat que nos possiera e puso la menor. Otrossi sey por verdat quel bispo Don Martin Rodriguez e el cabildo enviaron otra vegada al arcidiano Don Monio Alvarez he ami conel al rey Don Fernando sobre pleytos dela iglesia he axemoslo en Estremadura he se yua pora Cordova e daquella hyda preso Sevillia, e dio el bispo Don Martin a elle e ami CCCC maravedis pora despender. Otrossi sey por verdat quel bispo he el cabildo sobredichos enviaron al dean Don Pedro Arias e ami conel al rey sobre pleitos aela yglesia e axemoslo en Toledo, he el bispo Don Martino devandicho nos dio todas las despesas he yua conel dean Martin Perez cotisso e Pelay Petite que yera estuencia muy mal rapaz he agora muy mal villano. Et otrossi sey por verdat e vilo quando este dean escapo dela prision del emperador vino aqui ala terra e demandava al bispo Don Monnio Alvarez quele diesse las despesas que feziera porque fura en servicio dela yglesia. He puso conel al bispo dele dar XL marcos, e diole IIII mulas por XXV marcos e vi quando yelas dio e quando las el dean recebio. He yo fuy tractador he componedor desta avenencia entrel bispo e el dean. Otrossi vi que Maestre Miguel hermano que fu del otro Maestre Miguel que fu canoligo gano carta del Apostoligo pora racion enesta yglesia he el bispo e el cabildo oposieron sele e segundo como cuido auia iuyzes en Salamanca, he el bispo solo dava todas las despesas pora seguir el pleito. Otrossi sey por cierto quel bispo Don Monio Alvarez fu a Valadolit al rey Don Fernando que yera hy sobre pleytos que avia conel conceyo de Leon, e yo fuy conel. He el bispo Don Monio fizo todas las despesas a hyr e a venir e a estar hy en corte. Otrossi sey por verdat quel bispo Don Monio fue a Cacaviellos sobrel pleyto del arcediaganado de Tria Castiella que avia ela yglesia de Leon cona yglesia de Lugo, e levo por avogados a Maestre Gil he a Maestre Pedro; he el bispo fizo todas las despesas yendo e veniendo he estando hy. He yera iuyz de Roma el bispo Don Pedro de Astorga. He otra vegada envio el bispo ami e a Maestre Gil he a Maestre Pedro e a Don Fernan Abril que

LA IGLESIA DE LEÓN A MEDIADOS DEL SIGLO XIII

estuencia non yera thesorero al bispo de Orens que yera iuyz entre la yglesia de Leon he ela yglesia de Lugo; he el bispo nos dio todas las despesas yendo e veniendo he estando hy. Et otra vegada envio el bispo a Maestre Gil he a Maestre Pedro e ami conellos sobre este pleyto mismo a Cacaviellos e yo por amor del bispo Don Monio que me fazia mucho bien e mucha merced fiz las despesas a todos estando hy e veniendo ca ala yda non fuy yo conellos. E en todos estos pleytos sobredichos nunqua vi nen odi nen creo quel cabildo ren diesse nen fusse requerido que hy diesse, se non el bispo Don Monio que demando una vegada quelo aiudasse el cabildo a seguir este pleyto e todo el cabildo fu contra el e non le quiso ren dar; e vi depues que elle vino al cabildo e quitosse de demandar ren al cabildo e reconoscio que el devia a fazer elas despesas e el cabildo non yera tenudo, e segundo como yo creo dio sobresto sua carta abierta seellada de so seyello colgado. E sobre todas estas cosas sobredichas demandado se el cabillo dio dalque en estas despesas dixo que nunqua vio ne odio nen creyia que hy nunqua diera neguna cosa.

Sancho Ysidrez iurado e preguntado dixo que vio entiempo del bispo Don Rodrigo quela yglesia de Lugo avia pleito conna yglesia de Leon sobrel arcidia-ganado de Tria Castiella, he yera ende arcidiano Don Lope Arnaldo, he el arcidiano fazia las despesas, he elo mas fazia el obispo Don Rodrigo. Preguntado como lo sabia dixo que enaquest tiempo estava conel bispo Don Rodrigo e quelo vio e quele odio. Preguntado se dava hy dalque el cabildo dixo que numqua lo vio nelo odio nelo cree que hy diesse ren. Preguntado quanto tiempo que fu esto dixo que ha bien xxx e vii annos. Otrossi dixo que vio quel arcidiano Don Fernan Garcia avia pleyto cona yglesia de Palencia sobre las yglesias del arcediaganado de Saldanna. Preguntado quien fazia elas costas dixo que el arcidiano Don Fernan Garcia. Otrossi dixo que en todos los otros pleytos que acaycian enna yglesia de Leon sobre calongias e raciones que nunqua vio entiempo del bispo Don Rodrigo que el cabildo hy diesse despesas nengunas, e diz que sabe que el bispo las fazia todas. He demandado quien defende elos prestamos quando pleyto dalguno hy acaeçe dixo quelos prestameros los defendian e fazian las costas; he el bispo aiudavalos con suas cartas.

Martin Perez sobrino del dean Don Flora iurado e preguntado dixo que vio que el bispo Don Martin Rodriguez envio al dean Don Pedrarias e al arcidiano Don R. a Toledo sobre pleito que avia la yglesia hy antel rey e que el bispo yes dio las despesas. Preguntado como lo sabia dixo quelo vio e fuy conellos. Preguntado se dio hy dalque de las despesas el cabildo dixo que nunqua vio ne odio nen creyia que hy numqua diessen ren. Preguntado del arcidiaganado de Tria Castiella quien fazia las despesas dixo quel arcidiano Don Lope Arnaldo he el bispo; e diz que nunqua vio ne odio nen cree que el cabildo hy diesse nenguna ren. Otrossi dixo que vio que el bispo Don Martino avia pleyto con Maestre Miguel sobre racion que demandava ena yglesia de Leon, e vio que el bispo fazia las costas e que el cabildo non dava hy nenguna cosa; e delos prestamos dixo assi como Sancho Ysidrez.

El arcidiano Don Adam iurado e preguntado dixo que vio quel arcidiano Don Lope Arnaldo avia pleyto conna yglesia de Lugo sobrel arcidiaganado de Tria Castiella, e non sabe se fazia el arcidiano elas costas se el bispo, mas diz que sabe por verdat que el cabildo non dava hy nenguna cosa. Preguntado perque sabe que el cabildo non dava hy nenguna cosa dixo que el yera estuencia companero dela yglesia e diz que nolo dio nelo vio dar al cabildo e cree que nunqua lo dio. Otrossi dixo que odio dezir a sos tios Don Martin Alfonso arcidiano e a Don Fernan Alfonso quel bispo Don Rodrigo opusoseye e seguio el pleyto per sua costa, e nunqua vio ne odio nen cree que el cabildo hy diesse nenguna cosa destas despesas. Otrossi dixo quel arcidiano Don Fernan Garcia avia pleyto cona yglesia de Palencia sobrelas yglesias del arcidiaganado de Saldanna, e non sabe quien fazia las costas e diz que sabe por verdat que el cabildo non dava hy nenguna cosa. He dixo que creyia que fazia las costas el bispo he el arcidiano. Otrossi dixo que vio quel bispo Don Martin Rodriguez avia pleyto conno conceyo de Leon antel rey Don Fernando que yera estuencia en Burgos, e sabe por verdat que el cabildo non dava hy costas nengunas. He diz que numqua yelas viu demandar nen cree que nunqua yelas diesse. Preguntado quien dava las costas dixo que creyia quelas dava el bispo. Otrossi dixo que vio quel bispo Don Monnio vino al cabildo demandar quele aiudassen ennas costas pora seguir el pleyto de Tria Castiella e que el cabildo non ye quiso ende nenguna cosa. E diz que vio otra vez venir el bispo al cabildo e reconecio que elle avia de fazer las costas he el cabildo non. Preguntado quien fazia las costas quando venia carta de Roma sobre calongias e raciones dixo quelos obispos que furon antal tiempo deste bispo que agora ye, he delos prestamos dixo assi como Sancho Ysidrez.

Don Fernando Abril thesorero iurado e preguntado dixo que enno pleyto de Tria Castiella fu tres vezes a Galicia sobrel pleyto e vio al arcidiano Don G. fazer las despesas en una de las carreras, he yera estuencia arcidiano de Maorga como agora ye; he otra vegada fue conno arcidiano Don Abril ha Orens e vio que este arcidiano fizo las despesas e non sabe selo aiudo hy el bispo mas creyia quesi. Otra vez fu a Orens elle a R. Iohannes e fizo el bispo las despesas. Preguntado se ei cabildo aiudo en dalguna cosa ennas despesas dixo que numqua lo vio nelo odio. He en otras duas vezes que fu a Cacaviellos fizo el bispo las despesas. Item dixo que fu a Valladolit conno chantre que yera estuencia canoligo sobre pleyto que avia el bispo conno conceyo de Mansiella, e diz que el bispo fizo las despesas. Item quando el arzobispo de Santiago fizo xamar todos los bispos sos sofragannos he elos otros bispos elos procuradores delos cabildos a Ponferrada tuvo el cabildo por bien de enviar alla, he envio a el e a Don Miyel Sanchez chantre que yera estuencia canoligo, he el cabildo yes dio las despesas. Item dixo que enno fecho de Aguilar fu elle al pleyto con Maestre Rodrigo e vio que el bispo fizo las despesas. Item dixo que enno playto de Maestre Miguel quando sele opuso el bispo e el bispo fizo las despesas. Item dixo que sabe persi e per otros quando algun conceyo faz tuerto al canoligo, specialmientre sobrel prestamo, que el canoligo faz las despesas. Item dixo que sobrel pleito del alfoz que ovo el conceyo conno bispo Don Martino que el bispo fizo las despesas, he el fu a Burgos sobrel pleyto.

Item Don Miyel Sanchez chantre iurado e enpreguntado dixo que acaecio una vez en Cacaviellos quando se tractava hy el pleyto sobre Tria Castiella e non sabe bien ciertamientre quien se fazia las despesas mas cree quel arcediano Don Abril las fazia assisse como a procurador e el bispo fazia alos iuyzes he alos avogados. Item enno pleyto de Valladolit e de Ponferrada e delos prestamos dixo como el thesorero. Item dixo quelo envio el cabildo a Toledo sobre pleyto de Lope Suarez e de Iohan Dominguez e que el cabildo ye dio las despesas. Item dixo que enno pleyto de Tria Castiella ne enno de Saldanna non vio nen creyia que el cabildo numqua hy diesse despesas nengunas.

LA IGLESIA DE LEÓN A MEDIADOS DEL SIGLO XIII

Don Alfonso Martinez iurado e preguntado dixo que sobre pleyto de Tria Castiella e del pleyto de Saldanna que el cabildo nunqua diera hy despesas dalgunas mas el bispo he elos arcidianos que estuencia tenian las terras fazian las despesas assi como se avenian entressi. Item dixo del pleyto de Maestre Miguel e del pleyto de Aguilar e del pleyto del alfoz que el cabildo numqua diera despesas nengunas. Preguntado como lo sabia dixo que enno pleyto del alfoz que vira a Iohan Cibrianez que yera maiordomo del bispo fazer las despesas polo bispo e que vira despues hyr al bispo persisse e del pleyto de San Fagun que odira que el bispo dio las despesas.

Pedro Gardo iurado e preguntado dixo que fu conno bispo Don Munio una vez a Cacaviellos sobrel pleyto de Tria Castiella e vio fazer las despesas al bispo, he el mismo despendio pollo bispo. Item dixo que fu otras duas vezes a Cacaviellos sien lo bispo, e que dio las despesas polo bispo alos que hy van al pleyto polla yglesia de Leon. Preguntado se vio que el cabildo aiudasse ennas despesas dixo que en estas tres vezes que el fu a Cacavielo o nunqua el cabildo hy dio nada que el sobiesse ne odio dezir que hy diesse nada. Item dixo que sobre pleito que avia el bispo Don Martino conno conceyo que Ruy Sanchez fizo las despesas al arcidiano Don Monio he el arcidiano Don R. por parte del bispo, he que non dio hy nada el cabildo. Item delos prestamos dixo como el tesorero.

Peley Fernandez iurado e preguntado dixo en todo como Pedro Gayardo.

Martin Dominguez iurado e preguntado dixo que odio dezir que enno pleito que el bispo don Rodrigo se opuso contra Maestre Rodrigo he contra Maestre Miguel que el bispo Don Martino fizo las despesas. Item dixo que odio dezir que enno pleyto de San Fagun que el bispo Don Rodrigo feziera las despesas. Item dixo que eno pleito de Saldanna el arcidiano Don Fernando se fazia las despesas. Preguntado como lo sabe dixo que yera so clerigo del arcidiano e quelo vio. Item dixo que odio dezir que enno pleyto de Tria Castiella el arcidiano Don Lope que yera estuencia fazia las despesas ennos iuyzes e ennos avogados. De los pleytos de Tria Castiella que furon en tiempo del bispo Don Munio dixo como Pedro Gayardo e dixo que el bispo Don Munio pedio al cabildo CCC maravedis en aiuda poral picyto e el cabildo nole quiso dar nada. Item delos prestamos dixo que se alguna cosa demandan al prestamero por rezon del prestamo que el prestamero lo defiende mas se bispo he ricomme demanda la propriadat del prestamo que el bispo deve tomar los fruchos del prestamo e deffendello dando parte delos fruchos al prestamero se pobre fur enque se mantienga.

Al dorso: Pelagius Fernandi undecimus testis — Martinus Dominici duodecimus testis.

14

1268, agosto, 20. León.

El testamento de Rodrigo Pérez, arcediano.

León, ACL, doc. 1.569.

In Dei nomine Amen. Notum sit omnibus per hoc scriptum quod ego Rodericus Petri Legionensis archidiaconus, sanus mente eger tamen corpore, testamentum meum ordino in hunc modum. Inprimis mando corpus meum sepeliri in claustro Sancte Marie. Mando pallium meum, gernachiam et capam pellem capitulo sicut moris est. Mando etiam capitulo lectum meum meliorem cum una culcitra et cum uno pulvinarii et cum coopertorio de bruneto et cum duabus cultris et cum duobus linteaminibus. Mando dari domino episcopo mulam quam ego equito et unum ciphum argenteum, et restitui sibi annulum dignitatis. Relinquo capitulo du[cent]os mor[abitinos] pro anniversario meo ita quod dicta peccunia in emptione prediorum collocetur de consilio domini P. decani, Luppi Suggerii canonici et Marci Dominici socii Legionensium. Hac redditus qui haberi poterit de possessionibus suppradictis distribuatur singulis annis inter canonicos et socios in die obitus mei. Mando Luppo Suggerii canonico Legionensi totam hereditatem et omnia alia que emi in Vallelilla a Facundo Petri nepoti magistri Facundi quondam archidiaconi Legionensis ut ipse habeat ea in vita dicti Facundi Petri secundum quod ego ea debebam habere. Relinquo conventui fratrum minorum Legionensium xx mor. et fratribus predicatoribus xx mor. Relinquo monasterio Sancti Claudii xx mor. pro anniversario meo. Relinquo bachallariis ecclesie Legionensis xx mor. pro anniversario meo. Relinquo monasterio Sancti Marchi xx mor. Item relinquo hospitali Sancti Marchi x mor. Relinquo hospitali Sancti Marcelli x mor. Relinquo fabrice ecclesie Sancte Marie xx mor. Relinquo hospitali Roscidevallis xx mor. Relinquo monasterio Sancti Ysidori xxx mor. Relinquo hospitali de Arvis xxx mor., de quibus emantur possessiones et fiat anniversarium pro anima mea. Mando solvi monasterio Sancti Isidori c et xii mor. pro anniversario Pelagii Martini nepotis mei secundum quod ipse legavit in testamento suo. Relinquo monasterio de Gradeses pro pitancia x mor. Relinquo monasterio de Carrizo pro pitancia x mor. Relinquo capitulo Astoricensi c mor. Relinquo capitulo Zamorensi c mor. Relinquo capitulo Ovetensi c mor. et mando quod predicta capitula emant possessiones de quorum redditu annis singulis pro anima mea anniversarium celebretur. Relinquo singulis cappellis civitatis binos mor. Lego Martino Gundissalvi nepoti meo canonico Astoricensi omnes libros legales et Summam Azonis, raciones super eis et Decretum et Decretales, quod ipse habeat eos si remanserit in clericatu. Relinquo Petro Martini cappellano meo unam asinam quam ipse elegerit. Relinquo Fernando Alfonsi roncinum meum nigrum. Relinquo Petro Dominici servienti meo xx stopos de pane, x de tritico, alios x de cera; Symoni servienti meo alios xx. Relinquo Petro dicto Amoroso alios xx. Relinquo Salvatori clerico (?) meo alios xx, Alfonso filio Petro Dominici alios xx, Johanni de Rota alios xx, Petro Xemenez decem. Relinquo etiam singulis servientibus qui custodiunt equituras meas quinque stopos cere. Mando quod vendantur armentum vaccarum et grex ovium et jumenta et asini et asini et boves aratorii et solvantur ccc mor. Petro Benedicti magistro scolarum Zamorensi quos recolo me a domino Egidio bone memorie Sanctorum Cosme et Damiani diacono cardinali mutuo recepisse. Ita tamen si habet specialem mandatum recipiendi predictam peccuniam a domino Johanne Gagitano vel a domino Egidio bone memorie diacono cardinali. Ante omnia volo quod solvantur debita mea et legatum quod lego capitulo Legionensi. Item mando quod annuli mei vendantur et peccunia pauperibus erogetur. Sunt autem annuli tot numero: i halax et ii zaphires de oriente et i adamante et ii iagonzas et ii thopazes et i cornerina.

Et si distractis bonis meis debita et legata solvi poterunt armentum vaccarum mearum relinquo Martino Pelagii filio Pelagii Martini nepoti meo. Comitto autem domino P. decano, Luppo Suggerii canonico et Marco Dominici socio Legionensi executionem huiusmodi testamenti ita quod omnes habeant potestatem exequendi et michi debita reppetendi. Quod si omnes interesse noluerint vel non potuerint duo vel unus qui voluerint et poterint suppradicta omnia diligencius exequntur. Si quid autem solutis debitis et legatis superfuerit de hoc pauperes vestiantur. Et ne hoc testamentum possit in dubium revocari ipsum sigillo proprio, domini decani, thesaurarii, Luppi Suggerii canonici et Marci Dominici socii Legionensium sigillari mandavi. Acta sunt hec apud Legionem XIII, dezembris era M.CCC.VI.

15

1284, agosto, 8. León.

Informe de cuentas entre el obispo Martín Fernández y el cabildo legionense.

León, ACL, doc. 1.603.

Connoscida cosa sea aquantos esta carta vieren que nos cabildo dela eglesia de Leon connoscemos e otorgamos que vos Don Martino porla gracia de Dios nostro obispo comprastes paralas oras una heredat en Villa Merel por los cccc maravedis de la bona moneda que fueron de Monio Velasquez que nos demandavamos e por otros cient maravedis que vos dio pora esto Johan Perez Bruxa el canonigo, e damos vos ende por quito.

Otrossi otorgamos que non podiemos saber por verdat que vos oviessedes recebidos enla Corte de Roma treynta marchos de plata que dizian quel obispo Don M[unio] hy lexara pora el pleito del arcidianadgo de Triacastella, e damos vos ende por quitos.

Otrossi otorgamos que Pedro Perez vuestro procurador e nostro enel pleito del arcidianadgo de Triacastella recebio del cardenal Don Johan Gueytan veynt e quatro marchos de plata que el cardenal Don Pelayo mandara porala su capiella de aquesta eglesia, e que reçebio del otros VI marchos de plata que esse cardenal Don Pelayo mandara al obispo e al cabildo de aquesta eglesia, e otorgamos que estos dineros sean entregados per vos e per nos enla manera que fallaren por verdat que vos e nos devemos pagar enlas despesas del pleito del arcidianadgo de Triacastella.

Otrossi otorgamos que vos posiestes mil maravedis dela bona moneda enel thesoro para comprar heredades pora la Salve Regina e que feziestes tomar depois del thesoro estos mil maravedis que valian enton al quatre conla moneda pequena dela guerra, e feziestes nos carta que entregarades enel thesoro IIII mil maravedis dela moneda pequena dela guerra por estos mil maravedis delabona moneda fata un çierto plazo e so cierta penna, e pora esto cumplir destes nos por fiadores el arcidiano Don Fernan Patino e Martin Perez el canonigo e vuestro mayordomo, e nos tenemos la carta desta obligacion destes IIII mil maravedis, e prometemos de vos la dar e de vos quitar estos fiadores luego que fezierdes entregar por estos IIII mil maravedis enel thesoro CCCCXXVII doblas que vos prometedes hy poner pora comprar heredades pora Salve Regina assicomo se devian comprar de los IIII mil maravedis sobredichos.

Otrossi otorgamos que Martin Diaz el canonigo recebio e tuvo por nos delos prestamos del arcidiano Don Alfonso Eanes e del arcidiano Don Ruy Martinez e del thesorero Don Diego Eanes sex mil maravedis dela moneda pequena dela guerra a VII sueldos medio el maravedi, e estos VI mil maravedis puestos por vos enel thesoro para comprar heredades pora aniversarios delos arcidianos e del thesoro sobredichos fezierades vos tomar del thesoro e diestes nos carta de obligacion pora entregar estos dineros enel thesoro a certo plazo e so cierta penna, e para esto cumplir destes nos por fiadores el arcidiano Don Fernan Patino e Martin Perez de susodichos e nos tenemos esta carta seellada con los siellos de vos e destes fiadores, e damos vos la luego e quitamos vos estos fiadores.

Otrossi otorgamos que avemos recebido de vos per Ruy G: el canonigo L marchos de plata que nos deviades dar por aniversario de Don Johan Alfonso arcidiano de Santiago e damos vos ende por quito. De los quales L marchos avemos ya comprada heredat en Antinno por ochocientos XX maravedis dela moneda pequena dela guerra a VIII sueldos el maravedi, e prometemos de comprar otras heredades enlos otros dineros que fincan delos L marchos sobredichos por aniversario del arcidiano sobredicho.

Otrossi otorgamos que non fallamos por verdat que Martin Perez vuestro mayordomo sobredicho oviesse recebido del thesoro trezientos e ochenta e IIII maravedis delas doblas de Martin Dominguez de Obiel el canonigo segunt que antes fezieran entender, e por aquesto damoslo ende por quito. Mas fallamos por verdat que vos recebistes destas doblas de Martin Dominguez cient meaias simples en oro del arcediano Don Adan e otros XXX alfonsines en oro del dean Don P[edro] Eanes e que entregastes depois per Martin Perez vuestro mayordomo en cabildo estas meaias al arcidiano Don Adan; et otrossi que entregastes per otorgamiento del dean estos alfonsines al prior Pelay Perez e damos vos ende por quito.

Et nos obispo e cabildo de susodichos faziemos desto fazer dos cartas seelladas con nostros siellos, e la una delas cartas finco a nos obispo e la otra a nos cabildo de susodichos.

Fechas fueron estas cartas ocho dias del mes de agosto era MCCCXX secunda.

16

1295, abril, 20. León.

Testamento de Fernán Patino, arcediano de Valderas.

León, ACL, doc. 1.630.

Enno nombre de dios amen. Conoscuda cosa sea a todos per este scripto que yo ffernan patino Arcidiano de Valderas enna Eglesia de Leon, puesto en mia enfermedat sano mio seso e mio entendemiento ordeno mio testamento en aquesta manera. Primeramientre revogo todos los otros testamentos quantos fiz o mandey fazer ante

LA IGLESIA DE LEÓN A MEDIADOS DEL SIGLO XIII

desta quier per escripto quier por palaura e confirmo este que mando fazer a Garcia gil notario publico e iurado del Rey enna Eglesia de Leon. Mando mia alma adios. E mando soterrar mio cuerpo apar con don ffernan guilelmes mio thio contra los pies, e que me fagan mia sepultura asicommo touieren por bien los mios testamentarios. Mando que canten buenas missas e onrradas el dia de mia soterraçion e al tercero dia e alas ses selmanas e a cabo del anno. commo mios testamentarios touieren por bien. Mando una mula al mio sennor el Obispo la meyor que yo ovier, e çient mor: por un vaso de plata. Mando el mio lecho asicommo lo yo tengo bueno e onrrado al Cabildo segundo alvidro de mios testamentarios. e por manto dozientos mor: Mando sessaenta mor: alos bacheleros por aniversario. Item çiento e vinte mor: ala confraria de santa Maria. Mando las Casas que conpre en quintaniella mando las todas al Cabildo por mio aniversario. Et mando las otras casas que tien Maria Martinez donna de Caruayar quelas tenga en sua vida e aso finamiento que finquen livres e quietas al Cabildo. Et una casa delas que compre de donna Estevania. Mando quela tenga Maria martinez poren sua vida e despues de so finamiento que finque livre e quieta al cabildo. Mando a Gomez patino de dos pares de decretales que yo ey las melores. e el digesto vieyo. e una instituta e un livro iulgo e que de buenos fiadores quelos non barate nin los malmeta. e a so finamiento quelos leyxa a fijos de Maria Yanes mia hermana. al que entendiren que sera mas guisado pora seer clerigo. Et mando quanta heredat yo ey en Gallizia a Maria Yuanes mia hermana. e a so finamiento que finque a Lorenzo. Mando a fernan patino elas otras decretales menores. Et mando a Ordono [1] el degredo e el

---

[1] Podemos identificar a este Ordoño y al Alviro, mencionado poco abajo, como hermanos de Teresa Fernáns, criada de Fernán Patino, que recibió del arcidiano una rica dotación detallada en un documento de 20-VII-1332 (ACL, doc. 1.672), cuando «Gomes Patino ffijo de Ffernand Alffonso de Castro Verde e de Teresa Ffernans sua muger criada que ffue del arçidiano Ffernan Patino» hizo hecha copia del documento fechado 22-VI-1292; «Connosçida cosa ssea a quantos esta carta vieren que yo Ffernan Patino arçidiano de Valderas en la eglesia de Leon aviendo volund de ffaser bien e merced a Teresa Ffernans mia criada dolle por iuro de heredamiento las mias casas que yo he en Valençia e todo el heredamiento que yo he aver devo en Gordonçiello e en sso termino que lo aya por iuro de heredat pora ssiempre. Otrossi lle do el heredamiento e los ssuelos e los predos e la vinna que yo he e aver devo en Trobaio del Camino çerca de Leon con todos ssus derechos e con todas ssuas pertenençias. Et otrossi lle do que tenga de mi en prestamo por en toda mia vida todo el heredamiento e las vinnas e los ssuelos que tengo en Valençia en prestamo dela eglesia de Leon. Et otrossi lle do dos mill maravedis de la moneda pequena dela guerra a ocho sueldos el maravedi e que los aya e se entregue horden de Ocles que estado todo arrendado por çient e ssetienta e duas cargas de dellas dela renta e del heredamiento que yo tiengo en Valençia e en Marin dela pan [.]çiado cada anno. Et otrossi lle do e lle otorgo que sse Maria Martines monja de Carvayal ffina (?) ante ella que essa Teresa Ffernans he ssos ffijos legitimos ayan despues de sso ffinamiento las casas e los hunereos (?) que yo agora he en Leon en la rua que dizen Quintaniella de mia conpra por iuro de heredamiento. Et todas estas cosas do aesta Teresa Ffernans en la manera de ssusodicha en casamiento con Ffernand Alffonso ffijo de Alffonso Mathes e de Martina Peres de Castro Verde...» En la ausencia de hijos legítimos, estas heredades habrán que revertir a Ordoño y Alviro, hermanos de Teresa, y entonces a la iglesia de León para la fundación de

apparado de Innoçencio e ela summa que dizen Martiniana [2]. e que de buen fiador quelos non malpare nin los malmeta. e aso finamento que finquen a Alffonso. Mando las duas mulas de syellas a alffonso. e mando los livros todos de fisica a Alviro. e que de bonos fiadores quelos non venda nin los malmeta. Mando a ffrey Martin ıohan guardian de Leon. mio confessor. çinquenta mor: e al Convento delos frades menores .L. mor: e al Convento delos frades predigadores otros .L. mor: Et deyxo por mios heredes al arcidiano don Monio. e Alffonso perez. companero dela eglesia de Leon. e deyxo por mios testamentarios con ellos. a don Pedro abbat de santisidro. e a don Ruy garçia prior e a frey M. iohan guardian. mio confesor e a don Iohan vimanez e rogolles commo yo ey fiuza enellos aiudem e aconsellem a mios herederos sobredichos commo se paguen mias debdas e se cumpla mio testamento. Et mando a mios herederos que pagadas mias debdas. et mio testamento conplido que delo al que remaneçir. fagan algo a mios criados segunt so alvidrio e me fezieron serviçio. Et rogo a mios sennores Cabildo dela eglesia de Leon. que se [...] de mi e del serviçio queles yo fiz e que me sean bonos amigos asicommo yo ey fiuza enellos. Et mando que selas mias bonas mandas. e lo al que se pague segunt [...] guisado e commo axaren por derecho. e este mio testamento que se cumpla perllos dineros blancos dela guerra a ocho sueldos el mor: perlo mio e sen dampno delos mios testamentarios. Et se non valir commo testamento. valga commo quodiçillo. e se non valir commo quodiçillo. valga asicommo ultima voluntat. fecho fue. veynt dias del mes de abril en era de mill. e trezientos e trenta e tres annos. Testes. don Pedro abbat de santisidro. ffrey M. iohannis guardian de Leon. El arcidiano don Monio. Alffonso perez companero. Iohan vi[manez].

---

aniversarios en memoria de Fernán Patino y de su tío Fernán Guillélmez; o, después de la muerte de sus hijos, a la iglesia de León para el mismo objeto. No se mencionan los padres de Teresa. El hecho de que su hijo se llamó Gomes Patino puede sugerir que ella se emparentó con el arcediano, y quizá fuese su hija.

† [2] «La summa que dizen Martiniana» no puede identificarse; pero me informa mi amable amigo y guía en esta materia, prof. Antonio García y García, de la Universidad Pontificia de Salamanca, que hubo un cierto *Martinus Petri* que escribió una summa para sacerdotes en lengua vulgar pero de fecha incierta, al que alude un manuscrito del siglo XV de la misma biblioteca leonesa.

VIII

The Gravamina *of the Castilian Church in* 1262-3[1]

IN the winter of 1262-3 a group of Castilian churchmen gave
Pope Urban IV a lesson in recent Spanish history.[2] Preferring to
die on their feet than to live on their knees, the Spaniards – they
reminded him – had fought their way down from the mountains to
which the Moors had confined them, and in 1212, led by Alfonso VIII,
had stood alone at Las Navas de Tolosa and stemmed the
Almohad counter-attack. The enemy had not passed, and the
credit for saving Europe belonged to Spain alone – a claim which
Spaniards at the time had been quick to make, some foreigners
had had the grace to concede,[3] and modern Spanish historians have
been tireless in reiterating.[4] But the Castilians had not been content
with this signal service to the Christian West. During the fifty
years since Las Navas Alfonso VIII's grandson and great-grandson,
Fernando III and Alfonso X, had pressed relentlessly on. They had
taken Seville in 1248, and more recently the capture of Niebla and
the occupation of Cádiz had provided the Castilian prelates with
further opportunities for distinguishing themselves in assiduous
service *Deo et regi*.

The principal concern of Urban's correspondents was not, however, to provide him with a progress report on the *Reconquista*.
Their survey of contemporary history was merely a prelude to
serious business. For they had just received a visit from Raymond,
a canon of Paphos who was collecting funds for the papacy's own
proposed Reconquest – that of the Latin Empire of Constantinople
which had been lost to Michael Palaeologus in July 1261 – and the
purpose of their letter to the pope was to remind him that on account
of their past and present services to the Christian cause they ought
not to be expected to provide financial assistance for that scheme
and, furthermore, to inform him that in any event their actual

1. I am grateful to Mr. J. A. Crook for his assistance with the Latin of the published
documents.
2. E. Benito Ruano, 'La Iglesia española ante la caída del Imperio latino de Constantinopla', *Hispania Sacra*, xi (1958), 5–20.
3. 'Cum ... nec extra Hispaniam recursum aliquem inveniret': *ibid.* p. 12. In the
chronicle attributed to Bishop Juan of Burgos (d. 1246) the victory of Las Navas was
credited solely to *Yspania*, 'et precipue regno Castelle': 'Une chronique latine inédite des
Rois de Castille (1236)', ed. G. Cirot, *Bulletin Hispanique*, xiv (1912), 357–8. *Cf.* D. W.
Lomax, 'The Authorship of the *Chronique latine des Rois de Castille*', *Bulletin of Hispanic
Studies*, xl (1963), 205–11. Bishop Sicard of Cremona (d. 1215) was not alone in the
opinion that the Almohad offensive had threatened 'non solum Yspaniam, set et Romam,
immo Europam capere universam': *Chronica*, ed. O. Holder-Egger, *M.G.H., Scriptores*,
xxxi (1903), 180.
4. M. Menéndez y Pelayo regarded Las Navas as 'la mayor victoria lograda por la
Cristiandad después de la de Carlos Martell en Poitiers': 'El siglo XIII y San Fernando'
in *Obras*, Ed. Nacional, xii (Santander, 1942), p. 51. Similarly, C. Sánchez-Albornoz
insists that even before 732 'los montañeses de Asturias salvaron a Europa en España,
en las montañas de Covadonga': *España y el Islam* (Buenos Aires, 1943), p. 19.

penury prevented them from doing so. Having therefore introduced the subject with some account of their heroic activities, they proceeded to acquaint Urban with their current woes, with the *gravissima afflictio* by which the entire country had been struck down. Famine and drought[1] had wrought tremendous desolation everywhere. Neither could sons assist their fathers nor fathers their sons. People watched helplessly as their relations and friends perished: in a single year eleven thousand were said to have died in the city of Palencia alone *mediante fame,* as had previously been made known to Alexander IV and the cardinals. The rich had got poor and the poor had been killed off in the process. And the effect of all this upon the Church had been even more crippling, for it depended for its survival upon its income from tithes which, having been seriously affected by the general mortality, were then further reduced as the survivors abandoned the land and moved to the area of the frontier 'quia ibi habent possessiones pro nihilo et quia ibi tributa non solvunt'. Parish churches which in the past had supported many clerics were now unable to sustain even one, while, merely in order to remain alive, the clergy were reduced to working the land themselves or, if to dig they were ashamed, to other secular (and therefore shameful) pursuits.[2]

These gloomy reflections brought them to their third and last point: 'item, ecclesie et prelati Hispanie temporibus nostris per Sedem Apostolicam sunt gravati, scilicet quod gravamina appellentur', and there followed a partial catalogue of the demands made upon them by the Roman Church in recent times. The bitter memory of the fate that had overtaken the prelates *en route* for Gregory IX's 1241 Council[3] recalled them to the point at issue: the Latin Empire. Innocent IV, it was alleged, had received upwards of forty thousand *aurei* from them for the Emperor Baldwin II, and precious little good it had done: 'quod ipse imperator operatus est cum ipsa pecunia omnes sciunt.'[4] They could still recall the names of some

---

1. 'Tanta fames et tam *valida* ibi per continuum septennium viguit', according to Benito, p. 14, though his eighteenth-century MS. (B[iblioteca] N[acional, Madrid], MS. 13071, fo. 7r) reads *arida*. There is another copy of the letter, which Prof. Benito did not consult, in the Biblioteca de la Real Academia de la Historia, Madrid, MS. 9-25-1-C-19, fos. 237r-40v. This MS. might have enabled him to improve his not altogether convincing rearrangement of the text (especially pp. 13-14).

2. Benito, pp. 14-15. In 1264 a distinguished Jew of Navarre wrote of every man being 'poverty-stricken by the wrathful rod of fate' and of 'hardship and misfortune' everywhere: Yitzhak Baer, *A History of the Jews in Christian Spain*, trans. L. Schoffman, i (Philadelphia, 1961), p. 203. And there is English and Italian evidence that these were difficult years elsewhere too.

3. Benito (p. 15, n. 30) mentions those who escaped Frederick II's clutches. One who did not, and was imprisoned, was the dean of León, Master Juan: A[rchivo de la] C[atedral,] León, doc. 1564.

4. *Ibid.* p. 16. Benito (n. 32) regards this as 'una nueva aportación hispánica a la defensa del Imperio Latino hasta ahora totalmente desconocida'. The reference, however, is almost certainly to the general tax prescribed by canon 14 of the Lyons Council in 1245: C. Hefele and J. Leclercq, *Histoire des conciles*, v. ii (Paris, 1912), pp. 1651-2.

of the nuncios by whom they had been pestered since Innocent's pontificate, and their memory of one in particular – the patriarch of Grado 'qui inauditas exactiones ibi fecit' – was particularly vivid.[1] Finally, they referred to the refugees from the Italian wars whom Alexander IV and Urban had wished upon them, and concluded with a plea for clemency, recommending themselves to the tender mercies of the College of Cardinals.

There the letter ends, as we have it. And we have it because in the year 1750 Ascensio de Morales was commissioned to visit some of the country's ecclesiastical archives on behalf of Fernando VI and to make copies of any documents which touched on the regalian controversy.[2] The copy of the episcopal letter[3] which he found at Cuenca Cathedral struck him as being worth the trouble of transcribing not for its intrinsic interest and the account which it contains of an economy in collapse, but rather for the papal response that it produced. For, in Professor Benito's words, 'tan argumentada y angustiada súplica no halló en los ambientes romanos el eco o los valedores apetecidos'.[4] Apparently quite unmoved by their plight, Urban IV reacted in October 1263 by sending them yet another collector, Master Garinus, dean of Châlons-sur-Marne, and warning them that if they failed to provide an appropriate subvention promptly and voluntarily an even larger sum would be wrung from them *per coactionem*.[5] The juxtaposition of the impoverished bishops' plea and the implacable pontiff's reply appeared to provide timely and graphic justification for the *idée fixe* of that staunch regalist: the Romans' invariable practice of draining Spain's lifeblood to the very last drop.[6]

1. Benito p. 17. For information about the other five nuncios whom they mentioned and who are unknown to Benito, and about various others, see P. A. Linehan, *Reform and Reaction: the Spanish Kingdoms and the Papacy in the Thirteenth Century* (unpublished Cambridge Univ. Ph.D. dissertation, 1968), pp. 246–303.

2. Manuel Abella, *Noticia y plan de un viage para reconocer archivos y formar la colección diplomática de España* (Madrid, 1795), pp. 23–7; A. R. Rodríguez Moñino, 'Una visita de archivos en el siglo diez y ocho: Ascensio de Morales en Plasencia, 1753', *Revista del Centro de Estudios Extremeños,* iv (1930), 327–44.

3. The document itself does not mention that the protest was specifically 'episcopal', though that was the interpretation of Morales. Benito Ruano refers to it as 'la carta del *clero* castellano-leonés', *ubi supra*, pp. 10, 17, n. 38. However, it is described hereafter as 'the episcopal letter' in order to distinguish it from the other documents discussed.

4. *Ibid.* p. 17.

† 5. [*Les*] *Reg[istres d']Urbain IV,* ed. J. Guiraud (Paris, 1901), no. 740: publ. Benito Ruano, pp. 19–20.

6. In the covering letter which he sent with the Cuenca transcripts to the minister Carvajal, Morales alluded to 'la antigua tiranía con que hemos sido tratados de la Corte Romana y sus ministros' who 'han mirado siempre a un fin, que es el sacar hasta la última gota de sangre a nuestros naturales', 10 Feb. 1751: BN, MS. 13072, fo. 2ᵛ. 'La desgracia' of the loss of Constantinople, he suggested to King Fernando, was 'quizá causada por culpa de los Romanos': *ibid.* fo. 62ʳ. Morales' co-religionist, Nicolás de Azara, opined that when Spain had been a Roman province its tribute had not amounted to half as much as the popes had exacted since its so-called independence: J. Sarrailh, *L'Espagne éclairée de la seconde moitié du XVIIIᵉ siècle* (Paris, 1954), pp. 624–5.

Throughout the two centuries that have passed since Morales visited Cuenca that interpretation has remained in vogue. By the *doyen* of Spanish medievalists the medieval Spanish Church is still pictured as Rome's meek and uncomplaining servant, the source of 'rivers of gold and silver' but of never a syllable of protest.[1] It is an interpretation against which there is a great deal to be said,[2] but the immediate task is a more modest one. For the cathedral and public archives of Spain and Portugal contain a number of documents bearing on the *gravamina* of the Spanish Church which neither Morales nor any subsequent historian has taken into account. Professor Benito properly emphasizes the interest and value of the letter which he published, but he was unable to locate the original version seen by Morales at Cuenca.[3] The present writer was no more successful in that quest, but both at Cuenca and elsewhere he did have the good fortune to come upon quite new material, of which a very small selection is published below. What follows immediately is a brief commentary on its connection with the letter already in print.

In the Arquivo Distrital at Braga in northern Portugal, the repository of part of the medieval archive of the archbishops of Braga, there is a contemporary (and not entirely legible) copy of Urban IV's commission to Raymond of Paphos.[4] Dated 26 July 1262, Raymond's instructions were carefully framed and, like the bishops' letter, they contained some recent history. The nuncio was directed first to pay a call on Alfonso X, flatter him into taking an interest in the relief of Constantinople, and secure permission to address the bishops of Castile-León in a body. (It does not seem to have occurred either to Pope Urban or to Professor Benito that the king may have objected to having his bishops confabulating about this or any other matter.[5]) When they were assembled Raymond was to deliver a lecture on the subject of the papacy's various sacrifices for the retention of the Latin Empire. The main themes were sketched out for him: the achievement of Innocent III; Rome's anxiety through the ages and selflessness in financing the project; the ecclesiastical organization of the surviving Latin outposts; and the strategic value of the area to the defence of the Holy Land (though at this point unfortunately the document

1. C. Sánchez–Albornoz, *España: un enigma histórico*, i (Buenos Aires, 1956), 356. The author knows of no Castilian parallel for the struggles of Henry IV and Gregory VII, Frederick II and Innocent III [*sic*], or Philip the Fair and Boniface VIII.

2. See my forthcoming book on Papal-Spanish relations in the thirteenth century.

3. 'Es uno de los documentos más explícitos e interesantes con que hemos topado': *ubi supra*, p. 9.

4. Braga, Arquivo Distrital: Gaveta dos Quindénios, Decimas e Subsídios, no 9 (Appendix I).

5. Benito, p. 10. For the king's reservations about convoking any 'sínodo o junta nacional', see P. A. Linehan, 'Councils and Synods in Thirteenth-Century Castile and Aragon', *Studies in Church History*, vii (forthcoming).

is very faded). Then, having added any further material that might recommend itself to his listeners, he was to come to the point: an appeal to their generosity for a subvention of unspecified size. But – and this was important – he was to move warily. Only if he received a favourable hearing and the king and bishops felt confident that those prelates who were not present would concur with them, was he to produce the papal letters defining his powers. In short, he was to unsheathe the sword of *ecclesiastica censura* only if it were clear that there could be no question of resistance. And the same considerations applied to the second set of executive letters with which he was provided, authorizing a tax of one half, one third or one twentieth on the benefices of absentees, along the lines of Innocent IV's levy at the Lyons Council of 1245.[1] If, however, it was thought there might be resistance to these levies, then he was to hold his hand, proceed with neither the general subvention nor the graded tax, and apply to the pope for fresh instructions.

But in the event there was no need for the nuncio to take soundings, for the bishops did not adhere to the scenario proposed by Urban. Raymond was given no chance to explain to them the purpose of his mission. They sensed it, and even before he had presented his credentials – even, perhaps, before he had made his little speech – they appealed to Rome on account of the *multa gravamina* that their churches had already borne.[2] The letter published by Professor Benito is one of their appeals. But there were others too, for, in defiance of his instructions and despite their bitter protests, the nuncio seems at least to have announced his intention of levying the income tax.

We do not know the whereabouts of this confrontation,[3] but it had certainly occurred by 8 December 1262 for on that day the chapter of Toledo, *sede vacante*, prepared a formal appeal on behalf of the whole province.[4] Their letter covered much the same ground as the episcopal letter, and the similarities are such that what might have been expected may be concluded, namely that the draughtsmen of the two documents were in close touch. However, the canons of Toledo did provide some new details about the effect on the Church of the seven lean years from which they were only just emerging

1. Hefele-Leclercq, v. ii. 1651–2. In 1262, as in 1245, the *vicesima* was to be exacted from resident clergy, though this letter does not mention them. *Cf.* Appendix II.

2. *Reg. Urbain IV*, no. 740: 'Vos autem, presentientes ipsum pro predicto negotio ad partes Ispanie pervenisse, cum debueritis eum . . . et vidisse libenter et honorifice recepisse, ante quam vobis apostolicas super hoc litteras presentaret, in appellationis vocem ad sedem apostolicam prorumpentes, nuntios vestros ad nostram presentiam transmisistis.'

3. The king's itinerary between July and December 1262 is uncertain: A. Ballesteros-Beretta, *Alfonso X el Sabio* (Murcia, 1963), pp. 329, 1084.

4. AC Cuenca, 8/34/678 (Appendix II). The archbishop-elect, Domingo Pascual, had died on 2 June 1262: D. Castejón y Fonseca, *Primacia de la Iglesia de Toledo* (Madrid, 1645), pp. 765–6.

with increased debts and reduced income. Funds were lacking even for the performance of their essential clerical duties; old churches were falling down and new buildings could not be begun; the clergy had sunk in some parts to begging their living. For corroboration of this not altogether unconvincing narrative they sent their letter to Bishop Pedro Lorenzo of Cuenca at Seville. Pedro Lorenzo, however, did not merely rubber-stamp their appeal. He appended a letter of his own which is, in itself, by far the more interesting document. It would appear that the bishop had not yet been troubled by the nuncio: he referred both to Raymond and to the Emperor Baldwin (who was in Spain at this time[1]) rather as future hazards.[2] He was convinced that Urban would never have made these demands had he known the difficulties which the Spanish Church was faced with, and he reminded the pope of a hitherto unmentioned cause of their misery: Alexander IV's grant of tithes from the whole province to the late Archbishop Sancho of Toledo. This grant – which in effect had been two grants, of the tithe revenue from an individual in each parish, and of two-thirds of the *tertie fabricarum*[3] – had imposed an 'intolerable burden' on the churches and by depriving them of as much as a quarter of their tithe income had caused the 'manifest destruction' of many of them. To illustrate this point Pedro Lorenzo might well have referred (as the episcopal letter did refer) to the example of Palencia, where the church was on the brink of financial disaster even before the eleven thousand alleged deaths. On hearing of the quinquennial grant to the archbishop, Bishop Fernando had written to Sancho on 1 November 1259 with the request that his income for that year

1. R. L. Wolff, 'Mortgage and Redemption of an Emperor's Son: Castile and the Latin Empire of Constantinople', *Speculum*, xxix (1954), 45-84. Wolff (pp. 71-72) shows that Baldwin was in Aragon in the first half of 1263, and the seventeenth-century catalogue of the archiepiscopal archive at Tarragona mentions a document which recorded his presence at an assembly at Lérida on 24 Apr. where an unnamed nuncio's request for funds for the Latin Empire was refused by the Aragonese Church. 'Un protest fet per part del archebisbe, bisbes, abats y capitols e de tot lo clero de la provincia de Tarragona a un nuncio del papa, estant en lo palau del bisbe de Lleyda congregats lo rey don Jaume de Arago, lo infant don Pere son fill, Baldovino emperador de Constantinopla y los dits bisbes, abats y capitols, a la demanda del subsidi que feya per a cobrar la ciutat de Constantinopla que havia perduda, excusant-se de que la provincia estava molt agrevada per la Sede Apostolica ab altres subsidis y per guerres entre lo rey y sos barons y per gran carestia y altres coses. Fet a VIII de las calendes de maig MCCLXIII': Tarragona, A[rchivo] H[istórico] A[rchidiocesano]: *Index dels Indices mei Moderns . . . 10 de juny 1679*, fo. 2ʳ·ᵛ. Since 1679, unfortunately, the medieval archive has been almost completely destroyed.

2. Appendix II.

3. AC Toledo, Z/3/D/1/15; 15bis (Appendix III). By Sept. 1260 Alexander IV had modified the grants, suspending the one and halving the other, *ex certa causa*. Perhaps this *causa* was the plight of Palencia about which the bishops in 1262-3 recalled having informed him: Benito Ruano, *ubi supra*, p. 14. In Jan. 1259 Sancho was at Anagni, and fifteen days before the *tertie* were granted him he was given permission to borrow up to 800 marks sterling: AC Toledo, I/5/C/1/67. He died in October 1261: Castejón, p. 764.

be spared since his church was so heavily in debt, 'as you well know'.[1]
It is however not known whether the archbishop relented, and even
if he did it made little difference, for the church of Palencia continued on its crash course and by June 1263 the bishop's Florentine
creditors had assumed complete control of his affairs and Fernando
was managing on a meagre allowance from them[2]: a fate which
many other Spanish prelates may have shared in 1266 when a whole
bevy of Florentine bankers transferred their Spanish bonds to
their own creditor, Cardinal Richard Annibaldi, and the cardinal
foreclosed on the debtors with remorseless determination.[3]

On 2 January 1263, when the bishop of Cuenca prepared his
appeal, these developments still lay in the future. Already, though,
there were troubles a-plenty. In most places, according to Pedro
Lorenzo, the Church's public ministry had ceased, as a result of
extreme poverty for which the 'continuous and immoderate
expenses' caused by papal legates were partly responsible. And
in strategic terms the condition of his own see was particularly
perilous. The bishops' remarks in their letter about the loss of
manpower to the frontier echoed a complaint frequently made by
landowners in the north.[4] But the settlers of Cuenca who were
provided with motives for moving on to Seville and other points
south were abandoning what was itself virtually a frontier area,
and creating thereby a vacuum behind the front line into which
the enemy might easily enter, as indeed they did enter in the following year during the revolt of the Moors of Granada.[5] Having
hinted at this danger, Pedro Lorenzo concluded on firmer ground
by reminding Urban, in the usual formula, of his own constant

1. AC Toledo, X/2/A/2/4. Sancho had returned to Toledo by 31 Aug., and knew all
about Palencia's difficulties because he had arbitrated various disputes of the bishop
and chapter in July 1258: AC Toledo, A/7/C/2/9; AC Palencia, 3–2–23.
2. 'Sustentatione tenui episcopo reservata': *Reg. Urbain IV*, cameral, no. 156. One
of his creditors was Dulcis de Burgo, from whom Archbishop Sancho also had borrowed in Feb. 1259: AC Toledo, I/5/C/1/104.
3. A[rchivo] H[istórico] N[acional], Madrid, Sección de Clero], 2263/12: an executive
copy of Clement IV's bull *Cum Castra Gualfredi*, addressed to the abbot and prior of
Ste-Geneviève, Paris, 2 June 1266. Among the twenty named Florentines were 'Dulcis
et Noccius de Burgo'. In Nov. 1267 Bishop Guillermo of Lérida was summoned to
Paris to account for a 300 mark debt (*ibid*).
4. Already at the beginning of the century this process was causing 'multa dampna',
and in 1204 Alfonso VIII promised that he would return various settlers 'ad loca sua':
F. Fita, 'Testamento del rey D. Alfonso VIII', B[oletín de la] R[eal] A[cademia de la]
H[istoria], viii (1886), 232–3.
5. Ballesteros, *Alfonso X*, pp. 367–76. Though Cuenca had been reconquered almost
ninety years before, Pedro Lorenzo's assertion was perfectly valid: D. Mansilla Reoyo,
Iglesia castellano-leonesa y curia romana en los tiempos del rey San Fernando (Madrid, 1945),
pp. 132–3. However, Spanish claims for rebate on account of the proximity of the
frontier were not always as justifiable as this. During the pontificate of Boniface VIII,
for example, the Roman proctor of the dean and chapter of Tudela rather dis-
ingenuously alleged 'quod ecclesia erat in malo statu propter guerram et quia est in
frontaria': AC Tudela, 41–26–19.

service to God and the king which was for the benefit not only of Spain but also of the whole Church.

These two appeals, together probably with that of the bishops, were entrusted for delivery to the pope to a pair of proctors, Master Vivián archdeacon of Guadalajara and Master Ramón Bernárdez canon of Toledo. Yet despite the apparent urgency of the matter, neither seems to have been in any great hurry to set off, and they were both still in Spain when, in May 1263, they made known the contents of a papal mandate which contained further evil tidings for the Castilian Church.[1] Issued only sixteen days after the bishop of Cuenca had prepared his appeal, it required the province of Toledo to supply a family of exiles from the Italian wars – Paolo di Sulmona a nobleman, his wife, daughter, aged uncle, female relation, two small nephews and establishment of five – with food and clothing for three years. The refugees ought already to have been provided for, but an earlier mandate in their favour which had been sent to the same addressees had produced nothing, in spite of its impressive array of *non obstante* clauses. For Ramón Bernárdez had been away and the rescript had contained a flaw, the Latin for 'Guadalajara' having proved to be beyond the powers of the papal scribe who had written it.[2] And now, since they were on the point of leaving for Rome with the capitular appeal, they both subdelegated to the archdeacon of Lara (Burgos), Pedro de Peñafiel.

The outcome of this act of subdelegation was a further spate of objections from the bishop of Cuenca because the first he heard of the affair (or so he said) was when he received at Seville a letter from his chapter, dated 11 August, informing him that Pedro de Peñafiel had charged Cuenca with 250 of the 2,050 *aurei* which, after some wrangling, Paolo di Sulmona had settled for.[3] Having ignored his summons to the business meeting of 1 July at which these arrangements were made, the bishop and canons of Cuenca had no cause for complaint, according to Pedro de Peñafiel. But there he had underestimated his quarry, and on 22 August, some five weeks before the deadline for payment, Pedro Lorenzo appealed again to Urban IV. He did so this time on two grounds: procedure and equity. He flatly denied the archdeacon of Lara's contention that he and his chapter had been summoned to the July meeting and that they had replied by sending a frivolous objection. After all, he told the

1. AC Cuenca, 8/34/679 (Appendix IV).

2. In Pedro Lorenzo's appeal the addressee of Urban's second bull appears, also incorrectly, as *archidiacono Guadalphararensi*. But this slip must have crept in somewhere along the line between Vivián and Pedro Lorenzo, for the bishop of Cuenca would not have wasted such an opportunity for further delay. Vivián's election had occurred sometime after 16 March: F. Bujanda, *Episcopologio Calagurritano* (Logroño, 1944), p. 17.

3. For the *morabitini aurei*, see O. Gil Farrés, *Historia de la moneda española* (Madrid, 1959), p. 204.

pope, he had been perfectly accessible if any such summons had
indeed been sent. He had not been in hiding. In fact – and here he
casually assumed his heroic pose – he had been engaged in the
sacred task of colonizing the frontier, 'circa rempublicam occupati
. . . et in cancellarie officio constituti'. His second *gravamen* concerned the unfairness of Pedro de Peñafiel's assessment of Cuenca's
share of the 2,050 *aurei*. Since Sigüenza was twice as rich as Cuenca,
and Toledo at least four times as rich, why had one been charged
the same as his church – 250 *aurei* – and the other only 150 more ?[1]

It is not known what became of Pedro Lorenzo's second appeal
but – since it appears that the Spanish churches had not borne a
disproportionate share of the cost of supporting refugees, despite
the bishops' assertion in their letter[2] – Urban IV was probably
not greatly impressed. Anyway, whether or not it received the same
unsympathetic treatment as the earlier appeals about Raymond of
Paphos is of less interest than the information which it produced and
the questions which it raises. In order to estimate the plausibility
of the *gravamina* of the Castilian Church it may be worthwhile to
consider, if only very briefly, some of these questions.

A statement of the Castilian Church's claim to exemption from
papal taxation was provided, in a personalized form, by the bishop
of Cuenca in his two letters. The plea of poverty was only incidental;
the essential argument was independent of short-lived economic
crises. Pedro Lorenzo maintained that because he was doing the
state some service ('circa rempublicam occupati et in cancellarie
officio constituti') and because that state was engaged in Holy
War ('occupati circa Dei et regis servicia'), it was iniquitous that the
pope should claim further financial assistance from him and his
colleagues. By scrutinizing these premises it should be possible to
gauge the validity of his conclusion. Pedro Lorenzo was certainly
correct in describing himself as a professional civil servant. Previously archdeacon of Cádiz, he was elected to Cuenca on 6 December 1261, but so indispensable was he to the king that in the

1. He expressed no concern for Palencia which had been charged at the highest rate.
2. Benito Ruano, *ubi supra*, p. 17. I have found references to only two such papal
grants of income in Castile-León: for the bishop of Bethlehem, Godefrido de Prefetti,
from the church of Astorga in March 1256 (A. Quintana Prieto, 'Registro de documentos
pontificios de Astorga', *Ant[hologica] Ann[ua]*, xi (1963), 219, no. 84; le Comte de Riant,
Etudes sur l'histoire de l'église de Bethléem, i (Genoa, 1889), pp. 34–38); and for Rainerio
di Messina, his servant and his horse 'pro eo quod extra solum proprium exulare dicitur,
ecclesie Romane pretextu', from the diocese of León in May 1264 (*Reg. Urbain IV*,
no. 1646); and of these the former is doubtful. In the kingdom of Aragon, Baldwin of
Messina and nine of his *familia* had a total annual pension of £15 *turonenses* from the
church of Urgel, July 1259 (AC Seo de Urgel, Col. lecció Plandolít, unclassified doc.);
and in March 1262 the nobleman Licasio 'comestabulus Fogitanensis' was being kept
waiting for payment of a papal grant of twenty-two months earlier (A. Durán Gudiol,
'La documentación pontificia del Archivo Catedral de Huesca hasta el año 1417', *Ant.
Ann.*, vii (1959), 367, nos. 81–82). Even allowing for the loss of documents, this
represents a very light burden; and it is significant that neither the chapter of Toledo
nor the bishop of Cuenca included this issue among their *gravamina*.

following March Alfonso X informed the archbishop-elect of Toledo that he would have to be consecrated at Seville, where the royal court was, rather than at Toledo, Cuenca's metropolitan see.[1] Even this had to await a lull in the affairs of state, and, as the Paolo di Sulmona affair showed, in the absence at court of the curial bishop the temporal welfare of his church was neglected. So also was his pastoral activity: in the dedication of his *Liber Septenarius* to Bishop Juan of Palencia, the archpriest Rodrigo accepted the fact that necessarily his patron would be away from his diocese for the greater part of the year.[2] But this arrangement could be justified, and the service was performed by Rodrigo's illustrious contemporary, Alvarus Pelagius, bishop of the Portuguese see of Silves. At worst he could salve his conscience by reminding himself that canon law provided a loophole for prelates who abased themselves before their king 'more in fear than humility'.[3] There was a better argument than that, though, the argument used by Pedro Lorenzo in the previous century about the king of Castile's very special merits, and Alvarus Pelagius stated it admirably in a sentence addressed to Alfonso XI: while other monarchs praised God with their voices Alfonso actually risked his neck for Him.[4]

Such was the saving grace of 'regni prelati quorum interest regnum et sacerdotium intueri'.[5] But only by deliberate confusion could *Deus* and *sacerdotium* be made to appear the equivalent of *ecclesia* and *Sedes Apostolica*. The *leitmotiv* of the various appeals of 1262–3 – that the king's signal services to the Almighty redounded to the advantage of the Castilian Church and thereby to that of the Universal Church – was deceptive because the concept of

---

1. AC Toledo, X/1/E/2/4; A. Ballesteros-Beretta, *Sevilla en el siglo XIII* (Madrid, 1913), p. cxxi: 'Les avemos mester pora nuestro servicio. Ca si por aventura se fuesen consagrar a Toledo o a otro lugar fuera de provincia de Sevilla non nos podriemos tan ayna servir de ellos.' The king's letter referred also to the bishop-elect of Osma, Agustín.

2. AC Burgo de Osma, cod. 17, fo. 1ᵛa: 'Quia fere pro maiori parte anni estis cum domino rege vel regina seu infante ab ipsis vocatus, et pluribus ibi suis et vestris ac subditorum vestrorum negociis et circa plurima occupatus, its quod non potestis, ut desideratis, insistere circa subditorum vestrorum salutem studio et labore. . . .' The Bishop Juan, 'maior cancellarius' of the Infante Pedro, was probably Juan de Saavedra (1325–42). *Cf.* T. Rojo Orcajo, 'Catálogo descriptivo de los códices que se conservan en la S. I. Catedral de Burgo de Osma', *BRAH*, xciv (1929), 728.

3. *De Planctu Ecclesiae,* ii (Venice, 1560), fo. 52/a: 'Et est argumentum expressum secundum Laurentium contra viles prelatos Hispanie qui osculantur manus regum. Fateor ego, vilis presul Silvensis ecclesie, scriptor huius operis, potius timore quam humilitate coactus sum osculari dexteram Regis Portugallie, quamquam ab eo non teneam regalia. Sed qui ex timore facit iam non facit, extra de reg. iii *qui ex timore.*' *Cf.* E. Friedberg, *Corpus Iuris Canonici,* ii (Leipzig, 1881), col. 928: *Decretal. Greg. IX,* V. xli. *de regulis iuris* c. 8.

4. 'Quomodo regnum Castelle praecellit alia: . . . Alii reges vocibus laudant Deum: tu pro eo corpus exponis': *Speculum Regum,* ed. M. Pinto de Meneses, i (Lisbon, 1955), 22.

5. Rodericus Toletanus, *De Rebus Hispaniae* (in *Patrum Toletanorum quotquot extant Opera,* ed. F. de Lorenzana, Madrid, 1793, tom. iii) p. 204.

VIII

the Church in a corporate sense was precisely what was absent from
Castilian ecclesiastical politics. Indeed, only four months after
Pedro Lorenzo's second letter, this lack of solidarity was illustrated
by Pedro Lorenzo himself. In January 1263 he had condemned Archbishop Sancho's receipt of ecclesiastical revenue under papal licence
at the expense of his province, and in August he had figured as a
peninsular Grosseteste, standing four-square with his chapter and
refusing to countenance a grant of income to a family of papal
pensioners. Yet in December he himself received papal permission
to override his chapter's right of collation in his own church and to
fill two canonries there with his own nominees.[1] The bishop was
beholden to the king for this papal concession.[2] This was one
method open to Alfonso of rewarding a faithful servant (who
happened to be a churchman) at the expense of the Church and at
no personal cost. And while the pope remained compliant, being
himself beholden to the king, there was no pressure on the king
to assign his own resources either to churchmen or to the Church.
Twice, at the end of the previous reign when the *Reconquista* was
in full cry, Fernando III had been gently chided by Innocent IV
for his failure to endow the newly re-established cathedral churches
of the south, and in particular the church of Jaén.[3] But because no
more energetic measures could conceivably be employed against
a monarch who was so manifestly engaged in the service of the
Church militant, both Fernando and Alfonso were able to ignore
these warnings with impunity, so that in 1263 Pedro de Peñafiel
found that the two sees which had least to contribute towards Paolo
di Sulmona's pension were the two most recent recruits to the
province of Toledo – Córdoba and Jaén.[4] And by then the king's
hold over the pope on account of the *Reconquista* had been re-
placed by the pressure that he was able to exert in his capacity as
candidate for the German Crown. It was for that reason that
Urban IV complied with Alfonso's request for the bishop of Cuenca
in December 1263, just as Alexander IV had complied by granting
ecclesiastical revenue to Alfonso's brother, Sancho of Toledo, in
1259.[5] Any palliative that would discourage the king from forcing
the imperial issue was acceptable to Urban. In July and August 1264
a dozen more benefices were assigned to royal clerks of Pedro

1. *Reg. Urbain IV*, no. 2346.
2. *Ibid.* (Reg. Vat. vol. 29, fo. 263, no. 1395): 'pro te quem suis obsequiis fideliter et
diligenter insistere asserit. . . .'
3. 'Propter temporalium rerum carentiam nimium indigentem', the bishops of
Jaén 'cogantur in obprobrium pontificalis digitatis egere', April 1251: *Reg. Innocent IV*,
ed. E. Berger (Paris, 1884–1921), nos. 5216 (publ. Mansilla, pp. 357–8), 3770 (=AC
Toledo, I/6/G/1/12), March 1248.
4. Appendix IV
5. Writing to the king in April 1259 Alexander described Sancho as 'negotiorum
tuorum promotor precipuus': AC Toledo, A/7/C/2/6 (publ. *Memorial Histórico Español*,
i (Madrid, 1851), 147–8).

Lorenzo's background through the agency of the archdeacon of Trastamar, Alfonso's agent at the Curia with responsibility for the German affair.[1]

The diplomatic leverage provided by Alfonso's imperial claim is the key to an understanding of the papacy's amenability during these years. It accounts for the marked contrast between the instructions given to Raymond of Paphos in 1262 and those with which Bishop Pietro of Rieti, Nicholas III's nuncio, was supplied in 1279, four years after the collapse of the king's German candidature. There was no need for the bishop of Rieti to court Alfonso's 'benevolence and favour', as Raymond had been charged to do, for he came to upbraid the king for his offences against *libertas ecclesiastica* and was provided with an entire dossier of Alfonso's misdeeds.[2] One of the issues which he was commissioned to raise was the king's illicit receipt of ecclesiastical revenue, the *tertie*, on the strength of a papal grant to his father which had long since lapsed.[3] That grant – of half the *tertie* for three years – had been made by Innocent IV in April 1247 as a contribution towards the costs of the Seville campaign.[4] But the temporary expedient was regarded by the king as a permanent source of revenue, and neither the bishop of Rieti nor any subsequent nuncio or pontiff would prove capable of recovering what was to become one of the bases of the Crown's control of the Castilian Church, the notorious *Patronato Real*, in defence of which Ascensio de Morales did his archival research in 1750.[5] By dignifying an old abuse[6] with his blessing, moreover, Innocent IV provided his successor Alexander IV with a precedent for his grant to the king's brother in 1259 about which Pedro Lorenzo complained four years later. And the pope's concession also explains why so many parish churches were in a state of collapse and why so many parish clergy were unprovided for in the early 1260s. The underlying reason was not, as the chapter of Toledo suggested in December 1262, the nation-wide famine of the previous seven years. For Innocent IV had been aware of their dilapidation and their woe at least ten years before and, better than

---

1. *Reg. Urbain IV,* nos. 1680, 1915, 2061, 2076–7, 2080–1–2, 2093, 2100, 2728. Ballesteros regards these grants as 'síntoma inequívoco de amable armonía' between pope and king: *Alfonso X,* p. 343.

2. Appendix I; *Reg. Nicolas III,* ed. J. Gay (Paris, 1898–1938), nos. 739, 743.

3. *Ibid.* no. 743: '... cum notorium sit per regnum suum quod tertias recipit, quas et si aliquando receperit pater suus ex concessione apostolica et ipse idem rex, concessionis tamen tempora sunt finita jam multis annis elapsis.'

4. *Reg. Innocent IV,* no. 2538.

5. Mansilla, pp. 56–58; T. de Azcona, *La elección y reforma del episcopado español en tiempo de los Reyes Católicos* (Madrid, 1960), p. 288.

6. In 1228 Fernando III had been reprimanded by Gregory IX for seizing the *tertie* without authority: AHN, 3019/5: publ. F. Fita, 'Madrid desde el año 1228 hasta el de 1234', *BRAH,* viii (1886), 402. *Cf.* F. Gallardo Fernández, *Origen, progresos y estado de las rentas de la Corona de España,* iii (Madrid, 1805), 34–46.

anyone else, he was also aware of the cause.[1] But neither in the
capitular nor in the episcopal letter was the royal scourge mentioned.
A natural catastrophe of biblical duration exacerbated by papal
extortion provided a more convenient scapegoat. Nor did Urban's
correspondents explain that it had been the king's European
ambitions rather than the pope's wolfish appetite that had brought
the venal patriarch of Grado, whose 'unheard-of exactions' still
rankled with them in 1262, to Spain four years before.[2] It would be
absurd to claim that this knowledge ought to have alleviated the
sufferings of the churches upon which he had battened; but the
fact should be recorded that at least Alexander IV had been no
less scandalized than they by reports of the patriarch's enormities
and, acting presumably on the principle that it takes a thief to catch
a thief, had ordered Archbishop Benito de Rocaberti of Tarragona
to investigate thoroughly all the circumstances of the case.[3]

Willy-nilly, Spanish churchmen financed the king's enterprises.
If their *gravamina* emerged in anguished tones from between the
papal and royal millstones, then it must be understood that it was
the movement of the latter, not that of the former, that was crushing
them. Moreover, it was precisely at this time, in the early 1260s, that
their royal master was considering new departures in foreign policy
which completely invalidated their objections as Spaniards to
financing the futile Emperor Baldwin II. For, not content with his
funesta ilusión of securing the German Crown[4] and heedless both of
his manifest destiny in the south of Spain and his crippled economy
in the north, Alfonso, in combination with other members of the
royal family, chose this moment to go dabbling in the muddy waters
of the Eastern Mediterranean. Historians have already commented
upon the project for the Order of Santiago to provide a task force for

1. In Aug. 1253 Innocent promised Bishop Pedro of Sigüenza that on the expiry
of the grant to the king (which had been made in 1247 for *three* years) his diocese, in
which the churches 'in luminariis, ornamentis ecclesiasticis ac etiam reparatione defectum non modicum patiuntur', would be allowed to enjoy its revenue unmolested for
a period of six years: AC Sigüenza, doc. pontificio, no. 22: publ. but misdated in T.
Minguella y Arnedo, *Historia de la diócesis de Sigüenza y de sus obispos*, i (Madrid, 1910),
571. Six years before that, Bishop Rodrigo of Palencia had been promised similar
financial relief 'cum ecclesia Palentina tibi commissa magno prematur onere debitorum',
but in March 1253 he had still to receive satisfaction: *Reg. Innocent IV*, nos. 2775 (AC
Palencia, 2–1–53), 6439.
2. *Supra*, p. 732. On 21 Oct. 1258 the king wrote from Segovia to inform his Sienese
allies of the patriarch's arrival with instructions from the pope. Angelus had been there
at least five days: E. Winkelmann, *Acta imperii inedita seculi XIII*, i (Innsbruck, 1880),
464; AHN, 1977/5. For previous manoeuvres, see C. C. Bayley, 'The Diplomatic
Preliminaries of the Double Election of 1257 in Germany', *ante*, lxii (1947), 457–83.
3. Tarragona, AHA: *Cartoral AB*, fo. 23ᵛ, bull *Quia Patriarcham Gradensem*, 22 Sept.
1259. For a contemporary estimate of the unsavoury Archbishop Benito, see Josep
Blanch, *Arxiepiscopologi de la Santa Església Metropolitana i Primada de Tarragona*, ed. J.
Icart (Tarragona, 1951), i. 162–6.
4. A. Ballesteros-Beretta, 'Alfonso X de Castilla y la corona de Alemania'. *Rev.
Archivos, Bibliotecas y Museos*, xxxiv (1916), 219.

Baldwin in the 1240s and the plan for a marriage between Baldwin's son, Philip de Courtenay, and Alfonso's daughter, Berenguela, in 1266. They have also traced the Italian career of Alfonso's turbulent brother, the Infante Enrique.[1] To this catalogue may now be added another item which is mentioned on a fragment of a papal bull in the Archive of Toledo Cathedral: a scheme being seriously considered in August 1264 for another of the king's brothers, the Infante Felipe, to lead an expedition to Romania and 'expunge the heretical Greeks'.[2] It was one of the commissions entrusted by Urban IV to Master Sinitius, the distinguished diplomat who had been sent to the four peninsular kingdoms in the spring of that year to collect the *census* and other debts owing to the Roman Church.[3] Though its future was destined to be less brilliant, in the early 1260s *l'orientation thalassocratique* of Castile was at least as decided as that of Aragon.[4]

It will have been noticed that, as far as can be deciphered from the damaged bull addressed to the Infante Felipe, the Spanish Church was cast again yet in the role of financial impresario. And although nothing seems to have come of this venture, the demand for funds (if it came to that) was doubtless viewed by Castilian churchmen, and would have been viewed by Morales, as further evidence of papal rapacity. Doubtless, too, they protested, and when protest proved unavailing they simply disobeyed. For their almost total indifference to papal fulminations is the principal conclusion to which a study of the thirteenth-century Spanish Church and the papacy leads. First, though, they would play the pope. They were past-masters at the judicial game of *appellationes* and *exceptiones*. Idiosyncratic interpretations of papal mandates – such as that of the archbishop of Braga who maintained that metropolitan churches

1. E. Benito Ruano, 'Balduino II de Constantinopla y la Orden de Santiago: un proyecto de defensa del Imperio latino de Oriente', *Hispania,* xii (1952), 3–36; Wolff, *ubi supra,* pp. 64–66; G. del Giudice, *Don Arrigo Infante di Castiglia* (Naples, 1875), esp. pp. 117–20.

2. AC Toledo E/7/C(XIII)/7/1; 'Urbanus ... dilecto filio nobili viro Philippo germano carissimi in Christo filii nostri Castelle regis illustris in regem Romanorum electi'— through his envoy, Andreas de Celano 'aule regie ostiarius', Felipe had expressed his desire to leave for 'partes Romanie ad expugnandas Graecorum gentes scismaticas'. At this point the document is torn, but at the end the following fragment is legible: 'Sinitio camere nostre clerico et nuntio quem ... Ispanie pro ecclesie Romane ... ut cum archiepiscopis et episcopis ... super congruo subsidio ... ministrando tractatum habeat oportu(num)', 6 Aug, 1264.

3. *Reg. Urbain IV,* cameral, nos. 455, 459, 465, 471. It is particularly interesting that the Eastern question did not figure in Urban's review of the Church's tribulations in the general letter which accompanied his request for a subsidy: *ibid.* nos. 463, 468. *Cf.* Wolff, *ubi supra,* p. 68. For Sinitius, see P. Fabre, 'La perception du cens apostolique dans l'Italie centrale en 1291', *Mél d'Archéologie et d'Histoire,* x (1890), 371; W. E. Lunt, *Financial Relations of the Papacy with England to 1327* (Cambridge, Mass. 1939), p. 617.

4. D. J. Geanakoplos, *The Emperor Michael Palaeologus and the West, 1258–1282* (Cambridge, Mass. 1959), pp. 175–80, 252–4. *Cf.* C–E. Dufourcq, *L'Espagne catalane et le Maghrib aux XIIIe et XIVe siècles* (Paris, 1966), p. 28; S. Tramontana, 'La Spagna catalana nel Mediterraneo e in Sicilia', *Nuova Rivista Storica,* l (1966), 549–56.

were exempt from provision rescripts addressed to the province at large[1] – were legion. Both clerics and laymen scrutinized papal letters for the smallest flaw: Paolo di Sulmona and his family were not the only sufferers. In Aragon the bishop of Vich was denied justice against Gaston de Béarn because the bull had a crack in it and in the text the word *matrem* had been written as *martrem*.[2] Occasionally their enthusiasm got the better of them: at a slightly later date the archdeacon of Tierrantona took exception to a provision mandate presented by Bernardo de Requesen on account of its 'manifesti et notorii deffectus ... tam in grammatica, in constructione et intellectu congruo quam etiam in *orthogrophia* (sic) ut cuicumque intelligenti potest liquide apparere'.[3] But when textual criticism failed them there was disobedience, which was especially prevalent during the late 1250s and early 1260s, when no fewer than ten peninsular churches were reprimanded for their failure to comply with provision rescripts.[4] The Castilian Church *en bloc* refused to pay the pensions (only one of which amounted to more than twelve marks a year) which Innocent IV had awarded to the vice-chancellor of the Roman Church and his nephew, and it was only by denying the mutineers all access to the Roman Curia that Alexander IV managed to bring them to heel in December 1255.[5] Five years later the chapter of Compostela vowed solemnly to reject all future papal provisions,[6] and for two and a half years Bishop Suero Pérez of Zamora – another habitué of the royal court whose consecration was delayed to suit the king's convenience – turned a deaf ear to Pope Alexander.[7] Not until May 1269 did retribution catch up with him.[8]

1. *Reg. Innocent IV*, no. 5377 (Dec. 1250). The provision had been made 'in aliqua ecclesiarum regni Portugalensis cathedrali vel alia': Reg. Vat., vol. 22, fo. 101, no. 643. Cf. *Liber Sextus*, III. iv. *de praebendis et dignitatibus* c. 4 (Friedberg, ii, col. 1021–2).

2. AC Vich, 37–6–37 (Feb. 1260). *Cf Decretal. Greg. IX*, I. iii. *de rescriptis* c. 11 (Friedberg, ii. col. 20).

3. AC Lérida, *Regestre de presentasions de prebendes* (Arm. AB, no. 53), fo. 2ᵛ (Feb. 1317).

4. Compostela (*Reg. Alexandre IV*, ed. C. Bourel de la Roncière, etc. (Paris, 1902 –59), no. 410); León and Oviedo (*ibid.* nos. 809, 2980–81; *Reg. Urbain IV*, nos. 2216, 2360); Lisbon (*Reg. Alexandre IV*, nos. 1861, 2764); Braga (*ibid.* no. 819); Calahorra (*ibid.* no. 2291); Salamanca (*ibid.* no. 2641); Corias, O.S.B. (*ibid.* no. 2920); Palencia (*Reg. Urbain IV*, no. 1831); Burgos (*ibid.* no. 2061).

5. *Reg. Innocent IV*, nos. 6615, 6623 (Feb. 1252); *Reg. Alexandre IV*, no. 1014.

6. A. López Ferreiro, *Historia de la santa iglesia de Santiago de Compostela*, v (Santiago, 1902), 158.

7. *Reg. Alexandre IV*, no. 306 (Mar. 1255); no. 1668: 'tu preces et mandatum nostrum pertransietis, aure surda id efficere non curastis' (Feb. 1257); no. 2309 (Nov. 1257). In Oct. 1255 he was permitted to postpone his consecration for a year, although Alexander IV had already issued an indulgence for those attending the forthcoming event, 'cum ... ex parte regis Castelle fuit propositum ... tua sit ei persona plurimum opportuna': *ibid.* no. 870; AC Zamora, 11.i/5 (July 1255). For details of the group of royal notaries of which he was a member, see E. S. Procter, 'The Castilian Chancery during the Reign of Alfonso X, 1252–84', in *Oxford Essays in Medieval History pres. to H. E. Salter*, ed. F. M. Powicke (Oxford, 1934), pp. 115, 120–1.

8. AC Zamora, 11. ii/6: wrongly ascribed to the year 1231 by A. Matilla Tascón, *Guía-inventario de los archivos de Zamora y su provincia* (Madrid, 1964), p. 141.

However, papal sanctions held as little terror for men of this stamp as did papal mandates. In 1307 a case was argued at Burgos about the rents of a benefice which Boniface VIII had awarded to an archdeacon of Oviedo six years before on promoting the previous incumbent to the see of Segovia.[1] For the chapter it was alleged by one witness that the income from Burgos benefices which had fallen vacant – whether they had fallen vacant at the Roman Curia, at Burgos or anywhere else, one year, two or twenty before – still remained at the disposal of the dean and chapter. This had been the rule for at least sixty years, he said, and in his sentence the judge agreed.[2] Evidently *Licet Ecclesiarum* had made as little impression at Burgos as it had further east at Tudela where, in 1299, the chapter were of the opinion that what prevented them from filling the benefice of a canon who has died at the Curia was not Clement IV's constitution but some new-fangled ordinance of Boniface VIII.[3] It is therefore difficult to echo the lamentations of Sánchez-Albornoz about the docility of the medieval Spanish Church in the face of a rapacious papacy. Nor, however, is it possible to subscribe to the belief of Andrés Marcos Burriel – the infinitely superior contemporary of Ascensio de Morales – that the unearthing of ancient documents, already then gathering dust in Spanish ecclesiastical archives, would provide 'invincible proof' of, among other things, the sentiments of respect and devotion which the Roman Church had inspired there since remotest times.[4] The pope may have provided the Castilian bishops with a convenient bogey in 1263-3, but he was not really their oppressor. The *gravamina* of the Castilian Church were caused by other agents much nearer home.

St John's College, Cambridge

1. *Reg. Boniface VIII*, ed. G. Digard, etc. (Paris, 1907–39), no. 4043.
2. The witness, 'Don Nuño racionero', maintained that 'los prestamos que vacavan en la eglesia de Burgos, soquier vacassen en la corte de Roma soquier en Burgos ho en etro logar, soquiera estoviessen vacadas un ano o dos o XX ho mas, quelos tovieran (?) el dean e el cabildo ho otro por ellos pora la mesa del communal.' The judge, Juan Fernández, archdeacon of Çea (León), ruled 'quod a LX annis hucusque fructus omnium prestimoniorum ad personas et canonicos et ceteros socios et beneficiatos ecclesie Burgensis spectancium, quamdiu vacaverint et quomodocumque vacaverint et ubicumque vacaverint, ad usus mense communis idem decanus et capitulum perceperant ... et quod predicta prestimonia confert Burgensis episcopus cuicumque ea duxerit conferenda cum vacant': AC Burgos, vol. 62. ii, fos. 85–113, at fos. 100, 112.
3. AC Tudela, 41–26–9: 'Intelleximus a personis gravibus et fidedignis sanctissimum dominum Bonifacium octavum collaciones beneficiorum in curia Romana vacancium reservasse simpliciter sue collacioni.' *Cf. Liber Sextus, III. iv. de praebendis et dignitatibus* c. 2 (Friedberg, ii. col. 1021), and G. Barraclough's remarks in *Papal Provisions* (Oxford, 1935), pp. 155–6.
4. Burriel to Castro, 30 Dec. 1754, ed. A. Valladares de Sotomayor, *Semanario Erudito*, ii (Madrid, 1787), 45.

APPENDIX I

Viterbo, 26 June 1262. Urban IV's instructions to his nuncio in Castile, Master Raymond (canon of Paphos) for the collection of a subsidy for the relief of the Latin Empire.

Contemporary, unauthorized copy; damaged and illegible in parts.

Braga, Arquivo Distrital: Gaveta dos Quindénios, Decimas e Subsídios, no. 9.

† Urbanus episcopus servus etc. dilecto filio Magistro Raymundo etc. Cum te in regnum Castelle et Legionis ac alias terras regiminis in Christo filii nostri illustris regis Castelle pro negotio Constantinopolitani imperii de fratrum nostrorum consilio destinemus, volentes ut in commisso tibi negotio cum omni providentia, circumspectione ac cautela procedas, infrascriptam viam procedendi in eodem negotio studeas observare. Volumus igitur, et presentium tibi auctoritate mandamus, quatinus carissimum in Christo filium nostrum illustrem regem Castelle primo et principaliter adeas, eique litteris apostolicis que super ipso diriguntur negotio presentatis, exponas eidem necessitatis articulum in quo est dictum imperium Constantinopolitanum, inducens eundem iuxta datam tibi a Domino gratiam ut etiam ipse, prout decet magnificum et christianissimum principem, imperio predicto subveniat regiumque tibi favorem impendat ad hoc, ut commissum in regno suo pro subventione dicti imperii negotium valeas efficaciter promovere. Obtenta igitur regia benivolentia et favore, terrarum prelatos eorundem regnorum in aliquo loco in quo dictus rex interesse commode valeat non differas convocare. Et postquam convenerint tu sapienter et discrete proponas et exponas eisdem qualiter felicis recordationis Innocentius papa tertius, predecessor noster, illam regiam urbem Constantinopolitanam et ipsum imperium ad unitatem catholicam conquesivit, et qualiter multo tempore agnoxie vigilavit Romana mater ecclesia laboriosa studia intentis vigiliis advertendo ut rem tam inclitam et tam caram tamque insignem et amabilem infra sua brachia salutaribus refovendam pabulis rehaberet, et qualiter innumeras etiam sollicitudines subiit multisque sudoribus . . .[1] apostolica sedes pro ipsius recuperatione imperii quod fuerat ab eius obedientia et devotione subtractum quodque Romani pontifices qui postmodum fuerunt pro tempore summa diligentia studuerunt prefatum manutenere et servare ac defensare imperium contra ipsius adversarios, opportuna semper illi non sine gravi sarcina expensarum subsidia ministrando. Exponas etiam ipsis quod predicta urbs Constantinopolitana duas in se excelsas et expectabiles dignitates patriarcales, videlicet (im)periales,[2] continens, in corpore generalis ecclesie sublimi auctoritate ac potestate coruscat, quodque in principatu Acaye ac Moree, quod latini in ipso imperio detinent quatuor sunt archiepiscopales et octo ad minus episcopales ecclesie quibus ipsius generalis ecclesie firmamentum velut quibusdam

---

1. One word of five letters: perhaps beginning *mand-*.
2. Presumably the churches of Constantinople and Antioch.

conspicuis luminaribus adornantur.[1] Etiam quod per idem imperium providetur non modicum   necessitatibus Terre Sancte quibus in ipsius conservatione magnifica ipsius Terre salus procuretur. Unde ad tutelam ipsius imperii[2] (exclusa penitus . . .[3] sompnaliter . . .[4] aperiendus est oculus ut ipsius reliquie ad munimen fidei et . . .[5] ecclesie conserventur, quia sine illo ecclesie ipsius . . .[6] formata . . .[7] videretur) eiusque valde declararet claritas si predictarum dignitatum sine spe recuperationis ex toto lumine amitteret et ipsa Terra Sancta si ei favor eiusdem imperii non adesset gravi periculo subiaceret. Quibus et aliis inductivis per te propositis, sicut videris expedire, eos efficaciter moneas ut predicto imperio de aliqua parte suorum ecclesiasticorum proventuum usque ad certum tempus annis singulis exhibenda, vel alias de aliqua summa pecunie prout necessitas exigat, liberaliter studeant subvenire. Si vero predictus rex et tot ex archiepiscopis et episcopis, abbatibus, prioribus aliisque prelatis et personis quos conveneris ad hoc consenserint quod de reliquo rum scandalo timeri non possit, tu, productis litteris nostris in medium per quas super executione huius negotii tibi gladius ecclesiastice censure committitur, per illas secure procedas iuxta traditam in eisdem litteris tibi formam. Nichilominus aliis utaris nostris litteris quas super colligenda medietate, tertia et vicesima proventuum beneficiorum personarum illarum qui in illis non resident, tibi duximus assignandas, proviso quod quidquid huius subsidii pretextu colligeris sub fidedignarum personarum testimonio deponas in aliquo tuto loco, rescripturus nobis fideliter quod et quantum et a quibus per te collectum fuerit et ubi illud duxeris deponendum. Si dictus rex et tot ex archiepiscopis et episcopis et aliis prelatis predictis in hac parte dixerint quod ex eorum dissensu et contradictione videas scandalum eminere, tu per predictas executorias litteras et per alias quibus collectionem medietatis, tertie et vicesime tue committimus providentie aliquatenus non procedas, set utique totaliter supersedeas nege (. . .[8]) seriem totumque ipsius negotii statum nobis fideliter intimare procures, ut nos ex tua insinuatione sufficienter instructi provideamus qualiter salubrius et utilius, auctore Domino, in eodem negotio procedatur. Dat. Viterbii, VI kal. julii pontificatus nostri anno primo.

APPENDIX II

Seville, 2 January 1263. Bishop Pedro Lorenzo of Cuenca appeals on behalf of his church against such demands for subsidy as might be made by Master Raymond or by any other agent for the relief of the Latin

1. The reference is possibly to the archbishoprics of Athens, Thessalonica, Philippi and Corinth, to the first of which eight suffragan sees were ascribed by the *Provinciale Romanum*. *Cf.* R. L. Wolff, 'The Organization of the Latin Patriarchate of Constantinople, 1204–61', *Traditio*, vi (1948), 57–58.

2. The following passage within parentheses is hardly legible at all, the document having been folded across and also stained.

3. One word of six letters: *plegencie*(?).

4. One word of six letters followed by *vigilancie*(?).

5. One word of five letters ending in *-orem*. Possibly *vigorem*.

6. One word of nine letters.

7. One word of six letters.

8. Two words, each of three letters.

Empire, and confirms the appeal of the Chapter of Toledo, dated 8 Dec.-
ember 1262.

Cuenca, Archivo de la Catedral: doc. 8/34/678

† In Dei nomine, nos Petrus, divina providencia Conchensis episcopus,
ratam habentes appellationem interpositam a venerabili capitulo Toletano
pro ecclesia sua, diocesi et suis suffraganeis, cuius tenor talis est:

Cum in oppressorum subsidium appellationis remedium sit inventum,
idcirco nos capitulum Toletanum, adiecto quod Magister Raymundus
capellanus venerabilis patris S(tephani) episcopi Penestrini[1] intendebat per
litteras apostolicas tam Toletanam ecclesiam et diocesim quam provinciam
multipliciter aggravare – primo quia intendit exigere vicesimam omnium
beneficiorum in quibus beneficiati faciunt residenciam corporalem;
secundo, quia medietatem beneficiorum intendit exigere in quibus beneficiati non sunt personaliter servientes – sencientes ex his nos et diocesim
ac totam provinciam intollerabiliter aggravari: cum quia propter in-
saciabilis famis voraginem, que fere per septem annos in regno Castelle
miserabiliter ac dampnabiliter invaluit, ita sumus exinaniti quod quasi de
ineffabilibus angustiis resurgentes vix adhuc possumus respirare; cum
quia, ipsa ineffabili famis media causam dante, gravibus premimur oneri-
bus debitorum ad quorum solucionem fructus beneficiorum non sufficiunt diu recepti; cum quia beneficia ita sunt exilia quod vix ad onera
procurationum prelatorum ac ad alia que de iure clerici subire coguntur
vix sufficiunt; cum quia, nobis pro paupertate nimia fabricis ecclesiarum
subvenire non valentibus, constructe corruunt et iniciate consummari non
possunt; cum quia nonnulli clerici parrochiales, derobatis ecclesiis ob
beneficiorum inopiam, nedum ad secularia se negocia convertentes mendi-
care coguntur publice in vituperium ordinis clericalis: ex his gravaminibus et ex aliis quos suo loco et termino exponemus, in scriptis pro nobis
et ecclesia et diocesi et clero civitatis Toletani necnon pro suffraganeis,
personis, canonicis, clericis et religiosis Toletane ecclesie subiectis Sedem
Apostolicam appellamus, nos, ecclesiam, clerum civitatis et diocesis ac
totam provinciam necnon ordines ac beneficia nostra protectioni Summi
Pontificis supponentes. Et ut de premissis nullomodo valeat dubitari,
huius appellationis cartam, lectam publice necnon in Fratrum Predi-
catorum ac Minorum conventibus publicatam, munimine sigilli nostri
fecimus communiri. Actum est hoc apud Toletum, VI id. decembris anno
domini MCCLX secundo.

Ratam, inquam, habentes appellationem predictam et eandem innovantes,
et timentes, immo sencientes, per dictum Magistrum Raymundum vel per
alium delegatum sive executorem vel per illustrem dominum Baldouinum
Imperatorem Romanie vel per quemcumque alium posse aggravari, cum
redditus nostri episcopatus sint tenues et exiles, propter diversas ecclesiarum Hispanie condiciones graves et nimium onerosas, quas si sciret
Summus Pontifex nullo modo alicui litteras concederet contra ipsas;

---

1. Stephen of Gran, cardinal-bishop of Palestrina. A Hungarian by birth, he had
various connections with the Spanish Church at this time. See P. A. Linehan, 'La
carrera del obispo Abril de Urgel', *Anuario de Estudios Medievales* (forthcoming).

et propter intollerabile onus provisionis quod fecit dominus Alexander bone memorie Sancio archiepiscopo Toletano, concedendo eidem unum decimarium   in singulis ecclesiis suorum suffraganeorum, quod inter omnes duceret acceptandum, in cuius acceptatione fere in quarta parte sui iuris et decimacionis singule ecclesie ledebantur, ex quo sequitur ecclesiarum destructio manifesta; et propter iuges et immoderatas expensas quas sustinent ecclesie diversis legatis Sedis Apostolice necessaria ministrando, adeo quod in tantis sunt debitis obligate quod in plerisque divina officia omittuntur propter nimiam paupertatem, et timetur ex dicto subsidio deterius dispendium provenire; et cum ecclesia nostra in confinibus paganorum sita non sit in firmo statu, et habitatores discurrunt undique depopulando nostram diocesim et cotidie transeundo ad inhabitandum Ispalensem et alias frontarias – quocirca loca singula plures de nostra diocesi, immo maior pars, inhabitat; et nos simus totaliter occupati circa Dei et regis servicia, contra Sarracenos tam Ispanie quam Affrice in guerra continua laborantes, eciam circa populacionem terre de novo reddite cultui christiano, circa quam necessarie intendentes cum exinde formidetur perniciosum periculum Ispanie et sancte Dei ecclesie provenire, et vix possimus, immo non possumus, nobis sufficere in expensis: ex his causis et aliis quas suo loco et tempore ostendemus, pro nobis et ecclesia nostra, canonicis, clericis, ecclesiis tam civitatis Conchensis quam diocesis et populo nobis commisso, in scriptis Sedem Apostolicam appellamus, nos et ecclesiam nostram, clerum et ecclesias et cetera nominata et omnia bona nostra et ipsorum spiritualia et temporalia Apostolice Sedis presidio supponentes. In cuius rei testimonium rogavimus venerabilem patrem dominum Raymundum archiepiscopum Ispalensem, et Petrum Petri Astigiensem[1] in ecclesia Ispalensi et Petrum Roderici Segobiensem archidiaconos, et Gundissalvum Dominici canonicum Ispalensem ut presentem instrumentum appellationis sigillorum suorum munimine roborarent. Et nos, dicti archiepiscopus et archidiaconi et G(undissalvus) canonicus vocati et rogati, presentem appellationem quam fieri vidimus coram nobis sigillis nostris pendentibus fecimus communiri in testimonium predictorum. Nos eciam Petrus Conchensis episcopus sigillum nostrum apposuimus ad maioris roboris firmitatem. Actum apud Ispalim IIII. non. januarii anno domini MCCLXsecundo. Ego Petrus Stephani Segobiensis canonicus, Romanorum et Ispanie serenissimi regis scriptor, rogatus ductatus, interfui et subscripsi.

(Four featureless seals remain, attached by discoloured silk threads. The fifth is missing.)

APPENDIX III

i. Anagni, 26 January 1259. Alexander IV grants Sancho, archbishop-elect of Toledo, two-thirds of the *tercie* of the province of Toledo for five years in order to reduce the debts of the church of Toledo. Original. Leaden bull attached *cum filo canapis*. Endorsed: Toletum.

1. Ecija.

ii. Subiaco, 6 September 1260. Having cancelled his previous grant to Archbishop Sancho of Toledo of the revenue from one *decimarius* in each parish of his province for five years, Alexander IV confirms him in his right to the *tercie* due from these *decimarii* throughout the province.
Original. No bull or attachment. Endorsed: Caputius.
Verso: *top left-hand corner:* dupl; *on fold at left:* mayf R/.R; Reč al piñ G.ar *on fold, at right:* R.G.

Toledo, Archivo de la Catedral
i. doc. Z/3/D/1/15

Alexander episcopus . . . dilecto filio Sanctio electo Toletano . . Affectu benivolentie specialis . . . Sane petitio tua nobis exhibita continebat quod Toletana ecclesia magno premitur debitorum onere a tuis predecessoribus contractorum. Ut autem eadem ecclesia possit a debitis huiusmodi facilius liberari, Nos tuis su(pplicationibus inclinati exigendi et percipiendi[1]) duas partes tertie decimarum ecclesiarum fabricis deputate in civitate ac diocesi et provintia Toletanis usque ad quinquennium in solutione debitorum huiusmodi convertendas . . . Dat. Anagniae, VII kal. februarii pontificatus nostri anno quinto.

ii. doc. Z/3/D/1/15bis
Alexander episcopus . . . dilecto filio Petro Martini canonico Palentino . . . Inter alia munera gratiarum quibus olim personam venerabilis fratris nostri . . . archiepiscopi Toletani Sedes Apostolica honorare studuit, eligendi sibi in singulis parrochiis ecclesiarum civitatis et diocesis ac provintie Toletane singulos parrochianos decimarios seu solventes decimas ipsis ecclesiis, unum videlicet in qualibet parrochia, et percipiendi ab eisdem parrochianis usque ad quinquennium decimas debitas ipsis ecclesiis, liberam ei concessisse dicimur nostris litteris facultatem. Nuper autem ex certa causa, de fratrum nostrorum consilio, inter cetera duximus ordinandum ut salvum eidem archiepiscopo remaneret quicquid de facta sibi gratia ipso decimario ante huiusmodi ordinationem percepit, gratia ipsa post eandem ordinationem penitus revocata. Verum cum tertia pars decimarum predictorum decimariorum dicatur esse deputata ecclesiarum fabricis earundem, et Nos per alias litteras nostras dicto archiepiscopo duxerimus concedendum ut tertiam partem omnium decimarum provintie supradicte fabricis deputatam eisdem posset usque ad certum tempus suis usibus applicare, ac huiusmodi concessionis gratia sit ei per eandem ordinationem cum quadam diminutione temporis reservata, nostre intentionis non extitit ut super eadem tertia parte decimarum decimariorum ipsorum per ordinationem seu revocationem huiusmodi aliquod sibi debeat preiudicium generari. Ipsius itaque archiepiscopi supplicationibus inclinati, ut ipsam tertiam partem decimarum decimariorum eorundem pro eo tempore quo prefata tertia pars omnium decimarum dicte provintie dictarum ecclesiarum fabricis deputata, iuxta formam eiusdem ordinationis reservata sibi esse dinoscitur, libere percipere valeat memorato archiepiscopo per nostras litteras concedendum. Quocirca

---

1. Over erasure.

VIII

discretioni tue per apostolica scripta mandamus quatinus prefato archiepiscopo vel eius procuratoribus suo nomine predictam partem decimarum
decimariorum ipsorum iuxta tenorem concessionis huiusmodi facias
per te vel per alium integre ministrari. Contradictores . . . Non obstante
. . . Dat. Sublaci, VIII id. septembris pontificatus nostri anno sexto.

APPENDIX IV

a. Orvieto, 18 February 1263. Urban IV commissions Vivián, arch- †
deacon of Guadalajara, and Ramón Bernárdez, canon of Toledo, to
provide food and clothing for three years from the monasteries and
churches of the province of Toledo for Paolo di Sulmona and his family.

b. Mayorga, 1 May 1263. Ramón Bernárdez subdelegates to Pedro de
Peñafiel, archdeacon of Lara (Burgos).

c. (Vitoria), 10 May 1263. Vivián, bishop-elect of Calahorra subdelegates
to Pedro de Peñafiel.

d. Seville, 22 August 1263. Bishop Pedro Lorenzo of Cuenca appeals to
Urban IV against the demand made on his church by Pedro de Peñafiel
for 250 *aurei* as Cuenca's share of the pension for Paolo di Sulmona.

Cuenca, Archivo de la Catedral; doc. 8/34/679

Noverint universi presentem litteram inspecturi quod anno domini
MCCLXtertio, XI kal. septembris, nos Petrus Dei gratia Conchensis
episcopus recepimus litteram capituli nostri, cuius data erat XI die
mensis augusti eiusdem anni, in qua continebatur quod receperat litteram
venerabilis viri Magistri Petri de Pennafideli, archidiaconi de Lara in
ecclesia Burgensi, cuius tenor talis est: Reverendo patri ac domino P(etro)
divina miseratione episcopo et viris venerabilibus capitulo Conchensi,
dompnus P(etrus) de Pennafideli archidiaconus de Lara, Burgensis diocesis, salutem in eo qui est omnium vera salus. Noveritis me recepisse
litteras super provisione facienda nobili viro Paulo de Sulmon cum octo
personis et tribus equitaturis in ecclesiis   monasteriis provintie Tholetane a venerabili patre Magistro Viviano, Calagurritanensi electo, et a
Magistro Raymundo Bernardi canonico Tholetano, provisoribus vel
exequtoribus a Sede Apostolica ei datis, sub hac forma. A Magistro
Viviano sic:

Vivianus, Dei miseratione Calagurritanus et Calciatensis electus, viro
provido et discreto domino P. de Pennafideli, archidiacono de Lara
in ecclesia Burgensi, salutem et mandatis apostolicis obedire. Cum
super provisione facienda nobilis viri Pauli de Sulmon nobis fuissent
litterae apostolicae presentatae, et nos variis negotiis impediti non
possimus exequi quod per litteras apostolicas demandatur, discretionem
vestram auctoritate apostolica qua fungimur in hac parte dignum
duximus requirendam attentius et rogandam quatinus, si places,
iuxta mandatum apostolicum nobis commissum in predicto provisionis
negotio procedatis, vobis nichilominus committentes totaliter vices

nostras, et ex hoc nobis reddetis Romanam curiam obligatam. Datum apud Bitorcam,[1] VI id. madii anno domini MCCLXIII.

A Magistro Raymundo sic:

Viro provido et discreto dompno P. de Pennafideli archidiacono de Lara in ecclesia Burgensi, Magister R. Bernardi canonicus Tholetanus salutem et mandatis apostolicis obedire. Cum super provisione nobilis viri Pauli de Sulmon reverendo patri electo Calagurritanensi et michi litterae apostolicae fuerint destinatae, et simus in procinctu adeundi Romanam curiam ad prosequendam appellationem quam nuper capitulum Tholetanum pro se et provincia sua interposuit contra provisionem Imperatoris Constantinopolitani, propter quod person-aliter non possum exequi quod mandatur, discretioni vestre auctoritate apostolica precipio atque mando quatinus in predicto provisionis negotio procedatis iuxta traditam nobis formam, vobis nichilominus committo vices meas. Datum apud Maioricum,[2] kal. madii anno domini MCCLXIII.

Forma vero sibi commissa hec est:

Urbanus episcopus servus servorum Dei dilectis filiis magistris Viviano, archidiacono Guadalphararensi (sic) in ecclesia Tholetana, et Raymundo Bernardi, canonico Tholetano, salutem et apostolicam benedictionem. Dilectus filius nobilis vir Paulus de Sulmon sua nobis petitione mon-stravit quod Nos vobis olim sub certa forma nostris dedimus litteris in mandatis ut eidem nobili, spoliato suis bonis omnibus ab inimicis ecclesiae, ac cum uxore, una filia, uno avunculo sene, una cognata ac duobus nepotibus parvulis exulati, vel procuratori suo eius nomine pro se, uxore, filia, avunculo, cognata ac duobus nepotibus predictis, duobus servientibus et tribus equitaturis, a monasteriis et ecclesiis civitatis et diocesis ac provintie Tholetane, Cisterciensis et Sancti Dominici ordinum dumtaxat exceptis, vos vel alter vestrum per vos vel per alium seu alios faceretis decenter in victu et vestitu ac aliis neces-sariis per triennium provideri; non obstante si monasteria vel ecclesiae predictae essent de mandato apostolico super aliorum provisione gravata, seu si personis ipsorum a Sede Apostolica fuisset indultum quod ad provisionem aliorum minime teneantur, quodque ad id conpelli vel interdici, suspendi vel excommunicari non possint per litteras apostolicas quae de mandato huiusmodi plenam et expressam non fecerint mentionem, sive qualibet alia indulgentia Sedis eiusdem de qua cuiusque toto   tenore oporteat in ipsis litteris plenam et expressam mentionem fieri et per quam effectus earum impediri posset seu etiam retardari, et constitutione de duabus dietis edita in concilio generali dummodo ultra tertiam vel quartam aliquis extra suam dio-cesim auctoritate litterarum nostrarum ad judicium minime traheretur. Verum quia in cognomine, fili, tui, archdiacone, erratum fuisse dignos-citur, in eo videlicet quod ubi scribi debuit *archidiacono Guadalphaiarensi* scriptum extitit *archidiacono Valsafaiarensi*, et tu, fili R(aymunde), tunc temporis in remotis agebas, nominatus Paulus nullum ex huiusmodi gratia commodum reportavit. Propter quod prefatus nobilis ad Nos non

---

1. Unidentifiable. Vivián can hardly have been at Bourges, unless his route to Rome was unusually circuitous. Possibly Vitoria which is situated in his new diocese.

2. Mayorga (León).

sine magnis expensis habens recursum, Nobis humiliter supplicavit
ut ei super hoc providere paterna sollicitudine curaremus. Nos itaque
volentes eidem nobili misericorditer misereri, discretioni vestre per
apostolica scripta mandamus quatinus si est ita, hoc non obstante, vos
vel alter vestrum per vos vel per alium seu alios ad provisionem eiusdem
nobilis procedatis iuxta priorum continentiam litterarum; contradictores per censuram ecclesiasticam appellatione postposita compescendo. Datum apud Urbemveterem (XV kal. februarii[1]) pontificatus
nostri anno secundo.

Quarum auctoritate vobis precepi quatinus in primo kal. julii per vos
vel per procuratorem ydoneum compareretis coram me tractaturi
super provisione ei facienda in episcopatu vestro pro rata vobis contingente; alioquin procederem contra vos prout requireret ordo iuris.
Adveniente vero termino misistis quandam litteram appellationem
frivolam continentem et, ea contempta, ego cum aliis procuratoribus
tractavimus cum predicto nobili viro Paulo et cum maxima difficultate
induximus eum ut esset contentus in hac provisione de duobus millibus
aureorum et quinquaginta aliis pro expensis. Quorum taxationem fecimus
in hunc modum: quod solvat quadringentos morabitinos ecclesia Tholetana et quadringentos ecclesia Palentina, Segobiensis et vestra et Segontina
et Oxomensis solvat quilibet ducentos et quinquaginta, et Jahenensis
centum quinquaginta, Cordubensis centum. Quorum solutionem taxa-
vimus fieri predicto Paulo in festo Sancti Michaelis proximo venturo.
Quapropter auctoritate qua fungor in hac parte vobis mando quantinus
faciatis istam solucionem fieri ei usque ad terminum pretaxatum. Alioquin
ab officio et beneficio vos suspendo, ad aliam penam nichilominus
processurus si meruerit procervitas contumacis.

Et idcirco nos supradictus episcopus Conchensis, sentientes nos ex
hoc non modicum aggravatos, in scriptis ad Sedem Apostolicam appellamus propter gravamina que sequuntur. Quorum primum est istud:
videlicet quod cum Magister Vivianus, archidiaconus Guadalphaiarensis,
et Magister Raymundus, canonicus Tholetanus, essent mixti exequtores,
et ipsi commiserint Magistro P. archidiacono de Lara totaliter vices suas,
nobis non citatis non convictis vel confessis, non potuit procedere contra
nos et ecclesiam nostram ad taxationem aliquam faciendam quamvis in
predicto transcripto contineatur. Quod cum alia vice citaverit nos et
capitulum nostrum ut coram eo compareremus, per nos vel per procuratores ydoneos primo kal. julii et adveniente termino miserimus, ut
asserit, quandam litteram appellationem frivolam continentem qua
contempta processerat contra nos, cum in veritate super hoc ad nos nulla
citatio pervenerit (vel monitio[2]) nec aliqua appellatio a nobis fuerit
interiecta. Et si ad ecclesiam nostram aliqua citatio pervenisset non tamen
ad nos pervenit, ad quos debuerat pervenire, cum essemus in regno et
non latitandi vel subterfugiendi causa, immo circa rempublicam occupati
populando de mandato domini regis terram a Sarracenis de novo acquisitam et in cancellarie officio constituti, de quo archidiaconus supradictus
erat vel poterat esse certus, vel nuntius qui citatorium deferebat. Secundum gravamen est istud: quod non fecit taxationem prefatis facultatibus

1. Over erasure.   2. Interlineated.

ecclesiarum sicut debuerat, cum ecclesie Conchensi imposuerit ad provisionem dicti Pauli faciendam ducentos et quinquaginta morabitinos et quadringentos ecclesie Tholetane que est ricior in quadruplum et ultra. Item cum ecclesia Segontina sit ricior in duplo quam ecclesia Conchensis et taxatio utriusque imposita sit equalis. Ex his vero et aliis causis quas suo loco et tempore proponemus in scriptis, inquam, ad Sedem Apostolicam appellamus, nos et ecclesiam nostram, bona nostra ecclesiastica et mundana protectioni Sedis Apostolicae supponentes. In cuius rei testimonium presens scriptum sigilli nostri fecimus munimine roborari. Et rogavimus venerabilem in Christo patrem fratrem Laurentium Septensem episcopum[1] ut presentem appellationem sigillaret. Et nos dictus Septensis episcopus rogati et vocati interfuimus et presentem appellationem sigillavimus. Carta ista est interlineata in XLIIII regula ubi dicit *vel monitio*. Actum apud Yspalim coram dicto Septensi episcopo et personis venerabilibus infrascriptis predictis, XI kal. septembris anno domini MCCLXIII. Ego Petrus Petri de Medina, domini pape capellanus et canonicus Palentinus, rogatus interfui et subscripsi. Ego Magister Dominicus Scalatensis[2] abbas, domini regis Castellae clericus, rogatus interfui et subscripsi. Ego Petrus Alvari, canonicus Astoricensis et clericus domini regis, rogatus interfui et subscripsi.

(The names of the three witnesses are autograph. There are two holes at the bottom of the document, but no traces of thread or of the seals of the bishops of Cuenca and Ceuta.)

1. Lorenzo O. F. M., bishop of Ceuta. His North African see was *in partibus infidelium* for the whole of his episcopal career, the dates of which have never been established. C–E. Dufourcq suggests that it began 'en 1260 au plus tard', and G. Golubovich 'verso il 1266': 'La question de Ceuta au XIIIᵉ siècle', *Hespéris,* xlii (1955), 77; *Biblioteca bio-bibliografica della Terra Santa e dell'Oriente francescano,* ii (Florence, 1906), 324. However, his assumption of office occurred sometime between Sept. 1256 (Bayley, *ante,* lxii. 477, n. 4) and March 1258 when 'L. Ceptensis' witnessed a document at Valladolid: publ. by E. Benito Ruano (who extends 'L' to L(upo), confusing Lorenzo with the bishop of Morocco, Lope), *La banca toscana y la Orden de Santiago durante el siglo XIII* (Valladolid, 1961), p. 113. Lorenzo was still alive and at Seville 'in his palace' on 5 July 1266: R. Ríu y Cabanas, 'El monasterio de Santa Fe de Toledo: indulgencias otorgadas en 1266 para la construcción de su iglesia', *BRAH,* xvi (1890), 53.

2. Possibly San Miguel de Escalada (Burgos).

IX

THE SPANISH CHURCH REVISITED:
THE EPISCOPAL *GRAVAMINA* OF 1279

IN OCTOBER 1310 Archbishop Rodrigo of Compostela and various of his suffragans assembled at Salamanca and agreed upon a number of measures designed to preserve *libertas ecclesiastica*. They bound themselves to make common cause should any of their number come under attack thereafter. They would establish a fighting fund and share the expense of legal representation at the papal curia, and they would hold annual councils; but they did not call them councils, preferring the vaguer *tractatus* and *congregationes*. Nor did they define the enemy, except to insist that their resolve to assist one another did not lead them to contemplate the use of canonical sentences against members of the royal families of Castile–León and Portugal. Indeed they specifically excluded the possibility of employing the canon law against their monarchs. Errant kings would be visited not with spiritual penalties but by persuasive prelates.[1] These then were the heirs to the achievements of the thirteenth century – the century of Innocent III, Innocent IV and Boniface VIII, and the century of false starts in self-defence for the peninsular churches. Before them lay an equally sombre future. They had accepted the royal view of ecclesiastical councils as mitred *hermandades*. Eugenius IV was preaching to the converted in the Spanish kingdoms when in 1436 he alerted the estate of Catholic princes to the dangerous implications of the conciliarism of Basle.[2] The kings of Portugal, Aragon and Castile had survived relatively unscathed the century which followed the Fourth Lateran Council. The king of Castile in particular had been spared an Archbishop Pecham.

[1] H. Flórez, *España Sagrada*, XVIII (Madrid, 1764), pp. 372 ff. Cf. A. García y García, 'La "Summa de Libertate Ecclesiastica" de D. Egas de Viseu', in *Estudios sobre la canonística portuguesa medieval* (Madrid, 1976), pp. 242–3.

[2] 'In exactly the same way their own peoples, by assembling together, could claim power over *them*. This would turn upside down at once the episcopal order and the Christian polity – which is both unspeakable and insufferable': cit. A. J. Black, *Monarchy and Community: Political Ideas in the Later Conciliar Controversy 1430–1450* (Cambridge, 1970), p. 88. Cf. J. Gimeno Casalduero, *La imagen del monarca en la Castilla del siglo XIV* (Madrid, 1972), pp. 193–200.

Control over potential political opposition, however, was only one
aspect of the Castilian monarch's mastery of his Church. The recently
discovered correspondence of Pedro de Casis, Alfonso XI's agent at
Avignon in the 1340s, has drawn attention to another enduring
feature – the king's remote control of the traffic in ecclesiastical
benefices – and has provided a reminder of the need always to distinguish the material well-being of individual churchmen from the well-
being of the Church at large.[3] As was shown in some of the reviews of
the work first done during that memorable period spent under Walter
Ullmann's supervision, the sombre side of the story – the getting and
spending, the illiteracy, the concubinage – was not the whole story.
Nor was it ever intended to be.[4] Rodrigo of Toledo's many and illustrious achievements as warrior and scholar may be taken for granted.[5]
The deplorable state of the peninsular clergy (deplored, that is, by
contemporaries, from Diego García to Álvaro Pais) did not hamper
unduly the careers of individual luminaries who distinguished themselves in the schools both at home and abroad.[6] Contemporary
criticism must be weighed, however, and in the weighing a historian
will ask questions about the assumed preponderance of churchmen
and of the Church during this period. It may be time to jettison, after due
scrutiny, the age-old assumptions which historians elsewhere have
questioned; in this case the view of the Age of the Reconquest as the
history of the Spanish Church militant, inexorably triumphant, and
richly rewarded for her efforts.[7] We stand in need of scores of local

[3] A. García y García, 'Notas sobre la política eclesiástica de Alfonso XI de Castilla', *Miscelanea José Zunzunegui (1911–1974)* (Vitoria, 1975), pp. 163–82.
[4] See the prefatory remarks to Linehan, *La iglesia española y el papado en el siglo XIII* (Salamanca, 1975).
[5] See now H. Grassotti, 'Don Rodrigo Ximénez de Rada, gran señor y hombre de negocios en la Castilla del siglo XIII', *Cuadernos de Historia de España*, LVII–LVIII (1973), pp. 1–302; M. Nieto Cumplido. 'La "Cronica Omnium Pontificum et Imperatorum Romanorum" de Rodrigo Jiménez de Rada', *Historia. Instituciones. Documentos*, 1 (1974), pp. 391–415. The attribution to Rodrigo of the authorship of the *Cronica latina anónima* (ed. M. D. Cabanés Pecourt (Valencia, 1964)) is, however, surely mistaken. Cf. Linehan, *La iglesia*, p. 18.
[6] Peter Linehan, *The Spanish Church and the Papacy in the Thirteenth Century* (Cambridge, 1971), pp. 12, 239–40. The strictures of Álvaro Pais are conveniently summarised in A.D. de Sousa Costa, *Estudos sobre Álvaro Pais* (Lisbon, 1966), pp. 41–51. One such figure who has recently been shown to have held the office of 'ultramontanorum scolarium rector' at Bologna in 1252 was Abril, archdeacon of Salamanca, and subsequently bishop of Urgel. See D. Maffei, 'Un trattato di Bonaccorso degli Elisei e i più antichi Statuti dello Studio di Bologna nel mano-scritto 22 della Robbins Collection', *BMCL*, n.s. v (1975), pp. 85–7; P. A. Linehan, 'La carrera del obispo Abril de Urgel: la Iglesia española en el siglo XIII', *Anuario de Estudios Medievales*, VIII (1972–3), pp. 143–97.
[7] Linehan, *Spanish Church*, p. 102; R. S. Lopez, 'Hard Times and Investment in Culture' in W. K. Ferguson, ed., *The Renaissance, a Symposium* (New York, 1953), pp. 19–32. Cf. M.

studies which are both institutional and revealing.[8] Meanwhile we may be confident that the hypothesis of a connection between the supine posture of the Spanish bishops and the reported condition of their dioceses is one which will not unduly disconcert the scholars on the spot. Although the coincidence of conciliar activity and pastoral activity (as in the province of Tarragona in the 1240s) would be difficult to explain away, it would be hazardous either to state it in simple terms of cause and effect, or without qualification to ascribe to the Aragonese prelates any measure of disinterested zeal for the notion of *libertas ecclesiastica*. The bishops present at the Tarragona Council of 1244 were anxious to defend the Aragonese Church against royal depredations, but they did not scruple to exempt themselves from the measures which they prescribed against *raptores ecclesiarum*.[9] Still, no such collective measures seem even to have been attempted during the 1240s in Castile, where, appropriately enough, it was the son of the man whose *Planeta* had subjected the bishops to such merciless criticism a generation earlier who superintended Fernando III's taxation of the churches for military purposes.[10]

Hernández Villaescusa, *Recaredo y la unidad católica* (Barcelona, 1890), p. 343, cit. Linehan, *La iglesia*, p. 1, n. 5. T. F. Ruiz has recently advanced, as if it were revolutionary, the proposition 'que l'expansion en Andalousie au xiiie siècle fut une cause majeure de la crise économique, sociale et institutionelle qui affecta la Castille pour la plus grande partie du siècle qui suivit la chute de Séville en 1248', and has chided historians for not having pursued this line of inquiry: 'Expansion et changement: la conquête de Séville et la société castillane (1248–1350)' *Annales – Économies – Sociétés – Civilisations*, xxxiv (1979), pp. 548, 549.

[8] See B. de Gaiffier, 'Hispania et Lusitana VII', *Analecta Bollandiana*, xciv (1976), p. 407, reviewing T. Villacorta Rodríguez, *El cabildo catedral de León: estudio histórico-jurídico, siglo XII–XIX* (León, 1974). T. F. Ruiz has traced the decline of the chapter of Burgos as a land-purchasing agent in the second half of the thirteenth century: 'The transformation of the Castilian municipalities: the case of Burgos 1248–1350', *Past & Present*, lxxvii (1977), pp. 14–15. A highly revealing study of conditions in the city of Toledo is that of R. González, 'El arcediano Joffre de Loaysa y las parroquias urbanas de Toledo en 1300', *Historia Mozárabe* (Primer Congreso Internacional de Estudios Mozárabes, 1975) (Toledo, 1978), pp. 91–148.

[9] A. Durán Gudiol, 'Vidal de Canellas, obispo de Huesca', *Estudios de Edad Media de la Corona de Aragón*, ix (1973), p. 285; Linehan, *Spanish Church*, p. 81, n. 7. An edition of the conciliar legislation of the Aragonese Church has been initiated by J. M. Pons Guri, 'Constitucions conciliars Tarraconenses (1229–1330)', *Analecta Sacra Tarraconensia*, xlvii (1974), pp. 65–128. Cf. J. A. Brundage, 'The Provincial Council of Tarragona, 1239: a new text', *BMCL*, n.s. viii (1978), pp. 21–7.

[10] P. Fernández Martín, 'El obispo de Osma Don Juan Díaz, canciller de Fernando III el Santo, no se llamaba Don Juan Domínguez', *Celtiberia*, xxvii (1964), pp. 90–5; Linehan, *Spanish Church*, p. 111, n. 8. Bishop Juan's role as prelate and royal chancellor is aptly illustrated by the terms of the letter sent to the chapter of Osma regarding the appointment of a successor as sacrist to Fr. Gonzalo: 'si possumus sacristaniam dilecto clerico nostro J. Guterii contulimus [et si non possumus commendamus: *insert*.] viro discreto. . .per quem speramus multa provenire ecclesie tam in temporalibus quam in spiritualibus profutura' (dated 7 April, no year, but 1234 × 1240): Burgo de Osma, Biblioteca del Cabildo, cód. 89, fo. 1r.

Throughout the century the papacy generally stood aloof from these events. Apprehensive of the dire consequences of Islamic counter-attack – an apprehension which the kings of Castile tended to encourage – successive pontiffs acquiesced in the fate of peninsular churches and churchmen. Castile's alleged vulnerability to the Moors was Alfonso X's surest safeguard against papal interference. Registered drafts of Clement IV's correspondence during the summer of 1265 when the king of Granada was in rebellion against Alfonso show the pope progressively de-emphasising the king's personal responsibility for the baneful effects of retention of the *tercias decimarum*.[11] So much a feature of the century was papal acceptance of royal control of the churches, and so intermittent the attempts to check it, that by 1328 Alfonso XI was able to represent his willingness to contemplate some limitation on his fiscal policies as a gratuitous concession and an act of royal magnanimity in favour of Pope John XXII. Because then, as in the later period investigated by Professor Domínguez Ortiz, papal–royal disputes so often had the appearance of mere family squabbles, signalising an underlying stability, any evidence of concerted papal-episcopal resistance to the king deserves very careful consideration.[12]

Episcopal opposition in the portentous decade after the reconquest of Seville was betrayed by the king's brother, Archbishop Sancho of Toledo in 1257–9. The story has already been told[13] and need be recapitulated only to indicate the effectiveness of royal subversion of ecclesiastical unity. Whether or not Alexander IV's quinquennial grant to Sancho in January 1259 of *duas partes tertie decimarum* of the city, province and diocese of Toledo (*Affectu benevolentie*) was held to extend to the tithe income of the cathedral churches,[14] none of the archbishop's neighbours and erstwhile friends was unaffected by Sancho's ecclesiastical imperialism and Alexander's acquiescence in

[11] E. Pásztor, 'Per la storia dei Registri Pontifici nel Duecento', *Archivum Historiae Pontificiae*, VI (1968), pp. 85–6; Linehan, *Spanish Church*, p. 208.

[12] L. Serrano, 'Alfonso XI y el papa Clemente VI durante el cerco de Algeciras', *Escuela Española de arqueología e historia en Roma: Cuadernos de trabajos*, III (1915), p. 4. Cf. A. Domínguez Ortiz, 'Iglesia y estado en el siglo XVII español', in M. Andrés *et al.*, eds., *Aproximación a la historia social de la Iglesia española contemporánea* (El Escorial, 1978), p. x: 'Incluso cuando más amargos eran los reproches entre los papas y los reyes de España no dejaron de tener un aire de disputas de familia, cuya unidad esencial no estaba en cuestión.'

[13] Linehan, *Spanish Church*, pp. 152–72.

[14] AC Toledo, V.3.A.1.7 (26 Jan. 1259). Cf. the view of Bonaguida de Aretio cited by G. Barraclough, 'The English royal chancery and the papal chancery in the reign of Henry III', *MIÖG*, LXII (1954), p. 376, n. 16.

it.[15] In April 1259 the grant of *tercias* was reinforced by a papal licence (*Inducunt nos*) entitling Sancho to the entire receipts of one tithe-collector of his own nomination in each and every parish of his province for the same five-year period, as a contribution towards the building expenses of Toledo Cathedral.[16] Alexander's prompt cancellation of *Inducunt nos* 'ex certa causa' and the reduction from five years to three of the terms of *Affectu benevolentie*[17] highlight the confusion and division fostered by recent events. So too does the recorded action of one of Sancho's suffragans, Bishop Fernando of Palencia, who while seeking exemption on his own account did not hesitate to instruct his diocesan clergy to comply with the terms of *Inducunt nos*.[18] As pope and primate combined against the churches of Castile the bishops exposed their flocks to the storm and blamed the tempest on the papacy.[19] Of their feelings towards the real cause of their misfortunes only meagre evidence has survived. Archbishop Sancho II of Toledo and his bishops met at Brioca in 1267, but the unique record of the *acta* of that assembly is barely legible.[20] It would of course be fanciful to associate Sancho II's willingness to allow dissent its voice with the fact of his Aragonese origin. However, eight years later he again protested, together with his episcopal colleagues, this time to Alfonso

---

[15] *Devotionis tue:* sole appointment of two clerics to Toledo benefices collation to which was shared *de jure* with the chapter: AC Toledo, Z.1.G.1.5 (22 Nov. 1257); *Cum sicut:* benefices for eight of his clerics in the churches of Castile-León: AC Toledo, V.2.D.1.5 (7 Feb. 1259). Objections were entered by both the archbishop of Tarragona and the bishop of Zaragoza to the inclusion of the church of Segorbe in Alexander's solemn privilege of 17 June 1259 confirming the rights of the church of Toledo: Linehan, *Spanish Church*, p. 170; Zaragoza, Archivo Diocesano, 2/2/13 (*Venerabili fratri nostro*, 29 July 1259 = Potthast, 17646 *mutatis mutandis*).

[16] AC Toledo, X.3.A.1.2 (2 April 1259). For some indications as to the mechanics of tithe-collection see José Luís Martín, 'Diezmos eclesiásticos: notas sobre la economía de la sede zamorana (s. XII–XIII)' *Actas de las I Jornadas de Metodología aplicada de las ciencias históricas*, II (Santiago de Compostela, 1975), pp. 69–78; A. García Sanz, 'Los diezmos del obispado de Segovia del siglo XV al XIX', *Estudios Segovianos*, XXV (1973), p. 14.

[17] AC Toledo, V.3.A.1.16: *Inter alia* (ed. of executor's copy in P. A. Linehan, 'The *gravamina* of the Castilian Church in 1262–3', *EHR*, LXXXV (1970), p. 750). On 7 Sept. 1260 Alexander decreed that the three-year period commence on 1 October next: *Cum sicut:* AC Toledo, V.3.A.1.22; O.12.A.1.27.

[18] AC Toledo, X.3.A.1.8; Linehan, *Spanish Church*, p. 171.

[19] Linehan, 'Gravamina', p. 731ff.

[20] AC Palencia, 4/1/3; Linehan, *Spanish Church*, pp. 175–6. The *Crónica del Rey Don Alfonso Décimo*, ed. C. Rosell (Madrid, 1953), pp. 22–3, while charging the prelates at the Burgos Cortes of 1272 with having sought to sow dissension between king and nobles, states that Alfonso 'quisiera los echar del reino', but that for certain reasons (including that of 'non aver contra sí al Papa') he held back from doing so. Cf. A. Ballesteros y Beretta, *Alfonso X el Sabio* (Barcelona, 1963), p. 584. Sancho II's role in these years remains enigmatic. Cf. R. Gonzálvez, 'El Infante D. Sancho de Aragón, arzobispo de Toledo (1266–1275)', *Escritos del Vedat*, VII (1977), pp. 97–121.

X's heir Fernando de la Cerda. Their complaints were certainly specific,
but they were directed at the secular authorities in the localities, not at
the king or his advisers, and the Infante's response – that custom be
observed – is not revealing.[21] For a clearer view of the churchmen's
case what is needed is an extended account of their *gravamina*, together
with some response from the king's side. A document which provides
some of this evidence has recently been discovered, and in view of its
singular interest it is published below.

The document belongs to the year 1279, when Nicholas III sent a
legate, Bishop Pietro of Rieti, to Castile to investigate a list of complaints against Alfonso X and his agents, which had been submitted by
Castilian and Leonese prelates, and notably by two exiles, Archbishop
Gonzalo García of Compostela and Bishop Martín Fernández of
León.[22] The Spanish Church was leaderless, the see of Toledo having
remained vacant since the death of Archbishop Sancho II in October
1275, with the pope refusing to approve the election of the abbot of
Covarrubias, Fernán Rodríguez de Cabañas, on the grounds that he
had alienated ecclesiastical property to, amongst others, Alfonso's
clerk – and his emissary to the Infante Sancho in July 1270 –.Pay
Dacana. Prelates who had been ousted from the positions that they
regarded as traditionally theirs looked on helplessly as Alfonso's
creatures – a French bishop, Fredulus of Oviedo, and a foreign medic,
'Maestre P. de Marsella cirurgiano dela camara del rey' – toured the
country unlawfully exacting *decima*. Two years earlier Alfonso had
threatened Nicholas's predecessor John XXI with the Moors; now,
with Alfonso's imperial ambitions liquidated, the pope felt able to
launch a frontal attack on the king's policy of exploiting ecclesiastics

21 R. Menéndez Pidal, *Documentos lingüísticos de España*, 1 (Madrid, 1919), pp. 300–2. The letter
transcribed in Madrid, Academia de la Historia, Col. Salazar, vol. 0–8, fos. 80v–81r, is a garbled
abbreviated version of this letter (dated 13 April 1275), and not as described in *Índice de la
Colección de D. Luís de Salazar y Castro*, formado por el Marqués de Siete Iglesias y B. Cuartero
y Huerta, 1–(Madrid, 1949–), no. 65977. (I am grateful to Miss Driana Wybourne for verifying
this for me.) See also J. L. Martín Martín, L. M. Villar García, F. Marcos Rodríguez, M.
Sánchez Rodríguez, *Documentos de los archivos catedralicio y diocesano de Salamanca (siglos XII–
XIII)* (Salamanca, 1979), no. 349.
22 For Gonzalo's exile see Linehan, *Spanish Church*, p. 140. That of Martín Fernández does not
seem to have been noticed previously. Twenty-five years earlier he had enjoyed Alfonso's
friendship, but since then he and his church had been at odds with the *conceio* of León over
rights of jurisdiction: P. A. Linehan, 'La iglesia de León a mediados del siglo XIII', in *León
y su historia: Miscelanea histórica*, III (León, 1975), p. 19; *España Sagrada*, XXXV (Madrid,
1786), pp. 323, 434–49. See also E. S. Procter, *The Judicial Use of 'Pesquisa' in Leon and
Castile 1157–1369* (London, 1966), p. 7, and sections B' and B" of the document published
below.

and ecclesiastical resources.[23] What was at issue, as Nicholas stressed in a letter addressed to the king's bastard son, Alfonso Fernández, was *conculcatio ecclesiastice libertatis*.[24] The king himself was treated to a letter of unexampled peremptoriness, *Prepara quaesumus*, and urged to provide real not fictitious remedies.[25] A text of the legate's commission entitled *Memoriale secretum* is preserved in the papal register, together with detailed tactical instructions which were evidently based on expert knowledge of the political realities of Alfonso's court and of the difficulties which the legate was likely to encounter there. But the *gravamina* are listed only summarily and in no logical order.[26] The *memoriale* (which was for the legate's eyes only) states that Bishop Pietro bore with him more detailed evidence relating to the charges against the king ('quosdam alios articulos prolixiores ... in quibus seriosius gravamina exprimuntur'). This more detailed evidence, if not the full charge-sheet, has now emerged in the archive of Toledo Cathedral. Written on paper, the *folleto* AC Toledo X.1.B.1.4 contains a Spanish translation of the *gravamina* together with the Latin text of some of these as sent by Alfonso with a covering letter, here transcribed, to the Infante Sancho of 29 July 1279, four months after the pope had despatched his legate.[27] The king was seeking his son's advice, and appended is what appears to be an incomplete draft, undated, of the reply prepared either by Sancho or on his behalf. It cannot be assumed that this draft, or indeed any later version of it, was ever sent to

---

23 *Reg. Nicholas III*, nos. 27–41, 649; L. Serrano, *Cartulario del Infantado de Covarrubias* (Valladolid, 1907), p. 119; Linehan, *Spanish Church*, pp. 214–15, 217–20; AC Toledo, V.3.A.1.31 (11 May 1277); J. M. E. de la P., 'Variedades', *Revista de Archivos, Bibliotecas y Museos*, II (1872), pp. 58–60; Ballesteros, *Alfonso X*, p. 837.

24 *Reg. Nicholas III*, no. 740. The address of this letter in the papal register (R.V. 40, fo. 55r) is, as given in the edition of J. Gay, 'dilecto filio nobili viro A. nato carissimi in Christo filii nostri . . . regis Castelle ac Legionis'. It is perhaps surprising that the pope should have written to Alfonso Fernández, for whom see H. Flórez, *Memorias de las reynas cathólicas*, 3rd edn (Madrid, 1790), pp. 537–9.

25 *Reg. Nicholas III*, no. 739: 'non verbalem tantummodo set realem . . . veritatem'.

26 *Ibid.*, no. 743; Linehan, *Spanish Church*, pp. 218–19.

27 'Don Alffonsso & c. avos Don Sancho & c. Sepades que el Legado me dio escriptos unos articulos en razon dequellas cosas por quel embio el papa ami. Et yo embio vos el traslado ende con maestre M. abbat de sant Quirze e con Gomez Garcia canonigo de Toledo vuestros clerigos. Onde vos ruego e vos mando por aquella fe que vos devedes adios e ami que vos que lo mostredes a essos omnes buenos que son y connusco tan bien clerigos como legos a aquellos que vos entendieredes que vos sabran conseiar en tal fecho como este. Et otrossi que lo embiedes mostrar alos prelados e alos otros omnes buenos dy dela tierra que ellos que vos consseien en esta razon, e aquell conseio que vos diese embiarme lo dezir por vuestra carta e gradescer vos lo e mucho. Dada en Sevilla. xxix dias de julio.' Cf. Ballesteros, *Alfonso X*, p. 1117. According to Gil de Zamora, *De Preconiis Civitatis Numantine* (ed. F. Fita, *Boletín de la R. Academia de la Historia*, V (1884), p. 146), Sancho 'incipit coregnare' in 1278.

Alfonso. Its presence in the archive of Toledo Cathedral (the repository, it may be conjectured, of sections at least of the 'lost' Castilian archives) is best explained in terms of its direct transmission thither by Sancho himself and, in view of its contents, probably before rather than after his accession to the throne in 1284.

The *Memoriale secretum* lists the charges against the king under five headings: 1. *tercias*; 2. royal custody of vacant churches; 3–4. the king's persecution of the prelates of Compostela and León; 5. *gravamina prelatorum*. (A sixth item, a request for Alfonso's good offices in securing the liberty of the Portuguese Church, is not mentioned in the Toledo document.) No response from Sancho to items 3 or 4 is preserved. He and his advisers refer only to 1, 2 and various of the issues raised under 5 which the scribe identifies by the letters A, B, C as far as K.[28] If what has survived is the complete dossier sent by Alfonso then it would appear that it was on item 5, the *gravamina prelatorum*, that he particularly desired advice, for only of item 5 is the Latin (*prolixior*) text of the legate's charges provided. The draft gives Sancho's answers on 1 (= A), 2 (= B) and part of 5 (= C–F), at which point it ends abruptly. On the last sheet of the *folleto* the *gravamina* G–K are stated, and after each there is a gap unfilled (except in the case of I) by any response or attempt at justification. Here then either the ingenuity of Sancho's advisers deserted them or their work was interrupted or abandoned. Whatever the reason, this is the more regrettable in view of the interest of these *gravamina*, and particularly of those collected under *M*.

Because it provides both an extended version of the episcopal *gravamina* expressing exceptional bitterness against Alfonso X, and a sketch of his son's handling of them, the document possesses a twofold interest and is doubly revealing of the condition of one sector of the kingdom of Castile on the eve of Sancho's rebellion against his father's rule. The Infante, on this evidence, wished it to be known that he shared the conventional and incorrect view that, by courtesy of *la eglesia* (undefined), Alfonso was entitled to the *tercias* for life,[29] as well as to the use of ecclesiastical property during vacancies (which in the recent past had become increasingly numerous).[30] Otherwise the tone,

[28] For convenience of reference the subsequent items have been lettered *L*, *M* etc. in the edition below.

[29] Item A. Cf. Linehan, *Spanish Church*, pp. 207–8.

[30] Item B. For the king's view of his rights during episcopal vacancies, see *Primera Partida*, *tit.* v, *ley* xviii in *Alfonso X el Sabio Primera Partida* (*manuscrito Add.* 20787 *del British Museum*), ed. J. A. Arias Bonet (Valladolid, 1975), p. 77. In January 1273 nine out of twenty-nine of the sees

where not positively evasive, is markedly conciliatory to the protesting churchmen, but conciliatory only as to principle and falling short of admission as to fact. On article C the text of the reply is not entirely clear. It seems to state that royal interference in episcopal elections ought to be discontinued. Similarly, with regard to D, the events of the previous thirty years notwithstanding, Sancho opines that *de jure* churchmen and their vassals could not be subjected to fiscal demands. The same bland response is given to the complaint regarding the excesses of the secular justices (E) which had been reported to Fernando de la Cerda in 1275.[31] It is perhaps only in the distinctions made in the carefully phrased treatment of item F relating to alleged infringements of churchmen's landed rights, with its reference to the much debated Ordenamiento de Nájera, that Sancho appears conscious of his responsibilities as a future ruler rather than of the advantages available to the party politician.[32] The reply to I amounts to no more than a statement of fact that any restriction on free episcopal assembly and movement[33] is 'contra libertad de sancta eglesia e grand servidumbre delos clerigos e grand periudicio dela eglesia de Roma' while offering no comment on the justice of the allegations themselves.

The remaining unanswered articles, intriguing though they are, may be rapidly reviewed. The reference (G) to 'novum ordinem *seu* religionem' is even more enigmatic in its translated form 'nueva orden *a* religion'.[34] The accusation of using papal privileges *ultra tempus* can be proved (H).[35] Mention of Jewish influence in public affairs (K) echoes

of Castile–León had been vacant: L. Sánchez Belda, ed., *Privilegios reales y viejos documentos de Baeza* (Madrid, 1964), doc. IV. The *gravamina* of 1279 do not, however, charge Alfonso with having a consistent policy on this score.

[31] Menéndez Pidal, *loc. cit.* For Alfonso's centralisation of law codes in the 1270s, and secular reaction to his policies, see A. Iglesia Ferreirós, 'Las Cortes de Zamora de 1274 y los Casos de Corte', *Anuario de Historia del Derecho Español*, XLI (1971), pp. 945–71.

[32] See C. Sánchez-Albornoz, 'Dudas sobre el Ordenamiento de Nájera', *Cuadernos de Historia de España*, XXXV–XXXVI (1962), pp. 315–36; idem, 'Menos dudas sobre el Ordenamiento de Nájera', *Anuario de Estudios Medievales*, III (1966), pp. 465–7 (jointly reprinted in his *Investigaciones y documentos sobre las instituciones hispanas* (Santiago de Chile, 1970), pp. 514–33). Cf. J. González, 'Sobre la fecha de las Cortes de Nájera', *Cuadernos de Historia de España*, LXI–LXII (1977), pp. 357–61.

[33] That Spanish churchmen did indeed travel abroad, and especially to the papal curia, cannot be doubted. See Linehan, *Spanish Church, passim*; idem, 'Spanish litigants and their agents at the thirteenth-century papal curia', *Proceedings of the Fifth International Congress of Medieval Canon Law 1976* (Vatican City, 1980), pp. 487–501; idem, 'Proctors representing Spanish interests at the papal court, 1216–1303', *Archivum Historiae Pontificiae*, XVII (1979), pp. 69–123.

[34] I am now doubtful whether this is a reference to the mendicant Orders. Cf. Linehan, *Spanish Church*, p. 223. †

[35] *Ibid.*, p. 243, n. 1; AC Toledo, O.4.L.1.10 (use by Sancho IV, 1288–90, of privileges of Innocent III, Clement IV and Innocent V: Potthast 5012, 21135, *Reg. Clement IV*, 15).

one of the complaints of the Brioca assembly of 1267.[36] It was precisely at this time that Alfonso's chief *almojarife* in León–Castile, Çag de la Maleha, fell from grace after the Infante Sancho had fraudulently appropriated the monies collected by him for the king's troops at the siege of Algeciras – a fall from grace which dragged his co-religionists down with him.[37] The allegedly false charges of usury brought by Alfonso as a further means of raising revenue (*L*) belong to the same context,[38] as presumably does that charge in *M* which appears to have been designed to draw attention to current theological controversy in terms which may have been calculated to remind the pope of recent events in the University of Paris.[39] Significantly perhaps, no translation is furnished of *M* which, reflecting as it does contemporary suspicions regarding the orthodoxy of Alfonso (and of Sancho for that matter),[40]

[36] AC Palencia, 4/1/3: 'nephas est ut blasfemantibus (?) Christi iudeis maior habeatur fides quam christifidelibus christianis'.

[37] Y. Baer, *A History of the Jews in Christian Spain*, I (Philadelphia, 1961), p. 129–30; Ballesteros, *Alfonso X*, p. 896. In May 1282 the rebellious Sancho adopted anti-Jewish measures apparently in order to attract churchmen to his cause: D. Mansilla Reoyo, *Catálogo documental del Archivo Catedral de Burgos (804–1416)* (Madrid–Barcelona, 1971), no. 855.

[38] Ballesteros, *Alfonso X*, p. 853; P. León Tello, 'Legislación sobre judios en las Cortes de los antiguos reinos de León y Castilla', *Fourth World Congress of Jewish Studies*, II (Jerusalem, 1968), p. 59. The legislation of the Zamora Cortes of 1301 refers (c. 11) to the other complaint ventilated in *L* – royal prohibition of spiritual penalties – during Alfonso X's reign: *Cortes de León y de Castilla*, I (Madrid, 1861), pp. 154–5. The bishops could not necessarily count on papal support in this matter: just two years later Martin IV instructed the dean of Ávila not to impose sentences of excommunication or interdict on the nobleman Martinus Aldefonsi, if convicted of property offences against the bishop of Zamora, 'nisi a nobis super hoc mandatum receperis speciale': rescript *Conquestus est*, 7 May 1281: AC Zamora, 11(D–1)i.10.

[39] Cf. Thomas Aquinas, *Summa Theologiae*, 1a2ae. 35, 6; J. Guttmann (trans. D. W. Silverman), *Philosophies of Judaism* (London, 1964), pp. 170, 212ff; D. J. Silver, *Maimonidean Criticism and the Maimonidean Controversy 1180–1240* (Leiden, 1965); M. Alonso, *Teología de Averroes* (Madrid–Granada, 1947), pp. 228, 283ff. For the genesis of the terminology employed, see H. A. Lucks, 'Natura Naturans – Natura Naturata', *The New Scholasticism*, IX (1935), pp. 1–24, and O. Weijers, ed., *Pseudo-Boèce: De Disciplina Scolarium* (Leiden, 1976), pp. 169–70, who traces it back to the *Liber Introductorius* of Michael Scot, *c*.1230. (I owe these references to the Rev. Dr Edward Booth O.P. and Dr Charles Burnett.) An unnoticed earlier usage of Spanish provenance occurs in a literary exercise of Archbishop Rodrigo of Toledo *c*.1218: M. Alonso, ed., *Diego García: Planeta* (Madrid, 1943), p. 463. For the condemnation of the naturalistic propositions at Paris in 1277 – especially regarding 'libros, rotulos seu quaternos nigromanticos aut continentes experimenta sortilegiorum, invocationes demonum, sive coniurationes in periculum animarum', see P. Mandonnet, *Siger de Brabant et l'averroïsme latin au XIIIe siècle* (Louvain, 1908), II, p. 176; R. Hissette, *Enquête sur les 219 articles condamnés à Paris le 7 mars 1277* (Louvain–Paris, 1977), esp. pp. 32–4, 147–60; J. F. Wippel, 'The condemnations of 1270 and 1277 at Paris', *Journal of Medieval and Renaissance Studies*, VII (1977), pp. 169–201, esp. pp. 175–6.

[40] In the mid-fourteenth-century Silos Chronicle (ed. D. W. Lomax, *Homenaje a Fray Justo Pérez de Urbel O.S.B.*, I (Silos, 1976), p. 335), Alfonso is alleged to have boasted that had he been present at the Creation 'muchas menguas se y fiçieron que non se fiçieran'. But our knowledge of the literary remains of the king's circle of translators (who were particularly active during the years 1276–9): M. Rico y Sanobas, *Libros del Saber de Astronomía del rey D. Alfonso X*, I

contains a hint of mounting hysteria. It was not the last time that Castilian churchmen would claim that royal policies were resulting in the promotion of totally unsuitable prelates ('immo viles et ydiote'): the clergy of Jaén had the same tale to tell in December 1283.[41] By then, however, they had at least learnt to remain silent on that other issue raised under *M, matrimonia illicita*: eighteen months earlier the Infante Sancho had openly contracted such a union, with no audible protest from his ecclesiastical supporters.[42]

Alfonso X's accusers represented him as a barely Christian tyrant manipulated by Jewish counsellors, intent upon subjecting churchmen to an intolerable yoke of persecution and servitude. In the recent past Alfonso had effortlessly shrugged off the occasional mild reproof from Rome. Now, however, he may have been conscious of the imminent risk of ecclesiastical sanctions – a risk the reality of which was confirmed by the pope's anxiety that no publicity be given to the episcopal *gravamina*.[43] (In neighbouring Portugal Afonso III had died only a month before the legate's departure for Castile, having incurred excommunication and brought interdict upon his kingdom by ecclesiastical policies hardly distinguishable from those of Alfonso X.[44] Afonso III of course no longer had the alibi of the Reconquest with which to

(Madrid, 1863), pp. lxiii–lxxxiv; v.i (1867), pp. 9–10; E. S. Procter, 'The scientific works of the court of Alfonso X of Castile: the king and his collaborators', *Modern Language Review*, XL (1946), p. 27) does not bear out the bishops' charge: see J. Fernández Montaña, ed., *Lapidario del rey D. Alfonso X* (Madrid, 1881), p. 1; J. A. Sánchez Pérez, 'El Libro de las Cruces', *Isis*, XIV (1930), p. 80; J. Domínguez Bordona, 'El "Libro de los Juicios de las Estrellas" traducido para Alfonso el Sabio', *Rev. de la Biblioteca, Archivo y Museo*, VIII (1931), p. 174 (AvenRagel's prologue). The testimony of *Partida*, VII, 23, 1 ('Adevinanza tanto quiere decir como quier tomar poder de Dios para saber las cosas que son por venir') is cited by A. G. Solalinde, 'Alfonso X astrólogo: noticia del MS Vat. Reg. Lat. 1283', *Rev. Filología Española*, XIII (1926), p. 354. Attention is drawn to 'the confrontation of Christianity with the apparently naturalistic interpretation of reality represented by Greek philosophy in Semitic dress' in the *Lucidario* attributed to Sancho IV ('Ca dos saberes son que son el vno contra el otro e estos son la theologia e las naturas . . .') by R. B. Tate and I. R. Macpherson in their edition of Juan Manuel *Libro de los Estados* (Oxford, 1974), p. xxx, n. 32.

41 Linehan, *Spanish Church*, p. 235.

42 A. Marcos Pous, 'Los dos matrimonios de Sancho IV de Castilla', *Escuela Española de arqueología e historia en Roma: Cuadernos de trabajos*, VIII (1956), p. 43. Cf. Flórez, *Memorias*, p. 548.

43 *Reg. Nicholas III*, no. 739: the legate would refer *viva voce* to various matters 'que propter honorem tuum et presentis conditionis regnorum eorundem qualitate pensata non inserere distincte patentibus nostris litteris ex cautela providimus nec illa in vulgarem voluimus notitiam derivare.' Cf. the note (not translated) which prefaces item C, below ('Hic intermititur . . .').

44 The Castilian *gravamina* of 1279 are evidently related to the Portuguese *gravamina* of 1268 and 1289–92. The nature of the relationship merits careful study. The Portuguese evidence is considerably more abundant than the Castilian. See García y García, *Canonística portuguesa*, pp. 222–6; Linehan, *Spanish Church*, p. 220; *As Gavetas da Torre do Tombo* (Centro de Estudos Históricos Ultramarinos, Lisbon, 1968), VII, pp. 23–36.

ward off a determined pontiff.) In seeking the assistance of Sancho, Alfonso betrayed a measure of anxiety upon which his son may well have chosen to capitalise. Sancho did not content himself with attempting to comply with his father's request for advice. As requested, he consulted widely. Thirty years ago Antonio Ballesteros published evidence of the Infante's activity in the autumn and winter of 1279 summoning meetings of the *conceios* of Castile 'sobre aquellas cosas que el legado dixo al rey de parte del Papa'. However, Ballesteros misunderstood the purpose of the bishop of Rieti's legation, assuming that it was connected with Alfonso's diplomatic conflict with France – despite the fact that the *Memoriale secretum* and the pope's letters had been in print since 1932.[45] A further piece of evidence, hitherto unnoticed, shows that Sancho was casting even further afield than Ballesteros knew. On a spare leaf of a manuscript of the *Panormia* of Ivo of Chartres in the cathedral library of Burgo de Osma is copied the reply of that church, dated 14 October 1279, to Sancho's invitation to comment on 'the articles sent by the pope to the king concerning the state of the Church and of the land'. Osma's reply breathes defiance of Alfonso. Their spokesmen were charged to bear witness to the truth of the *gravamina*, even if they found themselves alone in this.[46]

This further text should serve to remove the suspicion that the episcopal *gravamina* of 1279 were merely those of the prelates of

[45] A. Ballesteros y Beretta, 'Burgos y la rebelión del Infante Don Sancho', *Boletín de la R. Academia de la Historia*, CXIX (1946), pp. 141–5 (where a connection with the siege of Algeciras is suggested); idem, *Alfonso X*, pp. 909–12. J. F. O'Callaghan, although aware of the *Memoriale secretum*, interprets Sancho's autumnal activity as having to do with a projected campaign against Granada: 'The Cortes and royal taxation in the reign of Alfonso X', *Traditio*, XXVII (1971), p. 393, n. 54.

[46] Burgo de Osma, Biblioteca del Cabildo, cód. 8, fo. 201v: 'Anno domini M.CC. septuagesimo nono jueves, xiiij dias por andar del mes de Octubre. El Prior don Estevan e el Cabildo dela Eglesia de Osma ovieron su tractado sobre la respuesta e el Conseio que darien al Infante don Sancho en Razon delos Articulos que enbio el Papa al Rey por el estado dela Eglesia e dela tierra. E el acuerdo que ovieron e el mandamiento que dieron a los procuradores que dixiessen fue esto. Que bien sabien el Rey e don Sancho que lo que el Papa dizie que verdat era e derecho e pues que verdat e derecho era que les conseiavan e les pidien mercet que fiziessen lo que el Papa tenie por bien por que non pudiesse venir ende periglo. Aun dixieron mas a los procuradores que si todos los otros fuessen contrarios desto que ellos non mudassen esta respuesta. En esta acuerdo fueron presentes el Prior e don Garçi Uanes Arcidiano de Osma e don Julian Perez Arcidiano de Asça e don Domingo Miguel Capiscol que fue depues requerido e otorgo (sic) e don Fferran Abbat Sacristan que fue present e don Guillem Capellan mayor . . .' Notice of this document was provided by T. Rojo Orcajo, 'Catálogo descríptivo de los códices que se conservan en la Santa Iglesia Catedral de Burgo de Osma', *Boletín de la R. Academia de la Historia*, CXIV (1929), p. 715. Cf. Linehan, 'The Synod of Segovia (1166)', *BMCL*, n.s. X (1980). Economic pressures may have strengthened their resolve: for evidence regarding the rapid price rises of the years 1278–81, see M. del Carmen Carlé, 'El precio de la vida en Castilla del Rey Sabio al Emplazado', *Cuadernos de Historia de España*, XV (1951), p. 139.

Episcopal 'gravamina' of 1279

Compostela and León writ large. Coming from that area of the centre of the kingdom which for half a century or more had borne such heavy financial burdens, it represents the widespread discontent of precisely that region which Sancho would court in 1282, and was indeed already courting in 1279, by masquerading as the champion of *libertas ecclesiastica*.[47] At the very end of 1279 he was still at work collecting evidence bearing on the episcopal grievances, possibly with a view to preparing a consolidated reply for the pope. It is not known whether any such reply was ever sent. No trace of one has survived. What, however, is certain is that for all his feigned tenderness to churchmen, Sancho was already developing fast as his father's son, the man who as king would harass the Church quite as remorselessly as Alfonso had ever done.[48]

Recent work has represented the twenty to thirty years after the death of Alfonso X as a period during which the Castilian nobility recovered the share in government of which Alfonso had deprived it.[49] The record of the Salamanca assembly of 1310 suggests that churchmen experienced no such revival – if revival be the word.[50] The evidence presented by the bishop of Cuenca at the Council of Vienne in 1311–12 shows that little had changed since 1279.[51] And little would change thereafter, because the Vienne decrees concerning those very abuses which had been catalogued on the earlier occasion would remain a dead letter in Castile–León.[52] Although on his return from Vienne Arch-

[47] He arbitrated the Zamora dispute of the bishop and chapter who, through the exiled archbishop of Compostela, had complained to Nicholas III in May 1278 that sundry named civic officials were subverting *libertas ecclesiastica* by preventing them from tending their vines and selling their wine: a settlement from which the laymen subsequently resiled (AC Zamora, 11(D–1)i.13; 11(D–1)ii.10). See also Martín Martín *et al.*, *Documentos de Salamanca*, nos. 365–7, 369; A. López Ferreiro, *Historia de la Santa Iglesia de Santiago de Compostela*, v (Santiago, 1902), appendix, pp. 112–13; L. Fernández Martín, 'La participación de los monasterios en la *Hermandad* de los reinos de Castilla, León y Galicia (1282–1284)', *Hispania Sacra*, xxv (1972), pp. 5–35.

[48] An indication of future developments was provided as early as December 1279 by Sancho's demand that representatives of the *conceio* of Burgos should come to him with 'carta blanca seellada, con uestro sseello colgado, para afirmar las cosas que acá ffueren ffechas' (Ballesteros, 'Burgos y la rebelión', p. 144): the exaction of blank charters from the prelates had figured in the *gravamina* (item D), and the charge had elicited no response from Sancho. And by December 1284 Sancho IV was taking the part of the friars against 'los obispos e los clerigos': M. Rodríguez Pazos, 'Privilegios de Sancho IV a los franciscanos de la provincia de Santiago (1284) y de Castilla (1285), *Archivo Ibero-Americano*, xxxvi (1976), p. 534. Cf. H. Grassotti, *Las instituciones feudo-vasalláticas en León y Castilla* (Spoleto, 1969), pp. 789ff., 1000ff.

[49] Jimeno Casalduero, *La imagen*, pp. 45–62; C. González Mínguez, *Fernando IV de Castilla (1295–1312): la guerra civil y el predominio de la nobleza* (Vitoria, 1976), p. 205ff., 330ff.

[50] See above, n. 1.

[51] F. Ehrle, 'Ein Bruchstück der Acten des Concils von Vienne', *Archiv für Literatur- und Kirchengeschichte des Mittelalters*, IV (1888), p. 370. [52] Cf. J. Lecler, *Vienne* (Paris, 1964), pp. 113ff.

bishop Rodrigo of Compostela summoned a provincial council 'for the maintenance and defence of ourselves and of our churches' and – in a letter the tone of which was one of cautious daring – urged Gonzalo of Toledo to do likewise and to prepare for an imminent meeting of the Cortes by discussing with him matters of common concern,[53] it was not an updated version of the 1279 *gravamina* that occupied the attention of the Zamora Council of 1313, but the Jews and legislation for their containment allegedly promulgated at Vienne.[54] And it was backward, to that single dark detail, and forward, to the darker decades ahead that Rodrigo and his suffragans referred. Like most of his episcopal colleagues both then and earlier, Rodrigo represented the interests of his God and his king as coterminous,[55] and on this occasion as on so many others a king who was professedly committed to the task of extending the boundaries of Christendom declined to subscribe to this comfortable arrangement. For when, other than in such relatively rare circumstances as those that obtained in the early 1280s did kings, or would-be kings, or even child-kings, need to ingratiate themselves with Castilian churchmen? Evidently not in 1313 at the beginning of a period of royal minority the civil disorders of which rendered church-men particularly susceptible to secular attack.[56] Yet precisely what it was, in terms of political power and influence, that their predecessors may have possessed before it was lost by the churchmen of Castile-León in the course of the thirteenth century: that has yet to be established.[57]

† [53] 'Et creemos Sennor que sia bem que vos fezessedes con vossos soffragannos vosso aiuntamento ante das Cortes pora aver acordo sobraquellas cousas que fazian mester avos et anos et a nossas Iglesias desse mostraren ennas Cortes': Madrid, Archivo Histórico Nacional, 7216/2, *papel* unnumbered doc: publ. from a faulty eighteenth-century copy by J. Tejada y Ramiro, *Colección de cánones y de todos los concilios de la Iglesia española*, v (Madrid, 1855), p. 679. Note the terminology – *aiuntamento*: his own Zamora Council he describes as 'nosso ajuntamento et conçello provinçial'.

[54] Tejada y Ramiro, *loc. cit.*, pp. 674–8. Cf. C.-J. Hefele (trans. H. Leclercq), *Histoire des conciles*, VI.ii (Paris, 1915), pp. 672–717; E. Müller, *Das Konzil von Vienne 1311–1312: seine Quellen und seine Geschichte* (Münster in W., 1934), pp. 685–8.

[55] 'Et aeste tempo Sennor seiamos todos huna cousa pora sserviço de dios et del Rey': as n. 53 above.

[56] On 7 December 1312, six days after Rodrigo of Compostela wrote his letter, the regent María de Molina was pressing for a meeting of the Cortes: A. Giménez Soler, *Don Juan Manuel* (Zaragoza, 1932), p. 418. The Jewish legislation of the Palencia Cortes (June 1313) fell far short of what the Zamora Council had prescribed in the previous January. In the context of tax-collecting, indeed, the clergy and the Jews were lumped together with 'otros ommes rreboltosos': *Cortes de León y de Castilla*, I, pp. 224, 226ff.

[57] For some observations regarding the kingdom of León, see R. A. Fletcher, 'Regalian right in twelfth-century Spain: the case of Archbishop Martín of Santiago de Compostela', *JEH*, XXVIII (1977), pp. 337–60, esp. pp. 357–9, and the same author's *The Episcopate in the Kingdom of León in the Twelfth Century* (Oxford, 1978), pp. 80–1.

Episcopal 'gravamina' of 1279

APPENDIX

TOLEDO, ARCHIVO DE LA CATEDRAL, X.I.B.I.4

In the document the Latin *gravamina*, the Spanish translation of them, and the draft replies are all copied *seriatim*. In what follows I have rearranged the text for ease of identification by bringing together the Latin and Spanish passages bearing on each individual *gravamen*, and for the same reason have supplied further lettering – *B'*, *B"*, *L-P* – which is lacking in the text.

The following conventions have been adopted:

italic: doubtful reading

( ): word or words supplied

[ ]: word or words illegible

Deletions and insertions in the draft reply are not normally noted.

My thanks are due to Don Ramón Gonzálvez, canon archivist of Toledo Cathedral, for assistance in locating the document and for permitting photographs to be taken of it, and to Professor C. C. Smith (St Catharine's College Cambridge) for his help in deciphering the Spanish passages.

Este traslado nos dio el arcidiano Pay Dacana e*ᵃ* trexolo de casa del Rey e fue trasladado dela carta del papa que levo el obispo de Rieto por que sopiessemos meior guardar al Rey e tractar en la corte algunas cosas a su servicio.

Estos son los mayorales articulos sobre que el papa enbia al Obispo de Rieto al Rey de Castiella e de Leon.

A Primera mientre delas tercias delas eglesias que el Rey tiene por fuerça e a tenido ya muchos annos.

Al primer articolo esta podrie seer carrera de avenencia que aya el Rey las tercias en su vida por otorgamiento dela eglesia e depues de sus dias que nunquam por*ᵇ* sus herederos sean tomadas sin licencia dela eglesia de primera e de esto que assegure el Rey e Don Sancho en aquella manera que conviene.

B Lo segundo dela guarda delas eglesias que vagan e de algunas dignidades e delos bienes que tenia delas eglasias cathedrales e Reglares.

Al segund articolo semeiarie esto que otorgasse la eglesia al Rey por las necessidades en que es que en su vida oviesse por razon dela guarda delas eglesias que vagan los frutas e las rendas dela mesa delos obispos mas el mueble que finca del obispo muerto quier en sus casas quier en su camara, que non sea tomado mas sea todo guardado pora conplir manda del obispo o poral successor que uviere.

B' El tercero articolo es delos agraviamientos fechos por el e por razon del al Arcobispo e ala eglesia de Santiago en las tierras e en los vasallos en el qual se contienen estos articolos que son de suso escriptos, sacado otros muchos que serie grave cosa aver remembrança.

a The conjunctive τ has been rendered 'e' throughout.　　　　*b* por [el m: *del.*]

Primera ment que demanda el Rey omenage al Arcobispo de Santiago el qual non el nin los otros Arçobispos que fueron ante del nunquam fizieron.

Otrossi que el Arcobispo quiere aver la piertega que el Rey tiene por fuerça e contra derecho e en grande danno dela Eglesia de Santiago.

Otrossi que se tien por agravado sobre sennorio dela Çibdad de Santiago e que non puede usar del e sobre los dannos fechos al Arçobispo por razon dela discordia que fue entrel e el Rey e sobre otros dannos que fueron fechos al Arçobispo por razon dela discordia que fue entrel e los omnes dela Çiudat de Santiago, a sugestion delos quales el Rey fizo fazer dannos sin cuento non tan solament al Arçobispo e ala eglesia mas alos que tienen con ellos e los ayudan.

Otrossi que el Rey que agrava al Arçobispo e ala eglesia de Santiago en muchas guisas en los puertos e enlos vassallos e que fizo fazer muchos dannos e muchas fuerças alas eglesias e alas personas delas eglesias que son subiectas al Arçobispo e ala eglesia. Ca tiene el Rey enbargado e ocupado todo el Arçobispado o por si o por otro e a dos annos que fizo delas rendas asu voluntad.

Otrossi que los castiellos e las fortalezas e las villas e las possessiones e los Celleros que la eglesia de Santiago a en muchos logares que son ocupados e enbargados por el Rey o por su mandado. E çertas otra cosa que no semeia de creer que las offrendas que vienen o que vinieron al Abad de Santiago desdel tiempo que lo el Rey tiene enbargado en aca que las reciben los legos e que fazan dellas asu voluntad. Onde acaesce que los Romeros *despreçiando* esto assi como cosa desguisada dexan de aver devocion e de yr en Romeria ala eglesia sobredicha.

Otrossi que los bienes dela eglesia e los bienes de aquellos que tienen con la eglesia e que la ayudan e demas los fructos e las rendas delos personadgos e delas raciones e delos otros beneficios que vagaron e vagan del sobredicho tiempo a aca que estan enbargadas por mandado del Rey e fazen dello a su voluntad. E commo quier que sea de doler delas cosas sobredichas mayor mente es de llorar del periglo delas almas dela Çiudat e del Arcobispado sobredichos, las quales almas son por esta razon en periglo de perdicion perdurable. E por aventura muchos dellos son dannados por esta razon.

Estas cosas son sacadas breve miente de otras muchas e fastas sin cuento por que el Rey que deve seer çierto de su fecho non se morasse por muchas palabras o por grand escriptura, ala dignidad e ala persona del qual el Obispo aviendo reverençia en quanto ael conviene es apareiado de conplir por palaura lo que mingua en este escripto en logares e en tienpos convenibles.

B" El quarto articolo es delos agraviamientos e delos tuertos que son fechos por el Rey o por razon del al Obispo e ala eglesia de Leon, las quales cosas mas son manifiestas por fama publica e por vista del fecho la qual non se podrie encubrir por ninguna guisa, que por demonstramiento de çierto e de special demostrador, como el sobredicho obispo aviendo reverencia al Rey a ya avido verguença e temor de fazer appella del o de enbiarla por mandadero. En pero manifiesta cosa es que el fuyendo la persecucion del Rey que mendiga e anda desterrado en tierras estrannas, cuyos bienes e los dela eglesia sobredicha son enbargadas por mandado del Rey a muy grande danno del obispo e dela eglesia, e non se puede escusar delas cosas sobredichas *ante* es la

opinion del Rey muy agraviada porend que sea dicho que el aya puesto plazo sennalado al Obispo sobredicho que tornasse a su eglesia e sino dend adelante quel Rey yria
contra el. Como tales cosas como estas tengan e encierren en si servidumbre de la
persona e dela eglesia sobredichas.

Quintus articulus principalis est de [ ] forte in iniuriis gravaminibus et pressuris
prelatorum et clericorum personarum (ecclesiarum regu)larium et secularium vassal-
lorum et bonorum ad ipsas personas spectantium, de quibus gravaminibus iniuriis et
pressuris causa brevitatis et vitande prolixitatis quaedam presentibus duximus
annectenda.

Hic intermittitur grave iugum et honus populi ne hoc audito superbiat contra
regem; qui super hoc dicto regi plene locutus fuerit quod debebat, et rex respondit
quod non potuerat aliud olim facere quamvis proponeret corrigere in futurum.

El quinto articolo es de agraviamientos de muchos maneras e sin cuento de *punnas*
delos prelados e delos clerigos e delas personas delas eglesias reglares e seglares e delos
vassallos e delos bienes que pertenescen a estas personas, delos quales agraviamientos e
delos tuertos e delas punnas oir razon delo dezir mas breve ment de muchas que son
pusiemos aqui algunas.

Estas cosas son las que descenden delos sobredichos articolos mayorales.

C Primum gravamen est quod quamcito vacat aliqua ecclesia regni sui statim fundit
preces pro aliquo eligendo seu postulando, quod si preces non sufficiunt addicit minas
et tandem in ecclesiis regularibus vel secularibus inponit quos vult pro sue beneplacito
voluntatis. Et quod peius est intrusis vel impressis facit omnes proventus vacantis
ecclesie vel partem ipsorum ministrari, parte sibi altera reservata, et tali accione
ecclesie destruuntur.

El primer articolo es que luego que vaga alguna eglesia desu reyno enbiar rogar por
alguien quel eslean o que demanden por prelado, e si el ruego non abasta annade
amenazas, e ala postre mete en las eglesias reglares e seglares los que el quiere segund
la su voluntad. E lo que es peor cosa, que faze dar alos que assi son metidos todas las
rendas dela eglesia que vaga o partida dellas e la otra parte recabela pora si, e por tal
razon destruyense las eglesias.

Al otro articolo ⟨…⟩ que es que el Rey inecta por algunos que sean esleydos alas
eglesias e alas vezes que ameneça, non se otra avenencia sinno que si *non* es assi es bien
e si assi es non sea daqui adelant.

D Secundum est quod a prelatis et personis ecclesiasticis et vassallis colonis et serrariis
eorum per varios modos exactiones et subsidia extorquantur et ipsis frequenter onera
gravia, angarie et perangarie imponuntur. Facit etiam dominus Rex sigillari paginas
vacuas per prelatos et perhibere testimonium de hiis que nec viderunt nec sciverunt.

El segundo articolo es que delos prelados e delas personas delas eglesias e delos
vassallos de sus omnes por desvariadas maneras saca dellos por fuerça pedidos e
ayudas e muchas veçes son puestos a esto por fuerça e malament e en grand punna
muchos agraviamientos. E faze aun el Rey alos prelados que seellen cartas blancas e
que den testimonio delas cosas que non veen nin saben.

Al otro articolo que el Rey saca pedidos e ayudas de prelados clerigos e vassallos delas eglesias por muchas guisas e por fuerça, non se otra avenencia sinno que non se faga por ninguna manera. Ca esto es cosa que aun que los prelados fuessen requeridos e quisiessen consentir non lo pueden fazer menos de licencia dela eglesia de Roma. Ca los prelados non son sennores pora poder esto otorgar mas solament procuradores. Pues mucho menos se deve esto fazer los prelados non seyendo requeridos.

E Tertium est quod privilegia et libertates ecclesiarum et ecclesiasticarum personarum, sive habeant hec a iure sive a predecessoribus dicti Regis vel etiam ab eodem Rege concessa, per actum contrarium infringuntur. Ita quod frequenter dicte persone aliquando contra iura quandoque vero contra suorum privilegiorum tenorem trahuntur ad iudicium seculare, immo quod gravius est capiuntur et incarcerantur et occiduntur eedem persone per iudices seculares de mandato vel auctoritate regis predicti, et in tantum est in regno dicti regis libertas ecclesiastica cavillata quod thesauri ecclesie fracti sunt in locis pluribus violenter.

El tercero articolo es que los privilegios e las liberdades delas eglesias e delas personas dellas, quier los ayan de derecho o por los anteçessores del rey o que los aya el mismo otorgados, que son quebrantados por fecho contrallo e en tal manera que muchas vezes los clerigos e las personas sobredichas son traydas a juyzio delos seglares, alas vezes contra derecho, alas vezes contra sus privilegios. E çertas lo que mas grave cosa es que los juezes seglares penden e meten enlas carçeres e matan estas personas. E esto acaesce muchas vezes por pesquisas que fazen encubiertamente los Alcaldes seglares contra los clerigos e contra las personas delas eglesias por mandado del Rey, non lo otorgando ellos nin seyendo vençidos en juyzio. E assi es la franqueza dela iglesia minguada enlos reynos del Rey. E que los tesoros delas eglesias son quebrantados por fuerça en muchos logares e los conceios son lamados que vayan contra las personas delas eglesias e contra sus vassallos e contra aquellos que tienen con ellos assi como enemigos.

Al otro articolo quanto al pender delas personas delos clerigos non veo y avenencia si non que non se faga o sinno fuesse preso en el fecho e citacion que se de luego ala iustiçia clerigal e que nel Rey nin los legos *ensufran*, pues mucho menos en iusticiarle a menos de seer judgado e degradado por su prelado. Esso mismo en razon de llamar los clerigos ante juez seglar. Ca non sabemos caso ninguno en que esto deva seer, quier sea la demanda personal, quier real, quier sea mueble, quier rayz, quier sobre demanda *spiritual* quier episcopal. Ca todos los bienes delos clerigos aun que sean temporales todos son de suso dela eglesia sinon fuesse por aventura demanda de ffeudo e de particion entre herederos. Esso mismo en razon de fazer pesquisa contra los clerigos, ca quier non puede seer juez non puede pesquisa fazer. Esso mismo en razon de los thesoros delas eglesias que se quebrantan. Esso mismo en razon de llamar e assonar los conceios contra las eglesias. En todas estas cosas non ay avenencia otra sinon parar ende mano, mayormente que en todas estas cosas es fazer libertad dela eglesia e todos los que esto fazen son descomulgados.

F Item si ecclesie vel ecclesiastice persone *regulares vel secu*lares acquirunt vel acquisi-verunt vassallos possessiones et bona exempta *communia* prius ab omni fisco vel onere dominus rex facit quod dicti vassalli possessiones et bona fiunt sibi tributaria et censsualia. Nec obstat etiam si ecclesia super talibus sit legitima prescriptione munita vel habeant (*sic*) super eas idonea munimenta. Sed quod mirabilius est coget possessores titulum sue possessionis ostendere contra iura.

Otrossi que si las eglesias o los clerigos o las personas delas eglesias reglares o seglares ganan o ganaron vassallos possessiones o bienes que eran ante francos de todo pecho de Rey que faze e que costrinne que los vassallos e las possessiones e los bienes sean pecheros. E non lo dexa pora que la eglesia sobre tales cosas aya legitima prescripcion o aya sobrestas cosas convenibles cartas. Elo que es mayor maravilla que costrinne contra derecho los possessores que muestren el titulo de su possession.

Al otro articolo semeiarie esto que por razon delas possessiones que fueron ante liberas por passar ala eglesia non fiziessen los clerigos por ellas pechar nin aun por las otras que fueron pecheras, si por privilegio que oviessen las ovieron quier ante delas cortes de Naiara quier despues. Mas en razon delas pechas que passaron alas eglesias e alos clerigos sin privilegio semeiarie esta carrera que pues los otros reyes lo suffrieron fasta aqui e la eglesia fue *confirmada* en possession desta libertad fasta agora, mayor mient como estas possessiones sean muy pocas e todas las possessiones tales que agora han fincassen en las eglesias e en los clerigos liberas, e daqui adelant non pudiessen comprar sin mandado del Rey o si comprassen pechassen por ellas. Pero si alguno por su alma assi como por anniversario dexasse alguna rayz ala eglesia por reverencia dela eglesia e por favor del alma fincasse quita e libera ala eglesia. Otrossi la heredad que los clerigos ganassen por otra manera e non por compra assi como por herencia o por manda o por donadio de parient o damigo por que si las quisiessen mas vender que pechar por ellas recibien grand menoscabo en venderlas tan assi a essora^c pusieseles el Rey plazo fasta quando las deviesse*n* vender, e si las non vendiessen fasta aquel plazo que pechassen por ellas e encaramient non. E si en razon delas heredades que han por herencia de padre o de madre o de parient fuesse la merced mayor que en su vida non pechasse el clerigo por ella, razon que serie guisado, ca aun non ha grand tiempo que non solament su persona mas el padre e la madre escusava. Elo que dixo de suso que tales heredades como estas son muy pocas entendiesse e esto que todas las eglesias catedrales en Castiella han privilegia que ellas e los canonigos dellas puedan comprar e ganiar (*sic*) por quel quier titulo, pues non finca la gracia si non en las possessiones que ganaron clerigos parrochiales e aldeanos e por verdad estas son muy pocas en Castiella.

G Item instituit auctoritate propria novum ordinem seu religionem quod esse de iure non potest, cuius occasione ecclesie multipliciter aggravantur.

Otrossi que establesçio por su auctoridat nueva orden a religion, la qual cosa non pode seer con derecho por razon dela qual los clerigos son mucho agraviados.

El otro articolo dela orden nueva: *gap*

H Item impetratis ab apostolica sede privilegiis vel obtentis utitur etiam ultra concessionis tempus pro sue beneplacito voluntatis, non facta de ipsis originalibus copia illis ad quos privilegia dicta spectant, et ut ex talibus privilegiis maius commodum assequatur alias ordinariorum indulgencias in terra sua frequenter non patitur publi-

c tan assi era a so ora

cari. Decimas quoque ad tempus sibi concessas extorqueri facit ab illis personis qui ab ipsarum solutione per declarationem summi pontificis sunt exempte.

Otrossi que delos privilegios ganados del papa usa a su voluntad mayor tiempo de quanto los otorgado, non dando traslado dellos a aquellos aquien pertenescen. E por que de tales privilegios aya mayor pro non consiente algunas vezes que por su tierra anden otros perdones ordinarios. E las decimas quele son otorgados por tiempo sennalado toma las daquellas personas que son end quitas por la declaracion del papa.

El otro articolo en razon de usar delos privilegios mayor tiempo que deve, e otras delas decimas: *gap*

I Item prelatis et capitulis terre sue non est liberum[d] convenire ut tractarent de premissis at aliis gravaminibus quae ipsis et aliis personis ecclesiasticis pro tempore inferuntur, nec exire extra regnum vel extrahere inde pecuniam pro necessitatibus variis que occurrunt etiam de bonis ecclesiasticis acquisitam libere permittuntur.

Otrossi que los prelados e los cabildos de su tierra non se osan ayuntar pora fablar e tractar destas cosas sobredichas e de otros agraviamientos que los fazie a ellos e alas personas delas eglesias. E non osan nin pueden salir del reyno nin sacar el aver ganado delos bienes delas eglesias pora aquellas cosas que an mester.

El otro en razon delos prelados que no se osan ayuntar ni osan salir del reyno nin sacar aver, a que non se avenencia ninguna ca es contra libertad de sancta eglesia e grand servidumbre delos clerigos e grand periudicio dela eglesia de Roma a que han de venir liberament los prelados e los otros cristianos por sus necessidades e de sus eglesias e de sus almas: *gap*

K Item judei[e] christianis in officiis et exactionibus preponuntur, ex quo perveniunt multa mala inter que id est principuum (*sic*), quod christiani multi ut favorem habeant judeorum subiciuntur eis et eorum ritibus et traditionibus corrumpuntur.

Otrossi que los judios son puestos sobre los cristianos en los offiçios e enlas collechas,[f] dela qual cosa vienen muchos males entre los quales es mayor mal quelos cristianos son subiectos a ellos e son corrumpidos por sus costumbres e por sus malos husos. Al otro de los judios que se ponen sobre los cristianos: *gap*

L Item de spiritualibus causis et processibus se multipliciter intromittens et legata ad pias causas sine cause cognitione usurpans facit auctoritate propria inquisitiones fieri contra clericos et laycos de usuris et fere contractum quemlibet usurarium judicans extorquet a dictis personis pecuniam sicut placet, prelatorum vel interdicti sententias servari nec in certis casibus non permittans (*sic*) ita quod excommunicationis exceptio a paucis annis citra non admittitur in sua curia et suorum, et qui eam observant vel observari mandant spoliantur bonis et de personis aliquando capiuntur.

Otrossi que se entremete en muchas maneras delos pleytos spirituales e las mandas que se fazen a casas de piedad, tomalos contra derecho sin connoscimiento de pleyto. E manda fazer por su auctoridat pesquisas contra los clerigos e sobre los legos sobre fecho delas husuras e fastas cada un contracto judga por usurario e saca por fuerca delas dichas personas aver segund su voluntad e non dexa aguardar sinon en ciertas

d suppl. liberum   *e* judeis   *f* cogechas

cosas las sentencias que fazen los prelados de descomunion o de demedo de pocos annos en aca no es recebida en su corte e delos suyos sinon en çiertas cosas, e a aquellos que la aguardan o que mandan^g guardar tomanles lo que an e alas vezes pendenlos.

M Item propter auctoritatem ecclesiasticam modis premissis et aliis impeditam, nam (*sic*) prelati non possunt suum officium libere exercere immo viles et ydiote penitus in: *gap*. Matrimonia multa in casibus illicitis contrahuntur, claves ecclesie contempnantur. Attribuuntur non Deo qui est natura naturans sed *nature* ab ipso naturate fere omnia a quibusdam qui, asserentes deum non esse ad fallax astronomorum et augurum vel aiusperitum judicium, procedunt quasi in omnibus factis suis.

Otrossi por que la auctoridad dela eglesia es enbargada por las maneras sobredichas e por otras los prelados non pueden de su officio usar libre mente, mas viles e non letrados son metidos enlas eglesias. E fazen se casamientos e matrimonios en casos non convenibles e que son menospreciados las laves dela eglesia e que se fazen otras cosas non convenibles.

N Item privilegia etiam ab ipso et predecessoribus suis ecclesiis et personis ecclesiasticis vassallis colonis et serrariis eorum concessa non observant eisdem et exigens a talibus martinega compellunt eos ad exercitium et ad diversas tallias et exactiones et censsus solvendos, ita quod vassalli et huiusmodi serrarii et coloni coguntur dimittere dominium prelatorum et exire regnum vel subicere se dominio laycorum.

Otrossi segund que sobredicho es non aguarda los privilegios que el e los otros sos antecessores dieron alas eglesias e alas personas delas eglesias e asus vassallos e asus omnes demandandoles martiniega o costreyendo les yr en hueste e pechar pechos de muchas maneras por que estos sus vassallos e sus omnes an de dexar el sennorio delos prelados e salir del reyno a meter en sennorio delos legos.

O Item clerici et ecclesiastice persone trahuntur frequenter in petitorio et possessorio ad seculare judicium violenter nec ibi possunt si aliquos conveniant expediri et fere in omnibus tributis et exactionibus sicut laici talliantur.

Otrossi los clerigos e las personas delas eglesias non tan solamente son traydos muchas vegadas a juyzio delos seglares por fuerça en razon desus possessiones e de otras demandas que les fazen. Mas si ellos demandan alli a algunos non son librados. E fastas en todos los pechos son pecheros assi como los legos.

P Item imponit nova pedagia et tributa locis et portibus spectantibus etiam ad ecclesias pleno iure.

Otrossi pone nuevos peages e pechos alos lugares e alos puertos que pertieniscen (*sic*) de derecho ala eglesia.

g madan

ADDENDA ET CORRIGENDA

STUDY I

P.161 n.3   Volume II of the Historia - J.Fernández Conde (ed.), La Iglesia en la España de los siglos VIII-XIV - covering the period considered here, was published in 1982. See my review of the work in Times Literary Supplement, n.4166, 4 Feb.1983, p.117.

P.169ff   What follows regarding the Chronicle of Alfonso III should now be compared with the suggestions and conclusions in Jan Prelog's edition, Die Chronik Alfons' III. Untersuchung und kritische Edition der vier Redaktionen (Frankfurt-am-Main/Bern/Cirencester 1980) which reopens many questions regarded as settled by Sánchez-Albornoz and others.

P.193 n.132 Cf Jacques of Vitry's similar but far more limited observations on the subject: Historia Occidentalis ,c.7,ed.J.F. Hinnebusch (Fribourg 1972) 92; L.Schmugge,'Uber "nationale" Vorurteile im Mittelalter', Deutsches Archiv 38 (1982)455-6.

STUDY II

P.43 lines 6,11   Is 'in requiem' conceivably a scribal error for 'in regem'? Cf Conc. Coyanza (1055),c.VI, listing the purposes for which travel on Sunday was permitted - prayer, burial of the dead, visiting the sick, royal business, resisting 'Saracen' attacks: García Gallo /above, Study I,p.182 n.85/ 297.

STUDY IV

Of the papers reproduced in this volume, this one - written in 1968 - stands in greatest need of revision in the light of subsequent research. In 1975 Domenico Maffei's discovery of the earliest statutes of the University of Bologna revealed Abril's whereabouts during the 'lost years' (cf p.180). Knowledge of the affairs of the church of Salamanca has been substantially advanced by the publication of J.L. Martín Martín et al. (eds), Documentos de los archivos catedralicio y diocesano de Salamanca (siglos XII-XIII) (Salamanca 1977). A.García y García (ed.), Synodicon Hispanum, I: Galicia (Madrid 1981) and the works of A. Paravicini Bagliani (cited below) have added considerably to our understanding of the history of the church of Compostela and of the college of cardinals respectively.
P.Baraut's kindness in correcting certain of my transcriptions, acknowledged by the editor of Anuario de Estudios Medievales

(p.197), having been rendered without my knowledge, I take this opportunity of restoring readings which after renewed study of photographs of the documents I believe to be preferable, as well as of rectifying the larger number of errors of my own making.

P.148 n.26 penultimate line For limitaría read forzaría.

P.148 line 10 Martín, Documentos de Salamanca, reveals no subsequent appearance of Abril at Salamanca after 1243.

P.149 line 7 He was at the University of Bologna as 'ultramontanorum scolarium rector': see Maffei /Study IX, p.128 n.6/.

P.154 n.58 For Juan Arias's council and synod, see Linehan, Spanish Church and the Papacy,172; Synodicon Hispanum, I,266-7.

P.159 n.92 Pedro Pérez's earliest appearance as dean can now be dated to February 1265: Documentos de Salamanca, 307.

P.159 n.93 The reference should read ACS, 20/1/33=Marcos 315.

P.159 n.96 The quoted passage should read "...prometer por nostra carta, e mandamos que lo aya pelo otro pan·de los otros çeleros del bispado."

P.160 n.102 For Cardinal Stephanus, see now A. Paravicini Bagliani, Cardinali di curia e 'familiae' cardinalizie dal 1227 al 1254 (Padua 1972) 349ff; idem, I Testamenti dei cardinali del Duecento (Rome 1980) 18,127ff.

P.162 n.120 The author's name should read A. Paravicini Bagliani.

P.163 n.129 In the first line of the document cited the word 'Urgellensi' has been omitted after 'episcopo';in line 4 'sana' should read 'sacra';'sacri' in line 5 is possibly the beginning of 'sacrista' repeated in error. The text of another letter of the cardinal,said in Spanish Church and the Papacy,56 n.5, to be published here, was by inadvertence omitted. It is as follows: Venerabili in Christo patri Dei gratia episcopo Ylerdensi J. eiusdem permissione Sabinensis episcopus salutem et sinceram in domino caritatem. Noverit vestra caritas nos per Dei gratiam corporea perfrui sanitate paratos semper ad vestrum commodum et honorem. Ad hec cum nostra sollicitudine venerabili patri Tarraconensi archiepiscopo et vobis comissa fuerit si capitulum non concordaverit provisio ecclesie Urgellensis, caveatis ne si providere vos contigerit ille Urgellensis archidiaconus qui fuit archidiaconus Narbonensis per vos preficiatur ecclesie supradicte. Insuper de statu persone vestre quam sincera in domino caritate diligimus etiam terre vestre nos velitis cumprimum poteritis sepius reddere certiores (ACU). Although undated, the letter unquestionably belongs to the year 1230 (cf Villanueva,11.72-3). Who the archdeacon of Urgel was,who was to be avoided at all costs, I have been unable to discover. If, however, it was none other than the eventually triumphant Ponce (as it may well have been:cf Villanueva,74n.), then it would appear that the cardinal was insufficiently aware of the ramifications of Catalan ecclesiastical connexions: for Ponce was the nephew of Berenguer de Eril, the bishop of Lérida to whom the letter was addressed.

P.166 line 2   Was Ponce's nephew, described in the letter published by Villanueva (p.222) as 'P.G.', really P.B. - i.e. Petrus Berengarii, of whose proctorial activities on behalf of the bishop of Zaragoza and others in the later 1250s trace has survived? Cf Linehan, 'Proctors representing Spanish interests at the papal court,1216-1303', <u>Archivum Historiae Pontificiae</u> 17 (1979) 91,119.

P.167 n.157   <u>contradictorum</u> misprint for <u>contradictarum</u>.

P.171 The identification proposed here of Juan Domínguez requires reconsideration in the light of the material published in <u>Documentos de Salamanca</u> where no fewer than thirty-five individuals of this name are separately indexed.

P.171 n.194   The text reads: ...sum cum archiepiscopo et teneo sigillum suum...

P.172 n.200   See now C. Batlle,'La Seu d'Urgell a la segona meitat del segle XIII,segons els testaments',<u>Urgellia</u> 3 (1980) 371-2,401 (Juan Domínguez's will).

P.179 n.241   A letter in ACU, dated 'die martis post cineres'(no year), from Abbot M. of S. Maria de Appamia and in response to a letter from Abril, apparently soon after the latter's election to Urgel, is largely concerned with the activities of Count Roger. 'Dolorem qui nostrum animum continue affligebat pro obpressione Urgellensis ecclesie repellendo que longuo (<u>sic</u>)tempore fuit afflicta pariter et attrita ab hiis a quibus deberet recipere consolationis et adiutorii fulcimentum', the news of Abril's election prompts the abbot to express the hope that 'iacula que previdentur minus feriunt' and that Abril will be wary 'a sagacitatibus nobilis viri Fuxensis comitis qui multa promittet quamvis non propona(t) ducere ad affectum set ut possit que detinet Urgellensis ecclesie retinere sine relaxatione aliqua tempus suum preteriens alliciens vos promissis.' S. Maria de Appamia OSB (on Lake Fucino, Abruzzi) was directly subject to the Roman Church (P.F. Kehr, <u>Italia Pontificia</u> ,IV (Berlin 1909)249.) Did the international friendship of bishop and abbot have its beginnings at the papal curia , or at Bologna ?

P.181 bottom line; p.182 line 10, line 10 up, bottom line; p.184 line 1: <u>Abril</u> (in italics).

4

Apéndice 1, line 2 for osculamen read osculum; line 4 for eam read eum.

Apéndice 2, line 2 for osculam read oscula; line 3 for incessantes read incessanter; line 7 for cor reserant read ocareserant (?).

Apéndice 4, p.192, bottom line delete comma after 'incontinenti'; p.193, line 1 read ipsius. Qui sub quadam conniventia; line 2 for Johanni read Johannes; line 12 read archiepiscopus respondit dicens quod non conferebat sibi canoniam licet dominus papa sibi per

Apéndice 5, line 9 for salutis, propter read salutis.Propter

Apéndice 9, line 9 for dominum read dominus (sic); line 12, for iuvenem (?) read virum; bottom line for lunis read lune; p.196, line 11 up for vos (?) read nos; p.197, line 8 up for instrante read intrante; line 9 up delete (?); for Raimundus de Uliola, canon of Lérida and scriptor of King Jaime I, see R.I. Burns, 'Canon Law and the Reconquista:convergence and symbiosis in the kingdom of Valencia under Jaume the Conqueror (1213-1276)', Proc.Fifth International Congress of Medieval Canon Law, Salamanca, 21-25 Sept.1976, ed. S. Kuttner and K. Pennington (Vatican City 1980)416,417.

STUDY V

P.482ff See now R. Pastor, Resistencias y luchas campesinos en la época del crecimiento y consolidación de la formación feudal. Castilla y León, siglos X-XIII (Madrid 1980) cap.4, esp.pp 156ff, 188ff, 206ff.

P.487 n.1, line 8 González's source is the so-called Crónica latina de los reyes de Castilla, cit. C. Sánchez-Albornoz, 'La Sucesión al trono en los reinos de León y Castilla', repr. Viejos y nuevos estudios sobre las instituciones medievales españolas, II (Madrid 1976) 1145.

P.501 n.10 contd., line 9 Cf Study VII p.31 n.108.

STUDY VI

As noted (p.205), further work on the subject of the economy of the diocese of Segovia was published after these papers (V, VI) had gone to the printers. In addition to the work of García Sanz et al., mention should be made of M. Santamaría Lancho, La gestión económica del cabildo catedralicio de Segovia (ss.XII-XIV), Memoria de Licenciatura, Univ. Complutense Madrid 1980. Parts of Santamaría's thesis have been published, and of especial interest to the present topic are 'La organización de la gestión economica del cabildo catedralicio de Segovia. Siglos XIII-XIV', Estudios en memoria del Prof. D. Salvador de Moxó, II (Madrid 1982) 505-40; 'Una fuente para el estudio del poblamiento y la

distribución de la renta agraria en la Castilla del s. XIII: la
distribución de los "prestamos"', unpubl. paper pres. at Jornadas
de Metodologia y Didáctica de la Historia, Cáceres 1981. I am
much obliged to the author for providing me with copies of these
papers. Prof. Angel Barrios García and his colleagues are engaged in research on Cardinal Gil's distributions at Salamanca,
Segovia, Burgos and Ávila. See also M. Barrio Gozalo, Estudio
socio-económico de la iglesia de Segovia en el siglo XVIII (Segovia 1982), and for Zaragoza in the 1290s, M.R. Gutiérrez Iglesias, La mensa capitular de la iglesia de San Salvador de Zaragoza en el pontificado de Hugo Mataplana (Zaragoza 1980).

STUDY VII

The massive work of C. Estepa Díez, Estructura social de la ciudad de
León (siglos XI-XIII) (León 1977) should be consulted for further
information on sundry individuals mentioned below.

P.24   Fernán Patino: see now Estepa Díez, Estructura, índice.

P.31 n.108   Mag. Melior. Cf Reg. Greg. IX,2431,4550 (Feb.1235, Oct.
1238).

Apéndice 1, line 6 for statum read statutum.

Apéndice 10,p.46,lines 25-6 read per ipsos vel eorum alterum sive
substitutos seu substitutum ab ipsis vel eorum altero gestum fuerit procuratoris officio habiturus...

Apéndice 16,p.76 n.2 Prof. Domenico Maffei suggests that 'la Summa
que dizen Martiniana' may have been the 'Margarita Decreti seu
tabula Martiniana' of Martinus Polonus (d.1279):J.F.v. Schulte,
Die Geschichte der Quellen und Literatur des Canonischen Rechts,
II (Stuttgart 1877) 137.

STUDY VIII

P.732 n.5   Master Garinus was at Toledo on 4 Feb.1264:AC Toledo,
V.12.X.1.1.

Appendix 1   p.746 n.1 the word is insudavit;p.747,line 7 for declararet
read declaresceret;p.747 possibly negotium .

Appendix 2   p.748,line 25 for termino read tempore;line 35 read eandem
etiam innovantes;p.749,line 2 read bone memorie domino Sancio.

Appendix 4 p.751,date:for 18 February 1263 read 18 January 1263;
p.752,line 15 read committo totaliter vices meas.Datum Maioricum...;line 22 for dedimus read dederimus;line 29 for Dominici read Damiani;p.753,line 20 insert ecclesia before vestra.

6

STUDY IX

P.135 n.34 J.O'Callaghan is surely correct in interpreting this as a
reference to the Military Order of Santa María de España,foun-
ded by Alfonso X in 1272 : 'The ecclesiastical estate in the Cortes
of León-Castile,1252-1350',Catholic Historical Review 67 (1981)
196. By the Ordenamiento de Zamora of 1274, moreover,members
of the Order had been granted a privileged role at the royal court
on being constituted the sole channel to the king for petitions 'que
non sean de justicia' (Cortes de los antiguos reinos de León y de
Castilla, I (Madrid 1861) 91-2): episcopal access to the king's
favour was thus blocked. To what degree was episcopal pressure
in 1279 responsible for the merging of the Order with the Order
of Santiago in the following year ?

P.140 nn.53, 55 Archbishop Rodrigo's letter is ed. in F.Fita, Actas
inéditas de siete concilios españoles celebrados desde el año
1282 hasta él de 1314 (Madrid 1882)150-51.

INDEX

Twelfth- and thirteenth-century pontiffs and monarchs who appear repeatedly in the preceding pages are not listed here. Nor are the hundreds of place-names of the diocese of Segovia which occur in Study VI. The usage of Latin and of vernacular forms of names has not been regularised. References to material in the Addenda and Corrigenda are indicated with an 'A' following the entry.

Segovia (cont.):
  Guillelmo,bp: II 34n;V 488n
  Martín,bp: V 499
  Pedro de Agen,bp: II 37; V 485
  Pedro de Cuéllar,bp: V 500
  Raimundo de Losana,bp: V 497f;
    VI 199f
  J., dean: V 485
  Nicolás, archd. of Cuéllar: V 488,
    491n,493n,494n;VI 165-6
  Petrus Roderici,archd.: VIII 749
  Petrus Stephani,can.,royal scriptor:
    VIII 749
Segura, card. Pedro: I 198
Sepúlveda: V 484-5
Seville,ch. of: V 501,504n
  Isidore,St,bp: I 173f,175,179
  Oppa,bp: I 170f,179
  Raimundo de Losana,abp: VIII 749
    (see Segovia)
  Gundissalvus Dominici,can.:
    VIII 749
  Petrus Petri,archd.Écija: VIII 749
Sigüenza,ch.of: VIII 738
  Cerebrun,bp: II 34
  Pedro I,bp: II 37,38n
  Pedro II,bp:VIII 742n
  Rodrigo,bp: I 193:V 484,486n,504
  G., archd. of Molina: V 484n
  P., archd. of Almazán: V 484n
Silves,siege of: I 189
Sinitius, collector: IV 166n;VIII 743
Stephanus dictus Surdus, Roman cleric:
  VII 16n,35
Stephanus Ungarus, card.: IV 159n,
  160f,167,172;VIII 748
Stephen,nephew of card. Stephanus
  Ungarus: IV 161

Tarragona,ch. of: I 185
  Council of (1244): IX 129
  Benito de Rocaberti,abp: IV 166,168,
    174,175;VIII 742
  Pedro de Albalat,abp: III passim ;
    IV 163f
Teobaldo II,kg of Navarre: I 177
tercias decimarum: VIII 735f;IX 130f
Thomas,mag., rector of ch. of S.
  Médard (Soissons): VII 51
Thompson, E.A.: I 173
Toledo:
  Bernardo,abp: I 184
  Cerebrun,abp: II 38
  Eulogius,bp: I 178-9
  Gonzalo I,abp: VII 24n
  Gonzalo II,abp: IX 140
  Juan,abp: II 33,34,37
  Juan de Medina,abp: X 492

Martín López,abp: V 483,497
Rodrigo Ximénez de Rada,abp: I 178,
  184,191,195;II 33;V 487;IX 136n
Sancho I,abp: VIII 735;IX 130-1
Sancho II,abp: IX 131-2 ;(as abt of
  Valladolid: IV 172)
Gómez García,can.: IX 133n
Ramón Bernárdez,mag.,can.:
  VIII 737
Vivián,archd. Guadalajara:VIII 737
Torres,card. Gil: IV 157-8,159f;V
  487f,505-8;VI 164-5;VII 15,17-18,
  36-7,61,72
Tortosa,ch. of: IV 168n
Toulouse, Council of (1119):II 40
Tours, Council of (1163): II 34
Tuy, Subgerius Gundisalvi,can. of:
  II 34

Ubaldini, card. Ottaviano: IV 173;
  VII 42f,45f
Umana, Arnulfo,bp of:VII 64
Urban II,pope: I 183,187
Urgel,ch. of: IV 162f
  Abril,bp: IV passim
  Guillermo,bp: IV 164n
  Pedro de Puigvert,bp: IV 163
  Pedro de Urg,bp: IV 176,179n
  Ponce de Vilamur,bp: IV 161n,162f
  Juan Domínguez,can.:IV 171-2,178,
    179
  Juan Peláez (Páiz),archd.: IV 147-
    148,162,170
  Ricardo,archd. Aristot: IV 174-6

Valencia,ch. of: I 185;III 10
  Andrés de Albalat,bp: III 11-12,14;
    IV 165,167
  Jazpert,bp: IV 174n
  Ramón Despont,bp: III 13n
Valladolid:
  Sancho,abt: IV 172
  Council of (1143): II 36
  Council of (1155): I 190n;II 35n,36
Venerabilem : I 192
vernacular: I 194
Veruela, O. Cist.: III 10
Vienne, Council of (1311-12):IX 139
Villanueva,J.: IV 145-6
Vincentius Hispanus: I 192
Vitas SS Patrum Emeretensium:I 173

Wamba, Division of: I 185

Zagreb,ch. of: IV 161,173
Zamora:
  Council of (1313): IX 140
  Ordeniamente de: IX 135nA